BED & BREAKFAST CAN BE FOUND IN:

a **FISHERMAN'S COTTAGE** on the east coa_____highest tides.

a **MOUNTAIN CHALET** on the west coast with an everchanging panoramic view of the Pacific Ocean and mountain ranges.

a **PRARIE RANCH** near the Rocky Mountains foothills where you can watch the annual round-up and branding.

a **SPECIAL NEEDS HOME** designed and equipped to meet the needs of the disabled traveller, where there is a ramp and wheel-chair van for transportation. Hosts have information on accessible places to go.

a **HISTORIC FARM HOME**, on the former property of one of the Fathers of Confederation and the only farm to contain a village.

a **DOWNTOWN METROPOLITAN RESIDENCE** where they serve champagne in bed for breakfast and the *New York Times* along with it.

an **ORGAN HOME** where hosts will give guided tours of the on-site organery which consists of 98 antique reed organs. Guests are invited to view and play.

a **FLOATING HOME** on the west coast in a snug and cozy boat-house which rises and falls with the tides.

a **TYPICAL CANADIAN FARM** where guests are invited to help with chores and feed animals, and where the hosts serve huge homecooked meals from their own produce.

a **BOOK-LOVER'S HOME** with thousands of books in the parlour/library and in the spacious barn, including a large section for children.

a **CYCLIST'S HOME** where guest bicycles are available and where you may join hosts on guided cycling tours.

a **MODERN WEST COAST RESIDENTIAL HOME** with private beach and boat for charter.

a **HISTORIC RELIGIOUS HOME**, once a frequent stop by Brother André, the founder of the famed Oratory in Montreal. Guests may request to stay in the room where he slept.

a **SKATING HOME** where you can put on your skates inside the back door and walk over to the longest outdoor skating rink in the world.

an **EAST COAST FISHERMAN'S HOME**—a base for deep sea fishing, clam digging and enjoying lobster suppers. Guests may join the hosts with hauling in lobster traps and preparing fishing nets.

a **GOLFING HOME** situated on a regulation golf course overlooking the 10th fairway.

an **ISOLATED PRAIRIE FARM** where you can sit and relax in wide open spaces and tranquil surroundings and listen to the wheat grow.

a **CHURCH HOME** in a converted Catholic church with the living room in the former church hall, high ceilings, stained glass windows and unique atmosphere.

a **HIKER'S HOME** on the famous Bruce Trail where they may offer to move your car to the end of your hike or drop it off at some other B&B location along the hike.

a **NORTHERN HOME** where you may be served smoked salmon, moose sausage or sourdough pastries for breakfast

an **ISLAND HOME** accessible only by ferry. Spend a busy or quiet island day.

an **INDIAN HOME** owned by a family specializing in Indian lore. Guests may sleep in a teepee or a trapper's tent.

a **THEATRE HOME** around the corner from Shakespeare or Shaw Festival theatres where you can walk home after a late performance.

a **SKI HOME** at the base of a ski hill or close to major slopes and groomed trails. Sip hot cider by the fireplace after a day on the slopes.

an **AUTHENTIC NORWEGIAN LOG HOME** in nature's paradise, where alfresco dining on the beach and a singalong around the bonfire is a regualr event.

a **STATUTORY HOLIDAY HOME** where guests are welcome to enjoy a Victorian Christmas.

a **NATIVE HOME** on an Indian reserve, where one can experience Iroquois culture and a different historic theme in each guest room.

a **CABOOSE** of a converted railway car, where you can enjoy the view from the cupola and have breakfast in the hosts' home.

a **FRENCH-SPEAKING HOME** of a Quebec family. An ideal place to brush up on or to learn the language.

a **HEALTH HOME** where there is a health centre for total mind and body rejuvenation on the premises.

a **PARK HOME** situated at the gateway of a Canadian national park. An ideal place for hikers and nature lovers.

a **PIANIST'S HOME** where guests may enjoy an impromptu recital by the host.

an **EMBROIDERY HOME** where both hosts are cross-stitch enthusiasts and finished artwork is displayed throughout the house.

a **DOCKED SHIP** (former Coastguard icebreaker) with cabin bunks, ideally suited for families and guests who like to experience rustic accommodation.

a **PET'S HOME** where guest pets are welcome amd sleep in heated kennels.

a **MUSEUM HOME** where the host will be proud to show guests the on-site museum of early Canadian artifacts and tools.

a **WILDERNESS HOME** where guests are taken on trail rides, canoeing, kayaking and overnight trips into the mountains.

a **SEA HOME** where the fisherman-host can tell sea tales from his 30-year involvement in the local fishing industry.

a **QUILTER'S HOME** where you can take lessons and browse in the on-site quilt shop for fabrics and supplies.

a **BRIDGE PLAYER'S HOME** where the host is involved in the local duplicate bridge club and loves to play a hand with guests.

a **MILITARY HOME** where the host will offer professional expertise in the region's military history.

an **ARTIST'S HOME** where the resident host artist will give lessons and where guests can watch her work at her easel.

a **5TH GENERATION FARM HOME** in a pretty fishing village, where the hosts will tell ghost stories about the lighthouse on the property.

a **BOAT CHARTER HOME** where the host will take guests on his sailboat for whale-watching and sailing trips.

a **TEA ROOM HOME** where guests enjoy teas and clam chowder in the Victorian tea room located in the large pleasant sun porch.

The Canadian Bed & Breakfast Guide Gerda Pantel

Fourteenth Edition

Penguin Books

PENGUIN BOOKS
Published by the Penguin Group
Penguin Books Canada Ltd, 10 Alcorn Avenue, Toronto, Ontario, Canada M4V 3B2
Penguin Books Ltd, 27 Wrights Lne, London W8 5TZ, England
Penguin Books USA Inc., 375 Hudson Street, New York, New York, 10014, U.S.A.
Penguin Books Australia Ltd, Ringwood, Victoria, Australia
Penguin Books (NZ) Ltd, cnr Rosedale and Airborne Roads, Albany, Auckland 1310,
New Zealand

Penguin Books Ltd, Registered Offices: Harmondsworth, Middlesex, England

First published in Penguin Books, 1998

1 3 5 7 9 10 8 6 4 2

Acknowledgments
Waterford Manor, St John's, Newfoundland

Manufactured in Canada

Typesetting E. H. Pantel

14th edition

Canadian Cataloguing in Publication Data

The National Library of Canada has catalogued this publication as follows:

Pantel, Gerda
The Canadian bed and breakfast guide

Began with 1983 ed.
Irregular.
Issues for 1983-1984 have title: Canadian bed & breakfast guide
Description based on 3rd ed. (1987).
Includes some text in French.
ISSN 0836-5717
ISBN 0-14-027493-6 (14th ed.)

1. Bed and breakfast accommodations - Canada - Directories. I. Title.

TX910.C3P35   647'.9471   C88-039020-4

Visit Penguin Canada's web site at **www.penguin.ca**

To my parents,
the late Alfons Kemper and Hedy Kemper,
who brought their family to Canada,
but themselves never had an opportunity to discover
how beautiful this country really is.

Contents

What is Bed & Breakfast?

Bed & Breakfast is the next best thing to staying with relatives or friends!

Bed & Breakfast is a pleasant alternative to staying in a hotel rooom. In an age of expensive travelling, one can find comfortable and reasonable accommodation located in private homes across Canada. These homes offer a short-term stay for a paying guest in comfortable, cosy, friendly surroundings, close to travel routes and places of interest. And they offer a hearty breakfast!

Bed & Breakfast is geared to that certain type of traveller who is interested in getting to know people and places through personal contact. This all amounts to a unique change of pace and a more original way of travelling. It provides adventure and a relaxed atmosphere. Above all, it provides assistance and advice on a personal basis and an opportunity to make new and lasting friends.

In Canada, the Bed & Breakfast concept was pioneered by farmers and rural families offering their home atmosphere to city travellers for a rest and a change away from the rat race. Bed & Breakfast flourished in Montreal during Expo, and arose in Cape Breton Island around 1972. Over the years, the concept has grown immensely and become very popular. Today, there are Bed & Breakfast places in or near virtually every city and town from coast to coast. Bed & Breakfast is still growing rapidly in Canada. More and more people are taking advantage of this phenomenon, while others are being introduced to it by chance, and they love it.

Typical Bed & Breakfast hosts are people who are interested in sharing their genuine hospitality in a family atmosphere, and at the same time enriching their own lives through cultural exchange and friendship. Most B&Bs are hospitality oriented, not purely service oriented like a hotel. The hosts' main concern, above all, is to make guests feel welcome and comfortable and to help them have a wonderful holiday. Many hosts give a complimentary snack and coffee or tea upon arrival or in the evenings. Their homes are neat, clean and cosy, but not necessarily luxurious. Places to stay range widely, from a modest fisherman's cottage to a metropolitan apartment suite, from a historic rural mansion to a contemporary residence in suburbia, from a prairie ranch to a cosy mountain chalet.

New Bed & Breakfast homes are opening every year – you can even find B&B homes that have been bought or built especially for that purpose. And because some of these B&B's are run in the style of a hotel or inn, the hosts have completely separate quarters. These homes are usually decorated beautifully and furnished especially for guests. Breakfast may be served in a special guest breakfast room. These B&B's usually have more than 3 rooms for guests. These hosts are also very interested in their guests and certainly will give them as much attention as they can. However, in these larger B&B's, guests socialize mostly with each other, and less with the hosts.

Several attempts to establish a B&B Grading System have been made with criteria similar to that used in the hotel industry. This is a very difficult thing to do, as each B&B is so unique and cannot be "compared" with another. Some provinces have awarded "stars" to those B&B's who have chosen to join their grading system. Many B&B's however, cannot afford the extra cost involved. At this time, *The Canadian Bed & Breakfast Guide* does not indicate any "grade star" awards until a National criterion suitable for B&B accomodation is established and accepted from coast to coast.

Many B&B's are members of a local Bed & Breakfast organization or agency or may be affiliated with the local Chamber of Commerce or Provincial Department of Tourism. These organizations establish guidelines and standards for B&Bs, and also provide a referral system within the local area for guests who need a room.

About The Canadian Bed & Breakfast Guide

The *Canadian Bed & Breakfast Guide* has been compiled for quick and easy reference for use with official Standard Canadian Road Maps. These maps are available FREE from Tourist Departments in each province, or from the Canadian Government Office of Tourism in Ottawa.

Visitors to Canada will find that mileage shown on road-signs and on Canadian maps is in kilometres (1 km = 0.6 mile). Distances to each individual B&B home are shown in approximate kilometres in *The Canadian Bed & Breakfast Guide*.

Most B&B homes *operate year-round*, but some homes do not offer B&B during every month of the year. Seasonal availability is listed.

Guests are responsible for contacting individual hosts or agencies – the author does *not* arrange for reservations. Most hosts would appreciate advance notice. It is suggested that *guests contact the hosts ahead of time*, either by letter or phone. When enroute, travellers should stop early in the afternoon and decide how far they will travel that day, choose a B&B from the *Guide* and phone ahead. Hosts will appreciate the consideration and if they are booked for the night, they may refer the traveller to another B&B in the vicinity.

E-mail addresses are shown when they have been given to the author.

Arrival and departure times vary & should be arranged by the guests/hosts at first contact.

Many of the homes have been visited by the author on her personal travels from coast to coast. However, listings should not be taken as a recommendation. All the information in *The Canadian Bed & Breakfast Guide* was supplied by hosts in response to a questionnaire, and has been transcribed as accurately as possible. All the hosts have provided essential information about their home, but some have provided more description than others.

Rates are shown in Canadian currency. These rates are set by the individual hosts or local B&B organization, and are subject to change from year to year. The rates shown in this edition were supplied in the fall of 1996. There may be a small variance in the rate, as it is difficult for the hosts to anticipate changes in the next season.

When a reservation is made well in advance, a *deposit* for one night is usually expected. Host will generally refund the deposit if a cancellation is necessary and is made at least 48 hours in advance.

A *tax charge* may be added to the room rate according to local, provincial or federal regulations, but this varies with hosts and with areas. Some hosts are required to collect taxes, but this is shown in their listing only if the hosts have notified the author.

It is appreciated if parents bring sleeping bags as bedding for small children. When hosts have provided information about the *pets they keep in the house*, it has been indicated in this publication. If allergies are a concern, travellers should check beforehand when they make their reservation. Some *rooms may be in the basement* of the house. These are shown in the listing as "lower level, below ground or ground level". This should be clarified by asking about the layout of the house. *Accessibility* is indicated where applicable.

The *photos* included in *The Canadian Bed & Breakfast Guide* were supplied by the hosts and should only be regarded as a quick reference, since a black & white reproduction of an exterior photo cannot reveal a B&B's beautiful interior and ambience.

Maps shown for each province are not to scale. They are meant to be used for quick reference and show only relative locations that feature B&B's listed here.

If there is no listing in a place of your choice, write or drop in to the local Chamber of Commerce office or the local Tourist Bureau and inquire about any B&B's in that area.

The *Guide* is updated and revised regularly. Many entries could not be included in this edition due to limitations of space and late questionnaire returns.

The author would like to hear about travel experiences with *The Canadian Bed & Breakfast Guide*, as well as any suggestions that might make the *Guide* more useful.

How to use The Canadian Bed & Breakfast Guide

1) Refer to the Official Standard Canadian Road Map of the province you are visiting for the route you plan to take.

2) Determine where you would like to stay in a Bed & Breakfast or, decide how many kilometers or miles you want to travel on a specific day and then choose a B&B in the place or area.

3) Consult the indiviual maps shown at the beginning of each Province for locations listed in this edition of The *Guide*.

4) Look for your chosen location in *The Canadian Bed & Breakfast Guide*, referring to the PROVINCE ON THE BOTTOM of each page.. All locations are listed in alphabetical order within each province. This eliminates the need of an index. Nearby larger places are shown in brackets throughout the *Guide* for each listing.

   If your chosen B&B is booked and you need somewhere else to stay in that immediate or general geographic area, follow the "see also" reference to other choices listed in this edition of the *Guide*. "See also" is listed under most locations. For example: Hamilton (south-west of Toronto; see also Burlington, Dundas, Ancaster....)

5) If there is no reference to a town you are looking for, consult your Provincial map again and look for a nearest larger community. Once you've found it in the book, use the "see also" reference as a guide to a place nearby. It could be that a small change in your route will find you other accommodations and perhaps a look at an interesting part of the country you had not thought of visiting.

6) Refer to the handy key on the front flap for interpretation of signs and symbols in each individual listing, and use the key for a handy bookmark.

7) Where available, use the toll-free number for reserving B&B accommodation.

If you would like to be included in the next edition of *The Canadian Bed & Breakfast Guide*, please write for a Questionnaire to:

Gerda Pantel, 270 Juniper Ave., Burlington, ON L7L 2T3
Phone (905) 632-1996   Fax (905) 632-7686

Please submit cancellations, corrections or new entries
before Dec. 1, 1999

Find out more about Bed & Breakfast - send for the booklet:
"ALL ABOUT BED & BREKAFAST - Questions & Answers" 2nd ed.
by Gerda Pantel

This booklet will help you decide if B&B travelling or B&B hosting is for you. It is the result of collecting many inquiries each year, while preparing and updating the Canadian Bed & Breakfast Guide. Gerda answers questions about travelling the B&B route and about being a B&B host.
Please send cheque (or Int.money order) for Can.$7.00 to
Gerda Pantel, 270 Juniper Ave., Burlington, ON L7L 2T3
(not available from Penguin Books or in book stores)

British Columbia

(including Queen Charlotte Islands)

Tourism British Columbia   1-800-663-6000
1117 Wharf St., Victoria, BC   V8W 2Z2
Travel Information Center
562 Burard St., Vancouver, BC   V6C 2J6   (604) 683-2000

For ferry crossing schedules and information to Vancouver Island, Gulf
Islands and Queen Charlotte Islands contact:
B.C. Ferries Corporation
818 Broughton St., Victoria, BC   V8W 1E4   (250) 669-1211

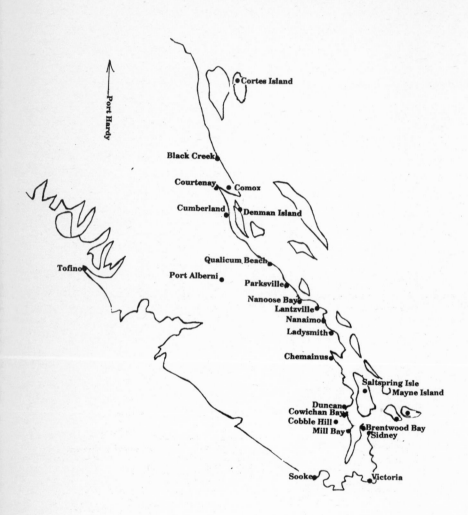

Port Hardy

Cortes Island

Black Creek

Courtenay • Comox

Cumberland • Denman Island

Qualicum Beach
Port Alberni •
Parksville
Tofino •
Nanoose Bay
Lantzville
Nanaimo
Ladysmith

Chemainus

Saltspring Isle
Mayne Island

Duncan
Cowichan Bay
Cobble Hill
Mill Bay
Brentwood Bay
Sidney

Sooke • Victoria

B.C Mainland

Smithers
Prince Rupert
Burns Lake
Francois Lake
Prince George

Valemount

Williams Lake

LacLaHache
Clearwater
Golden

Sorrento
Revelstoke
Parson

Sicamous
Invermere
Windermere

Kamloops
Mara
Fairmont

Pritchard
Nakusp

Salmon Arm
Cherryville

Powell River
Vernon

Merritt
Oyama
Lumby

Sechelt
Kelowna
Winfield
Kaslo
Kimberley

Roberts Creek
Whistler
Crawford
Fort-Steele

Gibsons
Brackendale
Summerland
Winlaw
Cranbrook

Penticton
Procter
Fernie

Vancouver
Nelson

New Westminster
Surrey
Kaledon
Castlegar
Jaffray

Richmond
Oliver
Creston

Delta
Osoyoos
Greenwood
Christina I.

Mission
Abbotsford
Langley
White Rock
Tsawwassen

Abbotsford
(east of Vancouver; see also White Rock, Langley, Mission)

Lutz, Brad & Wendy (Blackberry Brambles B&B)   ☎ (604) 855-1702
3433 Juniper Cr., Abbotsford, BC   V2S 7R1

From Hwy 1 take Exit 92 and follow signs toward Mission. Turn right at Hazelwood Ave, left at Juniper and proceed to end.
$45S $60D $15Add.person   ⬛ Meals   ▶ 9
🍴 Full, homebaked   🏠 Res., view, deck, quiet   ■ 1D,1F (main & ground floor)   ⊨ 1S,1D,1Q,futon for larger groups, crib
🛏1Private, 1sh.w.h.   ★ KF,LF,F,TV, ceiling fans, wheel-chair access, off-street parking   🚫 No smoking
🏃 Shops, restaurants, city bus, playpark in middle of crescent

☛ Modest home backing onto Greenbelt (blackberry bramble and blueberry field) with a view of the majestic Lion Mountain Range. Relax on the shady deck. There are pre-school children in the host family. Enjoy a hearty breakfast before a busy day of sightseeing or travelling. Visa ⌇B&B

Black Creek
(on Van.Isle; south of Campbell R.;see also Courtenay,Comox,Cumberland)

Bohn, Elaine and Ron (Country Comfort)   ☎ (250) 337-5273
8214 Island Hwy, Black Creek, BC   V9J 1H6

Located midway between Courtenay & Campbell River on Hwy 19. and 1 block south of Black Creek Country Market.
$55S $60D (Family & extended stay rates available)   ▶ 6
🍴 Full, homebaked   🏠 Rural, split-level home, sunroom   ■3D
⊨2D,1Q   🛏1Sh.w.g.   ★ TV,VCR,F,LF, freezer for fish
🚫Restricted smoking, no pets
🏃 Country market, coffee shop, gift & candy shop, bus stop, video rental, ski bus at door

🚗 Prov.parks & beaches, excellent hiking, golfing, stock-car racing, churches, trail riding, fishing, restaurants, skiing, scenic island drives
☛ Self-designed home with tasteful handcrafted decor, nestled among a variety of trees/gardens on 50 acre hobby farm. Hosts have welcomed B&B guest for over 10 years. Guest are invited to browse in the gift shop on site. ⌇CC

Brackendale
(north of Vancouver; see also Whistler)

Vanderhoef, Sue & Marty (Glacier Valley Farm)   ☎ (604) 898-2810, Fax (604) 898-2844
Mile 16.5 Upper Squamish Valley Rd., Box30, Brackendale, BC   V0N 1H0   Cell (604) 892-7533

Phone for directions.
$60-70S $75-90D $15 Add.person   ⬛ Meals   ▶ 6-8
🍴 Full (farm-style)   🏠 Working farm, quiet, glacier-views from guest rooms   ■ 3(upstairs)   ⊨2D,4T,1Q,cots   🛏1Sh.w.g.   ★ F
🏃 Hiking trails, bird watching, fly fishing, river rafting, creek fishing
🚗 Squamish, shops, pubs, restaurants, buses, trains
☛ Large, rambling wooden farm house on working farm with sheep, horses & farm animals, located in a very private and scenic valley, surrounded by snow-capped mountains, waterfalls & green hillsides. Relax in the cozy guest sitting nook. A perfect place to unwind. Visa,MC

Brentwood Bay

(Victoria; see also Sidney)

Cooper, Gwen & Tom (The Shires B&B)　　　　　☎ (250) 652-1421
6924 Wallace Dr., Brentwood Bay, BC   V8M 1G3

From Swartz Bay Ferry Terminal follow signs for Butchart
Gardens & onto Wallace Dr (app.30km)
$50S $60D $10Child $95F $15Add.person　　　　▶ 4
🍴Full,homebaked 🏠Res.,bungalow,patio,deck,quiet ▦1Ste(2D)
(lower level walk-in) ⊨2S,2D(P) ⊟1Sh.w.g. ★F,LF,TV,
off-street parking, private entrance, wood burning stove
🖐Designated smoking area, no pets, children min. age 6
🚗 Butchart Gardens, Butterfly World, downtown Victoria

🚶 Restaurants and marina facilities, bus stop at doorstep (for Victoria & Sidney)
📣 Warm and friendly welcome and the finest English hospitality in comfortable home. Relax in
the sunroom or on the deck overlooking the garden with many flowers & fruit trees. Breakfast is
served in the sunroom. 2-nights minimum. ✒B&B

Robinson, Faye & George (Garden Cottage B&B)　　　　☎ (250) 652-0392
1031 Parkway Dr., Brentwood Bay, BC   V8M 1C8

$55S $65D $15child (over age 5)　$75-95F　$15Add.person　　　▶ 6
From Victoria travel north on Hwy 17 to Keating Rd & follow signs to Butchart Gardens. Turn
north on West Saanich Rd to Brentwood Bay village. Turn left at Clarke Rd, left again on Lucille &

right on Parkway Dr.
🌞 Summer only 🍴 Cont., homebaked 🏠Rural, village, view,
patio,deck,quiet,secluded ▦Detached studio cottage ⊨D,Q,R
⊟Ensuite ★ TV(upon request in cottage), separate entrance,
room air-conditioner 🖐Designated smoking area, no pets
〰some French
🚶 Butchart & Butterfly Gardens, beach, waterfront restaurant
(overlooking Brentwood Bay), shopping, hiking trails, bus No75)

🚗 Airport, ferries, downtown Victoria, Royal BC Museum, Empress Hotel, Whale Watching
Charters, sailboat & kayak rentals
📣 Sunny, cozy guest cottage nestled amongst trees & flowers in secluded private back garden
(completely fenced in & safe for children). Young host family has 6-year old twins. Breakfast is
served in the studio or on the mountain-view sundeck. There are 3 beautiful cats. ✒B&B

Burns Lake

(west of Prince George; see also Francois Lake, Smithers)

Davidson, Sharon & Bill (Davidson's Tchesinkut Lake B&B)　　☎ (250) 695-6434
Box 1306, Burns Lake, BC   V0J 1E0

Located 16km south of Burns Lake on East Tchesinkut Lake Rd. From Prince George, take Hwy 16
west, turn south on Hwy 35 at Burns Lake. Watch for B&B signs.
$50S $60D $10Add.person　　　　　　　　▶ 7
🍴 Full, homebaked 🏠 Rural, 2-storey, lakefront, deck, quiet
▦ 3D main & lower level ⊨ 1S,1D,2Q ⊟1sh.w.g.,1ensuite
★F,LF,TV in guest sitting room, separate entrance, guest
quarters are separate 🖐 No smoking
🚶 Great walking area, x-c skiing from house, level lake access
with dock and decks
🚗 Omineca x-c ski trails, Eagle Creek Opal Beds, fishing lakes
📣 Warm welcome in newly renovated cozy lakeshore home with quiet, peaceful atmosphere.
There is an outside dog. Families welcome. Visa ✒CC

Castlegar   *(east of Penticton; see also Christina L., Greenwood, Nelson, Winlaw)*

Mason, John & Carolynne (Hope's End Plantation B&B)   ☎ (250) 365-3206
887 Waterloo Rd., RR1,S4,C25, Castlegar, BC   V1N 3H7

Take Hwy 3 towards Salmo proceeding past Weigh Scales. Turn right at West Arm Trucking, right again at Waterloo Rd, then left at bottom of steep hill and watch for B&B sign.

$50S $65D $15Child $85F   ▶ 6+
🍳 Full, homebaked   🏠 Res., 2-storey, view from guest rooms, acreage, riverfront, patio, deck, quiet, secluded   ■ 3(upstairs)
⊨ 2T,1D,1Q,crib, futon   🛏 1Sh.w.g.   ★ F,TV in one guest room, ceiling fans, guest balcony, off-street parking
👑Designated smoking area, pets outside only
🏃 Cycling/hiking, Columbia R. fishing, country restaurant
🚗 Dukhobor hist.village, golfing, marinas, excellent powder skiing at Red Mountain & White Water Ski Resorts, guided Fishing Tours to Arrow Lakes, airport
🐾 Antebellum-style home, tastefully decorated to evoke an English Cottage atmosphere. Located in a small peaceful valley on Columbia River's east bank in the heart of the Kootenays. Wake up to the song of the Meadow Lark, then savour a gourmet breakfast in a romantic garden setting, on the balcony or in bed. Free pick-up/drop-off at Castlegar Airport. There is a dog outside. ✓CC

Miller, Linda & Rick (Robson Homestead Bed & Breakfast)   ☎ & Fax (250) 365-2374
3671 Broadwater Rd., RR3,S4,C23, Castlegar (Robson), BC   V1N 4H9

From Hwy 3A take Robson Access Rd, turn right towards Syringa Prov.Park and drive 4.8km. Or go north through Castlegar, take Robson/Castlegar Bridge, turn left into Robson and follow Broadwater Rd for 4.8km

$45S $55D $10Add.person   🍽 Meals (plus tax)   ▶ 3A,2Ch
🍳 Full, homebaked   🏠 Rural, 3-storey, hist., acreage, porch
■ 1D,1F (upstairs)   ⊨ 2D,1S   🛏 1Sh.w.g.   ★ Air,F,LF,TV
♥   👑 Smoking outside only, no pets   〰 French
🏃 Columbia River, hiking, cycling
🚗 Zuckerberg Island Heritage Park, Hugh Keenleyside Dam, airport, Doukhobor Museum, Arrow Lakes, golfing, marinas, City of Castlegar, excellent downhill & x-c skiing, horseback riding
🐾 Restored 1909-built home situated on 3 acres in the beautiful scenic West Kootenays. Relax in the antique furnished rooms or on the porch and try the special blend of Kootenay coffee. Special diets on request. "Randy" and "Sheeba", the resident dogs, love to greet guests. There are horses & goats on the property. Children welcome. Airport pick-up available. ✓CC

Chemainus   *(on Vanc.Isle, south of Nanaimo; see also Saltsprings Isle, Ladysmith, Duncan)*

Plater, Jane & Roy (Terrace Gardens Guest House)   ☎ (250) 246-2815
3114 Sunset Dr., RR1, Chemainus, BC   V0R 1K0

$50S $55-65D $10Child(under age 13)   (2nd night 25% discount)   ▶ 4
Phone for directions.

🍳 Full, homebaked   🏠 Village, 2-storey, view from guest rooms, deck, quiet   ■1D,1F (ground level)   ⊨1D,1Q   🛏1Private
★F,separate entrance, private hot tub(spa)   👑One party only, children & pets welcome, designated smoking area   〰some Russian
🏃 Downtown Chemainus and 33 world famous murals
🚗 Nanaimo, ferries to Thetis/Gabriola/Saltspring Isls, Victoria
🐾 Spacious, beautiful home in "a hollow on a hill" overlooking Georgia Strait & mainland mountains. Breakfast is served in the dining room or adjacent upper deck. Relax in the hot tub and watch the moon rise over the water and the lights of Vancouvers' ski lifts in the background. Well travelled hosts enjoy music, theatre, books, golfing. ✓CC

Stegemann, John and Christa (Sea Breeze)   ☎ & Fax (250) 246-4593
2912 Esplanade, Box 1362, Chemainus, BC   V0R 1K0

Phone for direction.
$45S $55D $15Add.person   ► 6A,3Ch
🍲 Full, homebaked   ♥   🏠 Res., village, hist., patio, oceanfront,
old-fashioned porches, views from guest rooms   ■D,Ste (main and
upper floor)   ⊨3Q,2R   ⬙1Private, 2sh.w.g.   ★TV ᴡᴡGerman
🏃 Waterfront,boating, swimming, fishing (fresh and salt water),
downtown Chemainus ("the little town that did" with murals
portraying the history of the area, antique stores, art galleries
🚗 Duncan (City of Totems), Nanaimo (famous bath-tub races)
🐾 Spacious, turn-of-the Century home restored to its old splendor, yet with modern comfort, is
located just steps from the beach and boat-ramp. Enjoy beautiful views, watch sails & seals from
the veranda or from the guest rooms. There is 1 resident cat. ⮑CC

Cherryville   *(east of Vernon)*

DeVries, Dave & Jill (Cherry Ridge Crafts & B&B)   ☎ (250) 547-2257, (250) 547-8919
648 North Fork Rd., RR1, Cherryville, BC   V0E 2G0

Located 59km east of Vernon. From Hwy 6 turn onto North Fork Rd and go 6km to B&B on right.

$45S $55D $15Add.person   ► 6
🍲 Full, homebaked   🏠 Rural, ranch-style, acreage, view from
guest rooms, porch, deck, quiet, isolated   ■ 2F (main level)
⊨2S,2Q   ⬙ 1Private, 1ensuite   ★TV,LF, tea/coffee making
in room, parking   🖐 No smoking, no pets   ᴡᴡ Dutch
🏃 "Quilt & Craft" store on property, 10 acres of forest with deer
🚗 Vernon, Arrow Lakes, golfing, gold panning, fishing, Silver
Star Ski Resort, Monashee Wilderness Park
🐾 Semi-retired congenial couple in bright, new home with 1907 working wood cook-stove in
kitchen and Pellet Stove in living room, situated in mountain-view forest at the foothills of the
Monashee Mountains. Great birding area. Hostess is a quilter and host makes rustic twig furniture
(both give classes). Browse in the quilt shop on property and watch hostess demonstrate or work
with beautiful fabrics. Enjoy the Monashee calling - a wilderness experience with luxury too. ⮑CC

Christina Lake   *(east of Grand Forks; see also Greenwood, Castlegar)*

Albright, Patricia (Royal Inn B&B)   ☎ (250) 447-9090
1 Chase Rd, Box 262, Christina Lake, BC   V0H 1E0

Located 5 blocks from Hwy 3 in the village townsite.

$50S $75D $10Add.person   ► 4
❇ May-Oct.   🍲 Cont., homebaked   🏠 Village, bungalow, view
from guest rooms, deck, quiet, secluded   ■ 1F(ground level)
⊨1D,1P   ⬙ 1Ensuite   ★ TV in guest room, fridge,
microwave, coffee maker, separate entrance, off-street parking,
private covered deck   🖐Designated smoking area
🏃 Warm tree-lined lake, public beach
🚗 Golf Courses, marina, kayak/canoe/bike rentals
🐾 Spacious, luxurious guest accommodation. Hostess is a Certified TFH Practitioner/Instr. and
operates The Royal Health Therapies Clinic on site. There are 2 cats and a dog. Visa,MC ⮑B&B

Clearwater

Fischer, Joe & Monika (Trophy Mountain Buffalo Ranch B&B)   ☎ (250) 674-3095,
Box 1768, RR1, Clearwater, BC   V0E 1N0   Fax (250) 674-3131

In Clearwater, turn at the Tourist Info Centre and proceed 20 km up Wells Gray Pk Rd.
$35-55S $50-60D $15-25Add.person   (plus taxes)   (packed lunches)   ▶ 13

🐄 Full, homebaked   🏠 Farm, log house, view, quiet, 70 acres
■ 8D (main & upper level)   ⊨ 3S,2D,3Q   🚗 2Private,
4ensuite   ★Air,F,LF, horse/bike/canoe rental, sep.entrance
🖐Smoking outside, pets outside   ∾ German
🏃 Horseback riding, hiking and x/c ski trails, mountain biking
🚌 Wells Gray Provincial Park, Trophy Mountain hiking area,
Helmcken Falls, canoeing, river rafting, skiing, Clearwater
🐾 Hobby bison/horse farm with old log house built in 1926,
completely restored for B&B. Hosts are outdoor adventure guides and well informed about the area
and its manyexcellent outdoor activities. Visa,MC ✓CC

Kintzinger, Henry and Erika (Omas Bed & Breakfast)   ☎ (250) 674-3467
229 Schmidt Rd, Box 4074, RR2, Clearwater, BC   V0E 1N0

On Hwy 5 (Yellowhead) West 310 km from Jasper. From Vancouver take the Coquihalla Toll Hwy
East. From Kamloops take Hwy 5 North. Located in Clearwater off the old North Thompson Hwy.

$35S $45-50D $20 Deposit   ▶ 6A,2Ch
🐄Full,homebaked   🏠Rural,acreage,quiet,large sundeck,heated
swimming pool ■3D(main & upper level)   ⊨6T   🚗1Private,
1sh.w.g ★TV,F,LF ♥ 🖐Restricted smoking ∾German
🏃 Walks in woods or x-country skiing, Clearwater Shopping
center, Dutch Lake, canoeing
🚌 Wells Gray Wilderness Park, Trophy Mountains, Alpine Area,
downhill skiing, Spahats Falls
🐾 Old fashioned hospitality in new house set in a quiet wooded area close to the famous Wells
Gray Park. Ideal stop between Edmonton, Jasper and Vancouver. Well travelled hosts are
knowledgeable about the area and have been welcoming B&B guests since 1986. Pick-up from bus
and train station. (Children's rate available) ✓CC

Pirart, Chris & Jim (Wooly Acres Bed & Breakfast)   ☎ (250) 674-3508, Fax (250) 674-2316
Box 1739, RR1, Clearwater, BC   V0E 1N0

From Vancouver follow Coquihalla Toll Hwy east. From Kamloops take Hwy 5 east and Clearwater
Valley Rd north to Greer Rd. Turn right and right again on Bo Hill. Located at 1030 Bo Hill Place.
$40S $50-65D $10Child(under age 12) $15Add.person   ▶ 6A,4Ch

🐄 Full, homebaked   🏠 Farm, rural, 3-storey, view, quiet
■3(upstairs)   ⊨2T,2Q,1D,playpen   🚗1sh.w.g.,1ensuite
★F(gas)in guest sitting room with a beautiful view, high-chair,
large parking area   🖐 No pets, smoking outside
🏃 Walks in countryside, pet sheep, enjoy flower gardens
🚌 Spectacular water falls in beautiful Wells Gray Park, tennis,
golfing, hiking, canoeing, horseback riding, whitewater rafting,
downhill & c-x skiing, snowmobiling, ice-fishing, wildlife viewing
🐾 Country comfort in new home with large yard/gardens surrounded by 20 acres of wooded
farmland. The sheep have names; "ask for an introduction". Watch for hummingbirds at feeders
and enjoy the peace & quiet of the serene country farm atmosphere. A convenient stop between
Vancouver - Jasper - Edmonton. There are 2 cats & 2 dogs (but not in guest quarters). ✓CC

Cobble Hill
(south of Duncan; see also Cowichan Bay, Mill Bay)

Simpson, Vicki & Gordon (Heron Hill Bed & Breakfast)　　　☎ (250)743-3855,
3760 Granfield Place, RR2, Cobble Hill, BC　V0R 1L0　　　　　Fax (250)743-5821

From Hwy 1, north of Mill Bay, turn east on Hutchinson Rd
towards Arbutus Ridge. Turn left onto Telegraph, then right onto
Aros to Granfield.
$55S　$65-75D　$15Add.person　　　　　　　► 6-8
🍴Full 🏠Rural, 2-storey, deck, view, quiet ■3D ⊨2T,1D,1Q,1R
🚪3Ensuite ★Fridge/microwave in guest sitting room, separate
entrance to one room Ⓦ No smoking, no pets
🚶 Access to rocky beach, country roads
🚗 Arbutus Ridge Golf course, Shawnigan Lake, Cowichan Bay, Mill Bay Centre shopping, Duncan
Native Heritage Ctr, Chemainus Murals, Nanaimo, Victoria
☛ Relax with a sea view of Gulf Islands and Mt. Baker. Hosts have been welcoming B&B guests
for many years and assure a friendly approach and easy-going service. Enjoy the rural atmosphere
with good access to shops and attractions. Home of the world famous "Cobble Cake". ✔B&B

Vermegen, Ingrid & Simon (Cobble House B&B)　　　☎ & Fax (250) 743-2672
3105 Cameron-Taggart Rd., RR1, Cobble Hill, BC　V0R 1L0　　E-mail: vermeges@brentwood.bc.ca

Located south of Duncan, west off Trans Canada Hwy. Phone for direction.

$55-65S　$74-84D　$20Add.person　　　　　　► 6A,2Ch
🍴Full, homebaked 🏠Rural, one-level, acreage, deck, quiet
■3D,guest quarters are separate ⊨2T,2Q,1P(futon)
🚪Private ★TV,LF, guest bicycles, parking Ⓦ No smoking,
not suitable for small children ⌇ Dutch, some German
🚶 Walk/cycle in 38.5 forested acres in rural areas or along creek
🚗 Shawnigan Lake, Cowichan Bay, Duncan (city of Totems)
Chemainus (city of Murals), wineries, golf courses, Victoria
☛ B&B specifically designed & built by long time experienced hosts. Enjoy the cozy home, and
rural atmosphere. Special weekend packages available with Saturday dinner prepared by Simon,
former Exec Chef of Vancouver TCC. There are 2 dogs in residence. ✔B&B

Comox　*(on Vancouver Isle east of Courtenay; see also Cumberland, Black Creek, Denman Isle)*

Hendren, Dove & Michael (Foskett House Bed & Breakfast)　　☎ & Fax (250) 339-4272
484 Lazo Rd., Comox, BC　V9M 3V1　　　　　　E-mail: foskett@island.net

Located 5.2 km from Comox. Follow boat launching signs on Lazo Rd. Turn left at green gate.
$65-75S　$80-90D　$15Add.person　(reservation recommended)　　► 5
🍴 Full, homebaked 🏠 Rural, ranch-style, hist., acreage, view
from guest room, oceanfront at end of driveway, deck, veranda,
quiet, secluded ■2D (main level) ⊨2Q,1P 🚪 Ensuite
★TV,F, separate entrance Ⓦ Designated smoking area
🚶 Surrounding forest, boat launch, birdwatching, beachcombing
🚗 Skiing/hiking (Mt.Washington & Forbidden Plateau), fishing,
ferry to Powell River
☛ 1920-built South African-style rancher with wrap around
verandas, finished inside with cedar and a large beach stone fireplace in the great room, filled with
collectibles and antiques, and a view of the Straits of Georgia. Located on 5 acres of forest in the
Point Holmes area, retired hosts returned to the Comox Valley after years of city life in politics and
Industry. Ideal spot for painters & photographers. There is a dog and a cat in residence. Golf &
Heritage Tourism packages available. Visa,MC ✔B&B

Robb, Shirley & Alan (Levenvale B&B)   ☎ (250) 339-3307, Fax (250) 339-4036
2081 Murphy Ave, Comox BC   V9M 1V4

Enter Comox, turn right on Rodello just past Hospital. Look for 3rd street towards water.
$40S $55D $5-10Child   ► 4
🍴 Full(Gourmet)   🏠 Res, split-level, view, patio, very quiet   ■ 2D (main & ground level)
⊨2T(K),1Q,1P   ⊡2private   ★ F,LF, separate entrance, TV in suite sitting room, off-street
parking   Ⓦ Designated smoking area
🏃 Hospital, restaurants/pubs, marina/beach, shops, Filberg Lodge
🚐 Campbell River
🔫 Well travelled hosts in central home overlooking Comox Bay, furnished with interesting
memorabilia/antiques. Enjoy the lovely garden & pond. Gourmet breakfast served with a flair on
deck or in the formal dining room both with a glorious view of ocean, mountains & marina. ⌐B&B

Cortes Island   *(near Campbell River)*

Hansen, Emilia & Gunnar (Blue Heron Bed & Breakfast)   ☎ (250) 935-6584
Potlatch Rd., Box 23, Manson's Landing., Cortes Island, BC   V0P 1K0

Take ferry from Campbell River (Vancouver Island) to Quadra Island. Drive to Heriot Bay and take
ferry to Cortes Island (45min). (20km from Whaletown Ferry Ldg near Smelt Bay Prov.Park).
$40-60S $45-70D $15Add.person   ► 4A,2Ch

🍴 Full, homebaked   🏠 Rural, res., ranch-style, acreage, view
from one guest room, oceanfront, patio, quiet   ■ 1D,1F (main
level)   ⊨ 2T,1K,2R   ⊡ 1Sh.w.h., 1ensuite   ★ TV, separate
entrance, parking   ⓌNo pets, restricted smoking   〰 Danish
🏃 Beach and tide pools
🔫 Spacious country home situated in garden setting on Potlatch
Rd. overlooking Sutil Channel toward Vancouver Island. Relax and
enjoy the special sunsets. There are pets. ⌐B&B

Courtenay   *(on Van.Isle; south of Campbell R.; see also Black Creek, Comox, Cumberland)*

Shipton, Mike & Mo (Greystone Manor)   ☎ (250) 338-1422
4014 Haas Rd., RR6, Site 684, C2, Courtenay, BC   V9N 8H9

Located 3km south of Courtenay in Royston.Right on Hilton, left on Haas Rd
$55S $75-80D $20Add. person   ► 8A
🍴 Full, homebaked   🏠 Rural, older, view, waterfront, 1.5 acres, beautiful
flower gardens ■3D)upstairs)   ⊨1D,2T,1Q   ⊡ 2Ensuite, 1private   ⓌNo
smoking,no pets,child min age 12   ★Guest sitting room & open fire.
🏃 Walking trails, rural setting, beach
🚐 Hiking, Denman/Hornby Islands, x/c & downhill skiing, ferry to Powell
River & Sunshine Coast
🔫 Warm welcome in charming 1918-built waterfront home, with
breathtaking views across Comox Bay to the coastal mountains. Hosts came
from England in 1990 and have brought with them their love of gardening
and created an outstandingly beautiful English Flower Garden, which is a photographer &
Gardener's delight. Visa,MC ⌐B&B

Cowichan Bay
(north of Victoria; see also Cobble Hill, Duncan)

MacFarlane, Barbara & George (Old Farm B&B)   ☎ & Fax (250)748-6410, 1-888-240-1482
2075 Cowichan Bay Rd., Cowichan Bay, BC   V0R 1N0

From Victoria on Hwy 1 go 50km north to Cowichan Bay Rd. Turn right 4km through the seaside village of Cowichan Bay and another 1km to Old Farm B&B on right.

$65-110S $75-120D $20Add.person   ► 11
🍴 Full, homebaked   🏠 Rural, hist., 3-storey, acreage, view from guest rooms, waterfront, quiet ■4F(upstairs) ⊨2T,4Q,2R,1P ⊨4Ensuite   ★ 2F/TV/KF in one suite, guest lounge & reading room, host quarters are separate, gas barbeque, gazebo, dock ⓌSmoking outdoors,no pets,child min.age10 ～min.French
🕴 Quaint seaside village (boutiques, marine facilities & excellent seafood restaurants), secluded dock (tidal water) on property
🚗 Victoria, Duncan, Chemainus, Forest Museum, Indian Cultural Center, totem poles
🐾 Large restored family home built by well-known architect Samuel Maclure, ca1908 surrounded by fruit trees and berry bushes for picking. House specialty is gourmet breakfast served in special guest breakfast area, as well as coffee/tea delivered to the rooms before breakfast. There is a dog and a cat (not in guest areas).Visa,MC ⌐B&B

Cranbrook
(south-east BC; see also Kimberley, Ft.Steele, Jaffray, Fernie)

Johnston, Anita (Anita's Old Fashioned B&B)   ☎ (250) 426-7993, Fax (250) 426-7965
110-12th Ave South, Cranbrook, BC   V1C 2S1   1-888-452-2221

From Hwy 3/95 proceed to downtown area. Turn left at 1st St South, then right onto 12th Ave S.

$60-70S $70-80D $10Child/Add.person 🍴Meals   ► 6A,2Ch
🍴 Full, homebaked   🏠 Res, hist., patio, porch, quiet ■2D,1F (upstairs) ⊨ 2D,1Q,1P(T) ⊨ 3Ensuite   ★ TV,bar fridge, microwave, coffee/tea pots in each room, off-street/street parking ♥   Ⓦ Smoking outside, no pets, children min.age 5
🕴 Baker Hill Historic neighbourhood, Canadian Museum of Rail Travel, shops, theatres, restaurants
🚗 Fort Steele Heritage Town, Wasa Lake, Trout Hatchery, Cranbrook Heritage Tour, golfing, trail rides, boating, skiing
🐾 Uniquely renovated heritage-style home located in a quiet neighbourhood of "sunny" little town (more sunshine than any other city in BC). Energetic hostess and young daughter provide friendly hospitality. Breakfast is served in the "one-of-a-kind" dining room or on the sundeck. Relax in the front parlour with eclectic library. Honeymoon and special occasion packages available. School-age children welcome. There are cats in residence and a dog outside. Visa,MC ⌐B&B

Murray, Gloria (Cranberry House Bed & Breakfast)   ☎ & Fax (250) 489-6216
321 Cranbrook St.N., Cranbrook, BC   V1C 3R4

Located right on the strip in Cranbrook. From Hwy 3/95, turn at Van Horne St to Cranbrook St. Turn right to 3rd house on right. From Hwy 3/95 (Crowsnest Hwy) stay on Cranbrook St, continue past Sandman Inn and proceed to B&B on right.

$60S $65-70D   (plus taxes)   ► 8
🍴 Full, homebaked   🏠 Downtown, res., 2-storey, hist., patio, porch ■4D (upstairs) ⊨ 4T,2Q ⊨ 2Sh.w.g.   ★Air,F,TV in guest rooms, phone hook-ups, purified water, hot tub, off-street parking Ⓦ Smoking on patio, no pets, children min. age 12
🕴 Railway Museum, Cranbrook Heritage Walk, downtown core
🚗 Kimberley Ski Hills, Fairmont Hot Springs, Kootenay Trout Hatchery, Fort Steele Heritage Town, Moyie Lake
🐾 Beautifully, refurbished, award winning Heritage home with antiques & quality decor. Longtime hostess formerly operated a B&B in Moyie. Fax access available. Visa,MC,Amex ⌐CC

Crawford Bay
(west of Cranbrook; see also Proctor, Kaslo, Creston)

Huiberts, Joan (Wedgwood Manor)   ☎ & Fax (250) 227-9233
Box 135, Crawford Bay, BC   V0B 1E0

From Nelson go east on Hwy 3A cross Kootenay Lake by ferry (free) and drive 7km east to Crawford Bay. From Creston go north on Hwy 3A along Kootenay Lake to Crawford Bay

$79S $79-115D $20Child $20Add.person   ▶ 12A,2Ch
🍳Full, homebaked   🏠Rural, hist., acreage, view, patio, quiet
■6D(main & upper level)   ⊨1D,5Q   🛁6ensuite   ★3F,
2private guest lounges, guest bicycles   🚫No pets, no smoking, children min.age 4
🚶 Crawford Bay beach on Kootenay Lake (water still pure enough to drink), canoe along pristine shoreline, golf at Kokanee Springs, excellent walking/hiking from doorstep, Harrison Memorial Church next door (handy for wedding party)

🚗 Kootenay Lake Ferry (longest free ride in NA), Ainsworth (sumptuous hot springs and cavern)
☛ Historic, 1900-built Manor is situated on a 55-acres estate overlooking a small valley at the foot of the Purcell Mountains and is furnished with pieces from the Victorian era with a library lounge and front veranda. Honeymoon/anniversary/golf packages available. Visa,MC ✔B&B

Creston
(south-west of Cranbrook; see also Crawford Bay)

Allmeritter, Gertrud and Werner (Goat-River Lodge)   ☎ (250)428-7134,Fax(250)428-4713
1108 Lamont Rd, RR1,S40,Box8, Creston,BC   V0B 1G0   E-mail: allmi@kootenay.awinc.com

Located in Erickson, 0.5 km from Creston or 2km from Hwy 3W.
$45S $60-75D $10Add.person   E-mail: ✔ 6
🍳 Full (European)   🏠 Rural, res., bungalow, 7acres, view, patio, heated swimming pool,riverfront   ■ 3D (main level)
⊨2D,2Q   🛁 Private   ★TV in guest room, LF, sep.entrance, private porch   🚫No smoking,no pets   ⚬German
🚶 Wayside Gardens, museum, golf course
🚗 Kootenay Lake, Wildlife Center, golfing

☛ Home is located in the middle of 1000 fruit trees and cherry orchard with a beautiful view over the Goat River Valley. Enjoy the special honeymoon suite. There is a resident dog, cat & bird. ✔CC

Baumann, Martin & Susan (Rising Sun Guest Ranch)   ☎ & Fax (250) 428-4886
3246 Riverview Rd.,S7F-2,RR1, Creston, BC   V0B 1G0

From Creston take Hwy 21 to Mallory Rd. Turn left and continue to ranch. Look for Hwy signs.
$45S $55-60D $10Child   🍽 Meals   ▶ 8A,6Ch
🍳Full,homebaked   🏠Ranch, quiet, patio, isolated   ■4(main level)   ⊨2T,3Q,1D,R   🛁4Private   ★F,LF,TV,private balcony, sep.entrances   🚫No smoking, no pets   ⚬German
🚶 Restaurant, golf course, hiking in private and secluded woods, cross country skiing, birdwatching
🚗 Kootenay Lake, fishing, boating, Kootenay Skyway Summit, swimming, Ghost towns, Ainsworth Hot Springs, Creston

☛ Guest ranch offers country atmosphere (3km south of Creston). Newly decorated guest rooms, each with private entrance.

Doull, Gilbert & Elspeth (Sweetapple Bed & Breakfast)   ☎ & Fax (250) 428-7205
3939 Hwy 3 East, Creston, BC   V0B 1K0

Located on Hwy3 (Crowsnest Pass) at the east end of Creston.
$40S $55D $5Child $10Add.person   ► 5
🍲 Full, homebaked   🏠 Rural, ranch-split, acreage, view from
guest rooms, balcony, quiet ■1D,1F(lower level) ⊨1S,1D,1Q
🛏1Private,1sh.w.g.   ★ TV/VCR and woodstove in large guest
sitting room, separate entrance, guest space is selfcontained, guest
fridge, library ⓌDesignated smoking area ∾ Italian
🚗 Creston Wildlife Centre, Kootenay/Moyie Lakes, Salmo Pass,
US border & Bonners Ferry, Creston Golf Club, Crawford Bay Ferry, hiking trails, river fishing
☛ House is situated on 10 acres of original forest above the Goat River, facing the Skimmerhorn
Range of the Purcell Mountains. Enjoy the breathtaking view down the Creston Valley from south
facing balconies and the extensive in-house art collection. Golf packages, senior discounts and
family rates available. There is a cat named "Sam" in residence. ∼CC

Cumberland   *(south of Courtenay, Denman Island, Comox)*

Davis, Shelagh & D.Jackson (Wellington House B&B)   ☎(250)336-8809,Fax(250)336-2321
2593 Derwent Ave, Box 689, Cumberland, BC   V0R 1S0   E-mail: cma-chin@mail.island.net

Take Hwy 19 to Royston & continue 7km to Cumberland. Proceed through the village, turn left
towards Comox Lake and first right onto Derwent Ave.

$50-55S $65-75D $90F $20Add.person   ► 8
🍲Full,homebaked 🏠Village, hillside, small acreage, patio, deck
porch, quiet, secluded   ■ 2D,1Ste(upstairs & garden level)
⊨1S,3D,1Q   🛏 2Private,1sh.w.h.   ★TV/VCR in private guest
sitting rooms, KFin suite,ceiling fans, separate entrance, guest
quarters are separate Ⓦ Smoking on patio, children min. age 12
⚡ Original Mining Weigh Scale on property, village shops, Comox
Lake, restaurants, museum, hiking trails from property
🚗 Mt.Washington & Forbidden Plateau Ski Resorts, Filberg Lodge (Comox), golfing, ferries to
Powell River, Nanaimo and islands, sport fishing
☛ Warm welcome in large modern home situated in a park-like setting in historic mining village
located in the foothills of the Beaufort Mountains. A perfect spot to relax and unwind. Breakfast is
served in large country kitchen. Hostess hails from England and enjoys sharing the peaceful
surroundings with guests. There is a dog in residence. Visa ∼B&B

Dawson Creek   *(north of Prince George near Alberta border)*

Janssen, Wim & Marilyn (Cedar Cottage B&B)   ☎ (250) 782-3556
2013-89 Ave, Dawson Creek, BC   V1G 4S2

From Alaska Hwy, turn north on 17St, then left at 93Ave, which
runs into 89Ave.
$40S $50D   🍽 Meals   ► 2
🍲 Full, homebaked   🏠 Res., 2-storey, view, porch, deck, quiet
■1D(upst) ⊨1D   🛏1Private ★TV,F,LF,off-street parking
ⓌNo smoking, no pets, not suitable for children ∾Dutch
⚡ Pioneer Village, town center, park
🚗 Airport, Fort St. John
☛ Warm welcome in cozy country-style home with Canadiana antique furniture, backing onto a
quiet park. Well travelled hosts have model trains and a doll collection on the premises (some for
sale) and hostess designs Teddy Bear patterns. Relax on the back deck and enjoy the flowers
everywhere. There are 2 cats and a dog in residence. ∼B&B

Delta

Taylor, Jon & Margaret (The Ranch House)   ☎ (604) 946-1553
7061 Ladner Trunk Rd., Delta, BC   V4K 3N3

Located on Hwy 10 (Ladner Trunk Rd) in Delta, betw.Hwys 17/99.
$75S $85D $20Add.person   ▶ 8
⬤ Full, homebaked   🏠 Farm, ranch-style, acreage, view, porch
deck, quiet   ■ 3D,1F (main floor)   ◄ 1D,2Q,crib, playpen
⚑2Sh.w.g.   ★ LF,F,TV in guest living room, private entrance,
off-street parking, guest quarters are separate   ⓦ Designated
smoking area, no pets
🚗 Tsawwassen Ferries to Victoria & Nanaimo, US border,
downtown Vancouver, Grouse Mountain skiing, Vancouver Int. Airport
🏃 Reifel Bird Sanctuary, Burns Bog, hiking trails, bus to all areas of lower mainland
☛ Friendly country-style hospitality on small hobby farm with large backyard and located in the
Ladner area of rural Delta. There are 2 horses for viewing and petting. Relax in the hot tub on the
sundeck overlooking farmland and the captivating views of coastal mountains. For those guests
arriving and departing through Boundary Bay Airport, complimentary transportation is available.
There is a small resident dog. Visa ✓B&B

Denman Island   *(south of Comox; see also Courtenay, Cumberland)*

Helps, Mary (Hawthorn House Bed & Breakfast)   ☎ & Fax (250) 335-0905
3375 Kirk Rd, Denman Island, BC   V0R 1T0

Take Island Hwy north to Buckley Bay Ferry for Denman Island (15 min). On Denman, take ferry
road up hill, turn left on Northwest Rd and left on Kirk Rd. Look for signs up ferry hill.

$60S $75-85D $15Add.person   🍽 Meals   ▶ 6A,2Ch
⬤ Full, homebaked   🏠 Village, 2-storey, older, view from guest rooms,
patio, porch, deck, quiet   ■ 2D,1F (upstairs in main house & in separate
studio)   ◄2T,1D,1Q,1P,crib   ⚑ 3Private   ★ F,LF,TV in guest room,
sep.entrance, wheel-chair access, hot tub, off-street parking   ⓦNo smoking
🏃 Denman Island town centre, craft shops, library, art gallery, restaurants,
artist studios, cycling, kayaking
🚗 Sandy beach (Hornby Island), craft studios, hiking trails, fishing, cycling
☛ Beautifully renovated turn-of-the-Century farmhouse (built in 1904),
furnished with Canadiana pine antiques and overlooking Baynes Sound and
the Beaufort Range, an idyllic seaside setting near the ferry landing.
Discover the "undiscovered islands" with secluded beaches & trails. Island studio tours can be
arranged. There are 2 small friendly dogs in residence.✓B&B

Duncan   *(on Van.Isle; Cowichan B., Cobble Hill, Saltspring Isle)*

Gunnlaugson, Marjorie (Country Gardens B&B)   ☎ (250) 748-5865
1665 Grand Rd., Duncan, BC   V9L 5N7

From Swartz Bay Ferry, proceed on Hwy 17 to Hwy 1 and then north to Duncan. Turn right on
Trunk Rd (first light after Silver Bridges) and follow Maple Bay signs to Grant Rd.

$45S $60D   ▶ 4A,1Ch
⬤Full, homebaked   🏠Rural, ranch-style, lake view, 2patios
■1S,2D   ⚑Private   ★F,TV, wheel-chair access. ⓦNo
smoking, no pets, children min. age 13   ～Dutch
🚗 Chemainus ("the little town that did") famous for its murals,
Native Heritage center (with magnificient world of North-west
Coast Indians) Whippletree Junction (crafts and antiques), ferries
☛ Country charm in lovely cedar log home on private acreage.
Enjoy breakfast on the patios overlooking beautiful Quamichan Lake or tranquil garden with lily
ponds. There is a pool with a waterfall & goldfish and there is a Briard in residence. ✓CC

14   BRITISH COLUMBIA

Fairmont Hot Springs   *(south of Golden; see also Invermere, Windermere)*

McMillan, Bonnie & Ken (McMillan Chalet Bed & Breakfast)   ☎ & Fax (250) 345-9553
Box 989,5021 Fairmont Close,Fairmont Hot Springs,BC V0B1L0   E-mail: kenmcm@rockies.net

Take Hwy 93 to Fairmont Hot Springs. Turn east off Hwy at large Fairmont Resort sign,
left behind Fairmont Grocery, then two immediate right turns.
$44-59S $54-69D $20Add.person   ▶ 6A,2Ch
🍴Homebaked (gourmet)   🏠Resort,Chalet-type, 3-storey, quiet,
mountain view,deck   ■3D(loft & lower level) ⊨3Q,1P(Q),cot
⊲1Sh.w.g.,1ensuite   ★F,TV in guest rooms   ⦿Smoking outside
on deck, no pets
🐾 Two major golf courses, large natural hot spring pools,
recreational activities in Resort town
🚗 Scenic roads, fine dining, Windermere Lake, swimming, boating, Invermere, Kimberley
🔫 Professional couple in comfortable chalet with large cathedral windows, situated in popular
resort area. Relax on the deck and enjoy the beautiful mountain scenery. Convenient location near
major route. Cheese cake & other homemade goodies served in evening.Reservations
please.Visa,MC

Fernie   *(east of Cranbrook; see also Jaffray, Fort Steele, Kimberley)*

Bowles, Barbara (Barbara Lynn's Country Inn B&B)   ☎(250)423-6027,Fax(250)423-6024
691-7th Ave, Box 1077, Fernie, BC   V0B 1M0   E-mail: barnsinn@cancom.net 1-888-288-2148

$35-55S $50-75D $60-90F $5-15Child $20Add.person (Group/Senior/Cyclist rates)   ▶ 12-14
Located at Hwy 3 & 7th St. Phone for directions.
🍴 Cont.(plus),homebaked   🏠Res, in town, view from guest
rooms, private deck, veranda   ■ 5D,1F(upstairs) ⊨2T,1D,3Q,
bunk,futon sofa bed   ⊲2Sh.w.g.,2ensuite,1private
★KF,F,thermostats in rooms, private entrance & parking,
barbeque, guest TV room with full kitchen, hot tub   ⦿No
smoking, no pets
🐾 Restaurants, pubs, stores, golfing, x-c ski/bike/walking trails,
tennis courts, Elk River abounds with fish
🚗Fernie Alpine Resort, Golf & Country Club, mountain climbing, Cranbrook Airport, fish
hatchery, historic Fort Steele, Crowsnest Pass, Frank Slide
🔫 Warm and friendly welcome in new home with country charm, situated in the scenic Canadian
Rocky Mountains. Hostess is a bicycle tourist and loves to share experiences with other cyclists. Ski
packages available to ski ultimate snow in an area which is quickly becoming one of the great ski
destinations in the world. (Average snowfall is 750cm and liftlines are almost non existent). Relax
in the hot tub after an active day and enjoy the congenial atmosphere. Ski & Golf packages and
extended stay rates available. Visa,MC ✓B&B

Coombes, Peter (Fernie Westways Guest House)   ☎ (250)423-3058, Fax (250) 423-3059
202-4A Ave, Fernie, BC   V0B 1M0   E-mail: westways@telusplanet.net

From Hwy 3 go onto 2nd Ave Fernie & right on 2nd steet. Look for house on corner of 4th Ave.
$40-70S $60-100D $10Child $10Add.person   ▶ 8
🍴 Full   🏠 Downtown, res, 2-storey, hist., views from guest
rooms, porch, deck, quiet   ■ 3D(upstairs & ground level)
⊨2Q,1K,R,P,cot   ⊲ 2Private, 1sh.w.h.   ★ LF,F,TV in guest
rooms, hot tub on deck, storage garage, off-street/street parking
⦿Pets welcome, desig.smoking areas, children min.age 8
🐾 Downtown, Elk River, Court House, Art Center, museum,
golfing, restaurants, craft shops
🚗 Fernie Alpine Ski Resort, Fort Steele Heritage Center, Frank Slide, USA border, Cranbrook,
Mt.Fernie Prov. Park, Crows Nest Pass, winter and summer activies
🔫 1908-built, spacious Heritage home with high ceilings and hardwood. Enjoy the comfortable
elegance and friendy ambiance. Relax in the hot tub with beautiful mountain views or curl up in
front of the wood burning fireplace. There are 2 dogs. MC,Visa,Amex ✓CC

Johnson, Elsie & Bob (Canadian Spruce B&B)   ☎ & Fax (250) 423-6445
661-4th Ave, Box 57, Fernie, BC   V0B 1M0   E-mail: cdnsprbb@cancom.net

From Hwy 3 turn to city center on 7th St. Turn right at 4th Ave to second house on right.

$40-58S $55-75D   ▶ 7
🍽 Full   🏠 Downtown, hist., view from guest rooms, porch,
quiet   ■ 1S,2D,1Ste (main & upper level)   ⊨ 1S,2D,.1Q
🛏1Ensuite, 1sh.w.g.   ★ F,TV in guest sitting room, private
entrance, off-street & street parking, secure storage for skis &
bicycles, host quarters are separate   Ⓦ No smoking, no pets, not
suitable for children
🏃 Downtown historic area, golfing, biking, fly fishing, walking and
x-c ski trails along Elk River, Aquatic and Arts Centers, restaurants, coffee shops, theatre
🚗 Fernie Ski Resort, Island Lake Lodge, Fernie Prov. Park (hiking, biking, cat skiing) Lake
Koocanusa Recreation Area, mine tours, Fort Steele historic site
☛ Spacious, bright and cheerful historic home (1909) complete with relaxing veranda, main level
entrance antique staircase and open foyer, situated in upcoming tourist destination town. Relax in
the sitting room and enjoy the library and TV. Retired couple with many travel experiences and
interests to share are able to provide an unhurried restful B&B stay. ✍B&B

Lewis, Donna & Larry (Mountainside Inn B&B)   ☎ & Fax (250) 423-3754
50 Timberline Cr., West Fernie, BC   V0B 1M1

On Hwy 3 and 5km west of Fernie, turn right and go up ski hill road. Take
second left on Timberline Cr. to 2nd house on left.
Winter:$70S $90D   Summer:$50S $65D $10-20Child/Add.person ▶ 10
🍽 Cont.plus   🏠 Village, ski-resort, split-level, view, deck   ■ 3D,1F
(lower/ground/upper level)   ⊨ 2T(K),3Q,1P   🛏 1Private with double
jacuzzi, 3ensuite   ★ F,TV in guest living room, private entrance, guest
quarters are separate, off-street parking   Ⓦ No smoking, no pets
🏃 Ski-lift access, downhill & x-c skiing, hiking & biking trails, Elk River
🚗 Fernie, US & Alberta borders, lakes for boating & fishing, Cranbrook
and airport, 3 golf courses, Lake Koocanusa
☛ Spacious, modern home tastefully decorated, located at the base of the
Fernie Snow Valley Ski Hill, nestled in Timberline village with spectacular
views of the surrounding peaks and gorgeous Elk Valley. Relax in the forest-secluded 10 person
hot-tub on the deck behind the house after a day of deep powder skiing (from the door). Congenial
hosts enjoy helping guests with holiday requests & activity plans. Visa,MC ✍B&B

Fort Steele   *(north of Cranbrook; see also Kimberley, Fernie, Jaffray)*

Emery, John & Joanna (Emery's Mountain View B&B)   ☎ & Fax (250) 426-4756
Box 60, 183 Wardner-Fort Steele Rd., Fort Steele, BC   V0B 1N0

Located 2 km off Hwy 93/95. In Fort Steele, turn at Esso Stn. onto Wardner-Fort Steele Rd.
Proceed down hill over small bridge and continue 1 km to house on right.

$50-85S $60-95D $20Child $20Add.person   ▶ 9
🍽 Full   🏠 Rural, 2-storey, acreage, view from guest rooms,
riverback, patio, porch, quiet, secluded   ■ 3D,1F (upstairs)
incl.separate cabin   ⊨ 1S,2T,1D,1Q,1K,4R,cots   🛏 1Private in
cabin, 2sh.w.g.   ★ Ceiling fans, KF & separate entrance in cabin,
off-street parking   Ⓦ Smoking outside, no pets
🏃 Observe wild animals and birds in the marsh, stroll along the
Wild Horse River on north side of property
🚗 Golfing, skiing, Hot Springs, historic sites, mountain trails
☛ Country home located on 14 scenic hectares along Wild Horse Creek and away from the
highways. Enjoy the breathtaking panoramic view of the majestic Canadian Rocky Mountains.
Hosts are well informed about the area and will provide directions to interesting historic sites.
Breakfast is served in main building dining room. There are 2 dogs in residence. Visa ✍B&B

Francois Lake

(west of Prince George; see also Burns Lake, Smithers)

Opas, Meg & Ron (Little Madness on Francois Lake B&B)   ☎ (250) 695-6673
Box 606, Francois Lake, BC V0J 1R0

From Prince George take Hwy 16 (Yellowhead) west for 215 km to Burns Lake. Take scenic Hwy 35 south for 30 km. Continue west past the northside terminal of Francois Lake Ferry 4km and look for B&B on Colleymount Rd. (just past VanZanten Pit Rd).

$50S $60D $80F   ► 6A,2Ch
🍴 Full, homebaked   🏠 Rural, 2-storey log house, acreage, view, lakefront, patio, porch, deck, quiet   ■ 3D (lower level)
🛏1D,2Q   🚿 1Sh.w.g., sep. shower   ★ F,TV,LF, parking
🚭Smoking and pets outside   〰 some French
🎯 Spectacular lake (100 km long, fishing/boating/swimming), horseback riding, hiking, cycling, walks, nature watching, skiing
🚐 Tweedsmuir Prov. Park, Nadina River nature interpretive guiding, Native Communities
🚩 Log home situated in typical rural BC surrounded by fantastic lakes, forests, distant mountains and rolling ranch lands. Hosts offer traditional European style hospitality. Relax in the comfortable character living room or enjoy the active seasonal outdoor pleasures. Wheelchairs can be accommodated with some assistance. There is a resident dog and cat. ✍B&B

Gibsons

(north of Vancouver; see also Roberts Creek, Sechelt, Powell River)

Bailey, Sue & Gord (Marina House B&B)   ☎ (604) 886-7888
546 Marine Dr., Box 1696, Gibsons, BC V0N 1V0

From Horseshoe Bay, take ferry (40min) to Langdale Ferry Terminal and proceed 4km south on the lower road. Located on the Sunshine Coast north of Vancouver.

$80S $90D $20Add.person   ► 6A
🍴 Full, homebaked   🏠 Res, hillside, 3-storey, hist., view from guest rooms, oreanfront, porch, quiet   ■3D(street level & upst.)
🛏2T(1K),2Q   🚿1Private,2ensuite   ★TV in common lounge, private entrance, off-street parking,boat ramp/mooring
🚭Smoking on porches, no pets, not suitable for children
🎯 Beach walks, Gibsons Ldg & Molly's Reach (of "Beachcomber" Fame), museum, shops, restaurants, mountain hiking, Sunshine Coast Transit Bus
🚐 Trails & coastal beachwalks, golfing, fly fishing, secret coves, x-c skiing, Skookumchuck Rapids
🚩 Heritage home (1931) restored to its original charm. A perfect destination for a weekend cycling trip or stop-over on route around the inner-coast loop or home-base for kayak/canoe day-trips up the Sunshine Coast. Breakfast is served in the sunny breakfast room with exceptional ocean views. Breakfast picnic packages for early departure. Ferry pick-up avail.Visa,MC ✍B&B

Verzyl, Dianne and Bert (Ocean-View Cottage B&B)   ☎ & Fax (604) 886-7943
1927 Grandview Rd., RR2, S46-C10, Gibsons, BC V0N 1V0   1-800-231-9122

From Vancouver take ferry at Horseshoe Bay to Langdale (35 min). Proceed along scenic drive up the Sunshine Coast Hwy. Turn left at lower Rd, left on Pine Rd, right on Grandview Rd (#1927).
$70S $80D $115D(Cottage) $10Child $20Add.person   ► 4,2Ch

🍴 Choice, homebaked(gourmet) 🏠Rural, acreage, view,quiet
■1D,plus self-cont. cottage 🛏2T,1K,1Q 🚿2Private, soaker tub in cottage ★F,KF,TV in room 🚭No pets,no smoking
〰French, Dutch
🎯 Beaches, walking and hiking trails, restaurants
🚐 Ferries to Vancouver, Powell River, Vancouver Island, golfing
🚩 New home situated on the beautiful Sunshine Coast in quiet rural setting with a panoramic view of the sea/mountains. Relax on the deck & watch the Alaska cruise ships go by. Visa,MC ✍B&B

Golden
(near Alberta border/Banff National Park; see also Parson, Revelstoke)

Baier, Hubert & Sonja (Hillside Lodge)   ☎ & Fax (250) 344-7281
1740 Seward Frontage Rd., Box 2603, Golden, BC   V0A 1H0

$65-75S $70-85D $10-15Child $20Add.person $98Chalets 🍽 Meals (plus tax)   ▶ 20

Located 13km west of Golden and 500m off TCH1.Follow signs.
🍲 Full, homebaked 🏠 Rural, Black Forest house & brand new
chalets, acreage, patio, quiet, riverfront ■2D,5chalets ▬10D
🛏7Private ★TV,F, private balconies or terrace, parking
〰German
🚶 Blaeberry River, hiking trails, bird/game watching, Wildlife
Nature Reserve, fishing, whitewater rafting, kayaking, trail riding,
golfing, Whitetooth ski-hill, x/c skiing, dog-sledding trips
🚐 Banff/Lake Louise Nat. Park, Rogers Pass, Glacier Nat.Park, Mummery Glacier, Kootenay &
Yoho Nat.Parks, Radium Hot Springs, Columbia Icefields
🏹 Quiet get-away home situated on 60 acres at Blaeberry River in the heart of the Rockies.
Enjoy a brand new chalet or a room in the charming lodge. Relax on the porch, balconies or in the
dining room with a spectacular view. Fresh, healthy meals are prepared by host chef in the evening
and by the hostess for breakfast. There is a family dog; llamas, horses & goats are outside.
Visa,MC,Interac ✓CC

Kowalski, Ruth & André (H.G. Parson House)   ☎ (250) 344-5001, Fax (250) 344-2900
815-12th Street South, Box 1196, Golden, BC   V0A 1H0

$60-65S $80-85D $10-20Child $10-20Add.person (plus tax) 🍽 Meals   ▶ 6A,3Ch

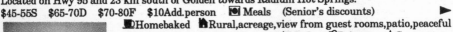
Phone for directions.
🍲 Full, homebaked (buffet) 🏠 Res., 2-storey, hist., view,
porch ■ 3D(upstairs) ▬ 2T,2Q 🛏 1Private, 2ensuite
★F,TV,off-street parking 🅦 Designated smoking area, no
pets 〰 French, Polish
🚶 Town walking trails, downtown area, summer/winter activities
🚐 Kootenay & Yoho Nat.Parks, Lake Louise, Radium Hot
Springs, Rogers Pass, Emerald Lake
🏹 Comfortable home built in 1893, completely furnished with antiques and collectibles and
theme guest rooms; surrounded by beautiful Rocky Mountain scenery. Town is situated in the last
of the natural wetlands. Relax on the front veranda or in the large private yard. Hosts know the
area well and will plan personal activity packages for guests. Dog in residence. Visa,MC ✓B&B

Perzinger, Erwin (Columbia Valley Lodge)   ☎ & Fax (250) 348-2508
Box 2669, Golden, BC   V0A 1H0

Located on Hwy 95 and 23 km south of Golden towards Radium Hot Springs.
$45-55S $65-70D $70-80F $10Add.person 🍽 Meals (Senior's discounts)   ▶ 35

🍲Homebaked 🏠Rural,acreage,view from guest rooms,patio,peaceful
■12units(main & upper floor) ▬T,D,Q 🛏Private ★Sep.entrance,
licenced dining room, parking 🅦No pets 〰German
🚶 Columbia River, birdwatching, canoeing, photography, x-country
skiing, horseback riding (on request)
🚐 Golden, Radium Hot Springs, Yoho, Banff & Glacier Nat.Parks
🏹 European-style lodge with its unique touch and relaxed
atmosphere, situated in a countryside setting surrounded by Rocky and Purcell Moutains and by the
Columbia Valley Wetlands. Host is an Austrian Chef and serves European cuisine. Visa,MC ✓CC

Greenwood
(south-east of Penticton; see also Osoyos, Oliver, Christina Lake)

Dixon, Keith & Marilyn (Forshaw House B&B) ☎ (250) 445-2208
197 Kimberley Ave.S, Box 288, Greenwood, BC V0H 1J0

From east or west, take Hwy 3 into Greenwood. At museum, turn uphill to 1st house on left.
$38S $50D $10Add.person (Child free under age 6) ▣ Meals ►8

♨ Full, homebaked ♠ Downtown, hist., 3-storey, quiet, porch, deck ■3(main & upper level)incl.suite ⊨2D,3S,2R ⊒2Sh.w.g ★F,TV,KF,one guest balcony, street parking ✋No smoking ⋀ Walks in old mining town with interesting Japanese history, horseback riding, Greyhound bus stop ⛟ Phoenix, old site of Coppermine, Grand Forks with Russian history, hiking, canoeing, fishing, golfing ☛Stately,1902-built Victorian-style home situated across from City Hall (&old Supreme Court & Jail) of the smallest city in BC. Join the walking tour offered by the museum. House specialty is sour-dough bread made with a 100-year old starter. ✔B&B

Invermere
(south of Golden; see also Windermere, Fairmont Hot Springs, Parson)

Dittmann, Joan & Hubert (Haus Dittmann) ☎ (250) 342-9706
126-7th Ave., Box 414, Invermere, BC V0A 1K0

Phone for directions.
$55S $65D ►2A

♨ Full, homebaked ♠ Res., 2-storey, view from guest rooms, patio, quiet ■ 1Ste (street level) ⊨ 1Q ⊒ 1Private ★TV/fridge/coffee maker in suite, off-street parking, private entrance ✋No smoking, no children, no pets ⋙German ⋀ Shopping, restaurants, Lake Windermere (beach, swimming) ⛟ Radium & Fairmont Hot Springs, Panoroma Alpine Res.
☛ New home with warm atmosphere in quiet location with spectacular mountain scenery all around. Guest suite is totally separate from main house. After a day in the mountains, relax in one of the nearby hot springs. An ideal place for a longer stay and from which to explore the beautiful and interesting area in summer and winter.

Gramlich, Heather & Garth (Primrose Manor) ☎ & Fax (250) 342-9664
Box 2937, 1512-9th Ave., Invermere, BC V0A 1K0 E-mail: primrose@rockies.net

Take Hwy 95 (north or south) to Invermere. Follow main street (7th Ave.) through town, past Invermere Inn, around turn and down Beach Dr. Before RR track, make a sharp right turn on 17th St and continue up to 9th Ave (not a through road). Turn right to 4th house on left side.
$50S $65D $15Child $95F $20Add.person $5crib (plus tax) ▣ Meals, box lunches ►15

♨ Full, homebaked ♠ Res, village, tudor-style, quiet, sundeck ■ 2D,1F,1Ste (main & upper level) ⊒1Sh.w.g., 1private,1ensuite ⊨3D,1Q,1K,2R,2P, 1crib ★F,TV, separate entrance, parking ✋No pets, no smoking ⋙ Russian (when available) ⋀ Kinsmen Beach on Lake Windermere (2.5 blocks), tennis courts, Pynelogs Cultural Center, museum, charming village with shops and excellent restaurants ⛟ 5 golf courses, 2 Hot Springs (Radium/Fairmont), 2 Ski Resorts (Panorama/Fairmont) ☛ European-style Manor nestled among the pines in a quiet neighborhood. Hosts have travelled extensively. Relax on the outdoor deck and expansive lawns or in the entertainment room after a day of golfing, skiing, whitewater rafting, or sightseeing in the Columbia Valley. CCards ✔B&B

Jaffray

% (south-east of Cranbrook; see also Fernie, Ft.Steele, Kimberley)

Lyon, Doris & Doug (The Three Bears B&B)
Box 209, Sand Creek Rd., Jaffray, BC V0B 1T0

☎ (250) 429-3519
E-mail: threebears@cyberlink.bc.ca

From Hwy 3 south of Jaffray, turn onto Sand Creek Rd. Look for B&B sign at property entrance.
$45S $60D $10Child/Add.person   🍽 Meals   ▶ 8

🍲 Full, homebaked   🏠 Rural, split-level, acreage, view from guest rooms, patio, porch deck, quiet, secluded   ■ 4   ⊨ S,Q   🛁 2Sh.w.g.   ★ F,TV,LF,separate entrance, canoe/kayaks and bikes for rent   🚭No smoking   ∼German   🏃 Hiking, birding, tennis, golfing, fishing, kayaking, wildlife viewing, cycling, bus to Cranbrook airport   🚗 Downhill skiing, canoeing, x-c and snocat skiing, hunting, rafting, Jaffray, Cranbrook, US border

🐾 Comfortable home on 5 acres of landscaped and forested land situated in the "South Country". Relax on one of several decks or in the yard. Enjoy good conversation and cozy evenings around the firepit or fireplace. Kennel provided for visiting pets. Picnic & packed lunches available. A perfect 4-Season destination. Visa ✓CC

Kaleden

(south of Penticton; see also Summerland, Oliver, Osoyoos)

Smith, Les & Diane (Smith & Wife Bed & Breakfast)
230 Ponderosa Ave, S12, C11, Kaleden, BC V0H 1K0

☎ (250) 497-5536

From Penticton, follow Hwy 97 south 7km to Kaleden sign. Turn east onto Lakehill Rd and right on Ponderosa Ave, proceed to house on right.
$50S $65-75D $25Add.person   ▶ 4A,1Ch

🍲 Full   🏠 Village, split-level, view from guest rooms, lakefront, patio, decks, quiet   ■ 1D,1F (main & ground level)   ⊨2Q,1P   🛁2Private   ★Air,F,TV,LF, off-street parking   🚭Smoking on covered deck, no pets, one child only (min. age 13)   🏃 Beach, walking trail, gourmet restaurant, boat launch, crafts   🚗 Numerous wineries, world famous game farm, bird sanctuary, golfing, Apex Ski Resort, potteries, Penticton, Oliver, Kelowna

🐾 New, modern country home with gorgeous lake views and quiet surroundings located in the heart of the Okanagan wine country. Enjoy a peaceful rest after a day at the beach, on the ski slopes, on the wine trail, hiking or bird-watching. Breakfast features fresh Okanagan fare. Guests are invited to relax in the lounge, on the decks and patio. Airport and bus pick-up. Visa ✓CC

Kamloops

(see also Pritchard, Salmon Arm)

Bentz, Lynn and Trevor (Park Place B&B)
720 Yates Rd., Kamloops, BC V2B 6C9

☎ & Fax (250) 554-2179

From Jasper Hwy 5 turn at signage for Airport & North Shore. Cross North Thompson River, take right hand ramp onto Westsyde Rd, then 5th right again on Yates.
$40S $55-75D $95Cottage   ▶ 4

🍲 Full   🏠 Sub., acreage, river view, swimming pool, patio   ■3D(main floor)   ⊨1Q,2D   🛁1Ensuite,2sh.w.g.   ★Air,LF,TV in guest room   🚭No smoking, child min. age 14, pets outdoors   🏃 Boating, hiking, fishing, swimming, shopping, tennis courts   🚗 Waterslide, lakes, paddle-wheeler river boat cruise "Wanda Sue", Provincial Parks, Indian Pow Wows, Salmon Run   🐾Warm and friendly hosts in delightful Santa Fe style riverfront home with antiques, breakfast solarium & in-ground pool. House motto: "Come as a guest, leave as a friend". Cottage is private & self-contained. ✓CC

MacQueen, Jack & Pat (MacQueen's Manor)
1049 Laurel Place, Kamloops, BC V1S 1R1
☎ (250) 372-9383, 1-800-677-5338

Going east on Hwy1, take Exit 367 Pacific Hwy (going west take Exit 368), Proceed to Hugh Allen

Dr, turn onto Gloaming and then onto Laurel Place.
$50S $55D $10Child $85F   ► 4A,1Ch
✳ Apr1-Nov1   ◗ Homebaked   ♠ Res., split-level, view, 2
private decks, quiet   ■2Ste(upstairs & ground level)   ⊨1D,1Q
⏛1Private,1ensuite   ★ KF,LF,F,TV & coffee bar in guest room,
off-street parking   ⊛ Designated smoking area, no pets
☆ Aberdeen Mall, restaurants, pub, golfing
🚗 Merritt, Salmon Arm, Vernon, Ashcroft Sun Peaks Ski Resort
🐾 Warm welcome in new home filled with collectibles and friendly hospitality. Breakfast is
served in antique furnished dining room overlooking the beautiful Kamloops Valley, or may be
served in guest rooms. There are 2 dogs. CCards ✓CC

Matter, Kitty (Matter House)
225 McGill Rd., Kamloops, BC V2C 1M2
☎ (250) 374-8011

Travelling on TCH Hwy1 from west, take Columbia St Exit. From east or north, take Exit 370 to

Columbia St. Proceed to 3rd traffic light, right onto McGill Rd.
$40S $65D $15Add.person   ► 5-6
◗Full,homebaked   ♠Res., split-level, view, patio, quiet   ■2D
(ground/upper level) ⏛2Private ⊨2T,1Q,1S,1P ★Air,TV,
guest living room,parking   ⊛ No smoking, no pets ⋙German
☆ Restaurants, shopping center
🐾 Cozy home in quiet residential area with beautiful view of
Kamloops river and the mountains. ✓CC

Kaslo
(north-west of Cranbrook; see also Crawford Bay, Nelson)

Saffran, Denis & Marion (Morningside Bed & Breakfast)   ☎ & Fax (250) 353-7681
670 Arena Ave., Box 1055, Kaslo, BC V0G 1M0   E-mail: msaffran@netidea.com

Phone for directions.
$40S $50-55D   ◙ Meals   ► 4A
◗ Full, homebaked   ♠ Village, bungalow, patio, view from
guest rooms, deck,quiet   ■2D   ⊨2T,1D ⏛Sh.w.g. ★TV in game
room, sep entrance, patio access, antique Brunswick pool table,
reading corner ⊛No smoking,no pets,children min age 13
☆ Golf course, S.S.Moyie (restored Sternwheeler), fishing,
swimming, boating, hiking trails
🚗 Ainsworth Hot Springs, Nelson, Duncan Dam, hiking to Kokanee Glacier, Sandon ghost town
🐾 Early retired Professional couple in new home overlooking Kootenay Lake situated in a
peaceful forested setting on a quiet street in a picturesque village, with view of the Purcell
Mountains, lake and surrounding cedar forest. There is a cat in residence. ✓B&B

Kelowna
(see also Winfield, Oyama)

Breitkreuz, Bernie & Bettina (Bluebird Beach House B&B)   ☎ & Fax (250) 764-8992
3980 Bluebird Rd., Kelowna, BC   V1W 1X6

Approaching Kelowna in the Okanagan Valley from Hwy 97, turn onto Pandosy to Lakeshore, then right onto Bluebird (dead end). Located 4 hours drive from Vancouver.

$85S $95-120D $15Add.person   ► 8-10
🌷Spring/Summer/Fall 🍴Full(Gourmet) 🏠Res., lakefront,
2-storey, view from guest rooms, quiet   ■ 3Ste (upstairs)
🛏1D,2Q,2P   🛁3Ensuite   ★ TV/fridge in guest rooms,
private patios facing lake, separate entrance, off-street parking
👋Smoking area, no pets, children min. age 10 ᴡᴡGerman
🧍 KF & barbeque in Beach Cabana (on property), private sandy
beach & dock at back, 711-store, family restaurants, bus stop
🚗 Town Centre, shopping malls, Okanagan wineries, golfing, biking/hiking, horseback riding
📢 Well travelled hosts in spacious custom-built home with tasteful, deluxe decor and located on beautiful Lake Okanagan. Ideal location for a restful luxury retreat and a paradise for swimmers, hikers and golfers. Enjoy gourmet breakfast at the beach Cabana. There is a resident old dog. Golf tee-time may be pre-arranged. ✓CC

Comben, Cathy & Herb (Point-of-View B&B)   ☎ (250)764-7378(REST),Fax (250)764-0920
378 Sandpiper St., Kelowna, BC   V1W 4K7

Phone for directions.
$60S $75D   ► 4
🍴 Full, homebaked   🏠 Res., ranch-style, lakeview from guest
rooms, inground swimming pool, patio, deck, quiet   ■ 2D (lower
level) 🛏2T(K),1Q 🛁2Private ★Air,LF,TV in guest lounge,
off-street parking, indoor hot tub for 8, barbeque, mountain bike
rentals, host quarters are separate 👋No smoking,no pets
🚗 Downtown, Kettle Valley Steam Railway, major ski resorts,
Myra Canyon, hiking/biking on old rail road bed, wineries
📢 Charming & comfortable home with a spectacular view of Okanagan Lake. After a day of sightseeing or travelling, enjoy an invigorating swim in the pool, lounge in the sun admiring the beautiful view or browse in the telephone museum on site. Private scenic tours or wine tours can be arranged. Experience the Okanagan lifestyle in an ambiance of comfort & charm. There is a small resident dog. CCards ✓B&B

Durose, Paul & Lynda (Yellow Rose B&B)   ☎ & Fax (250) 764-5257
504 Curlew Dr., Kelowna, BC   V1W 4K9   E-mail: yelorose@awinc.com

Take Pandosy to Chute Lake Rd and turn right on Curlew Dr.
$55S $70-85D   ► 7
🍴 Full   🏠 Res., 2-storey, porch, quiet, deck, secluded
■1S,2D(ground & upper level) 🛏 1S,1D,1Q,1P 🛁 1Private,
1sh.w.g.   ★ Air,F,LF, ceiling fans, separate entrance, off-street
parking   👋 No smoking, no pets
🧍 Park, paved walking paths in well-lit safe neighbourhood
🚗) Downtown, restaurants, shops, golfing, excellent downhill
skiing (Big White), winery, airport, Vernon
📢 Lovely Victorian-style home in quiet residential area. Hostess is a caterer who loves to entertain and serves delightful meals. Relax in the gazebo after a busy day. Breakfast is served in special guest breakfast room. There is a cat in residence. Visa,MC ✓B&B

Farries, Dorothy & Gordon (Wedgwood House B&B)
1281 Rio Dr., Kelowna, BC   V1V 1E3

☎ (250) 762-6503,
Fax (250) 762-6598

$50S $60-80D $7.50-10Child(age 2-12) $110F   ► 4A,2Ch
From Hwy 97 (Harvey Ave), turn north on Gordon Dr to High Rd. Turn right & proceed to Clifton

Rd. Turn left 2.2km to Rio Dr, turn right to last home on right.
🍽 Full   🏠 Res., hillside, view from guest rooms, patio, quiet
■2D(ground level   ⊨2T,1Q,R   ⬛ 1Sh.w.g.   ★ Air,LF,
separate entrance, off-street parking, guest sitting room, fridge
🚭 Designated smoking area, no pets
🏃 Hiking/cycling trails at doorstep, Okanagan Lake viewpoints
🚗 Wineries, golfing, beaches, skiing, shopping
🐾 Newer home in a quiet area, close to nature and overlooking
Blair Pond, were birds are active. Hosts are knowledgeable about the area, local happenings and
where to dine. Enjoy a gourmet breakfast on the deck or in the formal dining room with a view of
the Pond. There is a dog in residence.Visa ✔ B&B

Geismayr, Fred and Gaby (Crawford View)   ☎ (250) 764-1140/Fax (250) 764-2892
810 Crawford Rd., Kelowna, BC   V1W 4N3

In Kelowna, turn off Hwy 97 onto Gordon Dr S, then left onto Casorso. Keep right at stop and left
after bridge. Turn right onto De Hart, left onto Crawford Rd. Watch for driveway on left side.

$40-55S $55-68D $7.50Child   ► 6A,2Ch
🍽 Full   🏠 Rural, hillside, balcony, acreage, view, swimming
pool, patio, tennis court   ■ 3 (upstairs in separate building)
⊨2T,2Q   ⬛3Ensuite ★F,LF,TV & fridge in guest rooms,
sep.entrance, parking 🚭Smoking outside ᗯGerman,French
🏃 Golf course, orchards
🚗 Downtown Kelowna, Okanagan Lake, hiking trails, wineries,
Big White Ski area, Airport
🐾 Enjoy Austrian hospitality on 6 acre country estate within city limits and outstanding
panoramic view of lake, city and orchards. Breakfast is served in main building dining room
overlooking the pool. MC ✔B&B

Grube, Kurt and Edith (Augusta View Bed & Breakfast)   ☎ & Fax (250) 763-0969
998 Augusta Ct., Kelowna, BC   V1Y 7T9   1-800-801-2992

Phone for directions.
$65-79S $75-89D $10Child $20Add.person   ► 8
🍽 Full, homebaked   🏠 Res., 2-storey, hill-side, view from guest
rooms, patio, quiet   ■2D,1F (ground level) ⊨2T,3Q,1P
⬛3Ensuite   ★ LF,TV/phone/library/wood stove in cozy guest
sitting room leading onto patio, separate entrance, parking
🚭No smoking, no pets   ᗯ German
🚗 Lake/beaches, wineries, various ski hills, Fruit Packing Plant,
Recreation Centre, shopping, water sports, fishing
🏃 Golf course (surrounds property), hiking in the hills/along ravine, birdwatching
🐾 Well travelled hosts in new hillside home with European atmosphere, antiques, collectibles
and artists' touch. Built with B&B in mind and situated in established Glenmore area, just above
the Kelowna Golf & Country Club. Breakfast is served on the garden deck with a breathtaking view
of city, mountains and lake. Off-season rates available. ✔B&B

O'Toole, Johanne & LLoyd (Wicklow Bed & Breakfast) ☎ (250) 768-1330,
1454 Green Bay Rd., Westbank, BC   V4T 2B8 Fax (250) 768-1335

In Kelowna, cross bridge, turn left off Hwy 97 at 2nd light to Boucherie Rd, proceed 5km to Green
Bay Rd. From Peachland turn right off Hwy 97 at Gellatly Rd, left on Boucherie Rd to Green Bay Rd

$70-80S $80-90D $20Add.person   ▶ 6A,4Ch
🔟 Full   🏠 Sub., 2-storey, view from guest rooms, lakefront,
patio, porch, quiet   ■ 2D,1F (upstairs & ground level)
⊨3Q,1P(Q)   ⚷1Private, 2ensuite   ★ Air,F,LF,TV in guest
rooms, wheel-chair access, private entrance, RV parking   Ⓦ No
smoking, no pets   ⋙ French
🏃 Private sandy beach, boat dock, adjacent bird sanctuary
🚗 Downtown Kelowna, Mission Hill/Quail's Gate Wineries

📣 6-year old waterfront home with classic English decor facing Green Bay and Okanagan Lake.
Hosts are retired Health Care Professionals, have travelled worldwide and are avid birdwatchers.
There are eight birdfeeders scattered throughout the garden attracting more than 50 varieties.
Enjoy breakfast in the sunny dining room or the covered veranda with a bay view either location.
Complimentary boat tours available for 2day stay. Visa,MC ╰B&B

Puderbach, Jo & Willi (Bird's Eye Bed & Breakfast) ☎ (250) 764-2480
5142 Lark St., Kelowna, BC   V1W 4L3 Fax (250) 764-8497

Located in the Upper Mission area off Hwy 97. Travel south onto
Dandosy/Lakeshore to Chute Lake Rd. Turn right on Lark.
$40S $58-68D $15-25Child   ▶ 4
🔟Full, homebaked   🏠Res., 2-storey, patio, deck, quiet   ■2D
(1Ste)(ground level)   ⊨2Q,1R   ⚷2Private   ★TV in guest sitting
area, off-street parking   Ⓦ No pets, smoking outside
⋙German
🏃 Walks in nearby woods with view of Okanagan Lake

🚗 Beaches, wineries, Mission & Orchard Park Shopping Centres, downtown, restaurants/fine
dining
📣 Contemporary home with terraced rock garden and large patio in a quiet prestige area.
Children welcome. Visa ╰B&B

Rentmeister, Gisela & Gunther (Lakeview Mansion) ☎ & Fax (250) 768-2205
3858 Harding Rd., Westbank, BC   V4T 2J9

In Kelowna, cross Okanagan Lake Bridge. Turn left at McDonalds Restaurant (7th traffic light) and
continue towards Lake. Turn right onto Angus Dr and then right on Harding Rd (cul-de-sac).
Coming from Vancouver/Penticton, go through Westbank and turn right at McDonalds.

$60S $70-80D $10Child $20Add.person   ▶ 4-6
🔟Full, homebaked (Gourmet)   🏠Semi-rural, res., sub., 2-storey,
very quiet, Spanish-style, view from guest rooms   ■ 2-3 (upst)
⊨3Q,1-2 cots   ⚷1Private, 1sh.w.g.,1ensuite   ★Air,TV/phone in
guest roosms, TV/VCR, guest library, parking, 6 jet Hydro-Spa
ⓌNo smoking inside, no pets   ⋙German
🏃 Stroll down the road to the beaches
🚗 Superb dining, waterslide, swimming pool, wineries (tours)

golf courses, shopping centre, downhill & x/c skiing, Paddlewheeler, fruit processing plant
📣 Warm German hospitality in large, elegant Spanish-style home with park-like grounds &
breathtaking panoramic view of lake/mountains. Situated just above Okanagan Lake. Enjoy a
delicious beverage upon arrival, have a dip in the Jacuzzi, watch one of a collection of 70 movies in
the cozy library, or just relax on 2000 sq ft of covered/open sundecks. Visa,MC ╰B&B

Ruf, Eva-Maria & Michael (Apple Blossom B&B)
3582 Appleway Blvd, Kelowna, Westbank, BC   V4T 1Y7

☎ & Fax (250) 768-1163
Toll free 1-888-718-5064

Located off Hwy 97, below Mission Hill Winery.
$60-65S $65-75D   ►4A
🕮Full, homebaked 🏠Res., hillside, lakeview from guest
rooms,patio, quiet ■2D(ground level) ⊨2T,1Q,1P ⏎2Ensuite
★Air,F,LF,KF,TV in guest rooms, air-conditioners, sep.entrance,
off-street parking   🖑Desig.smoking area, no pets, children min
age 10 ⌇ German
🚗 City bus No20, shopping malls, restaurants, hiking in
Kalamoir Reg.Park, walking trails along Okanagan Lake, beaches, swimming, water sports rentals,
Mission Hill & Quail's Gate wineries (tours), golfing, downhill & x-c skiing
🐾 Bavarian hospitality in new house built for B&B and supreme comfort for guests. Enjoy the
panormaic views from large picture windows throughout the house. Rest in the comfortable lounge
or on the patio or by the waterfall. Hostess is an experienced cook. House specialty is "German
apple souffle". Breakfast is served in the formal dining room. Ideal place for a romantic get-away or
special occasions. Visa ⌁B&B

Schwab, Otto & Ella Van Dinther (Otella's Guest House)
42 Altura Rd., Kelowna, BC   V1V 1B6

☎ (250) 763-4922
1-888-858-8596, Fax (250) 763-4982

From Hwy 97, turn north on Spall (London Drugs).At Summit/High turn left on High, then right
on Clifton, right on Caramillo and left on Altura.
$65-85S $75-95D 🍴 Meals   ►8
🕮 Full, homebaked 🏠 Res., 3-storey, hillside, view from guest
rooms, 3patios, porch, deck, quiet ■ 4D (main & upper level)
⊨ 2T,3Q ⏎ 1Sh.w.g., 2ensuite ★ Air,F,separate entrance,
room keys, off-street parking, host quarters are in lower level,
guest lounge on main floor   🖑 No smoking, no pets, children
min.age 12 ⌇Dutch, German
🏃 Hike/jog/mountainbike or x-c ski into adjacent forest with many trails, Knox Mountain Park
🚗 Agricultural Research Station, Kelowna downtown, wineries/orchards (tours), golf courses,
restaurants, sandy beach with park, Kettle Valley Railway hiking, downhill ski resorts, art galleries
🐾 Large comfortable home with serene valley and mountainviews. Relax by the stone fireplace in
the beautiful guest lounge. Well travelled hosts are experienced in the food/wine and hospitality
industry and are very fond of Okanagan wines and enjoy sharing this interest with their guests.
Gourmet breakfast is prepared by host Chef and served in the elegant dining room or on one of the
charming patios outside. Fax service available. Visa,MC ⌁CC

Szita, Andy & Marilyn Rae (The Grapevine B&B)
2621 Longhill Rd.,Kelowna,BC V1V 2G5

☎(250)860-5580,1-800-956-5580,
E-mail: grapevin@silk.net, Fax(250)860-5586

In Kelowna turn north off Hwy 97 on Dilworth Drive to Longhill
Rd. Turn right onto Monford Rd for parking at entrance.
$65-75S $75-85D $20Add.person (plus taxes) 🍴 Meals ►10
🕮Full, homebaked 🏠Rural, 2-storey, acreage,patio,porch,quiet
■3D,1F(upstairs) ⊨2Q,2K(T),1P ⏎2Private,2ensuite ★Air,LF,
TV in guest rooms, sep.entrance, F (in guest living room) 🖑No
pets, smoking outside, children minimum age 10
🏃 Hiking trail, cycling, walks
🚗 Wineries, golfing, skiing, hiking, hot air ballooning, restaurants, shopping centres, beaches
🐾 Cape Cod-style home situated on 1 acre in the wine region of the beautiful Okanagan Valley.
Relax and enjoy the peaceful country setting and friendly hospitality. Delight in the many birds as
they feed in the hillside garden. Hosts are gourmet cooks and serve unique, creatively presented
breakfasts. Convenient location for business travellers. CCards ⌁CC

Kimberley

(north of Cranbrook; see also Fort Steele, Fernie, Jaffray)

Moore, Robert (Bob) & Mary Lue (The Moores Bed & Breakfast)   ☎ (250) 427-7092
104 Levirs Ave., Kimberley, BC   V1A 1X5

From Hwy 93, take Burdett St and the Levirs Ave on right.
$45S $55D   ▶ 4
🍲 Full, homebaked   🏠 Res., split-level, view, quiet, deck   ▪2D
(upstairs) ⊨2Q ⊒1Sh.w.g. ★ TV, parking Ⓦ No
smoking, no pets, children min. age 11
🧍 Centre of town, long walking trails, Bavarian Theme Platzl
(plaza), restaurants, shops
🚗 Kimberley Ski Hill (5km-with night skiing), x-c skiing, golfing
(P.G.A. & Kimberley courses), Fairmont Hotsprings, Purcell Mountains, US border
🐻 Spacious home with large back deck, glorious views of the Rocky Mountains and quiet,
relaxing atmosphere; located in interesting mountain town (highest city in Canada). Hosts enjoy
meeting people and spending time with guests. ✓B&B

Wheatcroft, Gerry & Dorothy Robinson (Boundary Street House)   ☎ (250) 427-3510,
89 Boundary St., Kimberley, BC   V1A 2H4   Fax (250) 427-3528

In Kimberley on Wallinger Ave, go 3 blocks north of Post Office to Boundary St. Turn left. Watch
for sign on right.

$50-55S $65-70D $15Add.person   ▶ 6A
🍲Full,homebaked   🏠Downtown, older, 1.5 storey, patio, quiet
▪3D(main & upper floor) ⊨1D,2Q ⊒1ensuite,1sh.wg. ★F,LF,
sitting area in rooms, parking �Ⓦ Smoking outside, no pets
🧍 Downtown Kimberley, Pedestrian Mall, unique shops, galleries,
restaurants & coffee houses, nature trails, Cominco Gardens,
Presbyterian and United churches
🚗 Fort Steele Heritage Town, Canadian Museum of Rail Travel, St. Eugene's Mission & Church
🐻 Pretty (c1920) cottage-style home lovingly restored, furnished with comfortable period
antiques & family heirlooms & a wonderful view with rock gardens and Tamarack covered hillside.
Explore Kimberley and the area, soak in a claw-foot tub, read in the sitting room or day dream on
the patio. Enjoy a fresh wholesome breakfast. Visa ✓CC

Lac la Hache

(south of Williams Lake; see also Clearwater)

Skyers, Carmen & Aubrey (Forbes Landing Sunset Lodge)   ☎ (250) 396-4984
Box 160, 3621 Forbes Rd., Lac la Hache, BC   V0K 1T0

Located 10km north of the townsite of Lac la Hache. From Hwy 97, turn onto Forbes Rd.

$65-85S/D 🍽Meals   ▶ 6A
🍲 Cont.   🏠 Rural, res., ranch-style, acreage, view, patio,
quiet ▪ 3D ⊨4T,1Q ⊒2sh.w.g. ★ F,private entrance,
off-street parking, guest quarters are separate Ⓦ No smoking,
no pets, not suitable for children
🧍 Scenic lakeview walkabout, in-house Yellow Bird Tea Room
🚗 Downhill & x-c skiing, fishing, historic attractions, rodeo (July
& Aug), horesback riding
🐻 Enjoy a relaxing Cariboo experience in quiet surroundings. Hosts will offer evening sing along
entertainment for guests and live Calypso music in lounge. Pet resort nearby. Visa. ✓CC

Ladner
(Vancouver; see also White R, Delta, N.Westmin, Surrey, Richmond,Tsawwassen)

Dillman, Carol & Irene Scarth (Our House B&B)   ☎ (604) 946-2628, Fax (604) 946-6869
4837-44A Ave., Delta (Ladner), BC   V4K 1E3

Phone for directions.
$50S $70D   ▶ 5A
▯Full (cater to special diets) ▮Village, res., 2-storey, patio, quiet
▮3(upstairs), host quarters are separate ⊨1S,2Q ⇱1Sh.w.g.
★F,TV/VCR in guest living room, off-street parking
Ⓦ Designated smoking area ⌒some French
ⵜ City parks, excellent restaurants specializing in fish dishes,
library, museum, village shops, bus route to airport, birdwatching
🚗 Richmond, downtown Vancouver, Bird Sanctuary, International Airport, beaches, ferry
🐾 Warm welcome in home situated in a quiet area of a friendly fishing and farming-oriented
community. Upper floor is entirely for guests. Hosts are world travellers and have lived in other
countries. Airport, and ferry pick-up available for a small fee. Special rates for long term stays. Also
available furnished Condos. Visa,MC ⌁B&B

Ladysmith
(on Vancouver Island south of Nanaimo; see also Chemainus, Duncan)

Merrill, Bill & Jo (The Secret Garden)   ☎ (250) 245-3578
3511 Paulson Rd., RR3, Ladysmith, BC   V0R 2E0

Located off Yellow Point Rd, between Nanaimo & Ladysmith. Phone for directions.

$55S $60D   ▶ 4
▯ Choice, homebaked   ▮ Rural, 2storey hillside house with 2
ground levels, acreage, view, patio, quiet   ▮ 2D (main & ground
level) ⊨2Q ⇱2Private ★F,KF, 2 sep.entrances, parking
ⵜ Blue Heron Park, Roberts Park, Yellow Point Park
🚗 Beach & woods trails, many craft & souvenir shops, easy day
trips to Victoria, Chemainus & north Island sites, notable dining
🐾 Unusual home with antiques & artwork and lovely secluded
garden & forest setting in beautiful Yellow Point. There is a small gallery featuring hosts' paintings
and stained glass. Rooms look out on garden pond and beaver pond and with luck, assorted wildlife.
There is an inside dog and an outside cat.

Langley
(Vancouver); see also Surrey, White Rock, Delta, Ladner, Abbotsford, Tsawassen)

Dean, Heather & Darrell (Tramore House B&B)   ☎ (604) 857-2618, Fax (604) 857-4918
26261-64B Ave., Langley, BC   V4W 3M7   E-mail: yodan@bc.sympatico.ca

From TCH1 east of Vancouver, take 264th St Exit North and travel 2km. Turn left onto 64B Ave
and to B&B on right. Located 13km north of the Canada/Lynden US border crossing.

$60S $70D   ▶ 4A
▯ Full   ▮ Rural, 2-storey, view from guest rooms, acreage,
deck, quiet   ▮ 2D(upstairs) ⊨ 2T,1D   ⇱ 1Sh.w.g.
★F,LF,TV in guest rooms, game room, off-street parking
Ⓦ Designated smoking area, no pets, no children
🚗 Regional parks, BC Game Farm, US border, antique stores,
Fort Langley, golfing, downtown Vancouver, Abbotsford airport
🐾 Retired Military couple in lovely new English Tudor house,
filled with fascinating memorabilia of travels & foreign countries where hosts have lived. Situated
on 5 acres, an ideal place for those searching for a peaceful & serenic setting. Full English breakfast
is served in the formal dining room. There are 2 dogs & a Parrot. ⌁ B&B

Jarvis, Elaine & Ray (Spring Brook Meadows B&B) ☎ (604) 856-3032
25420-64th Ave., Aldergrove, BC   V4W 1H3   E-mail: jarsaw@uniserve, Fax (604) 856-4509

Phone for directions.
$55S $69D $10Child $20Horses   ► 6
🍳 Full, homebaked   🏠 Farm, 2-storey, hillside, view from guest
rooms, patio, deck, gazebo, garden pond   ■ 1D,1F (upstairs &
ground level)   ⊨1D,1Q(waterbed),1P(double futon)
🛏2Private   ★F,TV in guest rooms, air-conditioners, ceiling
fans, hot tub, separate entrance   ⓌDesignated smoking area
🚗 Fort Langley, US border, City of Vancouver, island ferries
🕏 Tranquil gardens with gazebo & pond (watch fish feed), bike to the Vancouver Zoological Centre
🐾 Cheerful home on 5acre farm with cows, horses, cats & dogs, located in the central Fraser
Valley. Relax by the cozy fireplace or in the hot tub off large sundeck with a wonderful view of
Golden Ears Mountains and surrounding fields. Hosts are experienced bakers and serve delicious
goodies for breakfast. RV parking & 6-stall barn for horses available. There is a cat. ✒B&B

Schwertner, Sylvia & Alan (Traveller's Joy B&B) ☎ (604) 533-2696, Fax (604) 533-3480
59 Wagonwheel Cr., Langley, BC   V2Z 2R1

From Hwy 1 take Exit 66 south onto 232St. Follow the signs and turn left off Hwy 10 to stay on
232St. Turn left on 56Ave then first turn right onto Clovermeadow and Wagonwheel Cr.
$40S $60D $15Child $80F $15Add.person   ► 4A,2Ch
🍳 Full, homebaked   🏠 Rural, res., 2-storey, acreage, quiet, secluded   ■ 1D,1F(main & upper
level)   ⊨2Q,1P   🛏1Private, 1ensuite   ★ LF,F,TV in guest lounge, ceiling fans, balconies,
off-street parking, guest quarters are separate   Ⓦ Designated smoking area
🕏 Small Lake and park trail, golf course, shuttle service to airport, downtown bus/skytrain
🚗 Int. Airport, downtown Vancouver, beaches, Provincial parks, historic sites, museums,
mountains, horse riding trails
🐾 Peaceful and comfortable home with large country garden situated in a quiet residential area
of small acreages. Friendly and informal hosts can provide information about day trips in the Fraser
Valley or Vancouver area. Parking space for RV & house trailer. There is a cat. ✒B&B

Wong, Nola and Joseph (Nola's Garden B&B) ☎ (604) 533-3348
4675-209th St., Langley, BC   V3A 7E7

Tak 232 St exit south off Hwy 1 to Langley. Turn left on Glover Rd, then left on No10 bypass, cross
Fraser Hwy (becomes 208St). Proceed to 47Ave. Turn left to house/3rd cul-de-sac right.

From Vancouver or USA border phone for directions.
$50-60S $60-70D $15Add.person   ► 6
🍳 Full, homebaked(after 8am)   🏠 Res., sub., multi-storey, view
from guest rooms, patio, quiet   ■1F,1D(upst)   ⊨2Q,1P(D)
🛏 1Private, 1ensuite   ★ F,LF,KF, TV in guest room,
sep.entrance, parking   Ⓦ Smoking outside only
🕏 Newlands Golf Club and restaurant, corner store, several
churches, bus stop
🚗 Downtown & historic Fort Langley, Cloverdale Rodeo, Vancouver, ferry to Vancouver Island,
airport, Game Farm, Abbotsford Air Show, Harrison Hot Springs, US border, Milner Downs
🐾 Australian hostess in casual friendly home with gardens of riotous colour, birds and fish pond.
Relax and enjoy the quiet area away from the sound of traffic. Information and maps supplied for
guests' continuing journey.

Lantzville

(north of Nanaimo; see also Nanoose Bay, Parksville)

Martin, Sue & Dave (Home Again Bed & Breakfast)   ☎ (250) 390-3863
6773 Philip Rd., Lantzville, BC V0R 2H0

North of Nanaimo, turn off Island Hwy onto Aulds Rd. Proceed to stop sign (3km), turn left onto
Ware Rd, then right onto Philip Rd to house on left half-way down the hill.

$40S $55D $10Add.person $5Hot Tub   ▶ 4A,1Ch
🔌 Full   🏠 Rural, res., split-level, view, quiet   ■2D(upstairs)
⊨2T,1D,1P   ⌐Sh.w.g.   ★F   ⓦDesignated smoking area
🏃 Winchelsea View Golf Course, beach (see seals, sea lions)
🚐 Ferries, airport, hiking, boating, theatres, restaurants
☛ Comfortable and cozy home with view of the Winchelsea
Islands, Georgia Strait and mainland mountains in the background.
Good old English breakfast is served in the dining room off the
guest lounge. Relax by the fireplace after a walk on the beach or in the secluded ivy-surrounded hot
tub. There is a dog "Bill" and a cat "Smudge" in residence. ⟋B&B

Mara

(east of Salmon Arm; see also Sicamous,Vernon)

Bender, Fred & Anne (Lakeview Bed & Breakfast)   ☎ & Fax (250) 838-2283
92 Davy Rd., RR1, S2, C2, Mara, BC V0E 2K0

From Sicamous, follow Hwy 97A south for 17 km. Look for B&B signs or phone for directions.

$40S $55D $10Child $15Add.person   (weekly rates)   ▶ 6
🔌 Full, homebaked   🏠 Rural, bungalow, acreage, view from
guest rooms, quiet, isolated   ■ 1D,1F (upstairs & lower level)
⊨ 2S,1D,1Q   ⌐ 1Private, 1ensuite   ★TV, separate entrance
ⓦNo smoking, no pets   ∾ German
🏃 Hiking from back door
🚐 Beaches, golfing, fishing, boating, x/c skiing, hang-gliding,
Salmon Arm, Vernon
☛ Quiet mountain home with breathtaking view of Mara Lake and Shuswap River situated on
wooded acreage. Relax and enjoy a wonderful breakfast served with warm hospitality in the
solarium with view. ⟋B&B

Mayne Island

(east of Ladysmith; see also Saltspring Island)

Engelhardt, Jurgen & Judith Solie-Engelhardt (The Tinkerer's B&B)
C31 Miners Bay, 417 Georgina Pt Rd., Mayne Island, BC V0N 2J0   ☎ & Fax(250)539-2280
Take BC Ferry from Tsawwassen on the mainland (near Vancouver) or from Swartz Bay on

Vancouver Island (near Victoria).
$35-60S $70-90D $25Add.person   (plus tax)   ▶ 10
❎ Apr15-Oct15   🔌 Full, homebaked   🏠 Village, rural, older, view
from two guest rooms, multi-storey, oceanfront, quiet, wrap-around
decks   ■2D,1F (main, upper & ground levels)   ⊨ 5S,2D,1Q
⌐1Sh.w.g., 1ensuite   ★F,TV in guest room, 2 separate entrances,
parking   ⓦSmoking outside only, no pets   ∾German, Spanish
🏃 Miners Bay Village, government wharf, pub, restaurants
🚐 Georgina Point Lighthouse, Dinner Bay Park, Campbell & Bennet Bays, artists home studios
☛ Home is one of the most colorful and whimsical buildings on the Island, surrounded by
wonderful organic gardens of edible & medicinal herbs, flowers & fruit trees with magnificient
views of Active Pass. Bicycle, hike, paddle, ramble through the idyllic landscape and marine scenery.
Visit with Island artists in their home studios. Groups and families welcome. Visa,MC ⟋B&B

Merritt

(south-west of Kamloops)

Grant, Luke and Gale (Merritt's Finest B&B)   ☎ (250) 378 9865,
Grant Ranches, Aberdeen Rd., Box 4040, Lower Nicola, BC   V0K 1Y0   Fax (250) 378-4004

From Merritt, take Hwy 8 west toward Spences Bridge. Phone for detailed directions.

$50S $60D   ► 9A
🍳 Full, homebaked   🏠 Ranch, 2-level ranch-style, view from
guest rooms, large covered decks, patio, quiet, isolated ■2(ground
level) ⊨1S,2T,2D,1Q,1P 🛁2Sh.w.g., 1sh.w.h. ★TV,F,LF,
separate entrance, parking 🐾 No pets (boarding kennel next
door), restricted smoking, adults preferred
🧍 Nature trails along creeks with beaver ponds, fish feeding
station, adult horseback riding (by arrangement), bicycling
🚐 Merritt, scenic lakes ("A lake a day for as long as you stay"), x-country skiing, hiking, fishing
🐎 Genuine cow/calf working ranch located in the Nicola Valley with spacious rooms and
surrounded by beautiful mountain scenery. Guests are welcome to watch or take part in ranch
activities at own risk. House specialty: Belgian waffles. There is an open fire area in the house yard
for wiener roasts and relaxation. ⊶CC

Mill Bay

(south of Duncan; see also Cobble Hill)

Beevor-Potts, Carole & Bob (Arbutus Cove B&B)   ☎ (250) 743-1435, Fax (250) 743-1410
2812 Wiltshire Rd., RR2, Mill Bay, BC   V0R 2P0

From Victoria take Hwy 1 north through Mill Bay to 2nd traffic light (past Mill Bay Centre). Turn
east on Kilmalu Rd and proceed 2 km to Whiskey Pt.Rd. Turn left to Wiltshire Rd.

$60S $80-85D   ► 4A
🍳 Full, homebaked   🏠 Rural, ranch-style, acreage, view from
guest rooms, oceanfront, patio, deck, quiet ■ 2D (ground level)
⊨2Q   🛁2Ensuite ★ F,TV in guest lounge, sep.entrance,
canoe & bicycles for guests 🐾 No smoking, no pets, no children
🧍 Nature Park with walking trail, exploring beach frontage on
Saanich Inlet, swimming
🚐 Three public golf courses, fishing charters/boat rentals, wineries, BC Forest Museum, Victoria
🐎 Spacious, new westcoast-style home situated on 2 wooded acres on the water with southerly
view of beautiful Mill Bay. Relax in guest lounge, explore the area by bicycle, or use the canoe.
Congenial hosts are knowledgeable of the local scene and can recommend good restaurants and
activities. Breakfast is served in modern kitchen or on the spacious sundeck. Visa,MC ⊶B&B

Garbet, Dot & Jim (Maple Tree Lane Bed & Breakfast by the Sea))   ☎ (250) 743-3940
440 Goulet Rd., RR2, Mill Bay, BC   V0R 2P0   Fax (250) 743-3959

From Hwy 1, turn east onto Hutchinson Rd towards Arbutus Ridge, right onto Telegraph Rd, left
onto LaFortune Rd, right onto Kilip Rd and left onto Goulet Rd. Look for signs on all corners.
$60S $85D $20Add.person   (winter rates & 3days-plus discounts) 🍴 meals   ► 5A,3Ch

🍳 Full, homebaked   🏠 Rural, 3-storey chalet-type, acreage,
view, oceanfront, swimming pool, patio, porch, deck, quiet ■1D,1F
(main & lower level) ⊨2T,1Q,1P,crib 🛁2Private ★F,LF,TV
in guest room, separate entrance (lower level), facilities for
handicapped 🐾Designated smoking area
🧍 Arbutus Golf & Country Club, path leading to beach, canoeing
🚐 Mill Bay (shopping centre, marina, Chemainus (famous
murals, dinner theatre, craft shops), Duncan (totem poles)
🐎 Quiet oceanfront home. Enjoy the restful area and relax in the garden gazebo. Breakfast is
cheerfully served in country kitchen, on deck, by the pool, on the patio or under the Old Apple Tree.
Host will be delighted to have guests join him in a fishing venture. There are 2 cats. MC ⊶B&B

Moulton, Harold & Carol (Lee Wind Bed & Breakfast)   ☎ (250) 743-4363
646 Frayne Rd., RR1, Mill Bay, BC V0R 2P0

Located approx. 58km north of Victoria. Phone for directions.
$45S $75D   ► 6
🍽 Full, homebaked   🏠 Rural, res., 2-storey, small acreage, patio,
oceanview, quiet   ■ 1S,2D (main & upper level)   ⊨ 2S,1D,1Q
🛏1Private, 1sh.w.g.   ★ Air,TV,LF   🚭 No smoking, no pets
🕺 Marina (Mill Bay), shopping center, salt water beach, restaurant
🚗 Victoria, Nanaimo, Airport, ferries to mainland, hiking trails
🔫 Retired couple in comfortable fairly new home built by the hosts, situated in a country setting
and filled with beautiful handmade quilts/pictures/needlework. Hosts run fishing charters. ✓CC

Norton, Clifford & Mary (Norton's Green Bed & Breakfast)   ☎ (250) 743-8006
663 Frayne Rd., RR1, Mill Bay, BC V0R 2P0

Take Island Hwy into Mill Bay, turn left on Frayne Rd. Driveway is
on left before green mail boxes.
$50S $55D   ► 4
🍽 Full   🏠 Res, porch, quiet   ■ 2D (main floor)   ⊨1D,1Q
🛏 1Sh.w.g.   ★ F,LF,guest terry robes, off-street parking
🚭No smoking, no pets
🕺 Bay/beach/marina/waterfront park, restaurants, quaint shops
🚗 Victoria, Chemainus & Murals, Ladysmith, Duncan, Totems,
Native Heritage Centre, Brentwood College, Duncan, Victoria, Cowichan Valley wineries, Arbutus
Golf Course, Cowichan Bay (fishing & sailing)
🔫 Warm welcome and friendly hospitality in new house in old-fashioned style with wrap-around
balcony and pretty garden. Enjoy the relaxed atmosphere and 4 o'clock Tea. Longtime hosts enjoy
welcoming people from all over the world. ✓B&B

Salmon, John and Emmi (Billion $ View)   ☎ (250) 743-2387
610 Shorewood Rd., RR1, Mill Bay, BC V0R 2P0

From Victoria, travel north over the Malahat Mountain to Mill Bay. Turn right on Frayne Rd and
proceed to Mill Bay Rd. Turn left and then right again on Shorewood Rd (house on corner).

$55S $60D $15Add person   ► 6A,2Ch
🍽 Full   🏠 Rural, Bay view from suite, patio, oceanfront,quiet
🛏1Private   ■2D,1Ste (ground level)   ⊨2T,1D,1Q   ★Separate
entrance, TV/VCR/kettle in suite   🚭No smoking, no drinking, no
pets   🗣Spanish, German, Italian
🕺 Beach, pleasant walks along oceanside road, marina
🚗 Bemberton Park and beach, Native Centre, Hanging Bridge
and walks, Forest Museum, Duncan
🔫 Warm welcome in contemporary waterfront home overlooking Mt Baker and surrounded by
large landscaped gardens. Hostess, originally from Paraguay & teaches languages. ✓B&B

Mission
(east of Vancouver; see also Abbotsford)

Perdue, Fran & Martin (Fence Post Lane B&B)   ☎ (604) 820-7009, Fax (604) 820-4974
8575 Gaglardi St., Mission, BC   V4S 1B2

$50S $60-75D $10Child(under age 12) $15Add.person   ► 4-5

From Lougheed Hwy No7 at 6.6km west of Mission, turn right on Chester, then left on Silverdale and right on Gaglardi St.
🍴 Full, homebaked (special diets accommodated)   🏠 Rural, ranch-style/back-split, acreage, view, patio, porch, deck, quiet, secluded   ■ 2 (main & lower level)   ⊨ 1Q,1D   ⊿2Private
★F,separate large TV room, fans in guest rooms, quiet reading area   ⍓ Smoking outside, no pets
🏃 Back-yard strolling (with bridge over creek), Community Hall
🚗 Restaurants, shops, golfing, Mission Raceway, Westminster Abbey, Harrison Hot Springs, hiking at Rolley Lake, Ruskin, Mission & Stave Falls Dams, Vancouver (commuter trains)
☛ Longtime B&B hosts in new, lovely decorated quiet country home, surrounded by beautifully landscaped acreage with creek and bridge in backyard. Guests can relax in the large entertainment room or enjoy the outside patios. Ideal place for anniversaries, special occasions or weekend get-aways. There is a resident cat. Visa

Nanaimo
(on Vancouver Island; see also Lantzville, Nanoose Bay)

Craig, Carol & Jack (Jake and The Weaver's Bed & Breakfast)   ☎ (250) 756-1223
4111 Salal Dr., Nanaimo, BC   V9T 5L2

From Nanaimo Parkway, exit at Mostar Rd, which becomes Rutherford Rd. From Island Hwy, turn onto Rutherford and proceed to Uplands Dr. Turn right to Collishaw Rd, right to Ross Rd and right to Salal Dr.

$50S $60D   ► 2-4A
🍴 Full, homebaked   🏠 Res., 2-storey, small acreage, view from guest rooms, deck, quiet   ■2D(upst)
⊨2T,1Q   ⊿1Private   ★TV & ceiling fans & individual heat controls in guest rooms   ⍓No pets, no smoking, not suitable for children, only one party at a time
🏃 Executive par 3 golf gourse, Rutherford Village Mall, restaurants, Long Lake, bus service
🚗 Parks with trails in greater Nanaimo area, Chemainus (crafts/murals), Coombs Market
☛ Retired professional couple in custom designed Cape Cod-style white stucco house surrounded by trees, shrubs and flower beds, with large deck overlooking a green belt bordering the golf course. Second floor is dedicated to guests. Ideally situated for trips north, south & west to many Island attractions. Hostess is a weaver and spins/knits quality crafted clothing. Pick-up/deliver to Departure Bay Ferry, train or bus. Add.charge to Duke Point Ferry or Airport. ✓B&B

Gardiner, Fred & Elizabeth (Seaview Panorama B&B)   ☎ (250) 756-3152
5380 Kenwill Dr., Nanaimo, BC   V9T 5Z9

Phone for directions.
$40S $55-70D $70+F $10Airport pick-up   ► 9
🍴 Full   🏠 Res., 2-storey, hillside, view from guest rooms, patio, deck,quiet   ■1S,2D,1F(main & ground level)   ⊨1D,2Q,1K,1R
⊿1Private, 1sh.w.g., 1ensuite (jacuzzi tub)   ★F,TV, billiard room, parking   ⍓ Designated smoking area, no pets
🏃 Two shopping malls, restaurants
🚗 Scenic area, beaches, forest, waterfalls, ferry docks
☛ Fairly new rancher house with a majestic view of Georgia Strait/mainland/mountains and fantastic sunsets. House specialty is "Pecan waffles by Fred". There is a cat in residence. MC ✓B&B

Dillon, Darlene & Russ (The Island View B&B)   ☎ & Fax (250) 758-5536
5391 Entwhistle Dr., Nanaimo, BC   V9V 1H2

From Departure Bay Ferry Terminal follow Island Hwy 19A to Rutherford Rd. Turn right to
Hammond Bay Rd, right to Entwhistle Dr. Turn left and down hill to B&B on left side. From Duke
Point t Ferry Terminal take Hwy 19 to Mostar Rd., turn right and follow through lights at Hwy
19A. Road name changes to Rutherford Rd. Proceed as above.

$50S $60D $85Apt $20Add.person   🍽Meals   ►6A,2Ch
🍷Full   🏠 Res., 2-storey, view from guest rooms, patio, quiet,
deck ■1D,1F(ground level) ➥2T,1Q,1P(Q),2cots ⛱2Private
★ F,KF,LF,TV in guest rooms, private entrance, guest quarters
are separate, off-street parking ✋ No smoking, no pets
🚶 Walks along rocky shoreline, park, pub, No2 bus in next block
🚗 Departure Bay Ferry Terminal, Parksville, Coombs Market
Place, Cathedral Grove, Nanaimo, Chemainus

🔫 Warm & friendly hospitality in newly renovated home in a quiet area on 0.5 acre garden
paradise. Relax on the deck, enjoy the beautiful sunsets & spectacular views. Breakfast is served in
the main floor dining room at guests' convenience. Free pick-up & delivery in Nanaimo.✍B&B

Grogan, Gloria & Gene (Beach Drive B&B)   ☎ (250) 753-9140
1011 Beach Dr., Nanaimo, BC   V9S 2Y4

Phone for directions.
$35S $50D $25Add.person   n/c (Child under age 6)   ►4
🍷 Homebaked   🏠 Res., split-level, oceanview   ■ 2D (ground
level)   ➥ 2T,1D   ⛱ Sh.w.g.   ★ TV,LF,separate entrance,
parking   ～ Ukrainian, Irish
🚶 Beach access & beach combing, waterfront promanade to
downtown, Castle & Protection Islands (short boat trips for island
nature trails & Canada's only floating pub "Dingy Dock Pub")
🚗 Golf courses, Cathedral Grove with 1000 year-old trees, Indian shops with native works,
Chemainus Murals, Parksville, Salmon Charter fishing, kayaking, Adventure Tours
🔫 Home overlooks Departure Bay Ferry Terminal on the Strait of Georgia. Enjoy the distant
view of the Sunshine coast from the big bright sunroom where breakfast is served. Well travelled
retired hosts enjoy golfing and are active with volunteer work and many hobbies. Free ferry pick-up
at Departure Bay Ferry Terminal only. ✍CC

Turgeon, Ivan & Audrey (Jingle Pot B&B)   ☎ (250) 758-5149
4321 Jingle Pot Rd., Nanaimo, BC   V9T 5P4   E-mail: jpotandb@nisa.net

From Hwy 19 take Exit 24 and proceed north to Mostar, to Boban and to Jingle Pot Rd. From Hwy

19A, turn left at Jingle Pot Rd after Country Club Mall.
$75S $85D $15Child/Add.person   (plus tax)   ►6
🍷Full   🏠Rural, ranch-style, deck, fishing pond, quiet,secluded
■1Ste(ground level) ➥2Q,2R ⛱1Ensuite ★Air(air
cleaner), LF,F,KF,TV in guest suite, ceiling fans, separate
entrance, ramp & wheel-chair access, steam bath, mountain bike &
fitness equipment available for guests, guest quarters are
separate ✋Designated smoking area ～ French
🚶 Numerous parks, lakes, golf courses, shopping malls, hiking trails, bus Rte No4 (Bowen Rd)
🚗 Parksville, Coombs Market Place, Cathedral Grove, Chemainus, ferries to Mainland
🔫 Fairly new contemporary rancher nestled in 0.5 acres of beautiful landscaped property. Host is
a retired Sea Captain with a great deal of knowledge about the West Coast and always willing to tell
a story or two. Extra wide doors and overhead lift capability for wheel-chair access. Breakfast is
served in the solarium or patio or private dining area in suite. Diets catered to by request. Ideal
place for honeymoons/special occasion. Ferry/airport pick-up can be arranged. CCards ✍B&B

Whyte, Nancy (Gateshead B&B)　　　　　　　　　☎ (250) 754-3362
551 Nanaimo River Rd., Nanaimo, BC　V9X 1E2

From Nanaimo follow signs to Bungy Zone. Located off TCH south of Nanaimo.
$40S　$55D　$10Child　$10Add.person　🍽 Meals　　　　　▶ 7A,1Ch

🏠 Full, homebaked,　🏠 Rural, 2-storey, acreage, patio, porch, deck, quiet　■ 2D,1Ste (main & ground level)　⊨ 1S,2T,2Q
🛏 1Private, 1ensuite, 1sh.w.h.　★ LF,TV in guest room, hot tub in solarium off one room, off-street parking　🖐 Smoking on deck, no pets　⌇some French
🏃 Nanaimo River and swimming, shuttle available
🚗 Bungy Zone, Ladysmith, Chemainus and famous murals
🐎 Olde English hospitality in park-like setting. Hostess is a former Chef. Relax in the patio hot-tub after a day of sightseeing or travelling. ⌐B&B

Nanoose Bay　　　*(on Vancouver Island south of Parksville; see also Lantzville, Nanaimo)*

Hoglund, Knut & Marg (Court-Yard B&B)　　　☎ & Fax (250) 468-1720
Box 53, RR1, 1569 Madrona Dr., Nanoose Bay, BC　V0R 2R0

From Nanaimo on Island Hwy 19, turn at Parksville Exit and proceed north on Hwy 19A. After Tourist Office, turn right on Franklin Gull Rd, which becomes North West Bay Rd. Turn left at Beaver Creek Wharf and right at Madrona Dr.
$65S　$75D　$20Add.person　　　　　　　　　　　　▶ 6A
🍽 Cont., homebaked, buffet　🏠 Res., raised bungalow, view, deck, quiet　■ 2(ground level)
⊨ 2Q,1P　🛏 Ensuite　★ Air,LF,F in guest lounge, TV in guest room, off-street parking
🖐No smoking, no pets, no children　⌇ Norwegian
🏃 Access to beach areas, beach-walking, scuba diving, observe marine wildlife (seals/sea lions)
🚗 Fairwinds Golf Course, fishing, boating at Schooner Cove
🐎 Scandinavian warmth and charm in modern, new home, tastefully decorated and situated in central Island location. A good place from which to explore Vancouver Island. Hosts are knowledgeable of area sites and establishments and gladly assist with itineraries. There is a Toy Poodle in residence. Visa,MC ⌐B&B

Wilkie, Marj and Herb (The Lookout at Schooner Cove)　　☎ & Fax (250) 468-9796
Box 71, Blueback Dr., RR2, Nanoose Bay, BC　V0R 2R0

Location: 3381 Dolphin Drive. Phone for directions or follow signs to Schooner Cove at Fairwinds.
$50S　$60-90D　(weekly rate for vacation suite)　　　　　▶ 12A

🏕 May1-Sept30　🍽 Choice　🏠 Res., view, wrap-around decks,quiet, ■3D,plus vacation suite　⊨3Q,1P,1R,air mattress　🛏1Sh.w.h.,2ensuite
★F,KF,LF,TV in each guest room, balconies, rowing machine, parking, golf clubs, pullcart　🖐No pets, smoking on deck, children min.age 7
🏃 Delightful walks through woods or by the ocean, Schooner Cove Resort and Marina, Fairwinds Golf Club at doorstep, beaches, fishing, tennis, sailing, kayaking, riding stables, gourmet restaurants
🚗 Nanaimo, Parksville, Qualicum Beach, Courtenay
🐎 West Coast contemporary cedar home in natural rocky woodland setting with a spectacular panoramic view of Georgia Strait and the majestic mountains beyond. Enjoy an everchanging water spectacle of passing boats, Alaskan cruise ships, eagles, Orca whales, otters and sea lions. Hosts can book tee times at the many nearby courses. Fishing charters can be arranged. Mid-way between Victoria & Tofino. ("A little bit of heaven"). Ideal for longer stays/discounts for 2 or more nights.

Nelson

(north of Castlegar;see also Proctor, Kaslo, Winlaw)

Maloff, Harry & Verna (Verna's Country Kitchen B&B)   ☎ (250) 229-4961
6497 Erindale Rd., Harrop, Nelson, BC   V1L 5P6

Located 22km north east of Nelson. Take 5min "Harrop" Ferry. Turn left on Erindale Rd.
$65S $97D $4Child $30Add.person   🍽 Meals   (plus tax)   ► 4A,4Ch

🍲 Full, homebaked   🏠 Rural, back-split, acreage, view from
guest rooms, lakefront, patio, porch, deck, quiet, secluded   ■2
(main and ground level)   ⊨ 1D,1K,1P,cot,crib   ⊟ 2Private
★KF,LF,F,TV in guest rooms, ceiling fans, hot tub, private
entrance, guest quarters are separate   🖐 Designated smoking
area, no pets   ⚘ Russian
🕴 Private sandy beach, fishing, wharf, x-c skiing, snowshoeing,
swimming, firepit/bonfires, hiking
🚗 Nelson (ride the old street car), Ainsworth Hot Springs, Kokanee Glacier, longest "free" ferry
🐾 Beautiful beachfront home on Kootenay Lake surrounded by breathtaking panoramic views of
snowcapped mountains and everlasting sun exposure. Breakfast is served in guest breakfast room.
Full menu available for additional meals, lunch to go or a romantic al-fresco dinner on the beach.
After a hectic day of travelling or sightseeing, relax in the hot tub or by the fireplace to ease tired
bones and watch the sunset on the lake, ending yet another wonderful day. ✍CC

Mather, Janeen & Mark Giffin (Emory House B&B)   ☎ & Fax (250) 352-7007
811 Vernon St., Nelson, BC   V1L 4G3

From Vancouver take Hwy 1 to Hope and Hwy 3 east to Castlegar, then Hwy 3A north to Nelson
and follow signs to City centre. Proceed to one street north of Baker St (main street in town).
$65-85S $70-90D $15Add.person   (plus taxes)   (off-season rates avail)   ► 11

🍲 Full   🏠 Downtown, 2-storey, hist., view from guest rooms
■ 2D,1Ste,1F (main & upper floor)   ⊨ 1S,1D,3Q   ⊟ 1Sh.w.g.,
2ensuite   ★ Air,TV,F, guest quarters are separate, off-street
parking   🖐 No smoking, no pets, children min. age 10
🕴 Downtown Nelson, Aquatic & Fitness Centre, shopping mall,
Nelson Museum, heritage sights, restaurants, movie/live theatre
🚗 Granite Point Golf Course, Whitewater Ski Resort, hiking
trails, Kootenay Lake (fishing, beaches), Kokanee Glacier Nat.Pk
🐾 1926-built Heritage home furnished with restored antiques & local arts/crafts and nestled in
the centre of scenic town. Hosts have extensive experience in the hospitality industry (former Chef
& Restaurant Mgr). The convenient location makes exploring Nelson's heritage sights easy and
enjoyable. There are 2 resident cats. Golf & Ski Packages available. Visa,MC ✍CC

Stevens, Lynda & Jerry VanVeen (Inn the Garden B & B)   ☎ (250) 352-3226,
408 Victoria Street, Nelson, BC   V1L 4K5   Fax (250)-352-3284

Located 1 block south of Baker St. between Stanley & Ward Sts and across from Capitol Theatre.
$70S $150D $20-25Add.person   (plus taxes)   ► 20

🍲 Full, homebaked   🏠 Downtown, historic, view from guest
rooms, patio, porch, deck, terraced front gardens with steps
■5D,1Ste (2nd & 3rd levels)   ⊨2T,1D,5Q,1P,cot   ⊟3Private,
2sh.w.g.,1ensuite   ★Separate entrance, off-street parking,
ceiling fans, guest lounge, bicycle/ski storage   🖐No smoking, no
pets, children min. age 15(except in cottage)   ⚘Dutch
🕴 Heritage buildings and walking tours, parks, restored trolley,
arts & craft stores, restaurants, live theatre, museum
🚗 Kokanee Glacier Park (hiking, skiing), Whitewater Ski Resort, Ainsworth Hot Springs, Caves
🐾 Friendly and relaxed atmosphere in beautifully restored Victorian home with comfortable
decor of plants, wicker & antique furniture, located in picturesque Selkirk Mountain city with a
breathtaking view of lake and mountains. Enjoy the beautiful high terraced front garden with patio
and summer porch. Golf and Ski packages available. Also self-cont cottage available. Visa,MC.Amex

New Westminster *(Vancouver); see also Surrey, Richmond, Langley, White Rock, Delta)*

Field, Ethel (Royal City Bed & Breakfast)　　　　　☎ (604) 521-5733
127 Queen's Ave., New Westminster, BC　V3L 1J4

Located in Queen's Park area. Phone for directions.
$55-60S　$70-75D　$15Child　　　　　　　　　▶ 4A,1Ch
🕮 Full, homebaked　🏠 Res., hist., river view, sundeck　■ 2D
(upstairs)　🛏 2Q　⚓2Private,　★TV, parking, grand piano
for musical guests　🐾 Pets
🏃 Rapid Transit to downtown Vancouver, shopping mall,
Adventure Playground
🚗 International Airport, beaches, V.Island Ferry, Deer Lake

🐾 Grand old Heritage home, formerly the N.Nelson Mansion and built in 1913, with beamed
ceilings, stained glass windows. Hosts enjoy sharing their comfortable home with guests. Delicious
muffins are a house specialty. There is a resident dog and a cat. ✒CC

Oliver　　　　　　　*(south of Penticton; see also Osoyoos, Kaleden, Greenwood)*

Haak, Ruth & John (Wildflower B&B)　　　　　　☎ (250) 498-4326
RR2, S53A, C6, Oliver, BC　V0H 1T0　　　　　E-mail: j_haak@bc.sympatico.ca

On Hwy 97, proceed 4km north of Oliver. Turn west on Seacrest Rd and follow signs. Located at
38950-149th St (White Lake Rd).
$45S　$55-65D　$20Add.person　🍽 Meals　　　　　▶ 4A
🕮 Full, homebaked　🏠 Rural, 3-storey, acreage, view, patio,
deck, quiet　■ 2D(ground level)　🛏 1D,1Q　⚓ 2Private
★Wood stove, outdoor hot tub, piano, library, table tennis,
off-street parking　🐾 Smoking outside, no pets, not suitable for
children　⚒ German
🏃 Hiking & biking (easy to strenuous) on paved roads or trails
🚗 Beaches, golfing, skiing, horseback riding (summer only), many wineries
🐾 Long-time local residents in new comfortable home surrounded by everchanging nature and
wildlife in an environmental reserve. Hosts are "empty nesters" and enjoy outdoor sports activities,
as well as gardening. Relax with good conversation and food at the kitchen counter or in the dining
room or patio. There is an outside cat. ✒B&B

Nicholas, Judy (The Happy Quail B&B)　　　☎ (250) 498-3538, Fax (250) 498-0842
RR2, S52, C34, Oliver, BC　V0H 1T0

From Hwy 97 south of Penticton, turn onto Green Lake Rd at Okanagan Falls and proceed to
Willowbrook Community.
$55S　$60D　$15Child/Add.person　🍽 Meals　　　　▶ 4
🕮 Full　🏠 Rural, loghouse, 2-storey, 2acres, quiet, secluded
■ 2D (main & ground level)　🛏 2T,1Q　⚓ 1sh.w.g.　★ LF,F,
outdoor hot tub　🐾 Designated smoking area
🏃 Biking, hiking, beaver pond and wilderness park, bus service
🚗 Golf courses, Estate wineries, White Lake Observatory, fruit
orchards, Okanagan beaches (boating, swimming), scenic drives
🐾 Warm welcome and friendly hospitality in peaceful and cozy log home, situated in beautiful
Okanagan Valley town surrounded by fruit orchards, providing endless supply of fresh fruits and
vegetables. Relax in the hot tub, star gaze and enjoy the tranquil atmosphere. ✒CC

Osoyoos
(south of Penticton; see also Oliver, Greenwood)

Wallace, June and John (Haynes Point Lakeside B&B)   ☎ & Fax (250) 495-7443
RR1, S93, C2, Osoyoos, BC V0H 1V0

Located at 3619 Jasmine Dr. Take Hwy 97 south 3 km from Husky Stn or Control Light to Haynes Point Provincial Park sign (on right). Turn onto 32nd Ave, travel down hill to Jasmine Dr. Turn left to white rancher house on right.

$60-70S $70-85D   (off season rates available)   ► 6
🍴Full, homebaked 🏠Res., hillside, 2-level rancher, view,deck, quiet
■3D(main level)   ⊨1D,2Q   ⬦ 1Ensuite, 2sh.w.g. (jet tub)
★Air,TV,F,LF,guest lounge, purified drinking water, off-street parking 🚭Restricted smoking, no pets, no children
🏃 Haynes Pt Prov.Park sandy beaches, swimming, boat launch & rental canoes, town shops, restaurants, cycling, museum, Art Gallery
🚗 Golf courses, 14 wineries, museum, tennis, hiking, water slide, Desert Park Racing, Penticton, Grandforks, Oroville (WA)

📣 Hillside home overlooking Lake Osoyos situated in the "quiet end" of the Okanagan Valley. Seasoned Canadian hosts enjoy meeting and assisting fellow travellers. Relax on the large deck or read in the hammock under the patio umbrella or by the big campfire at night with the stars overhead and the moonlit lake. ↙CC

Oyama
(north of Kelowna; see also Winfield, Vernon, Cherryville)

Parker, Yvonne & Elgin (Orchard Lane Bed & Breakfast)   ☎ (250) 548-3809
13324 Middle Bench Rd., Oyama, BC V4V 2B4

Located 5.5km east of Hwy 97 (across the lake) at 13324 Middle Bench Rd. Phone for directions.
$45S $55-75D $10Child $15Add.person   ► 6
🍴 Full, homebaked   🏠 Farm, 2-storey, view from guest rooms, deck, quiet, verandas, secluded   ■ 3D (upstairs)   ⊨ 1S,3Q, portable crib   ⬦ 1Private, 1ensuite (sink in one room)
★Air,F,TV,LF, outdoor hot-tub, craft display room on site
🚭Designated smoking area, no pets
🏃 Orchard & tours, range land for hiking, biking, country walks
🚗 Lake access (swimming/boating), Silver Star (Vernon)/Big White (Kelowna) Ski Resorts & summer chairlift, golfing, fishing, winery tours
📣 New Victorian-style home, beautifully designed and decorated with large sprawling verandas & spiral staircase, with a panoramic view of the Central Okanagan Valley, nestled in a lush orchard surrounded by flower gardens, rockery and paths. Enjoy a tranquil retreat and breakfast served in the formal dining room or on veranda. Special diets on request. ↙B&B

Parksville
(on Van.Isle; north of Nanaimo; see also Qualicum B., Nanoose Bay, Lantzville)

Chilton, Bob and Marg (Parksville Bed & Breakfast)   ☎ (250) 248-6846
19 Jenkins Place, Parksville, BC V9P 1G4

From Island Hall go north to lights at Pym St.Turn left to Jenkins Place, and left again.
$45S $50-60D $15Add.person   (off season rates avail) (Reservation please)   ► 6

🍴 Choice, homebaked 🏠 Downtown, res., patio, quiet ■3D (upstairs) ⊨2T,1D,1Q,cot ⬦1Private,1sh.w.g. ★TV,LF,F, parking 🚭No pets, no smoking ♥
🏃 Wembley Mall, Community Park, tennis court, excellent fishing, beach, marina
📣 Cozy home with country tranquility located in town. Hosts welcome guests over for a cup of tea. Enjoy the tasty breakfast. Families welcome. ↙B&B

Hutchins, Jeanne (Hutchin's French Creek B&B)   ☎ (250) 752-5146
1280 Gilley Cres., Parksville, BC V9P 1W5

From Sandpiper Estate, off Island Hwy, go up Drew Rd, turn right on Gilley.

$50S $60D   ▶ 4A
✖Feb.-Oct. ◐Choice ♠Res., patio, quiet,balcony ■2D(upst)
⊨2T,1Q ⌐2Ensuite ★TV,F, parking, balcony 🖐No pets,
restricted smoking
⋔ French Creek Marina, beach, arts/craft shops, 5 golf courses
🚐 Cathedral Grove with huge trees, Englishman River Falls,
Coombs Country Market (with goats on roof), Rathtrevor Beach
☛ Located in the Sandpiper subdivision of French Creek in
garden setting. There is a blue-eyed pussycat called "Sheba" in residence. ✓B&B

Kern, Dea and Art (Marina View B&B)   ☎ (250) 248-9308 Fax (250) 248-9408
895 Glenhale Cr., Parksville, BC V9P 1Z7

Travel through Parksville on Hwy 19A past French Creek Market and turn right at light on Wright

Rd and left on Glenhale Cr. Look for flag on top deck.
$65S $75-80D $20Add.person   ▶ 6-7
◐ Full, homebaked ♠ Res., split-level, view, oceanfront, quiet,
covered deck ■3(upst) ⊨2T,2Q,R ⌐2Ensuite,1private ★TV in
guest lounge,sep entrance, parking 🖐No pets, no smoking,
children min. age 10 ~French, some German
⋔ French Creek Marina, excellent fishing, beachcombing,
restaurant, store,
🚐 Englishman River & Qualicum River Falls, Cathedral Grove Prov. Park (large trees), beaches
☛ Spectacular waterfront setting in the heart of vacationland with large deck overlooking the
Strait of Georgia, islands and mountains beyond. Relax in the large solarium and watch the Alaska
Cruise Ships sail by and catch a glimpse of seals and otters frolicking near the shore, as well as
shorebirds & eagles. Savour a delicious breakfast of homemade preserves & fresh-baked goods
served in gracious surroundings.Visa,MC ✓CC

Weber, John & Bea (Warwick Manor B&B)   ☎ (250) 248-8645, Fax (250) 248-1206
517 Pym St., Parksville, BC V9P 1B6

Located 0.4km from Hwy 19A North and Pym St. intersection.
$49S $65-75D $20Add.person   ▶ 6
◐ Full ♠ Res., 2-storey ■ 4 (main & upper level)
⌐1Sh.w.g., Private ⊨2Q,1K ★ Spacious quiet lounge,
private patio 🖐Designated smoking area,no pets
⋔ Shopping, golfing, tennis, fishing, boating, all amenities, beaches
☛ Charming traditional English Tudor Manor set in delightful
gardens and convenient surroundings. Relax in the hot tub or
private lounge. Breakfast served in breakfast room. CCards ✓CC

Parson
(south of Golden; see also Invermere, Windermere, Fairmont Hot Springs)

Dunphy, Brian and Suzette (Dunphy's B&B)   ☎ (250) 348-2394
Box 22, Parson, BC   V0A 1L0

Located right on Hwy 95 and 3.2 km south of Parson. Watch for sign.
$40S $50D   🍽 Meals   ▶ 6A,2Ch
🍵 Full, homebaked   🏠 Farm   ■ 2S,3D (upstairs)   ⊨2T,3D
⬛1Sh.w.h.,1sh.w.g   ★TV,F,LF   ✋ Restr.smoking, no pets
🏃 Many types of farm animals to enjoy, large yard/creek on door step,
back country hiking
🚗 Heli/x-c skiing/snowmobiling, Radium/Fairmount Hotsprings,
Golden Dist.Museum, Invermere Ski Resort, Bugaboos Alpine rec area
🔫 Large farm house in excellent location from which to experience the majestic Canadian Rocky
Mountains during summer and winter time. Hosts are avid outdoor enthusiasts. ✍B&B

Penticton
(s.of Kelowna; see also Summerland, Oliver, Osoyoos)

Buchanan, Ruth (Paradise Cove)   ☎ and Fax (250) 496-5896
Box 699, Penticton, BC   V2A 6P1

Located at 3129 Hayman Rd., Naramata. From Westminster & Main Sts in Penticton, take the
Naramata Rd East. Follow for 13km to DeBeck Rd, left before the Fire Hall, right at Hayman Rd.

$60-65S $70-75D $95-115Ste $15Add.person   ▶ 6A
🍵Full   🏠Rural,res,two-storey,lake view,patio,quiet   ■3D,1Ste
(main & lower level)   ⊨4Q   ⬛3Private,1sh.w.g.   ★TV/fridge &
beverage service in all rooms,F/KF/hot-tub in suite, wheel-chair
access   ✋No smoking, no pets,
🏃 Manitou Beach, Okanagan Lake, Riding Academy, 5 wineries
🚗 Kettle Valley Railway Tunnels, Country Squire Restaurant
🔫 Deluxe accommodation in modern home with panoramic view
of Lake Okanagan and situated in rural orchard surroundings. Very quiet. Widely travelled hostess
is a writer/editor. Ideal spot for honeymooners. Visa,MC ✍B&B

Lejeune, Ghitta & Ulric (God's Mountain Crest Chalet & B&B)   ☎ & Fax (250) 490-4800
RR2, S15, C41, Penticton, BC   V2A 6J7   1-888-490-4800

Phone for directions.
$95D $20Child   🍽 Meals   (plus tax)   ▶ 14
🍵 Full (buffet)   🏠 Farm, view from guest rooms, patio, porch,
deck, quiet, secluded   ■ 3D,4Ste(main & ground floor)   ⊨7Q
⬛7Private   ★ F,kitchenettes,separate entr., wheel-chair access,
guest quarters are separate   ✋Designated smoking area
〰German, French
🚗 Kelowna, Oliver, Osoyoos
🏃 100 acres of mountain park and vineyards, hiking, mountain biking, helicopter landing
🔫 European-style chalet located high above Skaha Lake with majestic cliffs and magnificient
views. Relax around the pond and patios and watch as wildlife wanders through nearby vineyards.
Hearty breakfasts & candle-lit dinners served with special European flair. Ideally suited for
conferences and private parties. Bus tours welcome. There is a resident dog & cat. Diners ✍CC

Port Alberni   *(on Vancouver Isle, west of Parksville; see also Qualicum Beach, Nanaimo)*

Visee, Dick and Jane (Lake Woods Bed & Breakfast)   ☎ & Fax (250) 723-2310
9778 Stirling Arm Cr., S339,C5,RR3, Port Alberni, BC   V9Y 7L7

From Hwy 4 west of Port Alberni, turn left on Faber Rd. Travel 4.8 km, turn right at stop sign.

$55-75S/D   ► 6
🍵 Full, homebaked   🏠 Rural, multi-storey, view, lakefront, patio, quiet   ■ 3D (main and ground floor)   ⊨ 2Q,1K
🛁1Sh.w.g., 1ensuite   ★ F,TV, parking   ⊛ Smoking outside only, no pets   〰 Dutch
🏃 Day trip on M.V. Lady Rose on Barclay Sound, forest & mill tours, salmon fishing, walking trails
🚗 Pacific Rim National Park, Long Beach, Tofino, Ucluelet

📢 Peaceful waterfront home overlooking the lake and expansive landscaped garden, situated on the shores of beautiful Sproat Lake and easy distance for daytrips to the Westcoast and Pacific Rim National Park. Enjoy a swim before turning in, or before breakfast. ✎CC

Port Hardy   *(on northern tip of Vancouver Island)*

Glynn, Rosaline (Rocklands B&B)   ☎ (250) & Fax 949-7074, 1-888-766-ROCK (7625)
Box 1145, 5096 Peel St., Port Hardy, BC   V0N 2P0   E-mail: dfaber@direct.ca

From Hwy 19 take Fort Rupert Rd. Turn right on Byng, left on Beaver Harbour Rd, left on Peel St.
$60S $70D $15Add.person   ► 6
🍵 Cont., homebaked   🏠 Res., 2-storey, view, deck, quiet   ■ 3D(main floor)   ⊨ 2T,2Q
🛁1Sh.w.g.   ★ Guest robes/slippers & hair dryer, private entrance, off-street parking, guest quarters are separate   ⊛ No smoking, no pets, children min. age 5
🏃 Beautiful sandy Storey's Beach
🚗 Port Hardy, Prince Rupert Ferry, Seven Hills Golf Course, Forestry Tours, whale watching, lake, stream and ocean fishing
📢 Ocean-view home, tastefully decorated with antiques, art and family heirlooms, creating a relaxing comfortable environment. Breakfast is served in the dining room and afternoon tea in the guest lounge. Ferry shuttle service available. Hosts are originally from England.Visa ✎CC

Hamilton, Lorne and Betty (Hamilton B&B)   ☎ (250) 949-6638
Box 1926, 9415 Mayor's Way, Port Hardy, BC   V0N 2P0

Travel up Hwy 19 past Petro Canada Gas Station on right. Turn next left (Granville St - has hospital sign) and continue to Mayor's Way. Turn left to first house on left.

$45S $55-60D   ► 6
🍵Cont,homebaked   🏠Res., split-level, view, quiet   ■3(main & lower levels)   ⊨2T,1D,1Q   🛁2Sh.w.g.   ★TVin one guest room, separate entrance   ⊛No smoking, no pets
🏃 Sea wall walk with lovely view of islands/mountains, downtown park, museum, fishing dock
🚗 Storeys Beach, Telegraph Cove, Marble River, whale watching at Port McNeil, charter fishing

📢 Active host family enjoys fishing, hiking and meeting people. Friendly hospitality in area with many attractions, lakes and rivers and year-around fishing. ✎CC

Powell River   *(north-west of Vancouver; see also Gibsons, Sechelt, Roberts Creek)*

Hollmann, Nancy and Alexander (Herondell B&B)   ☎(604)487-9528,Fax(604)487-1465
RR1, Black Point #29, Powell River, BC   V8A 4Z2   E-mail: herondel@prcn.org

Located halfway between Saltery Bay Ferry Terminal and Powell River City limits. From Vancouver, leave the bus at Lang Bay.
$40S $50D $15Add.person ⭐Meals   ▶ 8A,4Ch
🍲 Full (Lumberman's b'fast) 🏠Rural, older, 40 acres, front yard wildlife pond, isolated ■5D,1F(main & lower level) ★F,LF, separate entrance, parking ⊨4T,2D,1K,1R,1P ⚫1Private, 3sh.w.g., 1ensuite 🌙No smoking, children welcome ᰍGerman
🏃 Nature trail through woods, saltwater beach, river swimming
🚐 Powell River, scuba diving, salmon fishing, Powell River Forest Canoe Route (5-day trip)
🐾 Very private wildlife refuge with visible waterfowl (occasionally bear, deer, cougar etc.) Early breakfasts only. Breakfast specialty is Eierkuchen and sour dough products (the "starter" has been in the family for over 50 years). Canoe/camping rentals/charters avail. MC,DC,Amex ∼CC

Randall, Roger and Shirley (Beacon B&B)   ☎ (604) 485-5563/Fax (604) 485-9450
3750 Marine Ave., Powell River, BC   V8A 2H8

Take Langdale Ferry from Horseshoe Bay (Vancouver) and drive along the Sechelt Peninsula to Earls Cove. Take Saltery Bay Ferry and drive 29.5 km north. Watch for Beacons.
$65-125S/D $20Add.person   ▶ 10A
🍲 Full, homebaked 🏠 Res., view, oceanfront, patio, quiet, hot tub ■1D,1F,1Ste (main & ground level) ⊨2T,4Q ⚫3Private ★F,LF,TV in guest room, wheel-chair access to suite, parking
🌙 Smoking outside only, children min age 12
🏃 Walk and explore nearby beaches and sea life
🚐 Canoe route portage 8 lakes (4-5 days), new golf course, biking
🐾 Tranquil and congenial family surroundings in modern, waterfront setting. Enjoy the everchanging sights of Malaspina Strait, and the panoramic ocean views, including Vancouver Island's snowcapped mountains, from your breakfast table. Fishing, dinner, sightseeing charters can be arranged. There is a friendly cat. Ideal for groups or family reunions. Soothing hot-tub and on-site massage available. Visa,MC ∼B&B

Schulz, Erwin and Renate (Cedar Lodge B&B Resort)   ☎& Fax (604) 483-4414
C-8 Malaspina Rd, RR2, Powell River, BC   V8A 4Z3

Located near Okeover Arm Provincial Park and 26 km north of Powell River on BC Sunshine Coast. The drive from Horseshoe Bay in West Vancouver to the lodge includes 2 ferry crossings and is a 6 hour journey featuring spectacular scenery.
$40-50S $45-60D $65-75Ste $15Add.person   ▶ 14A
🍲 Cont. 🏠 Rural, 3-storey, acreage, view, patio, tranquil ■4 with sinks & toilets (on 2nd & 3rd floor), 1Ste (ground level) ⊨1S,2T,3D,2Q,1P ⚫2sep.shower rooms 🌙No pets ★TV, games room, power/sail/sea kayaks avail. ᰍGerman
🏃 Okeover Arm Prov. Park, Gateway to Desolalation Sound, boat rentals, scuba diving, guided fishing, restaurants, fjords, Sunshine Coast Trail (direct access from back door - built by hosts)
🚐 Powell River
🐾 Experience the Pacific Coastal Wilderness surrounding beautiful lodge with a European touch and situated in a rural area on acreage with a view. Located at the entrance to Desolation Sound Marine Park, an area with awesome tranquility and scenic beauty near the coastal village of Lund. Boat charters, ocean cayak rentals, guiding fishing trips and Adventure Tours into a Wilderness Camp provided (by prior arrangements). Visa,MC ∼ CC

Prince George

Beattie, Maxine & Bob Clayton (Emmet Park B&B)   ☎ (250) 562-4689,
2939 Spruce St., Prince George, BC   V2L 2S3   E-mail: rclayton@mag-net.com, Fax (250) 562-7899

Phone for directions.
$40-50S $50-60D $60Ste $5Child $10Add.person ► 4A,2Ch
🍳Full, homebaked   🏠Res.,bungalow,older,quiet   ▰1D,1Ste
(main & lower floor)   ⊨1D,1Q,1P   ⌁ 1Private, 1sh.w.h.
★LF,KF,TV, separate entrance,off-street parking, plug-ins
🖐No smoking, no pets
🚶 Walking near Fraser River, park, museum, shopping
🚍 Bus Depot/Rail Station, Civic Centre, College, University, airport, trails
🐾 Comfortable newly renovated home on large treed lot, with easy access to hwys 16/97. Special diets can be accommodated. Hosts enjoy helping guests with sightseeing plans. Guest pick-up available from various arrival points. Phone & fax machine access for business travellers. ✍B&B

Bowden, Glenn and Adrienne (Adrienne's B&B)   ☎ (250) 561-1662, Fax (250) 562-6699
1467 Fraser Cres, Prince George, BC   V2M 3Y4   E-mail: glennb@solutions-4U.com

Located 3 blocks west from intersection of Hwy 97 and 15th Ave. in the center of Prince George.
$40S $50D   ► 4A
🍳 Choice   🏠 Res., bungalow, quiet   ▰ 2D (main and lower level)   ⊨2D   ⌁1 Private, 1Sh.w.h.   ★F,TV, off-street parking 🖐 No smoking, no childern
🚶 Restaurants, shops, art gallery, museum, University
🐾 Quiet adult atmosphere. Longtime B&B hosts (since 1988)
love to play bridge and are well informed about the area; will gladly assist with sightseeing and other plans. Computer, phone & fax facilities available for the business traveller. ✍B&B

Coles, Cynthia & Dave (Tangled Garden B&B)   ☎ (250) 964-3265, Fax (250) 964-3248
2971 Sullivan Cr., Prince George, BC   V2N 5H6   E-mail: dpcc@mag-net.com

From Hwy 16 west, turn on Tyner Blvd and turn right on Baker, then left on Sullivan.

$50S $60D $15Add.person   ► 5
🍳 Full, homebaked   🏠 Res., 2-storey, view from guest rooms, porch, deck, quiet   ▰ 1D,1Ste(upper & lower level) ⊨1T,1D,1Q
⌁1Private, 1Ensuite   ★ F,LF,KF,TV in guest room, separate entrance, off-street parking, outdoor hot tub, guest quarters are separate 🖐 Smoking outside, no pets, children min. age 12
🚶 Nature trails, shopping, tennis, restaurants
🚍 Downtown, UNBC, golfing, x-c skiing, theatre, airport, railway
🐾 Attractive modern home with award-winning garden and view of distant Rockies, backing onto a Greenbelt. Relax on the flower-filled sundeck or in the terraced garden (a hummingbird paradise). Unwind in the hot tub under the stars. Train pick-up available. Breakfast is served in the dining room or on the sundeck. There is a cat "Emma" in residence. ✍B&B

Mead, Bob & Laura (Mead Manor Bed & Breakfast)   ☎ (250) 964-8436, Fax (250) 964-8449
4127 Baker Rd., Prince George, BC   V2N 5K2

Phone for directions.
$5060S/D   (Seniors Discounts avail)   ► 4A,2Ch
🍲 Full, homebaked   🏠 Res., split-level, deck   ■ 2D (main &
ground level)   🛏 2Q   🛁 2Private   ★ F,TV,LF, off-street
parking   🚬 Designated smoking area
🕇 College Heights Shopping Plaza
🚗 Downtown, Barkerville historic site, Fort St.James and
museum, lakes, trails (hiking, x-c skiing, snowmobiling), Tabor
Mountain Ski Resort, University of Northern BC, golfing
🔫 Warm, friendly hospitality in home tastefully decorated and situated in quiet location. ⌐CC

Van Peenen, Anneke & Adrian (Beaverly Bed & Breakfast)   ☎ (250) 560-5255,
12725 Miles Rd., Prince George, BC   V2N 5C1   Fax (250) 560-5211

From P.G. take Hwy 16 west for 18 km. Watch for sign on highway. Turn right on Hooper Rd.
Proceed to end and turn right on Miles Rd. (Chilako area).
$45S $55D $10Child   🍽 Meals   ► 4A,2Ch
🍲 Full, homebaked   🏠 Rural, res., ranch-style bungalow, view
from guest rooms, acreage, patio, porch, deck, quiet, secluded
■1D,1Ste (main floor)   🛏 1Q,2S(K)   🛁 1Private, 1ensuite
★TV,LF   🚬Designated smoking area, no pets   〰 Dutch
🕇 Watch 60 different species of birds, abundant wildlife/flowers
🚗 P.George, many lakes, golfing, UNBC, museums, hiking trails
🔫 Comfortable new house with a "Dutch touch", situated in a park-like setting and surrounded
by beautiful BC wilderness country. Breakfast is served in the country kitchen or on the deck
(weather permitting). There is a dog in residence. ⌐B&B

Bed & Breakfast Association of Prince George   ☎(250)561-2337(BEDS),Fax 2603
Box 2693, Stn B, Prince George, BC   V2N 4T5   E-mail: bedandbreakfastassoc@pgonline.com,

Rates: $35S(and up) $45D(and up)   1-888-266-5555
The Association represents over 15 homes offering warm and friendly central interior hospitality.
Accommodation varies from rustic to exquisite and each offers its own flavour of hospitality. Hosts
homes have been selected for cleanliness, comfort and courtesy. Breakfasts range from light
continental to gourmet-cooked.ph or fax the above for information and reservation.

Prince Rupert   *(central BC on west coast; see also Smithers)*

Buchholz, Hans & Irmgard (Pineridge B&B)   ☎ (250) 627-4419, Fax (250) 624-2366
1714 Sloan Ave., Prince Rupert, BC   V8J 3Z9   E-mail: pineridge@citytel.net 1-888-733-6733

Follow Hwy 16 through town, turn onto Smithers St and right on Sloan Ave to B&B on right.
$70S $80D   ► 6
🍲 European-style   🏠 Res., 2-storey, waterview from guest rooms, deck, quiet   ■ 3D(main &
upper floor)   🛏 2T,2Q   🛁 1Private, 2ensuite   ★ F,TV in guest lounge, ceiling fans, separate
entrance, off-street parking, host quarters are separate   🚬 Designated smoking area, no pets, not
suitable for children   〰German
🕇 Downtown, library, tennis, Performing Arts Centre, BC Packers Plant (largest fish plant in
N.A.), Northern Museum, BC Ferries Terminal, Fairview docks, Morse Creek & Totem Parks, bus
🚗 North Pacific Cannery Museum, Seal Cove Sea Plane Base, hiking trails
🔫 Large, newly renovated home in a quiet neighborhood with large rooms and decorated with
fine arts and crafts. Hosts are knowledgeable about local attractions and can assist in arranging
fishing charters, whale watching and Eco Charters etc. Observe the busy harbour from private
deck. There is a dog in host quarters only. Visa,MC,Amex

Cox, Bryan and Mary Allen (Eagle Bluff Bed & Breakfast))
201 Cow Bay Rd., Prince Rupert, BC   V8J 1A2

☎ (250) 627-4955/7052
Fax (250) 627-7945

$45-55S $55-75D $5Child $15Add.person (plus tax)(weekly & winter rates avail)   ►10A,7CH

Located next to Cow Bay wharf across from P.R. Yacht Club.
🅂Cont. 🏠 1922-built downtown, older, waterfront,pier structure
🛏4(main & upstairs) ⊨4T,3D,5Q,crib,cot ⚌3Private,1sh.w.g.
★ LF,TV/phone in guest room, exit to patio from each room
🚭Restricted smoking, no pets
🕴 Path along waterfront, downtown area, Northern Museum,
Mariner's Park, library, tennis courts, Performing Arts Centre,
Smile's Seafood Restaurant (a Prince Rupert landmark), fishing off
docks, Allied Pacific Processors (largest fish processing plant in
N.A.), Rushbrooke Floats (public boat launch and boat mooring at
entry to the Sea Walk hiking trail)

☛ Renovated fishing home overlooking harbour, dock and yacht club, located on the shore in an
older area of town. Observe freighters, cruise ships and sail boats come and go, as well as
commercial fishing boats delivering and gearing up to depart. Knowledgeable hosts will gladly help
with itineraries and sometimes offer barbeque and fresh sea food meals. Families welcome.

Pritchard

(east of Kamloops; see also Salmon Arm, Sorrento)

Isaac, Lorne & Lynn (Alpine Meadows Bed & Breakfast)
RR1, McKim Rd., Pritchard, BC   V0E 2P0

☎ (250) 577-3726,
Fax (250) 577-3654

Located east of Kamloops off TCH 1. Turn onto Hwy 97 (Vernon/Falkland), then left onto Duck

Range Rd and right onto McKim Rd. Watch for signs.
$35-45S $50-60D   ► 4
🅂Full,homebaked 🏠Farm,2-storey log home,view,patio,deck,
quiet 🛏2D(walkout entry lower level) ⚌1Sh.w.g. ⊨2D
★2F,TV in guest lounge,private entrance, ample parking
🚭Designated smoking area, no children ～ some German
🕴 Walking/hiking/cycling/x-c skiing/tobogganing on ungroomed
trails, large well sheltered dog kennel

🚗 Downhill skiing at Sun Peaks Resort, city of Kamloops, wildlife park & water slides, hunting
☛ Unique log home with large rock fireplaces, nestled in 20acres of pines & meadows. Enjoy the
breathtaking view of the South Thompson River & Lake Kamloops and the beautiful sunsets.
Tranquility at its best. Breakfast is served in the dining room or on covered deck. House specialty is
wildflower honey from own honey bees. There is a very friendly dog and a cat in residence.

Procter

(north-east of Nelson; see also Crawford Bay, Kaslo)

Ray, June (Kootenay Lake Homestays)
RR3, S26, C10, Nelson BC   V1L 5P6

☎ & Fax (250)229-5688, 1-800-256-8711

Located at 7459 Mauriello Rd, Procter. Phone for directions.
$70D $85F $10Add.person   ► 4
🅂 Self-serve (cooked) 🏠 Rural, 2.5-storey, log home, view from
guest rooms, waterfront, patio, porch, quiet, secluded, private
beach 🛏 1Ste (ground level) plus loft ⊨1D,1P,1D,cot
⚌Ensuite (jacuzzi) ★ TV,KF,LF, work-out space in loft suite,
mountain bikes, fishing gear & small boat available for guests,
separate entrance, private parking & walkway, guest quarters are
separate 🚭 Smoking on covered patio, pets accepted with damage deposit
🕴 Fishing, biking, horse-back riding, boating, kayaking, swimming, campfires on the beach
🚗 Golfing, restaurants, Kokanee Glacier Park, Ainsworth Hot Springs, Cody Caves, Ghost town
☛ Large log home with wrap-around patio and superb views, nestled on the shores of beautiful
Kootenay Lake in the southern Selkirks. Hosts have travelled worldwide and know the area's
hiking trails well. There is a tipi available for those guests who would like to stay in it and enjoy the
novelty. There is a dog and a cat (not in guest quarters). Visa ✓CC

Qualicum Beach *(on Van.Isle, north of Parksville; see also Nanoose Bay, Lantzville)*

England, Arlene & John (Blue Willow B&B) ☎ (250) 752-9052 Fax (250) 752-9039
524 Quatna Rd., Qualicum Beach, BC V9K 1B4 E-mail: bwillow@qb.island.net

From Nanaimo travel north on Hwy 19 and Qualicum Beach Exit. Follow Hwy 4A through the
village to waterfront. Turn right on Hwy 19A to Qualicum Rd. Turn right again at Quatna Rd. Or
via scenic route: take Parksville Exit from Hwy 19 nad continue north to Qualicum Rd. Turn left,
then right at Quatna Rd.

$70S $85-95D (Reduced rates Nov1-April 30) ► 6
Full, homebaked Res., 2-storey, quiet 2D(main level)
plus garden suite (sep from house) 1K(2T),1Q(house),
1Q,1D,2S(Ste) Private ★ TV in guest lounge, LF No
smoking French, German
Beach, golf course, restaurants
French Creek Marina, Denman/Hornby Islands, Cathedral G.
Elegant old Tudor home with leaded glass windows and beamed ceilings, amidst a show garden
of flowers, shrubs and tall West Coast conifers (featured on local Garden tours). Sumptuous
breakfast is served on hosts' collection of "Blue Willow" China. There is a long haired Dachshund.

Ross, Bill and Betty (Quatna Manor) ☎ (250) 752-6685 Fax (250) 752-8385
512 Quatna Rd., Qualicum Beach, BC V9K 1B4

From Island Exp'way (Hwy 19) take Qualicum Beach turn-off (Memorial Ave) through village to
waterfront. Turn right on Hwy 19A, proceed to Hall Rd. Turn right, then 1st left on Quatna Rd.

$60S $65-85D ► 9
Full, homebaked (English) Village, patio, quiet,
Tudor-style, acreage 2D,1Ste(upstairs) 2T,2Q,
1Private, 2sh.w.g. ★F/TV in guest lounge, separate
entrance, parking No smoking, no pets some French
Memorial & Eaglecrest golf courses, public access to beach
Fairwinds, Morningstar & Glengarry golf courses, Little
Qualicum Falls, Cathedral Grove, Rathtrevor Prov. Park, marina
Peacefull luxury in charming Tudor home tastefully decorated with quality European and
English antiques. Enjoy cozy warmth under European white goose-down duvets. Relax in the
comfortably furnished guest lounge with fireplace. Hosts will arrange tee-time at nearby golf
courses with reduced rates for house guests. Also new self-catering carriage house available for
longer staying guests. There is a Dachshund in residence. Visa,MC CC

Revelstoke *(west of Golden; see also Sicamous)*

Astra, Joan and Olympe (Smokey Bear Campground & B&B) ☎/Fax(250)837-9573
Box 1125, Revelstoke,BC V0E 2S0 1-800-710-9573

Located 5 km west of Revelstoke on Hwy 1.
$35S $50-60D $10Child $15Add.person ► 10A,5Ch
Full Rural, 5 acre, patio 3D,1F (upstairs & ground level) 1D,5Q,1crib
2Sh.w.g., 2ensuite ★F,TV,LF, hot tub No smoking Russian
Flower Gardens, hiking, x-c skiing & snowmobiling
Mt.Revelstoke Nat.Park, Revelstoke Dam, Begbie Falls, Glacier National Park, Hot Springs
Inviting country home. Hosts are knowledgeable of the area. Ideal place for snowmobilers and
groups. There is a dog & a cat. RV Park & hostel on property. Visa,MC CC

Blackwell, Syd (Wintergreen Inn)
Box 1260, 312 Kootenay St., Revelstoke, BC   V0E 2S0

☎ & Fax (250) 837-3369, 1-800-216-2008
E-mail: wintergreen@bctravel.com

$65-80S $75-90D $10Child (over age 6) $10Add.person   (plus taxes)   ► 24

Phone for directions.
🍲 Full   🏠 Res, 3-storey, view from guest rooms, patio, porch,
deck quiet   ■8D,2F (main & upper level)   ⊨ 8T,7Q,1P
🛏Private, ensuite   ★F,guest common area, ceiling fans,
separate entrance, off-street parking, wheel-chair access, host
quarters are separate   ⍝Smoking outside on deck
🕴 Historic Court House, downtown shops & restaurants, Railway
Museum, riverside trails
🚌 Mt.Revelstoke & Glacier National Parks, Revelstoke Dam, historic "Last Spike of CPR" site
☛ New B&B Inn, designed especially for guests' privacy and situated amid the splendor of
majestic mountains at the gateway of 2 National Parks. World travelled host is a former educator.
Free pick-up/delivery for buses. Visa, MC ✓CC

Ingram, Cliff and Donna (Alpine Lane Bed & Breakfast)
Box 1973, 487 Alpine Lane, Revelstoke, BC   V0E 2S0

☎ (250) 837-6106

Located on TC Highway and 3km east of the lights. OR 1km west of eastern access to city.

Phone for directions.
$40-55 $45-60 $10Child   ► 6
🍲Full,homebaked   🏠 Rural,split-level,acreage,decks,mountain
view ■1D,1Ste (upst) ⊨1D,1Q,2S 🛏1Ensuite,1sh.w.g.(bidets)
★F,TV, sauna, parking
🕴 Hiking and x-c ski trails
🚌 Mt Revelstoke National Park Summit, ski hill, Hydro Dam,
golf course, snowmobile trails, Railway Museum
☛ Home is situated at the base of Mt. Revelstoke on Hwy 1 and surrounded by mountains
offering plenty of sightseeing year around. Relax by the fire or on the outdoor deck. Enjoy a friendly,
casual atmosphere and the picturesque view of Mt Begbie Glacier. Breakfast is served in the dining
room. There is a resident cat. ✓CC

Nelles, Rosalyne (Nelles Ranch B&B)
Hwy 23 S, Box 430, Revelstoke, BC   V0E 2S0

☎ & Fax (250) 837-3800, 1-888-567-4177

Located 2.2 km off TCH 1 at Revelstoke on Hwy 23 South.
$35-65S $45-75D $10Child $15Add.person   ► 22+
🍲 Full(hearty ranch-style)   🏠 Rural, large Horse-Ranch,
acreage, view, patio, quiet   ■6 plus 1F (main & upper level)
⊨ 5D,4Q,3T,1R   🛏 3sh.w.g., 4private   ★ F,TV in guest
family room, sinks in some guest rooms, separate entrance,
overnight horse accommodation available
🕴 Trail rides (horses), riding stables, x-c skiing, hiking
🚌 Revelstoke Dam, Mt Revelstoke Nat.Park (scenic drive) Williamsons Lake, Railway Museum
☛ Congenial hosts have been welcoming guests for 11 years in spacious ranchhouse on working
horse ranch, set amid the majesty of the Selkirk Mountains. Enjoy the fresh mountain air and
breathtaking scenery. There is a small pet poodle called "Handsome". Wilderness trail rides (hours
and day rides) offered for experienced and inexperienced riders. Reservations recommended. ✓CC

Richmond   *(Vancouver); see also N.Westmin, Delta, White R, Surrey, Ladner, Tsawwassen)*

Enno, Gloria & Tim (Gloria's Bed & Breakfast)   ☎ (604) 277-7097
6191 Madrona Cr., Richmond, BC   V7C 2T3

Phone for directions.
$60S $65D $15Add.person (min. 2 nights)   ► 8
📺 Full, homebaked   🏠 Res., 2-storey, patio ■2Ste (street level) ⊨2Q,2P ⫔2Ensuite ⫔Separate entrance, TV/fridge in guest room, street parking   ⊛ No pets, smoking outside, children min. age 12
🕴 Major Shopping Mall, park, Richmond Sports Complex, Senior's Activity Center, Gateway Theatre of the Arts, hospital, bus stop
🚗 Steveston Fishing Village, Buddhist Church, Airport, Vancouver
🐾 Modern home in quiet residential neighborhood. Enjoy the convenient location and proximity to the airport and the big City. There is a small dog in residence. ✔B&B

Hamilton, Tom (Brigadoon B&B)   ☎ (604) 271-7096, Fax (604) 271-7099
4180 Lancelot Dr., Richmond, BC   V7C 4S3

From Hwy 99, exit westbound on Steveston Hwy. Turn right at Gilbert Rd, then left at Francis Rd.

Proceed to Lancelot Gate, turn right after crossing Railway Ave.
$55-75S $65-95D $20Add,person   ► 6
📺 Full, homebaked   🏠 Sub., split-level, porch, quiet, garden terrace ■3D(upstairs) ⊨2T,1D,1Q ⫔1Sh.w.g.,1ensuite
★F,TV in guest ground level sitting room, guest quarters are separate, off-street parking   ⊛ No smoking, no pets, children min. age 14
🕴 Walk or cycle on ocean dyke and trails, pitch & putt, tennis, shopping centre, bus #406 & connection to downtown Richmond and Vancouver
🚗 Downtown Vancouver, Horseshoe Bay, Int. Airport, Queen Elizabeth Park, Granville Island, Stanley Park, Grouse Mountain, BC Ferry Terminal, US border
🐾 "BC Superhost hospitality" in comfortable home. After a busy day enjoy the terrace garden or relax in the guest sitting room with fireplace and a large collection of books. Breakfast is served in guest dining room or terrace garden. There is a resident Corgi called "Lady".Visa,MC,Amex ✔B&B

Lewis, Joyce and Bob (Joyce's B&B)   ☎ (604) 278-8584
10880 Granville Ave., Richmond, BC   V6Y 1R4

Located between No 4 and No 5 Roads.ph for directions.
$40S $45-55D   ► 5
📺 Full, homebaked   🏠 Res., sub., split-level, acreage, patio, quiet ■ 2D ⊨ 2T,1D,1R ⫔1Ensuite, 1Sh.w.g. ★TV in guest room, separate entrance, prarking ⊛Restricted smoking, no pets, children min age 6
🕴 Aquatic center, jogging track, shopping malls, live theatre, restaurants, bus routes
🚗 Downtown Vancouver, International Airport, Ferries, easy access to Hwy 99
🐾 Warm and friendly hospitality in comfortable home situated in quiet and convenient location. Hosts will pick up at airport. ✔B&B

Roberts Creek
(north of Vancouver; see also Gibsons, Sechelt, Powell River)

Gaulin, Loragene and Philip (Country Cottage B&B)　　　　☎ (604) 885-7448
1183 Roberts Creek Rd., Box 183, Roberts Creek, BC　V0N 2W0

From Vancouver, take Hwy 1 and Horseshoe Bay-Langdale Ferry (40 min), and continue on
Sunshine Coast Hwy 101 through Gibsons to Roberts Creek Rd. Turn left.

$95-105Cottage $115-125Lodge $50Add.person　　　► 8A
🍴 Full, homebaked (gourmet)　🍴 Farm, older acreage, quiet
■ Cottage & lodge with cabin　⊨4Q　⊴3Private　★KF,wood
heater, River Rock fireplace in lodge, wood-fired sauna, campfire
circle, bicycles for guests　🚳No smoking, no pets, no children,
one party only in lodge & cabin.　⌇French
🏃 Bicycling on beautiful beach avenue, golf course, French
Gourmet restaurant, beach walks

🚗 Scenic coastline, hiking, swimming beaches, c/c skiing, fly-fishing, kyaking, mountain biking
☛ Totally restored farmhouse, rustic cottage and lodge (a few steps away) surrounded by English
Country style gardens and lawns. Breakfast is served in the main house kitchen for all guests and
cooked on antique wood stove. Hostess is a spinner and weaver and raises sheep for fine spinning
wool. Tea and scones served at 4pm either on the lawn or inside the parlor in front of the fire.
Advance reservation necessary. ⌐B&B

Salmon Arm
(east of Kamloops: see also Pritchard, Sorrento)

Bodnar, Gisela (Silver Creek Guest House)　　　　☎ (250) 832-8870
6820-30 Ave SW, Salmon Arm, BC　V1E 4M1

At Flashing light west of Salmon Arm, turn off to Salmon River Rd. Follow road for 2.5 km, turn

right on 30th Ave SW and drive for 1.5 km. Look forsign on left.
$25-30S　$40-45D　$5-10Child　　► 6A,2Ch
🍴 Choice　🏠 Small ranch, patio　■ 3D(main level)　⊨ 3D,
cots　⊴ 1Sh.w.h.,1private　★TV,F,LF　♥　🚳 Restricted
smoking　⌇ German
🏃 Bicycling, cross-country ski trails
drive Large Community center with swimming pool and hot tub,
Shuswap Lake, beaches, boating, fishing, Salmon Arm, canoeing
☛ Charming log house with beautiful view from deck of Mount Ida and Salmon River Valley. For
a delicious breakfast, enjoy fresh farm eggs, homemade buns and jams and fruits in season. ⌐B&B

Cruickshank, Barb & Don (Cinnamon Stick Bed & Breakfast)　　☎ (250) 832-4808
1801-28th Ave NE, Salmon Arm, BC　V1E 3X2　　　　　　　　　　(250) 833-8877

From East on Hwy 1, turn right at 30th St (1st lights), left at 20th Ave, right on Lakeshore Rd and
left on 28th Ave. From West on Hwy 1, turn left at McDonalds, immediately right on Lakeshore.
Continue approx. 3.5 km, then left on 28th Ave.

$40S　$50-55D　　　► 6
🍴 Full, homebaked　🏠 Res., split-level, view from 2 guest rooms,
patio, deck, quiet　■3 (main & ground level)　⊨ 2T,2D,1R
⊴1Private, 1sh.w.g.　★F,TV in guest rooms, off-street
parking　🚳 No smoking
🏃 Bird Sanctuary
🚗 Downtown Salmon Arm, golfing, hiking, swimming, fruit
stands, houseboating, boat launch, x-c skiing, sleigh rides
☛ Rustic log home with antiques and dried flower decor, nestled in the rocks and trees with
sweeping view of downtown & Shuswap Lake. Breakfast and evening tea is served on the patio or
beside wood burning 2-storey rock fireplace. There are lots of stairs. Pick-up from bus station or
airport. There is an English Setter called "Toffy" in residence. Pets and children welcome.

Evans, Marnie & Bob (Sherwood Forest Bed & Breakfast) ☎ & Fax (250) 832-1863
2511-4th Ave.NE, Salmon Arm, BC V1E 2A7 E-mail: mcurle@mail.shuswap.net

Arriving from west, turn right, from east turn left at 30th St.NE & TCH. Proceed to 5th Ave NE, turn right to 27th St, turn left to 4th Ave NE. Turn right to house on right.

$50S $55D $10Child (under age 12) $15Add.person ▶ 4
Full,homebaked Res., back-split 3-storey, quiet, view, deck
1Ste(ground level) Private 1Q,2P ★F,TV,small guest patio, guest sitting room, off-street parking, sep.entrance, separate guest quarters No smoking,no pets
Video store, restaurants, swimming pool, curling rink, hiking trails, bus to downtown, College, bowling
Downtown Salmon Arm, Shuswap Lake (many beaches & picnic areas), winter sports & x-c skiing, great little fishing lakes, golf courses, Vernon, Kamloops
Comfortable, multi-level home in a quiet, private setting. There is a 25ft hibiscus tree in the solarium adjacent to the living room. Host loves to show off his airplane under construction in the garage. Relax on the sunny little patio off the guest suite or join the hosts for interesting conversation in the large bright kitchen with a beautiful view of Shuswap Lake and where a wholesome breakfast is served. ✓CC

Oberholtzer, Carol (The Trickle Inn) ☎ (250) 835-8835, Fax (250) 835-2284
Box 96, 5290 Trans Canada Hwy, Tappen, BC V0E 2X0

Located 11km west of Salmon Arm on Trans Canada Highway. Phone for directions.
$90-140S $100-150D $20Add.person Meals (plus tax) ▶ 12

Full, homebaked Rural, 3-storey, hist., acreage, view from guest rooms, patio, porch, deck 4D,2F,1Ste (2nd & 3rd floor) 4T,2S,2Q,R 1Sh.w.g., 3ensuite ★ LF, hot tub, private entrance, guest quarters are separate No smoking, no pets, children min. age 6
Lake Shuswap, antique shop on site
Points of interest around Lake Shuswap, Salmon Arm, hiking trails, excellent skiing
Historic Heritage house built in 1908, recently renovated and with beautiful decor, graces the hillside overlooking the beautiful Shuswap Lakes. Enjoy the elegant cozy atmosphere and silver service breakfast in the formal dining room with a magnificient oak dining table. Menu available for fine dining. Visa,MC ✓CC

Rietzler, Kerry & Helmut (Pheasant's Roost B&B) ☎ (250) 832-4866, Fax (250) 832-6527
Box 211, 3971-30th St.NE, Salmon Arm, BC V1E 4N3

From East on Hwy 1 turn right on 30St NE (first traffic light in S.A.)and proceed 2.4km to B&B on the left. From West on Hwy 1, go all the way through S.A on Hwy 1, up the hill, turn left on 30St NE. Proceed 2.4km to house on left. Look for sign.

$45-60S $60-70D (plus tax) ▶ 5A
Full (healthy buffet) Sub, 2-storey, acreage, heated swimming pool, patio, deck, quiet 1S,2D,1Ste (main floor) 1T,1D,1Q 1Private,1sh.w.g. ★ TVin one guest room, separate entrance, off-street parking Smoking outside, not suitable for children German
Country walks and jogging routes, explore the property
Beaches & marinas on Shuswap Lake, golfing, riding stable, x-c skiing, downtown shopping, Bird Sanctuary, nature trails, downhill ski resorts
Warm hospitality in unique setting. Hosts are active outdoor enthusiasts and operate a small Dried Flower Farm on property. Stroll through the flower garden, little orchard, vineyard or the barn. Breakfast is served in the country dining room. There is a dog and a cat outdoors. ✓B&B

Roberts, Nelson and Claire (Auntie Claire's B&B)   ☎ (250) 832-2421
2930-5th Ave SE, Salmon Arm, BC   V1E 2H1

From Hwy 1, turn south at Super 8 Motel and go for 1 km on 30th
St to 5th Ave SE. Turn right to 2nd house on left.
$45S $55D $5-10Child(age 6-12)   ▮Meals   ► 5
🍲 Choice, homebaked   🏠 Res., split-level, deck, mountain view,
quiet   ■2D(lower level)   ⊨1Q,2T,1P,cot,crib   ⊒ Sh.w.g.
★TV,VCR, semi-private entrance, parking   ⊛No smoking.
🕴 Beautiful Shuswap Lake, downtown, Community center
(swimming, dancing, aerobics), fruit stands, house boating, hiking
🚗 Championship 18-hole golf course, salmon spawning and fishing, Silver Star Ski Resort
🐾 Early retired hosts in lovely quiet home filled with many railroad memorbilia and situated in
excellent neighborhood. Hostess is a landscape artist and former rodeo rider. Breakfast is served on
deck or in the dining area. Pick-up from train/plane at nom.charge. Families welcome. ✓CC

Scherba, Lillian & Paul (Apple Blossom B&B)   ☎ (250) 832-0100, Fax (250) 832-0101
3531-10th Ave SE, Salmon Arm, BC   V1E 1W8

Entering Salmon Arm from east, turn left at 30th St NW (traffic light) and proceed to 10th Ave SE,
turn left. Look for lighted sign.
$60-72S $75-90D $15Add.person   ► 4A
🍲 Full, homebaked   🏠 Sub, small acreage, 2-storey, patio,
quiet   ■1Ste(2D-ground level)   ⊨ 2T,1Q   ⊒ 1Private
★TV in guest rooms, private guest patio & entrance, small alcove
eating area with fridge/sink unit, coffee maker, guest quarters are
separate, off-street parking   ⊛No smoking, no pets
〰German, Ukrainian
🕴 Hiking trails on Little Mountains to Rec.Centre (swimming), restaurants, store
🚗 Downtown Salmon Arm, numerous golf courses, parks, museum, historic sites
🐾 Friendly, long-time hosts on small acreage within town limits at the foot of "Little Mountain",
and surrounded by panoramic Shuswap scenery. Enjoy the comfortable and tranquil atmosphere.
An abundant breakfast is served in the dining room. There is a cat in residence. ✓B&B

Van Huigenbos, Henrietta & Henk (The Inn at the Ninth Hole)   ☎ (250) 833-0185
5091-20th Ave SE, Salmon Arm, BC   V1E 1X6   1-800-221-5955

From Hwy 1 go south on Hwy 97B for 3km. Turn right onto 20th Ave SE and to last house on right.
$80-125D $15Add.person   (off-season rates available)   ► 6+
🍲 Full   🏠 Rural, 2-storey, acreage, golf course view from guest
rooms, quiet   ■ 3Ste (main & upper level)   ⊨ 2Q,1K,1P(D)
⊒3ensuite (with jet tub)   ★ Air,3F,LF,TV in guest rooms,
private entrance, guest quarters are in separate wing of the
building, off-street parking   ⊛ No smoking, no pets ˙   〰 Dutch
🕴 18 and 9-hole Championship Golf Courses, concession stand
🚗 Salmon Arm, x-c skiing at Larch Hills
🐾 Young host family in new beautiful Colonial-style home, especially built with B&B in mind)
located on the greens of Salmon Arm Championship Golf & Country Club. "A place for all seasons".
Relax in the peaceful surroundings. Visa,MC,Amex ✓B&B

Saltspring Island *(east of Duncan; see also Mayne Island)*

Bolton, Terry & Bev (Beddis House B&B)   ☎ (250) 537-1028, Fax (250) 537-9888
131 Miles Ave., Salt Spring Island, BC   V8K 2E1   E-mail: beddis@saltspring.com

From Ganges, take Fulford-Ganges Rd south to Beddis Rd. Proceed 6 km to Miles Ave, turn left.
$135-165S $150-180D   (plus tax) (weekly & seasonal rates available)   ▶ 6A
❄ closed Dec15-Jan31   ☍ Full, homebaked   ♠ Rural, hist.,
view from guest rooms, acreage, oceanfront, porch, deck, quiet
■ 3D (main & upper floor in new addition)   ⊨ 2T,1Q,1K
⊴3Ensuite ★F/library in parlour, sep.entrance, oceanfront
private decks/balcony, woodstove in each room, host quarters are
separate   ⓦ No smoking, no pets, no children
🕇 Private clamshell beach in sheltered cove, prolific wildlife, many
outdoor areas to relax, walks on quiet rural roads
🚗 Ganges Village, art galleries, craft studios, boating, Ruckle Provincial Park, Mount Maxwell
🐎 Restored Century Heritage farmhouse nestled peacefully beween the sea and an apple
Orchard. Savour luxury oceanfront accommodation in a truly magical setting. Well travelled hosts
enjoy sharing the diverse wonders of their island. Compl.afternoon tea/homebaking.Visa,MC ⌐CC

Broad, Rick & Ruth-Anne (Anne's Oceanfront Hideaway)   ☎(250)537-0851
168 Simson Rd,Salt Spring Isle,BC V8K 1E2   E-mail: annes@saltspring.com,Fax(250)537-0861

Located on the north-west side of the Island off Sunset Drive.
$135-185D (off season) $175-220D (Summer)   ▶ 8A
☍ Full (4-course Island b'fast)   ♠ Rural, res, 3-storey, acreage,
view from guest rooms, oceanfront, porch, guest balconies, quiet,
sandstone beach   ■ 4D(upstairs)   ⊨ 2T,3Q (incl canopy bed)
⊴ 4Ensuite (double hydromassage tub & shower in one ensuite)
★F,TV,Air(indiv.), balconies in 3 guest rooms, separate entrance,
wheel-chair access, exercise room, elevator, outside hot tub, library,
canoe & bicycles for guests, host quarters are separate   ⓦ No smoking, no pets, no children
🕇 Ocean, fishing, swimming, canoeing, kayaking, bird watching, cycling, craft/pottery studios
🚗 Golf course, tennis courts, movie theatre, swimming pool, shopping, restaurants, Art
Galleries, sailing charters, kayak rentals, hiking trails, pubs, Ganges, Vesuvius
🐎 Luxurious, spacious, newly-constructed home overlooking an everchanging panoramic
seaview. Enjoy the beauty and tranquility and unwind among the Arbutus and Oak. Allergy aware
and special diets can be accommodated with advance notice. Enjoy morning coffee on the sun deck.
Ideal place for special occasion, get-away or honeymoon. Visa,MC ⌐CC

Dexter, David & Marilyn & Haden (Mountain Aerie B&B)   ☎ & Fax (250) 537-5720
401 Wilkie Way, Salt Spring Island, BC V8K 2J4   1-888-332-3742

Located 5km from Ganges.
$150S/D $200Cottage $40Add.person   ▶ 8
❄ Apr15-Oct15   ☍ Full(Gourmet)   ♠ Rural, 2-storey,
hillside, acreage, view from guest rooms, decks, quiet, secluded
■ 1D,1Ste(inhouse/upstairs),plus cottage(for4) ⊨4Q
⊴2Private,1ensuite ★ LF,TV,KF,fans in guest rooms, 2 hot
tubs, separate entrance, guest quarters are separate   ⓦ No
smoking, no pets, no children
🕇 Six hiking trails on 15 forested acres, trail up Mt Erskine
🚗 Ruckle & Mt.Maxwell Parks, 4 lakes, Ganges (village & Saturday market), 3 ferries
🐎 Large custom-built secluded mountain hide-away, located 1000 ft high on Mt Belcher with a
spectacular panoramic view of ocean, islands and coastal mountain range. Retired hosts have
travelled extensively worldwide and love to entertain. Relax in the sitting room with Grand Piano,
or on one of the decks or in the hot tub and enjoy the serene and quiet atmosphere. Breakfast is
served in guest breakfast room. Guest cottage is located in secluded quiet area. Massage Therapist
on call. Weekly rates available. Visa,MC ⌐CC

Eastman, Paul & Michael McLandress (Summerhill Guest House)　　☎ (250) 537-2727
209 Chu-An Drive, Salt Spring Island, BC　V8K 1H9　　　　　　Fax (250) 537-4301

Located near Vesuvius Bay and 6km from the main village of Ganges.
$90-115S　　$95-120D　　　　　　　　　　　　　　　　　　　　　► 6A
🍳 Full, homebaked　🏠 Rural, 2-storey, view from guest rooms, onceanfront, deck, quiet
■3D(upstairs)　⊨2T,2Q　🛏1Private, 2ensuite　★ F,separate entrance, guest quarters are
separate　⊕ No smoking, no pets, not suitable for children
🔥 Nearby beach access, water activities, walking trail, Vesuvius Village, galleries, craft studios
🚗 BC Ferry dock at Vesuvius Bay, Long Harbour, Fulford Harbour, good car ferry & float plane
connections to Vancouver, Victoria & Seattle
📣 Tasteful and understated home evoking peace and tranquility. Relax in the garden on the
decks or in the spacious sitting room by the fire overlooking magnificient Sansum Narrows. A
tantalizing breakfast is served at water's edge in the special guest breakfast room. Visa,MC ✓CC

Evans, Susan & Ted Harrison (Weston Lake Inn B&B)　　☎ (250) 653-4311
813 Beaver Point Rd., Salt Spring Island, BC　V8K 1X9　　　　Fax (250) 653-4340

From Swartz Bay (Victoria), take ferry to Fulford Harbour on Salt Spring
Isle, proceed 3.6km tow.Ruckle Prov.Park on Beaver Pt. Rd.
$85-105S　$95-120D　$25Add.person　　　　　　　　► 7A
🍳 Full, homebaked(Gourmet)　🏠 Hobby farm, tudor-style, acreage,
waterview, quiet　■3D(upst)　⊨1T,3Q　🛏3Private ★TV,VCR in guest
lounge, library & refreshment area, hot tub, woodstove, sailing charters,
parking　⊕No smoking, no pets, child min.age 14　〰French
🔥 Weston Lake, swimming, fishing, biking, extensive gardens
🚗 Ruckle Park, Ganges (Canada's pottery capital) with craft shops featuring high quality works
📣 Comfortable contemp.farmhouse full of art & fine needlework overlooking Weston Lake.
Hosts are well informed about the area activities, eating places and quiet entertainment. Relax in
the hot tub (built into a mountainside). There is a cat. Weekly/off-season rates. Visa,MC ✓CC

Leader, Harry and Ilse (Ocean Spray B&B by the Sea)　　☎ & Fax (250) 653-4273
1241 Isabella Pt.Rd., Salt Spring Island, BC　V8K 1T5

Take ferry from Victoria (Swartz Bay) to Fulford Harbour on Saltspring Island. From Vancouver,
take ferry from Tsawwassen to Long Harbour and drive through Ganges to Fulford Harbour.

$85D　$10-15Child　$20Add.person　　　　　　► 4
🍳 Full (provided, but not served)　🏠 Rural, acreage,
oceanfront, 3-level, quiet　■Ste　⊨2T,1P,cot　🛏Private
★Sep.entrance, KF, parking　⊕Restr.smoking　〰German
🔥 Ecological Reserve, back country roads and forest trails
📣 Roomy cedar home (built by architect of Frank Lloyd Wright
School), is located on Satellite Channel with a panoramic view of
the Gulf Islands and Mount Baker, situated on 5 acres of forested
waterfront with the sea a stone's throw away from the bedroom deck, offering an ever changing
scene of marine life. Visa/MC ✓CC

McLean, Imme (Captain's Hideaway)　　　　　　　☎ (250) 537-9595
162 Harrison Ave., Salt Spring Island, BC　V8K 2N3

Phone for directions.
$55S　$65D　$10Add.person　　　　　　　　► 4
📅 March-Oct.　🍳 Full, homebaked　🏠 Rural, res., ranch-style,
acreage, view from guest rooms, quiet, tidalfront　■1Ste　⊨2D
(main level)　🛏 Private　★KF,LF,TV in guest living room,
wheel-chair access　⊕Children min. age 6　〰 German
🔥 Golfing, tennis, store, berry picking, explore inlet by rowboat
🚗 Lakeshore, ocean and beaches, village of Ganges, restaurants
📣 Quiet waterfront retreat on sunny Booth Inlet and a bird watcher's paradise. ✓CC

52　BRITISH COLUMBIA

Partridge, Lynne (The Partridge House B&B) ☎ (250) 537-2822, Fax (250) 537-1443
131 Salt Spring Way, Salt Spring Island, BC V8K 2G3

Located 3km south of Ganges village just off Fulford-Ganges Rd.
$55-80S $65-85D $165Ste(2rooms)   (weekly rates available. 7th night no charge)   ► 6

🍴 Full   🏠 Rural, 2-storey, hillside, view from guest rooms,
porch, quiet   ■ 2D (studio suite - main floor)
⊨2T,1Q,1P(Q),cot   ⬛ 1Sh.w.g.   ★ F,KF,TV in guest rooms,
private entrance & porch, off-street parking, hot tub on deck, guest
quarters are separate   ⚓ Designated smoking area, no pets
🏃 Cusheon Lake (fishing & swimming)
🚐 Central to all Island activities & sights, hiking, boating,
artisan studios, golfing, horseback riding, shops, galleries, Victoria
🐎 Warm hospitality in spacious island home with outstanding ocean & islands view. Enjoy a
busy or quiet island day and end it with a relaxing soak in the hot tub or snuggle by the fire. Whole
floor is suitable for family up to 6 persons. There is a resident dog. Visa,MC ✐B&B

Tara, Helen (Water's Edge B&B)   ☎ (250) 537-5807, Fax (250) 537-2862
327 Price Rd., Salt Spring Island, BC , V8K 2E9

Take any one of 3 ferries to Saltspring Island and then Fulford-Ganges Rd to Beddis Rd. Turn
southeast for 2km to Price Rd and left 1km to waterfront. Located 4.2km south of Ganges Village.

$95-120S $115-135D $35-45Add.person   ► 7
🍴 Full, homebaked   🏠 Rural, waterfront on Ganges Harbour,
2-storey, seaview from guest rooms, patio, quiet   ■1D,1Ste
(ground level waterside)   ⊨3Q,1S   ⬛ 1Ensuite, 1Private
★F,KF, rowboat, guest sitting room, separate entrance, parking
⚓Smoking outside only
🏃 Shore walk at down tide, rowboating over magic chain of islands
in the harbour, clam digging, beachcombing, country walks
🚐 Village of Ganges, shopping, restaurants, 3 ferries, golfing, swimming, horseback riding
🐎 Long-time island residents in contemporary home with country gardens and covered patio
facing waterfront. Relax in the quiet comfort, watch the sun rise over the water, see the abundant
birds & sealife and marine traffic in the harbour. ✐B&B

Sechelt
(north of Vancouver; see also Gibsons, Roberts Creek, Powell River)

Fedor, David & Brenda Wilkinson (Four Winds B&B)   ☎ (604) 885-3144
5482 Hill Rd., RR1, Blacks Site C33, Sechelt, BC V0N 3A0   Fax (604) 885-3182

From Langdale (ferry from Vancouver), take Sunshine coast Hwy 101 through Sechelt and proceed
past Wakefield Inn to Hill Rd. Turn left.

$85-105S $100-120D $20Child   ► 4A,2-3Ch
🍴Full, homebaked   🏠Rural, view from guest rooms, deck, quiet,
oceanfront   ■ 2D (ground level)   ⊨ 2T,1Q   ⬛Sh.w.g.,
1ensuite   ★ Guest robes, hot tub   ⚓ No smoking, no pets
🏃 Rocky beach
🚐 Skookumchuk Rapids, kayak & canoe rentals, boat charters,
hiking trails, mountain biking, art galleries
🐎 Architecturally designed home sitting on rocky oceanshore. Curl up in a window seat with the
sea just ten feet away. Join the host family in the spectacular living room surrounded on three sides
by the ocean. Relax in the outdoor hot tub, fall asleep to the sound of waves lapping lazily on the
rocks below. Breakfast is served on the deck or in dining room. Hostess is a Registered Massage
Therapist and will take advance bookings for treatment and workshops. Ideal place for a weekend
retreat or a special occasion. There is a dog and a cat in host area. Visa,MC ✐CC

Sicamous

(west of Revelstoke; see also Mara)

Meyers, Ray & Phillis (Rainbow Valley B&B) ☎ (250) 836-3268
Box 343, Sicamous, BC V0E 2V0   E-mail: rainbowv@shuswap.net, Fax (250) 836-3008

Located at 1409 Rauma Rd and 2 blocks north of TCH.
$75-110S/D $20Child/Add.person   ▶10
🍴 Full, homebaked 🏠 2-storey ■ 1D,2F(upstairs ⊨ 5Q
🛏 3Private ★ F,KF,LF,TV in guest rooms, separate entrance,
ceiling fans, off-street & street parking 🚭 Designated smoking
area, no pets,
🧍 Beaches, shopping places, houseboating, gifts/crafts,
restaurants, fruit stands, museum, golfing, Zoo, lake cruises
🚗 Scenic drive along Mara Lake to city of Vernon, large shopping malls, excellent downhill skiing
🎯 Newly-built house located with view of beautiful Canadian Rockies and Shuswap Lake and
located in a quiet area. Breakfast is served in special guest breakfast room. Ideal place for weddings
or family reunion-type gatherings and special occasions. Children welcome. Visa,MC

Sidney

(north of Victoria; see also Bretnwood Bay)

Christensen Kirsten & Leif (Little Mermaid B&B) ☎ (250) 656-4377, Fax (250) 656-0949
11064 Chalet Rd., Sidney, BC V8L 5M2

Phone for directions. Map will be faxed/send with reservation.
$85D   ▶4A
🍴 Full, homebaked 🏠 Rural, view from guest rooms, 2.25acres,
hillside, quiet, secluded ■ 2D(ground level) ⊨ 4T(2K)
🛏2Private ★KF,TV in guest sitting room, separate entrance
🚭No smoking, no pets, not suitable for children 〰Danish
🚗 Sidney, world famous Butchart Gardens, ferry to Vancouver,
Victoria Airport, Victoria downtown
🎯 Warm, Danish welcome in spacious waterfront home. Watch the sun go down over the ocean
from the waters edge garden and relax in the friendly atmosphere. Patio doors from all rooms lead
to private deck. Breakfast is served in ocean-facing breakfast room. 〰B&B

Clegg, Averil & Maurice (Mandeville - Tudor Cottage by the Sea) ☎ (250) 655-1587
1064 Landsend Rd., Sidney, BC V8L 5L3   Fax (250) 655-3993

Located at north end of Saanich Peninsula, at intersection of
Landsend Rd & West Saanich Rd. Phone for specific directions.
$75S $95D $15Child $25Add.person   ▶4A,4Ch
🍴 Full(West coast cuisine) 🏠 Rural, oceanfront forest acreage,
2-storey, hist., view from guest rooms, patio, porch, deck ■2Stes
(upstairs & ground level) ⊨1S,2Q,1R,1P(D),crib 🛏2Private
★TV,LF,F in one suite, kitchenette, private entrances, private
patio, guest quarters are separate 🚭Smoking outside, no pets
🚗 BC & Washington State Ferry Terminals, airports, Victoria, hiking trails (with excellent ocean
views from higher points), Butchart Gardens, Vancouver Island attractions and virgin forests,
Pacific Rim Nat.Park (with unspoiled beaches), good skiing
🎯 Retired Professional couple in picturesque classic English Tudor Cottage home with lawns &
gardens leading to the beach. Enjoy the breathtaking views across the Satellite Channel to
neighbouring Saltspring Island. Hosts are interested in the arts, music, travel, gardening and are
active at the local Anglican Church. Breakfast is served in guest dining room. 〰B&B

Lightbody, Glenda & William (The Log House Bed & Breakfast)   ☎ & Fax (250) 656-4421
1510 Sylvan Place, RR3, Sidney, BC   V8L 5L5   E-mail: lightbod@octonet.com

Phone for directions.
$95S/D(and up) $25Add.person   ▶ 4A,2Ch
🍴 Full, homebaked   🏠 Rural, 2-storey, log house, 1 acre,
panoramic view from all rooms, patio, quiet   🛏 2 (patio level)
⊨D,Q,K   🛁 2Private   ★ TV/VCR,F,LF,KF, wheelchair
access, separate entrance off large patio with barbeque, guest sitt.
room ⍖Smoking ouside only   〰 Spanish, German, French
🕊 Neighborhood Stonehouse Pub,marina,kayaking,sailing,beach
🚗 Swartz Bay/Anacortes Ferries, Victoria, airport, Butchart Gardens
🐾 Retired couple in beautiful, spacious country home furnished with family heirlooms and large
wrap-around deck, nestled in woodland on a ridge off Lands End Rd. Enjoy the sweeping view of the
Gulf Islands & Mount Baker with the marine traffic 400 feet below. Breakfast specialty is eggs
benedict with smoked salmon. Hosts are knowledgeable about local attractions and will gladly give
guidance. Pick-up on request. There is a Golden Labrador outdoors. ⌒CC

Monahan, Nancy & Kevin (Boldrewood Cottage B&B)   ☎ (250) 655-6767
1780 Dean Park Rd., Sidney, BC   V8L 1C1

From Victoria go north on Hwy 17, west on McTavish, south on E.Saanich & west on Dean Park.
$75S $85-110D $10Child (under age 12) $25Add.person   ▶ 5A

❊ May-Oct   🍴 Full, homebaked   🏠 Rural, res., 1.5-storey,
older, acreage, view, porch, deck, quiet   🛏 1F,2D (main floor)
⊨ 2T,1Q,cot   🛁 1Private, 1sh.w.g.   ★ TV in guest lounge,
private entrance for guests, off-street parking, guest quarters are
separate   ⍖ Designated smoking area, no pets
🕊 Dean Park, hiking trails, bus No70 to downtown and ferries
🚗 Sidney-by-the-Sea, Butchart Gardens, BC Ferries, Victoria
🐾 Charming older home set in a wooded hillside furnished
with art and antiques (both collected and inherited) and filled with books reflecting hosts many
interests and passions. Relax on the covered porch and enjoy the views of the Strait of Georgia.
Host is a Coast Guard captain and knowledgeable about the BC Coast and he is in the process of
publishing a book on satellite navigation. There is a cat in residence. Visa,MC,Amex

---

Siems, Susan (Borthwick Country Manor B&B)   ☎ & Fax (250) 656-9498
9750 Ardmore Dr., Sidney, Victoria, BC   V8L 5H5   E-mail: msiems@sutton.com

From Victoria travel 25 km north on Hwy 17A. Turn left on 2nd Ardmore Dr.

$85-130D $20Add.person   (Deposit required)   ▶ 10
🍴 Full, homebaked   🏠 Rural, 2-storey, acreage, view from guest
rooms, quiet   🛏3D,1F(upstairs)   ⊨3Q,1K,1R,1P   🛁4Ensuite
★TV, outdoor hot tub, guest bicycles, off-street parking   ⍖ No
smoking, no pets, children min. age 12
🕊 Beach, golf course
🚗 Butchart Gardens, Butterfly Gardens, Airport, Vancouver
ferries, Anacortes/Seattle-US ferries, sailing, boating, scuba diving
🐾 English Tudor Country Manor house, tastefully decorated with some antiques, set in one acre
of gorgeous landscaped gardens, and located in the beautiful Patricia Bay area of the Saanich
Peninsula. Relax in the outdoor hot tub or stroll to the nearby beach. English hosts serve breakfast
in the formal dining room or outside on the covered stone patio. CCards ⌒CC

Shrimpton, Josie & Malcolm (Cartref Bed & Breakfast)
1345 Readings Dr., Sidney, BC   V8L 5K7

☎& Fax (250) 656-1247
E-mail: cartref@islandnet.com

Phone for directions.
$60S $75-90D $10Child $15Add.person   ▶ 4A,2Ch
🍳Full, homebaked   🏠Rural, 2-storey, acreage, ocean view from
guest rooms,patio,quiet   ■1D,1F(upstairs)   ⊨1T,1D,1Q,crib
🚪Private   ★ LF,TV/VCR in guest sitting room   ✋No pets, no
smoking, only one party at a time
🚶 Nature trails, viewpoints
🚗 BC/US ferries, Sidney, Butchart Gardens, airport,Victoria
🐾 Warm and friendly welcome in new home (name is Celtic for "home") situated on a tranquil
sunny hillside with view of Sidney Channel. Breakfast is served in the Conservatory or on the
terrace by an ornamental waterfall. Recently retired hosts have travelled extensively and are
knowledgeable about southern Vancouver Island. Extra space available for family & friends.Visa

Silverton   *(north of Castlegar; see also Winlaw, Nelson)*

Iverson, Sue & George (Mistaya Country Inn & B&B)   ☎ (604) 358-7787
Box 28, Silverton, BC   V0G 2B0

Located north of Castlegar Airport or Nelson on Hwy 6.
$45-50S $60-65D $15Add.person   🍽 Meals   (plus tax)▶ 13
🍳 Full, homebaked   🏠 Rural, 2-storey ranch-style, acreage,
view from guest rooms, porch   ■ 4D,1F (upstairs)
⊨4S,1D,3Q,1P,1R, cot   🛁 2Sh.w.g.   ★ F,LF, guest lounge,
outside firepit   ★ Smoking on porch, no pets
🚶 90 acres of forest and pasture land, walking & x-c ski trails
🚗 Nakusp & Ainsworth Hot Springs, Sandon Ghost town,
Idaho Peak lookout, Unique village of New Denver, Valhalla Prov.& Kokanee Glacier Parks
🐾 Spacious, comfortable country home overlooking a forest meadow and the Valhalla Wilderness
Park. Experience a quiet vacation in the Slocan Valley, enjoy the wild flowers, magnificient scenery
& wildlife or relax by the fireplace. Trail rides, riding lessons and overnight pack trips into the
Selkirk Mountains, and wildlife viewing/canoe/kayak trips offered. Packed lunches & evening
barbeques available. ✓B&B

Smithers   *(east of Prince Rupert; see also Francois Lake, Burns Lake, Smithers)*

Davey, Margaret and Dave (The Ptarmigan B&B)   ☎ (250) 847-9508
Box 2439, Willow Rd., Smithers, BC   V0J 2N0

Located 6 km west of Smithers at junction of Willow & Lake Kathlyn Rds (just off Hwy16).

$35-55S $45-60D $75F(in 2rooms)   ▶ 6
🍳 Full   🏠 Rural, Alpine-style 2-storey, acreage, view, patio,
quiet   ■ 2D,1St   ⊨ 3Q   🚪2Private   ★ TV in guest rooms,
VCR/Video library, separate entrance, ski storage, car plug-ins
✋ Smoking outside
🚶 Airport, Adams Igloo (renowned Wildlife Museum), Twin Falls
& Glacier Gulch, Lake Kathlyn
🚗 K'San Indian Village, Moricetown Falls (historic native
fishing site), Tyee Lake Pro.Park, Hudson Bay Mt Ski Resort, Bulkley River (Steelhead fishing)
🐾 Bavarian-style home with Canadiana decor, nestled romatically among evergreens in a pristine
wilderness atmosphere. Situated on 5 acres with spectacular mountain & glacier views. ✓CC

Sooke
(south-west of Victoria)

Evans, Robyn (Gordon's Beach Farm Stay B&B)   ☎ & Fax (250) 642-5291
4530 Otter Point Rd., Sooke, BC   V0S 1N0

From Hwy 1 take the Sooke-Colwood Exit following Hwy 14 to Sooke. Proceed through traffic lights
and continue on the West Coast Rd for 10km. Turn right up Otter Point Rd to 2nd house on left.
$60D $80-175Ste $15Child $15Add.person   🍽 Meals (lunch)   ► 6A,3Ch

🍴 Full   🏠 Farm, 3-storey, hillside, acreage, view from guest
rooms, patio, quiet, secluded   ■ 3(main & ground level)
🛏3Q,1R   🛁 2Private, 1ensuite   ★ TV/coffee makers in guest
rooms, private patios, beach hot tub and gazebo, separate entrance,
guest quarters are separate   🖐 Smoking outside
🏃 Beach across road, whale watching, windsurfing, kyaking,
fishing, hiking, Storm Watch (winter)
🚗 Straight of Juan de Fuca (Gateway to Pacific Ocean), West
Coast Trails, marine parks, Botanical Beach, restaurants, Sooke & S.Potholes, Victoria
🏴 Custom-designed, contemporary home with an artistic blend of old and new and allergy-free
environment, situated on 10 acres in pasture with 180 degree view of the Juan De Fuca Straights
and Olympic Mountains. Guests may be surprised to see whales pass by during breakfast time.
Relax in the hot tub and watch the Sherringham Lighthouse as the sun sets. Breakfast is served in
the dining room, on the patio or in guest rooms. There is a resident cat and dog. Visa,MC ✍B&B

Lee, Daphne & Peter (Manzer Lodge)   ☎ (250) 642-6632
3007 Manzer Rd., Sooke, BC   V0S 1N0

From downtown Victoria, go over Johnson St Bridge to Tyee Rd. Turn right and follow all the way
to Sooke. Look for 17-Mile-House Pub on right and then Manzer Rd 3rd road on left.
$95S/D   ► 4

🍴 Full English   🏠 Lodge-style, peaceful, 1-acre ■2D 🛏2Q
🛁2Ensuite   ★ F in guest lounge, private balcony, hot tub on
large deck   🖐 No smoking, no pets, no children
🚗 Galloping Goose Trail, Sooke Potholes, kayak & bike rentals
🏴 Comfortable home, tastefully and recently renovated and
nestled high amongst the trees. Ideal place to explore the coastline
with its bays, lakes and trails - or for a peaceful and tranquil rest.

Price, Helen & Gord (Water's Edge Cottage & B&B)   ☎ (250)642-5716,Fax(250)642-4864
5641 Sooke Rd., Sooke, BC   V0S 1N0

$95D(Ste) $150D(cottage) $15Add.person(Child free under age 6)   ► 8A,1Ch

Located on Hwy 14, 4km east of Sooke.
🍴 Full, homebaked   🏠 Rural, 2-storey, older, 3acres, view from
guest rooms, harbourfront, deck, quiet, secluded   ■ 1Ste, plus
private guest house   🛏 1S,1D,3Q   🛁 1Ensuite, 1private
★F,TV,KF,LF, ceiling fans, cozy wood stove, wheel-chair access in
cottage, private hot tub   🖐 Designated smoking area, no pets
🏃 Galloping Goose Trail (hiking/biking), fishing & whale
watching (tour charters), beach, City Transport No 61
🚗 Sooke village, shops, unique dining places, Victoria, Port Renfrew, West Coast Trail/beaches
🏴 Quiet country home with newly renovated suite & charming, waterfront cottage. Relax on the
large deck or in the private hot tub, just feet from the water, and enjoy the magical views of water &
Olympic Mountains. A perfect spot for touring the incredible scenic Sooke area and the West Coast.
Photograph otters & seals from the beach. A hearty delectable breakfast is served in the sunroom.
Cottage guests may prefer dining on private deck. Children welcome. Visa ✍B&B

Rolston, Marion (Ocean Wilderness Inn & Spa Retreat) ☎(250)646-2116,
109 West Coast Rd., Sooke, BC V0S 1N0 Fax 250)646-2317,1-800-323-2116

$65-140S $85-175D (Off-season discounts & winter specials available. ► 12

From Victoria, take Hwy 14 along West Coast Road to Sooke
Village, go past the only traffic light and continue 13 km.
🍽 Full, homebaked (also served in guest room) 🏠 Rural, hist.,
acreage, view, patio, quiet, oceanfront, isolated ■ 9(main and
upper level - all bed/sitting) ⊨6Q,2K,2T(some canopy)
⊰9Private (3 soak-tubs for two) ★Separate entrance, facilities
for the disabled, parking, outdoor reading areas, jetted hot tub in
garden Japanese gazebo ⓦ No smoking

🯅 5 acres with ocean beach and marine life and forest trails, beachcombing, birdwatching, surfing
🚗 Victoria, Botanical Beach, Sooke River swimming, fine dining, wild west coast beaches
🐾 Old log house (authentic Norwegian cabin) with modern addition for luxurious guest
accommodation, furnished with antiques and with beautiful ocean and mountain views. "Where
eagles soar and old growth forest meets the sea". Massage, ocean nutrient treatment and seaweed
wrap for relaxation and revitalization. Salmon fishing and whale watching guides available.

Yates, John and Muriel (Harbour Villa) ☎ & Fax (250) 642-7506
Box 1223, 1946 Murray Rd., Sooke, BC V0S 1N0

From Trans Canada Hwy 1, take Sooke Colwood Exit to Hwy 14.
Drive to center of Sooke. Turn left at traffic light at Murray Rd.
$70-115S $85-145 $15Add.person (Res.preferred) ► 7
🍽 Full, homebaked (English-style) 🏠 Village, multi-storey,view
from guest rooms,patio, oceanfront, quiet ■3D(upstairs) ⊨2Q
(brass),1K(2T) ⊰3Private ★F,TV in large guest lounge, guest
phones,separate entrance, parking ⓦRestr.smoking, no pets

🯅 Beach access from property, Government dock, Sooke Museum, shopping plaza, restaurants,
hiking trails, salmon fishing
🚗 Sooke Potholes Prov.Park, Sooke Harbour House Restaurant, Whiffin Spit, Butchart Gardens
🐾 Modern waterfront home with rose garden and breathtaking views of Sooke Harbour, Whiffen
Spit, Strait of Juan de Fuca and Olympic Mountains. Centrally located, yet very private. ✒B&B

Sorrento *(north of Salmon Arm; see also Pritchard, Kamloops)*

Langevin, Verna & Linda Eberle(Evergreens B&B) ☎ (250) 675-2568, Fax (250) 675-3188
Box 117, Vimy Rd., Sorrento, BC V0E 2W0

Located in west end of village. Phone for directions.
$45S $55-65D 🍴 Afternoon Tea ► 14
🍽 Full 🏠 Res., large sundeck, mountain view, acreage
■2D,1F(ground & upper levels) ⊨ 4D,2Q,R ⊰2Private,
1Sh.w.g. ★KF,TV lounge, separate entrance, 2 guest kitchens,
dry heat sauna, wheel-chair access ⓦRestricted smoking,
controlled pets

🯅 Small shopping center, restaurants, Shuswap Lake, boat trips,
tea garden with gazebo (for 15 people) in back yard, small bird aviary on site, Country Chapel
🚗 Golfing, Adams River Salmon Run, x-c skiing, Okanagan Fruit Valley
🐾 Cottage-style home surrounded by evergreens in picturesque historic village. Congenial hosts
will serve breakfast in large guest breakfast room. Ideal place for small group, private retreats,
special occasions and weddings. ✒B&B

Summerland   *(south of Kelowna; see also Penticton, Kaledon, Oliver, Osoyoos)*

Clark, Marsha (Heritage House)   ☎ (250) 494-0039
11919 Jubilee Rd., Box 326, Summerland, BC   V0H 1Z0

Located 1 km west of Hwy 97. Phone for directions.
$40S $60D $15Child $15Add.person   ► 6A,2Ch
🍴 Full, homebaked   🏠 Res., village, 2-storey, view, acreage,
quiet, wrap-around veranda   ■2D,1F(upstairs) ⊨3T,2Q,1R
🛁 2Sh.w.g. ★ TV,LF, off-street parking ⓌRestricted
smoking, no pets
🚶 Downtown Summerland (Tudor theme)
🚗 Penticton, Kelowna, wineries, golf courses, superb beaches
🐎 Beautiful large heritage home situated on small acreage among gigantic pine and maple trees
with informal friendly atmosphere in quiet country setting. Hostess is willing to make "early bird"
breakfast for skiers who are anxious to get to the slopes or those wishing to take day trips. ✔CC

Raymond, Betty (Lakeshore Memories B&B)   E-mail: gary_raymond@bc.sympatico.ca
12216 Lakeshore Dr., RR1,S14,C9, Summerland, BC   V0H 1Z0   ☎ & Fax (250) 494-5134

From Hwy97, at south end of town, turn on Lakeshore Dr at bottom of hill (house on left corner)
$55S $65-80D   ► 6A
🍴 Full, homebaked   🏠 Res., 2-storey, hist., view from guest
rooms, lakefront, porch, deck, quiet   ■ 3D(upstairs), host
quarters are separate   ⊨ 2T,1D,1Q   🛁 1Sh.w.g., 1ensuite
★ Air,TV,sun room, parking   Ⓦ Designated smoking area, no
pets, children min. age 10   ➳ French
🚶 Public beaches, yacht/sailing club, popular restaurant/pub, fish
hatchery, spawning fish in nearby stream
🚗 Wineries, golf courses, tennis, downhill/x-c ski resorts, shopping, excellent dining, Bird Sanct.
🐎 Lovingly restored, turn-of-the-Century home located in the original Summerland townsite,
furnished to provide an atmosphere of comfort and romance. Well-travelled hosts have a particular
knowledge of local history, the local art scene, about hiking (particularly Kettle Valley Railway) and
fishing of lakes & creek.Visa,MC,Amex ✔B&B

Surrey   *(Vancouver); see also White R, Langley, Delta, N.Westmin, Tsawwassen)*

Bury, Chuck and Glad (White Heather)   ☎ (604) 581-9797
12571-98th Ave., Surrey, BC   V3V 2K6

Follow Hwy 99 to 96th Ave. Travel west to 126th St and north to
98th Ave. Turn left.
$45-55S $55-65D $15Child(under age 12)   ► 4A,2-3Ch
🍴 Full, homebaked   🏠 Res., sub., view from guest rooms, patio,
quiet, sunroom   ■ 2D(main floor) ⊨ 1Q,1D   🛁1Sh.w.g.,
2ensuite ★F,parking Ⓦ No smoking, no pets
🚶 Local bus routes connecting to all Vancouver bus lines and
sky-train, good restaurants
🚗Sky Lift, downhill skiing (Seymour/Grouse Mt/Cypress Bowl)
🐎 Panoramic view of North Shore Mountains. Well-travelled hosts are knowledgeable about
local area, as well as Vancouver Island. Breakfast is served in garden-like sunroom with a beautiful
view. Pick-up from cruise ships and airport. ✔B&B

Fennell, Dale & Mary (Bed & Breakfast on the Ridge)   ☎ (604) 591-6065
5741-146 St, Surrey, BC   V3S 2Z5   E-mail: fennell@planeteer.com, Fax (604) 591-6069

From Hwy 1, take Exit 66 onto Hwy 10. Turn right on 146 St. From Vancouver on Hwy 99, take
Exit 16 to Hwy 10 (Surrey). Turn left on 146th St. From US border, ferries take Exit 10 to Hwy 10.
$45-75S $50-80D $10Child(under age 6) $10Add.person   ▶ 10A,3Ch

🍲 Full, homebaked   🏠 Sub., 2-storey, contemporary, acreage,
deck, quiet   ■ 4 (main & upper level - includes honeymoon
room)   🛏 2T,3Q,2P,2R,crib, cot   🛁 1Private, 3ensuite
★TV/VCR in guest sitting room, use of fridge in garage, facilities
for the handicapped, off-street parking   🖐Designated smoking
area   🌬 Hungarian
🏃 Animal Farm, bus stop, Surrey City Hall & Court House, open
roads for cycling/running/walking
🚗 US border, Crescent & White Rock beaches, BC ferries, Airport, Skytrain to Vancouver,
Cloverdale Rodeo, Abbotsford Air Show, golfing, antique shops, race track, Sunday flea market
📣 Large, contemporary home with high cathedral ceilings & skylights, an architectural treasure
in a country setting, with an ambiance of sterling hospitality. Hosts have welcomed guests from all
over the world and love to plan itineraries with them. Breakfast is"silver-service" in guest dining
room. Large number of family members can be accommodated at one time. ✎B&B

Tofino   *(on Vancouver Island's west coast)*

Barton, Lynn (Clayoquot Retreat)   ☎ (250) 725-3305, Fax (250) 725-3300
Box 292, 120 Arnet Rd., Tofino, BC   V0R 2Z0

In Tofino, turn left on First St and right on Arnet Rd.
$65-80S $70-95D   ▶ 6
🍲 Full, homebaked (buffet-style)   🏠 Village, 2-storey, acreage,
view from guest rooms, oceanfront   ■3(ground level)   🛏2D,2Q
🛁3Private   ★ TV/fridge in guest rooms, hot tub, off-street
parking, private entrances/patios   🖐 Designated smoking area,
small pets considered
🏃 Tonquin Beach, town centre   🚗Pacific Rim National Park
📣 Warm welcome in very quiet waterfront home with spectacular views of ocean and islands
from every room. Hosts are long-time residents of this quaint small West Coast village. Enjoy a
delicious buffet-style breakfast in your own room. Watch boats, eagles and occasional whales pass
by, and relax in the oceanfront hot tub overlooking the surf. There is a cat and a dog. Two-day min
in high season (July1-Oct15). Visa,MC ✎B&B

Burgess, Ralph & Wendy (Wilp Gybuu - Wolf House B&B)   ☎(250)725-2330
311 Leighton Way, Box396, Tofino,BC V0R 2Z0   E-mail: wilpgybu@island.net,Fax1205

Take Hwy 4 across Vancouver Isle to Tofino. Phone for directions.
$75S $80-90D (off-season rates available)   ▶ 6A
🍲 Full, homebaked   🏠 Village, res., multi-storey, view, quiet
■3D(ground level)   🛏2Q,2T   🛁3Ensuite   ★2F,TV,in guest
lounge, library, piano, F in guest rooms, private entrance,
parking   🖐 No smoking, children min. age 12, no pets
🏃 Tonquin Park, ocean beach, whale watching, scenic cruises,
canoeing, kayaking, sport fishing, beachcombing, seaplane tours,
restaurants, gift shops, bus to/from east side of Island
🚗 Pacific Rim National Park & ocean beaches, golf course, airport
📣 Contemporary, artistic West Coast cedar home overlooking Duffin Passage and the inside
waters and islands of Clayoquot Sound. Host is a native Artist. Pick-up and delivery to bus/airport.
There is a resident cat. Visa,MC ✎B&B

Ironside, Ed & Mary Ellen (Water's Edge Bed & Breakfast) ☎ (250) 725-1218
Box 635, Tofino, BC V0R 2Z0

Follow Hwy 4 west across the Island to Tofino. Located at 331 Park St.
$70-90S $75-95D $20Child $20Add.person   ▶ 6
🔲Full, homebaked 🏠Village, 2-storey, view from guest rooms, oceanfront,
deck, quiet ■ 3D(main floor) ⊨ 2T,2Q,R   ⚷ 1Sh.w.g., 1ensuite &
jacuzzi   ★ Air, off-street parking   ⊛ No smoking, no pets
🚶 Tonquin Park (boardwalk through rainforest to superb sandy beach)
Tofino centre with restaurants, galleries, Tour Companies (boat trips to Hot
Spring Cove, whale watching, Meares Island (big tree walk), scenic flights
🚗 Golf Course, Pacific Rim National Park (beaches, rainforest trails)
📢 Cliff-side home with a spectacular sweeping views of several islands and
the open Pacific Ocean. There is access to the water by stairway to the rocks
and beautiful tidal pools. Well travelled hosts have lived in other countries, are knowledgeable
about the area and its attractions. Relax in the living room or on the deck and spot whales during
spring migration. Breakfast is served in the dining room, while watching many passing boats.
Pick-up from airport or bus. Visa,MC ✓B&B

Kirste, Christa (Christa's Bed & Breakfast)   ☎ (250) 725-2827, Fax (250) 725-4416
1367 Chesterman Beach Rd., Box 517, Tofino, BC V0R 2Z0

Located 4.5 km from the end of Pacific Rim National Park. Phone for directions.

$85S/D   ▶ 2A
🔲 Cont.(deluxe) 🏠 Res., 2-storey, view from guest rooms,
oceanfront, quiet ■ 1Ste (main floor) ⊨1Q ⚷ Ensuite
★ KF, separate entrance, off-street parking ⊛ No smoking, no
pets, not suitable for children ⌁ German
🚶 Beautiful sandy beach/open ocean, surfing, kayaking,
beachcombing, cycling, hiking
🚗 Magnificient Pacific Rim National Park, Tofino village
good restaurants, art galleries/shops, whalewatching/ float plane tours, scuba diving
📢 "Wake up to the sound of the ocean and experience the beautiful beach". Relax or take the
cycle path to Tofino. Breakfast is served on a service cart to the suite at guest's convenience.
Pick-up from airport and bus stop.

Lecavalier, Marc (BriMar B&B on the Beach)   ☎ & Fax (250) 725-3410, 1-800-714-9373
Box 739, Tofino, BC V0R 2Z0

$110-160S/D $15Add.person   (Discounts for longer stays)   ▶ 6A,2Ch

Located at 1375 Thornberg Cr. From Pacific Rim Hwy, turn left on
Chesterman Beach Rd. Turn left on Thornberg Cr.
🔲 Full 🏠 Village, 3-storey, view from guest rooms, oceanfront,
quiet ■ 3D (2nd & 3rd floor; incl."loft" for honeymooners)
⊨2Q,1K,1P,2cots ★ 1Private,2ensuite ★ F,TV, off-street
parking ⊛No pets, smoking outside, children min. age 14
⌁French, Spanish
🚗 Edge of Pacific Rim National Park
🚶 Fine sandy beach (2km), surfboarding, seakyaking, rain forest walks, whale watching
📢 New, elegant home with unique character situated at Chesterman's Beach. Enjoy the beautiful
panoramic ocean view and the relaxed atmosphere. Warm up by the wood stove in the huge
sitting/reading room. Capture the everchanging sights and sounds of the Pacific Ocean from the
guest rooms. Hearty home-cooked breakfasts are served in the cozy kitchen. A friendly Cocker
Spaniel is the mascot of the home. Seasonal rates available from Sept15. Visa,MC,Interac ✓B&B

Sloman, Val & James (The Tide's Inn on Duffin Cove)　　　☎ (250) 725-3765
160 Arnet Rd., Box 325, Tofino, BC　V0R 2Z0　　E-mail: tidesinn@island.net　Fax: (250) 725-3325

On Vancouver Island, follow Hwy 4 west. Phone for direction.
$65-85S　$80-95D　$140F　$20Add.person　　　► 7
🍲 Full, homebaked　🏠 Village, 2-storey, small acreage, view
from guest rooms, oceanfront, seaside deck ■1D,1Ste ⊨2T,3Q
⟋3Ensuite　★Hot tub, jaccuzzi tub, F,TV/fridge, beverage bar,
pool table, cozy sitting areas in guest rooms, private entrances,
host quarters are separate　Ⓦ No smoking, no pets, children
min. age 12

🕴 Explore shoreline & tidal pools, stroll along sandy Tonquin Beach, harbour docks, village centre
(with shops, restaurants, galleries), whale watching tours, Hot Spring tours, kayaking, bus
🚌 Long Beach, Pacific Rim National Park, golfing, beaches,
🐾 Commerical fishing family and lifelong Tofino residents in waterfront home with beautiful
view of Duffin Cove Passage, Meares Island, ocean and mountains. Large windows capture the
ever-changing shoreline, views and sounds of the sea. Ideal place for 2 couples or a family in
2-bedroom suite. Enjoy the beautiful views from the seaside decks or the relaxing hot tub. 2-night
minimum in peak season & long weekends. There is one cat (in host quarters only).

Wood, Janine (Solwood B&B)　　　　☎ (250) 725-2112, Fax (250) 725-2284
Box 468, Tofino, BC　V0R 2Z0

From Port Alberni travel west to Tofino. Located at 1298 Lyn Rd.
$55S　$75-125D　$10Child(free under age 5)　$15Add.person　　　► 8
🍲 Full, homebaked　🏠 Rural, res., 3-storey, view from guest rooms,
oceanfront, deck, quiet　■ 1F,1Ste(main & upper floor)　⊨ 2D,2Q,1P
⟋Private, 1sh.w.h.　★ KF,private entrance, off-street parking, guest
quarters are separate　Ⓦ No smoking　⌁ Spanish
🕴 Pathway to beautiful Chesterman's Beach from front of house
🚌 Pacific Rim Nat.Park, hiking, whale watching, Hot Springs, fishing, arts
festivals, village center, shops, restaurants
🐾 Neo-Eastern longhouse with vaulted ceilings, large cedar beams, many
windows overlooking the surrounding gardens, and nestled in the forests of
Chesterman's Beach. Enjoy the relaxing atmosphere in the cathedral room, which receives the
sunrise through it's 9ft windows overlooking the forest. There are cats in residence. Visa ⌐B&B

Tsawwassen　　　*(Vancouver) see also Delta, Richmond, Surrey, White R., Ladner)*

Troniak, Lyla-Jo & Bruce (Southlands House "on the Park")　　☎(604)943-1846,Fax 2481
1160 Boundary Bay Rd, Tsawwassen, BC　V4L 2P6　　　E-mail: btron@bc.sympatico.ca

Take Hwy 99 to Hwy 17 (to ferries) in Delta. Proceed on 56St in
Tsawwassen. Turn left at 12Ave and continue to the water.
$125-155D　$10Add.person　(plus tax)　　　► 14
🍲 Full, homebaked　🏠 Rural, 3-storey lighthouse tower and
2-storey carriage house, acreage, view from guest rooms, hot tub,
oceanfront, patio, porch, deck, secluded　■ 5D,1Ste(2D) main &
upper level)　⊨ 4Q,2K,1P　⟋ 1Private, 4ensuite,
1sh.w.g(Ste)　★ LF,F&TV in guest room, ceiling fans, hot tub,
guest room patios/decks, private entrance ⓌNo smoking, ask about pets, children in suite only
🕴 Beachcombing in Boundary Bay Park, walking, biking, excellent bird watching (Pacific Flyway),
great restaurants, world known Reifel Bird Sanctuary
🚌 Ferries to Vancouver Island & Gulf Islands, US border, International Airport, downtown Van.
🐾 Friendly hosts in beautiful sprawling West Coast country estate, located in the Sun Belt of
Vancouver (35% less rain) with beautiful views overlooking ocean and mountains. West Coast
breakfast is served in the special guest breakfast room. Relax in the large commercial hot tub or
socialize in the Great Room morning or evening. Visa,MC,Amex ⌐B&B

Valemount
(south-east of St.George)

Achterberg, Bill & Connie (Summit River B&B)   ☎ (250)566-9936,Fax:(250)566-9934
Box 517 Valemount BC   V0E 2Z0   E-mail: sumriver@vis.bc.ca

Located on the west side of Hwy 5 in Albreda and 22 km south of Valemount. Look for sign.
$50-60S $60-75D $12-15Add. person (plus tax) 🍽 Meals (group rates available)   ▶ 12-20A

🍲 Full, homebaked   🏠 Rural, riverfront, acreage, view, quiet,
isolated ■3D,3F(main & upper level) ⊨2S,8D,1R 🛁5Private
★VCR,LF ⓌRestricted smoking ∾Dutch
🏃 Fishing hole in glacier fed river, hiking, gold panning, x-c skiing
snowmobiling, horseback riding, frequent sightings of wild animals,
golfing
🚗 Village of Valemount, Mt Robson Prov.Park, Moose Marsh
canoeing, rafting float trips, heli skiing with expert ski guides

☛ Old fashioned, cosy log house with country-style decor, surrounded by 40 acres of woods, fields
and stream, located in mountain valley with a beautiful view of the Albreda Glacier. Pick-up service
from train/bus in Valemount available. There is a resident cat & a dog. Also 12 camp-sites
available. Seniors discounts. Visa,MC ⌁CC

Brady, Mavis and Al (Brady's Bed & Breakfast)   ☎ (250) 566-9906
Box 519, Valemount, BC   V0E 2Z0

Coming north from Valemount or west from Jasper on Hwy 5, take
Blackman Rd. Turn on Buffalo Rd & continue to B&B.
$50S $60D   ▶ 4A,4Ch
🍲Full 🏠Rural, 160-acres, log house, view, inground swimming
pool, quiet, isolated   ★TV,F,parking ■2 ⊨2Q 🛁Sh.w.g.
ⓌNo smoking
🏃 Hiking/x-c ski (outside back door), variety of wildlife/birds

☛ Comfortable, quiet mountain log home, built by the host family, situated on wooded acreage
with river (Salmon route) running through the property. Enjoy the sundeck for morning coffee and
the hearthstone fireplace at night. Relax in the gazebo or under a shade tree and take in the
magnificient panoramic scenery. ⌁B&B

Vancouver   *(see also N.Westmin, Richmond, Surrey, Delta, Tsawwassen, White R., Ladner)*
(see also **North Vancouver & West Vancouver**)

Barr, Jennifer & Larry (Kitsilano Point B&B)   ☎ (604) 738-9576
1936 McNicoll Ave., Vancouver, BC   V6J 1A6

Located at north end of Cypress St & 1 block west of Burrard St.
$70-80S $80-90D $35Add.person   ▶ 4A
🍲 Full 🏠 Res., older, quiet ■ 2D (upstairs) ⊨ 4T 🛁1Sh.w.g.,
private basin & shower in each room   ★ TV,F Ⓦ No smoking, no pets,
no children ∾ some French
🏃 Kitsilano Beach with parks and pool, Vanier Park with museums,
Planetarium and Observatory, Short-cut to downtown, restaurants, stores,
English Bay, Granville Island & market (by foot ferry near house)
🚗 Stanley Park, Science Centre, Grouse Mountain, Airport, U of BC
☛ Quiet, friendly hospitality in 1911-built house with secluded shaded
garden situated in very convenient location. Off-season rates available. ⌁B&B

Cudney, Amy (Dunbar Area Bed & Breakfast)　　　　　　　☎ (604) 263-5428
3716 West 37th Ave., Vancouver, BC　V6N 2V9

Located 1/2 block west of Dunbar St. Phone for directions.
$65S　$85D　$5surcharge (for 1 night only, special long-stay rates)　　　　▶ 4A
❊ May15-Sept30　🍳Full,homebaked　🏠Res., older, balcony, quiet, deck　■2(main floor)
🛏2T(K),1D　🛁1Private, 1sh.w.h.　★ F,TV,piano,games table in guest living room, front
parking　🖐 Guest bring clean sport socks/slippers, no smoking, no pets, children min. age 12
🧍 Lovely quiet walks near UBC endowment lands, restaurants, theatre, shops, public transportion
to downtown and sea-bus/skyway train, bus stop
🚐 Beaches, parks, gardens, downtown Vancouver, Airport, UBC, Stanley Park Van Dusen
Gardens Botanical Gardens
🗨 Quiet, classic bungalow, beautifully renovated, extended with balcony off dining room and a
lovely English country & organic garden. Relax and enjoy adult oriented environment. Breakfast is
served in dining room. Special diets are accommodated. ✔B&B

Egan, Cara (English Country Garden B&B)　　　☎ (604) 737-2526, Fax (604) 737-2750
3466 West 15th Ave., Vancouver, BC　V6R 2Z1　　　　　　　E-mail: english@uniserve.com

Take Hwy 99 into Vancouver & continue north on Oak St to W33rd Ave. Turn left to Blenheim St.

right to W15th Ave, left to house on left side.
$95-120S　$105-130D　$20Add.person　　　　　▶ 8
❊ May-Nov　🍳 Full, homebaked　🏠 Res., hillside, 3-storey, view from
guest rooms, deck, quiet, secluded　■ 1D,2Ste (main & upper level)
🛏2T,2Q,2P　🛁 Private, ensuite　★ F,TV in guest rooms, ceiling fans,
off-street & street parking, host quarters are separate　🖐No smoking, no
pets, ask about children
🧍 Downtown, UBC, beaches, cafes, restaurants, boutiques, bus stop
🚐 North Shore Mountains, US border, Fraser Valley, ferries
🗨 Lovely view home, brightly decorated with antiques and world wide art
and gorgeous views of Vancouver Skyline and mountains. Located
in tree-lined neighbourhood of Kitsilano. Relax on the sun drenched deck surrounded by English
Garden or in the large guest sitting room. Breakfast is served in guest breakfast room. There are 2
English cats and a Canadian dog outside. ✔B&B

Hainstock, Lyn (Penny Farthing Inn)　　　　☎ (604) 739-9002, Fax (604) 739-9004
2855 West 6th Ave., Vancouver, BC　V6K 1X2　　　　　　　E-mail: farthing@uniserve.com

From airport drive towards downtown. Turn left on W12St, right on
MacDonald St and left on W6Ave. Look for house on north side.
Summer: $75S　$140D　$15child　$15Add.person　(plus tax)　　　▶ 8
🍳 Full　🏠 Res., hist., view from guest rooms, porch, quiet, secluded
■2D,2Stes (upst)　🛏 2T,1D,2Q,1K,2P　🛁1Sh.w.g., 2ensuite　★F,
TV/coffee/bar/phones in guest rooms, fax/Email access, ceiling fans, street
parking, guest quarters are separate　🖐 Designated smoking area, no pets,
children min. age 12　〰 some French
🧍 Beach, museums, UBC, bus stop
🚐 Downtown, Northshore, Grouse Mtn, Fort Langley, US border
🗨 Heritage house with antiques and stained glass, situated on a quiet
street in Kitsilano district. Enjoy the friendly and relaxed atmosphere. Hostess (originally from
Africa) was a potter/weaver/quilter and arranges art shows. Two college-attending daughters help
out as relief hosts. Weather permitting, breakfast is served in the garden surrounded with herbs
and fragrant flowers. There are 4 friendly cats. ✔B&B

Harkley, Janice & Bill (River Run Cottages)　☎ (604) 946-7778, Fax (604) 940-1970
4551 River Rd.W., Ladner, BC　V4K 1R9　　　　　E-mail: riverrun@direct.ca

From Hwy 99 take Exit 28 going west. Then take Hwy 17 to 1st right turn onto Ladner Trunk Rd.
Continue, following 47A Ave (name change only) which becomes River Rd West.

$140-175D(cottage) $20Add.person 🍽 Meals (plus tax)　▶ 8
📖 Homebaked (delivered & served in cottage)　🏠 Sub,view,
decks ■4 guest cottages, one that floats, 3 on riverbank ⊨4Q
⊒4 Private ★ F, KF,Soaker tub, riverrock double cascade
shower, woodburning stove, off-street parking, wheel-chair
access 🖐Smoking outdoors
🏃 Downtown Ladner, Delta museum, jog/walk the dike, fresh
seafood dinners (from local fishermen), rowing, kayaking, bicycling
🚗 Victoria, Stanley Park, Granville Market, George Riefel Waterfowl Refuge, Int.Airport
🐎 Enjoy relaxation and romance in private waterfront cottage on the Fraser River with beautiful
view of North Shore Mountains, glowing sunsets, soaring eagles, crackling fireplaces and gourmet
breakfasts. Experience the cascade shower (like a waterfall in a river grotto). Kayak or bike or relax
on private guest deck. Perfect for a meeting place, small retreat or workshops. Reduced rates for
longer stay and in Jan/Feb. Visa,MC ↙CC

Holm Elke (B&B by Locarno Beach)　　　　☎ (604) 341-4975 (Cell)
4505 Langara Ave, Vancouver, BC　V6R 1C9

Phone for directions.
$70S　$95D　$25Add.person　(off season rates available)　▶ 6
📖 Full　🏠 Res., 2-storey, quiet　■ 2F(upst ⊨1T,1D,2Q, cot
⊒2Ensuite　★TV, street parking　🖐No smoking, no pets,
children min. age 12　〰German, French
🏃 Park opposite house, long sandy beach & beachside cafe,
walking trails, boat rental, tennis, elegant dining, shopping street,
direct bus line to UBC and City Center
🚗 UBC, City Centre, Airport, Stanley Park, northshore mountains
🐎 White Character home with newly renovated guest rooms, located opposite park on a quiet
side street in an exclusive residential neighbourhood, just 200m from beach with panoramic views.
Breakfast is served in guest breakfast room. ↙B&B

Jess, Kim & Bob (Chelsea Cottage)　　　☎ (604) 266-2681, Fax (604) 266-7540
2143 West 46 Ave, Vancouver, BC　V6M 2L2　　　E-mail: chelsea@bc.sympatico.ca

Phone for directions.
$80-110S - $90-120D　$15child　$15Add.person　　　　　▶ 8A,1Ch
📖 Full(Gourmet), homebaked　🏠 Res., 2-storey, older, deck, quiet　■ 3D,1F(main & upper
level)　⊨ 2T(1K),3Q,1R　⊒ 1Sh.w.g., 2Ensuite　★ F,TV in guest room, ceiling fans, private
entrance, street & off-street parking　🖐 No smoking, no pets, children min. age 12
🏃 Local shops and restaurants, No16 bus to downtown, No41 bus to UBC, No49 bus to Skytrain
🚗 Beaches, downtown, UBC, airport
🐎 Friendly and helpful hosts in character home surrounded by large trees and beautiful gardens,
located in well established neighbourhood of prestigious Kerrisdale. Relax by the fireplace in the
comfortable guest lounge. There is a dog in host's private quarters. Visa,MC ↙B&B

Johnson, Sandy and Ron (The Johnson House)　　　　☎ & Fax (604) 266-4175
2278 W34 Ave, Vancouver, BC　V6M 1G6　　　　E-mail: johnsonbb@bc.sympatico.ca

Located near 33rd & Arbutus Sts in the Kerrisdale/Shaughnessy area of Vancouver's West Side.

$65-135S　$75-145D　$25Add.person　　　► 6A,2Ch
🍳Full, hombaked　🏠Res., hist. older, quiet, large porch, partial
view from guest rooms　■ 3 (upstairs)　⊨ 2Q,1K,1D(including
brass iron beds)　🚽1Private,2ensuite　★ TV,F,LF, parking,
fans ⚓No smoking,children min age 10　ⱳFrench
🏃 City transportation to downtown, restaurants, Kerrisdale &
Arbutus Shopping centres
🚗 U.B.C.,Granville I.,China & Gastowns,Van Duesen Gardens
🐾 Restored 1920 Vancouver craftsman home, furnished with delightful antiques and collectibles,
including brass beds and carousel horses. Centrally located on a quiet street in one of Vancouver's
best neighbourhoods. Enjoy a bountiful breakfast and relax in the rock & rhododendron garden with
ancient sculptures. Recommended by Frommers & Fodors & "Best Places to Kiss". ⌐B&B

King, Anne & Christopher (King's Corner)　　　☎ (604) 879-7997, Fax (604) 879-2982
4006 Glen Dr., Vancouver, BC　V5V 4T3　　　　　　Cell (604) 218-2649

Summer:$70-100D　$10Child　$10Add.person　Winter:$65-85D　$5Child　► 4A,2Ch

Phone for directions.
🍳 Homebaked　🏠 Res., hist., deck, large hot tub, quiet
■1D,1F　⊨2Q,1P,1cot　🚽 1Sh.w.g.　★ F,KF, separate
entrance, street parking, quest quarters are separate　⚓ No
smoking, no pets　ⱳ French
🏃 Multicultural restaurants, Antique Row, Queen Elizabeth Park,
bus connecting to downtown/ferries/airport
🚗 Downtown, Whistler, Golden Ears Prov. Park, Bowen Island
🐾 Heritage home (1912) completely renovated and filled with an unusual mixture of antiques
and contemporary art, located across from lovely Glen Park in one of first settled neigbourhoods of
Vancouver. Relax on the deck or splash in the hot tub. Ideal place for special events. There are 2
cats and a dog (in hosts' quarters only). Children welcome. ⌐B&B

Kulash, Alida (Twin Hollies B&B)　　　　☎ (604) 876-1017, Fax (604) 876-1029,
604 East 23rd Ave., Vancouver, BC　V5V 1X8　　　　Cell (604) 916-1546

From TCH1 take Grandview Hwy, turn left on Fraser St, right on 23rdAve.
$85S　$95D　$10Child　$20Add.person　　　　► 8
🍳 Full　🏠 Res.,hist., view, patio, porch, quiet　■ 2D,1F(upper level)　⊨ 1S,2Q,1K,1R
🚽2Private, 1sh.w.g.　★ TV in guest rooms, ceiling fans, off-street parking, guest quarters are
separate　⚓ Designated smoking area, children min. age 14　ⱳ Russian, Croation, Dutch,
German, Spanish, Afrikaans
🏃 Queen Elizabeth Gardens, Antique Row, ethnic restaurants, Oakridge Shopping Mall, Van
Dusen Gardens, buses to downtown and skytrain
🚗 Whistler Mountain Resort, Harrison Hot Springs, Mount Baker, Hell's Gate
🐾 Charming Heritage home decorated with west coast art and artifacts and surrounded by large
trees. Enjoy the magnificient views of Vancouver night lights and spectacular North Shore
Mountains. Breakfast includes westcoast salmon among other specialties. Hosts speak many
languages and enjoy communicating with people from different cultures. Visa,MC,Amex ⌐B&B

Manering, Heath & Loesha (The Shamrock's Nook B&B)   ☎ (604) 329-9535
8234 Argyle St., Vancouver, BC V5P 3M2   E-mail: shamrock@istar.ca, Fax (604) 327-6744

Take Hwy 1 to Grandview. Proceed south on Knight St, exit to Marine Dr. Turn right on Argyle St.

$85S $95D $25Add.person   ► 5A
🍺 Full 🏠 Res., 2-storey, view from guest rooms, deck ■2F
⊨2S,2D,1R ⊐ 2Ensuite ★ F,TV, jaccuzzy on deck, off street
& street parking, guest quarters are separate Ⓦ Designated
smoking area, not suitable for children ⌇Portuguese
⃛ Promenade along the Fraser River, tennis courts, Fraserview
Public Golf Course, No20 bus connecting to sky train for downtown
🚗 Downtown, Whiterock, Richmond, Int.Airport, Horseshoe Bay
📣 Friendly welcome in charming spacious home with unique blend of European hospitality, a
cheerful place featuring skylights and bright open spaces throughout. Enjoy a gourmet breakfast
and complimentary expresso and cappucino bar. Relax in the natural waters hot tub under the stars
or curl up by the fireplace and listen to favourite Irish tunes. Guest are invited to use the baby
grand piano. Visa ⌐B&B

Peloquin, Eugene and Janet (Peloquin's Pacific Pad)   ☎(604)874-4529,Fax 6229
426 West 22nd Ave., Vancouver, BC V5Y 2G5

From Hwy1 use Grandview Exit and travel to Cambie St. Turn left, proceed to 22nd Ave. Turn left.
$65-75S $75-85D $15Child $20Add.person   (Reserve please)   ► 4A,2Ch
🍺 Full 🏠 Res., quiet ■ 1S,1D ⊨ 1D,2P,baby travel bed ⊐ 1Sh.w.g. ★ KF, TV in
guest rooms, garden entrance, off-street parking Ⓦ No smoking, no pets ⌇French, Ukrainian
⃛ Popular restaurants, shops, Q.E. Park, Bloedel Conservatory, seabus/skytrain, bus to
downtown. GM Place, Ford Centre (Theatre), hospitals
🚗 U.B.C., Horseshoe Bay Ferry Terminal, Oakridge Shopping center, downtown, Stanley Park
📣 Welcome to cozy comfortable home, situated in a quiet central residential area with easy
access to Hwy 99, from USA, Airport and Ferry Terminals. Hosts enjoy sharing helpful information
about their picturesque city.

Sanderson, Corinne (Beautiful Bed & Breakfast)   ☎ (604) 327-1102, Fax (604) 327-2299
428 West 40th Ave., Vancouver, BC V5Y 2R4

Located on the first block east of Cambie Street.
$95-210S $110-210D $135-210Ste $15Add.person   ► 10
🍺 Full 🏠 Res., sub., 3-storey, view from all guest rooms, patio,
porch, deck, quiet ■1S,3D,1Ste(upst) ⊨2T,2D,1Q,1P,1R
⊐2Sh.w.g., 1ensuite ★3F(pink-marble in suite), TV in some
guest rooms, parking, large balcony Ⓦ No smoking, no pets,
children min.age 14 ⌇French
⃛ Major tennis court, 2 golf courses, Queen Elizabeth Park, large shopping center, VanDusen
Gardens, hospitals, Vancouver's best restaurants, downtown bus
🚗 Grouse Mountain, Stanley Park, Reifel Bird Sanctuary, beaches, University, Airport, US border
📣 Gracious, new Colonial home with a view of north shore mountains & Vancouver Island,
furnished with antiques,fresh flowers, and situated on a quiet street in central location. Enjoy the
lovely garden incl. mini Japanese garden, pond & waterfall. Breakfast is served in formal dining
room with silver, linens, antiques and great coffee. Luxurious suite has pink fireplace, large balcony
and North & South view. Hosts are well informed about the area & happy to help with plans.
⌐B&B

Selvage, Bob & Barb (Treehouse B&B)   ☎ (604) 266-2962, Fax (604) 266-2960
2490 West 49th Ave., Vancouver, BC V6M 2V3

$110-140Ste $20Child $25Add.person   (Off-season rate available)   ►8

Located on the west side near UBC and west of Granville St.
🍴 Full, homebaked   🏠 Res., 3-storey, view from guest rooms,
deck, quiet   ■ 1D,2Stes (street & upper level)   ⊨ 3Q,1P,1R
🛁1Private,2ensuite ★F,TV/VCR,fridges, guest robes/tea
kettles/dryers/phones in guest rooms, 2jacuzzis, street parking
Ⓦ Smoking outside, no pets, children min. age 10 or infants
🏃 Kerrisdale (shopping, restaurants), parks, golfing
🚗 UBC, downtown, ferries to Victoria

🐾 Contemporary, multi-level home decorated with modern art and sculpture and located in one
of the city's most prestigious neighborhoods. Relax in 2nd floor guest living room with marble
fireplace or on the covered deck. Enjoy a calm, peaceful setting offering both privacy and
hospitality. Breakfast is served in special guest breakfast room. ✏B&B

Whitehead, Darlene (The Whitehead House B&B)   ☎ & Fax (604) 736-3050
901 West 23 Ave., Vancouver, BC V5Z 2B2

Located 1 block east of Oak St on corner of Laurel & 23rd Ave.
S70S $85D $15Child $15Add.person   ►5
🍴 Homebaked   🏠 Downtown, res., 3-storey, hist., porch, quiet   ■ 1D,1F
(street level)   ⊨ 2T,1Q,cot   🛁 1Sh.w.g.   ★ Private entrance, TV in
guest room, street parking, guest quarters are separate   Ⓦ Designated
smoking area, no pets   ⚬ some French
🏃 Park, gardens, market, restaurants, hospitals, coffee shops, bus 1 block
🚗 Downtown Vancouver, airport, Stanley Park
🐾 1910 Vancouver "A" Heritage home with pleasant decor and warm
hospitality. Enjoy a healthy west-coast breakfast served in the guest room, if desired. There is a dog
in residence. Visa ✏CC

Williams, D.& H. (Kenya Court Ocean Front Guest House)   ☎ (604) 738-7085
2230 Cornwall Ave., Vancouver, BC V6K 1B5

Located betw. Yew/Vine Sts, facing Kitsilano Beach. Phone for directions.
$85-130D   ► 16A
🍴 Full   🏠 Downtown, apartment, view, patio, oceanfront, quiet   ■4
waterfront suites (main & upper floor)   ⊨T,Q,K   🛁 4Sh.w.g.
★F,TV in guest room, separate entrance, music room with grand piano
Ⓦ No smoking, no pets   ⚬ Italian, French, German
🏃 Large heated outdoor salt-water swimming pool, English Bay, Kitsilano
Beach, tennis courts
🚗 Vancouver Island and Gulf Island ferries (Horseshoe
Bay/Tsawwassen), Stanley Park
🐾 Spacious three-storey Heritage building with gracious antique
furnishings and spectacular ocean view from penthouse solarium, where breakfast is served.

B&B Innkeepers Association (Western Canada)   ☎ (604) 255-9199
Box 74534 Kits Postal Outlet, 2803-W4th Ave, Vancouver, BC V6K 4P4   Fax (604) 926-8073

Rates: $45-100S $50-200D (including full breakfast)
Call for the list of inspected Inns. The B&B Innkeepers Assoc. was formed by Inn owners to
establish standards for the industry and promote independently inspected, quality B&B's
throughout Western Canada. Only Inns meeting the exacting standards of cleanliness and
hospitality are included. The Associations's "Quality Assurance Program" leads the industry.
Deposits may be required. Send for the brochure & book directly with the chosen inn.

North Vancouver
(see also **Vancouver & West Vancouver**)

Adems, Collin and Terrisa (Rockland House) ☎ (604) 987-5885
141 West Rockland, North Vancouver, BC V7N 2V8

From TCH1 (on City's north side), take Lonsdale Rd north to West Rockland Rd. Turn left.

$55S $65D $80F $20Add.person ▶ 4
🌙 Full   🏠 Res., 2-level ranch-style, ocean view, deck, quiet
■2(ground level) ⊨2T,1Q ⌐1Sh.w.g. ★TV,KF, sep.entrance
🤸 Play park outside back garden, public bus transit to Seabus and Lonsdale Quay, hiking paradise
🚗 Downtown Vancouver, ski slopes, suspension bridge.
🔫 Retired hosts in home is situated on the quiet slope 1000 ft up Grouse Mountain overlooking the city and the surrounding waters. Enjoy the magnificient view from upper sundeck in the fresh mountain air. Children very welcome. ✏B&B

Chalmers, Sue (Sue's Victorian Guest House - ca1904) ☎(604)985-1523,1-800-776-1811
152 East 3rd, North Vancouver, BC V7L 1E6

From Hwy 99, go over Lion's Gate Bridge and take North Vancouver exit (Marine Drive becomes West 3rd) and look for house 1/2block east of Lonsdale. From Hwy 1, go over 2nd Narrows Bridge

(Main becomes Cotton) then to East 3rd. Parking behind #152 & #158.
$60-75S $70-85D $25Add.person ▶ 7
🌙Not incl. 🏠Hist.,highrise area,full width veranda at front ■2(upst)
⊨1Q,1S,2D ⌐Sh.w.g.,Victorian Soaker Baths,no showers ★TV,video, indiv. keys,guest fridge,phone in guest rooms 🚭No smoking
🤸 Harbour (4blocks), Lonsdale Quay/restaurant on the water's edge, seabus terminal to downtown, Alaska cruiseship departure, restaurants, bus stops
🚗 Chinatown, Gastown, Stanley Park, Conference Center, IMAX Theatre
🔫 Lovely carpenter-gothic, modest sized, 1904-built home with original staircases, gingerbread on the front veranda, restored and upgraded for modern comfort. Bring own slippers. Very convenient & central location. Long term/off-season rates available. Deposit required.

Elliot, Joan (Mousehole Waterfront Bed & Breakfast) ☎ & Fax (604) 929-0347
2558 Panorama Dr., North Vancouver, BC V7G 1VS   E-mail: mousehle@axionet.com

From Hwy1 West, take Exit 22 to Seymour Parkway. Travel 5km east to Deep Cove Rd, turn left and proceed 1.5km north to Panorama Dr and turn left. Look for B&B on right (200 yds).
$125S/D ▶ 2A
🌙Full,homebaked 🏠Sub.,3-storey,view from suite,oceanfront,patio,deck, quiet ■1Ste(ground level) ⊨1D ⌐Ensuite ★Sep.entrance, TV/coffee maker/iron/hairdryer, seaside patio access from guest room, off-street parking 🚭No smoking,no pets,no children
🤸 Private dock & float on property, Panorama Park, canoe/kayak/skidoos/ boats rental, Deep Cove Cultural Centre with live theatre, hiking (Baden-Powel-Trail) Mount Seymour, restaurants, pubs, scuba diving,
🚗 Downtown Vancouver, Susp.Bridges, Grouse Mountain, ferry terminal
🔫 Home is named after a Village in Cornwall/England, and situated at the edge of the water on picturesque Indian Arm. Hosts are keen gardeners & fresh herbs are featured at breakfast. Enjoy the large library of gardening books and take home a special "seed package for guests" from the garden. Guests may be treated to a zodiac ride around Indian Arm. There is a blind Cocker Spaniel "Bobby" in residence.

Gruner, Sylvia & Gerhard (Pacific View)   ☎ & Fax (604) 985-4942
139 West St.James Rd., North Vancouver, BC   V7N 2P1

From Hwy 1 take Exit 18 (Lonsdale Ave) north, to St. James Rd.
$65-80D   ►4A+
🍽 Full   🏠 Res., 2-storey, view, backporch, patio, deck,
swimming pool, quiet, panoramic view from some guest
rooms ■2Ste (upper level) ⊨2Q   ⊒2Ensuite   ★F,TV,
spacious lounge with balcony, host quarters are separate, off-street
& street parking   🚭No smoking, no pets   ⌇⌇ Polish, German
🏃 Shopping, restaurant, parks, public indoor pool, local buses/sea bus connecting with Skytrain
🚗 Whistler Mountain Ski Resort, downtown Vancouver, Stanley Park, Horseshoe Bay
☛ Home is situated in quiet residential neighbourhood. Breakfast is served in glass enclosed
patio looking out on garden and heated pool. Families welcome. ✔B&B

Macek, Stefka (Mountain Bed & Breakfast)   ☎ (604) 987-2725, Fax (604) 987-2171
258 East Balmoral Rd., North Vancouver, BC   V7N 1R5

From Hwy 1 take Lonsdale Ave Exit.ph for directions.
$45-50S $75-80D $15Child $20Add.person 🍽Meals   ►6A,4Ch
🍽 Full, homebaked   🏠 Res., split 2-storey, view, balcony, patio,
quiet   ■ 2D(main floor) ⊨ 1D,2Q,2P   ⊒ Private
★F,LF,TV in guest room, separate entrance, jaccuzi in suite,
parking   🚭 No smoking, no pets   ⌇⌇ German, Slovenian
🚗 Grouse Mountain, Capilano Suspension Bridge, Stanley Park,
downtown Vancouver
☛ Modern, newly renovated house with a friendly atmosphere and a beautiful view of the city of
Vancouver. There is a cat in residence. Visa

Masterton, Delphine (Laburnum Cottage B&B Inn)   ☎ & Fax (604) 988-4877
1388 Terrace Ave., North Vancouver, BC   V7R 1B4

From Lions Gate Bridge take Exit for North Vancouver and travel east 1 block to Capilano Rd.
Turn left 1 km north to Paisley. Turn right, then to Philip. Turn right on Woods Dr, then left on

Terrace Ave and 350 yards to B&B.
$145-275D $30Add.person   (plus tax)   ► 16A
🍽 Full (gourmet)   🏠 Res., sub., acreage, patio, quiet ■4D,2Ste
(upst), small summerhouse cottage in garden for honeymooners
⊨2T,1D,4Q,1R,1P   ⊒5Private   ★very large flood-lit parking
lot, hook-up for large RV   🚭No smoking, no children
🏃 Capilano Fish Hatchery, Suspension Bridge, Grouse Mountain
Tramway, many tennis courts, Par-3 Pitch & Putt, two bus routes
🚗 City of Vancouver, Lonsdale Quay (sea bus), Q.E.Gardens, fabulous restaurants
☛ Charming home with Victorian air and antiques is surrounded by virgin forest (parkland), and
beautiful award-winning English Garden. Gourmet breakfast is served in guest breakfast room and
in large country kitchen with AGA stove. Relax in the charming Victorian drawing room. Home
has been featured in several Magazines. There is a cat "Geraldo". Visa,MC ✔CC

Bed & Breakfast Reservation Service for Vancouver & Whistler BC
404-1650 Grant Ave., Port Coquitlam, BC   V3B 7V2   ☎ & Fax (604) 552-0157

Sibylle Goebel, President
$75-130D(low season) $85-185D(peak season)   (including breakfast)   (some hosts charge tax)
The B&B Reservation Service for Vancouver & Whistler BC serves over 20 host homes throughout
Vancouver and B&B Lodges in Whistler. Most have spectacular mountain views and are situated in
quiet areas, in walking distance to bus and near major tourist attractions. All homes are
non-smoking. Some hosts have in-house pets and may speak other languages. Many homes have
private bath for guests and some have telephone & bar fridge, robes & slippers in guest rooms and
access to computer & fax. For reservation call the above.

Murphy, Anne & Michael (Mountainside Manor B&B at Grouse Mtn) ☎ (604) 990-9772
5909 Nancy Greene Way, North Vancouver, BC   V7R 4W6   E-mail: mtnside@ibm.net, Fax 8484

From downtown take Hwy 99 N over Lion's Gate Bridge & N.Van Exit. Turn left at Capilano Rd.
Continue up hill to B&B. From Hwy 1 take Exit 14 (Capilano Rd)
and continue up hill.
$75-135S/D $20Add.person   (plus tax)   ► 8A,2Ch
🍴 Full   🏠 Res., 3-storey, view from guest rooms, patio, decks
■ 4D (upstairs)   ⊨ 1Q,3K (2T),2R,crib   ⌐ 1Sh.w.g.,
2ensuite   ★F in guest sitting room, TV in guest rooms, hot tub,
off-street parking, host quarters are separate   Ⓦ No smoking
〰 some French/German/Italian
🏃 Grouse Mountain & Skyride (all year activities), Grouse Nest Restaurants with panoramic
views of city & Pacific sunsets, bus #236 to Seabus & downtown
🚗 Lynn Canyon Ecology Centre, Stanley Park, downtown Vancouver & attractions, Mt.Seymour
🐾 Spectacular west-coast contemporary view-home set in a beautiful garden and nestled on the
wooded slopes of Grouse Mountain with views of the City, Harbour & Stanley Park. Hosts have vast
experience in world travel and local knowledge/enthusiasm about the city and its surrounding area.
A B&B "spectacular by design and hospitable by choice". There are 2 cats. Visa,MC,Diners ✓B&B

Nelson, Roy and Charlotte (The Nelson's B&B)   ☎ & Fax (604) 985-1178
470 St.James Rd. West, North Vancouver, BC   V7N 2P5

From TCH #1 turn north at Westview Exit 17, right 1block on Windsor, then left on St.James.
$50S $65-80D   ► 7
🍴Choice(Gourmet) 🏠Res., quiet, heated swimming pool
■3D,1S   ⊨2D,1Q,1S   ⌐3Private Ⓦno pets, no smoking
🚗 Grouse Mountain Chairlift, Cleveland Dam, Fish Hatchery,
Capilano Suspension Bridge, par 3 golf course, Lonsdale Quay,
Gastown, Whistler Village Ski Resort, beaches, restaurants,
shopping, Island ferry, Stanley Park
🐾 Home is situated in garden setting on quiet tree-lined residential street.

Poole, Arthur and Doreen (Poole's Bed & Breakfast)   ☎(604)987-4594,Fax 4283
421 West St. James Rd., North Vancouver, BC   V7N 2P6   E-mail: rapoole@lightspeed.bc.ca

From Vancouver (Route 1), turn north onto Westview, right on Windsor and then left on St. James.
$45S $60D   ► 4A,2Ch
🍴 Choice, homebaked   🏠 Res., sundeck, patio, quiet garden
■3D (garden level)   ⊨1D,1Q,1T,cot,crib   ⌐1Sh.w.g.(additional
upst)   ★TV,LF,F   ⓌNo smoking, no pets
🚗 Grouse Mountain Skyride, Capilano Suspension Bridge, Royal
Hudson Train, Lonsdale Quay, Sea Bus to City Center Stanley Park
& Aquarium, Gastown, Ferry to Vancouver Island
🐾 Colonial-style home in quiet, lovely residential district. Convenient location to city center and
attractions of Vancouver area. Retired hosts are happy to assist visitors with information about the
city and area. Family/Children welcome. Winter Rates available. ✓B&B

Old English Bed & Breakfast Registry (since 1985)   ☎ (604) 986-5069, Fax (604) 986-8810
1226, Silverwood Cr., North Vancouver, BC   V7P 1J3

(Owner: Vicki Tyndall)
Rates: $85-175D   (including a hearty breakfast)
Good locations and easy access. Each individually inspected European style accommodation offers
unique, friendly, West Coast ambience. The Registry can provide the perfect place. Visa,MC

Sucloy, Clare & Kelly ("A Touch of English" B&B)   ☎ & Fax (604) 985-5380
3483 Chesterfield Ave., North Vancouver, BC   V7N 4M7

From Hwy 1, take Lonsdale north, left on Osborne to Chesterfield.
$75S $85D $15Child   ► 9
🍲 Full   🏠 Res., 2-storey, view from guest rooms, patio, deck,
quiet   ■ 3D(main & upper level)   ⊨ 2Q,2T(K)   🛏 1Ensuite,
1sh.w.g.   ★ F,TV in one guest room, ceiling fans, off-street &
street parking, guest quarters are separate   🚭 Smoking outside,
no pets, children welcome
                        🧍 Strolls through parks, public trails, Queens Cross Pub, transit
🚗 Downtown Vancouver, Grouse Mountain, Capilano Suspension Bridge, Sea Bus across Inner
Harbour, fine dining, ferries
📷 Large Tudor home located in beautiful North Shore area surrounded by trees, mountains and
scenic water views. Enjoy arrival-refreshments either in the fragrant Rose Garden, in the secret
English Garden or in the south veranda with the vistas of Vancouver. Breakfast is served in dining
room or verandas. There is a cat and a hamster in the house. ✓B&B

Walkley, Mavis (Mavis' Bed & Breakfast)   ☎ (604) 986-9748
No1-269 East Keith Rd., North Vancouver, BC   V7L 1V4

From Trans Canada Hwy 1 in North Vancouver take Exit 18 south on Lonsdale Ave to Keith Rd.

Located between St. Georges and St. Andrews Aves.
$50S $80-90D   ► 4
🍲 Cont, homebaked (full on request)   🏠 Res., townhouse, modern duplex,
view, patio   ■2D(upstairs)   ⊨2T,1Q   🛏2Ensuite(1 jacuzzi)   ★TV in
guest rooms, private patio, street parking   🚭No pets   💬some French
🧍 Lonsdale Quay and sea bus to Vancouver, many restaurants, shops
🚗 Horseshoe Bay and ferries, Grouse Mountain, Stanley Park
📷 Attractive and comfortable home with friendly hosts in convenient
location. Enjoy the view of the city and Grouse Mountain. Children welcome.
There is a resident cat. ✓B&B

Canada West Accommodations B&B Reservation Agency
Box 86607, North Vancouver,BC   V7L 4L2   ☎(604)990-6730,Fax(604)990-5876,
(Owner: Ellison Massey)   E-mail: ellison@b-b.com 1-800-561-3223
Rates: $50-85S $75-125D   (including breakfast)   (Deposit required)
A B&B reservation service covering British Columbia and Alberta, and including Greater
Vancouver, Victoria, Vancouver Island, the Okanagan, Whistler, Jasper, Banff, Calgary. The B&B's
offer one to three rooms, private, bath, breakfast. Accommodation for skiers at Whistler, Sun
Peaks, Big White, Silver Star, Apex and the Rockies. Credit card payment required to hold a
reservation. Cancellation notice seven days or, during ski season at Whistler, thirty days.

Town & Country Bed & Breakfast Reservation Service   ☎ & Fax (604) 731-5942
Box 74542, 2803 West 4th Ave, Vancouver, BC   V6K 1K2

(Helen Burich, Manager)
Rates from $85-225D   (Deposit required)
Town & Country B&B in B.C. is a reservation service for Vancouver and Victoria (established in
1981). Homes have been inspected and vary from city townhomes to family homes in residential
areas to self-contained suites and even a few cottages, modest to luxurious, with both shared and
private baths. Rates vary according to location & facilities. Most homes are within 10-20 minimum
drive to city center. The Town & Country Reservation Service does not mail a list of B&B homes.

West Vancouver
(see also **Vancouver & North Vancouver**)

Boden, John & Hawrelko, Donna (Creekside B&B)   ☎(604)926-2599/(604)328-9400
1515 Palmerston Ave., West Vancouver, BC   V7V 4S9   Fax (604)926-7545

Take Exit 11 off Hwy 1 and proceed down 15th St to Palmerston. Turn right to house on right.

$100-145D   (2-day minimum stay)   ► 4A
🍳 Full, homebaked   🏠 Res., sub., acreage, patio, quiet
■2D(upstairs)   ⊨1K,1Q   ⊴1Private,1ensuite (with marble jacuzzi and glass roof)   🚫No smoking, children min. age 10, no pets ★F/refrigerator/coffeemaker in suite, LF, guest balcony, complimentary guest robes & beverages, off-street parking
🏃 Shops, boutiques, parks, dining, beaches, skiing, hiking, boating, natural wilderness, bus stop
🚗 Downtown, major shopping centres, summer and winter recreation, art galleries
📢 Contemporary Heritage home, architecturally designed, in one of Canada's most prestigious communities. Totally private creek flowing through property among lofty native cedar trees. A very natural setting tucked away in the centre of the city. Ideal for honeymooners. Dining & Entertainment coupons available. Enjoy the wines and snacks in the guest rooms. Visa,MC

Gibbs, Gordon and Joan (Beachside B&B)   ☎ 1-800-563-3311, Fax (604) 926-8073
4208 Evergreen Ave., West Vancouver, BC   V7V 1H1   E-mail: beach@uniserve.com

Take Hwy 1 to West Vancouver, drive west along Marine Dr to Ferndale, turn left, then left on Evergreen. From Horseshoe Bay, go East on Marine to Ferndale, turn right.
$125-200S/D $20Child(over age10) $30Add.person   (winter rates avail.)   ► 8
🍳Full, homebaked   🏠Res., sub., view from guest rooms, oceanfront, patio, quiet, isolated   ■3D,1F(main level)   ⊨4Q
⊴3Ensuite,1sh.w.h.   🚫No pets, no smoking   ★TV,KF,2F, off-street parking, separate entrance
🏃 Sandy beach at doorstep, Lighthouse Wilderness Park, excellent gourmet restaurant, shopping mall
🚗 Gleneagles oceanside public golf course, Stanley Park, U.B.C. downtown, Museum of Anthropology, Grouse Mtn, Sea-to-Sky Hwy
📢 Beautiful luxury waterfront home situated on a quiet cul-de-sac in an exclusive area of the city, tastefully decorated in Spanish-style structure with stained glass windows and a panoramic view of Vancouver's busy harbour. Enjoy the jaccuzzi on the beach, sit at the water's edge and watch Alaska Cruise Ships pass by daily en-route to Vancouver Harbour. Hosts are world travellers and certified tour guides. There is a resident dog. 50% Deposit required. Visa,MC ⌒CC

Vernon   *(north of Kelowna; see also Cherryville, Oyama, Winfield)*

Brookes, Keith & Colleen (Richmond House 1894)   ☎ & Fax (250) 549-1767
4008 Pleasant Valley Rd., Vernon, BC   V1T 4M2

From Hwy 97 in Vernon, turn right on 39St and left on Pleasant Valley Rd.

$65S $75D $15Add.person (longer stay rates available)   ► 6
🍳 Full, homebaked   🏠 Downtown, res., 2-storey, hist., view from guest rooms, covered veranda, deck, quiet   ■ 2(upstairs)
⊨ 1D,1Q,1R   ⊴ 1Private, 1ensuite   ★ F,TV, outdoor hot tub, ceiling fans, off-street parking, bicycles for guest (at nominal cost), guest quarters are separate   🚫 No smoking, no pets, children min. age 12, two night stay min. on weekends   〰 Spanish
🏃 Downtown shopping, antique stores, heritage walk, museums, art galleries, Winter Carnival, wine tours, Agrotourism, inhouse artist's studio and art gallery
🚗 Beaches, fishing, water sports, golfing, excellent downhill and x-c skiing at Silver Star Resort
📢 Victorian Heritage home with antiques and elegant lounge situated on the East Hill of Vernon, surrounded by spectacular scenery. Relax in the outdoor hot tub. Gourmet breakfast is served with house-special blend coffee in the elegant dining room. Rooms named Tennyson & Emily Dickinson reflect the host's interest in literature. Hostess is an artist and her original paintings are displayed throughout the house. Dietary needs considered with prior notice. There are 3 cats and a dog kept separate from guest quarters. ⌒B&B

Cushing, Ruth-Maria and Peter Filas (The Maria Rose B&B) ☎ (250) 549-4773
8083 Aspen Rd., Vernon, BC V1B 3M9   Fax (250) 549-4789

Located off Silver Star Rd and 9 km from the city. From Hwy 97 in town, take Silver Star Rd all the
way up to Aspen Rd. Turn left, look for house on immediate right.

$40-60S $60-75D $20Add.person (plus tax) ► 10
Full, homebaked Rural, 2-storey, separate guest house,
acreage, view from guest rooms, patio, deck, quiet 4D (main &
upstairs) (2 upst.rooms make a suite) 2T,1D,1Q,1K,1R No
smoking, small pets by arrangment 2Ensuite, 1sh.w.g. ★F,
separate entrances,TV/VCR in 3 guest rooms, LF for longer
staying guests, sauna (winter only) German, Slavic understood
X-c skiing, hiking, country road walks, birdwatching
Silver Star Mountain Resort, downtown Vernon, Okanagan beaches, wine tours
Enjoy Royal treatment in mountain-side Coach House, situated among 7 acres of peaceful
treed seclusion with a fabulous panoramic view. Located halfway between the city and Ski Resort.
Guest rooms are named King, Queen, Prince and Princess, each with distinct character and
elegantly furnished. There is a small charge for coffee/tea & warm-up kitchenette. Breakfast is
served in main house guest breakfast room. ‿B&B

Dooling, Peter J. & Eva Frybes (Lakeside Illahee Inn) ☎ & Fax (250) 260-7896
15010 Tamarack Dr., Vernon, BC V1B 2E1   1-888-260-7896

From Hwys 97/6 follow Kalamalka Lake Prov.Park signs toward Jade & Juniper Bays. Turn right
on Kidston Rd and follow yellow center line, turn right onto Tamarack Dr to end.
$64-129S $74-139D $156-196Ste $15-30Add.person Meals ► 10

Full, homebaked Res, hill-side back-split, lakefront,
acreage, view from guest rooms, quiet,deck,secluded 4D,1Ste,1F
(ground level) 2T,3D,2K,1R 2Private, 2ensuite
★F,LF,KF,TV in large lakeview guest lounge, room keys, separate
entrances, mountainside hot tub, host quarters are separate
Smoking outside, no pets German, French
Sandy beach, kayaking, free canoes, fishing, outdoor firepit,
Kalamalka Lake Prov.Park entrance
Downtown, Silver Star Ski Resort, 5 golf courses, Grey Monk Estate Winery
Exquisite contemporary lakeside home, with cathedral high red cedar ceilings located on
Kalamalka Lake. A place "where mankind & nature meet" in a serene lakeside setting. Each guest
room is named for a wild flower. Professional hosts are well travelled and of Canadian & Swiss
origin. Hostess offers Estheticare services by appointment. Breakfast is served in large Grand
room. Pick-up & drop-off from Kelowna Airport can be arranged. Visa,MC ‿B&B

Larson, Eskil & Sharon (Castle on the Mountain) ☎ (250)542-4593,Fax(250)542-2206
8227 Silver Star Rd, Vernon,BC V1B 3M8   1-800-667-2229

Located 10 km east of Hwy 97 on 48th Ave (Silver Star Road). Phone for directions.
$65-135S $75-165D $10-20Child $30-45Add.person ► 14A,2Ch

Full, homebaked Rural, acreage, spectacular view, patio,
quiet, isolated 5 (on 3 levels including luxury suite) T,Q,K
5private,1sh.w.g. ★KF,F,TV in guest lounge, sep.entrances,
outside hot tub (open year-round),playground No smoking
Mountainside hiking, camp/fire pit area for guests, art gallery
and work studio on site, toboggan run
Silver Star Ski Resort (major x/c & Alpine ski area), Vernon
Long-time B&B hosts in spacious Tudor home with large deck situated on mountainside
offering fabulous views over lakes & city. Enjoy the sunny south exposures in allergy-free
environment. Ideal place for groups, honeymooners and special occasions. Hosts are artists and
crafts people and have filled their home with art and handcrafted woodwork. The new luxury
"Stargazer's Tower" provides a wonderful retreat for that special occasion. CCards

MacIntyre, Randy & Kathi (Gecko Lodge B&B)   ☎ (250) 545-8356
8726 Forsberg Rd., Vernon, BC   V1B 3M6

In Vernon from Village Green Hotel, follow Silver Star Rd for 12km. Turn right at Gecko Lodge sign on Forsberg Rd and proceed 1 km down road to B&B.

$40S $70D   ► 8
�狂 Nov-April (Ski Season)   🌑 Full   🏠 Rural, rustic log
ski-lodge, 2-storey ranch-style, acreage, quiet   ■ 1D,2F
(upstairs)   ⊨ 1S,3D,2Q   🚿 3Sh.w.g.   ★ F,LF,TV, poolroom,
outdoor hot tub, off-street covered parking, games room with pool
table, library   ⓦ Smoking outside, no pets
〰 Creek (runs year round), forest, excellent x/c-skiing
🚐 Silver Star Mountain Resort, downtown Vernon

📢 Large, rustic log house close to popular Ski Resort and Nordic trails, catering to skiers of all kinds. Enjoy the relaxing experience and a long soak in the hot tub or apres ski activities after a wonderful day on the slopes. There are ski tuning, ski waxing and ski storage facilities. "A B&B run for skiers by skiers". There is a toddler, a dog and a cat in residence.

Nicholls, Eileen and Michael (Coldstream Cottage)   ☎ & Fax (250) 545-2450
266 Cypress Dr., Vernon, BC   V1B 2Y1

From Vernon on Hwy 6, travel 4 km east to Aberdeen Rd. Turn
left, then right on Buchanan Rd and 2 km to Cypress Dr. Turn left.
$35S $45-55D $15Add.person   ► 6
🌑 Full, homebaked   🏠 Rural, res., large grounds, view from
guest rooms, patio, quiet   ■3D(ground level)   ★TV,F
⊨2T,1D,1Q,cot   🚿1Private, 1sh.w.g.   ⓦNo smoking, no pets
🚶 Walk on rural roads and classic Okanagan grass land slopes
🚐 Downtown Vernon, Silver Star Ski, Prov. Park, golf courses

📢 Contemporary, hillside home with a panoramic view of Coldstream Valley and Kalamalka Lake area. Well travelled hosts are interested in wine, weaving, collecting old glassware, creating beautiful hand-made Teddy Bears, and sell them at local markets and they are knowledgeable of the surrounding area and points of interest. Enjoy the congenial hospitality and cozy surroundings.

Schulte, Gisele & Frank (Wildwood B&B)   ☎ (250)545-2747, Fax (250) 545-0518
7454 Wildwood Rd, Vernon, BC V1B 3N8   E-mail: wildwood@junction.net, 1-800-545-1558

From Hwy 97 in Vernon, go up Silverstar Rd (48th Ave) for 6.5 km and turn left on Wildwood Rd.

$35-55S $45-75D $20Add.person   ► 8A,2Ch
🌑 Full, homebaked (Gourmet/vegetarian & special need diets)
🏠 Rural, acreage, Alpine-style, hillside, view from guest rooms,
patio, quiet, isolated   ■3(main & ground level)   ⊨3Q,2P
🚿Private, ensuite   ★Air,KF,F/TV/VCR in guest lounge, hot
tub, slippers & robes, separate entrance, parking   ⓦ No smoking,
no pets   〰German, French
🚶 Bird Sanctuary, hiking trails, x-c skiing, biking

🚐 Downtown Vernon, Silver Star Ski Resort, Okanagan wineries, golf courses, beaches, canoeing
📢 Quiet Alpine country home with panoramic lake & mountain views. situated on wooded acreage next to Sanctuary. Relax in the hot tub under the stars after driving or skiing. Enjoy the gourmet or vegetarian breakfast. Guest are welcome to use the canoe or mountains bike. Hosts are avid skiers and canoeists. Visa,MC

Tullet, Bill & Irene (The Tuck Inn Bed & Breakfast)　☎ (250) 545-3252, Fax (250)549-3254
3101 Pleasant Valley Rd., Vernon, BC V1T 4L2

In Vernon, take Hwy 97 to 30Ave. Turn east to point where 30Ave becomes Pleasant Valley Rd.
$40S　$65-75D　$15Child　$20Add.person　🍽 Meals　(plus taxes)　　　► 10A,2Ch

🍲 Full　🏠 Downtown, res., 2-storey, hist., view from 3 guest rooms　■2D,2F(upstairs)　⊨2T,1D,3Q,2R,crib　⊲2Sh.w.g.
★Air,TV,LF,F, off-street and street parking　🖐Designated smoking area, no pets
🏃 Restaurants, movie theatre, live Playhouse, shops, museum, art galleries, churches, new Tea Room on premises
🚐 Silver Star Ski Resort, Kalamalka/Okanagen Lakes, beaches, water skiing, fishing, golfing
📷 Award winning Heritage Home built in 1906 in very central location and furnished with antiques and collectibles from all over the world. Relax and enjoy the congenial hospitality and take a walk through town. Breakfast is served in the Tea Room. There is a cat. ✓CC

Turney, Judy & David (Paradise Ridge Bed & Breakfast)　☎ & Fax (250) 545-9093
8080 Jackpine Rd., Vernon, BC V1B 3M9

From Hwy 97 in Vernon, take Silverstar Rd (48th Ave) for 10 km to Aspen Rd. Turn left up Aspen to Jackpine Rd.
$49-69D　$10Child　　　　　　　　► 8A,2Ch
🍲 Full, homebaked　🏠 Rural, 3-storey, acreage, view, quiet, large deck　■ 2D,1Ste (main & ground level)　⊨2T(1K),2Q,1P, crib　⊲1Sh.w.g., 1private　★ F,LF,TV in guest family room, ski room, outdoor hot tub, separate entrance　🖐No smoking
🏃 Hiking, mountain biking, bird watching
🚐 Downtown, Silver Star Ski Resort, wineries, scenic drives, golfing, swimming
📷 Beautiful, new chalet-type home designed and built by hosts - a peaceful retreat on Silver Star Mountain - nestled in the trees with a breathtaking view of Kalamalka & Okanagan Lakes and the City of Vernon. Enjoy a full Okanagan breakfast. Relax in the hot tub under the stars, or on the large deck and view the spectacular sunsets. Hosts are avid skiers & gourmet cooks, well travelled and knowledgeable of the Vernon area (owners of Carlson Wagonlit Travel). There is a very friendly Golden Retriever "Prince". Pets & children of all ages welcome with prior notice.Visa,MC ✓B&B

Wray, Irma & Gord (Wray's Lakeview Bed & Breakfast)　☎ (250) 545-9821,
7368 L & A Rd, Vernon, BC V1B 3S6　　　　　　　Fax (250) 545-9924

Phone for directions.
$49S　$69D　　　　　　　　　　► 8A
🍲 Full(Gourmet)　🏠 Rural, 3-storey, view from guest rooms, patio, porch, deck, quiet　■ 4D(ground & upper level)　⊨4T,2Q　⊲1Sh.w.g., 2ensuite　★ Air,F,TV,LF, separate entrance, off-street parking　🖐No smoking, no pets, not suitable for children　〰 German
🚐 Silver Star Mountain Ski Resort, golfing, boating, fishing, hiking, downtown Vernon, shopping, fine dining & restaurants
📷 Warm and friendly welcome in contemporary, spacious new home, tastefully decorated and with a panoramic view of mountains Swan Lake and valley. Retired hosts love meeting new people, gardening and decorating. Hostess will give craft & floral arrangment lessons for longer staying guests. Enjoy the genuine & friendly Okanagan hospitality.Visa,MC ✓B&B

Victoria
(on Vancouver Isle; see also Sooke, Sidney, Brentwood Bay)

Adamek, Christine & Peter (Pacific Sunrise B&B) ☎ & Fax (250) 474-3373
3631 Park Drive (Upper) Victoria, BC   V9C 3W3

Phone for directions.
$70-75S $75-80D $15Child(free under age 6) $15Add.person   ▶ 4A,2Ch
🍳 Full, homebaked   🏠 Rural, split-level, acreage, oceanview from guest rooms, porch, deck,
quiet   ■ 3F(upstairs)   ▭ 1D,1Q,2cots,crib   ▱ 2Private   ★ TV,LF,fridge, microwave,
private entrance, off-street parking, guest quarters are separate   ⓦNo smoking, no pets
🎿 Beach, first growth Douglas Fir Forest on property
🚐 Several golf courses, salmon fishing, Wildlife Sanctuary, biking trails, Butchart Gardens
🌊 Newer house with rooms designed for B&B situated in classic West coast setting, nestled in a
mature Douglas Fir Forest and central location. Relax on the private decks. Breakfast is served in
separate guest breakfast room. Hosts will be happy to arrange for fishing charters. There are two
young children in the host family. Visa,MC ✓CC

Arlidge, Rose Marie and Bruce (Charlotte's Guest House) ☎ (250) 595-3528
338 Foul Bay Rd., Victoria, BC   V8S 4G7

From downtown Victoria follow Fairfield Rd east to Foul Bay Rd, turn right.
$70 per room $10Extra(one-night stay)   ▶ 4
🍳 Choice, homebaked   🏠 Res., sub., split-level, view, quiet   ■ 2D
▭2T,1D   ▱2Private   ★ F,KF,LF, TV in guest room, separate entrance,
ample parking, phones, fully equipped snack room for guests   ⓦ No pets,
no children, 2 persons in room only
🎿 Gonzales Bay, sea & "view" walks, Oak Bay Village, Sealand & marina
🚐 Butchart's Gardens, downtown Victoria, Beacon Hill Park, breakwater
🌊 Warm and attractive contemporary West Coast Garry Oak-shaded
house with spectacular views over the Straits to the snow-capped Olympics
in Washington State. Hosts operated a B&B in Ottawa for many years before
early retiring to their "beloved roots" on the West Coast. ✓CC

Banta, Gordon & Marilyn (Ambleside Bed & Breakfast) ☎(250)383-9948,Fx(250)383-9317
1121 Faithful Street, Victoria, BC   V8V 2R5   E-mail: hosts@amblesidebb.com, 1-800-916-9948

Proceed south on Cook St (bordering east side of Beacon Hill Park). Turn left on Faithful St

$95-150S $110-160D $30Add.person (off-season discounts) ▶ 6A
🍳 Full, homebaked   🏠 Central, res., 2 blocks to ocean, hist.,
quiet   ■ 2D,1Ste (main & upper level)   ▭2T(K),2Q,1P
▱3Ensuite   ★F,TV/VCR piano, parking   ⓦNo smoking, no
pets,children min. age 14   〰 French
🎿 Oceanside pathways & Olympic Mountain vistas, Beacon Hill
Park, Empress Hotel, Royal BC Museum, Parliament Bldg.,
downtown shops, Inner Harbour, Seattle/Port Angeles ferries
🚐 Butchart Gardens, Vancouver & Anacortes ferries, airport, University, Sooke
🌊 Tranquil retreat in one of the city's most scenic and walkable heritage neighbourhoods. Classic
1919 Arts & Crafts home with large front porch, beamed ceilings, vintage woodwork, leaded glass,
traditional furnishings and antique beds. Balconied south-facing suite is ideal for honeymoons or
three-some. Enjoy tasty, convivial breakfasts in the sunny dining room. Hosts are happy to help in
discovering Victoria's true charms. Visa,MC ✓B&B

Barber, Brian & Yoshiko (Cocoro Bed & Breakfast)   ☎ & Fax (250) 595-4779
1883 Taylor St., Victoria, BC   V8R 3G3

From Hwys 17/1 turn east on Hillside Ave/Lansdowne Rd. Right on Richmond and left on Taylor.

From Downtown go east on Fort, left at Richmond, right on Taylor.
$45S $65D $10Child   ▶ 5A,2Ch
Full, homebaked 🏠Res., 3-storey, quiet ■1D,1F(upst. & lower level) 1Sh.w.h.,1ensuite ◀1S,1D,1Q,1P,2R,crib
★F,TV,LF,off-street pkg Ⓦ No skg,no pets ⌇Japanese
🚶 Hillside Shopping Centre, restaurants, Camosun College
🚗 Downtown Victoria, University, beaches and many attractions
☞ Quiet family character home in convenient location for those
travelling by car, bus, taxi and bicycle. Well travelled hosts welcome guests and give friendly advice on local attractions, restaurants & outdoor activities. Enjoy "service from the heart". Spirited breakfasts are never dissapointing. There are young children in the host family.

Bender, Glenda (Bender's B&B)   ☎ (250) 472-8993, Fax (250) 472-8995
4254 Thornhill Cr., Victoria, BC   V8N 3G7

Phone for directions.
$40S $60D $15Add.person   (plus tax)   ▶ 10
🔅 Full 🏠 Res., bungalow, patio, quiet ■ 4D,2F
◀2T,3D,1Q,1R,crib,cot 4Sh.w.g., 2private ★ TV in guest room, facilities for the handicapped Ⓦ No smoking, no pets
🚶 K-mart shopping center
🚗 Uptown and Main Street, Butchart Gardens, ferries, airport
☞ Warm & friendly hospitality. Breakfast served in solarium.

Bowles, Gary & Oleen (Cordova Beach B&B)   ☎ (250) 658-1700
5137 Cordova Bay Rd., Victoria, BC   V8Y 2K1   Fax (250) 658-5955

From Swartz Bay ferry follow Hwy 17 to Sayward Rd. Turn left on Fowler Rd to Cordova Bay Rd.
$80-165S $90-175D   ▶ 4A
🔅 Full, homebaked 🏠 Res., ranch-style, view from some guest rooms, oceanfront, patio, porch, deck, quiet ■ 2D (main floor)
◀ 3Q 1Private, 2ensuite ★ F,TV, separate entrance, off-street parking Ⓦ No smoking, no pets, no children
🚶 Beachcombing, restaurants, shopping, golfing, tennis, trails
🚗 Butchart Gardens, Gulf & San Juan Isles, downtown Victoria,
☞ Friendly & informative hosts in West-coast-style home with
incredible views of San Juan Isles, Mt. Baker and Haro Straits in quiet location, yet close to all amenities & downtown. Enjoy the relaxed atmosphere & breakfasts from "Hearty to Heart smart".
↩B&B

Garden City Bed & Breakfast Reservation Service   ☎ (250) 479-1986 Fax (250) 479-9999
660 Jones Terrace, Victoria, BC   V8Z 2L7   E-mail: dwensley@vanisle.net

(Owner-Operator Doreen Wensley)
Rates: $45-90S $55-185D   (no booking fee charged)
The Service represents over 80 inspected and approved choices. Cottage, heritage, seaview, farm seclusion, are just a few of the amenities available at varied Island locations. Couples & singles are given the same courteous consideration as itineraries, weddings & group accommodations. All homes are non-smoking, many welcome children. Excellent breakfasts included. Reservations advised. Office open most days 7:30am to 10pm. Free catalogue on request. Have a pleasant stay!
Visa,MC,Amex

Boytim, Pauline (The Sea Rose B&B)　　　　☎ (250) 381-7932, Fax (250) 480-1298
1250 Dallas Rd., Victoria, BC　V8V 1C4　　　　　E-mail: searose@compuserve.com

$105-160S　$115-170D　$10-20Child　$15-20Add.person　(plus tax)　　　▶ 8+

From BC Ferries, follow Rte 17 to Mile 0. Turn left on Dallas Rd.
🛏 Full　🏠 Res., 3-storey, hist., view from guest rooms,
oceanfront, porch　■ 4Stes(main/upper/lower levels)
⊨2T,3Q,1K,3P,crib　🛁 4Private　★ KF,LF,TV in guest
rooms, private entrance, off-street parking, guest quarters are
separate　Ⓦ No smoking, no pets
🕴 Clover Point, Beacon Hill Park, Cook Street Village, seafront
parkway with walking and benches, Bus No5
🚗 Downtown, Butchart Gardens, Craigdarroch Castle, Butterfly Gardens, Anne Hathaway
Thatched Cottage, Miniature World, Wax Museum, ferries to mainland and islands
🔫 Comfortable large home built in 1921, recently completely renovated and located on scenic
marine drive with un-interrupted sea and mountain views. Relax in the common area sunroom
overlooking the Strait of Juan de Fuca & Olympic Mountains. Breakfast is served in manager's
dining room. Visa,MC,Amex

Davis, Joanne & Arnie (Abbey Rose B&B)　　☎ (250) 479-7155, Fax (250) 479-5422
3960 Cedar Hill Cross Rd., Victoria, BC　V8P 2N7　　　　　1-800-307-7561

From Swartz Bay ferry terminal on Patricia Bay Hwy 17 take McKenzie St Exit. Go left on
McKenzie for 2km to Cedar Hill Cross Rd. Turn right to house on right.

$65S　$80-90D　$20Child/Add.person　　　　　　▶ 7
🛏 Full, homebaked　🏠 Res., split-level, 3-storey, deck, quiet
■ 2S,3D(upstairs)　⊨ 1S,2T,2Q,1K,crib　🛁 2Private,
1ensuite　★ F,LF,TV in guest rooms, off-street parking, guest
quarters are separate　Ⓦ No smoking, no pets, all children
welcome　ᴡ French
🕴 Galloping Goose Trail - bike trail, Cedar Hill Golf Course, Swan
Lake, University of Victoria, shopping centre, strip mall, bus No25
🚗 Downtown, Inner Harbour, BC ferries, airport, Butchart Gardens, up-island attractions
🔫 Comfortable home surrounded by beautiful oak trees and located in quiet residential
community 5 km from Victoria's city centre. Breakfast is served in central dining room. Relax in
the common room by the fireplace and enjoy the large library. House specialty is homebaked fruit
scones. Visa ⮌B&B

Denniston,Drew & Rosemary (The Denniston By The Sea)　　☎(250)385-5195,Fax1962
430 Grafton St., Victoria, BC　V9A 6S3　　　E-mail: dennisto@datapark.com, 1-888-796-2699

$79-105S　$85-115D　$20Add.person　　　　　　▶ 10
Phone for directions.
🛏 Homebaked　🏠 Res., 3-storey, cliffside, oceanfront, older,
view from guest rooms, patio, porch, deck, quiet　■4 (upstairs)
⊨ 1S,2Q,2K,1R,1P　🛁 2Ensuite, 1private　★ F,KF,LF,TV &
coffee/tea maker in guest rooms, fax, piano, ext.library, games,
host quarters are sep.　ⓌDesignated outside smoking areas, no
pets, conscientious parents required
🕴 Waterfront walkway, picnic tables, Saxe Point Municipal Park,
Canadian Forces Base Esquimalt, Recreation Centre, complete shopping complex, restaurants
🚗 Inner Harbour, Empress Hotel, Parliament Bldgs, Royal BC Museum, Butchart Gardens
🔫 Cozy, comfortable, 1929-built waterfront Tudor-style home on a hill, once owned by famous
concert pianist Madam Huntley Green, with a beautiful view across the ocean of Washington State
snowcapped Olympic Mountain Range. Enjoy the quiet & serene surroundings and watch the
activities of bird/sea life along with the coming and going of ferry boats & other ocean ships. Gift
Certificates available. ⮌B&B

Dineen, Tana (Scholefield House B&B) ☎ (250)385-2025, Fax(250)383-3036
731 Vancouver St.,Victoria, BC   V8V 3V4   E-mail: mail@scholefieldhouse.com, 1-800-661-1623

Located 4 blocks east of the Inner Harbour, 4 blocks south of Fort
St, between Richardson and McClure.
$125-190S $140-205D $40Add.person   (plus tax)   ▶ 7
🍽 Full   🏠 Downtown, hist., 3-storey, patio   ■ 2D,1Ste
(upstairs)   🛏 2Q,1K,1R   🛁 3Ensuite   ★ F,TV in library,
ceiling fans in guest rooms, separate entrance, street & off-street
parking, guest quarters are separate   Ⓦ No smoking, no pets,
children min. age 12

🚶 Inner Harbour, Empress Hotel, Royal BC Museum, Parliament, Old Town, Beacon Hill Park,
whale watching, salmon fishing, ferries, shopping, restaurants, bus to downtown
🚗 Butchart Gardens, Goldstream Park, Sooke & West Coast trails, golfing, sailing, kayaking
🐾 Heritage house built in 1892, authentically restored and decorated with antiques and classic
furnishings, situated on a quiet tree-lined street. Step back in time to the refined elegance of a
by-gone era. A delectable 5-course champagne breakfast is served by the fireplace in the parlour and
highlighted by herbs and edible flowers from the English Country Garden. Special off-season
discounts up to 50%. There are 3 resident cats. Visa,MC ✔B&B

Dubien, Wayne (Craig House B&B)   ☎ (250) 383-0339. Fax (250) 383-0349
52 San Jose Ave, Victoria, BC   V8V 2C2   E-mail: craighouse@craighouse.bc.ca

From Victoria Airport or Swartz Bay ferry terminal, take Hwy 17 to end.
Turn right on Dallas Rd, continue 8 block to San Jose Ave.
$65-110S $70-120D $5-15Add.Person   ▶ 7
🍽 Full   🏠 Res, 2-storey, guest sundeck   ■ 4   🛏 1D,2Q,2T(K)
🛁2Sh.w.g.   ★ KF,F in one guest room, TV, parking   Ⓦ Smoking on
guest deck, no pets, children enquire
🚶 Inner Harbour & ocean, Beacon Hill Park, Empress Hotel, downtown
core, shopping, dining, public transportion
🚗 Downtown, cruise ship landing, ferry to Seattle on Dallas Rd
🐾 Warm and friendly welcome in cozy home with traditional furnishings
& elegant decor located in the James Bay community. Watch horse drawn carriages wind their way
through the streets and past Emily Carr's house and gardens along the streets of Victorian Homes.
Guest rooms are called "Charles Dickens", "Wellington", "Alexandra" etc. Visa,MC

Hansen, Henry and Pat (Top o'Triangle Mountain)   ☎ (250) 478-7853, Fax (250) 478-2245
3442 Karger Terrace, Victoria, BC   V9C 3K5   1-800-870-2255

Take Hwy 1 north from Victoria and Colwood/Sooke Exit. Follow Hwy 14 to Fulton Rd and turn
left. At top of hill, follow Fulton Rd to left and then turn left on Karger Terrace.

$55S $70-90D $75-120F $20Add.person   ▶ 8A,3Ch
🍽 Full, hombaked   🏠Res., sub, view, large deck on 3 sides,
quiet   ■3 (upstairs & ground floor)   🛏3Q,2R,1P, crib
🛁3Ensuite   ★3TV, parking, wheel-chair access, if requested
ⓌNo pets, no smoking   ☟Danish
🚶 Lovely wooded area for walking, small mountain lake,duck pond.
🚗 Royal Roads University, Inner Harbour, Butchart Gardens
🐾Spacious solid cedar home on top of mountain, nestled into a
backdrop of fir trees, spectacular view of Victoria/Juan De Fuca Strait/Olympic Mountains. Enjoy
the view while eating breakfast in the solarium or dining room. Visa, MC ✔B&B

Harris, Gail (Lilac House Country B&B)　　　　　　　☎ (250) 642-2809
1848 Connie Rd., Victoria, BC　V9C 4C2

Take Hwy 14 west from Victoria towards Sooke and watch for "entering Sooke Disctrict" sign. Turn left at Connie Rd to 3rd house on right before bridge up driveway to Connie Rd. Proceed across

private bridge to house on top of hill.
$50-80S　$70-95D　$25Add.person　　　　　　　► 6
🍲 Cont.(country breakfast on weekends)　🏠 Rural, acreage, quiet, view　■ 2(main & upper floor)　🛏1Q,1D,2cots
🚿1Private, 1sh.w.h.　★ Woodstove, hot tub, off-street parking　🚭No smoking, no pets, children min. age 12
🚶 Trails through woods/hills on property, Galloping Goose Trail
🚗 Matheson Lake, East Sooke Park, Sooke Museum, Potholes
& Harbour, historic 17 mile House Pub, French Beach, West Coast Trail
☞ Graceful, new custom home combining traditional architecture with modern skylights and vaulted ceilings. Set on 5 acres with creek and surrounded by beautiful Sooke Hills. Relax and enjoy the antiques, art and Pre-Raphaelite library, covered veranda, gardens and hot tub. Honeymoon suite with large soaker tub. After 13 years of operatating Lilac House B&B in the city, hostess offers the same charm and hospitality amid the natural splendor of the countryside. Advance reservation required. Visa,MC

Hunt, Noreen & Garry (Medana Grove B&B)　　　☎ (250) 389-0437,Fax (250) 389-0425
162 Medana St., Victoria, BC　V8V 2H5　　E-mail: medanagrove@pacificcoast.net, 1-800-269-1188.

$85-100D　$20Add.person　(off-season rates Sept-May)　(plus tax)　► 4A
From Bellevue St travel south on Menzies to Simcoe. Turn left and then first right on Medana to

2nd house on right.
🍲 Full, homebaked　🏠 Downtown, res., 2-storey, older, porch, quiet　■ 2D(main & upper level)　🛏 1Q,1K,1R　🚿2ensuite
★ F,TV in guest room, street parking, guest quarters are separate　🚭 Designated smoking area, no pets
🚶 Inner Harbour, downtown, shopping, restaurants, Royal B.C., Museum, Parliament Buildings, Empress Hotel, Ferry Terminal, oceanfront trails, whale watching tour operations, bus Rte 5
🚗 Butchart Gardens, golfing, Provincial parks, Vancouver & US ferry terminals, airport, beaches
☞ Lovingly restored 1908 character home, carefully decorated and furnished in keeping with the period, including antiques and stained glass windows. Located in James Bay, a quiet neighbourhood of mostly older homes. Hostess is the proud receiver of "Victoria Hospitality Award for Service Exellence". Breakfast is served in the dining room.Visa,MC

Kennedy, Elva and Skip (Wooded Acres B&B)　　　☎ (250) 478-8172/474-8959
4907 Rocky Point Rd., Victoria, BC　V9C 4G2

Located in the rural municipality of Metchosin between Victoria and Sooke.
$110S/D　(plus tax)　🍴 Meals　　　　　► 4A
🍲 Full, homebaked (hearty country-style)　🏠 Rural, log home, acreage, patio, quiet, veranda　■2D　🛏2Q　🚿Private　★TV, off-street parking, private hot tub　🚭 No smoking, no pets, not suitable for small children
🚶 Wilderness hiking trail, beaches, birding, tennis court, fishing, whale watching, variety of golf courses with beautiful facilities
🚗 Sooke Harbour House, elegant & pub-style dining, art shops
☞ Comfortable home is situated on over 3 acres of secluded "wooded park-like setting", which guarantees tranqility and relaxation. Enjoy candlelight, a touch of wilderness & complete privacy in hot-tub spa. Popular with honeymooners and for other special occasions. House specialties are "privacy and good food". 🖋B&B

Lin, Lily (Lily House B&B)   ☎ & Fax (250) 920-0891
143 Government St., Victoria, BC   V8V 2K6

Located between Simcoe & Niagara Streets.
$69-89S $69-120D $15Child/Add.person   (plus tax)   ► 12
🍽 Full   🏠 Downtown, res., 2-storey, hist., quiet   ■ 5(main & upper levels)   ⊨
3S,3Q,1P,1K   ⊿ Private   ★ F,KF,TV in guest rooms, off-street & street parking   ♨
Designated smoking area, no pets, inquire about children
🖈 Oceanfront, Parliament Bldg., Royal BC Museum, Inner Harbour, Beacon Hill Park, Market
Square & Chinatown, downtown area, restaurants, shops, buses No5/2/30
🚗 Butchart & Butterfly Gardens, Government House, Craigdarroch Castle, Royal Roads
University & Harley Park, Duncan, Chemainus, ferries
🖝 Warm welcome and friendly hospitality in comfortable home with large classic rooms and
surrounded by heritage buildings on quiet beautiful historic street. Breakfast is served in guest
breakfast room. Visa,MC ⌐B&B

Markham, Lyall & Sally (Markham House Bed & Breakfast)   ☎ (250)642-7542
1853 Connie Rd.,Victoria, BC   V9B 5B4   Fax(250)642-7538,1-888-256-6888

Located halfway between Victoria and West Coast beaches. From ferries or Airport, take Hwy 17 to
Hwy 1, and to Hwy 14. Then all the way to Connie Rd (approx.45km). Turn left.

$95-175D   (reduced rate for one person) $20Add.person   ► 8
🍽Full,homebaked(4-course)   🏠 Iris Farm, tudor-style, view, patio,
quiet   ■4D(deluxe cottage)   ⊨1K,2Q,2T   ⊿4Private
★Woodstove, hot tub   ♨Restricted smoking, no pets, children
minimum age 12
🖈 10 landscaped acres of exquisite Iris gardens (140 varieties) and
woodland paths, trout pond
🚗 Superb West Coast beaches, long hiking trails & bike paths
🖝 Quiet country living in spacious custom-built home situated on a knoll at the outskirts of the
City, surrounded by a huge splash of colours, especially from end of May to 1st week of July. Enjoy
afternoon tea in the lounge or terrace overlooking garden/pond. CCards,JBC ⌐B&B

McCarthy, Paul & Diana (Pitcairn House Bed & Breakfast)   ☎ & Fax (250) 384-7078
1119 Ormond St., Victoria, BC   V8V 4J9   E-mail: ptcairn@victoriabc.com, 1-800-789-5566

From Fort & Government Streets, travel east on Fort St for 6 blocks to
Ormond St, turn left to house on right.
$65S $80-140D $20Add.person   ► 8A,2Ch
🍽 Full, homebaked   🏠 Downtown, hist., patio, quiet   ■2D,2Ste
(upstairs)   ⊨ 2T,2Q,1K,cot   ⊿ 1Sh.w.g., 1ensuite   ★ Parking
♨Smoking on patio, no pets, children min. age 10   ⌇ French
🚗 Butchart Gardens, University of Victoria
🖈 Major downtown tourist attractions & harbour, bus (No11/14)
🖝 Victorian Heritage home (built in 1901) filled with period furniture, lace curtains, and stained
glass windows. Located centrally on Antique Row. Enjoy a hearty breakfast in the cozy dining room.
There are 2 small dogs in residence. Visa,MC

Merritt, Harvey and Jean (The Boathouse)   ☎ (250) 652-9370
746 Sea Drive, RR1, Brentwood Bay, BC   V8M 1B1

Located 1.5 km west of Brentwood Bay off Wallace and Woodward Drives.
$120S $130D   ► 2
🍽 Cont.   🏠 Rural, near village, res., acreage, view, patio, quiet, oceanfront   ■ Separate
cottage   ⊨ 1Q   ⊿ Private   ★ Separate entrance, parking, rowing dinghy for guests   ♨No
smoking, no children, no pets   ⌇ German
🖈 Butchart's Gardens, Village of Brentwood Bay, marina, boat rental, salmon fishing
🚗 City of Victoria, Sidney, Malahat Drive, parks, southern part of Vancouver Island
🖝 Lovely waterfront Cottage & bathhouse completely refurbished. Ideal for a romantic get-away
& perfect setting for total relaxation. Private dock for sunbathing/swimming. Visa,MC ⌐CC

McGuire, Pat & Kathy (Eagle's Nest Bed & Breakfast) ☎(250)658-2002,Fax(250)658-0135
4769 Cordova Bay Rd., Victoria, BC   V8Y 2J7

From Victoria Int.Airport or Swartz Bay Ferry Terminal, follow Patricia Bay Hwy (#17) to Royal Oak Dr, then to Cordova Bay Rd. Look for long private driveway.
$75-135D   (weekly & seasonal rates available)   ► 6
🔟 Full   🏠 Res.   ■ 3D,1Ste   ⊨ 1D,2Q,1K   ⚨Sh.w.g.,
1private in suite   ★ private deck & entrance in suite, jacuzzi in one room   🖐 No smoking, no pets, children welcome
🏃 Ocean/beachcombing, city bus route city
🚗 Downtown, Commonwealth Pool & shopping centre, world famous Butchart Gardens, public golfing, scenic drives
☛ Quiet, cozy, spacious high-tech home with well-travelled, hospitable hosts ready to offer tips on sightseeing, places to eat.

Moen, Annette & Dieter Gerhard (Birds of a Feather Oceanfront B&B) ☎(250)391-8889
206 Portsmouth Dr., Victoria, BC   V9C 1R9   E-mail: nest@surf101.net, Fax(250)391-8883

From Hwy 1 exit onto Hwy 1A/14 (Colwood/Sooke) to Ocean Blvd. Proceed to Lagoon Rd, to Heatherbell and to Portsmouth.
$89-119S/D $15child $25Add.person   ► 6A,3Ch
🔟 Full, homebaked   🏠 Sub, ranch-style, view, oceanfront, deck, quiet, secluded   ■ 2(ground level)   ⊨ 1Q,1D,1R,cot,crib
⚨2Ensuite   ★ Air,F,TV/phone/mini fridge in guest room, off-street parking   🖐 Designated smoking area   〰 German
🏃 Ocean beach, historic Fort Rodd Hill & Fisgaard Lighthouse,
Royal Roads University, Hatley Castle & Gardens, Migratory Bird Sanctuary, bus routes
🚗 Butchart Gardens, East Sooke & Goldstream Pov. Parks, trails, museums, downtown Victoria
☛ Spacious home in exquisite waterfront setting with views of historic Hatley Castle on the grounds of Royal Roads University and Esquimalt Lagoon Migratory Bird Sancturay from the back yard. Breakfast is served in special guest breakfast room or on the oceanfront deck, while watching marine wildlife a few feet away. For a closer look guests are invited to take out the canoe, kayaks or row boat. Soak in the huge hot tub after a busy day. Honeymoon & other special occasion packages can be arranged. There is a dog and a cat in residence. Visa,MC ⌐B&B

Mollins, Vesta & Dave Wilkie (The Villa Blanca B&B) ☎(250)658-4190,Fax4120
4918 Cordova Bay Rd., Victoria, BC   V8Y 2J5   E-mail: vesta@villablanca.bc.ca

From Swartz Bay Ferry Terminal travel south on Hwy 17 to Sayward Rd which becomes Cordova Bay Rd. Turn left.
$90D   ► 4A
🔟 Full, homebaked   🏠 Res, 2-storey, view from guest rooms, patio   ■ 2D(upstairs)   ⊨ 1Q,1K   ⚨ 2Private   ★ F,TV,LF, sep.guest quarters, off-street pkg   🖐No smoking, no pets
🏃 Golf Course, Cordova shops, restaurants, downtown bus No31
🚗 Butchart Gardens, Int. Airport, US & Canadian ferries
☛ Warm & firendly welcome in spacious, elegantly furnished Mediterranean-style villa, conveniently located in beautiful Cordova Bay. Well travelled hosts have lived overseas and are both avid sailors. Enjoy the light, airy atmosphere which imparts a deep sense of peace. Browse through the impressive collection of handmade quilts and hand-crafted items. Breakfast is served in special guest breakfast room. Visa,MC ⌐CC

Monahan, Pat & Cathie (Benvenuto Bed & Breakfast) ☎(250)652-9254,Fx(250)652-4003
1024 Benvenuto Ave., Brentwood Bay, BC   V8M 1A1

$75S $85D $20Add.person   (long term rates available)   ▶ 4-5A,2Ch

Located beside Butchart Gardens. Phone for directions.
🍴 Full, homebaked   🏠 Rural, res., 2-storey, porch, quiet
■2D(ground level)   ⊨ 2S,1Q,2cots   ⊲ 2ensuite   ★F,LF,TV
in guest sitting room, VCR/movies provided, library   ⊛No pets,
smoking outside
🜨 Beautiful Waterfront Provincial Park with hiking/walking
trails, Butchart Gardens, Butterfly Gardens
🚗 Downtown Victoria, Sidney by the Sea, good restaurants
🐾 Newly renovated home for B&B with lovely decor and friendly atmosphere in a treed setting.
Guest area is on entry level, separate from household. Breakfast is served in the dining room. Ferry
pick-up by appointment. Children welcome. Visa,MC ✓CC

Morrow, Jaye & George (Friends B&B)   ☎ (250) 480-5504, 1-888-480-5504
651 Trutch St., Victoria, BC   V8V 4C3   Fax (250) 480-5288

$75-85S $85-115D $10Child(under age 12) $20Add.person   (plus tax)   ▶ 16
From Hwys 17/1 take Blanshard or Douglas to city centre. Turn left on Fort, right on Cook, left on
Richardson to Trutch. From Inner Harbour take Belville east, left on Blanshard, right on Fairfield,
left on Trutch.

🍴 May1-Sept30   🍴 Full, homebaked   🏠 Downtown, res., 3-storey, hist.,
porch, quiet, secluded   ■ 3D,3F(main & upper level)   ⊨ 3S,6Q,2R,crib
⊲6Ensuite   ★ LF,TV in guest room, street & off-street parking, guest
quarters are separate, main floor guest kitchen   ⊛ No smoking, no pets,
children min. age 4   ⌇ Mandarin
🜨 Empress Hotel, Royal BC Museum, Parliament, Antique Row, Beacon
Hill Park, Gvt.House Gardens, Craigdarroch Castle, Dallas Road waterfront,
whale watching, fishing, shopping restaurants, city bus route No1
🚗 City Centre, Butchart Gardens, International Airport, Vancouver Ferry
Terminal, Old England Inn, Oak Bay Village
🐾 Nicely restored 1912 Heritage house with elegant interior, and stained glass windows, located
on a beautiful tree-lined street. Afternoon tea served in the private secluded flower garden. Hosts
have been welcoming B&B guests from worldwide for many years. Breakfast is served in the
character dining room. Visa,MC ✓B&B

Peggs, Joan (The Inn on St. Andrews)   ☎ (250) 384-8613, Fax (250) 384-6063
231 St Andrews St., Victoria, BC   V8V 2N1   E-mail: joan_peggs@bc.sympatico.ca, 1-800-668-5993

Phone for directions (map will be mailed if time permits).
$65S $80-110D $20-30Add.person   ▶ 4
🍴Full,homebaked   🏠Downtown,res.,hist.,2-storey,city-view,quiet
■2Ste(upst)   ⊨2T,1Q   ⊲1sh.w.g.,1private, washbasin in one
room   ★F,TV, off-street parking   ⊛No smoking
🜨 "Schoolhouse" (once Emily Carr's Studio), Inner Harbour, ferry
and seaplane terminals, Parliament Buildings, Royal BC Museum,
the Empress Hotel, downtown shops, fine dining, ocean front
🐾 Historic home, built in 1913 on the Carr-family property, is a designated heritage property in
James Bay. Enjoy modern comforts, wholesome food & old-fashioned hospitality. Visa,MC,Enroute

Richardson, Olga & Ken (Cedar Shade Bed & Breakfast)   ☎ & Fax (250) 652-2994
6411 Anndon Place, Victoria, BC   V8Z 5R9   E-mail: krichards@tnet.net

From Swartz Bay BC Ferry take Hwy 17 (Patricia Bay Hwy) to Tanner Rd and turn right up hill to
Rodolph Rd. Turn right to Anndon Place and left to bottom of cul de sac. From Victoria take Hwy
17 past Sayward Rd and turn left on Tanner Rd - continue as above.
$50S $70-85D $20Add.person   🖾 Meals   (plus taxes)   ► 6A,2Ch

🍲 Full(Gourmet)   🏠 Rural, res., split-level, view, patio,quiet
■3(ground level) ⊨2T,2Q,1P   ⊒1Private, 21sh.w.g.   ★Air,F,
sep.entrance, facilites for the handicapped, off-street parking
🖐No smoking   〰 Ukrainian
🕴 Bear Hill Reg.Park, Rodolph Park, Central Saanich Valley,
Pederson' Berry Farm, Trails, Beach.
🚗 Butchart Gardens, Elk Lake, Commonwealth Pool, Island
View Beach, Butterfly World, Cordova Bay Golf Course

🐾 Savour a taste of tranquility in comfortable home in quiet, private residential cul-de-sac
amidst big old cedars and douglas fir trees. Relax by the terraced rock gardens, cedar shaded fish
pond, water fall with fountain and herb garden and enjoy genuine Ukrainian hospitality. Hosts
enjoy ballroom dancing, winemaking, flower & herb gardening.

Simms, Marion and Thomas (Marion's B & B)   ☎ (250) 592-3070
1730 Taylor St., Victoria, BC   V8R 3E9

Phone for directions.
$35-40S $50-60D $10Child $20Add.person (Deposit)   ► 7A,3Ch
🍲 Full, homebaked   🏠 Res., bungalow, view, patio, quiet   ■3
(main level) ⊨1S,1D,2Q   ⊒1Sh.w.g.,1sh.w.h.   🖐No
smoking   ★TV,F,LF,parking
🕴 Hillside Market Mall, Mount Tolmie, bus to downtown
🚗 Butchart Gardens, Empress Hotel, Oak Bay Village, China B.
🐾 Cozy home located on quiet street overlooking spacious open
field and Mount Tolmie in the distance. Relax in a shower or jacuzzi bath. Beds are covered with
handmade quilts and cozy comforters. Transportation to and from bus depot can be arranged.
Two-days cancellation required.

Thomas, Harold and Elizabeth (Mylfford Haven House)   ☎ (250) 383-0699
1239 Pandora Ave., Victoria, BC   V8V 3R3

Travel south on Blanshard to Johnson (one-way). Turn left to
Fernwood. Turn left, go 2 blocks to Pandora (one-way). Left again.
$85-95S/D   ► 4
🍲Full, homebaked 🏠Downtown,res.,hist. ⊨2Q ⊒2Private
■2D(upstairs) ★Parking 🖐No smoking,no child,no pets
🕴 Downtown, theatres, restaurants, antique shops, transit stop
🚗 World famous Butchart Gardens, Anne Hathaway Cottage
🐾 Quietly elegant home, built in 1915, with charming features
i.e. impressive open staircase and friendly atmosphere.Breakfast is served in bright and cheerful
dining room. Well informed hosts will gladly assist with itineraries. Visa,MC

Wait, Sally (Windlock on the Sea)   ☎ (250) 652-2079, Fax (250) 652-2169
8560 West Saanich Rd., Sidney, BC   V8L 5W1

From Swartz Bay travel south on Hwy 17 to 2nd traffic light (McTavish Rd), turn right to end, left
on West Saanich Rd, travel 2km. Located 27 km north of Victoria
$50S $85D $85Cottage   ▶ 6
🍴 Choice   🏠 Rural, acreage, view, oceanfront, large patio
■1D(main level), also separate selfcontained guest
cottage ⊨2Q,1P ⚊2Private 🐾No pets,no smoking
🏃 Beach combing on private beach, watch seals and otters playing,
good birding and fishing in Saanich Inlet
🚗 Butchart Gardens, airport, Sidney & ferries to mainland
Charming West Coast Cedar designed home located on beautiful Saanich Inlet with lovely
views & fabulous sunsets. Featured accommodation is a lovely patioed cottage, set in picturesque
and extensive xeriscaped (dry) garden. Hosts are in their 15th year of providing a unique B&B
experience to many satisfied guests. Enjoy the relaxing atmosphere. A " Jack Russell" in residence
(Marriage Commissioner next door!). ✓B&B

Walsh, Gini and Peter (Swallow Hill Farm B&B)   ☎ & Fax (250) 474-4042
4910 William Head Rd., Victoria, BC   V9C 3Y8   E-mail: swallowhill@pacificcoast.net

Take Hwy 1 to Colwood/Sooke Exit onto Hwy 1A, then Hwy 14, left on Metchosin Rd, then William
Head Rd. Please phone first.
$75S $85S $85-95D $20Add.person   (some discount rates
available)   ▶ 6
🍴Full, homebaked   🏠Farm, view, quiet ■2Ste ⊨2Q,2S,1P
⚊2Private   ★Private decks, (1 Ste very private with separate
entrance), sauna   🐾No smoking, no pets
🏃 Nature Sanctuary (birds, deer, seal, otters), ocean beach, 46km
hiking trail, historic (1870) church, museum & school, country
store, restaurant & gift shop. Bus route
🚗 Victoria, Butchart Gardens, Sooke, Gulf Islands, Chemainus murals, Duncan, beaches, golfing
Apple farm home with antiques and handcrafted furniture, in beautiful country setting near
city. Enjoy the spectacular ocean & mountain sunrise view and a delicious farm breakfast. There
are farm animals, a resident dog and wildlife. Friendly hosts love meeting people. CCards. ✓B&B

Wilde, Shirley (Gracefield Manor)   ☎ (250) 478-2459, Fax (250) 478-2447
3816 Duke Rd., RR4, Victoria, BC   V9B 5T8

Phone for directions.
$85-100per room   ▶ 6A
🍴Full,homebaked 🏠Farm, rural, hist. 3-storey, view, acreage
■3(main & upper level) ⊨2T,2D ⚊3Ensuite ★5F,parking
🐾No smoking, no children, no pets
🏃 Regional parks, beaches, golf courses, driving range
🚗 City Centre, fishing, golfing, hiking trails, Butchart Gardens,
Lester B.Pearson College, Fisgard Lighhouse
Hallmark Award winning home (a captivating landmark), situated on large acreage has
recently been fully restored, recapturing the Plantation inspired feel of the Old South. Retreat to
the serenity of the countryside and enjoy the ever changing views of the Olympic Mountains and the
Straits of Juan de Fuca. There is a resident dog. Visa. ✓B&B

Whistler

(north of Vancouver; see also Brackendale)

Gerig, Louise and Willy (Swiss Cottage)
mailing: Box 1209, Whistler, BC   V0N 1B0

☎ (604) 932-6062/Fax (604) 932-9648
E-mail: swiss@direct.ca

Location: 7321 Fitzsimmons Rd. In Whistler after 4th traffic light, turn right at White Gold Estate and cross wooden bridge to Fitzsimmons Rd. Turn right and proceed to end and to house on right.
Winter: $89-145D   Summer $85-98D $25Add.person   ▶ 8

🍴Full, homebaked   🏠Res., village, quiet, riverside   ■2D,1F (upstairs)   ⊨4T,1Q   ⊿3Ensuite   ★TV,F,outdoor jacuzzi, parking   🖐No smoking, no pets   ⋙ German, French
🎿 Ski lifts, cross-country trail starts at doorstep, Whistler Village, Lost Lake, golfing, tennis court by the house, biking, fishing, hiking, canoeing
🚗 Garibaldi National Park, Cheakamus Lake, Brandywine Falls
📣 Swiss Chalet situated in excellent location. Enjoy all the warmth and hospitality of a traditional Alpine B&B. Host's specialty is homemade breads. Hostess is a ski-instructor. MC ✓CC

Habkirk, Diana & Les (Brio Haus Bed & Breakfast)
3005 Brio Entrance, Whistler, BC   V0N 1B3

☎(604)932-3313,Fax(604)932-4945
1-800-331-BRIO

In Whistler look for large Brio sign. Turn on Brio Entrance to 2nd property on right.
$65S(Summer) $80S(Winter) $75-120D(Summer/Winter $20Add.person   (plus tax)   ▶ 8

🍴 Full, homebaked   🏠 Resort town, res., 3-storey, view from guest rooms, porch, decks, quiet   ■2D,1F(upstairs)   ⊿2Sh.w.g.   ⊨2S,2T,1Q,1K   ★ F,LF,TV in guest room, sep.entrance, guest kitchen, off-street parking, jacuzzi moon tub/sauna, ski storage
🖐Smoking on decks, no pets, children min. age 10
🎿 Across from Whistler Golf Course, on Valley (hiking) Trail, 0.5km to Whislter Village Centre, shops/restaurants/ski lifts
🚗 Brandywine and Narin Falls
📣 Charming European-style Alpine Home situated 0.5km south from Whistler Village town center. Guests may prepare their own dinners in the guest kitchen, then relax around the fire in the guest living room, or enjoy the moon tub and sauna. Hosts have been in the tourism business for many years. Visa,MC,Diners ✓B&B

Huber, Erwin & Lisa (Chalet Luise)
Box 352,7461 Ambassador Cr,Whistler,BC V0N 1B0

☎ (604)932-4187/Fax(604)-938-1531,1-800-665-1998
E-mail: 100276.300@compuserve.com

Take Hwy 99 from Vancouver to Whistler. Approx 1km north of the village, turn right into White Gold Estates on Nancy Green Dr. Right again on Ambassador Cr. Proceed 2 blocks to No. 7461.
$89-109S $95-179D $10Child $25Add.person   (plus tax)   ▶ 14

🍴 Full, homebaked(different specialties each day)   🏠 Res., view, patio, balconies, quiet   ■8D(main & upper level-incl. honeymoon suites)   ⊨4T,4Q,4K   ⊿ Private ensuite   ★LF,F's in rooms, whirlpool & sauna, parking, ski/bicycle storage, separate entrance, guest lounge, beautiful garden with patios   🖐No smoking, children min.age 3   ⋙German, Italian, French
🎿 Whistler Village, ski lifts, shops, restaurants, x/c skiing & walking trails, biking, fishing
🚗 Alpine hiking, windsurfing, canoeing, sailing, golfing, horseback riding
📣 Enjoy the authentic Swiss hospitality, ambiance and charm in a beautiful mountain setting. Ski and summer packages available. ✓CC

Langtry, Stan and Shirley (Stancliff House)   ☎ (604) 932-2393, Fax (604) 932-7577
3333 Panorama Ridge, Box 995, Whistler, BC   V0N 1B0

Take Hwy 99 north from Vancouver and drive through Whistler Creek area to "Brio" section (sign on Hwy). Turn right on Pan. Ridge to house on top of hill on right.
Summer $75-95D   Winter $85-120D   ► 8
🛏Full 🏠Village, view, quiet ■2(ground level) ⊨4T,1Q
🛁1Sh.w.h ★TV,F, piano, microwave, fridge, art collection, ski room, hot tub, ample parking ⓌRestr.smoking,no pets
🏃 Whistler Village, Blackcomb/Whistler Chairlift, Valley Trail (biking, walking, Golf Course, tennis, windsurfing, canoeing
🚗 Warm welcome in contemporary-styled comfortable home with magnificent mountain view. Enjoy relaxing in the hot tub or guest lounge with tea or coffee. Breakfast is served upstairs. Easy walking distance to village and ski lifts. Complimentary bus or train pick-up and delivery. ✔CC

Lieberherr, Heidi (Rainbow Creek B&B)   ☎ & Fax (604) 932-7001
Box 1142, Whistler, BC   V0N 1B0

Located at 8243 Alpine Way. Take Hwy 99 north to Whistler and continue 3 km north from the village to Alpine Meadows. Turn left on Alpine Way and proceed 3 blocks to house on right.
Winter: from $85-105S/D   Summer: from $65-85S/D $20Add.person   (plus tax)   ► 6
🛏 Full, homebaked 🏠Resort, log house, 2-storey, view from guest rooms, quiet, porch, large sun deck ■3(upst) ⊨2T,2Q
🛁Private, 1sh.w.g. ★F,TV, fridge/phone for guests, parking
ⒶNo smoking, no pets 〰 German
🏃 Ice Rink, swimming pool, beautiful Meadow Park, bus stop
🚗 Whistler Village, ski lifts at Whistler & Blackcomb mountains
🚗 Charming log home with breathtaking views in quiet setting among towering evergreens. Enjoy Swiss hospitality & a cozy atmosphere. Relax by the fireplace. Reservations recommended. There is a dog.Visa/MC ✔B&B

Manville, Tim and Yvonne (Alta Vista Chalet B&B Inn) ☎ (604) 932-4900, Fax (604) 932-4933
3229 Archibald Way, Whistler, BC   V0N 1B3   E-mail: aucb-bq.direct.ca

Summer: $79S $99D $10Child   Winter: $130S $145D $15Child (plus tax)   ► 16A,4Ch
From Vancouver, take Hwy 99 to Whistler. Turn left onto Hillcrest Rd (Alta Vista Area), right onto Alpine Cres and left onto Archibald Way.
🛏Full, homebaked 🏠Village,European Chalet,view,patio,quiet ■6D,2F (main,upper & ground level) ⊨6T,6Q,2R 🛁 6Private,2sh.w.g. ★F, guest lounge, games room with TV,VCR,guest fridge, jaccuzzi hot tub on guest deck, secured ski storage,parking ⒶNo smoking,no pets 〰French
🏃 Lake for swimming/canoeing/sailing/kayacking (rentals available), Valley trail (canoe & bike rentals available), Whistler Village shops/restaurants
🚗 Horseback riding, ski lifts to Whistler and Blackcomb Mountain
🚗 Spacious European chalet furnished with pine and located on the Valley Trail in a quiet forest setting overlooking beautiful Alta Lake. There is a dog in residence. CCards ✔CC

Myette-Spence, Ann (Golden Dreams B&B)   ☎ (604) 932-ANN'S(2667)/Fax (604) 932-7055
6412 Easy Street, Whistler, BC   V0N 1B6   1-800-668-7055

Take Hwy 99 north; once in Whistler, at 4th set of lights, turn left (Lorimer Rd) and follow to
Balsam Way. Turn right and then next left on Easy St. Look for gold mailbox and sign on archway.
Winter:$75-95S $95-115D Summer:$55-75S $75-95D $25Add.person $10Child   ► 6A

🍴Full,homebaked 🏠Resort village, mountainview, sundecks,
hot tub ■3 ⊨2D,2Q,1cot ⊒1Sh.w.g.,1private ★F,TV in
library lounge, kitchen 🚭No smoking, no pets
🏃 Valley trail & along golf course to village, x-c/downhill skiing,
restaurants,shops,hiking, bike trails at doorstep
📷 Uniquely decorated rooms in Victorian, Oriental and Aztec
themes with sherry decanter, cozy down duvets. Nutritious
vegetarian breakfast served in country kitchen, including
home-made jams. Residence of Ex-National Ski Team coach. Children welcome. Visa/MC.

Plachy, Stan & Eva (Lorimer Ridge Pension)   ☎ (604)938-9722,Fax(604)938-9155
6231 Piccolo Dr,Whistler,BC V0N 1B6   1-800-988-9002

Take Hwy 99 north to Whistler Village Centre. Proceed to Lorimer Rd. Turn left and then left
again on Piccolo Dr. Look for house on left.
$90S $125D(Summer) $125S $145D(Winter)   (plus taxes)   ► 16

🍴 Full, homebaked (buffet) 🏠 Res., West-Coast style 2-storey,
view from guest rooms, patio, deck, quiet ■ 8D(main & upper &
ground level) ⊨ 8T,4Q ⊒ 8Private ★ TV,F(2 in guest
rooms), separate entrance, off-street parking, hot tub, sauna,
billiard room, ski lockers/ sports equipment storage, guest
quarters are separate   🚭 No smoking, no pets, children min. age
10 ⌇ Czech
🏃 Whistler Village Ski Resort, biking trails, golfing, swimming,
downhill & x-c skiing, hiking, dining, restaurants, horse-back riding, village bus route
🚗 Pemberton, Squamish, Shannon Falls
📷 Cozy mountain lodge set in spectacular surroundings with a touch of West Coast architecture
and fine Canadian hospitality. Enjoy the magnificient views of Blackcomb, Fissile & Rainbow Mts.
Breakfast is served in guest breakfast room. There is a dog in residence. Visa,MC ↙B&B

Ruiterman, Paul & Helga (Renoir's Winter Garden B&B)   ☎ (604) 938-0546, Fax 938-0547
3137 Tyrol Cr., Whistler, BC   V0N 1B3   E-mail: renoir@dualmountain.com

$85-125D(Summer) $115-145D(Winter) $25Add.person (Single person rates avail.)   ► 6A,2Ch

Take Hwy 99 past Whistler Creek traffic lights for 3km. Turn left
at Blueberry Hill sign, left after 30 m and left after 250m.
🍴 Full, homebaked 🏠 Village, 3-storey, view from guest rooms,
deck, quiet ■ 2D,1F(main floor) ⊨ 2T,1Q,1K.R ⊒1sh.w.g.,
1ensuite ★ LF,TV/VCR in guest rooms, spa hot tub, private
entrance, off-street parking, guest quarters are separate 🚭No
smoking, no pets, children min. age 5 ⌇ German, Dutch
🏃 Golf Course (via trail), main village shops/restaurants
🚗 Black Comb & Whistler mountain ski lifts, hiking, biking, hangliding, canoeing, water-rafting,
📷 New modern home with large rooms, tastefully decorated and situated at the foot of Whistler
mountain overlooking Alta Lake. Enjoy the jacuzzi hot tub after a day on the slopes. Breakfast is
served in the treetop dining room. Hosts will give a lift to skiers in the morning to the ski area.
Extended stay & off-season rates available. Pick-up from bus loop/train station. Visa,MC ↙B&B

Stangel, Sue & Hal (Chalet Beau Séjour)   ☎ (604) 938-4966, Fax (604) 938-6296
7414 Ambassador Cr., Box 427, Whistler, BC   V0N 1B0

Take Hwy 99 from Vancouver to Whistler. At 1km north of the village, turn right into White Gold
Estates on Nancy Green Dr. Turn right again on Ambassador Cr to 3rd house on left.
Summer:$80-90S/D   Winter:$105-120S/D $10Child $20Add.person   ► 6

🍴 Full   🏠 Res., village, 3-storey, view, deck, quiet   🛏3D
(upstairs)   🛏 2T,2Q,1cot   🚿 3Private   ★ F,TV, ski storage,
hot-tub, lounge, off-street parking ⓦDesignated smoking area
〰German, French, Spanish
🧍 Ski lifts, Whistler Village, lake, golf courses, ski trails, shops,
tennis, biking, restaurants, Whistler Valley bus service
🚐 Alpine hiking, sailing, horseback riding, canoeing, windsurfing
🚍 Spacious new Alpine home with friendly Canadian hospitality
and relaxing atmosphere situated in central location. Complimentary transportation from bus or
train station and special off-season and ski packages available. Relax in the spacious guest lounge
with sundeck. Children welcome by special arrangement. Visa,MC 〰B&B

Weh, Doris and Willi (Haus Stephanie)   ☎ & Fax (604) 932-5547
7473 Ambassador Crs., Bx 1460, Whistler, BC   V0N 1B0

Winter: $100-120S/D $20Add.person   Summer: $80-95S/D   (Child free under age 5)   ► 6

Coming north on Hwy 99, drive past village entrance, take second
road on the right (White Gold Estates). Stay on Nancy Green Dr
until it becomes Ambassador Cr.
🍴 Full   🏠Res., balcony, quiet   ■3D,1F (main and upper
floor)   🛏 2S,2Q   🚿 1Pivate, 2ensuite   ★KF,separate
entrance, parking   ♥   ⓦ No smoking   〰 German
🧍 Ski lifts, Resort village, cross-country trails
🚍 Austrian-style house with European atmosphere and situated
in convenient location to the lifts and village activities.

White Rock   *(Vancouver);see also N.Westminster,Langley,Delta,Ladner,Tsawwassen)*

Baynes, Bonnie & Gordon (Georgian Bed & Breakfast)   ☎ (604) 541-9129
2132-131 B St., White Rock, BC   V4A 9J5

Phone for directions.
$65S $75D   ► 2
🍴 Full, homebaked   🏠 Res., 2-storey, swimming pool, quiet,
porch   ■ 1D(upstairs)   🛏 1Q   🚿 1Ensuite   ★ off-street
parking   ⓦ No smoking, no pets, no children
🧍 Park/walking trails, Mall, bus stop to downtown Vancouver
🚐 White Rock Beach & Crescent Beach with many fine shops &
restaurants, BC Ferries to Victoria & Gulf Islands, US border
🚍 Friendly atmosphere in new home situated in a quiet residential area with large yard. Enjoy a
refreshing swim in the outdoor heated pool or just relax on one of the verandas. Breakfast is served
in elegant antique furnished dining room. In winter, home is especially geared to people with dust
allergies. Please bring slippers. Visa 〰B&B

Hall, Iris and Bruce (Hall's Bed & Breakfast)   ☎ (604) 535-1225, FAx (604) 535-0088
14778 Thrift Ave., White Rock, BC   V4B 2J5   E-mail: halls@lifestyler.com

From Vancouver & airport go south on Hwy 99 to White Rock Exit (#10) onto King George Hwy

99A. Turn right at 148St & 32Ave. Continue on 148St (becomes Oxford in White Rock) to Thrift Ave. Turn right.
$45-60S $55-75D   ▶ 6A
🏩 Full   🏠 Res., ocean view, patio, quiet   ■ 3D(main/ground level)   ⊨3Q,1P   ⛵1Sh.w.g.,1ensuite   ★TV, kitchenette, separate entrance, parking   🚳No smoking, no pets
🏃 Ocean and beach with promenade, shopping centers, arena, curling rink, on bus route to Vancouver & surrounding areas
🚗 Downtown Van., Island ferries, Peace Arch Park, US-border
🚐 Warm & friendly hospitality in a bright, comfortable and spacious home. ✓CC

Gray, Pat (Dorrington Bed & Breakfast)   ☎ (604) 535-4408
13851-19A Ave, South Surrey, BC   V4A 9M2   Fax (604) 535-4409

Phone for directions.
$65-80S $75-90D   (minimum 2 nights)   ▶ 4A
🏩 Full, homebaked   🏠 Res., 2-storey, small acreage, patio, quiet   ■ 2D (upstairs)   ⊨ 1D,1Q   ⛵ 1Private, 1ensuite
★LF,separate entrance, outdoor hot tub, gazebo, tennis court & ball machine & equipment, jaccuzzi tub in one guest room   🚳No pets, no smoking, not suitable for children
🏃 Parks & heritage walking trails amid tall cedars/firs/maples
🚗 White Rock beach (with sun-hot sandy flats, promenade, sidewalk cafes), specialty shops
🚐 Stately and comfortable home with themed guest rooms. Breakfast is served in the stunning "Hunt Salon" with its river rock fireplace and 12 ft ceilings, or on the patio with cushioned rattan chairs, overlooking the peaceful garden, tennis court and hot tub. Elegant picnic basket provided and directions to gourmet markets. There is a miniature Dachshund in residence. Visa ✓CC

Williams Lake   *(south of Prince George; see also Lac La Hache)*

Rowat, Marg & Jack (Rowat's Waterside B&B)   ☎ (250) 392-7395
1397 Borland Rd., Williams Lake, BC   V2G 1M3

From Hwy 97 turn south on Hwy 20 and east on MacKenzie Ave toward lake. Continue on Borland

Rd past Scout Island Entrance.
$55-60S $55-65D $20Add.person   ▶ 8-10A
🏩 Full, homebaked   🏠 Res., 2-storey, view from guest rooms, lakefront, deck, quiet   ■4D(upstairs)   ⊨2T,1D,2Q,1R
⛵4Private   ★ Air,F,TV in fireside guest lounge, off-street parking   🚳 No smoking, no pets, no children
🏃 Scout Island Nature Centre & Sanctuary, Stampede Grounds, mini golfing, restaurants, beach
🚗 Downtown area, golfing, arena, theatre, horseback riding, x-c skiing at Bull Mountain
🚐 Warm and friendly Cariboo Hospitality in new home beside Wildlife Reserve. Breakfast served on deck overlooking the Nature Centre and marsh or in the dining room. Hosts are long-time residents of Williams Lake, very knowledgeable of the area and like to share their love of the Cariboo. Ideal place for nature lovers and birdwatchers. Visa,MC ✓CC

Windermere
(s/of Golden; see also Invermere, Fairmont Hot Springs, Parson)

MacDonald, Scott & Astrid (Windermere Creek B&B)   ☎ & Fax (250) 342-0356
Box 409, Windermere, BC   V0B 2L0

Location: 1658 Windermere Loop Rd. Phone for directions.
$60-75D $90cabin   (plus tax)   ▶ 15
🍴 Full, homebaked   🏠 Rural, ranch-style, acreage, view, deck,
swimming pool, quiet   ■ 3D(in main house), plus 3 log cabins
🛏6Q,3P 🛁1Sh.w.g.,4private with jacuzzi tub ★2F, private
entrance, host quarters are separate, parking 🖐Designated
smoking area, not suitable for children, pets outside
🕴 Miles of developed walking trails on property, many view points
& picnic spots with benches, non-sleeping (ca1880) pioneer log cabin open to guests, creekside
hammocks, beaver ponds, golf course across road, daily nature walks
🚐 Windermere (artist corner & public beach), Invermere, 2 Hot Springs (Fairmont & Radium)
🏹 Log cabin, dating back to 1887, is very well laid out for B&B and situated on 107 forested acres
backing on to crown land and the Kootenay Park. Breakfast is served in guest breakfast nook. Relax
in the sunroom or on the deck and enjoy the peaceful surroundings & beautiful views. Honeymoon,
golf & romance packages available. Visa,MC ✏B&B

Winfield
(north of Kelowna; see also Oyama, Vernon)

MacPherson, Phyllis and Ian (MacPherson Vacation Cottage & B&B)   ☎ (250) 766-3038
14151 Carr's Landing Rd., Winfield, BC   V4V 1A7

Located in Carrs Landing. From Hwy 97 in Winfield turn west on Oceola (Lakewood Mall) and right
on Carrs Landing Rd. Proceed on winding road for 2.5 km toward and along Lake Okanagan to first

driveway on right after fire protection signs.
Summer: $45S $60D   Winter: $35S $50D   ▶ 8
🍴 Full, homebaked   🏠 Rural, chalet-style home, acreage, view,
swimming pool, patio, quiet   ■ 1D(ground level, plus large
cottage)   🛁Private   🛏1S,2D,1Q,2cot,crib ★ Fully equipped
kitchen and TV in cottage, separate entrance, parking 🖐 No pets
🕴 Wooded acreage, peach orchard (pick your own), beaches,
fishing, boat launch, several wineries (tours)
🚐 Silver Star and Big White Ski Resorts, golfing, restaurants, skido rentals, horseback riding
🏹 Spacious cedar Chalet home, nestled in Jack Pines and fruit trees with large decks. Breakfast
foods provided in cottage. Relax by the pool or on the decks and enjoy the spectacular view of
Okanagan Lake. Children welcome. ✏B&B

Winlaw
(north of Castlegar; see also Nelson, Procter)

Savinkoff, Wayne & Family (Slocan Valley B&B)   ☎ Phone & Fax (250) 226-7276
RR1, S13, C18, Winlaw, BC   V0G 2J0

Located at 6351 Slocan River Rd. Take Hwy 3A and Hwy 6 to Winlaw. Proceed west on Slocan

Bridge Rd and 2km north to Slocan River Rd.
$40S $50D $10Child/Add.person   ▶ 6
🍴Cont.   🏠 Rural, 3-storey, hillside, view, swimming pool, patio,
deck, quiet   ■ 2(main floor)   🛏 2T,1Q,2cots 🛁 2Private
★ LF,TV in suite, separate entrance, off-street parking, mountain
bikes for guests, guest quarters are separate 🖐 Smoking
oudoors, children min. age 10   〰 Russian, French
🕴 Mountain hikes, 5 major ski resorts, golfing, cafés
🚐 Hot Springs, Ghost towns (incl. Sandon), unique shops, historic sites, restaurants
🏹 Uniquely designed A-frame home with antiques and situated on secure gated acreage. Silver
service breakfast served in guest breakfast room. Relax in the library, by the tropical-themed pool
or fireplace; end the day with a jacuzzi under stars. Airport/bus pick-up available. Visa,MC ✏CC

Northwest Territories
and
Yukon

Travel Arctic
Yellowknife, Northwest Territories   X1A 2L9
Tourism Yukon (CG)
Box 2703, Whitehorse, Yukon   Y1A 2C6

toll-free 1-800-661-0788

(867) 667-5340

Fort Smith NT
(south of Yellowknife, near Alberta boder)

Calder, Linda & Bill Wade (Linda's B&B)
13 Cassette Cr., Box 955, Fort Smith, NT   X0E 0P0

☎ (867) 872-5787, Fax (867) 872-2166

$65S $85D   🍽 Meals   ► 4
🍳 Full, homebaked   🏠 Res., round log home, porch, screend-in
deck, quiet ■2D(main floor) ⊨2T,1Q 🛏1Sh.w.g. ★F,TV,LF,
off-street parking, guest quarters are separate ✋ No smoking
🏃 Downtown, museum, many wooded areas, Slave River
🚐 Wood Buffalo National Park with Pine Lake & Salt River and
hiking trails
🔫 Enjoy warm northern hospitality in uniquely designed round
log home with open concept living area, skylights and stone fireplace, located in beautiful town at
the gateway to Wood Buffalo National Park. Log guest rooms are equipped with cedar panelled
bathroom. Relax in the new wood burning sauna situated just outside the house. Access to
computer training classroom, multimedia production & recording studio. There are dogs and a cat.

Haines Junction YT
(west of Whitehorse)

Butterfield, Pam (Laughing Moose B&B)
Box 5432, 120 Alsek Cr., Haines Junction, YT   Y0B 1L0

☎ (867) 634-2335

Located 100 miles north of Whitehorse on the Alaska Highway.
$60S $70D $10Child   ► 2A,4Ch
🍳 Cont., homebaked 🏠 Res., 2-storey, view from guest rooms,
quiet ■ 1D,1F (upstairs) ⊨2D,1Q 🛏 1Sh.w.g. ★ TV in
guest room, guest kitchen, separate entrance, guest quarters are
separate, off-street parking ✋ No smoking, no pets
🏃 Hiking/walking trails with beautiful views of Auriol Mts &
Park, swimming pool, ice rink, stores, Park Interpretive Centre
🚐 Hiking/ski trails, lakes & rivers for fishing, canoeing, Kluane National Park
🔫 Comfortable home with a spectacular view, situated in the Gateway town to Kluane National
Park. Enjoy the growing collection of Yukon & Northern books. Visa. ✓B&B

Whitehorse YT

Pitzel, Carla & Garry Umbrich (Hawkins House)   ☎ (867) 668-7638, Fax (867) 668-7632
303 Hawkins St., Whitehorse, YT Y1A 1X5

Take Whitehorse City Centre Exit on Alaska Hwy. Follow 2nd or 4th Ave to Hawkins St.
$98.45S $116.65D $10Add.person high season: $129S $139D)   ► 8A

⬛ Full 🏠 Downtown, 2-storey, view
■4(upstairs) ⊢3Q,2T 🛏4Private ★LF, jaccuzi, guest
parlour, TV & balcony & fridge in guest rooms, parking 🚭 No
smoking, no pets ♥ ⁓French, German
🏃 Restaurants, swimming pool, museums, shopping, riverboat,
parks, waterfront, Gov't offices
🚗 Miles Canyon, ski & hiking trails, dog sledding, fishing,
canoeing
🐀 Lavish, spacious and bright Victorian home with high ceilings
located 2 blocks from the Yukon River. Breakfast house specialty is smoked salmon, moose sausage
& sourdough pastries. Young host family with 2 children. Hostess is a life-time Yukoner who
weaves and studies languages. High season: May 1-August 31). Visa,MC,Amex,Enroute

---

Yellowknife NT

Bryant, Wayne & Mary (the Bayside B&B)   ☎ (867) 920-4686, Fax (867) 920-7931
3505 McDonald Dr., Yellowknife, NT X1A 2H2   E-mail: becl@internorth.com

Take MacKenzie Hwy north to Yellowknife (1750 km from Edmonton).
$60-65 $70-75D $10Add.person (plus tax)   ► 4A
⬛ Full 🏠 Town-res., 3-storey, view from guest rooms, lake at back,
decks ■ 1S,2D (main & upper floor) ⊢ 3T,1D 🛏 1Sh.w.g.,
1ensuite ★ Air,TV in one guest room, woodstove, private entrances,
ample parking (temp.parking for touring available) 🚭 Designated
smoking areas, no pets, not suitable for children
🏃 Centre of town/retaurants/stores, boating/fishing/canoeing and x-c
skiing from back door, Outfitters establishment, cozy neighborhood pub
"Wildcat Cafe", city bus route   🚗 Airport
🐀 Modern home with panoramic view, located at the foot of a prominent
piece of Precambrian shield and distinct landmark called "The Rock" on the shore of Yellowknife
Bay near many original buildings from the early days. Watch bush planes on floats/skies flying to
points north, and fishing boats leaving for their daily catch of Great Slave Trout/pickerel/Northern
Pike or Whitefish. Relax in the Northern library with actifacts or on the upper or lower deck and
enjoy the harbour activities. Professionsal hosts have travelled worldwide and are longtime
residents of the North. Mooring facilities for 2 small planes and power boats available. Ideal place
for "Bush-Plane-Fly-In" travellers. Airport pick-up offered at certain hours on week days. There is a
Standard Poodle in residence. Visa

MacIntosh, Tessa (Blue Raven Bed & Breakfast)   ☎ (867) 873-6328, Fax (867) 920-4013
37 Otto Dr., Yellowknife, NT X1A 2T9

Take Franklin Ave (main street) toward "old town". Cross bridge to
Latham Island and Otto Dr. Look for blue house on the hill.
$60S $75D $10Child $15Add.person   ► 6
⬛ Cont.plus 🏠 3-storey, view, lakefront, deck, quiet ■2D,1F
(main, lower & upper levels) ⊢2T,2Q,1P,cot 🛏1Sh.w.g.,
1sh.w.h ★F,LF,TV in guest rooms, off-street parking 🚭No
smoking ⁓French
🚗 City Centre, museum, Legistlature, airport, beach
🏃 Charming historic restaurants, intriguing Northern souvenir outlets, bush plane float bases
🐀 Beautiful home perched atop Old Town's Latham Island on the shores of Great Slave Lake.
Relax by the fireplace or on the spacious deck amidst pleasant family atmosphere and enjoy the
view of lake and Northern Lights. Informative hosts (Lodge owner & photographer) are longtime
Northerners. There are 3 children in the host family. ⁓CC

Alberta

Alberta Tourism
10155-102nd St.
Edmonton, AB T5J 4L6

toll free 1-800-661-8888

As of January 1999 telephone numbers for all locations north of Red Deer and Stettler are scheduled to change from area code 403 to 780.

Airdrie

(north of Calgary; see also Cochrance, Carstairs)

DeWitt, Irene & Wendy Kelly (DeWitt's B&B)
RR1, Airdrie, AB T4B 2A3

☎ (403) 948-5356, Fax (403) 912-0788
E-mail: dewitbnb@cadvision.com

Located 10.75 km west of Hwy 2/Airdrie on Big Hill Springs Rd.
$65-75S $75-85D $10Add.person   (plus tax)   ► 6
⬛Full, homebaked 🏠Farm, ranch-style, view from guest rooms, patio, quiet, secluded ▪1D,2F
(main & lower level) ⊨2T,1D,1Q,2R 🛁2Sh.w.h.,1ensuite ★TV 🖐No smoking,no pets
🚗 Airdrie, City of Calgary, airport, Stampede Grounds, Spruce Meadows Equestrian Center,
Glenbow Museum, Heritage Park, Canmore, Rocky Mountain Foothills
🐎 Warm welcome and friendly hospitality in typical farm home with view of the Calgary skyline
and scenic Rocky Mountains. A great place to begin or end a visit to Western Canada. Relax on the
enclosed patio filled with fragrant flowers. Breakfast is served in guest breakfast room. There is a
dog in residence. Visa ⌐B&B

Whittaker, Carol & Earle (Big Springs B&B)
RR1, Airdrie, AB T4B 2A3

☎ (403) 948-5264, Fax (403) 948-5851
E-mail: whittake@cadvision.com

$90S $100D(June-Aug) $75S $85D(other) $125Ste $15Child/Add.person (plus taxes)   ► 6
From Airdrie travel 12km west on Hwy 567, south 2.8km and west 7km. From Cochrane travel
8km north on Hwy 22 and east 14.4km on Hwy 567.

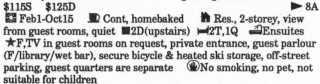

🍽 Full (Gourmet) 🏠 Rural, bungalow, hillside, acreage, deck,
patio, quiet, secluded ▪ 3D (ground level walk-out) ⊨1D,2Q
🛁3Ensuite ★ F,LF,TV in guest lounge, thermomasseur tub &
pedestral sinks, sep.entrance, sauna, piano, guest quarters are
separate 🖐 Smoking outside, no pets
🚶 From private nature path, take leisure walks on 35 pastoral
acres in hillside valley, exploring hillside rock outcroppings and
wild flowers, family photographing at the unusual rock formations
🚗 Calgary, Airport, Banff, Kananaskis Country, Banff-Canmore Corridor, Lake Louise
🐎 Luxury home with Victorian decor, surrounded by trees & lawns in private peaceful setting
overlooking the valley. Relax in the English Garden sitting room with furniture groupings arranged
so the garden atmosphere continues to the surrounding green of the outdoors. Silver service
gourmet breakfast is served in the dining room. Hosts are certified and experienced cooks. Ideal
place for first & last night stay for mountain vacations and insure quick & easy access to airport.
Romantic/corporate/weekend packages available. Visa ⌐B&B

Banff

(west of Calgary; see also Canmore)

House, Eleanor & Rick Kunelius (Eleanor's House B&B)
125 Kootenay Ave., Box 1553, Banff, AB T0L 0C0

☎ (403) 760-2457
Fax (403) 762-3852

In Banff, travel through town over bridge, turn left and follow signs to Hot Springs. Turn left on

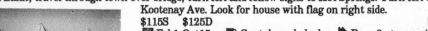

Kootenay Ave. Look for house with flag on right side.
$115S $125D   ► 8A
📅 Feb1-Oct15 ⬛ Cont, homebaked 🏠 Res., 2-storey, view
from guest rooms, quiet ▪2D(upstairs) ⊨2T,1Q 🛁Ensuites
★F,TV in guest rooms on request, private entrance, guest parlour
(F/library/wet bar), secure bicycle & heated ski storage, off-street
parking, guest quarters are separate 🖐No smoking, no pet, not
suitable for children
🚶 Banff Springs Hotel/spa/golf course, Banff Centre for Performing Arts, museums, Town Centre
🚗 Banff Upper Hot Springs Mineral Bath, Norquay/Lake Louise/Sunshine skiing
🐎 Newly renovated and enlarged mid-Century elegant home, situated within Banff Nat.Park
with mountain views from all windows and located in quiet prestigious neighbourhood. Breakfast is
served in large guest breakfast room. Former Nat.Park Warden & Hospitality/Travel worker, hosts
will provide personalized itineraries, to maximize important holiday time. Visa,MC ⌐CC

Riedinger, Herbert & Fannye (Haus Edelweiss) ☎ & Fax (403) 762-5660
120 Kootenay Ave., Banff, AB T0L 0C0 ☎(403) 762-3992

In town across Bow-River-Bridge, turn left after bridge and follow road to Upper Hot Springs. Look
for B&B on left, just before road make a right curve.
$90S $110D $25Child/Add.person (plus tax) ►6
◐ Full ♠ Res., back-split, view from guest rooms, deck, quiet ■2D (ground level)
⊨2T,1Q ⊒ 2Private ★ TV/indiv.heating in guest rooms, separate entrance, off-street
parking, host quarters are separate ⊛ No smoking, no pets ⌇ German, Spanish
☈ Banff Springs Hotel, Sulphur Hot Springs, Gondola & Sulphur Mt., Bow Falls, Indian Museum,
golf course, horseback riding, tennis, fishing, hiking, Mtn.biking, downtown, restaurants, shops
🚐 Cave & Basin (Birthplace of Banff & Banff Nat.Park), Lake Minnewanka, Lake Louise, Spiral
Tunnel, Great Divide, Canmore, Kananaskis Country, excellent downhill & x-c skiing
🖝 Charming Panabode house with gorgeous views across the valley to Banff Center.
Accommodations are very private and quiet. Long-time B&B hosts in new town location. Breakfast
is served in guest breakfast room. Relax on the private guest patio after an active day. ⌐B&B

Tarchuk, Clara (Cascade Court B&B) ☎ (403) 762-2956, Fax (403) 762-5653
2 Cascade Court, Box 883, Banff, AB T0L 0C0 E-mail: cascadecourtb&b@banff.net

Take Banff Ave over bridge, turn left, stay on Spray Ave, half a
block past YMCA and look for first court to right.
Summer:$95S $115D Winter:$50S $75D $20Add.person ►4
◐Full ♠Res., mountain views, patio,
quiet ■2D ⊨1Q,2T ⊒2Ensuite ★TV,LF,guest fridge, rumpus
room with pool table, use of phone, off-street parking ⊛No
smoking,no pets
☈ Banff Springs Hotel, Bow River Falls, Cascade Gardens, downtown, restaurants, golfing, tour
buses, x-c skiing/hiking trails
🚐 Major donwhill ski areas, Johnsons'Canyon, Lake Minewanka, Canmore, Kananaskis Country
🖝 Friendly western hopsitality in new executive home, located in a quiet court area. Relax in the
quiet library & sitting area and enjoy the beautiful panoramic mountain views. ⌐B&B

Bassano
(east of Calgary; see also Brooks, Duchess)

Bulger, Joel & Kathy (Bar B Guest House) ☎ (403) 641-4469
Box 126 Bassano, AB T0J 0B0

Located 12km west of Bassano and 6.5km east of the jct of Hwy 56.
$35-53 $42-60D $5-10Child (plus tax) ►6A,2Ch
◐ Full, homebaked ♠ Farm, 2-storey, older, view from guest
rooms, patio, quiet, isolated ■ 2D,1F(upstairs) ⊨2D,1Q,2R
⊒1Sh.w.g.,1ensuite ★F,TV, parking with plug-ins ⊛No
pets, smoking on open patio
🚐 Crawling Valley, Bassano Dam, Calgary, Drumheller,
Dinosaur Prov. Park, Tyrrell Museum, Sisika Blackfoot Reserve
🖝 Personally designed, unique, spacious (1950) farmhouse set in a large, well-treed, quiet yard
surrounded by prairie scenery and featuring decorative stonework & paintings by local artists. Host
is a historian specializing in ranching frontier history. There is a farm dog. Visa,MC ⌐B&B

Bentley
(north-west of Red Deer)

Christian, Evelyn (Ivy Chimney Bed & Breakfast)   ☎ (403) 748-2270
Box 588, Bentley, AB   T0C 0J0

Phone for directions.
$45S $65-90D $10Add.person   ►6A,2Ch
🌑Full 🏠Village, 2-storey, Cape-Cod-style, view, deck, quiet
■2D,1Ste (upstairs)   ⊨ 2S,2Q   ⊿ 1Sh.w.g.,
1ensuite   ★F,LF ⓌDesignated smoking area
🏃 Village center, 3 eating establishments
🚗 Bike path to beach, Gull Lake, Sylvan Lake (golfing, sailing, small ski hill with rope tow), shops, restaurants, theatres

📣 Quiet English country house, furnished with antiques situated at the edge of quaint Alberta village with pleasant quiet, well kept homes. Enjoy the wonderful view of the valley. Breakfast is served in the formal dining room with elegant setting. Expresso & Cappucino available, also evening tea by the log fire.

Blairmore
(west of Lethbridge near Alberta Borde; see also Coleman, Pincher Creek)

Matthews, Lyndsay (The Hearthside B&B)   ☎ (403) 562-7908, Fax (403) 562-8353
Box 1301, 12313-21Ave., Blairmore, AB   T0K 0E0   E-mail: hearthsi@telusplanet.net

From Hwy 3, take Blairmore Centre Exit & turn right on 21Ave.
$40S $55-65D $5-10Child   (plus tax)   ►8
🌑 Full   🏠 Village, 2-storey, hist., view, porch, quiet   ■2D,2F
(upstairs)   ⊨ 2T,2D,1K,2P   ⊿ 2Sh.w.g.   ★F,TV/piano in
guest lounge, private entrance, off-street & street parking
ⓌSmoking outside, no pets, children min. age 8
🏃 Pass Powder Keg Ski Hill, Crowsnest Pass Golf Club, public pool, tennis, shops, restaurants, churches, antiques, craft
🚗 Frank Slide Interp.Ctr, Castle Mountain, world class fly fishing, winter sports, hiking

📣 Heritage home, which has retained much of the original character and charm. Enjoy the picturesque beauty of the Crowsnest Pass, and experience the rich mining history of the area and relax in the cozy guest lounge by the fireplace. A full homecooked breakfast meal is served in special guest breakfast room. Visa,MC ✐CC

Brooks
(east of Calgary; see also Duchess, Bassano)

Conners, Judy & Fred (Conners' Country B&B & Bale)   ☎ (403) 378-4633,
Box 61, Patricia, AB   T0J 2K0   Fax (403) 378-4856

From Hwy 873 go east on Hwy 544 to 4-way stop and follow signs for Dinosaur Park and B&B.
$40S $50D $5-10Child $10Add.person $5Horse   🍽 Meals/Picnics   ►8A,3Ch

🌑 Full, homebaked   🏠 Farm, raised bungalow, view from guest
rooms, swimming pool, patio, porch, quiet, secluded   ■ 3F(main
& lower level)   ⊨ 3D,1Q,3P, playpen as crib   ⊿ 2Sh.w.g.
★LF,TV,wheel-chair access, snooker table, guest quarters are
separate   Ⓦ Smoking outside, pets welcome in insulated huts
🏃 Birdwatching (over 250 species nest in or pass through area),
explore the coulees of Little Sandhill Creek (also favorite camping
spot for Native tribes), berrypicking, hunting
🚗 Dinosaur Prov.Park (world heritage site - also bus tours for wheelchair), Tyrell Museum Field Stn, Brooks & District Museums, Aquaduct, golfing, rodeos, fishing at Lake Newell, Bassano Dam

📣 Warm welcome in comfortable, modern farm home fully wheelchair accessible. Enjoy the friendly hospitality and the large collection of Indian artifacts, fossils and dinosaur bones. Browse through the craft room on the premises, take a dip in the heated indoor swimming pool. Ask for brochure for visually impared. Cleaning and freezer facilities for hunters are available. ✐CC

Douglas, Doral and Ilene (The Douglas Country Inn) ☎ (403) 362-2873/Fax (403) 362-2100
Box 463, Brooks, AB T1R 1B5

Located 6.5 km north of the thriving town of Brooks on Hwy 873 and just off the TCH1.
$60S $77-99D   🍽 Meals (Corporate rate and Senior Citizens discounts available)   ► 14A

🍳 Full, homebaked   🏠 Rural, bungalow, quiet, separate facility
on acreage, isolated   ■7D (main level)   ⊨2T,5Q,1D
🛁7Private   ★Air,3F, soaker tub on deck in one guest room, TV
room and guest lounge area, separate entrance, freezer storage,
cleaning facilities for hunters   ✋No smoking, pets welcome in
heated kennels.
🏃 Hunting for pheasants, ducks, geese
🚗 Horticultural Research and Wildlife Centers, Dinosaur Prov.
Park (World Heritage site with guided tours to restricted areas) Brooks Aqueduct, fishing, golfing
🐾 "Rest easy in Casual Country Luxury" and enjoy a hearty country breakfast is served in the
solarium. There is a licensed dining room onsite with full menu. Visa,MC

Bruderheim

(north of Edmonton; see also Sherwood)

Kroker, Patricia (Gaeste-Haus Kroker)   ☎ (403) 796-3621, Fax (403) 796-3101
4511-48St, Box 202, Bruderheim, AB T0B 0S0   E-mail: pgkroker@compusmart.ab.ca

Phone for directions.
$45S $60D   ► 5
🍳Full   🏠Village, 2-storey, older, acreage, porch, veranda, quiet
■1S,2D(main & upper floor)   ⊨ 1S,1D,1Q   🛁1Sh.w.g.
★F(outdoor),LF,TV in guest room, separate entrance, off-street
parking   ✋ Designated smoking area, no pets
🚗 Elk Island National Park, observe wildlife, golfing, x-c skiing,
City of Edmonton, West Edmonton Mall, Muttart Conservatory
🐾 1927-built brick home turned into a charming Victorian guesthouse with the comfort of
yesterday and all the conveniences of today, surrounded by spacious lawn and garden. Breakfast is
served on fine china in the elegantly furnished dining room. Relax on the veranda, in the French
Provincial parlor or by the outdoor fireplace. Visa ✓B&B

Calgary

(see also Cochrane)

Brink-Scrimgeour, Helen G. (Brink Bed & Breakfast)   ☎ (403) 255-4523
79 Sinclair Cr SW, Calgary, AB T2W 0M1

Located in Southwest Calgary, Springwood off Elbow Dr. Phone for detailed directions.
$55-80S/D $5Extra(for 1 night stay)   🍽 Meals   ► 4
🍳Full,homebaked   🏠Res,split-level,patio,quiet   ■1D,1Ste
(main/upst.,incl. popular honeymoon suite)   ⊨1D,1Q
🛁1Sh.w.g.,1ensuite   ★F,LF,TV in guest room, barbeque
🏃 Direct bus route to Southland Station of LRT (Light Rail
Transit), walk & bike paths
🚗 South-Centre, Heritage Park, Fish Creek
🐾 Comfortable, country-style home with a relaxed atmosphere,
situated in quiet residential area. Congenial hostess is a retired
Nurse and a Teddy Bear Enthusiast. Breakfast served in dining room overlooking the large deck
and attractive landscaped back yard. Afternoon Tea and picnic baskets available. ✓B&B

Enyedvary, Thomas & Gabriella (Hot Tub Haven B&B)   ☎ (403) 281-8496
108 Woodglen Cr., SW, Calgary, AB   T2W 4G5   Fax (403) 258-1863

From Hwy 1, turn south on Hwy 2 and west on Anderson Rd. Proceed south on 24th St, west on
Woodview Dr and right 3 times to B&B.
$58S $75D $10Child   🍽 Meals   ► 2A,2Ch
🍲 Full, homebaked   🏠 Res.,sub., 2-storey, deck, quiet, secluded   ■ 1D(upstairs)   ⊨1Q,
2P(for children)   ⬛ 1Private   ★ F,LF, outdoor hot tub, off-street parking   ⓦ No pets,
children min. age 3   ᔆHungarianHungarian ~~Hungarian~~
🏃 Fish Creek Provincial Park with nature paths, horseback riding, x-c skiing, bus No56 to LTR
🚗 Downtown, Spruce Meadows, shopping centres, restaurants, Kananaskis Country (excellent
downhill/x-c skiing), Bragg Creek, Elbow Falls with spectacular view, Glenmore Reservoir & Park
🐾 Warm and friendly welcome in tastefully decorated home situated in quiet residential area.
Well travelled hosts may give daily piano entertainment upon request. After a hectic day of
travelling or sightseeing, relax in the hot tub on the deck. Breakfast is served in the dining room.
There is a dog in residence. ✍B&B

Jackson, Bill and Dorothy (The Robin's Nest)   ☎ (403) 931-3514
Box 2, S7, RR8, Calgary, AB   T2J 2T9

From Hwy 2 south of Calgary, go west on Hwy 22X for 16 km, turn left onto Hwy 22 and continue
for 6 km. Turn left and proceed east 1.6 km. Turn right and travel south 2.4 km to house on left.
$45-55S $60-85D   🍽 Meals (Picnic basket/backpack lunches)   ► 8A,4Ch

🍲 Choice, homebaked   🏠Farm, split-level, mountain view,
patio, quiet   ■2D plus 2 private luxurious new cedar log
cabins   ⊨4T,2Q,1D,2P   ⬛2Private, 1sh.w.g.   ★F,TV in
lounge, separate entrance, parking, extensive library, Indian
artifacts and butterfly collection   ⓦ No smoking
🏃 Interpretive nature trails through private wildlife sanctuary
with beaver ponds/nesting Canada geese), x-c ski/hiking trails
🚗 Golf courses, trail riding, fishing, Calgary
🐾 Environmentally conscious home with a collection of Western Heritage memorabilia and
pioneer farm machinery, surrounded by organic vegetable and flower gardens and located in the
beautiful Foothills. Pioneer farm family with a Saskatoon orchard, Scottish Highland cattle, Fjord
ponies and a small flock of sheep. Enjoy Rainbow Trout for breakfast (in season). ✍B&B

Knight, Kathryn & Ken (A Good Knight B&B)   ☎ (403) 270-7628, 1-800-261-4954
1728-7th Ave. NW, Calgary, AB   T2N 0Z4

From TCH1 (16Ave NW), turn south on 19th St NW, left on 8Ave NW
(bottom of hill), then right on 18St and left on 7Ave.
$60-85S $65-120D   ► 6
🍲 Full, homebaked(gourmet)   🏠 Res., 2-storey, porch, quiet   ■ 3D
(upstair)   ⊨3Q   ⬛ 2Ensuite,1private (1jacuzzi)   ★ F,LF, TV/coffee
maker in guest rooms, parking   ⓦ No smoking, no pets
🏃 L.R.T. station (Light Rail Transit to university, stadium, downtown and
stampede grounds), shopping, restaurants, parks
🚗 Stampede, Heritage Park, Spruce Meadows, Rocky Mountains
🐾 Newly-built, Victorian-style "In-Fill" home in quiet established
neighbourhood with custom pine and willow furnishings. Young hosts are
lifelong Calgarians and have a unique Teapot collection. Hostess is a Home-Ec teacher and serves
scrumptious and innovative breakfasts. There are two little girls in the family. Accommodation
includes a romantic suite with cathedral ceiling and private balcony. Visa ✍B&B

Larson, Valinda & Helmut Schoderbock (Inglewood B&B)   ☎ & Fax(403) 262-6570
1006-8thAve SE, Calgary, AB T2G 0M4

From TCH (16th Ave) go south on Centre St to Calgary Tower (9th Ave). Turn left (east) and proceed to 9th St, turn left again and continue 1 block to 8th Ave SE.

$60-100S $70-125D   ► 8A
🍴Full, homebaked 🏠Downtown, res, 2-storey, view from guest rooms, river at back, deck, quiet ■ 3D,1Ste(upst) ⊨4Q
🛏4Ensuite ★ TV, room keys, guest bike storage, off-street parking ⓦNo smoking, no pets ⚒ German
🕺 Calgary Stampede, Olympic Saddledome, Zoo, Calgary Tower & City Centre, Glenbow Museum, world class fly fishing on Bow River, bicycle/walking trails, light rail transit system (LRT)
🚗 Planetarium, Airport, Heritage Park, Olympic Park, City Look-Out
🐾 Young couple in large Victorian-style home built in 1992, situated next to the Bow River in very central location. Ideal place for scenic walks. Bring your own bike. ✏CC

Lloyd, Jonathon (Calgary Westways Guest House)   ☎ (403) 229-1758, Fax (403) 228-6265
216-25Ave SW, Calgary, AB T2S 0L1

$45-70S $60-100D $15Child $20Add.person ▣Meals (plus tax) (Deposit required)   ► 7
From downtown take McLeod Trail South access to 25Ave and continue past Elbow River to B&B on right side.

🍴Full(hearty) 🏠 Downtown, 2-storey, hist., porch, deck, quiet ■3 (upstairs) ⊨ 1D,2Q,R 🛏 3ensuite
★F,LF,KF,TV/phone & ceiling fans in guest rooms, hot tub on deck, street/off-street parking ⓦDesig.smoking area, children min. age 6, inquire about pets
🕺 Stampede Grounds, downtown, Lindsey Park Sports Arena, 4th Street restaurants, Mission Bridge Micro Brewery, LRT & busses
🚗 Kananaskis Nat.& Fish Creek Prov.Pks, Calgary Zoo, Calaway Pk, Olympic Pk, Int.Airport
🐾 1914-built Heritage home with original features & leaded glass windows, situated in the South West quadrant of the city, with elaborate new deco on the outside. Host has been in the hospitality business for over 20 years. Off-season & long-stay rates available. Visa,MC,Amex ✏B&B

MacNichol, Robin , L.J. (Bob)   ☎ (403) 243-0362
1639 Altadore Ave SW, Calgary, AB T2T 2P8

Located in the south-west part of the City. Phone for directions.
$30S $50D $10Child   ▣ Meals   ► 3
🍴Choice 🏠Res., older, quiet ■1D,1S (upst) ⊨1S,1D
🛏1Sh.w.h. ★Air,F,TV,KF,LF, parking ⓦNo smoking
🕺 Bus stop (15 min to downtown city center)
🐾 Quiet neighbourhood in residential area. There is a dog in the house. Retired, congenial and active host (formerly from Australia) enjoys showing off the beautiful city and sights to his visitors. House specialty is a delicious Australian omelet for breakfast.

McLeod, Karen (Sweet Dreams & Scones Bed & Breakfast)   ☎ & Fax (403) 289-7004
2443 Uxbridge Drive NW, Calgary, AB   T2N 3Z8

$65-75S $75-100D $10-15Child $120-160F/Ste $15Add.person   ► 8

From Hwy 1 (16th Ave NW), turn north onto Uxbridge Drive.
🍲 Homebaked (gourmet)   🏠 Res., 2-storey   ■3D,1Ste
(upstairs)   ⊨ 2T,1D,2Q,1K(four-poster)   ⌐1Private,
3ensuite   ★ F,TV,LF, off-street parking   ⓌNo smoking,
children min. age 3
🏃 University of Calgary, Olympic Skating Oval, Foothills
Hospital, restaurants, city bus #9 (2 blocks)
🚗 Downtown, LRT(Light Rail Transit), Calgary Zoo, Olympic Pk

☛ Spacious, elegant, residential home, "as close to country in the city as one can find anywhere",
full of antiques & quilts ("a feast for the senses"). Hosts are avid antique collectors, skiers and very
knowledgeable about the City. House specialty is breakfast scones. Relax in the spacious beautiful
backyard among the gardens and tall trees. Women's Get-aways can be arranged. ✍B&B

Moss, Hazel & Peter (the Cranberry Tree B&B)   ☎ & Fax (403) 225-1282
9928 Maplecreek Dr.SE, Calgary, AB   T2J 1T6

Phone for directions. Located 3 blocks from North/South Freeway.
$50-60S $55-65D $15child   ► 4A,1Ch
🍲 Full, homebaked   🏠 Res., raised bungalow, deck, quiet
■2D (main & lower level)   ⊨ 2Q,1cot   ⌐ 2Sh.w.h.
★Air,LF,F,TV, street parking   ⓌSmoking outside, no pets
🏃 Bus route to LRT and downtown
🚗 Downtown, Stampede Grounds, Calgary Zoo, Heritage Park,
Spruce Meadows, Kananaskis Country

☛ Friendly hosts in cheerful family surroundings located in established neighbourhood with easy
access to main highways. There is a dog called "Buffy" in residence.

Pantel, Evelyn (Evelyn's Bed & Breakfast)   ☎ (403) 286-5979
107 Silverbrook Rd NW, Calgary, AB   T3B 3H9

$30-35S $50-60D $10Child $15Add.person 🍴Meals (Off season rates avail)   ► 2A,2Ch

Phone for directions. Will mail map and meet guests if necessary.
🍲 Full (unique)   🏠 Res., bungalow, patio, quiet   ■3D(main &
lower floor)   ⊨2D,1Q   ⌐1ensuite, 1private, 1sh.w.h.
★KF,LF,TV in guest room, pool table, bar, parking   ⓌNo
pets   〰some French
🏃 Bow River with adjoining park & mountain view,
bicycle/walking path, bus service
🚗 LRT to downtown, University of Calgary, Olympic Park

☛ Country-style home, close to spectacular Rocky mountains, situated on a quiet pretty
residential street on the western side of the city fringe with quick access to Banff Hwy. ✍B&B

Pockar, Anna (Mountain View B&B)   ☎ (403) 246-4838
Box 6, S24, RR12, Calgary, AB   T3E 6W3

Located approximately 20km west of the City Center, 5km south of TCH. Phone for directions.
$60S $90D $15Add.person   ► 6A,4Ch
🍲 Full   🏠 Rural, bungalow, acreage, view, indoor swimming
pool, tennis court, patio, quiet   ■2(ground level)   ⊨ 3Q   ⌐
1Ensuite, 1sh.w.h.   ★ TV,F, games room   ⓌNo smoking
〰Italian
☛ Warm and friendly hospitality in hillside home near the Rocky
Mountain Foothills. Enjoy the magnificent views and relax in the
guest lounge around the pool and hot tub. ✍B&B

Romanzin, Valerie & Gerry (In Meadow Splender B&B)(pending) ☎ & Fax (403) 288-6902
Box 81, S20, RR2, Calgary, AB   T2P 2G5   E-mail: inmeadow@cadvision.com

Phone for directions.
$60S $75D   📷 Meals   (Reservations recommended)   ► 4
🍴 Full, homebaked   🏠 Rural, raised bungalow, acreage, view
from guest rooms, quiet   ■ 1D,1Ste (ground level)   🛏 2Q
🛁1Private,1ensuite   ★TV in great room, F/fridge & microwave
in guest library, separate entrance, guest quarters are separate
🚭No smoking   ～some French
🚶 Bow River, fishing, horseback riding, golfing & driving range,
country walks, small aircraft flights, local artisan crafts, landscaped garden
🚗 Calgary, Zoo, Olympic Venues, Western Heritage Centre, Bragg Creek & Cochrane village
shops, whitewater rafting, Kananaskis Country, Canmore, Banff, skiing, hiking
🐾 Bright & comfortable home, tastefully decorated with fine furniture and Western art and
country ambiance. Crafts & wares of local artisans are displayed throughout the house and are
available for purchase as keepsakes of a warm, comfortable & peaceful stay. Enjoy the tranquil
landscape of rural life and spectacular panoramic view of the Canadian Rocky Mountains. Breakfast
is served in guest dining area. There is a cat in residence. Visa,MC ✓B&B

Russell, Elva B. (Russell's Bed & Breakfast)   ☎ (403) 249-8675
2806 Linden Dr SW, Calgary, Alta   T3E 6C2

Located just north of Glenmore Reservoir/Glenmore Park and 8 blocks south of Crowchild Trail

and Glenmore intersection southwest.
$40-45S $70-75D   (winter rates available)   ► 7
🍴 Choice   🏠Res., 2-storey, quiet, covered or open patio
■4(main and upper floor)   🛏1S,4T,1D   🛁1Private,1sh.w.h.
★F,TV,LF, parking   🚭No pets, restr.smoking, child min. age 6
🚶 Glenmore Reservoir & Park, bus stops, restaurants, shopping
🚗 Downtown, Performing Arts Center, Glenbow Museum,
Heritage & Prehistoric Parks, Calgary Zoo, Kananaskis Country
🐾 Comfortable & spacious executive home, tastefully decorated, situated in quiet residential
area. Informed hosts can help with travel plans, tours, directions in this beautiful busy city and
interesting, picturesque areas nearby. Enjoy gracious Western hospitality. ✓CC

Trevitt, Bruce & Debbie (The Crescent B&B)   ☎ (403) 287-0654, Fax (403) 287-8009
635 Crescent Blvd. SW, Calgary, AB   T2S 1L1   E-mail: btrevitt@cadvision.com

Phone for directions.   ► 6A,2Ch
$75-125(S/D) $140-160(2couples) $10Child   📷 Meals
🍴Full(3-course gourmet)   🏠Sub, bungalow, deck, quiet   ■2Stes
(ground level)   🛏3Q   🛁2Ensuite   ★TV,LF,full kitchen in one
suite, separate entrances, private patios, jaccuzzi, fridges, sitting
areas, off-street parking   🚭No smoking, no pets
🚶 Stanley Park & Elbow River walkways, public swimming &
wading pools, River bikepaths, children's playground
🚗 Downtown, fashionable restaurants and shops, Calgary Stampede
🐾 Very private, contemporary accommodation in bright and spacious, luxury home located in a
quiet established area near heart of the City's Elbow River Valley and it's beautiful parks and
walkways. Ideal for couples/families. There are school children in the family. ✓B&B

Turgeon, Eileen and Denis (Turgeon's Bed & Breakfast - 1988)   ☎ (403) 288-0494
4903 Viceroy Dr NW, Calgary, AB   T3A 0V2   Fax (403) 286-9638

Situated between TCH 1 and Hwy 1A. Please call for directions.
$35S $55D   🍽 Meals   ► 4
🍴Full, homebaked   🏠Res., patio, bungalow, quiet   ■2D (main and lower level)   ⊨2T,1Q   ⊒2Sh.w.h.   ★Air,TV,F,LF, beverage station, street parking   🚫No pets, restricted smoking, children only by special request   ⌇French
🚶 Quiet park at end of street, three large shopping centres, bus line connecting with LRT (Light Rapid Transit) to downtown
🚐 Canada Olympic Park, Heritage Park, Calgary Zoo, Glenbow Museum, Kananaskis Country
🐾 Home is located in quiet north-west residential area. Warm and friendly Western Hospitality. Relax on the pleasant large bricked patio and enjoy homemade muffins, bread, scones and jams. Hosts have been welcoming guests for 10 years. There is a dog in residence. Tourist brochures & maps available. ✍B&B

Ullrich, Frank & Glenys (Evergreen on Fish Creek Park B&B)   ☎ (403) 256-2237,
1609 Evergreen Hill SW., Calgary, AB   T2Y 3A9   Fax (403 256-5676

Directions will be faxed.
$60S $75D   ► 4A,2Ch
🍲 Full, homebaked   🏠 Sub., new 2-storey walkout, view from guest rooms, patio, deck   ■ 3D(upper and walkout level)   ⊨ 2T(extra long),2Q   ⊒1Private, 1sh.w.g.   ★ F,TV,private entrance, off-street & street parking   🚫 Designated smoking are, no pets   ⌇ German
🚶 Largest urban (Prov) park in NA (walking paths, birdwatching, cycling), bus connecting to LRT for downtown
🚐 Downtown Calgary, Spruce Meadows, Badlands, Head-Smashed-in Buffalo-Jump, Canmore, Foothills of Rocky Mountains
🐾 Spacious, elegant home with contemporary decor and city view.
Enjoy the casual atmosphere. Well travelled hosts enjoy sharing treasures of the area with their guests. There is a cat in residence. Visa,MC ✍B&B

West-Daradich, Margaret & Philip (Riverpark Bed & Breakfast)   ☎ (403) 257-0757
86 Mountain Park Dr SE, Calgary, AB   T2Z 1S1

Phone for directions.
$60-65D   ► 2A
🍲 Full, homebaked   🏠 Res., 2-storey, view from guest rooms, patio, deck, quiet   ■ 1D (upstairs)   ⊨1Q   ⊒ Private
★TV in guest room, private sitting room, off-street parking
🚫No smoking, no pets, no children
🚶 Walking, cycling, lovely nature trails along the river with great abundance of Canada Geese, bus stop (#93) to Light Rail Transit
🚐 Downtown, Spruce Meadows Equestrian Center, Stampede Grounds, Canada Olympic Park
🐾 Spacious modern home with grounds bordering on park. Congenial hosts know the area well.

Wood, Dori (Lions Park Bed & Breakfast)
1331-15 St NW, Calgary, AB T2N 2B7

☎ (403) 282-2728, Fax (403) 289-3485
1-800-475-7262

Phone for directions. Located 2 block south from Trans Canada Hwy.

$50-65S $65-95D $10Add.person   ► 7
🍲 Full   🏠 Downtown, res., 2-storey, view   ■1D,1F(upstairs),
plus 1Ste   ⊨3S,1D,1K,1Q   ⌂1Private, 2ensuite   ★F,LF,TV
in guest living room, sep entrance, air filter, parking   🐾No pets,
restricted smoking
🧍 Jubilee Auditorium, S.A.I.T., University of Calgary , North Hill
Shopping Centre, Riley & Conf.Parks, Bus & Light Rail Train
Systems, Kensington
🚗 Kensington, Canada Olympic Park, Bragg Creek, Canmore, Kananaskis, Calgary Zoo, airport,
Calaway & Heritage Parks, Spruce Meadows, Banff
☛ Spacious executive home in central location. Enjoy a nutritious breakfast. Visa,MC ✒B&B

Zorn, Barb & Gary (Hilltop Ranch B&B)
Box 54, Priddis, AB T0L 1W0

☎ 1-800-801-0451

Located 25km south-west of Calgary on Hwy 22X.
$45-60S $65-80D $15Child $20Add.person   ► 8
🍲 Full, homebaked   🏠 Rural, bungalow, hillside, acreage, view,
patio, deck, quiet, secluded   ■ 2D,1F(ground level)
⊨2S,1D,2Q   ⌂2Ensuite,1private   ★ F,TV,KF,LF, guest
lounge, guest quarters are separate   🐾 Designated smoking area,
children min. age 4
🧍 Hiking, golfing, wildlife & bird watching
🚗 Banff, Kananaskis Recreation area & Park, Spruce Meadows, Calgary downtown, Stampede
☛ Warm welcome and Western hospitality in beautiful park-like ranch setting, with view of the
Rocky Mountains. Enjoy a hearty ranch breakfast in the morning and romantic walks under stars
and moon in the evening. Carriage & sleigh rides available. There is a Boxer dog and a cat in
residence. Horse stabling available in eight new box stalls with wood floors and there is room to
exercise horses. Visa,Amex ✒B&B

Camrose

(south-east of Edmonton; see also Wetaskiwin, Ripley)

Taylor, Elaine & David (College Lane B&B)
4602-49 St., Camrose, AB T4V 1M5

☎ (403) 672-2882
E-mail: drtent@telusplanet.net

$50-60S $65-75D $10Add.person   🍴Meals   (plus tax)   ► 6
From Hwy13(48Ave),south on 50St,east on 47Ave,south on 49St.
🍲 Full   🏠 Downtown, hist., porch, quiet   ■ 2D,1Ste(upst)
⊨2D,1Q   ⌂ 1Private, 2,ensuite   ★ TV,LF,separate entrance,
off-street parking   🐾No smoking, no pets
🧍 paved hiking trails (15km), x-c ski trails, Augustana University
College, shopping, Camrose Historical Museum
🚗 Edmonton, museums (Ukrainian Heritage, Reynolds, Donalda
Antique Lamps), Steam Train rides, world's smallest airport
☛ Fully renovated heritage (1912) home furnished with antiques and situated on large treed lot
bordering the College Campus. Well travelled hosts enjoy exchanging travel stories with guests
from around the world. Experience a small city in the unique parkland of central Alberta and learn
about the area pioneers. Breakfast is served in special guest breakfast room. Visa

Canmore
(west of Calgary; see also Banff)

Charczuk, Elizabeth (Welcome to our Home B&B)   ☎ (403) 678-3221, Fax (403) 678-0770
332 Canyon Close, Canmore, AB   T1W 1H4   E-mail: Eliz@expertcanmore.net

From Hwy 1A follow signs to Exshaw. Turn left onto Elk Run and proceed 0.5km to Lady
McDonald, follow to first right turn (Canyon Close).

$60S $85D $10Child $15Add.person   ▶ 2A,2Ch
🍽 Full   🏠 Res., 3-storey, hill-side, view from guest room, deck,
quiet   ■ 1Ste (ground level)   ⊨1Q,1P   🛏 1Ensuite
★KF,LF, ceiling fans, private entrance, off-street parking,
barbeque   🚭 No smoking, children min age 6   ⚬ Polish
🚶 Mountain walks/hikes, birdwatching, golfing, fishing, skating
🚗 Restaurants, galleries, gift shops, 5 major Ski Resorts, World
Class Golf Courses, Kananaskis Country, Banff & Banff Nat.Park
📢 Spacious mountain home with luxurious suite, including full kitchen and private garden
entrance, located in quiet north residential area. Relax on the deck and enjoy the beautiful flower
garden and panoramic mountain and valley views. There are young teenagers in the host family and
a dog in residence. ✓B&B

Ciaramidaro, Carmelo & Anneke (Stella-Alpina B&B)   ☎ & Fax (403) 678-2119
Box 2191, 1009-9th Ave, Canmore, AB   T0L 0M0   E-mail: martino@agt.net

Phone for directions.
$60S $75D $130F   ▶ 4A,2Ch
🍽Full   🏠Downtown, split-level, view from guest rooms,quiet
■1Ste,1F (lower level)   ⊨2S,2Q   🛏 1Private, 1sh.w.g.
★F,LF,TV in guest rooms, off-street parking, guest area is
separate, x-c ski waxing facility, outdoor fireplace   🚬Designated
smoking area   ⚬Italian/Dutch/German/French/Spanish
🚶 Bow River with great walking trails, excellent fishing & hiking
& mountain biking, public tennis court, downtown Canmore, excellent restaurants, art galleries
🚗 Banff, Banff National Park, Lake Louise, several major ski resorts, Nordic Ski Centre
📢 Quiet home with rustic interior, spruce woodwork throughout, located on a cul-de-sac across
from a wooded reserve. Hosts have a wealth of international hospitality experience, including on
cruise ships world-wide, and are very knowledgeable about the area's flora and fauna. Special
gourmet breakfast includes smoked salmon, wild mushroom/and or herb omelette with herbs from
own garden. There is a dog and a cat in residence. Children welcome. Visa, MC ✓B&B

Claxton, Kathy (Wedgewood Mountain Inn & B&B)   ☎(403)678-4494, Fax 5017
1004 Larch Place, Canmore, AB   T1W 1S7   E-mail: wedge@expertcanmore.net,

Follow Hwy 1A to 17St (turn at Boston Pizza - south-west). 17St becomes Larch Dr. At 700 block
Larch Place on right, turn left into 1000 block Larch Place and look for large cedar home (#1004).

$75S $85-125D $15Child/Add.person   ▶ 8
🍽 Full, homebaked   🏠 Res., Alpine-style, 2-storey, view from guest
rooms, deck, quiet   ■1D,1Ste,1F(upper & high lower level)   ⊨2T,2Q,1K
🛏3Private, 1jaccuzzi   ★F, cozy guest loft with TV,VCR & library,
off-street parking   🚬Designated smoking area, no pets
🚶 Network of walking and x-c ski trails at backdoor, Bow River & Forest
Reserve adjacent to backyard
🚗Kananaskis Country, Banff, Lake Louise, downhill resorts, Calgary
📢 Large country home - a unique warm & comfortable Rockie Mountain
hideaway - with relaxing atmosphere & romantic & elegant ambiance, located
in popular year-round resort town. Hostess is a quilter and her work is
displayed throughout the house. Relax on the deck or in the loft after a busy
day. Ideal place for honeymoon, family gatherings and special occasions.
There are 2 cats & a dog. Visa,MC ✓B&B

Cole, Alan & Sharon (McNeill Heritage Inn)　　　　☎ & Fax (403) 678-4884
500 Three Sisters Dr., Canmore, AB　T1W 2P3

From TCH travel through Canmore on 8th (Main) St.Turn left on 8th Ave, crossing the Bow River

on Rundle Dr., then right on Three Sisters Dr.
$75S　$85-145D　$25Add.person　(plus tax)　　　► 13
🍲 Full, homebaked (self-serve)　🏠 Village, 2-storey, hist., acreage,
view, riverfront, porch, quiet, secluded　■ 5D,1Ste (main & upper
level)　🛏1T,1D,5Q,1K,2R　🛁 6Private　★F,TV room, separate
entrance, off-street parking, guest quarters are separate　🖐 No
smoking, no pets, not suitable for children
🕴 X-c skiing/hiking from back door, fishing, golfing, restaurants
🚐 Banff, Kananaskis Country, Lake Louise, Calgary
🖐 Warm and friendly hospitality in historic home situated on the Bow River. Relax on the
veranda or by the cozy fireplace. Hosts are outdoor recreation oriented and can advise on good
places for activities. Breakfast is served in the old fashioned dining room.Visa,MC ⤶B&B

Dorsey, Marilyn & Dwayne (Alpine Quest Bed & Breakfast)　　　☎ & Fax (403) 678-2284
25 Ridge Rd., Canmore, AB　T1W 1G5

$65S　$75-95D　$10Child/Add.person　　　　► 5

Located at 25 Ridge Rd. Take Hwy 1A into Canmore, north on
Benchlands Trail, left on Canyon Rd, right on Ridge Rd.
🍲Full, homebaked　🏠Res.,bi-level,view from guest rooms,
quiet ■1D,1F(main floor)　🛏2T,1Q,1P 🛁1Sh.w.g.(private can be
arranged)　★F, host quarters are separate, off-street
parking 🖐No smoking, no pets, children min. age 10
🕴 Town of Canmore, shops, restaurants, galleries, hiking/biking,
canyon trails & mountain/sports climbing start at door
🚐 Banff Nat.Park, Kananaskis Ctry, Lake Louise, Nordic Centre (Winter Olympic site)
🖐 Spacious new mountain home with cathedral ceiling, feature fireplace and large windows with
wilderness mountain views. Enjoy the library of local history & mountaineering literature in the
spacious lounge. Young host family loves the outdoors & have special interest in hiking, x-c skiing,
photography, mountaineering, & local history. "Come by the hills to the land where legend
remains". Special diets available on request. Visa,MC

Gailus, Andrea & Fred (Cougar Canyon Bed & Breakfast)　　　☎ & Fax (403) 678-6636
3 Canyon Rd., Canmore, AB　T1W 1G3　　　　　　1-800-289-9731

Location: 3 Canyon Rd. From TCH1 exit at Hwy 1A Canmore & Exshaw. Follow Hwy 1A toward
Exshaw, turn left at Elk Run Blvd. Proceed to Canyon Rd and turn right. Look for house on left.

$75-95S/D　(plus tax)　　　　► 4
🍲Full(Gourmet)　🏠Res., 2-storey, view, patio, quiet, back creek
■2(upper level)　🛏 2T,1Q　🛁 2Ensuite　★F,TV/VCR,
library in guest loft　🖐No smoking, no pets　⤳German
🕴 Cougar Canyon hiking trail at back door
🚐 Town centre, shopping, casual/fine dining, galleries, Bow
River trout fishing, Mordic Center downhill/x-c skiing, mountain
biking, Banff Nat.Park, Sulphur Hot Springs, Kananaskis
🖐 Modern home especially designed for B&B, with beautiful mountain views, situated on the
north side of town. Tea & coffee are provided in the cozy guest loft. Share the fireplace at breakfast
around the dining room table. Well travelled family enjoys skiing & hiking. Calgary airport pick-up
available. There are resident pets. Visa,MC ⤶B&B

Guy, Frank (Spring Creek Bed & Breakfast)   ☎ & Fax (403) 678-6726
1002-3rd Ave., Canmore, Alta   T1W 2J8

Located on corner of 1st St and 3rd Ave.
$75-95D   (minimum booking 2 nights)   ▶ 6
🍽 Choice   🏠Res., view, patio, quiet, isolated   ▣2D(upstairs)
🛏2Q,2P   🛁 2Private   ★TV in guest sitting room, parking
🖐No pets, no smoking, no children
🏃 Bow River, dining, golfing, hiking, skiing, shops, watch wildlife
graze nearby, white water rafting, helicopter tours

🚐 Calgary, Banff, Chair-lift to Sulphour Spring, Lake Louise, Kananaskis Country, skiing, hiking,
📣 Bright, spacious home located on Spring Creek and nestled under picturesque Three Sisters
Mountain in the Bow Valley. Enjoy the fresh air and pure water and the beautiful mountain views
from guest room windows. Site of the 1988 Winter Olympics and Canmore Nordic Center. ✔CC

Hunt, Garry (Fjellhytten Bed & Breakfast)   ☎ (403) 678-4932
805 Larch Place, Canmore AB   T1W 1S4

Location: 805 Larch Place. Entering Canmore follow 17th St which becomes Larch Drive. Continue
past cul-de-sacs on right side of road starting with "100 Larch Place" and pass "Larch Close"
cul-de-sac on right to "800 Larch Place" cul-de-sac. Turn right.

$55-65D   (minimum booking 2 nights)   ▶ 5
🍽Full(nutrit.& energizing) 🏠 Res.,Chalet-type, panoramic
mountain views, patio, quiet   ▣2D(upstairs)   🛏1S,2T,1Q
🛁2Private   ★ TV,F, parking, private deck, sauna, extensive
library 🖐No smoking, no pets ∿French
🏃 Golf course, Recreation Centre, swimming pool, walkway and
bicycle path, Bow River, town of Canmore
🚐 Canmore Nordic Centre, hiking/cross-country ski trails,
downhill skiing, rock climbing, scuba diving, canoe and kayaking, fishing, Helicopter Tours
📣 Fjellhytten is Norwegian and means "Mountain Holiday Home". Rustic and unique, open-plan
home with post & beam construction and a wood stove backed by a floor to ceiling rock wall. There
are sheep/goat skins everywhere. Active out-door host (qualified x-c ski instructer and guide) will
gladly conduct tours. Summer hiking and winter x-c ski packages available.

Johnson, Jan & Bob (Moose Mountain Lodge B&B)   ☎ & Fax (403) 678-6469
701-2nd St., Canmore, AB   T1W 2K3

From TCH exit into Canmore. Proceed on 8th St to corner of 2nd St/6th Ave.
$85-120S/D $20Add.person   (children & longer-stay rates available)   ▶ 4

🍽 Self-serve   🏠 Downtown, 3-storey, view from guest rooms,
deck, quiet   ▣ 1D,1Ste (main & street level)   🛏 1Q,1K,1P
🛁 2Private   ★ F,KF,TV in guest rooms, ceiling fans, separate
entrance, off-street parking, guest quarters are separate   🖐 No
smoking, no pets, children min. age 12   ∿ some French
🏃 Bow River/hiking/walking/biking trails, quaint downtown area
(with shops, galleries restaurants, museums), x-c ski trails, golf
course, direct Airporter service

🚐 Five major downhill Ski Resorts, Banff, Kananaskis Country, 3 Nat.Parks, Lake Louise
📣 Bright log-style home with beautiful decor, enchanting surroundings, comfort, privacy and
panoramic mountain views, situated by the river in popular all year-round resort town. A perfect
place for longer stays. Breakfast is served in special guest breakfast room. There is a cat.✔B&B

Kamenka, Pat & Ann (Hidden Falls B&B) ☎ (403) 678-3604, Fax 6594
Box 8073, Canmore, AB   T1W 2T8   E-mail: info@hiddenfalls.com, 1888-678-3600

From Hwy 1 proceed to downtown (Main St). Turn left at 8th Ave and follow Nordic Centre signs. Look for house on right (sign). Location: 107 Three Sisters Dr..
$110S/D   (Special rates for 3nights min.)   ► 8
🍳 Full   🏠 Res., 3-storey, view from guest rooms, ravine at back, deck, quiet, secluded   ■4D(upstairs)   ⊨2T,3Q   ⊒4Ensuite
★F,TV in guest lounge, separate entrance, two guest rooms with balconies, outdoor firepit, off-street parking   🖐No smoking, no pets, children min. age 12
🚗 Banff, Kananaskis Country, Lake Louise, Calgary
🚶 Olympic Nordic Centre, Beaver dam, hiking/cycling and x-c ski trails, fishing, waterfall
📣 New, bright large home in unique setting with park-like privacy. Enjoy the stunning views and and soothing sound of the fal'ls at night. Hosts are longtime area residents and gladly help with sightseeing & activity plans. Rooms are named after area mountains. Relax on the lage property by the little brook or by the old barn - a painter's delight. Breakfast is served in special guest breakfast room. Spectacular scenery & frequent wildlife visits make this an ideal place for photography buffs.

Kranz, Astrid and Erhard (Astrid's B&B)   ☎ (403) 678-4718
1002-14th St., Canmore, AB   T1W 1V5

Phone for directions.
$50S $55-60D $10Child $15Add.person   ► 6
🍳 Choice, homebaked   🏠 Res., village, Alpine-style, balcony, view, patio   ■ 2   ⊨2S,1D,1Q   ⊒1Sh.w.g.   ★F,guest living room, parking   🖐No smoking, no pets   ᜌGerman
🚶 Bow River, excellent fishing, hiking trails, Nordic Center, gift shops, restaurants, golfing
🚗 Spray Lakes, Kananaskis Country, Calgary, Banff, L.Louise
📣 Beautiful, alpine chalet home featuring woodwork decorated with tole painting on cabinets and doors and with post-beam structure evident throughout its interior. Enjoy the magnificient mountain view. Excellent location for summer and winter activities. ↙CC

Marusaik, Shirley & Brian (A Shady Lane B&B)   ☎ (403) 678-5239
121 Rundle Plant Lane, Canmore, AB   T1W 2L6   E-mail: bmarusai@banff.net

From Hwy 1 turn onto 1A and follow signs to Nordic Centre. Proceed to 8thAve, cross Bow River bridge. Turn right on Rundle Plant Lane (gravel access).
$76-98D $20Add.person   ► 2
🍳 Homebaked   🏠 Res, 2storey, view   ■ 1D   ⊨ 1Q   ⊒ Private   🖐 No smoking, no pets, ask about children
🚶 Fishing in river, walking into town, white-water rafting
📣 New home with beautiful mountain views in quiet lane close to downtown. There is an artist in residence. Water color workshops can be arranged. Hosts are knowledgeable about hiking in the area and have many hiking books available to browse through.

Mazzucchi, Albert and Connie (Bird's Nest)   ☎ (403) 678-2294
1005-15th Street, Canmore, Alberta   T1W 1V3

Canmore is located 22 km east of Banff. Phone for directions.
$65D $15Add.person   ► 3
🍳Choice, homebaked   🏠Res., bi-level, view, patio, quiet
■1(lower level)   ⊨1S,1Q   ⊒ Private   ★TV,parking   🖐No pets, no smoking, child min age 8   ᜌItalian, German
🚶 Nordic Centre, museum, hiking trails, excellent dining facilities
🚗 Banff, Lake Louise, 5 major ski resorts, 200km x-c skitrails
📣 Friendly atmosphere in home located in new area abundant with recreational facilities and excellent services and circled by the rugged Rockies. Enjoy a hearty breakfast and watch the many different species of birds hosts love to feed.

Middleton, John & Joan (By The Brook B&B) ☎ (403) 678-4566, Fax (403) 678-4199
4 Birchwood Place, Canmore, AB T1W 1P9   E-mail: jmiddle@riscan.com

Phone for directions.
$85S $95D $10Add.person (Off-season rates available) ▶ 7A
🍴 Full, homebaked 🏠 Res., 3-storey, view from guest rooms,
quiet, 2 decks ■ 2F(main floor) ⊨ 1S,2D,2Q ⊒2Ensuite
★LF,F,TV/ceiling fans in guest rooms, off-street parking 🚫 No
smoking, no pets, not suitable for children
🚶 Downtown, restaurants, galleries, shops, walkway system along
mountain stream, golfing, x-c skiing, hiking, fishing
🚗 Five Ski Hills, Banff, Kananaskis Country, dog-sled rides, snowmobiling, white water rafting
🔫 Large modern home with Bay window sitting areas in guest rooms and tranquil environment.
Relax in the hot tub or sauna or by the fireplace. Experienced travellers (hiking, biking, skiing,
fishing in the area) hosts are happy to help with guests plans and itineraries. Breakfast is served in
special guest breakfast room. Special rates for two-night weekends on holidays and for special
occasions. Gift Certificates available. Visa, MC ✔B&B

Recompsat, J.D. ("A Room with a View" Bed & Breakfast) ☎ & Fax (403) 678-6624
711 Larch Place, Canmore, AB T1W 1S2   E-mail: bestbnb@telusplanet.net

Phone for directions.
$50-60S $85-110D (multi-night discount) ▶ 4-5
🍴Gourmet 🏠Res., view ■1D,1Ste (ground & upper level)
⊨3Q,baby bed ⊒2Ensuite ★Separate entrances, off-street
parking 🚫No pets no smoking 🗣French, Spanish
🚶 Foot/bicycle/ski trail to Golf course, Recreation Centre,
swimming pool, Bow River
🚗 Banff & Banff National Park, Icefields Parkway
🔫Quiet, traditional mountain chalet nestled adjacent to golf course and trails. First class
breakfast is served in glassed-in atrium with spectacular views by well travelled/gourmet chef
Jean-Daniel from France. There are 2 school-age children in the host family. Visa ✔CC

Robillard, Deborah (Cedar Springs B&B) ☎ (403) 678-3865, Fax (403) 678-1938
426-1st St., Canmore, AB T1W 2K9

Phone for directions.
$85-135D   ▶ 6
🍴 Full, homebaked (dietary needs accommodated) 🏠 Downtown, res., multi-storey, view from
guest rooms, patio, deck, quiet ■ 2Ste (incl turret 3rd floor) ⊨ 2T,2Q,1K ⊒2ensuite
★KF,TV/F in guest room, skylights, private entrance, off-street parking, guest quarters are
separate 🚫 No smoking , no pets, not suitable for children 🗣 French
🚶 Bow River scenic and quiet pathways, Town Centre, superb dining, shops, galleries, golfing,
fishing, horseback riding, x-c skiing
🚗 Canmore Nordic SkiCentre, world classe golfing, Kananaskis Country, Banff, Hot Springs
🔫 Award winning, spacious cedar Chalet with unique cosy country decor, huge windows and
beautiful views of the Rocky Mountains. Relax in the natural garden area and gazebo and enjoy
mountain hospitality at its best. Ideal for honeymooners and special occasion. On-site Marriage
Commisioner (mother) will perform mountain wedding ceremony. Breakfast is served in special
guest breakfast area. Visa,MC ✔B&B

Segstro, Jac and Sarah (Jac'n'Sarah's)   ☎ (403) 678-2770, 1-800-600-3816
10 Riverview Place, Canmore, AB   T1W 2B9

Please call for directions.
$50S $75-85D $20Add.person $5-10Child   ► 8
🍴 Choice, homebaked 🏠Res.,views,quiet cul-de-sac,large decks
■2D,1Ste ⊨3Q,2T ⊲1Sh.w.g. plus tub,1sh.w.h. ★F,LF,KF,
large skylights in 2 guest room for starlit views from beds, separate
entrance 🚭No smoking ⚓Dutch,some French & German
🏃 Quiet and scenic walks at the doorstep, restaurants, galleries, gift
shops, dike holding back the Bow River (at back door step)
🚗 Nordic Centre, Hot Springs, hiking, mountaineering, skiing, Banff Nat.Park, Kananaskis
🔫 "Rooms with a difference - Hospitality with a flair". House is situated on a quiet cul-de-sac
which backs onto the Bow River with a beautiful view of the Rocky Mountains and Foothills. Ideal
place to use as a base from which to experience the Kananaskis, Bow Valley, Banff & Lake Louise
areas of the Rocky Mountains. Hostess is a marriage commissioner and performs civil marriages.
Early reservation recommended. Two-day min. stay during high season. There is a dog in residence.

Tarnowski, Roseanne & Grant (The Quilters Inn))   ☎ (403) 678-6785
702-2nd St., Canmore, AB   T1W 2K7

From Main Street (8th St) in Canmore, turn left at 7th Ave. Proceed to 2nd St, turn left and
continue to house on left (at stop sign). Located at corner of 6thAve & 2ndSt.

$55S $70D   ► 4A
🍴 Full, homebaked 🏠 Downtown, 3-storey, view from guest rooms,
quiet ■ 2D (lower level) ⊨ 2T,1K ⊲ 1Sh.w.g. ★ TV in guest
sitting room, guest robes, separate entrance, off-street parking, guest
quarters are separate 🚭No smoking , no pets, not suitable for children
🏃 Downtown shops, restaurants, Bow River, extensive walking trail system,
helicopter tours
🚗 Nordic Center, Banff Nat.Park, Bragg Creek, Kananaskis Country,
Calgary, Sunshine & Lake Louise world class ski resorts
🔫 Warm welcome and friendly hospitality in contemporary-style home
decorated with family treasures, antiques and quilts. Hostess is a quilter
and Home Economist. Studio space and classes are available. Enjoy the beautiful mountain setting,
providing peace, serenity and inspiration. ✓B&B

Whitlock, Maureen & John (Ambleside Lodge B&B)   ☎(403)678-3976,Fax 3919
123a Rundle Dr., Canmore, AB   T1W 2L6   E-mail: amblside@telusplanet.net

From Hwy 1 turn onto Hwy 1A, follow signs to Nordic Centre and proceed to 8 Ave. Cross bridge
into Rundle Dr to barn-shaped house with River-Rock fireplace.
$70-110 $20Add.person   ► 8
🍴 Homebaked 🏠 Downtown, 2-storey, view from guest rooms,
deck ■ 4D (upstairs) ⊨ 2T,1D,1Q ⊲ 1Sh.w.g., 2ensuite
★F,TV, skylight windows in guest rooms, parking 🚬 Smoking
on deck, no pets, ask about children
🏃 Town of Canmore, stores, casual & fine dining, golfing, trout
fishing, hiking, x-c skiing, mountain biking
🚗 Kananaskis Country, Banff, Calgary, Hot Springs, hiking, boat tours, great skiing, Hoo Doos
🔫 Beautiful home, pine wood throughout, with 18-ton rock fireplace. Enjoy the warm and
friendly mountain hospitality. Hosts are avid walkers and hope to guide and join guests exploring
the area. There are 2 small friendly dogs and "Rasputin" the cat in residence. ✓B&B

Carstairs

(north of Calgary; see also Airdrie)

Carroll, Lynn & Terry (Gray Fox Ranch & Bed & Breakfast)   ☎ (403) 337-3192
RR2, Carstairs, AB   T0M 0N0

From Hwy 2 north of Calgary proceed on Hwy 2A, west on Rte 580.
$60S $70-85D   ► 8A
⊅ Full   🏠 Farm, ranch-style, 2-storey, porch, quiet   ■ 3D
(upstairs)   ⊨ 2T,2Q   ⊿1Sh.w.g,1ensuite (clawfoot soaking
tubs)   ★ F,LF, separate entrance, library, reading room, old
fashioned cookstove ⓦNo pets, desig.smoking area, no children
⌇ Sign Language
🏃 Nature walks on ranch

🚗 4 Golf courses, fishing, horseback riding, white water rafting, rodeos
🐾 Victorian-style farmhouse with special ambiance of Elegance & Romance on a working cattle
ranch. Decorated in English Country and situated in rolling farmland dotted with trees & wildlife
close to the mountains & Banff. A wonderful place to relax and rejuvenate while creating that very
special memory. Silver service gourmet breakfast served at guests' convenience.

Cochrane

(north-west of Calgary; see also Airdrie)

Degraw, Neil & Marilyn (Mountview Cottage B&B)   ☎ (403) 932-4586, Cell (403) 660-5268
Box 8,S4,RR1, Cochrane, AB   T0L 0W0

Proceed north through Cochrane on Hwy 22. Turn left at first road and drive 4.4km, turn left at
stop sign. Continue 1km, turn left at Mountview Estates. Look for B&B sign in front of house.

$45S $50-65D $10Child   ► 6
⊅ Full, homebaked   🏠 Rural, hillside, view, acreage, deck,
quiet   ■ 3D(main & ground level)   ⊨ 3Q,cot   ⊿ 1Sh.w.g.
★ TV,F, pool table   ⓦ Designated smoking area, no pets
🚗 Cochrane, rodeos, Calaway Amusement Park, Calgary,
Fortress Ski Resort, Kananaskis Country, craft & specialty shops,
Spruce Meadows horse jumping
🐾 Warm welcome and friendly hospitality in comfortable home,
situated in a park-like setting with a beautiful view of valley and mountains (180 degree on the
horizon). Stroll the large grounds, rest on a bench and take in the country atmosphere and "the
most magnificient view in the West". There is a corral for horses & a resident cat. ⌐B&B

Howell, Ray & Fran (Timber Trail)   ☎ & Fax (403) 932-4995
Box 1313, Cochrane, AB   T0L 0W0

From Calgary, take Hwy 1A west to Cochrane. Continue west on Hwy 1A for 7 km. Turn on Grand
Valley Rd and follow for 21 km. Turn at red barn mailbox and proceed 1km.
$35S $50-60D   ► 4
⊅ Full, homebaked   🏠 Farm, Cape Cod, 2-storey, acreage,
isolated   ■2D(upstairs)   ⊨1D,1Q   ⊿1Sh.w.g.   ★F,TV,LF,
front porch swing, parking
🏃 Farm animals & ostrich on grounds, birdwatching, walks & x/c
skiing on forested trails
🚗 Cochrane, craft & art shops, two golf courses, Banff, Calgary,
shopping, restaurants, Stampede, Kananaskis Country, Canmore
🐾 Warm welcome on horse,cattle & ostrich ranch with Cape-Cod country farm house nestled in
a spruce and pine forest. Breakfast is served on the front porch or back deck, weather permitting.
Relax on the front porch swing. Rooms are named "Cowboy's Roost" (old west-style) and "Cowgirl's
Dream" (flowers & country antiques). ⌐B&B

Peterson, Elsa & Mike Madsen (Dickens Inn Bed & Breakfast)   ☎ (403) 932-3945
RR1, Cochrane, AB   T0L 0W0

From Hwy 1, take Cochrane Turnoff (Hwy 22) and drive north to Hwy 1A. Go west 2 km to Horse Creek Rd. Turn north 7km.

$65-75S $75-85D   ►6
🍳 Full, homebaked   🏠 Rural, 2-storey, acreage, view from guest rooms, porch, quiet, isolated   ■ 3D (upstairs)   ⊨ 3Q (four-posters)   🛁 3Ensuite   ★ F,TV   ✋ Designated smoking area, no pets, no children
🚗 Town of Cochrane, Kananaskis Country, Canmore, Calgary, Banff Nat. Park (hiking, skiing)

🏹 Large, beautifully decorated Victorian-style home, designed and built as a B&B, with a panoramic view of surrounding mountains. Relax on the wrap-around porch. Well travelled and informed hosts enjoy crafts and woodworking. Ideal country getaway. Visa,MC ⌐B&B

Cold Lake   *(north-east of Edmonton near Saskatchewan border)*

Flebotte, Gayle (Harbour House)   ☎ (403) 639-2337, Fax (403) 639-2338
615 Lakeshore Dr., Cold Lake, AB   T9M 1A2

Located 280 km NE of Edmonton on Hwy 28 (ends at Cold Lake). Turn left 2 blocks.

$60-80S $70-100D $10Child $10Add.person   (plus tax)   ►30

🍳 Cont, homebaked   🏠 Downtown, suburban, multi-storey, view, lakefront, front porch, observation tower   ■11D(upstairs)   ⊨4S,2D,7Q,2R,2P,cribs   🛁Sh.w.g., private   ★F,TV,VCR, tapes, books and games in guest sitting room, separate entrance, beverage station, off-street parking, winter plug-ins   ✋No smoking, no pets
🕴 Playhouse in yard, Cold Lake Marina, Kinosoo beach and trail, bowling, mini-golf, restaurants
🚗 Cold Lake Provincial Park, M.D.of Bonnyville Campground.

🏹 Spacious, comfortable home designed and partially built by owners with rooms facing the lake. There is a large front porch and a Coast Guard-type Tower with Widows Walk and a view of town and lake. Homebaked breakfast served in guest breakfast room and varies each day. Bag lunches provided. Off-season rates available. CCards ⌐B&B

Coleman   *(west of Lethbridge, near Alberta border; see also Blairmore, Pincher Creek)*

Trotz, Billy & Chris (McGillivray Creek Hide-Away B&B)   ☎ (403) 563-5187
Box 192, Coleman, AB   T0K 0M0

From Hwy 3 in Crowsnest Pass, turn north on 61St (far west end in Coleman) and proceed 1km.

$45S $60D $85F $15Add.person   (Seniors discount)   ►6
🍳 Full, homebaked   🏠 Rural, 3acres, hillside bungalow, view, deck, quiet, secluded   ■3(main & ground level)   ⊨2T,1D,1Q 🛁1Sh.w.g.,1private   ★ TV in guest lounge, picnic area   ✋No smoking, no pets
🕴 Hiking/snowmobiling/x-c skiing from door, antique store, museum, restaurants, quiet walks in the country
🚗 Golfing, Mine Tours, Frank Slide Interpretive Centre, downhill skiing, shopping, fishing, theatre, art gallery, horseback riding, mountain climbing, Old Man River Dam, BC border

🏹 Charming country home surrounded by breathtaking scenery, located in the beautiful mountains of the Crowsnest Pass. Enjoy the quiet country lifestyle and relax after a busy day of sightseeing or outdoor activities. There is a horse and a dog outside. Children welcome. Visa ⌐B&B

Drumheller

(north-east of Calgary: see also Strathmore, Three Hills)

Barnes, Jack & Florence (The Victorian House Bed & Breakfast)   ☎ (403) 823-3535
541 Riverside Dr. W., Drumheller, AB   T0J 0Y3

Phone for directions
$40-50S $50-75D $5-15Add.person   ► 8
Full, homebaked   Res., 2-storey, view from guest rooms,
river across street, porch, deck, balcony, quiet   4(main, upper
level)   1S,1D,4Q   2Sh.w.g., 1private with jet tub ★LF,TV,
ceiling fans, one private entry way, guest quarters are separate,
off-street parking   No smoking, no pets
Downtown, swimming pool, arena, walking & biking paths
Royal Tyrrell Museum of Palaeontology, Rosebud Dinner Theatre, Alberta Steam Train Tours
Retired farmers in riverfront home with river/valley views from balcony and veranda. Hostess
enjoys making porcelain dolls and other crafts which give finishing touches to each guest rooms.
Breakfast is served from 6-10AM. ✔B&B

Cole, Mabel (Cole's Bed & Breakfast)   ☎ (403) 823-5844
Box 2114, Drumheller, AB   T0J 0Y0

Located at 529-2nd Ave in the village of Nacmine and 1km west of Drumheller on Hwy 575 (also
called South Dinosaur Trail).
$40S $50D $10Add.person   ► 5A,3Ch
Full   Village, urban, bungalow, view, patio, deck, quiet
3 (main floor)   3S,2D,crib   1Private, 1sh.w.g.   ★ TV,
off-street & street parking, guest quarters are separate   No
smoking, children and puppies welcome
Warm hospitality in comfortable residential home located in
unique Badlands, home of the Royal Tyrrell Museum. Relax and
enjoy the large deck. ✔B&B

Crawford, Marjorie and Lloyd (Riverside Inn Crawford's B&B Home)   ☎ (403) 823-4746
501 Riverside Drive West, Drumheller, AB   T0J 0Y3

Phone for directions.
from $40S   from $50D $10Child   ► 7
Full   Res., split-level, view, patio, quiet, riverfront   3D,1F
(main and upper floor)   3D,1S   1Ensuite, 2sh.w.g.   ★2 large
sitting rooms with TV and VCR, separate entrance, garage
&driveway parking, freezer available   No pets
Drumheller, churches, restaurants, shopping, swimming pool
World famous Tyrrell Museum of Palaeontology, Dinosaur Valley in Red Deer River Badlands
Young retired Professionals in modern, comfortable home situated in quiet location. Ideal
place to relax and enjoy a nice walk in the peaceful countryside. Visa ✔CC

Kashuba, George & Maureen (McDougall Lane B&B)   ☎ & Fax (403) 823-5379
71 McDougall Lane, Drumheller, AB   T0J 0Y1

Proceed over Gordon Taylor Bridge, turn left on Dinosaur Trail North, left on Poplar Cr., then

right on McDougall Lane.
$50S $55-85D $10Child/Add.person   ▶ 6+
🍴 Full   🏠 Res., acreage, quiet, patio, deck   ■ 1D,1Ste,1F
(upstairs)   ⊨ S,Q,cot   ⬛ 2Sh.w.g.,1ensuite   ★ Air,F,TV in
guest room, off-street parking, semi private guest entrance, guest
quarters are separate   Ⓦ Designated smoking area
🏃 Downtown, restaurants, Hoover Tours & Water Park, walking
trails, swimming pool   🚐 Royal Tyrrell Museum
🐾 Large, executive-style home overlooking the Dinosaur Trail (North), on a quiet lane in town
with mature trees, overflowing flower gardens & enroute to the Royal Tyrrell Museum. Breakfast is
served in private dining room. A "Pretty, peaceful & private place". There is a dog. ✓B&B

Lucas, Daniel & Michele (Pearl's "Cabin" Bed & Breakfast)   ☎ (403) 823-9263
Box 1558, Drumheller, AB   T0J 0Y0

From Drumheller proceed north on Hwy 9, turn right at top of hill. Turn left again, then

right into yard. Watch for signs.
$65S $65-85D $10-15Add.person   ▶ 6+
▦ March-Nov   🍴 Full, homebaked   🏠 Farm, guest cabin,
view, porch, quiet   ■Separate cabin   ⊨ 2T,1Q,2cots
⬛1Private   ★TV in cabin   Ⓦ Smoking on porch
🏃 Playground with playhouse, strolls on back country roads,
access to coulee's for hiking, biking, birdwatching, view sunrise &
sunsets, excellent star gazing
🚐 Royal Tyrrell Museum, golfing, Rosebud Dinner Theatre, HooDoo's, Swinging Bridge, Rowely
🐾 Third Generation grain and pheasant farm on the peaceful prairies. Cozy guest cabin with two
bedrooms, situated 100 yards from main house and nestled in trees. Breakfast is served in the guest
cabin. Ideal setting - fun for families, intimate for couples and quiet for business travellers. Early
booking is recommended for July & August.✓CC

Nimmo, Bryce & Rosalie (Taste The Past Bed & Breakfast)   ☎ (403) 823-5889
281-2nd Street West, Box 865, Drumheller, AB   T0J 0Y0

Located on Hwy 9 West (2nd St W).
$55S $65D $10-15Add.person   ▶ 9
🍴Full, homebaked   🏠Downtown, 3-storey, hist., porch   ■4D
⊨2D,2T,1Q,cot   ⬛ 2Sh.w.g.   ★F,TV in guest room, off-street
parking in rear   Ⓦ Smoking on veranda only
🏃 Dinosaur Empire, Red Deer River, waterpark, tennis court,
bicycle/walking paths, restaurants, shopping, trail rides
🚐 Royal Tyrrell Museum, scenic canyons, Hoo Doos, Badlands
🐾 Spacious turn-of-the-Century brick home, one of the areas original grand mansions, renovated
and restored with antique decor and romantic atmosphere. Breakfast is served in sunny breakfast
room. Energetic hosts are knowledgeable on local tourism. Visa,MC ✓B&B

Duchess

(east of Calgary; see also Brooks, Bassano)

Trimmer, Bob, Myrna & Kristy (Trimmer's Country B&B)   ☎ (403) 378-4216
Box 145, Duchess, AB   T0J 0Z0

Located 2.3km north of jcts Hwys 544/873; 13km north of Brooks.
$40S $55D $5Child $10Add.person   (plus tax)   ► 6
🍳 Full, homebaked   🐄 Farm, 2-storey, older, acreage, porch,
deck, quiet, secluded   ■ 1S,2D (upstairs in sep.guest house)
🛏1S,2Q,1R   ⬛1Shw.g.(on main floor)   ★ TV,KF, separate
entrance, 24hr beverage station, outdoor firepit   🚭No smoking,
no pets (outside dog-kennel by prior arrangement)
🕴 Farm grounds, 1940's 3-storey hip roof barn, park-like grounds
🚗 Dinosaur Provincial Park (World Heritage Site), Royal Tyrrell Museum Field Station
(Dinosaur Bones), golf courses, Brooks Aquaduct, Crop Diversification Centre, museum, hiking‛
☛ Newly renovated 1920's cozy guest house with antiques, quilts, wicker, hardwood and stained
glass windows. Hosts are 3rd & 4th Generation on working irrigation/cattle family farm and are
very knowledgeable about the area. Relax in the sunroom or on the seasonal front porch. Breakfast
is served in guest house. Parking space for motorhomes. Families welcome. Visa ↙B&B

Edmonton

(see also Sherwood Park, Spruce Grove)

Amyotte, Emil & Jeannine Roy (L'Amy du Roy B&B)   ☎ (403) 465-3225
8514-86 Ave, Edmonton, AB   T6C 1J5

Located in s/e Edmonton, beside Bonnie Doon Shopping Centre.
$50-55S $55-60D $10child   ► 4A,2Ch
🍳 Full, homebaked   🏠 Res., bungalow, deck, quiet   ■1D,1F
(lower level)   🛏1D,1Q,1R,crib   ⬛ 1sh.w.g.   ★ F,LF,TV in
guest sitting room, coffee/snack station for guests, off-street
parking   🚬Smoking on deck, no pets   〰 French
🕴 Shopping Centre, Old Strathcona, St.Jean Faculty (UofA),
Edmonton Transit
🚗 Downtown, Coliseum, Muttart Conservatory, West Edmonton Mall, Convention Centre
☛ Retired couple in new, spacious and sunny home situated in quiet cul-de-sac in the heart of the
Francophone area. French Canadian-style breakfast served in the spacious kitchen or on deck,
weather permitting. Guest accommodation is in bright full lower level. Children of all ages
welcome. MC ↙B&B

Brooks, Ernie & Ethel (Brooks Place B&B)   ☎ (403) 438-6048 Fax (403) 437-7889
3230-104A St., Edmonton, AB   T6J 2Z6   E-mail: brookspl@freenet.edmonton.ab.ca

Take Calgary Trail to 34Ave and proceed west to 106St. Turn south
to 32A Ave and east to 104A St, then north.
$45S $60-75D $10Add.person   ► 4A,1-2Ch
🍳 Full, homebaked   🏠 Res., sub., 2-storey, deck, quiet   ■1Ste
(upstairs)   🛏2Q(foam for child)   ⬛1Private,1Ensuite   ★F,LF,
ceiling fans, off-street & street parking, entire 2nd floor for guests,
TV-sitting area with coffee bar   🚭No smoking,no pets
🕴 Shopping Mall, restaurants, bowling, City bus
🚗 West Edmonton Mall, Airport, Old Strathcona & Fringe Festival, University, Coloseum
☛ "Empty-nester" hosts in modern southside home located on a quiet street with easy access to
all attractions in the city. Hosts have welcomed people from around the world for over 30 years and
draw on this experience to offer warm and sincere hospitality to their guests. Special dietary needs
will be considered with advance notice. Gourmet-style breakfast is served in the dining room. Relax
in the guest sitting room or join the hosts in the cozy family room featuring a Tyndel stone
fireplace. Families welcome. Visa ↙B&B

Carr, Ruth & Paul (Streetside Garden B&B)
11318-63rd St, Edmonton, AB   T5W 4E8

☎ & Fax (403) 474-7046
E-mail: streetsidebb@compusmart.ab.ca

Phone for directions.
$50-65S/D $10Add.person   ► 4A
🍲 Full, homebaked 🏠 Res., 2-storey, hist., view of garden from
guest rooms, veranda, patio ■ 2D (upstairs) ⊨1K,1P(D)
🛁 1Sh.w.g. ★ TV,LF,F, guest robes, 6-soaker tub, off-street
parking 🚭No smoking, no pets
🧍 Highland Historic Walking Tours (guided), panoramic
N.Saskatchewan River Valley, paved trail network (walking &
biking & x-c skiing), golfing, restaurants, unique shops, bike rentals, backyard art workshops
🚗 Downtown, fine dining, art galleries, Muttart Conservatory, West Edmonton Mall, Elk Island
Nat.Park (buffalo), Aagricom Trade Center, Citadel Theatre, Yellowhead (Jasper) Hwy 16
🐾 Friendly Heritage home with a unique blend of antiques and contemporary decor, set in a
well-treed neighbourhood. Special breakfast served in the dining room, tea on the veranda and
eveing dessert in the sitting room. Guest are welcome to stroll, sit or paint in the garden. Hostess'
interest include a passion for gardening, art, geneology and host's enthusiasm is for martial arts
and radio-control planes. Kitty Carr is the resident cat. Gift certificates available. Visa,MC ✒B&B

Champigny, Kathy & Paul (Kountry Komfort B&B)
4601-42 St., Beaumont, AB   T4X 1H1

☎ & Fax (403) 929-2342

Phone for directions.
$35S $45D $10Child $10Add.person   ► 4A,1Ch
🍲Full 🏠Res.,small town,1.5-storey,view,deck,quiet,swimming
pool, secluded ■1D,1F (upstairs) ⊨1S,1D,1Q 🛁1Sh.w.g.
★F,TV,LF, off-street parking 🚭Smoking outside 〰French
🧍 Town of Beaumont, hist.church, golfing, restaurants, shops,
parks, walking trail
🚗 City of Edmonton, Int.Airport, West Edmonton Mall, U of
Alberta, Old Strathcona Miquelon Prov. Park (swimming, boating, fishing), Ukrainian Village,
🐾 Comfortable new home backing onto a wooded area in quiet community with French Cdn
Village Theme evident in its architecture. Phone, fax, computer available for the business traveller.
Hosts are very helpful with information about area tourist attractions. Silver service breakfast
served in the dining room. Parking available for guests flying out of Int.Airport. Visa ✒B&B

Cooper, Linda & Alan (Memory Lane - West Edmonton Mall B&B)
8719-179th St., Edmonton, AB   T5T 0X4

☎ (403) 489-4161

$35-40S $45-65D $10Add.person   (off-season rates/Oct-Apr) 🍽 Meals   ► 10
From West Edmonton Mall drive to 178St and west on 89Ave. Proceed south on 180St. Follow loop
around to B&B.

🍲 Full, homebaked 🏠 Res., raised bungalow, view from guest
rooms, porch, quiet, deck ■2S,2D,1F(main level) ⊨2S,2D,1Q,R
🛁1Shw.g., 1sh.w.h. 1ensuite ★ F,TV,LF,KF, games & toys for
children, off-street parking, guest quarters are separate
🚭Designated smoking area
🧍 West Edmonton Mall, excellent restaurants, Dinner Theatre,
pubs, bus terminal & airport shuttle service
🚗 Space Science Centre, Fort Edmonton Park, Old Strathcona, Stadium, Coliseum, U of A
🐾 Large home with spacious grounds and relaxing deck, located in quiet neighborhood. Congenial
hosts are happy to please and help. "Give us just one night... we will give you a memory". Breakfast
is served in special guest breakfast room. Pick-up & return from airport/bus/train available
(nominal charge). There is a small dog and a cat in residence. ✒B&B

Croteau, Paul and Suzanne (Chez Suzanne B&B)   ☎ & Fax(403)483-1845,1-888-483-1845
18603-68 Ave., Edmonton, AB   T5T 2M8   E-mail: fils@connect.ab.ca

$50S $60D $80F   ►8
Phone for directions. (Car pick-up available at West Edm.Mall)
❄Mar1-Nov30 ◐Gourmet,homebaked ❒Res.,patio,quiet ■3
◄2S,2D,1Q ◰1Sh.w.g.,1private ★F,LF,TV/VCR & phone in
guest rooms, guest bev.station, off-street parking ⌇French
⚊ West Edmonton Mall, sports complex, restaurants
🚐 Elk Island Park, Storyland Valley Zoo, University of Alberta,
City Center, Muttart Conservatory, Ukrainian Village
🖝 Comfortable home, situated in residential area close to Jasper Hwy. Relax and enjoy the large
yard with garden after a full day of exploring world's biggest Mall (with indoor Fantasyland, beach,
waterpark & skating rink). Extended stay rates and motorhome rental available.

Hanlon-Karrel, Carol & Bryan Karrel (Karrel's Sleepover B&B)   ☎ & Fax (403) 456-5928
15615-81st St., Edmonton, AB   T5Z 2T6   E-mail: karrels@compcocity.com

Located north of 82nd St off Yellowhead Hwy.
$40S $50-60D $10Child $70-80F $20Add.person► 4A,3Ch
◐Full, homebaked ❒Res, split-level, quiet, deck ■1S,2D(upst)
◄1S,1D,1Q ◰1Sh.w.g.,1ensuite ★F,TV,ceiling fans, off-street
parking, guest quarters are separate ⊕Desig.smoking area
⚊ Small lake & park area, bus route & LRT (Light Rail Transit)
🚐 Coliseum & Agricom, golfing, City Centre, shopping mall,
restaurants, W.Edmonton Mall
🖝 Hearty welcome in deluxe, well appointed home in quiet residential of north end of the City.
Hosts are a retired Military couple and enjoy welcoming guests from worldwide. Enjoy the
comfortable ambiance. Relax on the deck in the pretty, secluded back yard. There is a cat. ⌐B&B

Iliffe, Monica (Sentimental Journey B&B)   ☎ (403) 963-3215, Fax (403) 963-6022
24, 53103 Range Rd. 14, Stony Plain, AB   T7Z 1X2

Location: 6 Diamond Dr., Hubbles Lake. Situated 8.5 km west of Stony Plain on Hwys 16A. Turn
north on Range Rd 14 to Diamond Rd. Turn right, then 1st left and proceed to 6 Diamond Dr

$40S $50D   ►4A
◐ Full ❒ Rural, cedar structure, view, lakefront, patio, quiet,
sun deck, spa, solarium ■2D ◄2D(main floor) ◰Sh.w.g.
★TV,F,LF, parking ⊕ No smoking, children min.age 12
⚊ Lakeside walking trails, swimming, cross-country skiing
🚐 West Edmonton Mall, charming town of Stony Plain, Andrew
Wolf Wine Cellars, Multicultural Heritage Centre, Victorian Tea
House, golfing
🖝 Unique accommodation in comfortable cedar cluster home with 5 roofs, built into the hillside
and situated on tranquil Hubbles Lake. Hostess is artist and Loon enthusiast and has been
welcoming guests in her home for many years. Relax in the spa and solarium. Canoes available to
observe loons. Picnic table at lake side. ⌐B&B

Krause, Brian & Yvonne (Crossroads B&B)   ☎ (403) 963-6095
RR5, Stony Plain, AB   T7Z 1X5

Located at the jct of Hwys 770 & 627. On Hwy 16 proceed west to Hwy 770 and left for 13 km to
Hwy 627. Look for house on southeast corner.
$40S $50D $60F $5Add.person   (plus tax)   ► 6
🍳 Full, homebaked   🏠 Farm, bungalow, ranch-style, patio, deck, quiet   ◼ 2S,2D (main and
ground floor)   ⊨ 2S,2Q   ⇶ 2Sh.w.g.   ★ Air,TV in guest rooms, private entrance, guest
quarters are separate, wheel-chair access
🚐 Multicultural Centre, Stony Plain Murals, Victoria Tea House, West Edmonton Mall, lakes and
friendly beaches, fishing, golf courses
🐎 Quiet, modern home on a working ranch with horses and cattle. A great place for summer
vacations. View the scenic country side or access the large covered arena. Breakfast is served in
dining room. Facilities for guest horses available. Families and pets welcome. Visa,MC ⌐B&B

Longley, Doug & Joan (Barratt House B&B)   ☎ (403) 437-2568
4204-115 St., Edmonton AB   T6J 1P4

From west travel to 119St, from north/south/east to 111St. Proceed to 49Ave, then to 115St,

north to 42Ave. Located 3 blocks south of Whitemud Freeway.
$45-55S $60-70D $10Add.person   ► 4
🍳 Full, homebaked (Gourmet)   🏠 Res., 2-storey, deck, quiet
◼ 2D(upstairs)   ⊨ 1D,1Q,cot   ⇶ 1Private, 1ensuite
★TV,LF, off-street & street parking   ✋ Smoking on deck
🚶 Park & ravine walks, bus No52 to Southgate Transit Centre
🚐 Downtown, Airport, West Edmonton Mall, Kinsman Aquatic
Centre, over 30km paved river valley trails, University of Alberta
🐾 Attractive spacious home in quiet residential south-west area of the city. Relax in the inviting
family room or outdoors on the flower filled deck overlooking a beautiful landscaped yard. Hosts are
friendly and caring Christian couple and enjoy a warm and relaxed atmosphere. Gourmet-style
breakfast is served in the dining room. Special dietary needs will be accommodated with prior
arrangement. There is a cat in residence. Visa ⌐B&B

Maitland C.& Konduc D.("This is it" Bed & Breakfast)   ☎ & Fax (403) 439-8481
11013-87th Ave, Edmonton, AB   T6G 0X5   E-mail: thisisit@icrossroads.com

Located in the University area. Phone for directions.
$80D $87D   🍽 Meals   ► 6
🍳 Full, homebaked   🏠 Res., 3-storey, porch   ◼ 3D (2nd floor)
⊨2Q,2T   ⇶ 2Private, 1sh.w.h.   ★F,LF,TV in guest room,piano,
ceiling fans, private art gallery, bathrobes, hair dryers, fax   ✋No
smoking, no pets, children min. age 12   ∿ French, Ukrainian
🚶 University Campus & Hospital, Olympic Fitness Centre, LRT and
bus to downtown, golfing, walking/x-c ski trails in river valley, fine
restaurants, Jubilee Auditorium (Symphony & theatre), Old Strathcona
🚐 West Edmonton Mall, Ukrainian Village, Provincial Museum,
Muttart Conservatory, Fort Edmonton Park, John Janzen Nature Ctr
🐾 Unique home, formerly a Fraternity House with turn-of-the-Century decor and elegant,
enchanting atmosphere, situated among majestic trees in the heart of the University. The creative
memorabilia, heirlooms, paintings & photographs done by the hosts are unique. There are clean,
friendly resident cats.Visa,MC,Amex ⌐B&B

Martel, Paul & Peggy (Alberta Setting Sun Bed & Breakfast)   ☎ & Fax (403) 468-3217
7911-98th Ave., Edmonton, AB   T6A 0B5

$40-50D $15Add.person   🍴Meals   (Picnic lunches)   ►6

Located at 79th St & 98th Ave. Phone for directions.
🍲Choice, homebaked   🏠 Res., raised bungalow, patio, quiet
■1D,1Ste(main & lower level)   ⊨1D,1P,1Q(antique brass)
🛁1Private, 1sh.w.h.   ★Separate entrance, LF,KF,TV in guest
room, parking, bev/snack station, bicycles available   🚭No
smoking, no pets, children welcome
🏃 City Centre, Alberta Legislature, Convention Centre, Muttart
Conservatory, Citadel Theatre, Art Gallery, beautiful river valley
parks, pools, golf course, ski/bicycle/nature paths & Paddle Wheel Riverboat), bus service
🚗 West Edmonton Mall, U.of Alberta, hospitals, Auditorium, museum, Northlands Coliseum
🐷 Relax in private apartment suite after a "shop-til-you-drop-day" at West Edmonton Mall.
Hosts have been welcoming B&B guests since 1987. House specialties are omelets & pumpkin
muffins served in suite, or in the dining room or on the patio surrounded by flowering plants &
towering spruce trees. There is a friendly cat named "Babykins" who greets guests on arrival.
Excellent location for long term stays/discounts. ✍B&B

Schnelle, Ursula (Cardiff Sunset Bed & Breakfast)   ☎ & Fax (403) 939-3568
62 Mill Rd., Cardiff Echoes, Morinville, AB   T8R 1N6   E-mail: csunset@telusplanet.net

Located just south of Morinville, 19km north of Edmonton. From Hwy 2 turn right on Cardiff

Rd, proceed 2km to Cardiff Echoes, right again at 2nd entrance.
$45-55S $55-65D   ► 4A
🍲 Full, homebaked   🏠 Res., bungalow, view from guest rooms,
patio, deck, quiet   ■ 2D (main floor)   ⊨ 2T,1Q   🛁 1Private,
1ensuite   ★ LF,F/TV in guest lounge, off-street parking
🚭Smoking on deck, no pets, children min age 6   〰 German
🏃 Golf course, lake, canoeing, fishing, walking trails
🚗 Edmonton, West Edmonton Mall, Elk Island Nat Park,
Coloseum, Space Science Center, museums, teahouses, shopping, restaurants
🐷 Quiet, comfortable home with country atmosphere and friendly neighbourhood. Enjoy
gourmet breakfast overlooking the garden and park. Informed hosts will assist with directions and
plans. Airport or bus pick-up can be arranged. ✍B&B

Young, Marion (Inglewood House B&B)   ☎ (403) 452-8679, Fax (403) 454-3360
11113-127 St., Edmonton, AB   T5M 0T5

Located in Inglewood Place. Phone for directions.
$38S $49D $10Add.child/person   🍴 Meals   ► 7
🍲 Full   🏠 Res., 2-storey, deck, quiet   ■ 1D,2Fupstairs)
⊨1S,1D,1Q,2R   🛁 1Sh.w.g.   ★ LF,F/TV/library in guest sitting room,
separate entrance, off-street parking, guest quarters are separate
🚭Designated smoking area, no pets, children min. age 5   〰some French
🏃 Space Science Centre, Westmount Shopping Centre, bicycle path,
restaurants, churches, excellent bus service
🚗 West Edmonton Mall, downtown, U of A, Valley Zoo, historic Fort Edmonton Park, Old
Strathcona (boutiques, cafés, unique restaurants), Provincial Museum, Municipal Airport
🐷 Charming spacious house (ca 1912) furnished with antiques, located in historic area of the city
with landscaped yard & cedar deck. Relax with a good book by the fireplace in the guest sitting
room. British-born hostess has extensive experience & knowledge with B&B establishments.
Families welcome. Visa,MC

Williamson, Tim & Dianne (Dianne's (West Edmonton) B&B   ☎ & Fax (403) 444-3749
7004-185 St., Edmonton, AB   T5T 2L8   E-mail: twilliam@oanet.com

Take 170 or 178 St Exit from Hwy 16 or Whitemud Dr. Proceed south to 69St and continue west to 184St. Turn right and then left.

$45-55S $55-65D $10Add.person (over age 5)   ► 4A,2Ch
🅳 Full, homebaked   🏠 Sub., res., 2-storey, deck, quiet
■1D,1Ste (main & upper level)   ⊨ 1Q,1K,1P   ⌐ 2Private
★ LF,F,TV/phone in guest room, ceiling fans, guest robes, off-street & street parking, host quarters are below
Ⓦ Designated smoking area
🏃 2 bus stops, quiet residential walks
🚌 West Edmonton Mall, Fort Edmonton Park (historic site), Devonian Botanical Gardens, downtown Edmonton, University, museum
📢 Comfortable Cape Cod style home in quiet upscale neighbourhood furnished with antiques and fine art. Breakfast is served in the family dining room or the suite sitting room. Hosts will pick-up guests at Airport, Bus/Train Station for a small fee. There is a 12-year old Cocker Spaniel "Max" in residence. Visa ⌐B&B

Fox Creek   *(north-west of Edmonton; see also Mayerthorpe)*

Deans, Grant and Diana (Grant & Diana's B&B)   ☎ (403) 622-3930, Fax (403) 622-2878
506-4th Ave., Box 466, Fox Creek, AB   T0H 1P0

Located half-way between Edmonton and Grand Prairie. From Hwy 43 exit onto Kaybob Drive. Turn right on Hammond Drive and left on 4th Ave. Proceed to house across from playground.

$30S $40D   (plus tax)   ► 3A
🅳 Full(buffet) 🏠Res., bungalow, patio, quiet ■2(main level)
⊨1S,1D ⌐1Sh.w.g. ⌐LF,KF,TV in guest room, parking, whirlpool tub, barbeque, fire pit Ⓦ No pets, no children
🏃 Golf Course (9-hole par 36), outdoor swimming pool, ball diamonds, tennis courts
🚌 lakes with small sandy beaches/boat launches/fishing, birdwatching/berry picking, x/c skiing/ice fishing/snowmobiling
📢 Adult accommodation in a quiet well established residential neighbourhood. Enjoy the forest wilderness, the backyard rock garden with fountain, and watch a variety of birds. Pick-up from the Bus Depot available. Located 2km from busy Alaska Hwy. There is a cat in residence. Visa ⌐CC

Granum   *(north-west of Lethbridge; see also Nanton)*

Lane, Keith & LeAnne (Willow Lane Ranch)   ☎ (403) 687-2284, 1-800-665-0284,
Box 114, Granum, AB   T0L 1A0   Fax (403) 687-2409

Located south of Calgary on Hwy 2. Turn west at Hwy 519 intersection (Granum) and follow signs.

$45S $70D $100D(cabin) $25Add.person 🍽 Meals   ► 8
🅳 Full, homebaked   🏠 Ranch, ranch-style 2-storey, view from guest rooms, 2 covered verandas, quiet ■ 2D,1F(upstairs on private floor in main ranch house plus self-cont.log cabin)
⊨4T,3Q ⌐1Sh.w.g., 1private, 1ensuite ★F,TV,LF, outdoor fire pit, outdoor cedar hot tub Ⓦ Desig.smoking area, no pets
🏃 Guided horseback riding & access to stocked trout ponds available at extra charge (seasonal), hiking, x/c skiing
🚌 Remington Carriage Centre, Head-Smashed-In Buffalo Jump, historic Fort MacLeod, golfing
📢 Enjoy a true Western adventure on working cattle and horse ranch with a relaxed, easy going atmosphere, nestled at the foot of south-western Alberta's Porcupine Hills. Relax and watch the ranch activities or take part in organized day rides, authentic cattle drives. Newly renovated cozy cabin is ideal for romantic get-aways. Package prices and room/board offered. Greyhound bus pick-up from Claresholm and Fort MacLeod available. Visa,MC ⌐B&B

Carter, Bob & Glenda (Wyndswept Bed & Breakfast)
☎ (403) 866-3950, (403) 865-8247
Box 2683, Hinton, AB T7V 1Y2
E-mail: wyndswep@agt.net

$70(and up) $25Add.person   (min.2 nights preferred/book early for June to Sept) ► 6
Located at 12 Folding Mountain Village, Jasper East. On Hwy 16E,
4km past Park East Gate, turn right at Folding Mt.Campground.
🍳 Full, homebaked 🏠 Village, 2-storey, hillside, acreage, view
from guest rooms, quiet, deck ■ 2Ste (main & garden level)
⊨ 1Q,2K,1T 🛁 2Private ★ F,LF,TV in guest room, guest
kitchen, billiard area, private decks ⓦ Smoking outside, no pets,
children min. age 12
🏃 Flower gardens, firepit, gazebo, viewing decks, bird watching
🚗 Town of Jasper & Nat.Park, Hinton, Columbia Icefields, Miette Hot Springs, Marmot Basin
📣 Large custom-built home, specially designed for B&B, the view, and to fit into the hill. Located
in the village on the side of Folding Moutain with a spectacular panoramic view - a painter's &
photographer's paradise. Hosts are avid naturalists, long time residents of the area, and willing to
share off beaten tracks to enjoy the mountains. Enjoy a heart/healthy/hearty breakfast in the the the
big country kitchen, while watching the clouds dance over the mountain ranges. Families welcome.
There is a Miniature German Schnauzer in residence.Visa ✓B&B

Kan, Mrs. Marilyn Leslie
☎ (403) 852-3009
Box 1940, Jasper, AB T0E 1E0

Located at 1222A Cabin Creek Drive. Phone for directions.
$35-50S/D $10Add.person ► 4
🍳NONE (Complimentary coffeee/tea, self-serve 🏠Res., quiet
■2D ⊨2T,1D 🛁Sh.w.g. ★Private entrance, handicap
access may be arranged ⓦNo pets, no smoking
🏃 Town centre, mountain lakes, hiking trails begin across street.
🚗 All the attractions in Jasper National Park (Columbia Icefields,
Miette Hot Springs, Maligne Lake), Mt Robson Prov Park (BC)
📣 Quiet comfortable residence, located at edge of town in new subdivision. Main floor guest
rooms have a southern exposure, with a view of the garden and the mountains along the Icefield
Parkway. Host's interests include local history, environmental issues and travel. ✓CC

Mellace, Wendy and Tony (Rocky Mountain "Hi" B&B)
☎ (403) 852-3851
Box 932, 907 Pyramid Lake Rd., Jasper, Alta T0E 1E0

Take Yellowhead Hwy 16 into Jasper. Turn onto Pine Ave for 5
short blocks and then left. House is 4th on left side.
$40S $50D ► 6
🍳 NONE 🏠 Res.,quiet ■2(downstairs) ⊨ 1S,1D,2Q
🛁Sh.w.g. ★Private entrance ⓦNo smoking, no pets ✍Italian
🏃 Downtown, restaurants, shopping. entertainment, hiking
🚗 Lakes, fishing, Jasper Sky Tram, horseback riding, excellent
downhill and cross-country skiing, hiking
📣 Centrally located home in beautiful, popular year-round resort town in Jasper Nat.Park. Long
time Jasper residents are well informed about the area.

Robinson, Mrs. Jean
Box 640, Jasper, AB   T0E 1E0

☎ (403) 852-4527

From Hwy 16 East or West travel into town. Look for 808Connaught Dr at west end of main street. $45S/D (off season rates available - Oct1-April30)   💷 $3Extra per person   ▶ 6

💷Not included 🏠Downtown, village, bungalow, quiet, view from guest rooms ■1D,1F(main floor) ⊨3T,1D,cot ⬛1Sh.w.g. ★F,lounge for guests, street parking ⑩No smoking, no pets 🏃 Town Centre, walks in forest across the street, ski bus for Marmot Basin pick-up, x/c skiing on groomed trails 🚗 Mount Edith Cavell with the hanging Angel Glacier, Maligne Lake, Columbia Icefields, world-class downhill skiing 🖝 Hosts, born and raised in Jasper, have welcomed B&B guests for a long time, are avid birders and have hiked all the trails and fished in most of the lakes. They will gladly share their local knowledge with visitors. Enjoy the breathtaking beauty and magnificient views in this active year round resort town. There is a resident dog. ✒CC

Swales, Tom & Ann (Annie's Abode B&B)
804 Patricia St., Box 2582, Jasper AB   T0E 1E0

☎ & Fax (403) 852-3975

Phone for directions.
$50-75D $15Child/Add.person   ▶ 5
💷 Homebaked, self-serve 🏠 Res., split-level, view from guest rooms ■ 1Ste(2D)(lower level) ⊨2T,1Q,1R ⬛ 1Sh.w.g. ★ KF,TV,private entrance, street parking, guest quarters are separate ⑩ No smoking, no pets 🏃 Downtown Jasper, Jasper Park Lodge, Old Fort Point, x-c skiing, hiking 🚗 Pyramid & Patricia Lake, Maligne Canyon, Maligne Lake, Athabasca Falls, Sunwapta Falls, Icefield, Miette Hot Springs, world class skiing 🖝 Comfortable & friendly home situated in central location. Relax in the cozy atmosphere after a day of hiking, shopping, skiing or sight-seeing. Enjoy a European style breakfast served in guest breakfast room. ✒B&B

Yates, Denise & Gordon (Mountain Splendour B&B English Style)
Box 6544, Hinton, AB   T7V 1X8

☎ (403) 866-2116

Located in Jasper East at #17 Folding Mountain Village on the Yellowhead Hwy 16 and 4 km east of Jasper Park. Phone for directions.
$75-118D $25Add.person   ▶ 7A
💷 Full 🏠 Rural, village, 3-storey, acreage, view from guest rooms, patio, wrap-around deck, private upper balconies, quiet ■ 2D ⊨ 2Q,3R ⬛ 2Ensuite ★ F,LF,TV in guest lounge ⑩ No smoking, no pets, no children 🚗 Town of Jasper, Miette Hot Springs, Athabasca Falls, excellent x-c & downhill skiing (Athabasca Lookout, Nordic Centre, Marmot Basin), Columbia Icefields 🖝 Lovely new home with beautiful panoramic mountain view in a peaceful setting where nature abounds. Relax and enjoy the warm English-style hospitality. Visa ✒B&B

Chell, Ruth (Chellsea House B&B)　　　　　　　　　☎ (403) 381-1325
9 Dalhousie Rd.W., Lethbrtidge, AB　T1K 3X2

Travel south on University Dr., turn right onto McGill Blvd.
Continue for 3 blocks to Dalhousie Rd. Turn right.
$45S　$65D　　　　　　　　　　　　　　　　　　▶ 4
🍳 Full, homebaked　🏠 Res., bungalow, patio, quiet　📷2D
(main floor)　🛏 2T,2Q,1P,crib　🛁1Ensuite, 1sh.w.g.　★F,TV,
parking　✋No smoking, no pets, no perfumes, ask re children
🕴 Two man-made fishing lakes and parks, U.of Lethbridge,
recreation/shopping centers, walking/hiking, city bus stop
🚗 Head-Smashed-in Buffalo Jump, Writing-on-Stone Archaeological Park, Dinosaur
museum/birds of Prey Sanctuary, Japanese Gardens, Remington Carriage House, Mormon Temple
🐎 Modern home with antiques and original oil paintings, situated in pleasant heart-of-Alberta
town. Enjoy the timeless elegance and comfort. Breakfast is served in antique furnished dining
room, or the country kitchen, or on the covered patio (weather permitting). ✒B&B

Haig, Joan and Bruce (Heritage House)　　☎ (403) 328-3824, Fax (403) 328-9011
1115-8th Ave. South, Lethbridge, AB　T1J 1P7　　　E-mail: haig@upanet.uleth.ca

Phone for directions.
$40S　$50D　$10Add.person　　　　　　　　　▶ 5
🍳 Full, homebaked　🏠Res., hist., patio, quiet　■2D(upst)
🛏1D,1Q　🛁 Sh.w.g.
🕴 Walking tour of Lethbridge, Japanese Gardens
🚗 Head-Smashed-In Buffalo Jump, hist. Ft. MacLeod, Mormon
Temple, Waterton Park, Remington Carriage Collection
🐎 1937-built home is a provincial historic resource, situated on
a large city lot not far from downtown area and designated because of its architecture and hand
painted inside decorations. Breakfasts reflect western Canadian taste. Hosts are knowledgeable
about western Canadian history. Reservations recommended. ✒B&B

Haynes, Helen (Forsyth House B&B)　　　　　　　☎ (403) 320-5344
715-3rd St.South, Lethbridge, AB　T1J 1Z4　　　E-mail: haynes@upanet.uleth.ca

From Calgary on Hwy 3 continue on Scenic Drive past 6th Ave South to 4th St South. Turn left to
7A Ave South, left to 3rd St South and left again to B&B.

$40-45S　$55-60D　　　　　　　　　　　　　　▶ 4A
🍳 Cont., homebaked　🏠 Downtown, 2-storey, hist., view from
guest rooms, deck, quiet　■ 2D(upstairs)　🛏 2D,1R
🛁1Sh.w.g　★ F,TV in guest rooms, separate entrance, off-street
& street parking, guest quarters are separate　✋ No smoking, no
pets, not suitable for children
🕴 Downtown, Gault Museum, Southern Alberta Art Gallery,
University of Lethbridge, Community College, YMCA, Coolie walks
🚗 Fort McLeod, Buffalo-Jump-Head-Smashed-In, Wakerton National Park
🐎 Tastefully restored 1906-built quiet home furnished with antiques througout, situated at the
edge of the Coolies looking over to the University. Formerly from Toronto, retired teacher has
many varied interests, including golfing, bridge playing. Breakfast is served in special guest
breakfast room. Access to computer available.

Mayerthorpe

(north-west of Edmonton; see also Fox Creek)

Allred, Donna Marie (Where Paths Cross - Bale & B&B) ☎ & Fax (403) 786-4972
Box 1372, Mayerthorpe, AB T0E 1N0 1-888-786-4972

From Edmonton, take Hwy 16 west to Hwy 22 and travel north to secondary Rd 647. Turn left
(west) 6.6km to Range Rd 92 and right (north) 2km.

$30S $40D $10Add.person $10(per horse) ⦿Meals (plus tax) ► 10

⬮ Full, homebaked 🏠 Rural, bungalow, acreage, view from
guest rooms, patio, quiet, secluded ▨ 2D,1F(main level)
⊨1T,3D,3air mattr. ⬯2Sh.w.g (one near office) ★ TV,LF,
large wood stove, off-street parking ⬤ Designated smoking area
🚶 Short paths through wooded area, log benches to rest and take
in the view or watch horses in pasture
🚙 Southills x-c ski area, Golden Triangle Trail (snowmobiling
350km long), ES Huestic Demonst.Forest, bow hunting & tours

🐎 Warm welcome in comfortable home with 19th Century furnishings and surrounded by quiet
scenic countryside. In the winter, the woodstove gives the whole house a toasty warm and cozy
atmosphere. Hostess is fond of the outdoors and likes to share "her little corner" with guests. Enjoy
pleasant conversation, good meals and a wonderful rest. There are 2 horses, 3 dogs and 3 cats.
Guest pets, including horses are welcome.

Nanton

(south of Calgary; see also Granum)

Gelden, Bill and Maria (Broadway Farm) ☎ (403) 646-5502
Box 294, Nanton, AB T0L 1R0

From Calgary take Hwy 2 south to Nanton. Turn east on Hwy 533 for 13 km. Turn south at sign
and travel 1.6 km. Then proceed east for 0.8 km.

$40S $50-60D 10Child ⦿Meals $100Homestead (Senior Discounts & weekly rates) ► 10A,2Ch

⬮ Full, homebaked 🏠 Farm, 2-storey, view, quiet, atrium
▨5(main & upper floor) ⊨4T,3D,1R,crib ⬯ Sh.w.g.
★TV,parking ⬤ Restricted smoking, no pets 〰 Dutch
🚶 Hiking, fishing, cross-country skiing, watch Swainson Hawks
nesting in back yard
🚙 Restaurants, swimming, tennis, golfing, museum, Magnetic
Hill, Little Bow & Chain Lake Provincial Parks, Olympic sites

🐎 1925-built and renovated brick farmhouse in a country setting of sunny Alberta. Located in
grainfields of the beautiful and spacious prairies with a panoramic view of the majestic Rockie
Mountains and lovely sunsets. Enjoy breakfast in the Atrium with large plants including a 10 ft
Palm tree. Hosts offer pig roasts for group functions. Fully licensed. There is a cat. Visa ⬿B&B

Squire, Sam & Rosemary (Turret House B&B) ☎(403) 646-5789
1911-26Ave, Nanton, AB T0L 1R0

At north end of Nanton, turn south off Hwy 2 at North Esso onto
26th Ave and to B&B.
$35S $55D $10-15child (babies free) ► 8
⬮ Full 🏠 Res., older, 2-storey, quiet, patio ▨ 2D(upstairs)
plus studio over garage ⊨1Q,1D,1P,cots ⬯ 2Sh.w.g. ★TV,
jacuzzi, off-street parking, sep.entrance ⬤No smoking, no pets
🚶 Downtown, antique shops, restaurants, Lancaster Air Museum,
swimming, park, churches
🚙 Golfing, horseback riding, Rocky Mountain Foothills, lakes, Calgary, Fort MacLeod
🐎 Friendly and helpful Christian hosts in new B&B location. Spacious, renovated home on
2-acres situated on the outskirts of small country town. Enjoy the lovely view of fields, mountains &
sunsets. Hosts have welcomed B&B guests for many years on their ranch outside of town. ⬿B&B

Peace River

Kelly, Irene (Kozy Quarters B&B)   ☎ (403) 624-2807
11015-99th St, Box 7493, Peace River, AB   T8S 1T1

Phone for directions
$50S $60D   ► 8A
🖭 Full, homebaked, self-serve   🏠 Res, hist., 2.5-storey, view,
frontriver, porch, quiet   ■ 4(upstairs)   ⊨ 2T,2D,1Q
🛁1Sh.w.h.   ★ F,TV, off-street parking   ⓌNo smoking
🏃 Downtown area, stores, restaurants
🚗 Museum, River Boat Tours, golfing, skiing, local arts & crafts,
trout farm, nature trails

🐾 Large home, tastefully renovated to enhance its historic character, located in a tranquil garden setting and the sole survivor of buildings constructed by the RCMP since 1916. Ideal place for business or pleasure stays. Bridal room on request. Breakfast is served in special guest breakfast room. There is a dog in residence. Visa ↙B&B

Pincher Creek

Lewis, Ken and Dorothy (Beau-K-Ranch)   ☎ Fax (403) 627-2234, Fax (403) 627-2276
Box 1720, Pincher Creek, AB   T0K 1W0

From traffic ligth in Pincher Creek, go 9km south on Hwy 6 to small cemetery on right. Turn

left and proceed .2 km to 1st house on right.
$35S $40-50D $5Child   🍽 Meals   ► 6A,4Ch
🖭Homebaked   🏠Farm, view, quiet   ■2D(main floor/ground
level)   ⊨1D,1Q,(1P/1R in ground level family room)   🛁2Private
★F,LF,wheel-chair access,trampoline,hot tub   ♥   ⓌNo smoking
🏃 Horseback riding, hiking,
🚗 Head-Smashed-In Buffalo Jump, Waterton Lakes Int. Peace
Park, Oldman River Dam, Frank Slide Interp.Center, Ft McLeod

🐾 Quiet country home on a working ranch in tranquil and very scenic surroundings, located in the Foothills. Relax in the open air hot tub after a busy day. Visa,MC ↙B&B

Ponoka

Storms, Jim & Doreen (Cranberry Creek B&B)   ☎ (403) 783-6123
RR2, Site 1, Box 15, Ponoka, AB   T4J 1R2   Fax (neighbor) (403) 783-2685

From Ponoka, go north on Hwy 2A for 12km, then east 3km and look for signs on highway.

$35S $45D $10Child(free under age 6)   🍽 Meals   ► 4
🖭 Full, homebaked   🏠 Farm, 3-storey, older, view, riverfront,
patio, deck, quiet   ■ 1F(lower level)   ⊨ 1D,1P   🛁1Private
★ Air,LF,KF,TV in guest room, coffee center & microwave
ⓌNo pets, designated smoking area, children welcome
🏃 Walks along riverside, large grounds with fire pit, frisbee golf
🚗 Ponoka Stampede, Wolf Creek Golf Course, Reynolds
Museum, Wetaskiwin, West Edmonton Mall

🐾 Senior hosts in comfortable Vintage 1922 house, situated on the banks of the Battle River. Relax on the deck while watching 40 species of wild birds (live/nest in the yard) and observe Canada Geese & beavers. Enjoy the award winning flower gardens. Pick-up & drop-off at airport available for a small charge. ↙B&B

Red Deer
(midway Calgary/Edmonton; see also Bentley, Ponoka)

Blake, Keith & Janine (McIntosh Tea House Bed & Breakfast)   ☎ (403) 346-1622
4631 Ross St.(50St), Red Deer, AB   T4N 1X1

From Red Deer city center go east on 49th St to 46th Ave, turn north and then west on Ross St.

$55S $65D $15Rollaway   (plus taxes)   ▶ 7A
🍳 Full, homebaked   🏠 Downtown, res, 3-storey, hist., view
■3D (2nd and 3rd floors)   ⊨ 3D,1R   ⊒ 3Private   ★ TV in
guest sitting room, separate entrance, off-street parking   🚭No
smoking, no pets, not suitable for children
🏃 Banks, shopping centre, restaurants, churches, theatres,
museum, 75 km walking and cycling paths leading to Fort
Normandeau and Heritage Ranch and excellent dining places
🐎 Stately Victorian home (1906), completely restored to it's original grandeur and furnished
with antiques. Hot breakfast with sweets and hot beverages served in the McIntosh Tea Room (on
premises), which also serves lunches & caters to small receptions. Visa, MC ✓B&B

Braun, Betty Ann & Ewald (Betty's B&B)   ☎ & Fax (403) 347-2465
RR1, Red Deer, AB   T4N 5E1

$40S $55D $20-25Child $5Pets   🍽 Meals   (plus tax)   ▶ 4A,2Ch

From Hwy 2 travel 6.7km west on Hwy 11 to Range Rd 284. Turn
north 0.8km to Twp Rd 384, then east 0.1km to B&B on left.
🍳 Full, homebaked   🏠 Rural, hillside, acreage, view from one
guest room, patio, porch, deck, quiet, secluded   ■ 2(lower
level)   ⊨2Q,1P   ⊒ 1Sh.w.g.   ★ LF,TV in guest family room,
private entrance, guest quarters are separate   🚬 Designated
smoking area, well-behaved children min. age 10   ∾ Slovak
🏃 Rainbow Trout Pond (fishing limit one a day per family)
🚗 Red Deer, Calgary/Edmonton Int. Airports, golf courses, Sylvan Lake Waterslides, Kerry Wood
Nature Centre (trails), Fort Normandeau (hist.site), 4 restaurants, shops, theatres, museums
🐎 Large, modern country home on 18 acres tree farm, easily accessible from major points. Enjoy
the comfortable and scenic tranquil surroundings and genuine Western hospitality. Breakfast is
served in the bright country kitchen. Corral facilities for visiting horses and kennels for dogs and
cats available. There are 2 dogs, 2 cats and 3 caged birds in residence. ✓B&B

Uiterwyk, Susan (Dutchess Manor Spa & Guesthouse)   ☎ (403) 346-7776
4813-54 Street, Red Deer, AB   T4N 2G5

Coming from south, proceed to city centre. Turn right on 55St, right on 48Ave and right on 54St.
From north take 67St turn-off to city entre. Turn left on 55St and proceed as above.

$50S $60D   (plus tax)   🍽 Meals   ▶ 6A

🍳 Full or Cont (caters to vegetarian diets)   🏠 Downtown, hist.,
2-storey, patio, porch, quiet   ■1S,2D(upstairs)   ⊨2T,1D,1K
⊒Sh.w.g.   ★ TV,LF, separate entrance, private deck, off-street
parking   🚭No pets, no children, designated smoking area
∾Dutch, French, German
🏃 City parks & Recreation areas, downtown, shopping, hospital
restaurants, theatres, museums, courthouse, bus stop across street
🚗 Golf courses, x/c ski trails, theatre
🐎 Cozy 1905-built home with lots of original woodwork, decorated in European style and located
in old area of city. Guest rooms have Dutch names. Hostess operates a full service aesthetic salon
and giftstore on main floor. Spa packages (evening, day or weekend) and steamroom/water massage
tub on premises available. "Come to Dutchess Manor for a Dutch Re-treat". ✓B&B

Ryley
(east of Edmonton; see also Sherwood Park, Camrose)

Meadley, Isabelle & Mick (Meadley's Bed & Breakfast)   ☎ (403) 663-2033
4832-54Ave., Box 224, Ryley, AB   T0B 4A0

Located 89km south-east of Edmonton on Hwy 14 ("the "Poundmaker Trail") to Sask.border.

$50S $55-65D   🍽 Meals   ▶ 6
🍲 Full, homebaked   🏠 Rural, village, bungalow, older, view,
deck, quiet   ■ 3(upper & lower level)   ⊨ 2D,1Q
🛁1Sh.w.g.   ★F,LF,TV in guest lounge, guest quarters are
separate, off-street parking   ✋ No smoking, no pets, children
min. age 12, quiet time after 11pm
🏃 George's Harness shop & working museum, Ryleys Cultural
Museum, indoor heated swimming pool, sausage making factory
🚗 Beaver Reg.Arts Centre (live theatre), Beaverhill Lake Shore Bird Reserve, Dodd's Coal Mine
📣 Relax on the lovely cedar deck and listen to the birds and water fountain, and watch the
goldfish in the pond. Or unwind by the fireplace with coffee and goodies. Entire cheerful downstairs
level has been renovated for B&B. Enjoy the wonderful Alberta hospitality. ↙B&B

Sedgewick
(east of Wetaskiwin; see also Camrose)

Trekofski, Mona & Joe (Ms Mona's Bed & Breakfast)   ☎ (403) 384-3936, Fax (403) 384-3730
Box 504, Sedgewick, AB   T0B 4C0

Phone for directions.
$45S $55D   🍽 Meals   (plus tax)   ▶ 6
🍲 Full, homebaked   🏠 Res., 2-storey, hist., porch, deck, quiet   ■ 3D
(upstairs)   ⊨ 2D,1Q   🛁 3Private   ★ Air,LF,F,TV in guest rooms,
separate entrance, off-street parking, winter plug-ins, large dining
room/gathering area with hot tub
🏃 Town of Sedgewick, archives, town park, Rec Centre, curling, bowling, hockey, golfing, x-c skiing
📣 Comfortable home (1912) on the highest point in town with Victorian-style decorated rooms.
Relax in the hot tub or by the fireplace & enjoy down-home country atmosphere.Visa,MC ↙B&B

Sherwood Park
(east of Edmonton; see also Ryley, Bruderheim)

Hendricks, Inge & Paul (Parklane Bed & Breakfast)   ☎ and Fax (403) 922-6143
#74 - 51047 Range Rd 221, Sherwood Park, AB   T8E 1G8

Take Hwy 14 east to Range Rd 221 and proceed south to 2nd entrance of Parklane Estates. Turn
left to 6th house on left.

$55S $65D $75Ste $10Add.person   🍽 Meals   ▶ 7
🍲 Full   🏠 Rural, hillside walkout, veranda   ■ 3 (ground
level)   ⊨ 2T,2Q,1R   🛁3Ensuite   ★Air,F,LF, guest lounge
(with TV,VCR, billiard table, exercise equipment, small bev.fridge),
hot tub ♥ ✋Smoking on veranda ∿German
🚗 Horseback riding, golfing, swimming, sailing, canoeing,
fishing, hiking, x-c skiing, shopping (West Edmonton Mall)
📣 Newer, elegant estate home with themed guest rooms including a honeymoon suite, situated
on 4 acres of rolling hills. Relax in the sun room, great room or in the guest lounge. Special events
packages (anniversaries/birthdays with customized menus, business meetings & retreats) offered.
Special diets considered. There are 2 outside cats. Visa ↙B&B

Newman, Vic & Marie (The Berry Inn B&B)   ☎ & Fax (403) 662-2595, (403) 662-3313
51271 Range Rd 203, Sherwood Park, AB   T8G 1E8

From Edmonton travel east 40km on Hwy 14E to Range Rd 203. Turn north 2km.
$55S $65D $10Child   🍽 Meals   (special rates available)   ▶ 8

🍲 Full, homebaked   🏠 Farm, 2-storey ranch-style, view from guest rooms, lakefront, porch, deck, quiet, secluded   ■4D(ground level) ⊨4S,2Q ⊿1Sh.w.g.,1sh.w.h. ★Air,F,KF,LF,TV in guest room,, separate entrance, wheel-chair access, pool table, reading area, indoor sauna, horse shoe pitch, large private guest area ⓌNo smoking, no pets
🏃 Strawberry/raspberry/saskatoon berry fields, in-house gift shop, excellent bird watching
🚗 Large wilderness rec.area (x-c skiing, cycling, hiking), Beaver Hill Lake Nature Centre
🚐 Large modern log home, fully accessible (Access/Level 3), located on functioning 160 acres berry farm at Hastings Lake. U-pick/we-pick available. Relax & enjoy an outdoor barbeque, wiener roast or a sing song at the fire circle. Breakfast is served in special guest breakfast room. Wheel chair van transportation available. Ask about longer stays/special needs. MC,Visa ✔B&B

Smoky Lake   *(north-east of Edmonton; see also Vilna)*

Plumb, Enid & Bob (Inn at the Ranch)   ☎ (403) 656-2474, Fax (403) 656-3094
Box 562, Smoky Lake, AB   T0A 3C0   1-800-974-2474

Travel northeast on Hwy 28 to secondary Rd 855 at Smoky Lake. Follow sign for 22 km to ranch.
$55S $70D $15Add.person   🍽 Meals   (Reservations required)   ▶ 13

🍲Full, homebaked 🏠Farm, ranch-style, 2-storey, view from guest rooms, porch, quiet, deck   ■3F(upstairs ⊨2T,1D,3Q,3P ⊿Ensuite ★TV in guest room, parking ⓌNo smoking, no pets
🏃 Walking and x/c ski paths (up to 13.5 km), tours to see large herd of bison, elk and minature donkeys on farm site
🚗 Lakes, antique shops restaurants, historic sites
🚐 Warm welcome on Bison-Elk ranch with newly-built home surrounded by bushland. Relax on the covered front porch or on the back deck. House specialty is bison roast or steak. ✔B&B

Spruce Grove   *(north of Edmonton)*

Babala, Anne & Dale (Annie's B&B Inn)   ☎ (403)459-9858,Cell914-4301,Fax459-2703
No15, 51214, Range Rd.260, Spruce Grove, AB   T7Y 1B1   E-mail: anniesinn@compusmart.ab.ca

From Hwy 16, go south on Winterburn Rd (215St). Go 16km to Twp Rd 512, west to 1st house.
$40S $55D $5Child $70F   ▶ 8

🍲 Full, homebaked   🏠 Rural, 2-storey, acreage, view from guest rooms, porch, quiet   ■2D,1F(upstairs) ⊨1S,1D,1Q,1R,1P,1D ⊿ 2Sh.w.g., 1powder room(main floor) ★ F,TV, ceiling fans, guest quarters are upstairs, host quarters on main floor   �ⓌNo smoking, pets accepted with prior arrangement
🏃 Excellent bird watching from screened veranda, meander in bush acreage on property, fire pits for wiener roasts/yarn spinning
🚗 University of Alberta, Devonian Bot.Garden, golf courses, West Edmonton Mall, Int.Airport
🚐 Bright, modern home in excellent countryside location. Hosts are enthusiastic hobbyists, enjoying woodworking, quilting, golfing, gardening and scuba diving in far off places and are experienced grandparents. Motorhomes, horse trailors etc. can easily be accommodated on large circular driveway. Plug-ins available. Children welcome. Visa ✔B&B

Henitiuk, Mike & Audrey (Stonesthrow B&B)　　　☎ (403) 962-0829, Fax (403) 962-9465
46 Fairway Dr., Spruce Grove, AB　T7X 3K3

Travel west from Edmonton on Yellowhead Hwy 16 to Century Rd (turn-off
at Spruce Grove). Proceed south on Century Rd to Grove Dr, west to Links
Rd, and north on Fairway Dr.
$45S　$60D　$5Child　$15Add.person　🎫 Meals　　　　▶ 4A,2Ch
🌞Summer only　🍞Homebaked　🏠Res., 2-storey, view from guest rooms,
patio, deck, quiet　■ 1S,2D(upstairs)　🛏 1D,1Q,2R　🛁1sh.w.g.
★F,KF,LF,TV　🖐 Designated smoking area, no pets　〰 French
🧍 Golf course at back, walking trails, shops, public swimming, restaurants
🚐 West Edmonton Mall (world's largest shopping Mall), downtown
Edmonton, Stony Plain Multicultural Centre, Devon Botanical Gardens,
Fairytale Grounds

☛ Quiet city place with a view of the Glory Hills north of Spruce Grove and golf course at back.
Watch the golfers on the links from the back yard or try a round or two. Well travelled hosts enjoy
exchanging travel experiences. Transportation to and from airport, train or bus terminal and City
of Edmonton available. ✏CC

Strathmore　　　　　　　　　　　　　　　　　　　　*(east of Calgary)*

Sproule, Winston and Vera (Sproule Heritage Place Bed & Breakfast)　　☎ (403) 934-3219
Box 43, S14, RR1, Strathmore, AB　T1P 1J6

Located east of Strathmore on TCH1. Travelling west go 7.8km
west from jct 561. From Calgary (going east) travel 14.5km east of
Strathmore. Watch for B&B highway sign.
$60-70D　　　　　　　　　　　　　　　　　　　　　▶ 6A
🍽 Full, homebaked　🏠Rural, hist., veranda　■3D(upst)
🛏2T,1D,2Q　🛁1Sh.w.g.,1private　★TV, separate entrance
🖐No pets, smoking on open veranda, not suitable for children
〰Russian, Ukrainian
🚐 Rocky Mountains, Tyrrell Museum, Drumheller, Calgary (40Km)
☛ Charming 1920 Heritage home surrounded by prairie scenery (an Alberta Registered Historic
Resource farmsite). House was chosen by Hallmark (USA) for 1987 Christmas & 1991 Alberta
Gov't Telephone for filming. Restored by the hosts to its original beauty and furnished with
antiques and replicas handmade by the hosts. Fine handwork/historic art are for viewing and sale.

Three Hills　　　　　　　　　　　*(north-east of Calgary; see also Drumheller)*

Vermeer, Gerrit & Mary (A Touch of Dutch B&B)　　　　　　☎ (403) 443-2709
820-8th Ave, Box 1363, Three Hills, AB　T0M 2A0

From Calgary, travel east on Hwy 1 to Hwy 21. Turn north to Three Hills, proceed on Hwy 583
west to 4-way stop. Continue north on 6Ave to 7St. Turn east to 8Ave.
$45S　$50D　$10Child/Add.person　🎫 Meals　　　　　　　　▶ 6A,2Ch

🍽 Full, homebaked　🏠 Village, raised bungalow, deck, quiet
■3D (lower level)　🛏 3Q,1P　🛁 1Sh.w.g.　★ F,TV in guest
lounge, separate entrance, off-street parking, guest quarters are
separate　🖐 No smoking, no pets　〰 Dutch
🚐 Prairie Bible Institute, Three Hills Aquatic Centre, Knee Hill
historic museum, Guzoo Animal Farm, golfing, Dry Isle Buffalo
Jump Prov. Park, Bleriot Ferry, Gopher Museum, Rosebud
Theatre, Hoodoos, Royal Tyrell Museum, Badlands
☛ Friendly Dutch hospitality in newly-built home with Dutch touches throughout. Retired hosts
have a large family (all away from home) and enjoy having a "full house". Breakfast is served in
family dining room. ✏CC

Turner Valley
(south of Calgary)

Gauger, Jutta & Peter (Nature's Nook B&B Retreat & Wellness Spa) ☎/Fx(403)933-4756
687 Royalite Way SE, Turner Valley, AB T0L 2A0

From Calgary, take Hwy 22 south to Turner Valley. Turn left at Decalta Dr and left at Imperial

Dr. Proceed to Royalite Way. Turn right.
$45-55S $60-70D   🍴 Meals   ► 6A
🍽 Full, homebaked   🏠 Rural, 2-storey, view from guest rooms,
patio, deck, quiet   ■ D,Ste (main & upper level)   ⊨ 4S,1Q
🛏 1Ensuite, 1sh.w.g.   ★ Air,TV in guest rooms, separate
entrance, private balconies, spa services/massage available
🚭Smoking outside, no pets 〰German
🏃 Golf course, horseback riding, hiking, fishing, golfing
🚐 Kananaskis Country, Spruce Meadows, City of Calgary, Calgary Stampede, Banff
🚐 Elegant country home situated on Golf Course. Relax in the garden hot tub. Fasting/detoxing
program & special meals available. ✓B&B

Vilna
(north-east of Edmonton; see also Smoky Lake)

Lavoie, Yvette & Robert (Country Garden B&B) ☎ (403) 636-2029
Box 545, Vilna, AB T0A 3L0

Phone for directions.
$35S $45D $15Add.person   ► 6
🍽 Full, homebaked   🏠 Rural, bungalow, acreage, deck, sun room, quiet   ■ 1S,2D(main
floor)   ⊨1S,2Q   🛏 2sh.w.h.   ★ KF,LF,TV   🖐 Designated smoking area   〰 French
🚐 Smokey Lake (World Pumpkin Weigh-off in Oct), great hunting and fishing areas
🚐 Warm welcome in spacious log-style home. Relax in the sun room off the kitchen or on the
deck. Hostess is well known for her cooking/baking and can usually be found in the kitchen.

Wetaskiwin
(south of Edmonton; see also Camrose, Ponoka)

Chamberlain, Sue & Tom (Karriage House 1908 B&B) ☎ (403) 352-5996
5215-47St, Wetaskiwin, AB T9A 1E1   1-888-352-5996

Follow Hwy 2A into Wetaskiwin. turn east on Main St at water-tower. Proceed through downtown
to 47St (old court house on corner). Turn north and look for B&B on corner of 53Ave.

$55S $65-85D $10Add.person   ► 8
🏕 guest cottage in summer only   🍽 Full, homebaked   🏠 Res.,
2-storey, hist., sunroom   ■ 3D(upstairs) plus guest cottage
⊨2T,2D,1Q,1P   🛏 1Sh.w.g., 1ensuite   ★ F,private entrance,
off-street parking, guests quarters are separate   🖐 No smoking,
no pets, children welcome by arrangement
🏃 Browse in the antique shop on premises, historic Court House,
downtown district, museum, recreation facilities, restaurants
🚐 Reynolds Alberta Museum (transportation), Cdn Aviation Hall of Fame, Railway Museum
🚐 1908-built home - a good place to rest after a day of museum trecking or a long journey.
Experience the intimacy of the Karriage guest cottage during the summer. Hosts are familiar with
local museums and interested in antique vehicles and collectibles. Breakfast is served in the dining
room or on the deck. Savour a cup of tea by the fireplace or in the Curio Sunroom. Visa ✓B&B

Saskatchewan

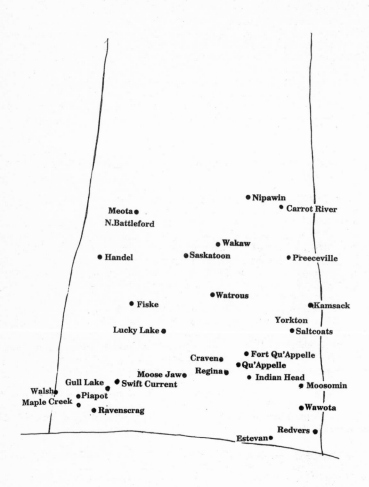

Meota●
N.Battleford

●Nipawin
●Carrot River

●Wakaw
●Saskatoon
●Handel
●Preeceville

●Watrous
●Fiske
●Kamsack

Yorkton
Lucky Lake●
●Saltcoats

Craven● ●Fort Qu'Appelle
●Qu'Appelle
Moose Jaw● Regina●
Gull Lake● ●Swift Current ●Indian Head
Walsh● ●Piapot ●Moosomin
Maple Creek●
●Ravenscrag ●Wawota

Redvers ●
Estevan●

Tourism Saskatchewan
1919 Saskatchewan Dr.
Regina, SK S4P 3V7

toll-free 1-800-667-7191

Carrot River
(east of Prince Albert)

Craig, Dorothy & Osborne (Craig's Pasquia Hills View Vacation Farm & B&B)
RR1, Box 2, S5, Carrot River, SK S0E 0L0 ☎ (306) 768-3637

Phone for directions.
$30S $50D $10Child   🍽 Meals   (plus taxes)   ►4A,2Ch
🍳 Choice, homebaked   🏠 Farm, bungalow, view, porch, deck, quiet, isolated   ▪2D(main floor) plus Dorm   ⊨ 2D,1P,4Din
Dorm   ⬛ 1Sh.w.h.,1sh.w.g in basement for Dorm
★F,TV,LF   ⓦ Designated smoking area
🕏 Buffalo Rubbing Rock, beaver dams, bird & wildlife watching, x-c skiing, organic garden & tree demonstrations & innovative farming practices, great snowmobiling (near Rtes 66/75 - groomed trails), horseback/trail rides
🚗 Pasquia Hills, shale bed rivers & fossil digging site, peat bog stripping & processing plant, Sask Forest Sawmill, grain elevators, Nipawin Golf Course, Tobin Lake (fishing, boating), hunting
🐾 Modern house on 675 acres homestead surrounded by orchard, garden and natural shelterbelts situated on the edge of tree-clad Pasquia Hills. Enjoy the tranquil, surroundings with fresh, clean & pollution-free air and watch the beautiful Northern Lights (when visible). Ideal place for wildlife enthusiasts and photographers. Special diets & picnic lunches provided. Located in hunting zone #59 (exp.hunter on premises). Powered camp sites available. There are outdoor pets. ✓B&B

Craven
(north of Regina)

Brennan, Carrie & Kelly (The Fieldstone Inn)   ☎ (306) 731-2369 (306) 731-2377
Box 26038, Regina, SK S4R 8R7   Fax (306) 731-2369

Located in the scenic Qu'Appelle Valley and approx. 45km north of Regina. Phone for directions.
$57S $75D   (plus tax)   ►6
🍳 Full, homebaked   🏠 Rural, 3-storey, fieldstone, acreage, view from guest rooms, riverfront, patio, quiet   ▪3D (2nd floor)
⊨3D   ⬛ 1Sh.w.g. 1sh.w.h.   ★ TV,F,LF, guest library
ⓦDesignated smoking area
🕏 Hidden Valley Nature Refuge, Qu'Appelle River, Kennel Historic Church, Buffalo Jump
🚗 Craven Big Valley Jamboree, Piapot Indian Reservation, Regina, Hutterite Colony
🐾 Cut fieldstone Heritage homestead (ca 1903) with country elegance, tranquility and a spectacular view of the beautifull Qu'Appelle Valley. Explore the unlimited trails and unsploiled prairie wilderness. A variety of optional tour programs are available, ranging from romantic get-aways to horse drawn sleigh and wagon rides. Winner of the Saskatchewan Architectural Heritage Society 1996/7 Vintage Building Award. ✓B&B

Estevan
(south east of Regina, near US border; see also Redvers)

Hemus, Kaye (Turn-of-the-Century B&B)   ☎ (306) 634-6405, Fax (306) 634-7456
1309-3rd St., Estevan, SK S4A 0S1

Located 10km from US border on Hwy 475. Phone for directions.
$45-50S $50-55D   (plus tax)   ►6
🍳 Full, homebaked   🏠 Downtown, hist., deck, quiet   ▪3D (main level)   ⊨ 2D,2T   ⬛ 1sh.w.g., 1ensuite   ★ Air,TV, off-street and street parking   ⓦ Smoking outside only
🕏 Heritage Town Walking Tour, Estevan Nat. Exhibition Centre, Aquatic & Leisure Centre, golfing
🚗 Rafferty/Alameda Dams, Shand Power Stn & Greenhouse
Estevan & area self-guided driving, mine & energy tours (free), summer theatre (July/Aug)
🐾 Heritage home with plenty of oak, brass, stained glass windows, antique furnishings and Victorian lace. Elegance & hospitality in the Energy City. Enjoy a peaceful, quiet and refreshing rest in beautiful surroundings. Family or group rates available. Visa ✓B&B

Fiske
(south-west of Saskatoon; see also Handel)

Siemens, Bob & Charlene (Longview Farm & B&B)   ☎ (306) 377-4786
Box 53, Fiske, SK S0L 1C0

From Hwy 1 at Swift Current, take Hwy 4 north to Rosetown, then Hwy 7 west to Fiske. Proceed

1.5 km south and 1.5 km east.
$35S $45D   🍽 Meals   (plus tax)   ►4
❄ Summer only   ⬤ Full, homebaked   🏠 Farm, 2-storey,
quiet   ■ 2D(main & upper level in guest house)   ⊨ 2Q,1S
🛁1Sh.w.g.   ★LF,KF, parking   ⛔ No smoking   ～ German
🚶 Nature walks through pastures, rustic cottage on property
🚗 Petroglyphs at Herschel
🐾 Warm welcome on working farm in western Saskatchewan
farm country. There are cattle, sheep and chickens. "Come, share our love of the land". Bring a
chicken ornamment to add to hosts' "roost" (collection) and get discount on first night. ✓B&B

Fort Qu'Appelle
(east of Regina; see also Qu'Appelle, Indian Head)

Whiting, Jill & Jerry (Company House B&B)   ☎ (306) 332-6333
Box 1159, 172 Company Ave., Fort Qu'Appelle, SK S0G 1S0   E-mail: chbbt@sk.sympatico.ca

Located 1 block from The Hudson Bay Store, next to Town Office.
$40S $55D   (Family rates available)   (plus tax)   ►6
⬤ Full, homebaked   🏠 Res., hist., older, sweeping veranda,
quiet   ■ 3D(upstairs)   ⊨ 2D,1K   🛁2Sh.w.g. clawfoot tub &
jacuzzi   ★Air,F,parking, TV in private guest lounge
⛔Smoking outside only, no pets   ♥   ～some French
🚶 Beaches, fishing, canoeing, birdwatching, tennis, shopping
🚗Mission Ridge golf club/skii hill,Echo Prov.Park,Ft Museum
🐾 Charming home, built in the early 1900, with 10 ft ceilings, chandeliers, bevelled glass
windows and ceramic cherry wood fireplaces. Enjoy friendly Prairie hospitality in a relaxed rural
setting of popular Saskatchewan resort town. Hosts have lived in many regions of Canada and are
delighted to welcome guests. ✓B&B

Gull Lake
(west of Swift Current; see also Piapot, Maple Creek)

Magee, Tom & Beatrice (Magee's Farm)   ☎ (306) 672-3970
Box 428, Gull Lake, SK S0N 1A0

Take Trans Canada Hwy west from Gull Lake for 13.3km. Turn left at "Carmichael" sign, then 6km
south to "Magee" sign. Turn left and go for 2.5km to 1st farm on left.
$25-30S $35-50D $10-15Child(under age 12)   🍽 Meals   ►6

⬤ Choice, homebaked   🏠 Farm, ■ Modern cabin   ⊨S,D
🛁 Sh.w.g.   ★ F,KF   ⛔ Pets welcome
🚶 Working grain and livestock farm grounds
🚗 Town of Gull Lake, Indian historic site, lookout, trout fishing
🐾 Mixed working farm. Hosts were involved in 4H and are very
interested in photography. Hunters welcome. There is a resident
dog and cat. Please phone ahead for reservation. ✓B&B

Handle

(west of Saskatoon; see also Fiske)

Schoeler, Howard and Shirley ☎ (306) 658-4347
Handle, Saskatchewan S0K 1Y0

From Saskatoon, take Hwys 14 and 51 past Biggar and continue on paved road.

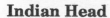

$30S $40D $3 Each   Meals   ▶ 4A,3Ch
Choice, homebaked   Farm, view   1S,2D   D,S
2Sh.w.h.   ★ TV,F
Towns of Biggar, Unity and Wilkie
Fully equipped working grain farm in wheat-farming centre
and situated in a quiet setting, excellent location for a night of
relaxation after a day's travelling. Enjoy the wide-open spaces.
Hosts delight in giving visitors a short tour of the area.

Indian Head

(east of Regina; see also Qu'Appelle, Fort Qu'Appelle)

Sanders, Murray & Christy (Manor House Bed & Breakfast)   ☎ (306) 695-3853
Box 159, 501 Woodward St., Indian Head, SK S0G 2K0

Phone for directions.
$35S $45D   Meals   ▶ 11
Cont., homebaked   Res., 2-storey, hist., above-ground
swimming pool, patio, porch, quiet   1S,5D(upst)   1S,5D
2Sh.w.g.   ★F, TV,LF   No smoking, no pets
Qu'Appelle Valley, PFRA Tree Nursery, PFRA Experimental
Farm, Regina
Comfortable home, built in 1904 as a Duplex was once a focal
point of the town renowned for its gardens and fish pond and situated in oldest town in
Saskatchewan. Now a single dwelling and upgraded to modern comfort retaining as much of the
original character & charm as possible. Relax and enjoy the congenial hospitality. Visa

Kamsack

(north of Yorkton; see also Preeceville)

Brock, Don & Marleen (Border Mountain Country B&B)   ☎(306)542-3072
Box 1233, Kamsack, SK S0A 1S0   E-mail: scott.tulloch@sk.sympatico.ca, Fax(306)542-2166

From Kamsack travel 7km east and 3km south on Hwy 5, 5km east on Side Rd.
$35S $45D $5-10Child(free under age 6) $10Add.person   Meals   ▶ 4A,4Ch
Full, homebaked   Farm, bungalow, view, porch, deck,
quiet,secluded   2F(lower level)   2T,1Q,3R,crib   1sh.w.g.
★LF,private entrance   Smoking outside
Scenic valley area for hiking, cycling, horseback riding (guest
owned horses), bird/wild animal viewing, hunting (Elk, moose,
deer, black bear, wolves, coyotes, fox, beaver), farm animals
including Arabian horses
Kamsack, Duck Mountain Prov.Park and Ski Area, National
Doukobour Heritage Village, museum, restaurants, golf course
Cozy, country-style bungalow with a pleasant mixture of old and new in scenic valley setting.
Property adjoins thousands of acres of accessible wildlife lands and gorgeous Duck Mountain
Prov.Park (Aspen forest gives way to Pine). All produce is home grown. "Empty-Nester" hosts are
familiar with the surrounding area and enjoy outdoors. Bed/Bale for guest horses. There is a small
resident dog. Visa,MC B&B

Lucky Lake

(north of Swift Current)

Gjertsen, Dagny & Harold (D & H Bed & Breakfast)   ☎ (306) 858-2102
107-2nd Ave.N, Lucky Lake, SK   S0L 1Z0

Phone for directions.
$25S $35D $5Child $15Add.person (plus tax)   ► 4A,2Ch
📞(provisions in room) 🏠Village,bungalow,hist.,quiet ■2
(main floor) ⊨4S,1R,cot ⌂2Private ★LF,KF,TV in guest
rooms,sep.entrance, parking 🚫No pets ⚬⚬Swedish
🚶 Museum, shopping, dining, hockey/curling rink, park
� 6000 acre Ducks Unlimited Marsh, fish hatchery & fish farm,
Lake Diefenbaker, exc.hunting (duck/goose/deer/antelope)
🐾 Friendly hospitality in large renovated school house. Hosts have been welcoming guests for
many years & are very knowledgeable about the area and willing to be tour guides.Visa,MC ✓CC

Maple Creek

(west of Swift Current near AB border; see also Piapot, Ravenscrag)

Sorensen, Bent & Karen (Cypress Hills Bed & Breakfast)   ☎ (306) 662-3377
Box 1090, Maple Creek, SK   S0N 1N0

Located 37 km south of Maple Creek on Hwy 21, then 2.5 km west and 2.5 km north. Look for signs
$30S $40D $5Add.person 🍽Meals   ► 4
📞 Cont. 🏠 Rural, 2-storey, 160 acres, deck, patio, quiet
■1Ste(main floor), host quarters are upstairs ⊨ 1D,1P,cot
⌂Ensuite ★ KF,TV in suite, guest lounge, separate entrance,
parking ⚬⚬ Danish
🚶 Hills and forests for walking, large vegetable garden, wild
berries in season, outdoor fire pit
🚗 Maple Creek ("Old Cow Town"), Cypress Hills Prov.Park
🐾 Situated on secluded large 160 acres of unspoiled nature with abundant wildlife. Hosts have
retired from Tourism business and travelled extensively. There is a "Kitty" in residence. ✓B&B

Meota

(north of North Battleford)

Sutton, June and Brian (Lakeside Leisure Farm)   ☎ & Fax (306) 892-2145
Box 1, Meota, SK   S0M 1X0

Located 28 km north of the Battlefords (Hwy 4) and 4.5 km west on Metinota Access Rd.
$50-79S/D   (Special rate for longer stays)   ► 12
✚ April-Nov 📞(health-smart) 🏠Farm, ranch-style, view,
lakefront, patio, quiet ■3D, plus 3D at poolside ⊨4Q,4T
⌂2Sh.w.g., 1private ★TV,F,LF, indoor swimming pool, private
entrance (2rooms) 🚫No smoking, pets welcome
🚶 Swimming Pool, Jackfish Lake, sandy beaches, fishing,
swimming, sailing, golfing
🚗 N/S Battleford, bird-watching, hunting
🐾 Spacious home overlooking Jackfish Lake with a spectacular view of the water, rolling
farmland and distant hills. Nature & Agriculture tours, experienced licensed guide for excellent fall
hunting available. Gift Certificates. Hosts are recipients of Sask. Business Hospitality Award for
Excellence (1996). Champagne & Roses packages available. Two nights stay min. on weekends
during June/July/August. Visa

Moose Jaw
(west of Regina)

Latimer, Bill (Latimer on Oxford Bed & Breakfast) ☎ (306) 692-5481
37 Oxford Street West, Moose Jaw, SK S6H 2N2

Phone for directions.
$55-65S $60-90D   (plus tax) ▶ 6A
🍴 Full, homebaked 🏠 Downtown, res., 3-storey, hist., city view
from guest rooms, porch, deck ■3D(2nd floor) ⊨1S,2D
🛏1Sh.w.g. ★Off-street parking ⓌNo smoking
🏃 Downtown, museum, Temple Gardens Mineral Spa
📣 1911 Heritage Neo-Greek Revival home with ten Corinthian
columns, Acanthus leaves on front oak door and leaded glass
windows. Hosts' interest include classical music, art & literature and are involved with the Heritage Board. There is a also a carriage house on property. Mineral Spa tickets available. ✓B&B

Thiele, Patricia (Redland Cottage B&B) ☎ (306) 694-5563
1122 Redland Ave., Moose Jaw, SK S6H 3P3

Phone for directions.
$45S $50D $5Vhild $75F   🍽 Meals ▶ 4
🍴 Full 🏠 Res., bungalow, hist., porch, quiet, veranda ■2 (main floor) ⊨3D 🛏1sh.w.g.
★KF,LF,F,TV, ceiling fans, off-street & street parking, guest quarters are separate
ⓌDesignated smoking area
🏃 Downtown, historic Mineral Water Health Spa, beautiful crescent Park, Civic Centre
🚗 Kinsmen Aquatic Centre, CFB Moose Jaw, Snowbirds Flying Team, Regina
📣 Restored home to reflect its Prairie beginnings with Prairie antiques in one guest room and Victorian decor in the other. Relax on the open veranda and enjoy breakfast (weather permitting). Complimentary Chokecherry Jelly Jar for guests. There is a poodle in residence. Also available Homesteader cabin quarters in back yard with very authentic decor. ✓CC

Moosomin
(south-west of Regina; see also Redvers)

Wright, Pat (Pat's Attic B&B) ☎ (306) 435-4196
708 Mark Ave., Box 214, Moosomin, SK S0G 3N0

Take Hwy 1 to Moosomin. Turn south on Hwy 8 (Main St) and
proceed 5 block to Mark Ave. Turn west.
$35S $45D $55F $10Add.person   (plus tax) ▶ 6A,2Ch
🍴 Full, homebaked 🏠 Res., 3-storey, quiet ■ 2D,1F
(upstairs) ⊨ 2T,2D,1P 🛏 1sh.w.g., 1sh.w.h ★TV,F,KF,
off-street parking ⓌNo smoking
🏃 Jamieson Museum, downtown (shops, restaurants, churches,
tennis, bowling)
🚗 Golf course, 6 lakes, Tea Houses, scenic Qu'Appelle Valley, Moosomin Reg.Park, plane landing strip, historic Cannington Manor, Potash Mine
📣 Recently retired hostess in turn-of-the-Century home with spacious grounds. Relax in the comfortable surroundings and cozy up to the fire place on a cool evening. Browse through the display of Art by local artists. Breakfast is served in special guest breakfast room. Inquire about the family lakeside cabin on Round Lake in the beautiful Qu'Appelle Valley. ✓CC

North Battleford
(north-west of Saskatoon; see also Meota)

Klassen, Irene (Irene's B&B)   ☎ (306) 445-4092
1402-98th St., North Battleford, SK   S9A 0M4

Phone for directions.
$25S $35D $5Child $10Add.person   ◙ Meals   ►6
⬛Full,homebaked   🏠Res.,2-storey,patio,porch   ■3(upstairs)
⊨ 2S,2D   ⬛ 1Sh.w.g., jacuzzi   ★TV,LF, street & off-street
parking   ⬤No smoking
🏃 Allen Sapp Gallery, downtown, Sports Arena, public pool
🚗 Western Development Museum, Fort Battleford, golfing, Table
Mountain & White Tail Ski Resorts, Provincial & Regional park
routes & scenic Saskatchewan River Valley drives, bus depot
☛ Friendly welcome in large "low key" family home, surrounded by unique blend of culture,
history and world class art. Over the years, hosts have welcomed many guests through Mennonite
Central Committee Exchange. Enjoy comfortable/homey & genuine Northern hospitality.

Piapot
(west of Swift Current; see also Gull Lake, Maple Creek)

Wright, Linda & Ken (Wright's Vacation Farm)   ☎ (306) 558-4611
Box 28, Piapot, SK   S0N 1Y0

Halfway between Tompkins & Piapot on TCH 1, turn south towards the town of Eastend to first
farm on west side of road.
$30S $40D   ◙ Meals   (plus tax)   ►8A
⬛ Homebaked   🏠 Farm, ranch-style, old   ■ 4 (main & upper
floor) in guest house & main residence   ⊨ 3D,1Q   ⬛Sh.w.g.,
sh.w.h.   ★ KF, TV in guest quarters, corral accommodation for
horses, camping area   ⬤ Smoking area
🏃 Walks in open native prairie land, bird watching, farm grounds,
custom saddle & leather work shop on premises
🚗 Various golf courses, museums, Cypress Hills Provincial Park, Fort Walsh Nat.Park, Piapot
☛ Mixed grain farm with Hereford cattle and horses. Guests can help with farm chores if they
desire. There are many opportunities to do things or just relax. Bus tours welcome for coffee break.
There is a resident dog.

Preeceville
(north-east of Regina; see also Kamsack)

Peters, Sally (The Red Willow)   ☎ (306) 547-3325, Fax (306) 547-2736
Box 954, Preeceville, SK   S0A 3B0

Located 1km north of Preeceville on Hwy 9. Look for big Lady & Teapot sign.
$30S $40D $60F   (Reduced rates for longer stay)   ►6
✚ May1-Oct.1   ⬛ Self-serve   🏠 Rural, separate guest cottage, 3acres, view from guest room,
patio, deck, quiet   ■ 2 in guest cottage   ⊨ 3D   ⬛ 1Private   ★ KF, wheel-chair access,
paddle boat for guests   ♥   ⬤ Designated smoking area   〰 some French
🏃 Small driving range, walks & trails, Teahouse and Courtyard on property, Preeceville, x-c skiing,
🚗 Hospital, Lady Lake Reg.Park (lake stocked with trout), Sturgis Station House Museum, Rama
Grotto, Doukhobor Heritage Village, Duck Mountain Prov.Park, antique machinery abound
☛ Retired Airforce couple in country home situated in park-like surrounding. Guest quarters are
in separate cottage with Victorian decor nestled on the shores of Annie Laurie Lake. Enjoy the
morning call of the loon and the peacefullness as the sun gives some of the most magnificient
display of its glory. Hosts enjoy walks in the woods and invite guests to join them. Excellent
birdwatching around the lake. Guests are invited to bring own canoe. Breakfast provisions supplied
in cottage. There is room for campers and trailers or tents.

Qu'Appelle
(east of Regina; see also Fort Qu'Appelle, Indian Head)

Mader, Ken and Jo (Bluenose Country Vacation Farm & B&B)   ☎ & Fax (306) 699-7192
Box 173, Qu'Appelle, SK S0G 4A0   ☎ (306) 699-2328

Located 4.8 km north of the Trans Canada Highway on Hwy 35. Watch for signs.
$48S $64D (or Family) $3Pets   ☒ Meals   (plus tax)   ► 12

🅳 Full, homebaked   🏠 Working grain farm, 3-storey, indoor heated swimming pool, quiet   ⬛ 3 (upper floor), 2Stes   ⊨3D,2Q cots   ⟿5private   ★Air,TV, separate entrance, wheel-chair access   ⓌRestricted smoking
🏃 Mini golf & children's playground on property, Bluenose Agriculture Interpretive Centre, farm animal zoo, nature trail
🚗 Qu'Appelle fishing lakes and resorts, boating, Regina, Dominion Experimental Farms, horseback riding

📷 Majestic fieldstone (turn-of-the-Century) English style home, built in 1904, with walls up to 3ft deep, with a striking silhouette - a landmark on the prairie landscape. There is a Country Tea Room on premises and a historic Church Hall for day bus tours, weddings, retreats. Relax and enjoy the fresh country air and beautiful sky-wide sunsets - an agriculture experience with country elegance. Saskatchewan hospitality award winners. Vacation packages available. Visa,MC ⟿B&B

Ravenscrag
(south-west of Swift Current near US border; see also Maple Creek)

Saville, Jim (Spring Valley Guest Ranch)   ☎ (306) 295-4124
Box 10, Ravenscrag, SK S0N 0T0

Call ahead for directions.
$35S $55D $15Child   ☒ Meals   ► 8
🅳 Full   🏠 Farm, older, quiet, isolated   ⬛ 4D (upstairs)   ⊨4D   ⟿1Sh.w.g.   ★ KF,LF   ⓌRestricted smoking
🏃 Pleasant wooded valley (exceptional in spring-time) and abundant wildlife, horseback-riding arranged, craft/leather shop
🚗 Cypress Hills Prov. Park (golfing, swimming, boating, craft shops), historic Fort Walsh

📷 Early-Century built home in ideal location for naturalists, photographers and those who can appreciate the beauty of total darkness, silence and solitude. Also available large log home with banquet facilities for weddings, family re-unions, retreats and workshops. ⟿B&B

Redvers
(south-east corner of Regina near MB border: see also Moosomin, Estavan)

Sylvestre, Lorna & André (Sylvestre's Bed & Breakfast)   ☎ (306) 452-3854
Box 429, Redvers, SK S0C 2H0   Fax (306) 452-6195

Located 14 km west of Redvers on Hwy 13. Phone for directions.
$35S $45D $10Child   ☒Meals   (plus Tax)   ► 10
🅳 Choice, homebaked   🏠 Farm, 2-storey, quiet, large yard   ⬛1D,2F(upstairs)   ⊨T,D   ⟿Sh.w.h.   ★ TV,LF, parking
〰 French
🏃 Quiet walks with clean prairie air in native grasses & wild flowers, abundant birds and some wild animals of interest to photographers and naturalists
🚗 Kenosee and White Bear Lakes (swimming, boating, golf courses, waterslides, entertainment)
📷 Enjoy the peace and tranquility of a rural Saskatchewan farm and relax in the old farm home and large yard. Hosts enjoy meeting people from all over the world and offer true & friendly Saskatchewan hospitality. Farm tours available. Visa ⟿B&B

Regina

Cryer, Lee & Denise Needham (Two Spirit Guest Ranch & Retreat) ☎ (306) 731-2200
Box 33084, Regina, SK. S4T 7X2

Take Hwy11 from Regina to Hwy54. Turn north for 9km, then west 1km. Watch for Rainbow Flag.

$40-45S $45-50D $8Add.person $5B&Bale   (plus tax) ► 8
Full   Farm, ranch-style, view from guest rooms, porch, deck, quiet   2D,1Ste(main floor) + bunkhouse   3Q,2cots
Private   LF,F,TV, ceiling fans, private entrance, jacuzzi, wheel-chair access, guest quarters are separate   Designated smoking area, dogs on leash outdoors
Original Prairie pastures, x-c skiing, nature walks, livestock & poultry, on-site craft shop
Regina Beach Resort on Last Mountain Lake, renowned Qu'Appelle Valley, downtown Regina
Newly-renovated home on 160-acres ranch provides a country haven for those who seek peace and quiet and the simple pleasures of getting back in touch with the natural world. The north wing of house is exclusive for guets. Dinners and sleepover's for 8 in "Harvest Bunkhouse" is a house specialty (guests bring own sleeping bags). Bed & Bale available. Children welcome. Plenty of unserviced campimg sites for tents or RVs (with solar shower baths & old-fashioned outhouse). There are 2 cats. Visa

---

Mogg, Cheryl, E. (Crescent House B&B) ☎ & Fax (306) 352-5995
180 Angus Cr., Regina, SK S4T 6N4   E-mail: cheryl.mogg@dlcwest.com

From Albert St., turn west on 15th Ave to Angus St. Turn south to College Ave, where Angus St becomes Angus Cres.
$40-45S $45-50D $5Add.person   (plus tax) ► 5
Full, homebaked   Res., 2-storey, hist., porch, deck, quiet 2 (upstairs)   1D,1Q,cot   1sh.w.g.   Air,LF,F,TV in one guest room, private entrance, off-street parking   Designated smoking area, compatible pets welcome
Wascana Park, Royal Sask.Museum, Albert Street Bridge, Legistlative Assembly, Devonian Pathway, Cathedral Shopping District, Collections Art Gallery, downtown business district
Exhibition Park, Taylor Field, RCMP Museum, Sask.Science Centre
1927-built character home with sunny south addition and many antiques, located in the prestigious Cresents area. Relax on one of the three decks or in the tree-shaded backyard. Modem & fax access for business travellers. Low fat and special diet available. Pick-up and delivery from airport can be arranged. Winter plug-ins for automobiles. Guests are welcomed by 3 very friendly non-shedding, retired champion soft-coated Wheaten Terriers. CC

Powell, Gail (Morning Glory Manor) ☎ (306) 525-2945, Fax (306) 352-6515
Box 1364, Regina, SK S4P 3B8

Phone for directions.
$45-85S/D   (Reduced rates for longer stay) ► 4
Cont.(extended)   Downtown, 2-storey, older, view from guest rooms 2D(upstairs)   4T   1Sh.w.g.   Air,F, off-street parking   Smoking on patio, no pets, children under 1 or over age 12
Downtown, Wascana Lake Park, performing arts centre, museum, art galleries, University of Saskatchewan, Science Centre, Imax-Theatre
Qu'Appelle Valley, lakes, nature preserve, sportsplex
Charming character home built in 1923 featuring plenty of oak, beveled glass and beautiful views. Relax by the fireplace or in the delightful sunroom and enjoy the tranquil surroundings.

Saltcoats

Farquharson, Joan & Walter (Blue Heron House)　　　　　　☎ (306) 744-2214
142 Crescent Lake Rd., Saltcoats, SK　S0A 3R0

Located on Yellowhead Hwy and 26 km from Yorkton. Phone for directions.
$35S　$45D　(Family rates available)　　　　　　　　　　　► 16

🍴 Cont(plus)　🏠 Village, 2-storey, view from guest rooms, deck, lakefront, patio, quiet　■2(ground level)　◄Q,T　🛏 Sh.w.g.
★Air,F,LF,TV in guest lounge, extensive library, limited wheelchair access, parking　🚭No smoking, no pets
🏃 Spacious garden, playground, public park, excellent birding opportunities, local museum and library, good cafes
🚐 Shopping Mall, antique and craft shops, Western Development Museum, Three Provincial Parks, golf course

🐾 Warm and friendly hospitality in home overlooking Anderson Lake. Enjoy good conversation and relaxed, peaceful surroundings. Spiritual guidance, opportunities for counselling and Thematic Retreats available. Hosts are knowledgeable about local and ethnic history of the province. By pre-arrangment National History guided tour with well-known Naturalist Guides may be booked. Also available: 2bedroom bungalow "Katies Cottage" and "The Guest House (for 8).

Saskatoon

Chaplin, Kathy and Ron (Chaplin's Country Bed & Breakfast))　　☎ & Fax (306) 931-3353
RR5, Box 43, Saskatoon, SK　S7K 3J8

From jct of Hwys16/11 proceed south of Saskatoon for 7km on Hwy11. Turn east on Baker Rd(Tsp354), go 7km to red mailbox.
$35S　$45D　　　　　　　　　► 6
🍴Full,homebaked　🏠Rural,view,quiet　■3D(upstairs)　◄2S,2D
🛏 1Sh.w.g　★TV,F, woodstove, off-road parking, guest quarters on 2nd floor with guest lounge　🚭No smoking, no pets, not suitable for small children
🏃 Explore the friendly barnyard, walks on quiet country lane
🚐 Saskatoon, museum, University campus, golfing, dining, famous Wanuskewin Heritage Park
🐾 Warm welcome in comfortable country home with pine intgerior, unique spiral staircase & prairie antiques. Relax in the guest TV lounge with panoramic view or rest on the covered veranda & enjoy the peace & quiet of country living and watch awesome sunsets. Hosts are knowledgeable about local tourism and attractions. ✔B&B

Clay, Barb and Lynne Fontaine (Brighton House)　　　　☎ (306) 664-3278
1308-5th Ave N, Saskatoon, SK　S7K 2S2　　　　　　　　Fax (306) 664-6822

Upon entering the City, take Circle Drive to Idylwyld Drive. Turn east on 33rd Street to 5th Ave North and look for house 2 blocks down Ave.
$35S　$45D　$55F　$10Add.person　　　　　　　► 8A,4Ch
🍴Homebaked　🏠Res., older, patio, quiet　■3D,1Ste (main & upper floor)　◄3Q,2D,3R,2cribs　🛏1Private,2sh.w.g.,1ensuite　★TV,KF,LF, elegant antique gas fireplace, facilities for disabled　🚭Smoking outside

🏃 River, University, YWCA, theatre, galleries, downtown, city bus route
🚐 Historic Batoche, Western Development Museum, Forestry Farm/Zoo, Wanuskewin Heritage Park
🐾 Gracious character home (affectionately known as the "Gingerbread House"), with the warmth of country and furnished with antiques, beautifully renovated to preserve it's original appearance & atmosphere of a by-gone era. A "beary" warm welcome for all ages. Complimentary use of bicycles. Relax in the outdoor hot tub after a long busy day. Ideal spot for honeymoon/anniversaries.Visa,MC ✔B&B

Dueck, Carry & Wayne (Windsong Acres B&B)   ☎ & Fax (306)373-1395, Cell(306)227-0350
Box 9, RR5, S506, Saskatoon, SK   S7K 3J8

In Saskatoon, travel south on Lorne Ave for 10.9km (becomes Hwy 219). Do not take curve -
proceed straight through for 2.5km to house with sign at end of driveway.

$40S $50D   ▶ 4
🍲 Homebaked   🏠 Rural, raised bungalow, acreage, deck, quiet
■ 1S,2D(one on lower level)   ⊨ 1S,2D   ⚄ 2Sh.w.g.,1ensuite
★F,TV,LF   ✋ No smoking, no pets, children min.age 10
〰some Dutch & German
🚶 Beaver Creek Conservation Area
🚐 Several golf courses, Western Development Museum, Seager
Wheeler Centre, Wanuskawin Center (Indian Heritage)

🐎 Quiet, friendly and accommodating home. Active hosts farm and breed/raise Arabian Horses,
and make stained glass handicrafts (available for sale). Join them for a buggy ride with the Arabian
filly Bint Gamilah (weather permitting). Breakfast is served in the dining room. ✍B&B

Dyck, Jed & Helen (Chic-A-D Acres B&B)   ☎ (306) 931-7119
GS 316, Box 21, RR3, Saskatoon, SK   S7K 3J6

From Saskatoon, travel west on Hwy 7, south on Hwy 60 for 10km, west on Vanscoy Rd (No762)

for 3km, and south on gravel road for 2.4km. Watch for sign.
$35S $45D   ▶ 4
🍲 Full, homebaked   🏠 Rural, 2-storey, acreage, view from guest
rooms, porch, deck, quiet, secluded   ■ 2D (upstairs)   ⊨ 2D
⚄ 1Sh.w.g.   ★ F,Air,TV in spacious lounge area, guest quarters
are separate   ✋ No smoking, no pets
🚶 Walks through natural woodland and virgin prairie and open
meadows (perchance observe white-tail deer)

🚐 Pike Lake Prov. Park, Moon Lake Golf & Country Club, downtown Saskatoon, Wildlife Art
Gllery & Tea Room, Saskatoon Berry Barn & Craft Shop, museums, parks

🐎 Newly constructed country home nestled among acres of natural trees with pastoral views of
sheep and horses and natural flora of the area. Ideal for a quiet country retreat. Nutritious
breakfast is served in the large country kitchen. Hosts are educators who enjoy meeting people and
they love the many aspects of country living. There is a dog in residence.

Petersen, Darryl & Lola Poncelet (Ninth Street B&B)   ☎ (306) 244-3754
227-9th St East, Saskatoon, SK   S7N 0A3

Phone for directions.
$40S $50D $100F   (plus taxes)   ▶ 6
🍲 Full, homebaked   🏠 Res., 2-storey, hist., view from guest
rooms, patio, deck, quiet   ■ 3D (upstairs)   ⊨ 2S,1D,1Q
⚄1Sh.w.g.   ★ TV,LF, ceiling fans, off-street & street parking,
compl. bicycles for guests   ✋ Smoking outside, no pets, not
suitable for small children
🚶 South Sask. River & Valley, Meewasin Valley Trails (20km),
Broadway shopping district, public tennis courts, downtown core, Exhibition Grounds, festivals
🚐 Wanuskewin Heritage Park (Nat.Hist.Site), Beaver Creek & Cranberry Flats Conservation
🐎 Light and airy home with a cozy atmosphere and eclectic mix of artifacts complimenting the
Victorian theme, situated in old Nutana, the city's oldest and unique heritage community. Hosts
have travelled extensively throughout Asia. Relax, read and contemplate in the quiet and private
garden with an English flavour. Breakfast includes locally grown, organic ingredients. "Latcho
Drom" (Safe journey).Visa ✍B&B

142   SASKATCHEWAN

Studer, Louise & Dan (Courtney Leanne Bed & Breakfast)   ☎ (306) 382-0444
3428 Dieppe St., Saskatoon, SK   S7M 3S9

In Saskatoon, take Circle Dr to 11th St, turn right to Elevator Rd,
turn left and proceed to Dieppe St and 5th house on left.
$36S $47D $57F   ▶ 4A,2Ch
🍲 Homebaked   🏠 Sub., 2-storey, large yard, deck, quiet   ■ 3
(main & upper floor)   ⊨ 2T,2D, crib   ⌁ 1sh.w.g.,1sh.w.h
📺F,TV, playpen/highchair/carriage for babies, piano, billiard
table, off-street parking Ⓦ No smoking, no pets, children welcome
🏃 Public transportation to downtown
🚐 Downtown, Via Rail Station, John G. Diefenbaker Airport
🏹 Comfortable chalet-type home decorated in a country theme with crafts displayed throughout,
situated in restful, quiet neighbourhood. Breakfast with homemade jams/jellies and berries (in
season) may be served on deck overlooking the flower beds, creek & pond. ↙B&B

Swift Current   *(west of Regina; see also Gull Lake, Piapot)*

Green, Dixie & Dave (Swift Current Heritage B&B)   ☎(306)773-6305,Fax(306)773-0135
Green Hectares Farm, Box1301, Swift Current,SK   S9H 3X4

From Hwy 1 exit at Swift Current Tourist booth (22nd Ave NE) and travel north on Hwy 4 to first

road at right (east) and proceed 1km to farm. Watch for sign.
$35S $50D   (plus tax)   (Child rate available)   ▶ 6
❎ April1-Nov1   🍲 Full, homebaked   🏠 Farm, at edge of city
limits, 2-storey, hist., view from guest rooms, creek at front, deck,
quiet   ■3D (main floor)   ⊨ 2T,2Q   ⌁ 1Sh.w.g., 1sh.w.h.
★ TV,F, guest quarters are separate, off-street parking
Ⓦ Smoking outside
🏃 Swift Current Petroglyphs 500 m from door (historic rock
carvings & paintings). Swift Current Creek flows through farm property (canoeing, fishing)
🚐 Swift Current & Wheatland Malls, museum, Frontier Days Fair, Doc's town, art gallery
🏹 Working cattle ranch and irrigation farm with comfortable farmhouse located near all
activities. Large host family (including visiting grandchildren in summer) are interested in
Archaeology and trail riding. Enjoy and relax in congenial surroundings. ↙B&B

Wakaw   *(north-east of Saskatoon)*

Kushneryk, Ron & Lucille (Wakaw Lake Country Hideout B&B)   ☎ (306) 233-4791
Box 430, Wakaw, SK   S0K 4P0

From Saskatoon, take Hwy 41 to Wakaw. From Jct 41/2 continue 2.5km east. Watch for road sign.
$35S $50D $5Child (under age 10)   (plus tax)   🍽 Meals   ▶ 12

🍲 Full, homebaked   🏠 Farm, older home with new addition, 15-20 acres,
view, patio, quiet   ■2S,3D and cottage   ⊨4D,2Q   ⌁1Private,1sh.w.h.
★TV,LF, parking, partial wheel-chair access, separate entrance   Ⓦ No
smoking, no pets 〰French, Ukrainian
🏃 Woodland walks on large property
🚐 Batoche and Fort Carlton Historic Sites, Duck Lake Interp.Centre,
Wakaw Lake Regional Park, museum, Diefenbaker House (Prince Albert),
Manitou Springs Mineral Spa (Watrous)
🏹 See nature at its best and experience a quiet get-away and a relaxing
stay. View the beautiful flower garden bursting with annuals and perennials
of the prairies, carefully and lovingly tended to for the enjoyment of B&B guests. Hosts are eager to
make new acquaintances & enjoy obtaining a deeper unterstanding of pecples from all nations.

Walsh
(west of Swift Current on AB border; see also Maple Creek)

Reesor, Scott & Theresa (Historic Reesor Ranch) ☎ & Fax (306) 662-3498
Box 83, Walsh, AB T0J 3L0 Cell (403 502-9026

$45S $55D $10Child(free under ge 2) $27.50Add.person (plus tax) 📷 Meals ▶ 6A,6Ch
From TCH 1 west of Walsh, turn south onto Graburn Rd (Range Rd 12). Drive 33km on gravel road

to B&B sign, then turn left (east) and go 3km to ranch.
🐖 Full 🏚 Ranch, 2-storey, hist., view from guest rooms, quiet,
secluded, piazza (front porch) ■ 3F(upstairs) - ⊨ 3D,1R, foam
matresses ⊶ 1Sh.w.g., 2sh.w.h. ★ LF,F,TV 🦌 Smoking
on front porch, pets outside only, children welcome ⋙ French
🕴 TCH Trail next to property, Conglomerate Rocks (spectacular
view of Cypress Hills), Indian teepee rings, buffalo wallows
🚗 Fort Walsh Nat.Hist.Park, Cypress Hills Prov.Parks
(Sask/Alta), Hidden Valley Ski Hill, fishing at Reesor Lake
🐎 Forth Generation family in 1916-built home on working cattle ranch close to highest point in
Saskatchewan. Guest rooms have historic theme of three previous generations. Host was raised on
the ranch and loves to recite cowboy poetry. Hostess is French-Canadian and of Ojibwa Native
descent. There are 3 children in the host family who enjoy making guests feel at home. Also
available, rustic s/c guest cabin (guests bring own bedroll & pillows). Guest horse accommodation
in barn and corral. There is a basement/outdoor cat. ⌐B&B

Watrous
(south-east of Saskatoon)

Munro, Alex and Esther (West Wind - The Graf House) ☎ (306) 946-3821
Manitou Beach, Watrous, SK S0K 4T0

Located 5 km north of Watrous. Follow signs to Manitou Beach, turn left at golf course.
$50S $55D $95Ste 📷 Meals (plus tax) ▶ 8

🐖 Full, homebaked 🏚 Village, hist., multi-storey, view, quiet,
decks ■ 4D (ground level) ⊨ 4Q ⊶ 4Private,2sh.w.g.
★TV in breakfast room, games room & pool table, parking
🕴 9-hole grass green golf course across the road, mineral water
spa, small mall, tennis courts, unique horse-hair floor dance hall,
picnic grounds, paddle boats, cross-country skiing
🚗 Town of Watrous, shopping, bowling, restaurants
🐎 Historic house (1917-built in a neighbouring town, recently
moved to its present location and extensively restored and enlarged) is nestled into a hill, just below
the golf course. Enjoy breakfast in the breakfast room with an incredible view, relax on the guest
deck. Host operates the local Specialty Meat Shop and hostess restores houses and furniture. ⌐CC

Yorkton
(north-east of Regina, near MBborder; see also Saltcoats, Kamsack)

Musey, Ann & Zenon (Lazy Maples B&B) ☎ (306) 783-7078
111 Darlington St.West, Yorkton, SK S3N 0E9

Located 2.5 blocks from jct of Hwy 16 & on the corner of Smith St.
$35S $45D $10Add.person 📷 Meals ▶ 7
🐖 Full, homebaked 🏚 Res., raised bungalow, patio, quiet ■2D
in suite (lower level) ⊨ 2D,1P,1R ⊶ 1sh.w.g.
★TV,KF,LF, use of bicycles/exercise cycle, off-street parking, plug
in 🦌Smoking outside, pets outside 🦌 Ukrainian
🕴 Anne Portnuff Theatre, Godfrey Dean Cultural Center, Deer Pk
Golf Course, Western Develop. Museum, corner store, bus route
🐎 Early retired couple in totally renovated home with large perennial glower garden. Hosts are
familiar with city and area tourist attractions/events and have conducted many church and area
tours. Hostess is involved in the local Cultural Center. Breakfast (incl. perogies) is served in the
dining room or in guest suite, if requested. Ukrainian souvenirs are available. Visa ⌐CC

Manitoba

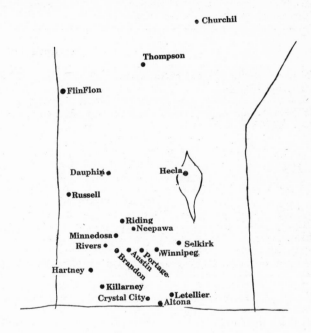

- Churchil
- Thompson
- FlinFlon
- Dauphin
- Hecla
- Russell
- Riding
- Neepawa
- Minnedosa
- Rivers
- Selkirk
- Winnipeg
- Portage
- Austin
- Brandon
- Hartney
- Killarney
- Crystal City
- Letellier
- Altona

Travel Manitoba (Tourism Dep't)
155 Carlton St.   7th floor
Winnipeg, MB   R3C 3H8

toll-free 1-800-665-0040

Altona

(south of Winnipeg near US border; see also Letellier)

Siemens, Ed & Ruth (Schwartz Heritage House B&B)   ☎ (204) 324-1233
Box 1671, No245, 10thAve NW, Altona, MB   R0G 0B0

From Winnipeg, travel 108km south on Hwy 75. Proceed west on
Hwy 14 for 18km, then south on Hwy 30 for 10km.
$45S $55D $15Child/Add.person   🍴 Meals   ► 8A,4Ch
🍶 Cont., homebaked   🏠 Res., hist., 3-storey, deck, quiet
▪4D,2F (upstairs)   ⊨ 2D,2Q,2P   ⌐ 1Sh.w.g.   ★ TV, street
parking   🕊 No smoking, no pets, children min. age 5   〰 some
German
🚗 Downtown Winnipeg, beach and campgrounds, golf course
🏃 Outdoor Community swimming pool, park, Nature Sanctuary, mini golf course next door
📣 Theme rooms enhanced with antiques add interest to recently modernized Heritage house
(built in 1902). Breakfast is served in the spacious dining room. Enjoy the spectacular Manitoba
sunsets from the 2nd-storey guest room and the warm friendly atmosphere. There is a dog and a
bird in residence. Visa,MC ✒B&B

Austin

(west of Portage La Prairie)

Jones, Cecil & Judith (The Oak Tree B&B)   ☎ (204) 637-2029
Box 35, Austin, MB   R0H 0C0

$40S $50D $65F $10Child/Add.person   🍴 Meals   ► 4A,2Ch

Located 5km south of TCH at east entrance to Austin.
🍶 Full, homebaked   🏠 Farm, bungalow, patio, deck, quiet,
secluded   ▪ 2(main & lower level)   ⊨ 2D,1P,1S,crib,bunkbeds
(children in sleep bags)   ⌐1Sh.w.g.(in lower level)   ★F,TV,LF,
some wheel-chair access   🕊No pets
🏃 Farm grounds, x-c skiing, snowshoeing
🚗 Golf courses, Manitoba Agricultural Museum (Pioneer village,
large display of agricultural machinery), Annual Threshermen's
Reunion & Rodeo (July), Spruce Woods Park, Carberry Desert
📣 Modern home full of family heirlooms and collectibles; surrounded by six golf courses. Enjoy
the shaded yard and landscaped gardens, where wildlife, birds & nature abound. Ideal place for a
short or longer golfing holiday. Tee time can be booked, if required. End the day with a weiner roast
at the outdoor fire pit. Breakfast is served in family dining room and bag lunches are available.
Semi-retired hosts are active in the community and involved with local historic book publishing.
Children welcome. ✒B&B

Brandon

(west of Portage La Prairie; see also Austin)

Janzen, Tana & Marv (West Meadows Bed & Breakfast)   ☎ (204) 725-0753
RR1, S145, Box16, Brandon, MB   R7A 5Y1

Located 5km from Hwy1A, 5km from Hwy10. Phone for directions.
$30S $40D $50F   🍴 Meals   ► 4
🍶 Full   🏠 Rural, 2-storey, hist., acreage, quiet   ▪ 2D (upst)
⊨2D   ⌐1Sh.w.g.   ★Air,TV,LF   🕊 No smoking, no pets
🏃 Explore 13 acres of yard and pasture and treeland
🚗 Golfing, Brandon Hills (hiking, biking, x-c skiing), Brandon,
large shopping mall, Keystone Center (agricultural fairs, trade
conventions and sports facilites)
📣 Warm & friendly hospitality in large Turn-of-the-Century home surrounded by the quietness
of a rural setting. Enjoy a homestyle breakfast in the farm kitchen overlooking the garden. ✒B&B

Relf, Ray & Betty Anne (The White House Bed & Breakfast) ☎ & Fax (204) 726-4280
1705-Middleton Ave., Brandon, MB   R7C 1A8

From TCH turn off at McDonalds Restaurant onto North Service Rd (Middleton Ave). Turn west to

Chalet Motel and look for white house on west side of Motel.
$40S $50D $5Child   🍽 Meals   ► 7
🍴 Full, homebaked   🏠 Rural, 2-storey, older, 2-acres, view from
guest rooms,patio,porch,quiet ■3D,1F(main & upper) ⊨1Q,3D
⌂1Sh.w.h.,1private ★Air,TV,LF ⓦNo smoking,no pets
🏃 9-hole golf course, restaurants
🚗 Riding Mountain National Park, International Peace Gardens,
Spirit Sands Desert
🔫 Warm and friendly hospitality in older home in quiet rural surroundings. Enjoy the putting
green (private for guest only). ✑B&B

Smith, Joy and Keith (Gwenmar Guest Home)   ☎ (204) 728-7339, Fax (204) 728-7336
Box 59, RR3, Brandon, MB   R7A 5Y3

Located northwest of Brandon and 4 km off Trans-Canada Hwy. Phone or fax for directions.
$35S $50D   (Reservations)   🍽 Meals   ► 8

🍴 Full, homemade breads   🏠 Rural, acreage, hist., quiet
■4D(upper & lower level)   ❤   ⊨3Q,2S   ★LF,TV,F,
wheel-chair access   ⌂1Sh.w.h.,1sh.w.g.
🏃 Creek with beaver dam, x-c skiing, hiking, berry picking
🚗 Brandon, shopping, restaurants, waterslide, air museum,
Brandon U., golf courses, airport, Agriculture Canada Research
Station, Neepawa (Author Margaret Laurence childhood home)
Riding Mt. Nat.Park, International Peace Gardens
🔫 Relax on the big screened porch in 1914 Heritage home built by former MB Lt. Governor J.D.
McGregor, and enjoy the beautiful grounds or pick asparagus, raspberries or wild fruit in season.
There is a Golden Retriever who will be happy to escort guests on secluded walks in the valley.
Hosts have been welcoming B&B guests since 1981. Special rates for children. Bus tours welcome.

Soloway, Ivan & Paulette (Casa Maley)   ☎ (204) 728-0812 Fax (204) 728-6287
1605 Victoria Ave, Brandon, MB   R7A 1C1

Located two blocks east of junction of Hyws 10/1A.
$35S $45D $55F 🍽 Meals   ► 4A,4Ch
🍴 Choice, homebaked   🏠 Downtown, res., older, patio, quiet
🍴 3D (upstairs)   ⊨2T,2D   ⌂3Sh.w.g.   ★ 2TV,3F,LF
parking for 4 cars, sinks in 2 guest rooms ⓦNo smoking
🏃 Brandon University, Daly House Museum, Architectural
walking tours, antiques, Keystone Recreation Center
🚗 Canada Winter Games Sportsplex, waterslides
🔫 Designated Heritage, 1912-built European-style, 3-storey Tudor house with red brick exterior,
fairy-tale Gingerbread-house appearance and spacious interior decor and beautiful quarter-cut oak
and wainscotting in foyer, dining room and grand staircase. Transportation and pick-ups by
appointment can be arranged. ✑B&B

Churchill

Gould, Donald (Polar Bear B&B)   ☎ (204) 675-2819
Box 41, 26 Hearne St., Churchill, MB   R0B 0E0

Accessible only by train or air. Fly in from Winnipeg or take the train from Thompson.
$30S $50D   (call ahead for Peak Season rates & reservation Oct15-Nov7)   ► 12
🏠 Full   🏠 Village, raised bungalow, view   ■4D,1F (main floor)   ⊨D   ⊿3Sh.w.g.
★LF, separate entrance   ⊛ No smoking   ⌇ French
🏃 Excellent viewing (Polar Bears, Cariboo, Beluga Whales, Northern Lights, Arctic Wildlife),
historic sites (Fort Prince of Wales, Ithica Shipwreck, Cape Merry, Sloops Cove, Rocket Range),
boat tours, bird watching, x-c skiing,
☛ Host is a world-wide traveller, has lived in Churchill for 18 years, and enjoys exchanging
experiences with fellow travellers.

Crystal City

Hildebrand, Judy (Poplar Lane B&B)   ☎ (204) 873-2194
Box 443, Crystal City, MB   R0K 0N0

Travel 7km south of Crystal City on Hwy 34, then 3km west to end of road.

$35S $45D $10Child   ► 8
🅳 Full   🏠 Farm, 2-storey, hist., view from guest rooms, quiet
secluded   ■ 3D (upstairs)   ⊨ 1D,2Q,1P   ⊿1Sh.w.g.,
1ensuite   ★ TV,LF   ⊛ No smoking, no pets   ⌇ German
🏃 Hiking along creek & ravine on property, x-c skiing
🚙 Holiday Mountain Ski Resort, golf courses, Rock Lake
(boating, fishing, swimming)
☛ Warm hospitality in recently renovated 1905 farm house,
enhanced with hardwood and character furnishings and situated on operating sheep farm. Feel free
to visit the sheep and goats and explore the valley of the meandering Cypress Creek. Experience a
relaxing country stay with abundance of home cooking and baking.

Dauphin

Jamieson, Virginia & Ken McCartney (Edgar House B&B)   ☎ & Fax (204) 638-7857
703 Main St N., Dauphin, MB   R7N 1E4

Phone for directions.
$40S $50D   ► 6
🅳Full   🏠Res, 2-storey, hist., veranda, deck   ■3D(upstairs)
⊨2S,2D   ⊿1Sh.w.g., 1sh.w.h.   ★ F,TV, separate entrance,
off-street parking   ⊛ Designated smoking area
🏃 Municipal Park, Fort Dauphin Museum & Gallery, shopping,
architectural walking tour
🚙 Lake Dauphin & beach, picnics, camping, Riding Mt.Nat.Pk
& Clear Lake, historic farm site (Ukrainian), Duck Mt. Prov. Park, fly/reel fishing areas
☛ Warm welcome in 1899-built home located in convenient proximity to Riding Mt.National
Park. Hosts are outdoor enthusiasts and knowledgeable about the area's recreation and sightseeing
opportunities. Matthew the cat is a lively conversationalist.MC ⌁CC

Flin Flon
(northern Manitoba on SK border)

Barabonoff, George (Yoho Bay B&B)
Box 427, Flin Flon, MB R8A 1N3

☎ (204) 687-3051, Fax (204) 687-8397
E-mail: yohobnb@mb.sympatico.ca

Located on Hwy 10, 15km from Flin Flon. Phone for directions.
$55S/D $15Add.person   ► 4+
🏠 Full   🏡 Rural, bi-level, deck   ■ 2D(ground level)   ⊨ 2Q
🛏1Sh.w.g.   ★ Private entrance   🖐 No smoking, pets &
children welcome   ∿ Russian, Ukrainian
🏃 x-c skiing/walks from back door and across the lake, Prov.Park
🚗 Town of Flin Flon, fishing, golfing, canoeing, berry picking
☞ Retired host in large cedar home located on the shore of
Lake Athapapaskow in Baker's Narrows Prov.Park. After a day of fishing or exploring the vast
wilderness, relax on the deck with a cup of tea and watch the sun set. Host has lived in town all his
life and is experienced in the hospitality buiness. There is a dog "Buddy" in residence. ✓B&B

Hartney
(south-west of Brandon; see also Killarney)

Whetter, Margaret (River Park Farm Guest Home)
Box 310, Hartney, MB R0M 0X0

☎ (204) 858-2407, Fax (204) 858-2390

Located on Hwy 21 and 1 km west of the town.
$30S $50D $10Child   🍽 Meals   ► 10
🏠Full,homebaked 🏡Farm,hist.,3-storey,view,quiet,riverfront
■4D plus attic suite (all upstairs) 🛏2Sh.w.g. ⊨8S,1D,1P,1R,
futon   ★Air,F,TV in guest room   🖐No smoking
🏃 Souris River, small dock with canoe, nature trails along river
bank, golfing, horseshoe pit, restored farm buildings (barn and
shop)part of a mixed farming operation
🚗 Lauder Sand Hills Wildlife Management area, Souris Agate pits, swinging bridge, Peace Garden
☞ Restored turn-of-Century house and farm buildings (built 1910-1913), furnished with period
antiques. Enjoy a vacation center and learn about country living at its best; a place of Canadian
culture and beauty in a very scenic setting. Abundance of wildlife can be seen on the property and
along the river. A great place for retreats and seminars. Hosts are involved with English as a
second Language Homestay program. Guided canoe trips available. ✓B&B

Hecla Island
(north of Winnipeg in Lake Winnipeg)

Holtz, Sharon and Dave (Solmundson Gesta Hus)
Box 76, Hecla Island, MB R0C 2R0

☎ & Fax (204) 279-2088
E-mail: holtz@mb.sympatico.ca

Located within Hecla Island Provincial Park in the heart of Lake Winnipeg, accessible via Hwy 8.

$55S $60-75D   🍽 Meals   ► 10A,4Ch
🏠 Full, homebaked   🏡 Village, hist., acreage, view, lakefront,
quiet, veranda   ■4(main & upper floor)   ⊨2D,2Q,2cots
🛏2Sh.w.g.,1ensuite   ★TV,KF,parking   🖐Smoking
🏃 Woodland lakeshore for walking, church & museums in historic
Icelandic fishing village. hiking, cycling, angling
🚗 18-hole golf course, beaches, interpretive programs, hiking and
x-c ski trails
☞ Luxurious European-style hospitality in newly renovated and completely modern comfortable
home located in an original Icelandic settlement. Each room has a view of the lake. Relax on the
veranda and enjoy the beautiful view of Lake Winnipeg and the tranquil and peaceful atmosphere.
Host is a commercial fisherman and dinner specialty is Manitoba Pickeral (Walleye). There are
cats, dogs, ducks. Visit the in-house gift shop. Off-season rates avail.Visa,MC

Killarney
(south of Brandon; see also Hartney)

Krueger, Linda & Henry (Country Comfort B&B)   ☎ (204) 523-8742   Fax (204) 523-8511
Box 808, Killarney, MB   R0K 1G0

Located 4km south of Hwy 3 between Killarney & Boissevain.
$40S $50-55D $10child   (Reservations appreciated)   ▶ 6
🅠 Choice   🏠 Modern ranch-style   ■ 2F (lower level with
entrance)   ⊨ 2T,2D,1Q,1R   ⌐ 1Sh.w.g.   ★ KF,TV in guest
sitting area, private entrance   ♥   🅦 No smoking, no pets
🕴 Quiet country walks, bird & animal watching, x-c skiing,
ski-dooing, biking
🚗 International Peace Garden, US border, Boissevain Outdoor
Art Gallery (murals), Killarney Lake, Bottineau Winter Park (downhill skiing), Brandon, Turtle
Mountain Prov. Park, golfing, water sports, excellent hunting for birds & deer, fishing
🐾 Warm welcome and friendly Manitoba hospitality in newly renovated farm house with cozy
comfort in a country setting. Relax after a day of sightseeing or travelling and partake in many
recreational and entertainment facilities provided. ⌐B&B

Letellier
(south of Winnipeg near US border; see also Altona)

Derksen, Dennis and Sheila (Fraser House)   ☎ (204) 737-2284/737-2361,
33 Main St., Letellier, MB   R0G 1C0   Fax (204) 737-2081

Located 16 km N of US border on Hwy 75. Phone for directions.
$35S $45-55D $7.50Child   (Children welcome)   ▶ 4A,2Ch
🅠 Homebaked   🏠 Rural, older, quiet, front porch   ■ 1D,1F
(upstairs)   ⊨ 2D,1P   ⌐ 1Sh.w.g.(no shower)   ★ TV,LF
parking   🅦No smoking, no pets, children welcome   ⌂ French
🕴 Park, tennis court.
🚗 Golfing, fishing, swimming, shopping
🐾 1916-built home, furnished with wonderful antiques
enhancing its Victorian decor and situated in the heart of Manitoba's bustling agricultural area in a
French community. Enjoy a quiet walk, cycle, or play a game of tennis. Visa,MC

Minnedosa
(north of Brandon; see also Rivers, Neepawa, Riding Mt)

Proven, Susan (Fairmount B&B)   ☎ & Fax (204) 874-2165
Box 633, Minnedosa, MB   R0J 1E0

From jct of Hwys 10/16 north of Minnedosa, proceed 6.6km north on Hwy 10 (towards Riding
Mt.Nat.Park). Turn west on Fairmount Rd and continue 6km to farm.

$35S $50D $10Child/Add.person   🍴 Meals   ▶ 7
🅠 Full   🏠 Farm, 3-storey, hist., view from guest rooms, deck,
lakefront, porch   ■ 2D,1F(upstairs)   ⊨ 1S,2T,2D   ⌐1Sh.w.h.
★ TV,LF   🅦 No smoking, no pets   ⌂ Spanish
🕴 Woodland and waterbirds, walking trail around Paririe Slough
(waterway), beaver house, x-c skiing, ox-cart historic trail
🚗 Brandon, Riding Mtn.Nat.Park, Margaret Lawrence Museum
(Neepawa), Rock Concert (Minnedosa), Agassiz Ski Resort
🐾 Restored 1914-built farmhouse with stained glass windows and furnishings in the style of
early Canadiana situated on third Generation working farm, on the edge of a slough and a sheltered
natural spruce grove. Relax while sheep graze on the pastures by the water. Spend summer
evenings around the bonfire or in the cozy attic rec-room in the winter. Hostess loves to cook for
guests, using natural farm products ("just like Granny"). Breakfast is served in special guest
breakfast room. There is a dog and a cat (Ralph and Frank) in residence. ⌐B&B

Yates, Richard & Mary Joyce (The Castle)   ☎ (204) 867-2830, Fax (204) 867-5376
149-2nd Ave S.W., Box 1705, Minnedosa SW, MB   R0J 1E0

From Hwy1 at Brandon, take Hwy10 north to Minnedosa. At Town Center, go west on 2nd Ave SW.
$40-45S $60D $90(Honeymoon Ste) $10Child   (plus 10% in July/Aug)   ► 8A,2Ch

🍴Homebaked 🏠Village,hist.,3-storey,quiet,riverlot ■2D,1F,1Ste
(upstairs),host quarters on top floor ⊡1Sh.w.g, 3ensuite
⊨S,D,Q,P,T,3cots ★F,bicycles for guests,parking ⓌRestricted
smoking ⌇French
🧍 Town center, restaurants, Lake Minnedosa with beach and
park, golfing, tennis, Pioneer Museum, bird walk,boating, skiing
🚗 Brandon, Neepawa (Margaret Laurence Museum), Clear Lake,
Riding Mountain Nat.Park

☛ Victorian home (ca1901) known locally as "the Castle", a redesigned and restored Heritage
landmark of Queen Anne architecture. Located on the Minnedosa River on a quiet street in a lovely
setting. Hosts are artists and display many of their own works around the home. Suitable for
retreats,honeymoon,anniversary and workshops There is a resident cat. MC ⌇MBB

Neepawa   *(north of Brandon; see also Minnedosa, Riding Mt)*

MacPhee, Joe & Glenda (The Garden Path B&B)   ☎ (204) 476-3184
Box 928, 536 Second Ave., Neepawa, MB   R0J 1H0

Located on the Trans Canada Yellowhead Hwy 16 at the corner of 2nd Ave in town.

$49S $59D $10Add.person   ► 7A,1ch
🍴 Full, homebaked, buffet 🏠Res., rural town, hist., 2.5-storey,
porch ■3D (upstairs) ⊨2T,2Q,cot ⊡1Sh.w.g.,
1Ensuite ★F,off-street parking Ⓦ No smoking, no pets
🧍 Margaret Laurence Home & Plains Museums, MB Holiday
Festival of the Arts (July), World Lily Capital Festival (July),
Plains Agricultural Society Fairgrounds, walking trail
🚗The Lily Nook, Neepawa Golf & Country Club, Mt Agassiz Ski
Centre, Riverside Cemetary, Riding Mt.Nat.Park, Minnedosa Classic Rock Festival (Aug)

☛ Spacious yellow brick home (ca 1903) completely renovated, containing much of the charm
and character of its early heritage, and situated in rural town, the proud receiver of "Manitoba's
Most Beautiful Town Award". Breakfast is served in the formal dining room or on the casual sun
porch. Leisure time may be spent in the spacious living room with its fireplace, piano, books and
garden view. The grounds are well suited for strolling. There are 2 resident cats "Tramp" &
"Nuisance". Visa,MC ⌇B&B

Portage-La-Prairie   *(west of Winnipeg; see also Austin)*

Rud, Marnie & Barry (Rud's on the Lake Bed & Breakfast)   ☎ & Fax (204) 857-9231
Box 974 Main Station, 10 Pine Cr., Portage-La-Prairie, MB   R1N 3C4   E-mail: brud@portage.net

In Portage turn south off Sask Ave (at any light) towards lake, turn right at lake and proceed past
Yellowquill School/College to Pine Cr. OR: From Hwy 1 east or west turn north from Portage

by-pass onto Yellowquill Trail, turn right onto Pine Cr at stop sign.
$45S $50-55D $10Add.person   (plus tax)   ► 6A,1Ch
🍴 Full 🏠Res, acreage, bungalow, view, lakefront, swimming
pool, patio, deck, quiet ■ 3(lower level) ⊨1S,1D,1Q,
cot,crib ⊡1sh.w.g. ★ Air,F,TV/VCR in guest room,
coffee/tea in guest lounge, off-street parking Ⓦ No smoking
🧍 Fishing in Assiniboine River, waterfowl & wildlife seen on
property, canoes/paddle/row boat available

🚗 Winnipeg, golfcourses, Delta Beach & Marsh, Austin Machinery & Fort La Reine Museum
☛ Comfortable home in park-like setting on the shore of Crescent Lake. Relax by the heated
pool. Enjoy the perennial flowers & beauty of the property over a homecooked Western breakfast.

Riding Mountain   *(north-west of Portage La Prairie; see also Minnedosa, Neepawa)*

Spafford, Thelma and Stewart (The Lamp Post)   ☎ (204) 967-2501
Box 27, Riding Mountain, MB   R0J 1T0

Located on west side of Provincial Hwy 5, north of Neepawa.
$30S $45D $10Child ☫Meals   ►7
⏧ Choice, homebaked   ♠ Farm, ranch-style, view,quiet
■3D   ⊨ 2Q(1waterbed),2D,2R ⊿1Sh.w.g,1sh.w.h ★LF,
separate entrance,TV in guest room, parking   ⍟ No smoking
♯ Restaurant, post office, excellent hiking/x-c skiing
🚗 Neepawa, Clear Lake Summer Resort, Mount Agassiz skiing
🔫 Farm home situated in the deer/elk/moose/bear country in the foothills of the spruce-covered
Riding Mountains, excellent for hunting as well as fishing. Lunches packed for
hikers/skiers/hunters and fishermen. Baked goods produced by the hostess are in great demand in
the area. Hosts are natives of the farming community and very knowledgeable of the local history.
Visa ✓ CC

Rivers   *(north of Brandon; see also Minnedosa)*

Kroeger, Lynn & Jake (Cozy River Inn B&B)   ☎ & Fax (204) 328-4457
Box 838, Rivers, MB   R0K 1X0

Take Hwy 1 west from Brandon to Hwy 270. Proceed north to Hwy 25 and west to Rivers. Look for
B&B 1km east of town.
$60S/D $10Add.person   ►4A,4Ch
⏧ Cont., homebaked (self-serve)   ♠ Rural, bungalow, view from guest rooms, riverback, quiet,
deck ■ 2Stes (in separate cottage) ⊨2Q,1P ⊿ 2Private ★ TV in guest room, separate
entrance, fridge/coffee maker/ toaster oven in each suite   ⍟ Designated smoking area, no pets
♯ Town of Rivers, gravel pit & dam
🚗 Watersports, fishing, hunting, wildlife, bird watching, x-c skiing, snowmobiling, curling,
tennnis, golfing, Lake Wahtopanah Provincial Park with sandy beach, Brandon, Souris, Minnedosa
🔫 Guest house with theme rooms is separate from main dwelling and situated on Little
Saskatchewan River surrounded by trees and park-like yard. Hosts enjoy music & crafts. Enjoy the
cozy and peaceful atmosphere and friendly surroundings. Crafts available by local crafters.
Breakfast is served in suites. There is an outside cat. Visa ✓B&B

Russell   *(north-west of Brandon, near SK border)*

Tweet, Ward & Linda (Boulton Manor B&B)   ☎ (204) 773-3267
Box 1468, 322 Memorial Ave. South, Russell, MB   R0J 1W0

Phone for directions.
$40-50S $50-60D $90Ste $10Add.person   ►11
⏧Full, homebaked ♠Res., 2-storey, hist., deck/balcony ■4D (incl
2Ste)(main & upper level)   ⊨ 2D,2Q,2R,1P ⊿2sh.w.g.
★F,LF,off-street parking ⍟Smoking on deck,no pets
♯ Restaurants, shops, public pool, Beth Naylor costume Museum
🚗 Golf course, historic sites, fishing, Asessippi Park with ski hill
(opening Dec98), Riding Mountain Nat. Park, air strip, Ukrainian and
Native Culture
🔫 Century home with spacious grounds & backyard wood. Browse through the collection of
antiques, books, letters and photos and imagine the trials of early Manitoba life. Breakfast is served
in the dining area or on the front deck. Hosts are knowledgeable about history of the area and about
nearby cultural and recreational sites. ✓CC

Selkirk

(north of Winnipeg)

Sarginson, Laurel & Robert (Evergreen Gate B&B)   ☎ (204) 482-6248
1138 River Rd., Box 68, G349,RR3, Selkirk, MB   R1A 2A8

Take Hwy 9 (Main St) north from Winnipeg, turn right on River Rd directly north of Lower Fort
Garry. From Selkirk follow Eveline St south. Look for No 4550.

$45S $55D $10Add.person   ► 4
🕮 Cont.(large choice)   🛏. Semi-rural, riverfront, acreage, quiet,
private, screened porch, deck ■2D(or Ste) ⊨2Q ⊐1Sh.w.g.
★TV lounge, kitchenette, bicycles available   ⊕No smoking, no
pets, families welcome   ⋙ French
🏃 Walking, cycling, fishing, Lower Fort Garry
🚗 Golfing, Oak Hammock Marsh, Selkirk Marine Museum, Lake
Winnipeg beaches, Bird's Hill Park, downtown Winnipeg

🦅 Warm welcome and friendly hospitality in unique contemporary home situated in peaceful
park-like surroundings high above the historic Red River. Ideal place for birdwatching (white
pelicans), for business travellers, weekend get-aways or visiting Manitoba's Interlake. ✔B&B

Thompson

(northern Manitoba)

Doorenbos, Anna and Robert (Anna's Bed & Breakfast)   ☎ (204) 677-5075
204 Wolf Street, Thompson, MB   R8N 1J7

Take Hwy 6 north from the Perimeter Rd in Winnipeg (760 km to Thompson).

$40S $50D   🍴 Meals   ► 2A
🕮 Full   🏠 Bungalow, quiet, deck, gazebo ■1Ste(self-cont -
main level)   ⊨2T ⊐Private   ★Parking,sep entrance, phone
& TV in den ⊕No smoking,no children,no pets ⋙Dutch
🏃 Northern Zoo, indoor swimming pool with waterslide, shopping
centers, Heritage Museum, on local bus route
🚗 Paint Lake Provincial & Pisew Falls Heritage Parks, Sasagui
/Odei River Rapids, Ospwagan/Troy Lakes stocked trout fishing

🦅 Thompson is the depot centre for travellers to Churchill, other Northern Communities and
fly-in fishing lodges. Enjoy true Northern Hospitality in spacious home with large guest suite.
There is a greenhouse connected to the cozy and informal living room. Hosts originally came from
Egypt and Indonesia and they enjoy cooking oriental foods. Airport, train and bus pick-up available
for a nominal charge. ✔CC

Winnipeg

(see also Selkirk)

Antymis, Ray & Linda (Southern Rose Guest House)   ☎ (204) 775-3484
533 Sprague St., Winnipeg, MB   R3G 2R9

$35S $48D   (Advance reservation recommended)   ► 4
Phone for directions.

🕮 Full   🏠 Res, 2-storey, older, patio, deck   ■ 2D (upstairs)
⊨2Q ⊐ 1Private, 1ensuite   ★ F,TV,LF, hot-tub, guest
quarters are separate, bicycles available, off-street parking
⊕Designated smoking area, no pets
🏃 Polo Park Shopping Centre, restaurants, cycling
🚗 Downtown, casino, The Forks Convention Centre, art gallery,
Winnipeg Folk Festival, Assiniboia Downs, airport, Via Rail

🦅 Red-brick residential home with warm woods, burnished brass trim, leaded glass and redwood
hot-tub. Experience the charm of decades past with a touch of Southern hospitality and relax in the
redwood hot-tub. Breakfast is served in formal dining room or on wrap-around sundeck.Visa✔B&B

Auriat, Anna (Aubrey B&B)   ☎ & Fax (204) 775-1433
292 Aubrey St., Winnipeg, MB   R3G 2J2

Located just south of Portage Ave (main street in City)
$35S $50D $10Child   🍽 Meals   (plus tax)   ▶ 4A,1Ch
📞 Choice   🏠 Downtown, 3-storey, porch, quiet   ■2D(upstairs)
q▬4S   🛏1Sh.w.g.   ★TV,KF,LF, ceiling fans, guest bikes available,
off-street & street parking   🚭 No smoking, no pets, children min. age 12
〰Ukrainian
🚶 Assiniboine River, shopping, bus stop for all routes
🚗 Beaches, horse races, Stadium, historic places, gambling casino
🔫 Comfortable home situated on a quiet street with mature elms/ashes.
Relax alone or join the family for a chit chat. Special rate for longer stays.
Pick-up from airport or bus depot.

Clark, John and Louise (West Gate Manor)   ☎ (204) 772-9788 Fax (204) 772-9782
71 West Gate, Winnipeg, MB   R3C 2C9   E-mail: jclark@escape.ca

Located in City Centre. Phone for directions.

$40S $50-58D $10Add.person   ▶ 8
📞Full,homebaked   🏠Downtown, hist., sunroom, quiet
■4D(upst)   ▬1Q,4D,1T,cots   🛏2Sh.w.g.   ★ F,1guest sitting
room, off-street parking   🚭 No smoking, children min. age 11
🚶 Antique shops, restaurants, shopping, bus depot, Winnipeg Art
Gallery, University of Winnipeg
🚗 Polo Park Mall, Winnipeg Arena/Stadium, Convention center,
CNR Station, The Folks Market

🔫 Situated in historic, picturesque Armstrong Point area of the city, where Winnipeg's elite
built during the turn of the Century. Home is decorated in Victorian splendour with each room
reflecting its own period and theme. Ideal central location from which to explore the city.

Ingalls, Ann & Ray (Prairie Charm Bed & Breakfast)   ☎ (204) 253-3636
Box 124, St.Germain, MB   R0G 2A0

$30S- $40D $10Child (age 5-12) (free under age 5) $10Add.person   ▶ 4

Located at 190 Greenview Rd. From South Winnipeg Bypass (Rte
100) go 5.5 km south on Rte 200, then east on Greenview Rd.
📞 Cont., homebaked   🏠 Rural, sub., split-level, acreage, porch,
quiet, secluded   ■ 2D (upstairs)   ▬2T,1D   🛏 1Sh.w.g.
★F,TV,LF   🚭 Smoking outside
🚶 Surrounding prairie farmland
🚗 University of Manitoba, downtown Winnipeg, restaurants,
shopping, Steinbach Mennonite Museum

🔫 Charming, modern home furnished comfortably with antiques and family heirlooms
surrounded by park-like setting condusive to relaxation. Located in the southeast corner of
Winnipeg with easy access from major routes. Enjoy gracious country living in the city. Tourists,
business and professional guests welcome. There is a dog in residence. Weekly rates available.

Jones, Arlene and Bob (Bannerman East B&B)   ☎(204)589-6449,Fax(204)528-5937
99 Bannerman Ave., Winnipeg, MB   R2W 0T1

Located close to Portage/Main Sts junction in North Winnipeg.

$38S $48D $10Child (under age 12)   ► 3
⚑Full 🏠Res.,patio,quiet ■1S,1D(upstairs) ⊨1S,1D ⌐1Sh.w.g.,
1sh.w.h. ★TV,KF,LF,parking ⓦNo smoking,no pets
🕴 Excellent ethnic and continental restaurants, public
transportation, historic St. John Park Anglican Church(1820),
historic "Forks" site, Museum of Man & Nature, Concert Hall,
Ukrainian Cultural center, shopping, theatres, Folklorama sites &
Rainbow Stage (July/Aug)
🚗 Lower Fort Garry, Steinbach Mennonite Museum, MB Stampede (Morris), Emerson (USA
border), Mint Factory, Lake Winnipeg, International Airporrt, Railway Station, Bus Depot
🐾 Well-traveled hosts (B&B in Europe and Eastern Canada) in comfortable home and pleasant
surroundings. Enjoy warm hospitality in convenient location. ✒B&B

Kauss, Sharon & Adolf (Shar-A-Cuppa B&B)   ☎ (204) 339-6270, Bus.Fax (204) 586-8425
257 Dougls Ave., Winnipeg, MB   R2G 0Y2

Located in n/e corner of the city, 1 block off Henderson Hwy & 2km from North Perimeter Hwy.

$40S $50D $10Child   ► 4A
⚑ Full 🏠 Sub.,raised bungalow, patio, deck ■2D(lower level)
⊨1D,1Q ⌐1Shw.g. ★F,TV,LF, off-street/street parking
ⓦNo smoking, no pets, not suitable for children 〰German
🕴 Large park with outdoor theatre & golf course on Red River,
hiking/x-c ski trail,bus Nos 11/77
🚗 Lower Fort Garry & Captain Kennedy Tea House (both on Red
River by Lockport), Birds Hill Park (horseback riding, ski trails
around small lake, Dugald Costume Museum, Canada Mint, Forks market, downtown Winnipeg
🐾 Warm welcome and friendly hospitality in modern home. Guest quarters are in complete
lower level of the home. Relax in the guest family room after a day of travelling or sightseeing.
Hosts are a retired cabinet maker and health field worker and enjoy welcoming guests from all
parts of the globe. Waffles are a house specialty. Airport pick-up can be arranged. There is a Lhasa
Apso dog "Peaches" in residence. ✒B&B

Lacroix, Marielle (Chex Marielle B&B)   ☎ & Fax (204) 452-7730
889 Jessie Ave., Winnipeg, MB   R3M 0Z8

Located between Corydon & Stafford. Phone for directions.
$38S $55D $110F 🍽Meals   ► 4
⚑ Full, homebaked 🏠 Res., 2-storey, sunporch, quiet ■ 2D
(upstairs) ⊨ 2T,1D ⌐ 1Sh.w.h. ★ TV, window air-conditioner in
one room, off-street parking ⓦ No smoking, no pets 〰 French
🕴 Quaint gift shops, cafes & boutiques along trendy Corydon Avenue, Grant
Park Shopping Centre, on bus route #18 (North Main)
🚗 Downtown, Forks Market, Assiniboine Zoo & Park, Manitoba Museum
of Man & Nature, airport, University of Manitoba
🐾 Warm welcome and friendly hospitality in character home located in the
City Centre district and exciting, charming and relaxing neighbourhood
known as Fort Rouge. Hostess enjoys gardening, cooking and golfing. Relax on the sun porch after a
day of sightseeing and travelling. ✒B&B

Lobreau, Francis and Anya
137 Woodlawn Ave., Winnipeg, MB R2M 2P5
☎ (204) 256-9789

Located in South Winnipeg, off St. Mary's Rd (Rt 52), with easy access to Trans Canada Hwy or
South Bypass (Hwy 100).

$35S $45-50D ▶ 4-6
🍽 Choice 🏠Sub.,4-level split-level,acreage,quiet ■3D(upst)
🛏1Q,2D 🚪1Private, 1Sh.w.g. ★TV,KF,LF,F, parking
🖐No pets, no smoking ᝰFrench,Polish
🧍 Major Shopping Centre, University of Manitoba, City transit,
St. Vital Park, Riel House
🚗 Quick access to downtown attractions, St. Boniface

🐾 Comfortable home with antique furnishings, located on a half acre of landscaped grounds in a
quiet neighbourhood near the Red River. Warm up by the fireplace on cool evenings. Relax in the
hammock or play a tune on the grand piano. Pick-up service available at added charge. ✍B&B

Taylor, Joe & Bev Suek (Twin Pillars Bed & Breakfast)
235 Oakwood Ave., Winnipeg, MB R3L 1E5
☎ (204) 284-7590,
Fax (204) 452-4925

Take Rte 16 & Osborne St south to Oakwood Ave (east off Osborne)
$35S $45D $50Ste $5Child ▶ 8A,2Ch
🍽Cont.(generous) 🏠Res., 3-storey, hist., porch, deck,quiet ■3D,1Ste
(2nd/3rd floor) 🛏2T,2D 🚪1Sh.w.g.,1sh.w.h. ★LF,KF,TV & balconies in
some guest rooms, separate entrance, off-street parking ♥ 🖐Designated
smoking rooms ᝰ some French
🧍 Old movie theatre, park across street, restaurants, public transportation
(bus #16), Municipal Hospital
🚗 Osborne Village shopping, downtown, Canoe & Golf Club, The Forks
Market, Winnipeg Zoo, Museum of Man & Nature
🐾 Turn-of-the-Century Heritage house with antique furniture and twin
pillars on front, situated in a quiet residential area. Enjoy a friendly, homey atmosphere and
conversation with congenial hosts. Only unscented, non-allergenic soap is used in the household.
Children welcome. There is a resident dog in host area only. Catering to groups available. ✍CC

Zonneveld, Mary Jane (Mary Jane's Place)
144 Yale Ave., Winnipeg, MB R3M 0L7
☎ (204) 453-8104

Phone for directions.
$35S $45D $10Child $20Add.person ▶ 6A,4Ch
🍽 Full 🏠 Downtown, res., 3-storey, hist., view, porch, quiet
■ 1S,1D,1F(2nd floor) 🛏S,T,Q 🚪Sh.w.g. ★F,TV,VCR in guest
den, separate entrance, clean radiation heat (no forced air), off
street parking 🖐No smoking ᝰFlemish & Dutch
🧍 Corydon Ave., Osborn Village, bike & jogging trails
🚗 The Forks, Assiniboine Park, Lower Fort Garry,restaurants
🐾 Spacious home (built in 1912 by same builder as Legislative Buildings) with ornate fire places,
beautiful chandeliers and situtated in quiet park-like surroundings. ✍B&B

Bed & Breakfast of Manitoba (Reservation Service)
434 Roberta Ave., Winnipeg, Man R2K 0K6
☎ (204) 661-0300

(Paula Carlson)
Rates:$35-50S $45-60D (including full breakfast. Advance reservation highly recommended)
Organized in 1980, Bed & Breakfast of Manitoba has a variety of friendly, knowledgeable hosts who
combine a unique flavour of ethnic and cultural heritage along with warm Manitoba hospitality.
The inspected homes are located in urban, rural and popular resort areas, open year-round. Call or
write for a full colour brochure with detailed listing and description of each home & current rates.

Ontario

Ontario Travel
77 Bloor St.West, 9th Floor,
Toronto, ON   M7A 2R9

(English) 965-4008
(French) 965-3448
toll-free (English) 1-800-668-2746
(French) 1-800-668-3736

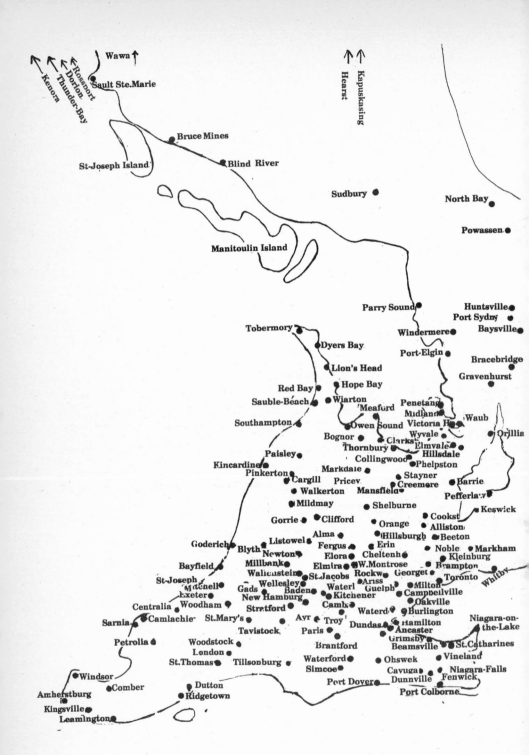

Kenora
Rossport
Dorion
Thunder-Bay
Wawa
Sault Ste.Marie

Hearst
Kapuskasing

Bruce Mines
St-Joseph Island
Blind River

Sudbury

North Bay

Powassen

Manitoulin Island

Parry Sound
Huntsville
Port Sydny
Baysville

Tobermory
Windermere
Port-Elgin
Bracebridge
Gravenhurst

Dyers Bay
Lion's Head
Hope Bay
Red Bay
Sauble-Beach
Wiarton
Meaford
Penetan
Midland
Victoria H
Waub
Orjllia

Southampton
Owen Sound
Bognor
Clarks
Wyvale
Elmvale
Thornbury
Hillsdale
Collingwood
Phelpston

Paisley
Markdale
Stayner
Kincardine
Pinkerton
Cargill
Pricev
Creemore
Barrie
Walkerton
Mansfield
Pefferla
Mildmay
Shelburne

Gorrie
Clifford
Orange
Cookst
Alliston
Keswick

Goderich
Blyth
Listowel
Alma
Hillsburgh
Beeton
Newton
Fergus
Erin
Noble
Markham
Bayfield
Millbank
Elora
Cheltenh
Kleinburg
St-Joseph
Walienstein
Elmira
W.Montrose
Rockw
Georget
Brampton
Mitchell
St.Jacobs
Ariss
Toronto
Whitby
Exeter
Wellesley
Baden
Waterl
Guelph
Milton
Centralia
Gads
New Hamburg
Kitchener
Campbellville
Woodham
Camb
Oakville
Stratford
Waterd
Burlington
Sarnia
Camlachie
St.Mary's
Ayr
Troy
Dundas
Hamilton
Niagara-on-the-Lake
Tavistock
Paris
Ancaster
Petrolia
Woodstock
London
Brantford
Grimsby
Beamsville
St.Catharines
St.Thomas
Tillsonburg
Waterford
Ohswek
Vineland
Simcoe
Cavuga
Niagara-Falls
Windsor
Dutton
Port Dover
Dunnville
Fenwick
Amherstburg
Comber
Ridgetown
Port Colborne
Kingsville
Leamington

158 ONTARIO

Ontario

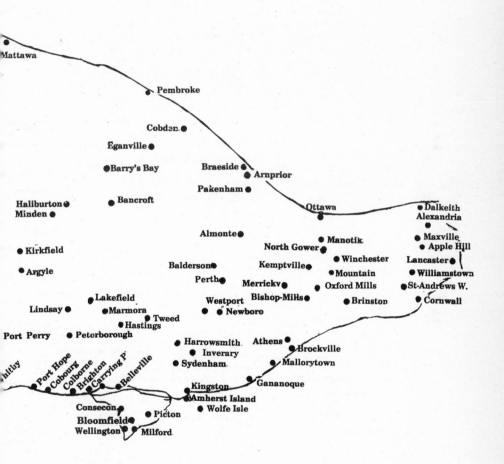

Mattawa

Pembroke

Cobden

Eganville

Barry's Bay

Braeside

Arnprior

Pakenham

Haliburton
Minden

Bancroft

Ottawa

Dalkeith
Alexandria

Almonte

Manotik

Maxville
Apple Hill

Kirkfield

North Gower

Winchester

Lancaster

Argyle

Balderson

Kemptville

Mountain

Williamstown

Perth

Merrickv

Oxford Mills

St-Andrews W.

Lakefield

Westport

Bishop-Mills

Brinston

Cornwall

Lindsay

Marmora
Hastings

Tweed

Newboro

Port Perry

Peterborough

Harrowsmith
Inverary
Sydenham

Athens

Brockville

Mallorytown

hitby

Port Hope
Cobourg
Colborne
Brighton
Carrying P.
Belleville

Kingston

Gananoque

Consecon
Bloomfield
Wellington
Milford

Amherst Island
Wolfe Isle

Picton

Acton

(west of Toronto; see also Rockwood, Georgetown)

Toth, Marg and Les
RR1, Acton, ON L7J 2L7

☎ (519) 853-1065

From Hwy 401, take Exit 320 (Hwy25) north and go 14km to Reg Rd12. Turn left (west) and continue to 6th Line. Turn right (north) and look for 6th house on left side.

$35S $45D $10Child   ►4
🍴 Cont.   🏠 Rural, acreage, ranch-style, huge deck, quiet ■2D
⊨2T,1Q   ⊐1Private,1sh.w.h.,whirlpool   ★Air,F,LF,KF,TV in guest rooms   ⊛ No smoking   ⌇ Hungarian
🏃 Walking, biking, (bicyles provided), Blue Spring Golf Course
🚗 Old Hyde House Leather Goods, Agricultural Museum, Mohawk/Woodbine Raceway, Glen Eden (downhill skiing), Kelso and Rockwood Conservation Areas, Bruce Trail (hiking, x-c skiing)

📣 Spacious, sunny bungalow situated in a park-like setting on 10 acres of quiet wilderness. There are two small house dogs (downstairs only). Well behaved pets can sleep in garage.

Alexandria

(n/of Cornwall; see also Apple H., Willamstown, Lancaster, Dalkeith)

MacDonald, Ed & Audrey (Maple Lane Guest Home B&B)
No.21320, RR2, Group Box129, Alexandria, ON   K0C 1A0

☎ (613)525-3205
(905)666-0517

From Hwy 401 take Exit 814 and go north to Alexandria. At 1st traffic light turn right at Lochiel St and proceed 6.5 km east to Gate Post 21320.

$35-40S $45-50D   🍴 Meals   ►6
✚ May24-Oct1 (other by special arrangement)   🍴 Full, homebaked   🏠 Rural, hist., view from guest rooms, porch, secluded, veranda   ■ 3D (main & upper level)   ⊨ 2T,2D
⊐1Sh.w.g.   ★ Air(partial), TV available for guests   ⊛ No smoking, no pets, children min. age 12   ⌇ French
🏃 Strolling through unspoiled nature trails, old sugar shack on property (at one time an award winning Maple Syrup producer)
🚗 Maxville Highland Games, Nor'wester & Dunvegen Museums, Ottawa, Montreal

📣 Century farmhouse with hand hewn beams, pine floors, loft and "Old Country" atmosphere, nestled among mature maples on 100 acres in a truly peaceful setting. Relax on the sun porch or in the evening around a crackling campfire (hostess frequently involves her well-known Marionettes to participate in the fun). Hostess teaches French (ideal place for French Immersion guests). There are 2 dogs kept in closed area away from the house.

Alliston

(north of Toronto; see also Cookstown, Beeton, Mansfield)

Davies, Valerie and Wally (Fintona Farm)
RR1, Alliston, ON   L9R 1V1

☎ & Fax (705) 435-5685

Located 6.6 km west of Alliston on Hwy 89 and 5.3 km east of Airport Rd on Hwy 89. Turn south onto dirt road on Con 3 of Adjala. Look for 1st house on s/e corner of 3rd Con & 30 SR (1km)

$45S/D   ►4
🍴Full   🏠197-acres farm, hist., view, patio, quiet ■2D(upst)
⊨2D   ⊐Sh.w.g.   ★Air,LF
🚗 Hiking, fishing, cycling, downhill or x-c ski Loretto/Mansfield
📣 Fully restored 1874-built farm house surrounded by mixed farm land. There is a north-south 2000ft grass runway with 2 tie-downs available, for those who would like to fly in. Ideal location for Bruce Trail hiking. Several good restaurants close by.

Alma

(north of Kitchener/Waterloo; see also Fergus, Elora, Elmira)

Driedger, Arthur & Irene (Sentimental Pathway with a Touch of Peace B&B)
7925 Wellington Rd. 7, RR1, Alma, ON   N0B 1A0   ☎ (519) 638-2399, Fax (519) 638-2499

Phone for directions.
$50-55S $55-60D   ►6
🍳 Full, homebaked   🏠 Rural, split-level, hillside, 2-acres, view
from guest rooms, on stream, patio, porch, quiet, secluded
■3(upstairs)   ⊨ 2S,1T,1D,1Q, crib   🛁 2Sh.w.g.   ★ Air,F,
large well stocked library, ping pong, volleyball, badminton, guest
quarters are separate   ⊛ No smoking, no pets   ᵥᵥ German
🎣 Natural woods with meandering brook and 3 wooden bridges, lit
pathway through woods, campfire area on island, bird watching
🚐 Drayton Festival, Elora Gorge, Elmira, St.Jacobs & farmers' market, Waterloo Universities
🚍 Semi-retired past farmers and Christian couple in Spanish-style Country home, nestled in 2
acres of wooded/valley setting, with plenty of tranquility and nature's beauty. Host is very musical
(having released Cd's of his own creation), and may entertain guests on his guitar, if they wish.
Hostess is a former Health Care worker and librarian. Relax on the balcony patio overlooking the
beautiful flower gardens/woods or browse in the Peace Arch Creations Gift Shop on the premises.
Breakfast is served in the living/dining area. There is a dog and a cat in residence. ↙B&B

Almonte

(south-west of Ottawa; see also Pakenham)

Matheson, Pat and Ian (The Squirrels)   ☎ (613) 256-2995
Box 729, 190 Parkview Dr., Almonte, Ont.   K0A 1A0

From Ottawa going west, follow Queensway to Almonte cut-off and then Hwy 44 for 14 km to house
situated diagonally opposite Almonte Community center.

$35S $50D   🍴 Meals   ►5
🍳 Full, homebaked   🏠 Village, ranch style,view,acreage,quiet
■1S,2D(main level)   ⊨1S,4T   🛁1Sh.w.g.   ★ TV, large
guest lounge, parking   ⊛No smoking   ᵥᵥsome French
🎣 Community center/park, public swimming pool, shops &
restaurants x-country skiing, Mississippi Valley Textile Museum
🚐 Downhill skiing, golfing, Tait MacKenzie Museum, Naismith
Basket Ball Museum
🚍 Unique very spacious home with cathedral ceilings surrounded by almost an acre of
landscaped gardens, providing plenty of privacy for guests. Hosts are world travellers and have
many interesting memorabilia around the house. Farm-style breakfast is served in sunroom. ↙CC

Amherstburg

(south of Windsor; see also Kingsville, Leamington, Comber)

Honor, Robert and Debra (The Honor's)   ☎ (519) 736-7737
4441, C4, RR2, Amherstburg, ON   N9V 2Y8

From Amherstburg, go out Simcoe St/Pike Rd to 4th Con., turn
right. Look for 13th house on east side. (send for detailed map)
$45-55S $55-65D $55Ste $5Child   ► 4A,2Ch
➕ July/Aug.(other by arrangement   🍴Choice   🏠Farm, view,
older, patio, quiet   ■2D(upstairs)   ⊨2D,cot   🛁1Private,
1ensuite   ★Air,TV   ⊛No smoking, no pets   ᵥᵥFrench
🚐 Historic Amherstburg, Fort Malden Nat. Hist. Park,
birdwatching, Black History Museum, Point Pelee, Windsor
🚍 Tree shaded cottage-style home in quiet and peaceful country setting, overlooking farm and
woods, but close to Metropolitan activities. There are 3 cats & a dog in the house. ↙B&B

Amherst Island

(west of Kingston; see also Wolfe Island)

Caughey, Susan and Bruce (Poplar Dell)
Amherst Island, Stella, ON K0H 2S0
☎ & Fax (613) 389-2012

From Hwy 401, take Exit 593 to Hwy 133 south to Millhaven Ferry Dock and ferry to Amherst Island. Drive 2 km east to Poplar Dell. Ferry makes round trip every hour (20min ride)

$45S $60-65D $15Child 🍽Meals ►9
� Full, homebaked 🏠 Farm, hist. large patio, lakefront, ■3D(upstairs) ⊨2T,1D,2Q,R ⊂Sh.w.g. ★TV,F
🏃 Swimming at back door, quiet country roads for hiking and biking, bay-water windsurfing
🚗 Historic Kingston or Napanee, 1000 Island boat cruises
🔫 170-year old stone farmhouse overlooking Lake Ontario and situated on the most westerly of the 1000 Islands. Relax or take part in dairy activities. Enjoy abundant homecooking and friendly island hospitality.✒B&B

Thompson, Bob & Corrinne (Anniversary House B&B)
RR1, Stella, ON K0H 2S0
☎ (613) 389-8190, Fax (613) 389-1858

From Hwy 401, take Exit 593 to Hwy 133 south to Millhaven. Turn right on Hwy 33 to Ferry dock.

Ferry leaves every hour on half hour. Drive 3km west to B&B.
$50-60S/D $10Child ►6A,2Ch
� Full, homebaked 🏠 Rural, 2-storey, acreage, view, lakefront, patio, deck, quiet ■ 3D(upstairs) ⊨2T,2Q,P,cot,crib
⊂1sh.w.g., 1ensuite ★ Air,TV 🖐 No smoking, no pets, inquire about children
🏃 Swimming at lakeside, bird watching, quiet roads for walking and cycling (guest owned bikes), x-c skiing, pond skating
🚗 Historic Kingston, 1000 Islands and daily summer cruises, Marine Museum of the Great Lakes
🔫 Large, modern designer waterfront home situated on a small island in Lake Ontario. Enjoy the peaceful island country atmosphere and a different sunset every evening. Relax on the dock, explore the island and its beautiful scenery, or read a favorite book in the den or in the great room. Breakfast is served in the Hearth Room. There is a dog outside. ✒B&B

Ancaster

(west of Hamilton; see also Dundas)

Samson, Betty & Doug (Windy Knoll Farm)
1116 Boock Rd.West, Ancaster, ON L9G 4X1
☎ (905) 648-3913

From Hamilton or Brantford take Exit 52 south and proceed on Trinity Rd to Book Rd. Turn left to 1st farm on right. From Hwys 2/53 go south on Trinity Rd to Book Rd.

$45-55S $55-65D ►6
� Full � Farm, 78-acres, 2-storey, hist., view from guest rooms, patio, porch, deck, quiet ■ 3D(upstairs) ⊨2D,1K
⊂ 1sh.w.g, 1ensuite ★ Air,TV,LF,F, boat for guests 🖐 No smoking, no pets, not suitable for children
🏃 1-acre man-made pond on property (not for fishing), golf course, ongoing tree nursery operation on grounds, walking path
🚗 Ancaster, War Plane Museum, downtown Hamilton, Bell Museum (Brantford), Kitchener/Waterloo and Mennonite Country, Toronto
🔫 Completely restored, Historic house was built between 1817/1825 from the lumber off the land, and once a stop-over on the trail from Middleport on the Grand River to Ancaster. Retired hosts are very familiar with local history and sites. Entire farmhouse is exclusive for guests. Hosts live in small bungalow on the property. Breakfast is served in the farmhouse dining room/kitchen. Guests are invited to take the boat out on the pond. There are 2 cats in hosts' residence.

162 ONTARIO

Wentworth, Dan and Dorothy (Duck Tail Inn Bed & Breakfast)   ☎ (905) 648-3596
1573 Butter Rd. West, Ancaster, ON   L9G 3L1

From Hamilton or Toronto on Hwy 403, take Copetwon Exit and continue south on Hwy 52, crossing Hwy 2/53 onto Trinity Rd. Proceed through 2 concessions, then turn right (west) onto Butter Rd. Go one concession and look for Duck mailbox and a cannon on front lawn.

$45S $55D   ► 4A
🦆 Choice   🏠 44-acre farm, view, ranch-style, patio, quiet, isolated, pond with ducks   ■ 2D(main level)   ⊨ 2T,1Q
⌐1Ensuite, 1sh.w.h., jacuzzi for guests   ★ Air,TF, separate entrance   ⓌRestricted smoking, children min. age 4
🕺 Private museum on property (Early Canadian Artifacts & Tools - free tours), quiet country roads
🚗 Mt.Hope Airport, Caledonia Boat Farm, Mohawk Chapel

🔫 Modern country home overlooking rolling fields and pond, situated near picturesque Niagara Escarpment. Enjoy the very restful country atmosphere. Hostess hatches ducks. There is tasteful duck decor all through the house. Relax in the large sunroom, furnished with wicker, overlooking the garden and pond. A cat lives in residence. ✓B&B

Woods, Shirley & Larry (Tranquility Base B&B)   ☎ (905) 648-1506, Fax (905) 627-2818
110 Abbey Close, Ancaster, ON   L9G 1K7

From Hwy 403 west of Hamilton, take Wilson St East Exit, then first turn left at fire hall on Meadowbrook Rd, and right on Abbey Close.

$50S $65D $20Child   🍽 Meals   ► 4A,1Ch
🦆Full, homebaked   🏠Res., 2-storey, deck, quiet   ■3(upstairs)
⊨1S,2T,1D   ⌐ 1Sh.w.g.   ★ Air,F,TV, off-street parking
ⓌNo smoking, no pets
🕺 Centre of old village of Ancaster, shops, restaurants
🚗 Downtown Hamilton, Copps Coliseum, Hamilton Place, Dundurn Castle, Canadian Heritage War Plane Museum, Mt.Hope Airport, Ancaster Old Mill, Niagara Falls, Kitchener/Waterloo Mennonite area, Toronto
🔫 Warm welcome and friendly hospitality in comfortable, large modern brick home located on a quiet cul-de-sac. Well travelled hosts have been collecting Victorian cranberry, crystal, dolls, art and other antiques for more than 25 years and these are displayed through the house. A justifiable fine local reputation as a talented cook is reflected in memorable breakfasts, served in guest breakfast room. The coffee pot is usually on. ✓B&B

Apple Hill *(north of Cornwall; see also Lancaster, Williamstown, Alexandria, St.Andrews W))*

McIntosh, Stewart and Christena (Tanglewood Farm)   ☎ (613) 527-2884
RR2, Apple Hill, ON   K0C 1B0

From Hwy 401 take Exit 789 & Hwy 138 north to Hwy 43. Travel east 5 km to Strathmore (Pidgeon Hill) Rd, then south 2 km to McIntosh Rd and left to first farm (5 km west of Apple Hill).
$25S $40D $10Child   🍽 Meals   ► 4A,2Ch
🦆 Full   🏠 Farm home   ■ 3D (upstairs)   ⊨ 2D,2T
⌐1Sh.w.g.   ★TV,F   ⓌNo smoking, no pets
🕺 Hiking, walking, cross-country skiing, maple bush
🚗 Glengarry Highland Games, Cornwall, Seaway Valley
🔫 Feel the warmth and welcome of country hospitality and relax in rural tranquility. Enjoy delicious homecooking and fresh vegetables from the garden.

Argyle
(west of Lindsay; see also Pefferlaw, Kirkfield)

Fleming, Rae (Argyle B&B)   ☎ (705) 439-2337
RR6, Woodville, ON   K0M 2T0

Located in the village of Argyle. From Toronto, take Hwy 404 (Don Valley Parkway) north to Davis
Dr, then right to Hwy 48. Continue all the way north to Beaverton and proceed 12km east.
$45S $60D $10Child $75F $20Add.person   ▶ 7-8

Full, homebaked Village, 2-storey, deck 1S,1D,1F(upst &
ground level) 2D,1Q,1P 1Sh.w.h. ★TV, off-street
parking Smoking outside, pets with special arrangement
only French
Casino Rama (Orillia), Kirkfield Lift Lock, Sir William
MacKenzie Historic Home, Trent Canal, Trent U., Peterborough,
Champlain Monument, Old Stone Church, Historic Jail, museum
& archives in Beaverton

Very cozy home decorated with prints, posters & carvings from local & international artists.
Host is a published writer of biography & local history and very knowledgeable of the area and its
geneology. House specialty is homegrown Mint Tea. Breakfast is served in special guest breakfast
room. There is a cat in residence.

Ariss
(west of Guelph; see also Rockwood, Elmira, Elora)

Bosma, Rita & Jim (Blossom Hill Bed & Breakfast)   ☎ (519) 836-2062
RR2, Ariss, ON   N0B 1B0

From Guelph take Hwy 6 north and turn left on County Rd7 to Elora. Turn right on RR51, left
on Side Rd2 to first house on left.
$45S $60D $100F   ▶ 6

Full, homebaked Rural, 2-storey, 1acre, patio, porch, deck,
quiet 2D,1Ste (upstairs) 1D,2Q,cot 1Sh.w.g.,
1ensuite ★ Air,F,TV, pool table, wood stove, separate entrance,
off-street parking No smoking, children min. age 10 (infants
accepted) Dutch
Walking & x-c ski trail
Elora Gorge, Elora shops & restaurants, Guelph, Fergus covered bridge, St.Jacobs
Warm & friendly welcome in large modern, tastefully decorated country home with friendly
English/Dutch atmosphere and beautiful prize winning gardens. Relax on the lawnswing/patio
under the trees. Breakfast is served in guest breakfast room. Crafts available. ✔B&B

Athens
(west of Brockville; see also Newboro, Westport, Mallorytown)

Thompson, Chris & Marie (The Apple Grove)   ☎ (613) 924-1463, Fax (613) 924-1417
10 Elgin St.S., Box 478, Athens, ON   K0E 1B0

From Hwy 401, take Exit 696 (Brockville) onto Hwy 29 and go north app. 24 km. At fork in road,
follow signs for Hwy 42 & Athens. At main intersection, turn left on Elgin St S to 5th house.
$45S $50-65D $10Add.person   Meals   ▶ 5A,2Ch

Full, homebaked Village, hist., 2-storey, quiet, sundeck,
Victorian veranda 2D,1F(main & upper level) 1S,2D,2Q
1Ensuite,1sh.w.g. ★Air,TV,guest parlour,sep.entr.,parking,
wheel-chair access in one room No smoking French
Walking tour of the Murals of Athens, restaurants, cycling
Charleston Lake & Prov.Park (year-around outdoor activities),
swimming, hiking, x-c skiing, Brockville, Thousand Islands
Gracious, circa 1886-built Victorian home with shaded front porches, white pillars, large back
sundeck and large quiet rooms. Situated on a shaded street of historic village; in the heart of United
Empire Loyalist country. Hosts have a motorboat at the lake for touring. There is a cat. ✔CC

Ayr

(south of Kitchener; see also Cambridge, Troy)

Bartholomew, Paul & Sharon (Bartholomew Cottage B&B)   ☎ (519) 632-8891
RR1, Reg.Rd 49 (Wrigleys Rd), Ayr, ON   N0B 1E0   Fax (519) 632-8375

From Hwy 401, take Exit 268, east on Hwy 97, right on 47 Rd, then right on 49 Rd. for 2km to house on left.
$45S $55D $15Child/Add.person   ► 6
🍴 Full   🏠 Rural, hillside, view, acreage, swimming pool, patio, porch, quiet   ■ 2D(main level)   ⊨ 1D,1Q,2R   🛁 1Sh.w.g.
★ TV,F, ceiling fans, host quarters are separate   🚫 No smoking, no pets
🕴 Quiet walks in rural countryside with gardens, flowers & birds
🚗) Pretty village of Ayr, St.Jacobs, African Lion Safari, Southworks Outlet Mall, Doon Heritage Crossroads, Kitchener Sportsworld, Adventures on the Grand River, hiking & ski trails
☛ Retired couple in comfortable home built in 1950 as a "retirement home for the farmer", furnished with a delightful mixture of new and old. Hosts are developing perennial gardens, including herbs, which are used in the preparation of breakfast. ╰B&B

Baden

(east of Stratford; see also New Hamburg, Wellesley, Tavistock, GadsHill)

Banbury, Michael & Mother Sarah (Banbury Farm B&B)   ☎ (519) 634-5451
RR2, Baden, ON   N0B 1G0   (519) 662-2707

Take Hwy 401 to Hwy 8 west towards Kitchener and continue on Hwy 7/8 west towards Stratford to Waterloo Reg Rd 12. Turn right (north) and travel through Petersburg and St. Agatha. Take 1st crossroad (Tsp Rd4) west to 1st farm on right.

$40S $60D $20Add.person   🍴Meals   ► 7
🍴 Cont., homebaked   🏠 Farm, older, pleasant view, veranda   ■1D,1F(upst)   ⊨1S,2T,1D,1P   🛁 2sh.w.h.   ★TV,F,LF
🚫No pets, smoking downstairs, child min. age 6   〰 French
🕴 Walking, cycling, cross-country skiing
🚗 Kitchener/Waterloo, Stratford, Golf courses, two Universities, farmer's markets, St.Jacobs Mennonite Country
☛ Attractive 86-acres farm with horses and emus. Enjoy the space, comfort & hospitality. Relax on the screened veranda overlooking paddocks with split rail fencing, fields & trees. Riding instructions available nearby. There are 2 dogs in residence. ╰B&B

Hill, Jane & Graham (Dappled Pegasus Bed & Breakfast)   ☎ (519) 634-8379,
RR2, Baden, ON   N0B 1G0   Fax (519) 634-8725

Located just west of St.Agatha. Take Hwy 7&8 west from Kitchener to RegRd12. Turn north through Petersburg to St.Agatha. Turn west on RegRd9 and look for B&B sign on left at long lane
$50S $65D   ► 7
✚ April-Dec   🍴 Full, homebaked   🏠 Farm, 2-storey, hist., 150 acres, view from guest rooms, heated swimming pool, porch, quiet, isolated   ■ 3 (upstairs)   ⊨ 1S,1Q,2D   🛁 1Sh.w.g.
🚫 No smoking, no pets
🕴 Nature Trails, restaurant, shops, churches, pub
🚗 Waterloo/Kitchener, Stratford Festival Theatres, Baden (Castle Kilbride), Elora, St.Jacobs, farmers' markets
☛ 1840-built stone farmhouse, lovingly restored, decorated with antiques situated amidst 150 acres of gently rolling rich farmland and forest. Unwind in a casual country atmosphere, sleep with the gentle sounds of wind sighing through the leaves & the soft nickering of horses; awaken to a dip in the sparkling pool followed by a hearty breakfast served in sunny windowed room resplendent with plants. There are 2 dogs & 3 cats. Enjoy a quiet get-away.

Balderson
(south-west of Ottawa; see also Perth)

Miller, Ann (Woodrow Farm & Guest Ranch)
RR1, Fergusons Falls Rd. Balderson, Ontario K0G 1A0

☎ (613) 267-1493, Fax (613) 267-1766
E-mail: whitedun@capitalnet.com

$60D 🍽 Meals ▶ 6

From Perth off Hwy 7, go north on Hwy 511 (app 6km) to Balderson village, right on Ferguson

Falls Rd and look for 3rd farm on left, an easy drive from Ottawa. 🏠Full, homebaked 🐄96-acre working farm ■3D(upstairs) ⊨K,D,T,2R ⬛Sh.w.g. ★TV,F,guest lounge & dining room 🖐No pets ♥
🕴 Village of Balderson, Prov. Parks (beaches, fishing, boating, fishing), x/c ski & snowmobile trails, nature trail to explore 🚗 Glenair Kitten Factory outlets, Heritage Silversmiths,Brown Shoes & Balderson Cheese Factory outlets, Ottawa, Kingston
📣 Century Victorian farmhouse, set in large country garden shaded by maples and overlooking horse paddocks. One, two and 4 day Horseback-Riding break-away packages offered. Craft workshops & Massage Therapy available. In winter enjoy the Country Retreats, x-c ski, take a sleigh ride or just relax. Visa,JCB ⮞CC

Bancroft
(N.of Peterborough; see also L'Amable, Haliburton, Barry's Bay, Minden)

Leenders, Kathleen & Albert (Leender's Lakeside B&B)
RR3, Bancroft, ON K0L 1C0

☎ & Fax (613) 339-1055
E-mail: leebb@mail.bancom.net, 1-888-255-8222

From Bancroft travel south 20km on Hwy 28. Located 2km north of Silent Lake Prov.Park.
$40S $50D $10Child $15Add.person 🍽 Meals ▶ 6
🏠 Full, homebaked 🏡 Rural, res., 2-storey ranch-style, 1.5acres, view from guest rooms, lakefront, patio, porch, quiet ■3D(upstairs) ⊨ 2T,1D,1Q ⬛ 2Sh.w.g. ★ F,KF,LF,TV, guest quarters are separate 🖐 No smoking ⮝ Dutch
🕴 Fishing on Paudash Lake, marina, boat launch, hiking, restaurants, Greyhound bus stop
🚗 Bancroft, Playhouse Theatre, "Gemboree", rock hunting
📣 Comfortable home located on Anderson Lake with beautiful decor and tanquil surroundings abounding in natural beauty. An ideal place for artists, photographer, bird watchers and nature lovers. Browse through the assortment of "Kathleen's Kreations" in the on-site studio. Scumptuous breakfast is served in large dining room with a view of the lake. Special package rates on request. Snowmobilers, hunters, skiers welcome. Visa ⮞CC

Barrie
(north of Toronto: see also Phelpston, Hillsdale, Elmvale, Stayner)

Blackstock, Hugh & Jane (Heavitree House B&B)
RR1, Shanty Bay, ON L0L 2L0

☎ (705) 721-0483

On Hwy 400, travel north from Barrie and continue on Hwy 11 north towards Orillia. Five km past junction, take Oro-Medonte Line 3 south to 2nd house on right.
$40S $55D ▶ 6
🏠Homebaked 🏡 Rural, 2-storey, hist., acreage, view, porch, quiet ■3D(upstairs), guest quarters are separate ⊨2T,2D ⬛2Sh.w.g. ★ TV,F & woodstove, separate entrance, parking 🖐 No smoking, no pets, children minimum age 12
🕴 Walk or bike on country roads, large perennial garden, croquet
🚗 St.Marie among the Hurons & Martyr's Shrine, Wye & Tiny Marsh Wildlife Centres, historic Naval & Military Establ., Leacock & Norman Bethune homes, boat cruises, theatre, fine dining
📣 1860's farm house with open vistas surrounded by rolling countryside. Relax in the parlour with fireplace, piano, games & books or on the screened-in porch. Well travelled hosts (including Nepal & Africa) enjoy hiking, gardening & birding. Breakfast is served in separate guest breakfast room. There is a very friendly cat in residence.Visa ⮞CC

Hosie, Sandy & Gina (Inn-Between B&B)
6 Maplecrest Court, Horseshoe Valley, RR1, Barrie, ON L4M 4Y8

☎ & Fax (705) 835-0047

From Hwy 400 take Exit 117 north of Barrie. Proceed east on Horseshoe Valley Rd and continue

east out of valley to Maplecrest Ct. Look for 3rd house on right.
$55S $65D $15Add.person   ► 4
🔲 Homebaked   🏠 Rural, 2-storey, view from guest rooms, deck,
quiet   ■ 2D(upstairs)   ⊨ 2D   ⊟ 1Sh.w.g.   ★ F,TV,
outdoor hot tub (for 6)   ♥   ✋ No smoking, no pets
🎿 Downhill & x-c skiing, golfing at Horseshoe Valley Resort,
Ganaraska Hiking Trail, mountain biking, snowshoeing &
snowmobiling, Copeland Forest

🚗 Moonstone/Mt St.Louis (downhill skiing), Hardwood Hills (x-c skiing & mountain biking),
horseback riding, Barrie/Orillia Theatre, Casino Rama, Canada's Wonderland, Toronto
🔫 Large chalet-type country home ideally situated in the popular Horseshoe Valley Resort area,
backing onto the 6th hole of the beautiful Valley Golf Course. X-c ski from the door or walk over to
lifts for downhill skiing. Hike the Ganaraska Trail nearby or enjoy the beauty of the fall colours in
Copeland Forest. Relax by the log fire or unwind in the hot tub. Babysitting can be arranged with
due notice & additional charge. Golf & Ski packages available. ✔B&B

Kirby, Charita & Harry (Cozy Corner Bed & Breakfast)
2 Morton Cr., Barrie, ON   L4N 2T3

☎ (705)739-0157,(705)323-3471

Take Hwy 400 north to Barrie and Exit 96A (Dunlop St). Turn left at Ann St and proceed to

Hanmer St and then to Morton Cr (4th St on left).
$55S $65D $110Ste   🍽 Meals   ► 6A
🔲 Full   🏠 Res., 2-storey, patio, porch, quiet   ■ 2D,1Ste
(upstairs)   ⊨ 2D,1Q   ⊟ 1Sh.w.g, 1ensuite   ★ Air,F,LF,TV
in guest rooms, jacuzzi in suite, guest quarters are separate,
off-street parking   ✋ Smoking on patio or porch, no pets, no
children   🗣Spanish, German
🎿 Downhill and x-c skiing on doorstep

🚗 Rama Casino, Georgian Bay & Wasaga beaches (world's longest fresh-water beach),
Saint-Marie-among-the-Hurons, Canada's Wonderland, Toronto
🔫 Charming brick home with old world ambiance reflecting hosts' European backgrounds.
Situated in a quiet residential area. Hosts are a former teacher & governess to Julio Iglesia's
children & a German/British-trained Chef. Gourmet breakfast is house specialty. Pick-up at
Toronto Airport & Union Station. Superb dinners with compl. wines available. Visa ✔CC

Murray, Diane C (Round Table Bed & Breakfast)
59 Kinzie Lane, Barrie, ON   L4M 6A1

☎ (705) 739-0193, Fax (705) 739-0145

From Hwy 400 in Barrie, take Duckworth cut-off. Turn left on Grove, right
on Hickling, then left.
$40S $60D $15Add.person   🍽 Meals   ► 4
🔲 Full, homebaked   🏠 Res, sub., multi-storey, patio   ■2D(upstairs)
⊨ 2T,1Q,1R   ⊟1Shw.g.   ★ F,LF,TV in guest room, hot tub
✋Children min age 6
🎿 Lakefront, beach, downtown, bus stop, golfing, Casino
🚗 Midland & Penitanguishene, Wonderland, Orillia, skiing
🔫 Award-winning home is furnished with antiques. Relax in the sun room
and enjoy the beautiful garden. There is a cat "Gweniviere" & a dog "Camelot" in residence. Short
stay & corporate rates available. ✔CC

Richmond, Pam & Bob (Richmond Manor)　　　　　　　　　☎ (705) 726-7103
16 Blake St., Barrie, ON　L4M 1J6

From Hwy 400, take Exit 96 (Dunlop St) & travel 3km east to Blake St. Look for first house on left.

$50-60S　$65-75D　$15Child　$125F　$20Add.person　▶ 5
🝓 Full, homebaked　🏠 Res., 3-storey, hist., acreage, view from guest rooms, porch, quiet　■ 2D(upstairs)　➤ 1D,1Q,1R
🛁 1Sh.w.g., 1sh.w.h.　★ F,TV in private sitting room, ceiling fans, off-street parking　🖐 Smoking on porch, no pets
🏃 Walking & bicycle trails along Kempenfelt Bay (Lake Simcoe), sandy beaches, marina, parks, downtown shopping & dining
🚗 Canada Wonderland, Rama Casino, skiing, Toronto

🐾 Ivy-covered Georgian-style home (ca 1911) with traditional elegance situated on forested property and waterfront. Home is included in local Christmas House Tour. There is an in-house folk artist. Breakfast is served in formal dining room. Enjoy many folk art treasures. ✓B&B

Barry's Bay
(southwest of Pembroke; see also rrEganville)

Deakin, Mary Helen & Don (Barry's Bay B&B)　　　　　☎ (613) 756-1023
Box 217, 29 Sandhill Dr., Barry's Bay, ON　K0J 1B0

Located in town just off Hwy 60.
$40S　$50D　　　　　　　　　　　　　　　　▶ 4
🝓 Full, homebaked　🏠 2-storey　■ 2D(upstairs)　➤ 2D
🛁 1Sh.w.g.　★ Private guest entrance　🖐 No pets, no smoking
🚗 Historic sites, art galleries, boating, kayaking, canoeing, rifer raft trips, fishing, tennis, artists' studio tours, craft shops, Pioneer Museum, heritage log structures, flaming leaf tours, downhill & nordic skiing, mountain biking

🐾 Comfortable home, tastefully decorated with Nottingham lace, cozy wool duvets, silver & fine china. Enjoy the friendly atmosphere and a hearty breakfast, walk around the spacious grounds or relax by the fireplace in the bright living room. Hostess designs Victorian gifts, nightwear and wool duvets - all displayed throughout the house and for sale. ✓B&B

Newing, Barb & Dave (Inglenook B&B)　　　　　　　　☎ (613) 756-0727
Box 234, Barry's Bay, ON　K0J 1B0

In Barry's Bay go south on Dunn St to Siberia Rd to hospital. Proceed 1.5km, turn left and go 0.7km

turn right and continue 5.2km to B&B.
$40S　$55D　$10Child　🍽 Meals　　　　　▶ 4
🝓 Full, homebaked　🏠 Rural, 2-storey, lakeview from guest rooms, lakefront, deck　■ 2D (lower level)　➤ 2T,1Q
🛁 1Sh.w.g., whirlpool tub　★ Air,F,TV,LF, private entrance, guest quarters are separate　🖐 No smoking, no pets
🏃 Trails (hiking, x-c skiing, snowmobiling), swimming, boating
🚗 Algonquin Park, whitewater rafting (Madawaska & Ottawa R)

🐾 Congenial couple in comfortable lakeside home overlooking beautiful Lake Kamaniskeg. Enjoy the warm and friendly hospitality, relax on the deck, paddle a canoe or swim off the dock. Breakfast is served in the sunny dining room or on outside deck. ✓B&B

Bayfield

(south of Goderich on Lake Huron; see also St.Joseph, Blyth)

Cassidy, Joan & Peter Karstens, (Brentwood on the Beach)   ☎ (519) 236-7137,
RR2, Zurich, St. Joseph Shores 1, ON   N0M 2T0   Fax (519) 236-7269

St.Joseph Shore Phase I is located off Hwy 21 between Bayfield &
Grand Bend. Look for sign.
$65S $135-225D $25Add.person   ► 20
🍴Choice, homebaked 🏠Village, ranch-style, indoor swimming
pool, lakefront ■10(incl.2honeymoon suites) 🛏1S,2T,4Q,3K
★Air,6F(incl in 2guest rooms),TV,LF,KF, whirlpool,sauna,
pingpong 🛁9Ensuite,1sh.w.g. Ⓦ No pets,no smoking
〰German,French
🏃 Sandy beach at back, golf course, tennis, x-c skiing
🚗 Pinery Prov. Park, marinas, shops, Stratford/Blyth theatres, Huron County Playhouse
🛏 Relax and escape the stresses of everyday life in a B&B with luxury Country Inn atmosphere.
Enjoy spectacular sunsets, walks, swimming in a spa-like environment. Breakfast served in large
sunroom overlooking Lake Huron. Ideal place for honeymooners & special occasions and winter
retreats. Rest and rejuvenate on the 60ft balcony and screened-in porch. Gift Certificates available.
Also available: (0.4km) 4 off-site condo-style cottages. Visa,MC 🛏B&B

Pakenham, Carol & Ted (Magnolia Manor Bed & Breakfast)   ☎ & Fax (519)233-3181,
RR1, Varna, ON   N0M 2R0   E-mail: magmanor@tcc.on.ca, 1-800-216-5968

Located on County Rd3 and 8km from either Hwys 4 or 21 and
approximately 8km from Bayfield.
$50S $75D $15Add.person   (winter rates avail.)   ► 10
🍴 Full, homebaked   🏠 Rural, plantation, 2-storey, hist., 3acres,
swimming pool, patio, porch, quiet ■ 4D(upstairs)
🛏1S,1D,3Q,1R, crib 🛁 1Sh.w.g., 1sh.w.h. ★ F, guest
parlour with TV, ceiling fans, plant-filled sun room, ample
parking   Ⓦ No smoking, no pets, children over age 5 welcome
🏃 Walking trail on property, village of Varna
🚗 Bayfield, Bannockburn Cons.Area, fine dining, Blyth Festival/Grand Bend Playhouse
🛏 Impressive Estate in a Southern Plantation setting, a haven of peace and tranquility far
removed from the hustle & bustle of city living. Languish in the shade of the weeping willows, have
a swim in the pool, or relax in front of the field-stone fireplace or plant-filled bright and breezy sun
room. There are a Cockatiel, a cat and 2 dogs in residence. A wonderful place for a rest. Winter-,
mid-week special and business rates available. Visa,MC 🛏B&B

Baysville

(n/of Bracebridge; see also Huntsville, Pt.Sydney, Windermere)

Burton, Robert and Shirley (Burton's B&B)   ☎ & Fax (705) 767-3616
Box 70, Bay Street, Baysville, ON   P0B 1A0

From Hwy 11 exit onto Hwy 117 East. Proceed 16 km to Baysville Village. Turn right on Bay Street

(last before bridge) and proceed to 3rd house on right.
$40S $55D $10Child   ► 4A,1Ch
📅 May-Oct. 🍴Full, homebaked 🏠Village, patio, quiet
■2S,1D(upst) 🛏2S,1Q,1cot 🛁1Private,1sh.w.g. ★TV in guest
room,parking Ⓦ Restr.smoking, well behaved child welcome
🏃 Craft shops, Muskoka River (south branch)
🚗 Lake of Bays, Algonquin Park, Muskoka Colour Tour
🛏 4th Generation Ontario family in quiet, 1872-built
Victorian home, always kept in good repair and located in center of the village. Enjoy breakfast in
the sunny all-season solarium. 🛏B&B

Beamsville
(west of St-Catharines; see also Grimsby, Vineland, Hamilton)

Coulson, Ethel & Paul (Inn on the Thirty)   ☎ (905) 563-6526
4502 Thirty Rd., RR3, Beamsville, ON   L0R 1B3

From QEW exit at Bartlett and proceed south towards the Escarpment to first stop sign. Turn left and follow Reg Rd 81 for 2.3km to Thirty Rd. Turn left to B&B on left.

$45-65S $45-75D   ► 6
🍴Cont. 🏠 Rural, 2-storey, hist., acreage, quiet ■3(upstairs)
🛏2T,2Q 🛁1Sh.w.g. ★Air,KF,F,private entr., host quarters are sep.,off-street parking ⓦNo smoking,no pets
🡒 Century Barn, natural wooded area & orchard-lined country roads for walking and hiking
🚗 Niagara Falls, Niagara-on-the-Lake & Shaw Festival, winery tours, historic village of Jordan, birdwatching (busy skyway)
🡒 Charming Heritage home, decorated with furnishings collected during worldwide travel and located in a country setting. 1805-built house once served as a Wayside Inn (1870 - two original carved stage coach steps remain). Host was born & raised in the Niagara Peninsula and is knowledgeable about the area and history. Breakfast is served in the guest dining room. MC ✓CC

Opperman, Norm & Jo Ann (The Vineyard B&B)   ☎ (905) 563-1052
4255 Mountainview Rd., Beamsville, ON   L0R 1B2

From QEW take Exit 64 (Ontario St/Beamsville) and proceed south to King St (Reg.Rd 81 - the Wine Rte). Turn right (west) to Mountainview Rd, then left (south) for 1km .
$45S $60-75D $105F $15Add.person   ► 8

🍴 Full, homebaked (self-serve before 7AM) 🏠 Rural, res., 2-storey, older, acreage, view from guest rooms, pond at back, porch, deck, quiet, secluded ■3(upstairs) 🛏2T,1D,1Q,1P,cot 🛁1Sh.w.g., 1sh.w.h. ★LF,TV in 2 guest rooms, off-street parking ⌇ some French
🡒 Bruce Trail hiking, Mountainview Conservation Area, Niagara Escarpment (World Biosphere Reserve), wineries, fruit & vegetable stands, restaurants/bars
🚗 Historic towns & villages, antique shops, flea markets, Niagara Falls, N-O-T-L (Shaw Festival)
🡒 Large home nestled on the scenic Niagara Escarpment, on the Bruce Trail & adjacent winery with magnificient views of Lake Ontario and southshore settlements. Ladybug Lounge features extensive information for travellers. Hosts offer Eco-agri tourism and golf excursions, as well as rides from bus/train stops or spots on the Bruce Trail. Campsites available. There is a cat. ✓CC

Beeton
(north Toronto; see also Alliston, Cookstown)

Clark, Bill and Ruth   ☎ (905) 729-2038
78 Center St., Beeton, ON   L0G 1A0

Take Hwy 27N from Toronto to .8 km north of Bond Head. Turn west to Beeton, right on center St
$35S $45D   ► 4
🍴Full 🏠 Village, hist., acreage, quiet ■ 2(upstairs)
🛏2D 🛁1Sh.w.g. ★ TV ♥ ⓦ No smoking, no pets
🡒 Tree-lined park, race track
🚗 Honda Plant, Wonderland, Midland Martyr's Shrine & Wye Marsh, swimming, fishing,skiing areas
🡒 100-year-old brick home is surrounded by many trees which attract over 20 different kinds of birds and is an Ornithologist's delight.

Belleville
(west of Kingston; see also Brighton, Carrying Place)

Anderson, Lana & Bob (The Moira B&B)
21 Elvins Gardens, Belleville, ON   K8P 2T2   ☎ (613) 967-7856

From Hwy 401, take Exit 543 and travel south on Hwy 62 (Front St) to College St. Turn left to Prince of Wales Dr and left again to Elvins G. Turn right & follow around to house on right.

$40S $45D   ▶ 4A
Cont.   Res., 2-storey, deck, quiet   2D(upstairs)   2D   1Sh.w.g.   ★ F, ceiling fans, off-street parking, guest quarters are separate   No smoking, no pets
Sports Centre, downtown area, Quinte Shopping Mall, Moira River, walking/cycling trail, Riverside Park, restaurants, bus stop
Kingston, Presqu'ile Prov.Park, bird watching, Picton & Prince Edward County, Sandbanks Prov.Park & clear sandy beach
Quiet home in a peaceful central neighbourhood. Enjoy a glass of wine (made by host) along with friendly conversation. Living room exclusive for guests. Breakfast is served in separate special guest breakfast room or outside on deck. There is a cat in residence. CC

Empey, Faye (Windcrest Farm B&B)
RR7, Belleville, ON   K8N 4Z7   ☎ (613) 962-5129

Phone for directions.
$45S $50-55D   ▶ 5A
Full, homebaked   Farm, 2-storey, older, acreage, quiet   3(upstairs)   3D,1Q   1Sh.w.g., 1ensuite, 1private   ★off-street parking   No smoking, no pets
Pioneer Cemetery on property (one of oldest in Prince Edward County), lovely walking trails
Bay of Quinte, Belleville, Glanmore House Museum, golfing, Trenton Air Base & Museum, walking & cycling trails, Picton, artisan studios, Loyalist College
Totally renovated old farm house on a working horse and boarding farm, located on offical tour route in picturesque Prince Edward County. A substantial country breakfast from local produce is served in dining room. Hostess operates a home-based Catering Business. Special dietary requirements should be given at time of reservation. Children welcome. CC

Bishops Mills
(north of Brockville; see also Merrickville, Oxford Mills)

Graham, Joyce and Bob (Graham's Pightle)   ☎ (613) 258-3753, Fax (613) 258-0392
Bishops Mills,391 Cty Rd 18,RR2,Oxford Stn,ON K0G 1T0   E-mail: bob.graham@sympatico.ca

Located 1 km south of Bishops Mills on County Rd 18 and 16km south-east of Merrickville.

$40S $55D $25Child   Meals   ▶ 6
Full   100-acres hobby farm, 2-storey, older, swimming pool, quiet   2S,2D(upstairs)   2S,2D   Sh.w.h.   ★ TV,F, parking   No pets   Spanish, some French
Nature trails, village of Bishops Mills
Merrickville, Ottawa, Upper Canada Village, 1000 Island boat cruises, Fort Wellington, Prescott, Kemptville (16.5km), Brockville
1850's stone house furnished with antiques typical of 19th Century rural living, near the picturesque community of Merrickville. Ideal place for a country get-away in historic Eastern Ontario. Relax by the pool, or explore the back roads for antiques & garage sales. Enjoy gracious hospitality & hearty gourmet meals. Retired hosts have travelled extensively & are continuously involved with Rotary & Forestry projects internationally. B&B

Blind River   *(east of Sault-Ste-Marie; see also Bruce Mines, St. Joseph Isle)*

Bohren, Yvonne (A Taste of Home B&B)   ☎ (705) 356-7165
29 Fullerton St., Blind River, ON   P0R 1B0

From east on Main St (Hwy17) in Blind River go north just after lights. From west look for house
before lights.
$40S $50D $5Child   ◨Meals   ⌐8A,1Ch
🍴 Full   🏠 Downtown, 2-storey, older, porch   ■ 1S,3D,1Ste
(upst) ⊨1S,4D,1R ⬛2Sh.w.g. ★Air,sitting room for guests,
separate entrance, off-street parking   ⊛ No smoking, no pets
🕴 Downtown, restaurants, shops, parks, marina
🚐 Blind River Museum (logging), scenic drives, golfing, Agawa
Tours (Sault-Ste-Marie)
🐾 Friendly welcome in comfortable ancestral home, situated in picturesque little town. House
has been in host's family since the early 1900. Good location for catching popular Agawa Canyon
Train leaving from Sault-Ste-Marie on day trips into the northern wilderness.⌐B&B

Bloomfield   *(south of Belleville; see also Wellington, Consecon, Picton, Milford)*

Evans, Frank and Bonnie (Cornelius White House)   ☎ (613) 393-2282
8 Wellington St., Bloomfield, ON   K0K 1G0

On Hwy 401 from Toronto, take Wooler Rd S to Hwy 33. Continue to Wellington, then Bloomfield.
From Kingston, take Hwy 401 west and Hwy 49 south to Picton, then Hwy 33 to Bloomfield.
$45S $55D $80F   ► 8A,2Ch
🍴 Full   🏠 Village, hist., acreage, patio, quiet   ■2D,1F(upst)
⊨4T,3D ⬛2Private, 1ensuite ★TV, parking
🕴 Restaurant, artisan studios, pottery/antiques and craft shops,
bicycling, cross-country skiing
🚐 Sandbanks Provincial Park, golf course, Lake Ontario
🐾 Early 1862-built house for a Dutch Quaker family is located in
quaint, quiet, but industrious farming community and close to
beautiful beaches & clear water. "Prince Edward County hospitality with European charm". ⌐B&B

Jamieson, Peter & Paulette (Bloomfield B&B)   ☎ (613) 393-1392
341 Main St., Box 153, Bloomfield, ON   K0K 1G0

From Hwy 401, take Hwy 33 south at Trenton, or take Hwy 49
south to Hwy 33 at Picton, then west to Bloomfield.
$50S $60D $110F   ► 5
🍴 Full, homebaked   🏠 Village, 2-storey, hist., 1.5acres, view
from guest rooms, porch, deck   ■ 1S,2D(upstairs)   ⊨S,2D
⬛1Sh.w.g.   ★ TV,separate entrance, off-street parking
⊛Smoking outside, no pets, not suitable for children
🚐 Picton, Sandbanks Provincial Park, scenic drives
🕴 Five restaurants, gift/artisans/antique shops, art galleries, museum, park, tennis courts
🐾 Classic 1870's Victorian home, furnished with warm country antiques and situated in the
middle of historic town (noted for its's many historic homes and gardens) and in the heart of Prince
Edward County. View the streetscape of a quaint old village from guest rooms. Relax on the veranda
or sundeck and enjoy the surrounding gardens while contemplating your next outing to the fabulous
beaches. Breakfast is served in guest breakfast room. Antiques are sold from the house. There are 2
dogs in residence. ⌐B&B

Blyth

(east of Goderich; see also Gorrie)

Mitchell, Phyllis and Emerson (Mitchell's Bed & Breakfast)   ☎ (519) 887-6697
RR3, Walton, Ontario N0K 1Z0

Take Hwy 86 from Elmira/Kitchener area and travel 20 km west of Listowel to County Rd 12. Turn left for 17 km and right at Walton (church) to 1st farm on left. From Stratford go west to Seaforth & take County Rd 12 at lights. Follow through to Walton and turn left at church.

$30S $40D $15Add.person   ►8
🏵 Full   🏠 600-acre farm, hist., view, quiet, deck, veranda   ■5
(down & upst)   ⊨ 3D,1Q,2T   🛏1Sh.w.g.,1sh.w.h.(downst)
★TV,LF,wheelchair access (1room)   🖐No pets, no smoking
🏃 Many farm animals, walking/hiking, x/c ski and snowmobile designated trails (250km), park, creek, church, store
🚗 Blyth Summer Festival, Goderich, Grand Bend beaches, trail & arena, riding horses, leather/wool outlet, Bayfield, Stratford

🐾 1889 English home with winding staircase, natural wood work, jacuzzi in wood-lined bathroom, and surrounded by large lawns, trees and many flowers. Hosts are interested in country western or old tyme music and dancing. There are pets outside. ✍B&B

Bognor

(south-east of Owen Sound; see also Clarksburg, Meaford)

Crawford-Weishar, Blue & David (Solstice B&B))   ☎ (519) 371-1440
RR1, Bognor, ON N0H 1E0

Take Hwy 6 north towards Owen Sound. Turn east at Rockford, Grey Rd18. Proceed 12km to Bognor/Walter's Falls turn-off. Turn south, following Grey Rd29 uphill, to B&B on left.

$55S $65D $10Add.person   🍽 Meals   ►5
🏵 Full   🏠 Rural, hist., former church, acreage, view from guest rooms, patio, deck, quiet   ■ 2(main floor)   ⊨ 1S,1D,cot
(incl.sleigh bed)   🛏1Sh.w.g.   ★ TV,F(sunken),ceiling fans, separate entrance, guest quarters are separate   ♥   🖐 Smoking outside, no pets, children welcome, peanut-free environment
〜Some French, sign language
🏃 Bruce Trail hiking (Sydenham Tract: map29), bird watching,
on-site artisan studio & gallery, outside children's play area, Spring migration of spawning fish
🚗 Golfing, horseback riding, excellent downhill & x-c skiing, Duncan Caves, Inglis Falls, museum, Symphony Series & Theatre, galleries, cycling trails, Georgian Bay/Lake Huron beaches, fishing
🐾 Renovated, spacious country church (ca 1868)perched atop a hill with a panoramic view of the Niagara Escarpment & Queens Valley and surrounded by flora/fauna and forests with abundant wildlife. Hostess is a stained-glass and bee's-wax candlemaking artist. Breakfast is served in one of many dining areas. Pick-up & drop-off service to points on Bruce Trail & Bus Terminal. There are three children in the host family and a resident goose "Gulliver" & a duck "Stanley".✍CC

Bracebridge

(s/of Huntsville; see also Gravenhurst, Baysville, Pt.Carling, Windermere)

Yudin, Sandy and Norman Yan (Century House B&B)   ☎ (705) 645-9903
155 Dill Street, Bracebridge, ON P1L 1E5   E-mail: cnturybb@muskoka.com

From Hwy 11, take Hwy 118 west towards Bracebridge. Go over the bridge at the first traffic light to Dill (2nd St on right). Turn right to B&B.

$40S $65D $10-15Child $20Add.person   ►6
🏵 Full   🏠 Res., older, patio, quiet   ■ 3(upstairs)
⊨2Q,1S,1R   🛏 Sh.w.g.   ★ Air,TV in guest living room
🖐No smoking, no pets
🏃 Waterfall, river beaches, picnic area, boat tour of Muskoka Lakes, shopping, canoe rentals
🚗 Craft studios & galleries, Summer Theatre, Provincial Parks
🐾 Restored Century home in Ontario's premier recreational
lakes district. Hosts are lovers of nature, conversation and fine food. A friendly dog. Visa ✍B&B

Bourdages, Marie & Gilles (Bourdages B&B-PTL Maple Syrup Farm)   ☎ (705) 645-3711,
Clear Lake Rd., RR3, Bracebridge, ON   P1L 1X1   ☎ (905) 728-4845

From Hwy 11, exit east on Hwy 118. Continue 25 km and turn left on Black River Rd for approx.
1km. Turn on Clear Lake Rd and follow signs to white bungalow.

$30S $45-50D   🍴 Meals   ►5
🔲 Choice, homebaked   🏠 Rural, bungalow, res., acreage, patio,
quiet   ■2 (ground level)   ⊨1S,1Q,1D   ⊴1sh.w.g.   ★TV/fridge
in guest living rooms, parking   🖑No smoking, no pets
∿English (household language is French)
🕇 Public safe sandy beach, boat ramp, ice fishing/nature
trails/cross-country skiing and skidoo trail in front of house, visit
sugar shack (when sap is running)

🚗 Bracebridge, Santa's Village, Lady Muskoka cruises, Algonquin Park, Fall colour cavalcade
🔫 Large, comfortable home situated on 28-acres of maple trees. Hosts produce maple syrup and
breakfast is always served with maple syrup. Relax, watch the birds and deer and enjoy the quiet,
invigorating country atmosphere "a home away from home". There is a dog & a cat in the house.
Also 27ft self-contained trailer available. Children welcome. ∠B&B

Streeter, Bob & Margaret (Streeters Landing B&B)   ☎ 1-800-300-6252, (705) 385-2131
RR2, Utterson, ON   P0B 1M0

From Bracebridge go north on Hwy 11 for 19 km to left turn on Hwy 141. Proceed 7km to stop sign
and turn left on Hwy 35, then right onto Muskoka Rd 4 West and 1km to B&B on right.

$60-70D $15Child $25Add.person   ►6A,3Ch
➕ Summer only   🔲 Full, homebaked   🏠 Rural, acres, view
from guest rooms, swimming pool, porch, deck, quiet, secluded
■ 3Ste (ground level   ⊨ 2T,1Q,1K   ⊴ 3Ensuite   ★ TV,
private parking, host quarters are separate   🖑No smoking,no pets
🕇 Nature trails, private ponds, birds sanctuary
🚗 Boat rentals, beaches, swimming, fishing, Algonquin Park
🔫 New, elegant country home with high vaulted ceilings and
large entertainment center, specifically built for B&B and situated on 5 acre parkland setting.
Breakfast is served in separate screened lani with a panoramic view of beautiful Muskoka pines,
soft wood maples and mighty oaks. Hosts are retired professionals and world travellers. Scottish
heritage house specialty is "eggs of any style" and other baked goodies. Visa.∠B&B

Yeo, Ruth and Len (Riverview B&B)   ☎ (705) 645-4022
420 Beaumont Dr., RR4, Bracebridge, ON   P1L 1X2

From Hwy 11 travel exit at Hwy 118 West to Beaumont Dr. Turn
left at traffic lights and follow the river to 420 Beaumont Dr.
$30S $60D   ►7
🔲 Full, homebaked   🏠 Rural, hist., multi-storey, acreage, view,
riverfront, patio, quiet   ■1S,3D(upstairs)   ⊨1S,2T,1D,1Q
⊴1Ensuite, 1sh.w.h.   ★TV,F, parking   🖑 No smoking.
🕇 Swimming at the dock area and riverfront, walking trails
🚗 Santa's Village, artisan studios, museums, cruises, craft shops
🔫 Spacious old farmhouse overlooks the Muskoka River and is situated on 3.5 acres of well
cared-for grounds. Relax by the fire upon return from cross-country skiing (right from door). Enjoy
breakfast around the harvest table in large country kitchen, where all baked goods and preserves
are prepared. Sally, the resident Golden Retriever is on hand to help welcome guests.

Brampton
(west of Toronto; see also Georgetown, Cheltenham, Acton)

DeRooy, Anna and Karl (Creditview B&B)   ☎ (905) 451-6271, Fax (905) 453-7831
RR10, 7650 Creditview Rd., Brampton, ON   L6V 3N2

From Hwy 401 take Exit 336 and Mississauga Rd north to
Halstone Rd. Turn right and proceed to Creditview Rd. Turn right.
$45S $50D $10Child 🍽 Meals   ► 4A,2Ch
🍴Full 🏠Rural, 2-storey, large acreage, view, quiet ■2D(upst)
⊨2S,1Q ⊐1Sh.w.h.(main floor) ★Air,F,KF,LF,TV 🖐No
smoking, no pets ⚬⚬ Dutch
🕺 Wonderful walks along Credit River
🚗 Airport, Brampton, shopping, dining, Go-Train to Toronto

🔈 Comfortable home, renovated by builder-host, is situated on a 2-acre property in Churchville
(Brampton), a small village which has "Heritage Village" status. Children welcome.✒B&B

Brantford
(west of Hamilton; see also Paris, Ohsweken)

Terhune, Liz & Harry (Yarrhill Farm & B&B)   ☎ (519) 753-8111
98 Pleasant Ridge Rd., RR2, Brantford, ON   N3T 5L5   E-mail: yarrhill@worldchat.com

Travel west of Brantford on Hwy 53, turn onto Cty Rd 7 (Pleasant Ridge Rd) before Brantford
Airport. Proceed 1.6km to Farm. From Hwy 403 take Rest Acres Rd Exit & past Airport on #53.

Then turn right on Pleasant Ridge Rd.
$32S $45D 🍽 Meals   ► 4
🍴 Full, homebaked 🏠 Farm, hist., 160acres, view, deck, porch,
quiet ■ 2D (upstairs) ⊨ 1D,1Q ⊐2Sh.w.g. ★Air,LF,TV
in guest rooms 🖐 Restricted smoking, kennels for dogs provided
🕺 Laneways and walking trails, Brantford Airport
🚗 Brantford (Bell Homestead, Sanderson & Gretsky Centres),
Six Nations Reservation, Port Dover, Lake Erie (beaches, fishing

🔈 1840's fieldstone farmhouse with large rooms and period decor, situated on 60 acres of rolling
farmland overlooking L'Aubigny Creek, the Grand River Valley and the city of Brantford. Hosts
operate a working cow/calf operation with friendly polled Hereford cattle. Enjoy the relaxed family
farm atmosphere. Full farm breakfast is served in the elegant dining room or on the deck at the
convenience of guests. Children welcome. There are outside dogs and barn cats.✒B&B

Brighton
(west of Trenton; see also Carrying Place, Colborne)

Dodds, Bob (Main Street B&B)   ☎ (613) 475-0351
Box 431, 96 Main Street, Brighton, ON   K0K 1H0

From Hwy 401 take Hwy 30 and continue south to traffic lights in village. Turn right on Main St

and continue 2 blocks.
$45S $55D $10Child 🍽 Meals   ► 6A,2Ch
🍴 Full 🏠 Res., village, older, 2-storey, above-ground swimming
pool, patio, quiet ■3D(upst) ⊨2T,2D,2R ⊐ 2Sh.w.g.
★F,LF,TV in guest room, parking 🖐Restricted smoking
🕺 Village shopping, farmer's market, Proctor House Museum and
historic site, antique barns and warehouses, cross-country skiing
and hiking trails, Applefest in September

🚗 Presqu'ile and Sandbanks Provincial Parks (fine beaches, guided bird-watching tours), boat
charters, Brighton Harbour, Trent Canal System, Bay of Quinte, Gateway to Prince Edward County
🔈 Gracious and elegant Century Home (built in 1843) with warm and friendly ambiance. Passes
for Presqu'ile Beach arranged. Bicycles for guests. Free transportation for boaters arriving at
Brighton Harbour, the Murray Canal and Trenton. Reservations recommended. ✒B&B

Friedrichkeit, Burke & Ken Bosher (Butler Creek B&B)　　☎ (613) 475-1248
RR7, Hwy 30, Brighton, ON　K0K 1H0　　　　E-mail: obbrs@mail.reach.net, Fax (613) 475-5267

Located 3 km south off Hwy 401 on Exit 509 to Brighton.
$45S　$55D　$75F　　　　　　　　　　　　　　　　　▶ 8
🚪 Full　🏠 Village, 2-storey, hist., 9-acres, view from guest
rooms, porch　■ 4D (upstairs)　⊨ 2T,2D,1Q　🛁 1sh.w.g.,
1ensuite　★ F,TV in guest lounge, off-street parking, ceiling fans
in each room, host quarters are separate　🖐 No smoking, no
pets　〰German, French
🚶 Hiking, x-c skiing on property & adjoining Prov. Park
🚗 Beaches at Presqu'ile Park, Sandbanks at Prince Edward County, Lake Ontario, antiquing
🚙 Long-time, experienced B&B hosts in new location (formerly Burken Guest House in
Toronto). White Victorian house with elegant furnishings, yet cozy atmosphere, perches over 9
acres of trees, meadows, gardens and bubbling brook (Butler Creek runs through property).
Breakfast is served in the formal dining room. Enjoy the congenial hospitality. There is a dog in
residence. MC/Visa ✓B&B

Le Ber, Elizabeth & Charles (Sanford House B&B)　　☎ & Fax (613) 475-3930
Box 1825, 20 Platt St., Brighton, ON　K0K 1H0　　　　E-mail: leber@connect.reach.net

From Hwy 401, take Exit 509 and Hwy 30 south for 5 km into town. At traffic light turn right onto
Main St. Go 3 blocks to Platt St, turn right to 2nd house on left.

$45S　$55D　　　　　　　　　　　　　　　　　▶ 6
🚪 Full, homebaked　🏠 Village, res., 2-storey, hist., view, porch,
quiet　■3D(upstairs), separate guest quarters　⊨2T,2Q
🛁Sh.w.g.　★TV/VCR/games in guest lounge, air-conditioned
guest rooms, ceiling fans, electronic air cleaner, off-street
parking　🖐No smoking, no pets
🚶 Restaurants, shops, farmers' market, antique auctions, Proctor
House Museum & Conservation Area, hiking/x-c ski trails
🚗 Presqu'ile Provincial Park (sandy beaches, swimming, birding, marsh board walk, cycling
🚙 Warm welcome in stately red brick Victorian home (ca1895) featuring large, comfortable,
bright rooms with period furniture and sunny round turret room with view of town & Presqu'ile
area. Delectable homebaked breakfast is served in separate dining room. ✓B&B

Muir, Eleanor (Applecrest House)　　☎ (613) 475-0538
61 Simpson St., Box 1106, Brighton, ON　K0K 1H0

From Hwy 401, take Exit 509 to Brighton. From traffic light on Hwy 2 in downtown go west. Then
turn north onto Simpson Street and look for 2nd driveway on right at top of hill (laneway leads to

house set among towering trees.
$45S　$55D　$5Child/Add.person　　　　　　　　▶ 8
🚪 Full, homebaked　🏠 Rural, 10 acres, quiet, hist.　■ 4D
(upstairs)　⊨4T,2D　🛁1sh.w.g., 1sh.w.h.　★TV　🖐no pets,
no smoking
🚶 Brighton, woodland walks. birdwatching
🚗 Presqu'ile Prov. Park, sandy beach, bird watching, antiques,
Trent Severn Waterway, Bay of Quinte
🚙 Relax in large, gracious restored 1868 home and spacious rooms filled with family antiques,
surrounded by quiet woodlands and apple orchards with a panoramic view of Lake Ontario and
Presqu'ile Park. Ideal place for a wonderful rest. ✓B&B

Payne, Linda & Jim (Harbour Haven B&B)
44 Harbour St., RR3, Brighton, ON   K0K 1H0

☎ (613) 475-1006

From Hwy 401 take Exit 509 to Brighton via Hwy 30 south. Go
south through village down Prince Edward St to Harbour St.
$45S $55D   ► 5
🍲 Full, homebaked   🏠 Rural, res., swimming pool, patio, deck,
quiet ■1S,2D(main floor) ⊨1S,1D,1Q ⫤1Sh.w.g. ★F,TV,
ceiling fans, separate entrance, guest quarters are separate
🚭No smoking, no pets, children min. age 12
🕴 Marina, Lake Ontario boating & tours, fishing, restaurants
🚗 Presquile Park, museum, skiing, tennis, golfing, CFB Trenton, Prince Edward County, beaches
🔫 Spacious contemporary home located by the Bay on the waterfront trail. Relax by the pool or
in the private sitting area or join the hosts in the cozy family room with fireplace. Breakfast is
served formally or by the pool. Hosts love to pamper their guests, particularily for celebrations and
special occasions. ✎CC

Wickens, Barbara & Elmer (Brownwick House B&B)   ☎ (613) 475-0916
35 Centre St., Box 1028, Brighton, ON   K0K 1H0

From Hwy 401, take Exit 509 and Hwy 30 south into town. At traffic light turn right onto Main St.
Proceed to Centre St, turn left and continue south to house on left.

$45S $55D   ► 6A
🍲 Full, homebaked   🏠 Res., village, 2-storey, hist., view, patio,
porch, deck, quiet ■3D(upstairs) ⊨2T,1D,1Q ⫤1sh.w.g.
★F,ceiling fans, bicycles & outdoor games available, guest TV &
hospitality rooms on 2nd floor, off-street parking 🚬Smoking
outside, no pets, not suitable for children
🕴 Proctor House Museum, walking & x-c ski trails, antique, wine
Café, restaurants, shops, churches
🚗 Presqui'le Prov. Park, sandy beaches, bird watching, Marsh board walk, cycling, marina, fine
dining, Bay of Quinte, Prince Edward County, auction sales
🔫 Turn-of-the-Century home with oak trim, stained glass windows and furnished tastefully with
antiques and elegant decor. Relax in the music room, fireplace sitting room, or TV room. Breakfast
is prepared by a professional baker and served in the formal dining room or on the spacious
veranda. Hosts are a retired couple who enjoy meeting people from all over the world. ✎B&B

Brinston
(north-east of Brockville; see also Mountain, Oxford Mills)

Westervelt, Gerry and Johanna (Westergreen Farm)   ☎ (613) 652-4241
RR2, 11245 Smail Rd., Brinston, ON   K0E 1C0

Take Exit 738 off Hwy 401 at Iroquois. Follow County Rd 1 north for 4 km to Irena Rd, turn right.
Continue 4 km to Brinston Rd (CRd 16), turn left. In Brinston turn right on Henderson Rd, right

on Bell Rd, left on Smail Rd to first farm (2nd house) on left.
$25S $35D $5Child (under age 12)   ► 5
🍲 Choice, Farm, patio, quiet, a small orchard ■1Ste,1F (main
floor) ⊨1S,2D ★TV, separate entrance ⫤1Private,
1sh.w.h. 🚭No pets ⚓Dutch
🚗 Upper Canada Village, Iroquois Seaway Locks, Fort
Wellington at Prescott, Thousand Islands vacation area, Ottawa
🔫 1825 grey stone house on a 60 milking cows dairy farm and located in the heart of Eastern
Ontario Vacation Wonderland. Hosts welcome young and old. ✎CC

Brockville

(see also Athens, Mallorytown)

Clarke, Keith & Sylvia (Underwood House B&B) ☎ (613) 345-2797
402 King St. West, Brockville, ON   K6V 3S6

From Hwy 401, take Exit 696 and follow signs to Hwy 2 (King St.West). Turn right for 1km.

$45S $50D $15Add.person   ⬛ Meals   ▶ 6
🍴 Full, homebaked   🏠 Downtown, res., 3-storey, older, porch,
quiet   ⬛ 3D(upstairs)   ➜ 2T,1D,1K,1R,1P   ⬛ 1Sh.w.g.
★TV,off-street parking, guest quarters are separate   🚫 No pets,
designated smoking area, children minimum age 12
🚶 Theatre, museum, harbour & 1000 Islands boat tours, shops,
Fulford House (museum), St.Lawrence River
🚗 Gananoque, Fort Henry (Kingston), Upper Canada Village
(Morrisburg), murals (Athens), Hershy's (Smith Falls), US border
🚌 Victorian home (ca 1895) comfortably furnished with family heirlooms and collections, located
on old Hwy 2 (King St) with many older homes. Breakfast is served in the dining room or in the
glass-enclosed front veranda. Retired from the hospitality industry, hosts are interested and active
in the "World of Dollhouse Miniatures" and welcome other enthusiasts. Free pick-up/delivery for
train or waterway travellers.

Logie, Dixie & John (The Calico Cat B&B) ☎ (613) 342-0363
193 Brockmere Cliff Dr., Brockville, ON   K6V 5T3

From Hwy 401, take Hwy 2 Exit (10km west of Brockville). Look for
B&B on Brockmere cliff Rd .5km from exit
$50S $65D   ▶ 3
🍴 Full, homebaked(gourmet)   🏠 Rural, 2-storey at back, 1acre, river
view from guest rooms, riverfront, patio, dock   ⬛ 1S,1D (ground
level)   ➜ 1S,1Q   ⬛Private   ★ F,TV in guest room, private
entrance, parking   🚫 No smoking, children min. age 12
🚶 Bicycle path (50 km on 1000 Islands Parkway),
🚗 Town of Athens (11 murals), Gananoque & 1000 Islands Boat Tours
🚌 Home is situated among lovely gardens with 50 varieties of hostas,
sculptures (by artist hostess) and a waterfall, looking across to NY State.
Located on the St. Lawrence River and surrounded by the
beautiful and popular 1000 Islands resort area, a convenient stopover for travellers from Toronto to
Montreal. Breakfast is served on the stone patio or dockside (weather permitting). Enjoy a cup of
tea while watching the boats go by. Hosts are world travellers and recently retired. Bicycle & boat
tours can be arranged. There is a cat.

Menard, Mike & Linda Evans (River Inn B&B) ☎ (613) 498-1580
173 King St. East, Brockville, ON   K6V 1C1   Fax (613) 345-4253

From Hwy 401 take Exit 698 (North Augusta Rd). Proceed south to King St., west to B&B.

$70S $90D   ▶ 10
🍴 Cont., homebaked   🏠 Downtown, res., 2-storey, older, view
from guest rooms, swimming pool, patio, quiet   ⬛2S,5D(upst)
➜2T(K),2D,2Q,1R   ⬛ 1Sh.w.g., 2ensuite   ★ F,LF,ceiling
fans, off-street parking, guest bikes, guest quarters are separate
🚫Designated smoking area, pets, children min. age 8
🚶 Historic tours, downtown shops/dining, 1000Isles Boat Tours
🚗 Merrickville, 1000 Isles & Ogdenburg Bridges, Kingston
🚌 Spacious Chateau-style stone house situated in downtown acreage with spectacular view of the
St.Lawrence River. Relax and watch the Lakers and Salties go by. Hosts are also available for
special events and gourmet dinners on weekends. Visa ⌐CC

Slack, Betty (Misty Pines B&B)　　　　　　　　☎ (613) 342-4325
1389 Heritage Hwy 2, RR3, Brockville, ON　K6V 5T3　　E-mail: bslack@recorder.com

From Hwy 401 take Exit 687 to Brockvile and proceed on Hwy 2 for 3km east to sign.

$30　$55-75D　(meals) Meals　　　　　　　　▶ 9
🍴 Full　🏠 Rural, 2-storey, acreage, view, riverfront, patio, quiet, secluded　■ 5(upstairs　⊨ 2Q,1D,2T,1S,cot
🛁2Sh.w.g.　★F,TV, ceiling fans, guest bikes available, off-street parking　🚭No smoking, no pets, check re children
🏃 Walking/biking path (begins at end of driveway) to St.Lawrence River, beaver dam, museum, Fulford Mansion, golfing, boat cruises, swimming, River Festival (June/July), lighthouse
🚐 Thousand Island Parkway, summer theatres, Capital City Ottawa, Fort Wellington, Kingston
📣 Warm welcome in modern executive French Provincial home with antiques and a tranquil view of Molly's Gut (a deep & narrow passage between island and mainland), situated on original homestead land owned by hosts' ancestors. Breakfast is served on the outside patio weather permitting or in the bright dining room. Browse through the display of cottage industry crafts. There is a resident cat calico "Patchie". Visa,MC ✒B&B

Bruce Mines　　　　　　　*(e/of Sault Ste Marie; see also St.Joseph I, Blind River)*

Kersey, Christine and James (Beacon Inn B&B)　　　☎ (705) 785-9950
Box 293, 5 Mitchell St., Bruce Mines, ON　P0R 1C0

Located in Bruce Mines behind the museum, one block off Hwy 17 (75 km east of Sault Ste.Marie)

$70-90D　　　　　　　　　　　　　　　▶ 8
🏖Summer only (Fall by special arrangement)　🍴Full　🏠Village, 2-storey, view, lakefront, large waterfront property, marina & private beach　■4D(upst)　⊨2T,3D　🛁4Ensuite(1jacuzzi)
★Air,F,separate entrance, parking, windsurfer/canoe/rowboat for guests,spa on waterfront deck, large waterfront gazebo, boat cruise (weather permitting)　🚭No smoking, no children, no pets
🏃 Extensive Museum/Archives next door, Simpson Mine Shaft (1840's CopperMine)
🚐 Agawa Canyon Train from Sault Ste. Marie, Fort St. Joseph, Lock Tours
📣 Young, active hosts in bright and airy, beautiful new home overlooking the Bay; decorated with antiques and original art throughout and an atmosphere of comfort and elegance. Rooms are named after the 4 seasons with 6ft high windows looking onto the water. Enjoy the romatic spa illuminated with oil lamps on deck posts. Breakfast is served on the veranda or in the gazebo and rumcake is served at 10pm. Ideal spot for honeymooners or special occasions. Visa ✒CC

Burlington *(west of Toronto;see also Waterdown, Hamilton, Oakville, Campbellville, Milton)*

Glatz, Arlene (Cedarcroft)　　　　　☎ (905) 637-2491, (905) 637-2079
3273 Myers Lane, Burlington, ON　L7N 1K6

From QEW take Exit 105 (Walkers Line) south to New Street. Turn right to Pine Cove Rd. Turn left to Myers Lane on right.
$35S　$50D　$10Child　　　　　　　　　　▶ 4
🍴 Choice　🏠 Res., quiet, swimming pool　■ 2D (upstairs)
⊨1Q,2T　🛁 1Sh.w.g.　★Air,F,TV in guest rooms,parking　·
🚭No smoking　　　　　　🏃 Small plazas, Lake Ontario
🚐 Burlington Shopping Mall, downtown Lakeside Park and trendy shopping, Royal Botanical Gardens, Toronto, NOTL
📣 Unique cottage-like home, beautifully decorated and situated on a quiet court. Relax in spacious cosy sunroom and enjoy the warm "Home-away-from-home" atmosphere. ✒B&B

Hoepp, Anneliese (Haus Anneliese B&B)　　　　　　　　☎ (905) 634-8918
970 Birchwood Ave., Burlington, ON　L7T 2H8

From QEW take Brant St(Exit101) south to Fairview St. Turn right and continue (west) on Plains Rd to Birchwood. Turn left.
$40S　$50D　🍽 Meals　　　　　　　　　　　　　　　　▶ 2
🛏 Full　🏠 Res., 2-storey, older, quiet, porch　■ 1Ste(upst)
🛏1Q　🚿 Private　★ Air,TV in guest sitting room, off-street parking, guest quarters are separate　🐾 No pets, designated smoking area, not suitable for children　🗣 German
🚶 Lake Ontario Waterfront Trail, lovely park & marina
🚗 Downtown, restaurants, Mapleview Shopping Mall, Botanical Gardens, Dundurn Castle, Go Train Commuter to Toronto, McMaster University, Niagara Falls
🐾 Warm and friendly welcome in older home with Canadian-German hospitality. Upper floor is exclusive for guests. Relax on the porch or in the large yard. Hostess is experienced in the catering industry and very active in the local ethnic community. ✔B&B

McDowell, Marjorie (The Painted Door Bed & Breakfast)　　　☎ (905) 639-3663
237 Strathcona Dr., Burlington, ON　L7L 2C7

From QEW take Exit 105 (Walkers Line) south to Lakeshore Rd (Hwy 2). Turn left & then 1st left onto Strathcona.
$40S　$60D　🍽 Meals　　　　　　　　　　　　　　　　▶ 3-4
🛏 Full, hombaked　🏠 Res., bungalow, patio, quiet　■ 2 (main level)　🛏1S,1D　🚿1Shw.g.　★T,TV,LF,parking　🐾No pets
🚶 Eastway (small shopping plaza), Lake Ontario, bus stop to downtown Burlington, Hamilton and Toronto
🚗 Downtown Burlington & lakeside park, 2 shopping malls
🐾 Cozy bungalow with large yard and garden. Well travelled hostess is active at the Burlington Art Centre and also operates a Catering Business "Amazing Grazing" out of her home. ✔B&B

Nash, Susan & Bill (Bellwood Place B&B)　　　　　　　☎ (905) 639-5038
2111 Bellwood Ave., Burlington, ON　L7R 1P9　　　　E-mail: whnash@istar.ca

From QEW take Brant St Exit 101 and proceed south 1km to Victoria St.Turn left 2 blocks to Emerald St, turn right, then left through the park to Bellwood Ave.
$35S　$50D　$75F　　　　　　　　　　　　　　　　　▶ 6
🛏 Full　🏠 Downtown, res., older, patio, quiet　■2D(upstairs
🛏3D　🚿 2Ensuite　★ Air,F,TV,off-street parking　🐾No smoking, no pets
🚶 Downtown core, restaurants, Lake Ontario and waterfront Spencer Smith Park, Joseph Brant Hospital & museum, YMCA, Senior Citizen Centre, tennis courts, Go Commuter Train to Toronto, local buses
🚗 Niagara Falls, Toronto, Elora Gorge, Shaw Festival, Kitchener/Waterloo, NOTL
🐾 Retired naval pilot host in comfortable home with large addition at back, and situated half-way between Toronto and Niagara Falls. Tour of Hamilton/Burlington Bay can be arranged on hosts' cruiser boat, weather permitting. Hosts' varied interests inlude music, theatre, skiing and golfing. There is a little resident dog called "Beau-Beau". ✔B&B

Quinn, Louise & Barry (Springer House B&B)　　　☎ (905) 335-5453, Fax (905) 335-0773
2373 Dundas St (Hwy 5), RR1, Burlington, ON　L7R 3X4　　　E-mail: quinn@worldchat.com

Located on the north side of Hwy 5, between Brant & Guelph Line. From QEW take exits 101/103.

$65S　$75D　$10Add.person　🖲 Meals　　　► 6A,4Ch
🌑 Full　🏠 Rural, hist., 5 acres, indoor swimming pool, quiet
■2D (upstairs)　🛏1K(2T), 1D(antique)　🛁 1Sh.w.g., 1ensuite,
1sh.w.h.　★Air,F,off-street parking, library & TV room for
guests only　🖐 No smoking, no pets, children min. age 6
🏃 Large grounds with 3 ponds and fruit trees, Bruce Trail and
Niagara Escarpment adjacent to property
🚗 Burlington, Botanical Gardens, golfing, Niagara Falls

🐾 Large 1835-built Georgian-style home tastefully furnished with antiques and a magnificent view of the Niagara Escarpment. Enjoy Old World Charm and New World Comfort. Hosts have travelled world-wide and are well informed about local history, community events and Japanese City Twinning. Separate rustic log cabin with pioneer family experience situated on hidden corner of property in future plan. Easy access to major highways. There are 2 cats & a dog.Visa ⌐B&B

Wilkie, Nancy & Peter (Wilkie House B&B)　　　☎ (905) 637-5553, Fax (905) 637-7294
1211 Sable Dr., Burlington, ON　L7S 2J7　　　E-mail: nancy.wilkie@sympatico.ca

From QEW, take Brant St Exit and proceed south. Turn right at Fairview St., left at Maple Ave, left on Maple Crossing Blvd and left on Sable Dr.

$50S　$60D　$5child　　　► 4A,2Ch
🌑 Full, homebaked　🏠 Downtown, res., 2-storey, swimming
pool, deck　■ 1D,1F(upstairs)　🛏 3D　🛁 1Private,1ensuite
★F,TV in guest room, ceiling fans, off-street parking　🖐No
smoking, no pets
🏃 Lake Ontario & Spencer Smith Park, Joseph Brant Mem.
Hospital, museum, Burl Arts Centre, Mapleview Mall, Burlington
Transit Buses and connection to GO Commuter Train (to Toronto)
🚗 Oakville, Hamilton, Dundurn Castle, Royal Botanical Gardens, Rockton Lion Safari, N.Falls
🐾 Large executive home located in the core of Burlington. Hosts have welcomed B&B guests for several years and provide a warm and friendly family atmosphere. Fax and computer access available. Ideal place for business travellers. Breakfast is served in special guest breakfast room. There are school children in the host family and 1 dog is in residence. ⌐B&B

Cambridge

(east of Waterloo/Kitchener; see also Troy, Ayr)

Barrie, Debra and Sandy (Spruceview Century Farm)　　　☎ (519) 621-2769
RR4, Cambridge, ON　N1R 5S5

From Hwy 401 take Exit 268 and go east on RegRd 97 for 5 km, pass Reg Rd 47 and look for 2nd farm on right.
$40S　$55D　$5Child　🖲 Meals　　　► 6A,5Ch
🌑Full　🏠Farm, hist., patio, quiet　■3(upst)　🖐No smoking,
no pets　★F,TV　🛏1S,2D,1Q,1R, crib　🛁 1Private,1sh.w.g.
🏃 Farm grounds, hiking (Grand Valley Trail through property)
🚗 Farmers'markets, African Lion Safari, Mennonite Country
🐾 5th Generation family field-stone house on 250-acre active
working farm (beef, sheep, corn, grains & maple syrup). Enjoy the warm hospitality and quiet relaxing atmosphere. There are three school children in the host family. ⌐B&B

Moyer, Joan (The Calico Cat Bed & Breakfast)   ☎ & Fax (519) 623-8689
42 Gilholm Ave., Cambridge, ON   N1S 1T4

Phone for directions.
$45S $55D   ► 4A
💷Full   🏠Res., older, quiet   ■2D(upstairs)   ⊨2T,1D   ⊐1Sh.w.g.
★ Air,TV in small guest sitting room, off-street parking   ✋No
smoking, no pets, not suitable for children
🕴 Downtown Cambridge (Galt), outlet stores, restaurants, hiking,
canoeing on the Grand River
🚗 Kitchener/Waterloo farmers' markets, Stratford Festival, Royal
Botanical Gardens, hiking trails, Mennonite Country, Bell Homestead, Doon Pioneer Village
🖐 Warm and friendly welcome in quiet home in the old part of town. Relax on the old-fashioned
veranda overlooking the garden and have another cup of coffee. Hostess is involved with
Soroptimist International Service Club. There is a Calico cat in residence. ✏CC

Okrafka, Paul & Dianne (Eagle Crest Bed & Breakfast   ☎ (519) 658-5313
RR22, Eagle Lane, Cambridge, ON   N3C 2V4

From Hwy 401 exit at Townline Rd (Cambridge). From the carpark travel down sideroad 32 past
Barber's Beach and past McClintocks Marina. At stop sign go right onto gravel road, take first
laneway on right (Eagle Lane) down long densly treed laneway (1km) to B&B. Look for No 4

$45-65S $55-75D $10Child/Add.person   ► 4A,2Ch
💷 Full   🏠 Rural, 2-storey, acreage, view from guest rooms, lakefront,
patio, porch, deck, quiet, secluded   ■ 2D (main & upper floor)   ⊨ 1D,1Q
(4-poster),2cots   ⊐1Private, 1ensuite   ★ Air,F,TV,LF, guest room
balcony, private entrance, large guest living room, host quarters are
separate   ✋No smoking, no pets, children min. age 6 ⌇French, German
🕴 Hiking/cycling & x/c-ski trails, swimming, fishing, waterskiing at
neighbouring marina, boat rental
🚗 Cambridge, downhill skiing, golfing, Kitchener/Waterloo markets
🖐 Large open-concept home designed to resemble a seaside Nantucket
residence with fieldstone fireplace and plenty of natural woodwork, furnished with Canadian
antiques. Relax inside with a beautiful view of Puslinch Lake and Blue Heron Bay, or in the
hammock by the water and enjoy the very restful atmosphere. Ideal place for honeymoons, retreats
or special occasions. There are schoolchildren in the host family and "Rover" the friendly dog.
Private, detached full-equipped guest house suitable for families also available. ✏B&B

Camlachie   *(east of Sarnia on Lake Huron; see also Petrolia)*

Hamilton, Bob and Audrey (Doon's Beach Bed & Breakfast)   ☎ (519) 899-2962
Box 18, Bonnie Doon, RR2, 3889 Ferne Ave., Camlachie, ON   N0N 1E0

Take New Lakeshore Rd (Cty Rd 7) north from Camlachie to Queen St. (Cty Rd 11). Turn left
(west) then immediately right on Bonnie Doon Rd to lake.
$55-65S $65-75D   ► 2
💷 Full, homebaked   🏠 Res., beach community, hillside, patio,
3-storey, lakeview, quiet   ■1Ste(ground floor)   ⊨1Q   ⊐Private
★F/KF in suite, sep.entrance, TV in private living/dining area,
wheel-chair access   ✋No smoking,no pets,no children
🕴 Sandy beach, variety of walking trails, x/c skiing
🚗 Huron Country & Victoria Playhouses, museum, golf courses
🖐 Enjoy a private get-away offering swimming and country walks, lovely gardens, privacy, music
and books. Well-travelled hosts in beautiful hillside home situated across the road from Lake Huron
in the beach community of Bonnie Doon. Breakfast served in dining room or veranda, or on the
sunny patio. "An evening walk down to the beach to view the sunset is a must". ✏B&B

Campbellville *(east of Toronto; see also Milton, Burlington, Oakville, Waterdown, Guelph)*

McPhee, Dave & Martha (Maranatha Log House B&B) ☎ (905) 854-0444, 854-0535
Box 340, 125 Main St S (Guelph Line), Campbellville, ON L0P 1B0   Fax (905) 854-3390

From Hwy 401, take Exit 312 and follow Guelph Line south through Campbellville. Look for house after railway tracks on left hand side. From QEW take Guelph Line North Exit 102.

$55-65S $65-75D   ▶ 5A
Full, homebaked Hist., log house, view from guest rooms,
deck 2(upstairs) T,D,Q 1Sh.w.g.with jacuzzi F,TV,
off-street parking No smoking, no pets, no children
Unique historic village with many artisans/antique shops and
tea rooms. several conservation areas (swimming, hiking, maple
syrup wagon rides, skiing etc), adjoining flower & gift shop
Burlington, Oakville, Guelph, Cambridge, Hamilton, Toronto

Historic log home with the charm of yesterday but with modern conveniences of today. Originally built around 1850, it was moved to its present location and has been featured on TV & magazines, photographed and painted by many artists over the years. Browse through the flower & seasonal decorating shop (hostess has won many awards for her unusual and beautiful designs) and enjoy the peaceful backyard from the deck. There are birds and a dog. MC,Visa ✓CC

Raithby, Nancy (Winklewood Lane)   ☎ (905) 854-0527
RR2, Campbellville, ON L0P 1B0

Phone for directions.
$65S $85D   (Reservation preferred)   ▶ 4A
Full Rural, ranch-style cottage, acreage, deck, quiet
2D 4T 2Private F,TV/VCR in guest rooms,
parking No smoking, no pets, no children
Kelso and Hilton Falls Conservation Parks for hiking & rock
climbing, birdwatching, Glen Eden ski hills, Bruce Trail hiking
Farm Museum (Milton), Aberfoyle Flea Market, U of Guelph

Enjoy a rural retreat with typical English cottage atmosphere among 8 acres of wooded bliss on 16-Mile Creek and backing onto Kelso Conservation Park. Part of property is classified as "natural". Relax on the gorgeous deck over the creek and partake in the rural tranquility. Well-traveled host enjoys theatre, music and nature. ✓B&B

Cargill   *(east of Kincardine; see also Pinkerton, Paisley, Mildmay, Walkerton)*

Moffatt, Elaine and John (Cornerbrook Farm B&B)   ☎(519) 366-2629,Fax(519) 366-2275
RR2, Cargill, Ontario N0G 1J0

From Hwy 21, take Co Rd 15 at Tiverton and go east 14.5 km through Glammis to farm on right side (well marked). Or travel 12 km north of Junction 4 and 9 on Bruce 20 to County Rd 15. Turn left, to first farm on left.

$35S $45D $65F Meals   (Children half-price)   ▶ 6
Full Farm 3D(upstairs) 2T,2D 2Sh.w.g.
TV, Air (on main floor) Smoking on patio, no pets
Hiking, skiing, woodland and maple bush
Saugeen River, canoeing, fishing, swimming, Lake Huron,
farmers' markets, museum, anitques

200-acre mixed farm with large modernized century-home with open staircases, restored hardwood and a spattering of antiques add a flavour of the past. Located in the heart of Bruce County in quiet, scenic surroundings with relaxed atmosphere. Enjoy Lake Huron's magnificent sunsets. Senior citizens, cyclists and canoeists especially welcome. Cycling packages available. Visa ✓OFCA

Carrying Place

(west of Trenton; see also Brighton, Consecon, Colborne)

Davis, Gisèle & Michael (The Quinte Anchorage)   ☎ (613) 394-5593
RR1, 254 Old Orchard Rd. Carrying Place, ON   K0K 1L0

From Hwy 401 take Wooler Rd (near Trenton) to Hwy 33 and follow directions to Picton. Cross Murray Canal, then left at County Rd 3 (Rednersville Row - Shell Station on corner). Continue 4km

to Old Orchard Rd. Turn left and look for small sign on mailbox.
$50-60S/D   ▶ 4A
🛏 Full 🏠Rural, back-split, waterfront, patio, quiet, water-view from suite ■1D,1Ste(main & ground level) ⊨1D,1Q
🚪1Private,1Ensuite   ★F,TV,F, private entrance, ample parking ⓦNo smoking, no pets ⤳French
🏃 Sailing, fishing, cycling, walking, x-c skiing, golfing
🚗 Presqu'ile & Sandbanks Provincial Parks, North Beach
🐾 Bright and contemporary home with a large deck and patio facing the Bay, located on a quiet road in a peaceful setting with lots of trees. Previous city dwellers, hosts are semi-retired and active with sailing/free-lance translations and enjoy the escape from the hustle and bustle of big city life. Breakfast is served dining-room, deck or patio.

Cayuga

(south of Hamilton; see also Dunnville, Ohsweken)

Belbeck, Frank & Helen (River Inn B&B)   ☎ (905) 774-8057
RR1, 759 Reg Rd17, Cayuga, ON   N0A 1E0   E-mail: riverinn@linetap.com

Take Hwy 56 south from Hamilton, then Reg Rd32 to Reg Rd19. Turn right 1.6km to B&B on left.
$55S $65D $20child/Add.person   ▶4A,3Ch
🛏 Full, homebaked   🏠 Rural, hillside, 2-storey, acreage, view from guest rooms, riverfront, swimming pool, porch, deck, quiet, secluded   ■ 1D,1F(upstairs)   ⊨ 2D,1Q,cot 🚪 1Private, 1ensuite   ★ TV,ceiling fans, air-conditioners, host quarters are separate ⓦDesignated smoking area, no pets
🏃 Grand River, enjoy a quiet stroll through natural parkland,

golfing, lake & stream fishing, boating, craft shops, tea rooms
🚗 Mount Hope Airport, Warplane Heritage Museum, Rosa Flora Greenhouses (tours), Six Nation Reserve, Hamilton, Lakes Ontario & Erie, Niagara Falls, Niagara-on-the-Lake, African Lion Safari
🐾 Comfortable home with country charm, decorated in Victorian style and situated in a 14-acres park-like setting on the banks of the beautiful Grand River surrounded by historic and scenic waterways. An excellent starting point for exploring Southwestern Ontario. Relax and enjoy the view from the deck or cool off in the solar-heated pool. Ideal place for a weekend get-away. There is a resident cat in hosts apartment. Visa ⤳B&B

Centralia

(nroth of Longon; see also Woodham, St.Marys)

Thompson, Carla & Wilson (The Shall B In B&B)   ☎ & Fax (519) 228-9969
RR1, Centralia,ON   N0M 1K0   E-mail: theshall-b-in.bb@sympatico.ca

Located 3km south of Exeter on the corner of Hwy 4/Credition Rd.
$65S $85D   🍽 Meals   ▶ 10
🛏 Full 🏠 Rural, acreage, indoor swimming pool, patio, quiet
■4D,1F (upstairs) ⊨ 3D,1Q,1K,1R 🚪 2Private, 3ensuite
★Air, well-stocked library, hot tub ⓦ Smoking outside, no pets
🏃 4 acres of land to stroll incl. 1-acre of gardens
🚗 Conservation Area for hiking & x-c skiing, live theatre in Blyth, Grand Bend, Stratford Shakespeare Theatres, golfing, museums, shops
🐾 Large home nestled among mature trees with a panoramic view of the wonders of the season, offering the pleasure of country elegance to the discriminating traveller. Relax by the fireplace in the great room or by the heated indoor pool or in the 4-persons hot tub. Breakfast is served in the pleasantly appointed breakfast/dining room. Ideal place for special occasions, business meetings and fine dining. Massage & Reflexology sessions can be administered. There are birds and a cat in residence. Children welcome. Visa,MC ⤳B&B

Cheltenham

(w/of Toronto; see also Brampton, Georgetown, Erin, Hillsburgh)

Craig, Stephen & Shelley (The Top of the Hill B&B) ☎ (905) 838-3790
14318 Creditview Rd., Cheltenham, ON L0P 1C0

From Hwy 401, take Mississauga Rd. north for 20km to King St. Proceed one road east to Creditview Rd.and turn left.
$50S $60D $5Child $10Add.person   ►4
🍺 Full, homebaked   🏠 Rural, village, 2-storey, hist., 2acres, view from guest rooms, swimming pool, patio, deck, quiet
🛏2D(upstairs)   🛏 2D   🚿 1Sh.w.g.   ★ Air,F,TV,LF, off-street parking   🚭 No smoking, no pets
🚶 Hiking (Bruce Trail or Caledon Trailway), scenic rural village (country store & dam), fishing & canoeing
🚗 Brampton Flying Club, skiing, golfing, cycling, Terra Cotta Inn & crafts, Belfountain
📢 Original famly homestead (1830-built heritage home) with rooms appointed in period decor, lovingly renovated and modernized; located in lush park-like setting of the beautiful Niagara Escarpment. Relax by the fireplace or on the patio by the pool and enjoy the unique pastoral atmosphere. Hostess is very knowledgeable of the area and will pick-up from Brampton Flying Club. Ideal place for cyclists and nature lovers. There are pets on premises.

Clarksburg

(east of Owen Sound; see also Meaford, Thornbury, Bognor)

Maitland, Don and Nan (Grape Grange) ☎ (519) 599-2601
Box 39, Marsh St., Clarksburg, ON N0H 1J0

Take Hwy 26 to Thornbury stop light, turn south 1.5 km to 4th house on left at top of hill. Look for Century Farm sign.
$35S $55-60D $15Add. person $15crib   ► 5A,1Ch
🍽Meals 🍴Choice, homebaked 🏠Farm, historic,older, patio, quiet
🛏1S,2T,1D,crib 🛏1S,2D(upstairs) 🚿2Sh.w.h. ★TV,F 🚭No pets, no smoking
🚶 Village shopping, art studios, Georgian Bay
🚗 Meaford, scenic caves, hiking the Bruce Trail and Georgian Trail, Blue Mountain & Beaver Valley popular Ski Resorts
📢 Comfortable, spacious 1860-built brick house, shaded by towering black walnut trees and large garden. Enjoy homemade preserves. ✒CC

Stewart, Karen & Norm (Hillside Bed & Breakfast) ☎ (519) 599-5523
Box 72, Clarksburg, ON N0H 1J0

From Hwy 26 in Thornbury, turn south at light and follow Bruce St to Clarksburg. Heading up hill, turn right on Brook St. Located at corner of Marsh St.
$45S $65D $20Add.person   ►7
🍺 Full, homebaked   🏠 Village, 2-storey, hist., acreage, view from guest rooms, porches, quiet   ■ 3D(upstairs), host quarters are separate   🛏2T,1D,1Q,cot   🚿 2Sh.w.g.   ★TV,F, separate entrance, off-street parking   🚭 No smoking, no pets, children minimum age 8
🚶 Walks on 3.5 acres of terraced lawns (natural streams, park benches, lookout over the pond), Village of Clarksburg (bridges over Beaver River & fish ladders)
🚗 Excellent downhill ski resorts, Bruce Trail hiking, fishing, boating, windsurfing at beaches of Georgian Bay, fine dining, antique shops, x/c skiing
📢 Warm and friendly atmosphere in stately Victorian home, overlooking the village, with spacious rooms, period furnishings, deep wood trim, chandeliers and fireplaces. ✒B&B

Walton, Tom & Grace (Walton's Country Home B&B)   ☎ (519) 599-3898
RR1, Clarksburg, ON N0H 1J0

Phone for directions.
$40S $55D   ► 6-8
🍳 Full   🏠 Rural, bungalow, acreage, view from guest rooms,
deck, quiet ■ 2F (upstairs) ⊨ 2D,1Q
🛁1Private,1sh.w.g.   ★TV/guest kitchen & living room, private
entrance, host quarters are separate   🚭 No smoking, no pets
🚗 Downhill & x/c skiing, Blue Mountain/Talisman Ski Resorts,
Wasaga Beach, Owen Sound, Georgian/Bruce Trails hiking
🐾 Retired farmers in new home with excellent view of Georgian Bay and mountains. Situated on
small acreage on the original farmland located in the popular Beaver Valley Resort and 4-season
recreation area. Guest rooms are in one part of the house. There is a dog Jasmen outside. ✓B&B

Clifford   *(north of Listowel, Mildmay, Gorrie, Walkerton)*

Hutchison, Georgie & Bruce (Country Lane B&B)   ☎ & Fax (519) 327-8236
9792 Creek Rd., RR3, Clifford, ON N0G 1M0   E-mail: hutch@wcl.on.ca

Follow Hwy 9 north to the south-end of Clifford. Turn right on Cty
Rd 2, then left on Creek Rd to first house on left.
$30S $45D $5Child 🍽 Meals   ► 8
🍳 Full, homebaked 🏠 Rural, bungalow, quiet, view from guest
rooms, porch, secluded ■2D,1F(main & lower
level) 🛁1Sh.w.g.1sh.w.h.
⊨2T,1Q,1D,bunks ★TV,LF,KF,house keys, ceiling fans
🚭Designated smoking area, no pets, children min. age 6
🚶 Country roads with little traffic, Wetlands
🚗 Mt.Forest, Hanover, Guelph, Owen Sound, Southampton, Lake Huron beaches
🐾 Warm welcome in comfortable home with large windows, situated amidst quiet farms, winding
streams and woodlands. Hosts are active in the community, local craft market, country jamborees,
historic fairs & church events and are very flexible to suit guests' schedules. Refreshments are
always available. Enjoy the congenial get-together in the kitchen or on the veranda and unhurried
atmosphere. Seniors' discounts available on Monday to Thursday.

Cobden   *(south-east of Pembroke; see also Eganville)*

Mackey, Anne and Doug (Cobden Bed & Breakfast)   ☎ (613) 646-2643,1-800-667-1028
26 Crawford St., Cobden, ON K0J 1K0

From Hwy 17 exit at Cobden Business Section sign. Proceed on Main St to Crawford. Turn left.

$40S $60D $5Child $10Add.person   ► 12
🍳Full 🏠Village,older,3-storey,large veranda,quiet ■3D,1F (2nd
& 3rd floor) ⊨2S,3D,1Q 🛁1Ensuite,2shw.g.
★Air,TV,LF,F, parking
🚶 Shopping, swimming, boating, ice fishing, snowmobiling
🚗 Whitewater Rafting, Logosland, Bonnechere Caves,
Calabogie/Candiac Ski Resorts, museums, Pembroke Murals
🐾 Restored older funeral home, with antiques & lots of
stained glass (designed by hosts). There are 2 quiet Yorkshire Terriers in residence. Hosts will take
guest on Ottawa & Valley tours. Free transportation provided to/from whitewater rafting. Hosts
are winner of 1995 Hosptiality Award. ✓B&B

Cobourg

(east of Oshawa; see also Port Hope, Colborne, Brighton)

Duncan, Jayne and John (Victoria View) ☎ (905) 372-3437
216 Church Street, Cobourg, Ontario K9A 3V9

From Hwy 401, take Exit 474 and Hwy 45 south to Cobourg and King St (Hwy 2). Turn left to Church St and right to 1st house on left.

$45S $65-75D   ► 5
🔲 Full   🏠 Downtown, hist.,3-storey, sunporch   ■3(upstairs)
🛏1D,1Q,2T   ⎠1Ensuite, 3h.w.g.   ★F,TV ⓦNo smoking
🏃 Town centre and town hall, Victoria Park across street with beach/boardwalk and Waterfront Trail, shopping, restaurants, theatre, library, churches, harbour
🚗 Toronto, Rice Lake, Bay of Quinte
📢 Historically designated house furnished with a mixture of antiques & period pieces, with a beautiful porch overlooking park & in the heart of town. ⤳CC

Thompson, Cathryn & Ian Woodburn (Mackechnie House B&B) ☎ (905) 372-6242
173 Tremaine St., Cobourg, ON K9A 2Z2

From Hwy 401 at Cobourg, exit on the Burnham St cut-off and follow downtown signs to King St. Turn right (west) and continue 2 blocks to Tremaine St. Turn left to 4th house on right.

$50S $75D   🍴Meals (plus tax)   ► 6
🔲 Homebaked   🏠 Downtown, hist., 2-storey, small acreage
■3 (upstairs), host quarters are separate   🛏1D,2Q(4-poster)
⎠1Ensuite,1sh.w.g ★LF,parking ⓦSmoking on porch
🏃 Sandy beach on Lake Ontario, multitude of south-eastern Ontario historic buildings, Cobourg main street & Victoria Hall
🚗 Antique shops, Toronto, Trent River, Rice Lake, fishing
📢 Bright, spacious 1843 home, one of the most interesting examples of domestic Greek Revival Architecture in Ontario, with most of the original features intact and beautifully decorated, surrounded by lovely gardens, maple & chestnut trees. Hostess is a prof. Caterer and serves interesting and above average meals. A friendly bagpipe playing "ghost" is occasionally present. There is an 11 year old boy in the host family and a friendly cat. Amex ⤳B&B

Colborne

(west of Trenton; see also Brighton, Cobourg, Carrying Place)

Lee, Roger and Margaret (The Maples) ☎ (905) 355-2059
Box 743, 119 King St. E., Colborne, Ontario K0K 1S0

From Hwy 401 take Percy St/Big Apple Dr Exit into village to King St (Hwy2), turn left.

$45S $55D $10Add.person   ► 6
✚ May-Oct. (other by prior arrangement) 🔲 Full 🏠Village,
acreage, older, veranda, quiet ■3D(upstairs) 🛏2Q,1D
⎠1Sh.w.g.   ⓦNo smoking, no pets
🚗 Antique and craft shops, local auctions twice weekly, Big Apple Restaurant, Theme Park and Bakery, Presqu'ile Prov. Park, "Apple Route" and Waterfront Trail
📢 Friendly hospitality in spacious red brick century home sitting well back from the road. Relax on the large porch and let the world go by. House is located on Waterfront Trail (Hwy 2).⤳B&B

Collingwood

(see also Bognor, Meaford, Clarksbur)

Szelestowski, Steve & Diane (Pretty River Valley Country Inn)   ☎&Fax(705)445-7598
RR1, Nottawa, ON L0M 1P0

Take Hwy 24 through Duntroon to Side Rd 30/31. Turn left and proceed 7.5 km to Inn on left.
$64-90S $79-120D $10Child $15Add.person   (plus taxes)   ► 16A,7Ch
🍴 Full   🏠 Farm, log board/batten house, acreage, view from guest rooms, patio, pond, quiet
■6plus 2Stes,(main & upper level) ⊨8Q,7P ⏚8Private ★Air,F(8 in guest rooms), guest
fridge's,sep.entrance,3in-room whirlpool baths,1 guest balcony 🚭No smoking, no pets
🕺 Scenic Bruce Trail (excellent hiking), Pretty River Valley Wilderness Park, farm ground
🚗 Village of Nottawa, Collingwood (excellent downhill & x-c skiing), Wasaga Beach Resort
🐎 Elegant Country Inn with traditional Canadian pine furniture nestled amidst 120 acres of
plateaus and forest in the scenic Blue Mountains overlooking the Pretty River Valley. After a day's
adventures relax in the whirlpool or sit by the pond and enjoy the view of Ontario's most lovely
unspoiled valley. Breakfast is served in the guest breakfast room, which can also serve as a seminar
room for groups of up to 16 people. CCards ✔B&B

Comber

(east of Windsor; see also Leamington, Kingsville)

Markham, Kathy (This Old House B&B)   ☎ (519) 687-3850, Fax (519) 687-6467
7005 County 46, Box 377, Comber, ON N0P 1J0   E-mail: thisold@1bm.net

Phone for directions.
$60S $70D   ► 8
🍴 Full, homebaked   🏠 Village, 2-storey, hist., acreage, patio,
porch, swimming pool ■4D(main & upper level) ⊨2T,2Q,1D
⏚2Sh.w.g, 1sh.w.h.   ★ Air,TV, guest bicycles, off-street
parking   🚭No smoking, no pets, children min. age 6
🕺 15 acres birding conservation area, Tilbury Golf & Curling
Club, Tilbury West Agricultural Museum, on-site gift shop
🚗 Windsor, Casino, Chatham, Jack Miners Bird Sanctuary Pelee Island, Point Pelee National
Park, Lake Erie fishing, excellent wineries, US border
🐎 119-year old Gothic-Victorian stately home, furnished with antiques and surrounded by 1.6
acres of parkland. A great place to unwind and relax. Enjoy historic charm combined with modern
convenience. Hostess is a Travel Agent and an excellent cook. Breakfast is served in special guest
breakfast room. Boxed lunches and dinner can be provided with notice. Visa,MC ✔CC

Consecon

(south of Trenton; see also Carrying Place, Wellington, Bloomfield)

Banks, Rosemary (The Marsh House B&B)   ☎ (613) 394-5319
Box 143, 60 Mill St., Consecon, ON K0K 1T0

$40S $55D $15Add.person 🍽 Meals   (Deposit required) (Winter rates available)   ► 6A
From Hwy 401 take Exit 522 at Wooler Rd and continue on Hwy 33 to Rte 29. Look for house

opposite Post Office.
🍴 Full, homebaked   🏠 Rural, village, hist., older, acreage,patio,
quiet ■ 3D   ⊨ 3D,1T,1R ⏚1Sh.w.h.,1sh.w.g.   ★ TV,F,
fans   🚭No pets, no smoking
🕺 Weller's Bay, Lake Ontario, Consecon village, United Church
(built in 1820)
🚗 North Beach Prov. Park and beautiful sandy beaches, fine
dining, Art studios, antique hunting, berry picking, museums.
🐎 Friendly hospitaly in "Queen Anne"style home (ca 1876) furnished with some antiques, set in
a large attractive garden on the north end of the village next to the old stone church. Relax on the
outside patio or in the cozy guest lounge. Visa ✔CC

Cookstown

(south of Barrie; see also Alliston, Beeton)

Baues, Gisele & Alfred (Victoria House B&B) ☎ & Fax (705) 458-0040
36 Victoria St.East, Cookstown, ON L0L 1L0

Phone for directions.
$50S $65D ► 4A,2Ch
Full · Village, 2-storey, view from guest rooms, deck, quiet ■ 2D(main & upper level) 2Q,2R 2Ensuite
★ Air,F,TV, off-street parking, private walkout deck, private sitting area in one room, guest quarters are separate Smoking on decks, children min. age 8
Cookstown village with antique/craft/artisan shops, retaurants
Cookstown Outlet Mall, Lake Simcoe, Wasaga Beach, Orillia (Casino, Opera House), Toronto
Bright Board & Batten home (too large for Empty Nesters) of older origin, nicely upgraded and furnished with traditional to eclectic pieces and situated on large lot close to village centre. Congenial hosts invite guests to relax on the private deck or join them in the living room with cathedral ceiling. Breakfast is served in guest breakfast room. There are cats in residence. CC

Cornwall

(see also St.Andrews W.,Lancaster, Apple Hill, Williamstown)

Biggs, Carol & Peter (Blakely House B&B) ☎& Fax (613) 933-6528
1712 Blakely Dr., Cornwall, ON K6J 5L3

From Hwy 401, take Exit 789 (Brookdale) to traffic circle. Take 7th St west straight onto Queen St, right on Riverdale, left on Grant then right on Blakeley Dr to 4th house on right.

$40S $50D Meals ► 4A
Full, homebaked Res., 2-storey, deck, quiet, secluded
■ 1D,1Ste(upst) 4T 1Ensuite,1private ★Air,LF,TV in upst.lounge, off-street parking No smoking, no pets, not suitable for children
Pitt Street shopping, Inverarden & Wood House Museum, scenic waterfront park with 35km recreational cycling path to Ingleside, public transportation to downtown
Morrisburg (upper Canada Village), Provincial parks and marinas, Montreal, Ottawa
Stylish home furnished with exceptional comforts, many collectibles and art. Located in a park-like setting near downtown. Well travelled hosts are former Toronto residents who enjoy meeting people from all over the world. There is a cat named "Smokey" in residence.

Johnson, Edward and Michelyne (Riverdale House B&B) ☎ (613) 933-0398
1002 Pescod Ave., Cornwall, ON K6J 2J9

From Hwy 401 take Exit 789 (Brookdale) and drive to traffic circle. Take 7th St west and continue onto Queen St. Turn right on Pescod Ave.

$40S $50D ► 4
Full Res., large cedar deck, quiet ■ 2D (upstairs)
T,Q,K 2Sh.w.g. ★Air,LF,TV in guest lounge French
Pitt Street Mall shopping, St. Lawrence Seaway, Wood House Museum, Inverarden Regency Cottage, Museum, bicycle path
Morrisburg (Upper Canada Village), beaches, Bird Sanctuary
Comfortable contemporary home, beautifully decorated including some antiques and conveniently located in quiet residential area of town. Well-travelled, retired hosts with many interests enjoy visitors and showing them around Ontario's most easterly City situated right on the St. Lawrence Seaway. More space available for special events.

Lounsberry, Darlene and John (By the Sea B&B)   ☎ (613) 931-3041
19000, Hwy 2, RR1, Cornwall, ON   K6H 5R5

Located on Hwy 2, west of Summerstown and 8 km east of Cornwall.
Exit 804 off Hwy 401. Phone or write for directions.
$40S $50D $10Add.person 🍽 Meals   ► 8
🍴Full 🏠Rural, 2-storey, hillside, view, patio, quiet, riverfront
■2(ground level) ➡1S,4D,1P ➡1Sh.w.g.,1private,1sh.w.h.
〰French ★TV,F,KF,LF, sep.entr., parking 🚭No smoking
🕴 Fishing/swimming/boating, St.Lawrence Seaway ships
🚗 Upper Canada Vill., Montreal, Coopers Marsh, Glengarry
🚩 Home is situated on the St. Lawrence Seaway. Watch International ships sail by and enjoy the
park-like surroundings on the Seaway. Boat tours (fishing charters, sightseeing to the islands) &
canoeing to sanctuary & marshes of the St.Lawrence with experienced guides available. ✍CC

Creemore

(south of Collingwood; see also Stayner)

Kashuba, Leona (Edenstone Bed & Breakfast)   ☎ (705) 466-3564
RR4, Creemore, ON   L0M 1G0

Located in Dunedin. Follow Airport Rd (Reg.Rd 18) from Mansfield to Cty Rd 9 and proceed west
through Creemore and Dunedin all the way to Con.9, then south to B&B stone gates. From Hwy 24
travel north from Shelburne to Simcoe Cty Rd 9, proceed east to Con.9 and south to B&B.

$50-60S $60-70D   ► 6
🍴 Full, homebaked 🏠 Rural, recreational farm, 2-storey,
acreage, view from guest rooms, river at back, patio, deck, quiet,
secluded ■ 3D (upper & walk-out lower level) ➡ 2T,1D,1Q
➡ 1Ensuite, 1private ★ Air,TV, spa & sauna 🚭No smoking,
no pets, children min. age 12 〰 Ukrainian
🕴 Bruce Trail hiking, back country roads for walking, Noisy River
🚗 Collingwood, Wasaga Beach, Georgian Bay, swimming, golfing
🚩 Large, tastefully decorated new home with landscaped terraces and large decks in popular four
season recreational area. Relax in the spa or sauna or in the large recreation/hospitality lounge
with billards & games facilities. Enjoy the seclusion and serenity of surrounding cedar groves and
meadow lanes. There is a cat in residence.

Smart, Jean & John (Blacksmith House B&B)   ☎ (705) 466-3373, Fax (705) 466-2886
7 Caroline St.W., Box 130, Creemore, ON   L0M 1G0   E-mail: jsmart@mail.transdata.ca

From Barrie, travel west on Hwy 90 and north on Simcoe Rd No10. At Simcoe Rd No9 turn left and
proceed to Creemore. Turn left at Mill St and right at Caroline St.

$48S $58D   ► 5A
🍴Full,homebaked 🏠Village,2-storey,hist.,patio,porch,deck ■2D
(upst) ➡2Q,1T ➡ 1Sh.w.g.,1sh.w.h. ★Air,F,LF,TV,ceiling fans, off-street
parking 🚭No smoking,no pets,not suitable for children
🕴 Antique shops, artist studios, quaint village shops, North America's
smallest Jail (1892), Creemore Springs Brewery (tours), unspoilt beauty of
Purple hills (walking, bicycling), Bruce Trail hiking, local auctions
🚗 Downhill skiing at Devil's Glen & Blue Mtn ski areas, golfing, swimming
& sailing on Georgian Bay, South Simcoe Railway steam train
🚩 Victorian home (ca 1895) located in a picturesque village nestled in the
valley of the Mad & Noisy Rivers. Relax and enjoy afternoon tea in the
cozy sunporch or on the back deck/patio overlooking the lovely private garden. Well informed hosts
will provide information/maps/brochures of the area. Breakfast is served in special guest breakfast
room. There is a friendly Siberian Husky "Taiga" in residence. Visa, MC ✍B&B

Dalkeith

(east of Ottawa near QC; see also Alexandria, Apple Hill)

Howes, Lillian & Murray (Glengarry Haven B&B)   ☎ (613) 525-3640
1700 Old Military Rd., Box 60, RR1, Dalkeith, ON   K0B 1E0

From Hwy 417 take Exits 27 or 35 and proceed south to Kirkhill and Old Military Rd.

$35S $45D $10Child $90F   🍽 Meals   ► 4
🍲 Full, homebaked   🏠 Rural, bungalow, acreage, view, porch,
quiet ■2(lower level) ⊨2S,1D, crib   ⌂1Sh.w.g. ★TV,
ceiling fans, guest quarters are separate   ✋No smoking, no pets
🔥 Two country churches, maple sugar bush
🚐 Maxville Highland Games, local fairs, Dunvegan Museum,
golfing, craft shops, Upper Canada Village, Rigaud Ski Hill,
restaurants, Ottawa, Montreal

🔫 Well travelled, semi retired couple in comfortable country home in a quiet rural setting of Glengarry County. Hosts are former farmers and were involved with the Nat. Holstein Association and related travels around the globe. Relax on the veranda and watch the birds in a small grove near the house. Visit a local pottery which makes beautiful pieces from Glengarry Clay. Breakfast includes maple syrup made in hosts' sugar bush. Host works at the Upper Canada Village.

Dorion

(east of Thunder Bay; see also Rossport)

Buckley, Kathy & Paul (Wolf Den Bed & Breakfast)   ☎ (807) 857-2913
Box 21, Dorion, ON   P0T 1K0

$38S $48D $10Add.person   (child free under age 6)   (groups rates available)   ► 6A,2Ch
Phone for directions.

🍲 Full, homebaked   🏠 Rural, 2-storey, acreage, deck, secluded,
quiet ■1D,1S,1F(main & upper floor) ⊨1Q,1D,1S + 1Dfuton
⌂1sh.w.g., 1sh.w.h.   ★ F,TV   ✋ Restr.smoking, no pets
🔥 Lake Superior and north shoreline, Wolf River, Coldwater
Creek, Dorion Bible Camp, trails through property
🚐 Ouimet Canyon, Amethyst Mines, downhill skiing, walking
trails in Nipigon Red Rock, golfing, Thunder Bay

🔫 Pleasant & comfortble open-concept home with screened summer sun room nestled in 109 acres of beautiful wooded area which borders the Wolf River. Hosts are outdoor enthusiasts. There are 3 small children in the host family & a Golden Retriever. Reservations appreciated. ✒B&B

Dundas

(west of Hamilton; see also Ancaster, Waterdown)

Pieper, Betty & J. (Walnut Grove Bed & Breakfast)   ☎ (905) 627-0578
Box 83, 219 Hwy 8, West Flamborough, ON   L0R 2K0

Phone for directions.
$330-40S $55-60D $10Child $20Add.person 🍽Meals ► 7A,2Ch
🍲 Full, hombaked   🏠 Rural, village, 2-storey, older, .5acre, view
from guest rooms   ■ 2D,1F(upstairs) ⊨1S,2D,1Q,cot
⌂1Sh.w.g.,1sh.w.h.   ★ LF,TV in guest living room, guest
kitchen with extra provisions, private entrance, wheel-chair access
to one room, host quarters are separate, window air-conditioners,
off-street parking ♥ ✋No smoking,no pets,children welcome

🔥 Webster's Falls & park, Borer's Falls, Christie Conservation Area (swimming, boating, picnics), charming rural walks & rugged hiking trails, interesting local village, Sulphur Springs Cons.Area 🚐 African Lion Safari, Flamborough Downs (harness racing), Dundurn Castle, hist. Whitehearn 🔫 1848 home, built in New England Salt Box- style with comfortable decor and peaceful surroundings. Hosts are B&B world travellers and will act as a guide and/or driver to local points of interest. Pick-up can be arranged. Meals are served in elegant and leisure manner and special diets can be catered. There is a budgie in the house. Specialty: catering to wedding guests. ✒B&B

Dutton
(south-west of St.Thomas near Lake Erie; see also Ridgetown)

Rowe, Mike and Bonnie (Dunwich Farm B&B)　　　　☎ (519) 762-3006
28620 Marsh Line, RR1, Dutton, ON　N0L 1J0

From Hwy 401, take Exit 149 and Dutton Currie Rd south through Dutton. Cross railway track, take 1st street right (Concession St). Proceed 2.5 km to farm on right with name on mailbox.

$40S　$45D　　　　　　　　　　　　　　　　　　　　　► 4
🍳 Full, homebaked　🏠 Farm, multi-storey, acreage, quiet
🛏2D(upstairs)　🛏1D,2T　🚿2Sh.w.h.　★TV,F, parking
🚭Restricted smoking, children and pets are welcome
🏃 Barn, farmyards, golf course
🚗 Talbot Trail (Lake Erie's historic highway), Swain's
Greenhouse in Eagle, nature walks, beaches, marinas, shops

📢 Easy-going young host family in Century home situated on a quiet country road, surrounded by a variety of trees/gardens, a haven in any season. There is a dog & a cat in residence. ✔B&B

Dyers Bay
(south of Tobermory; see also Lion's Head, Hope Bay)

Bowman, Ron and Tove (Craglee B&B)　　　　　　☎ (519) 795-7887
Dyers Bay, RR 1, Miller Lake, ON　N0H 1Z0

Located 13.5 km from Hwy 6. Take the Dyer's Bay Rd to the Hamlet of Dyer's Bay. Go up coast for 3.5 km to last house on the Bay. (Paved road ends at driveway).

$55S $60-65D $15Add.person　🍽 Meals (in off-season)　　　► 7
🍳Full,homebaked　🏠Rural,acres,view,lakefront,patio,quiet,
gazebo　🛏3D(upst)　🛏1S,3Q　🚿1Sh.w.g.,1sh.w.h.　★F,LF,
parking　🚭No smoking,no pets　💬Danish/Swedish,some German
🏃 Bruce Trail hiking, excell x-cskiing, walks along coastal road
🚗 Devils Monument, Bruce Peninsula Nat Park, singing sands at
Dorcas Bay - a Naturalists paradise & guided tours, ship wrecks at
Tobermory, ferry to Manitoulin Island
📢 Home is tucked into side of the Niagara Escarpment and
offers a magnificient view of Georgian Bay sunrises, moonlight glimmering in the water. Extremely peaceful, restful atmosphere. Listen to the loons while enjoying breakfast on the 30ft deck. ✔B&B

Girouard, Jean-Denis & Céline (Plumica B&B)　　　☎ (519)795-7499
RR1, Dyer's Bay, Miller Lake, ON　N0H 1Z0

Phone for directions.
$60-80S　$75-95D　$130F　🍽 Meals　　　　　　► 8
🍳 Buffet(hot & cold)　🏠 Rural, 2-storey, view from guest
rooms, lakeback, patio, porch, large deck, quiet, secluded　🛏2D,1F
(upstairs)　🛏4Q　🚿3Private　★ TV in guest living room,
small guest fridge, guest quarters are separate, private balconies,
gazebo　🚭No smoking, children min. age 14　💬English
(household language is French)
🏃 Bruce Trail hiking, Niagara Escarpment, Larkwhistle Gardens, Devils Monument (Flower Pot Rock), Cryptoendolithics (hidden inside-rocks-vegetation),
🚗 Tobermory, ferry to Manitoulin Island, Cabot Head Lighthouse
📢 Newly-built French Country-style home furnished with antiques/contemporary and rattan pieces and nestled between 300ft of shore (crystal water) and the 90ft cliff of the Niagara Excarpement & Bruce Trail. Ideal place for hikers, nature lovers and small seminars or workshops. Hosts are a retired Journalist (also Big Band musician) & Artist. After a day of hiking & exploring the Escarpment, relax with a book or magazine from the collection on Environment. There are 2 cats & a dog in residence (on the Welcome Committee). ✔B&B

Hawkes, Sally and Wes (Camariche)
RR1, Dyers Bay, ON   N0H 1Z0   ☎ (519) 795-7699

Travel north on Hwy 6 past Miller Lake to Dyer's Bay Rd. Turn right, proceed 4 km to house.

$35S $50-55D $10Add.person   ► 6A
🍳Full, homebaked 🏚Rural, hist., acreage, quiet ■3D(upst)
🛏2T,2D   🛁1Sh.w.g., 1sh.w.h.   ★ TV,2F, separate entrance,
parking   ⓦRestricted smoking
🚶 Bruce Trail hiking, bicycling, x/c skiing, snowmobiling
🚗 Georgian Bay and beaches, restaurants, Tobermory, National
Park, Tobermory Ferry, Griegs scenic caves
🚐 Rambling, turn-of-the-Century farmhouse, once a popular
Inn called the "Dew Drop Inn", surrounded by expansive lawns/, forest/fields and located close to
Georgian Bay with the Bruce Trail passing close by the property. Ideal location for hikers and ferry
travelers to Manitoulin Island. There is a cat in the house. ✓CC

Chapitis, Michael & Christian Nold (Applewood Inn Dyer's Bay)   ☎ & Fax (519) 795-7552
RR1, Miller Lake, ON   N0H 1Z0

From Hwy 6 North, take Dyer's Bay Rd for 5 km. At T-junction
turn right and proceed to first residence on right side.
$45S $60-70D $20Add.person   🍽 Meals   ► 6A,3Ch
🍳 Full   🏚 7 acre private estate, view, quiet   ■ 2F (main &
upper level)   🛏1D,2Q,2T   🛁1Sh.w.h.,1ensuite   ★F,
parking, bicycles & canoe for guests   ⓦ No smoking, no pets
〰 Swiss German, French, Italian
🚶 Georgian Bay and Dyer's Bay Docks, beautiful pebble beach,
Bruce Trail passes at front of door, (excellent hiking/bicycling/horseback riding)
🚗 Larkwistle Garden, Bruce Peninsula National Park, Tobermory Ferry to Manitoulin Islands
🚐 Serene, light-filled renovated log house (built in 1878 as a pioneer farm), in a park-like very
private setting, with grand sunset views of old apple orchard and sweeping fields. Artist hosts will
serve meals in a waterview rose garden cottage. Ideal for nature lovers and those seeking a quiet
retreat. ✓CC

Steckley, Bill and Merrill (Merrill's Upper Deck)
Dyers Bay, RR1, Miller Lake, ON   N0H 1Z0   ☎ (519) 795-7714

Phone for directions.
$45S $55D $70Ste   ► 6A
🍳 Full, homebaked   🏚 Rural, 2-storey, view, lakefront, patio,
quiet, decks   ■ 1D (main floor), 1Ste (upstairs)   🛏 2D,1P
🛁1Private, 1sh.w.h.   ★F,TV in guest room   ⓦ No smoking,
no pets, adult accommodation
🚶 Bruce Trail, Lake, swimming, country walks
🚗 Tobermory, ferry to Manitoulin, Lark Whistle Gardens, Cabots Head Lighthouse
🚐 Enjoy waterfront hospitality and a true retreat in quiet country home, designed built by host
family, elegantly furnished and tastefully decorated with beautiful quilts made by the hostess,
overlooking clean Georgian Bay. There is a private upper deck ensuite. Enjoy the most beautiful
view. A rock-lovers paradise. Specialty of the house is coffee cake, muffins and rice pancakes. ✓CC

Eganville

(south of Pembroke; see also Cobden, Barry's Bay)

Stewart, Terry & John (The 'Hobit' Bed & Breakfast) ☎ (613) 628-1173
176 Wellington St., Eganville, ON K0J 1T0

Located on the south side of Bonnechere River.
$35S $50D $5Chld $10Add.person ► 6
🍳 Full, homebaked   🏠 Village, 2-storey, hist., .6-acres, view
from guest rooms, patio, porch, deck, quiet   ▮ 2D(upstairs), plus
main floor bed sitting room   ⊨ 2T,1D   🛁 1Sh.w.g., 1sh.w.h.
★Air,F,TV, off-street parking, facilities for the handicapped
✋Designated smoking area   ⌇ German
🚶 Restaurants, churches, park, Tea Room, antique & craft shops
🚗 Bonnechere Caves, whitewater rafting, Logos-Land Resort, Madonna House Pioneer Museum
☞ Warm and friendly welcome in spacious Century home situated in picturesque Ottawa Valley
village. Relax on the cozy porches and in comfortable sitting areas, perfect for a short repose. Hosts
were recipients of O.V.T.A. 1993 top award for hospitality. There is a cat & a grandson. ✓B&B

Verch, Miss Beatrice (Stonehedge Bed & Breakfast) ☎ (613) 628-6901
RR2, Eganville, ON K0J 1T0

Take Hwy 512 off Hwy 41 at Eganville to IGA Supermarket. Then take Sand Road 5km to stop
sign. Turn right for 0.2 km and turn left at South Algoma Rd 9. Look for red plow at mailbox.
$20S $30D ► 5
🍳 Full   🏠 Farm, quiet, older, view   ▮1S,2D(upst)   ⊨2D,1S
🛁2Sh.w.g.   ★TV,KF   ✋no pets   ⌇ German (Flemish)
🚗 Bonnechere Caves, Golden Lake

☞ Gracious hostess invites guests to spend some time in quiet
and relaxed atmosphere and fall asleep to the tinkle of the cowbells
and awaken to the roosters crow. Long-time B&B hostess is
involved with Red Cross Home Support Work. There is a dog in the
house. Most easily reached in early morning or evening. ✓B&B

Elmira

(n/of Kitchener; see also Elora, Fergus, St.Jacobs, Alma)

Milliken, Rodger and Doris (The Evergreens) ☎ (519) 669-2471
RR1, Elmira, ON N3B 2Z1

In Elmira, take Arthur St. north towards Alma to Woolwich Rd 3, turn right to house on right.
$40S $50D $10Add.person/Child(age 5-16) ► 4A,2Ch
🍳 Full, homebaked   🏠 Rural (fruit farm), backsplit, acreage,
view, patio, inground swimming pool, quiet, isolated   ▮ 2D
⊨2D   🛁 2Sh.w.g.   ★ F,TV,LF, parking   ✋No smoking
🚶 Wooded walks, 300 acre forest, x-c skiing
🚗 Elmira, shopping, Elora, St.Jacobs, Stratford Festival,
Kitchener (Octoberfest and famous farmer's market)
☞ Retired hosts in quiet location in the heart of Old Order Mennonite Country. House is set
among large evergreens. Relax on the pleasant large covered porch (upper level). A great place to
rest and enjoy the country atmosphere. There is a dog in residence. ✓B&B

Smith, Vivian and Gerrie (Teddy Bear B&B Inn) ☎ (519) 669-2379, Fax (519) 669-3446
Wyndham Hall, RR1, Elmira, ON N3B 2Z1

From Elmira take Hwy 86 west 1.5 km to Road 19. Turn right and continue through Floradale to house on left.
$65S $75D (Reservations please) ► 6A
🏠Full 🏡Hist.,raised bungalow, acreage ■3D ⊨2D.2T(K)
⊷2Ensuite,1private ★TV in rooms ♥ 🖐No smoking
🕺 Antiques, Canadiana display, gift and collection shoppe, hiking
🚐 Elora Gorge, Fergus Highland Games, St.Jacobs
☛ Converted 1907 Schoolhouse with large inside entrance hall & a few steps, beautifully remodelled and uniquely decorated with many antiques and Teddy-Bear decor. Located in the heart of Mennonite countryside, portraying many of Ontario's heritage and cultural hideaways. B&B Workshops/Consultations available. Visa,MC ⊷B&B

Elmvale
(north of Barrie; see also Hillsdale, Phelpston, Wyevale)

Duhig, Peggy (The Homestead Bed & Breakfast) ☎ (705) 322-1334
40 Amelia St., Elmvale, ON L0L 1P0

In Elmvale after turning onto Hwy92 (Queen St), look for 2nd street on right.

$45S $55D (please reserve) ► 5
🏠Cont. 🏡Village, hist., res.,acreage,patio,quiet ■1S,2D(upst)
⊨1S,2D ⊷Sh.w.g. ★F,TVin guest room,grand piano,parking, lounge-library 🖐No smoking,no pets,children min.age12
🚐 Georgian Bay parks and beaches, wildlife centres, golfing, museums, St.Marie Martyr's Shrine, antique shops, ski shops, x-c trails, Horseshoe Valley ski area, Naval Establishment
☛ Enjoy the tranquil setting and relax in Century old Victorian home with Old World charm, furnished with antiques and located on acres of lawns and gardens on the Wye River at the outskirts of the village. There is a dog and a cat. ⊷B&B

Elora
(north of Kitchener; see also Fergus, Alma, Elmira, Rockwood, Ariss)

Campbell, Orval & Marjorie (Marj's B&B) ☎ (519) 846-5820
12 Wellington Dr., Elora, ON N0B 1S0

From Hwy 401, take Guelph cut-off (Hwy 6) to Elora Rd. Proceed 15km to McNab St. Turn right to stop sign then left and cross bridge. Proceed to Moir St, turn right to Wellington Dr.
$35S $50-60D ► 4
🏠 Full 🏡 Res., village, raised bungalow, deck, quiet ■ 2D (lower level) ⊨ 1D,1Q
⊷1sh.w.g. ★ F/TV in guest sitting room, off-street and street parking 🖐 No smoking
🕺 Boutiques/specialty shops, Three Centuries Festival (July/Aug), nature & x-c ski trails (Elora Gorge Park), Quarry (swimming)
🚐 St. Jacobs/Mennonite country, Kitchener farmers' market (Thurs/Sat), Waterloo Universities
☛ Warm and friendly welcome in artists' home. Well travelled hosts are a writer of poetry & children's stories and an artist. Relax and watch the hostess paint at her cottage studio in the backyard. There is a friendly dog called "Patch" in residence. ⊷CC

Hendriks, Margaret & Harry (Trail's End B&B)   ☎ (519) 846-5800
36 David St East, Elora, ON N0B 1S0

Phone for directions.
$65-85D   🍽 Meals   ▶ 6A
🔟 Full   🏠 Village, 2-storey, hist., 0.5acres, quiet ■3D(upst)
■3Q   🛏 1Private, 2ensuite   ★Separate entrance, guest room
air conditioners, off-street & street parking, guest quarters are
separate, spa (outside)   🤚No smoking, no pets, children by
special arrangement   ⤳ Dutch
🎣 Elora gorge, Irvin & Grand Rivers (fishing), Elora Cataract
Trailway, charming village shops, antique warehouse, Elora Festival, theatre, fine restaurants
🚗 Kitchener, Guelph, St.Jacobs Farmers Market, Elmira's Maple Sugar Festival, famous Kissing
Bridge, Stratford, Forks of the Credit, Hamilton, hiking trails
☞ Bright and cheery large Century Victorian home with warm simple elegance, some antiques
and a replica of an old cookstove in the kitchen. Breakfast (using herbs and garnishes from the
garden) is served in the bright sunroom or in the formal dining room. Ideal place from which to
explore the beautiful Mennonite countryside (watch out for horsedrawn buggies). There are two
Red Factor Canaries in the house, which like to entertain guests. Visa,Amex,Enroute ✍CC

Hornsby, Lewis and Ethel (Ethel's Bed & Breakfast)   ☎ (519) 846-9763
231 Queen Street N., Box 33, Elora, ON N0B 1S0

Travel north on Hwy 6 to Elora cut-off (County Rd 7). Continue across bridge in Elora. At flashing
light turn right onto David Street, then continue to Queen Street. Turn right to 2nd house on left.

$30-35S $40-45D $5Child $10Add.person   ▶ 6A,3Ch
🔟Full   🏠 Village, res., bungalow, patio, quiet   ■3D(main &
upper level)   ⤚2T,2D,1P,cot   🛏1Private,1sh.w.g.,1sh.w.h.
★Air,F,TV in 1 guest room, parking   🤚No smoking, no pets
🎣 Popular boutique and gift shops, Elora Gorge and park, Grand
& Irvine Rivers, Elora Community Centre, cross-country ski trails
🚗 Elmira/Floradale, St-Jacobs, Mennonite country, craft shops
☞ Well travelled hosts have stayed in many B&B's, are semi
retired and have lots of time to spend with guests. Children welcome. ✍B&B

Veveris, Ingeborg-Petra (Gingerbread House)   ☎ (519) 846-0521
22 Metcalfe St.South, Elora, ON N0B 1S0

From Hwy 401/403, take Hwy 6 north and then country Rd7 (Elora Rd) to Elora. At flashing light,
turn east (downtown) to B&B on left side.

$60S $70D $125-$200Ste $15Add.person   ▶ 20
🔟Full (Gourmet)   🏠Downtown, hist., 1 acre, quiet, 4 porches
■5D,2Ste (main & upper level)   ⤚ S,D,Q,P,R   🛏 2Ensuite,
4sh.w.g.   ★ Air,F,separate entrance, guest dressing gowns &
slippers, common areas, jacuzzi, parking   🤚No smoking, no
pets   ⤳ German
🎣 Downtown Elora with many craft/pottery/souvenir shops,
restaurants, Elora Gorge nature walks
🚗 Mennonite country & markets, covered bridge, Kitchener/Waterloo, Maple Syrup Festival
☞ Gracious Century Manor, filled with antiques (historic reg'd building and 1st prize winner of
the Home-builders Assoc in 1991) situated in quaint & cheerful town full of interesting limestone
architecture. Breakfast is served on fine china and linen. ✍B&B

Erin
(n/w of Toronto; see also Hillsburgh, Cheltenham, Brampton)

Edwards, Ginny & Gord (Cedarbrook Country Inn & B&B) ☎ (519) 833-1000,
5483 Trafalgar Rd.(Hwy 25 North), Erin, ON N0B 1T0 Fax (519) 833-1004

From Hwy 401, take Trafalgar Rd north. Proceed 1km past Hwy 24 towards Hillsburg.

$65S $85D $20Add.person 🍽 Meals (plus tax) ► 22
🍽 Full 🏠 Rural, hillside, 12acres, view from guest rooms,
patio, porch, deck, quiet, secluded ■ 2D,6F (upstairs & ground
level) ⊨ 4S,2T,2D,4Q,3R 🛁 Private ★ F(also in one guest
room),Air,LF,TV in guest lounge & in one guest room, sauna, large
& small meeting rooms, guest quarters are separate ⓦ Smoking
outside, no pets, children min. age 10 ⌇ French
🕴 Walking trails on property

🚗 Bruce Trail, Elora/Cataract Cycle Trail, theatres (Orangeville/Fergus), golfing
🗣 Warm, inviting, country mansion situated on wooded acreage overlooking the Caledon Hills &
Niagara Escarpment. Hostess is a Certified Reflexologist & Health Educator & artist, whose works
are displayed in-house. Treatments available, if booked in advance. Weekend workshops (wellness
education, quilting etc.) are available. Ideal place for a country wedding, conference, spa get-away or
a place to unwind. Breakfast is served in special guest breakfast room. Visa,MC ✔B&B

Fenwick
(south of St-Catharines; see also Port Colborne, Niagara Falls)

Schafer, Lore & Dieter (Schaferhof B&B) ☎ (905) 562-4929, Fax (905) 562-3028
2746 Moyer St., RR3, Fenwick, ON L0S 1C0

Phone for directions.
$45-55S $50-65D $15Child 🍽 Meals (plus tax) ► 6A
🍽 Full 🏠 Hobby farm, 15acres, raised bungalow, view from
guest rooms, patio, deck, quiet, secluded ■ 3D (main building)
plus 2D in sep building ⊨ 2D,1Q 🛁 2Sh.w.g. ★ F,TV,
barbeque, guest quarters are separate ⓦ No smoking, no pets
⌇German
🕴 Bruce Trail, golfing

🚗 Ball's Falls, wineries, Lakes Ontario & Erie, Niagara Falls, Niagara-on-the-Lake, Hamilton
🗣 A hearty European welcome in farm home, surrounded by extensively landscaped grounds in
the fruit and wine growing region of the Niagara Peninsula. A wonderful place to relax and
rejuvenate. Enjoy the bonfire and weekend barbeque, watch fabulous sunsets and humming birds
from the large deck. Breakfast is served in special guest breakfast room. Guided bicycle wine-tours
and eco-tours can be arranged in advance. Vegetarian meals available. Airport pick-up can be
provided. Visa,MC ✔B&B

Fergus
(north of Kitchener/Waterloo; see also Elora, Elmira, Alma)

Morrison, Douglas & Emily (Fergus Lee Bed & Breakfast) ☎ (519) 843-5936
RR4, Fergus, ON N1M 2W5

Located 3.3km east of Fergus. Phone for directions.
$50S $75D ► 6A
🍽 Full, homebaked 🏠 Rural, 2-storey, hist., patio, quiet ■3D
(upstairs) ⊨ 2T,1D,1Q 🛁 Sh.w.g. ★ F, off-street parking ⓦ No
smoking, not suitable for children
🕴 Stroll through downtown Fergus along the Grand River, tour historic
Templin Gardens, Fergus Market, Theatre on the Grand, Fergus Highland
Games (world known), Cataract Trail, fly-fishing
🚗 Wellington County Museum & Archives, Elora (Elora Gorge & Mill),
hiking, whitewater rafting, unique shops, Mennonite Country, Stratford
🗣 Century farm home appointed with antique furnishings, pine floors, located 2km east of
charming Scottish Town. Enjoy afternoon tea on the veranda or by the crackling fire. Hosts will
advise on sites to tour & arrange reservations at delectable eating estalishments or theatre. ✔B&B

Juergensen, Helen & Chris (Fly-in B&B)　　　　　☎ & Fax (519) 843-1487
RR1, Beatty Line 6868, Fergus, ON　N1M 2W3

From Fergus take Hwy 6 north (towards Arthur). Turn left on roadsign "Nichol SideRd 5" to Beatty
Line, then first left again and look for house on right.
$40S　$60D　$10Child(under age 12)　$20Add.person　◙ Meals　　　　　　▶ 6A,1-2Ch

✚ Not March　◑Full, homebaked　🏠Farm, rural, 2-storey
Cape Cod, 100acres, view from guest rooms, indoor swimming pool,
deck, quiet　■3(upstairs)　⊨2T,1Q,1P,cot　⊒1Sh.w.g.　★Air,TV
in guest room, sep entrance, guest balcony, sep guest quarters
⬤Designated smoking area, no pets　⤳German
🏃 Walking, skidooing, x-c skiing, airplane tours
🚙 Large variety of restaurants, Elora Gorge (Musical Festival,
antique stores), Fergus (week-end market, Highland Games)
🐾 Semi-retired farmers (cashcrop) in new farmhouse, an ideal place for relaxation. Enjoy the
year-round warm indoor swimming pool and the wind protected sundeck or balcony. Hosts offer day
tours in their private plane wherever guests desire to go (at hourly rate). Official registered runway
is on property (Fergus airport). Country supper on request. There is a cat (inside in winter).⤳B&B

Gadshill
(north of Stratford; see also Wellesley, Millbank)

Schlueter, Beth & Murray (Bluebird Meadow B&B)　☎ (519) 656-2731, Fax (519) 621-0405
RR1, Gadshill, ON　N0K 1J0　　　　　　　　　　　E-mail: stuie68@aol.com

From Hwy 401 take Exit 278 onto Hwy 8 to Kitchener. Proceed west towards Stratford on Hwy 7/8
to Shakespeare. Turn right on County Rd107 and continue 7km north to house on right.
$40S　$50D　$15child　(plus tax)　　　　　▶6A,2ch
◑ Full (self-serve on weekdays)　🏠 Farm, 2-storey, hist., view
■2D,1F(upstairs)　⊨2S,1D,1Q,1P　⬤No smoking, no pets
⊒1sh.w.g.　★Air,KF,F,TV
🏃 Wooded trails on Avon Trail and on private woodlot, bird
watching, hiking, farm animals
🚙 Stratford (theatres), Baden (Castle Kilbride), St. Jacobs
(Mennonites Heritage Community), Lake Huron
🐾 Experience the spectacular seasons of rural Ontario on 37-acres farm. Enjoy the comfortable
country hospitality in country-style surroundings. Breakfast may be served on the large deck,
weather permitting. Relax with a good book, watch the farm animals graze close to the building
(including "Bonnie" the retired Clydesdale mare from Black Creek Pioneer Village and her colt
"Princess"). Gluten-free breakfasts are available. Snowmobilers and x-c skiers welcome. ⤳B&B

Gananoque
(east of Kingston: see also Inverary, Mallorytown)

Austin, Liz & Ric (The Victoria Rose Inn)　　　　　☎ (613) 382-3368
279 King St.West, Gananoque, ON　K7G 2G7

$65-85S　$85-105D　$155-175Suite　$25Add.person　◙ Meals　(plus taxes)　　　▶ 18
Phone for directions.
◑ Full　🏠 Downtown, res., hist., 3-storey, 2-acre,verandas,
quiet　■ 7D2Ste(upstairs)　⊨2K,2Q,3D,　⊒Private,
(2jacuzzi & fireplace in 3suites)　★Air,3F in parlours,
LF/TV in common room, parking　⬤No pets, no smoking,
children min.age 10
🏃 Boat tours of 1000 Islands, Summer Playhouse, antique
shops, public golf course, marina (bike/boat/canoe rentals)
🚙 Beach, paved bicycle path (35km), Fort Henry, Queen's University (Kingston)
🐾 Stately mansion with tall central tower, high ceilings, lavish woodwork, marble fireplaces,
Canadiana antiques and picturesque Italianate architecture, situated on estate grounds with
tranquil gardens, close to the St.Lawrence River. Enjoy the charm of the past blending with
conveniences of today. Breakfast is served in elegant dining room (also open for lunch & English
Tea from May-Thanksgiving). ⤳CC

Bounds, Jocelyn & George (Manse Lane Bed & Breakfast) ☎ (613) 382-8642
465 Stone St. South, Gananoque, ON   K7G 2A7

From Hwy 401, take Exit 645 and go south to traffic lights. Then straight ahead for 4.5 blocks.
$48S $53-85D $105F $15Child   ► 8A,1Ch

🍽 Full   🏠 Res., hist., Century home, pool, quiet   ■4(upst)
⊨ 2T,2Q,1D,cot   ⊿1Sh.w.g., 2ensuite   ★ F,TV, sinks in guest
rooms, indoor bike storage, Air (window units), parking, swimming
pool   ♿ No smoking, no pets, children min. age 6   ⌇ some
French
🏃 1000 Islands boat tour & playhouse, Gananoque Museum, Wild
Kingdom Zoo, St.Lawrence River, marina, excellent dining, shops
🚗 Old Fort Henry, bicycle paths, Fort Wellington, Kingston
📢 125 year-old brick Victorian home with safe, relaxed atmosphere, warm hospitality in popular
vacation area. Hosts can provide theatre reservation/Boat Line tickets.Visa,MC,Amex ✓B&B

MacIntyre, Douglas & Linda (Seasons B&B Inn)   ☎ & Fax (613) 382-3822, 1-888-382-7122
95 King St.West, Gananoque, ON   K7G 2G2   E-mail: seasons@gananoque.com

From Hwy 401 take Exit 645 and Hwy 32 south to Hwy 2 (King St). Turn right, proceed across
bridge, then sharp right (still on Hwy 2) to B&B.

$60-145D $15Add.person   ► 12
🍽 Full, homebaked   ■ Downtown, res., hist., 3-storey, view
from guest rooms, porch, quiet ■6D(upstairs) ⊨2T,2Q,3K,1S
⊿4Private, 2sh.w.g.   ★ Ceiling fans, private entrance, off-street
parking, guest quarters are separate   ♿ No smoking, no pets,
children min. age 12
🏃 1000 Island Cruises, 1000 Island Playhouse, cycling, boating,
sailing, antiquing, ice fishing, museum, summer & winter festivals
🚗 Upper Canada Village, Fort Henry, Queen's University, Skydeck Tower, scenic drives
📢 Classic Turn-of-the-Century mansion complete with all the ambience of the period yet
comfortably appointed. The house boasts a grand entrance and staircase, rich wood panelling,
bevelled/stained glass and details found only in the finest homes of the era. Enjoy the cozy library
on the second floor the twin living rooms one of which has a grand piano. Congenial host may be
persuaded to play a selection on the piano for guests' pleasure. Cruise & theatre packages can be
obtained. Corporate/off-season & senior rates available. There is a resident cat, Visa,MC,Amex
✓CC

Georgetown   *(west of Toronto; se also Brampton, Acton, Rockwood, Cheltenham)*

Singleton, Ruth & Wayne (Victorian Rose Bed & Breakfast)   ☎ (905) 702-0166
34 Cindebarke Terrace, Georgetown, ON   L7G 4S5   E-mail: wayne@stn.com

From Hwy 401 take Trafalgar Rd north to Maple St in Georgetown. Turn right, then right on 8th
Line, right again on Cindebarke Terrace.

$45S $50-55D $75F   🍽 Meals   ► 4A,2Ch
🍽 Full   🏠 Res., village, 2-storey, acreage, view, river at back,
porch, deck, quiet   ■ 2D(upstairs)   ⊨ 1D,1Q   ⊿ 1Sh.w.g.
★ Air,, off-street parking   ♿ No smoking, no pets
🏃 Golf Course, hiking trails, trout stream
🚗 Scenic little hamlets, Int. Airport, Toronto, Lake Ontario
📢 Comfortable home decorated with traditional & carefully
blended Victorian-style accents. The house backs onto a meadow and bush area with a stream that
brings with it a feeling of peace and quietness. Relax in the large spa under the stars. Congenial
hosts enjoy helping guests with itineraries for theatre & events in southern Ontario. ✓B&B

Goderich

(on Lake Huron west of Toronto; see also Bayfield, Blyth)

Beyerlein, Kathi (Kathi's Guest House)　　　　　　☎ (519) 524-8587
RR4, Goderich, ON　N7A 3Y1

From Hwy 8, take Hwy 1 to Benmiller & Huron Rd31 for 1.5km to B&B on left past Benmiller Inn.
$50S　$60D　$5Child(free under age 2)　(Special longer stay rates)　　　► 4A,2Ch

🍽 Full　🏠Farm, separate guest house, patio, quiet
■2D(mainlevel)　⊨2Q,1R,crib　🚗2nsuite　★KF,separate
entrance, small guest veranda　🖐No pets　〰German
🧍 Village of Benmiller, Benmiller Inn & gift shop
🚙 Lake Huron & beaches, Goderich, Blyth Summer Theatre
👅 Separate and self-contained cottage on working farm situated
in beautiful rolling hill area. Suitable especially for families or a
group of four. Enjoy breakfast in guest house. ✔B&B

Darby, Kathryn (Colborne Bed & Breakfast)　　☎ (519) 524-7400, Fax (519) 524-4943
72 Colborne St., Goderich, ON　N7A 2V9　　　　　　　　　　　　　　1-800-390-4612

From the highway follow signs to downtown and look for Colborne St (between North & West Sts.)
$60-90D　🍽 Meals　　　　　　　　　► 8

🍽 Full, homebaked　🏠 Downtown, 3-storey, view, porch,
quiet　■ 4D (upstairs)　⊨ 2T,1D,2K　🚗 4Ensuite (2 with
whirlpool bath)　★F in some guest rooms,TV/VCR in guest
parlour, guest bikes & safe overnight storage　🖐No smoking, no
pets　〰French
🧍 Historic Town-Square with fine restaurants, museums and
shops, sandy beaches, golfing, historic homes
🚙 Blyth, Stratford, Grand Bend
👅 Large, well maintained turn-of-the-Century home (former Manse), situated on a quiet street
in pretty little town on Lake Huron. Enjoy the friendly hospitality, relax on the sunporch or explore
the town on foot or bicycle. Breakfast is served in the guest breakfast room. ✔B&B

Strote, Argelyn (Twin Porches)　　　　　　　　☎ (519) 524-5505
55 Nelson St.E, Goderich, Ontario　N7A 1R7

From the interesection of Hwys 8/21, go north 5 blocks to Nelson St (1st house west off Hwy 21).
$40S　$50D　$10Child (ages 5-12)　　　　　► 6A,1Ch

🗓 May-Oct.　🍽 Choice, homebaked　🏠 Downtown, res., hist.,
patio, quiet　■ 3D (upstairs)　⊨1D,2Q,1R　🚗 1Sh.w.g.
★Air,F,TV, guest lounge and piano, host quarters are separate,
in-house collectibles (for sale), street parking　🖐No smoking,
children minimun age 5
🧍 Tourist Bureau across street, Lake Huron beach and Harbour,
golfing, tennis, lawn bowling, horse races, public swimming pool
🚙 Blyth Theatre, Huron Country Playhouse, Benmiller, Stratford Festival
👅 Congenial hosts in gracefully refurbished Victorian home with antique furnishings and
beautiful landscaped gardens located in the heart of Goderich. Relax on one of the small porches
after a busy day of travelling. ✔CC

Tanguay, Kathy & Al (Maison Tanguay)　　　　　　　　☎ (519) 524-1930
46 Nelson St.W, Goderich, ON　N7A 2M3

From Stratford, take Hwy 8 to end (Goderich). Turn right on Hwy 21 and drive 5 blocks north to
Nelson St. Turn left 2 blocks to house on right.

$55(and up)　🍽 Meals　(Reservations recommended)　　▶ 6A
🛏 Full　🏠 Downtown, res.,quiet, large front veranda, deck (off
one guest room)　■ 3D (upstairs)　⊨2T,1D,1Q　⟋1Sh.w.g.,
1sh.w.h.　★F,TV,LF,library of videos & games & books,parking
🖐No pets, smoking outdoors　〰French
🏃 Unique Town Square, downtown, shopping, fine restaurants,
Lake Huron beaches and harbour, golfing, tennis, museums, x-c
skiing/biking trails (complimentary bikes available)
🚐 Stratford Festival, Grand Bend, Huron Country Playhouse, Blyth Theatre, Bayfield
🚩 Elegant, turn-of-the-Century Victorian home extensively renovated, tastefully decorated on a
quiet tree-lined street. Relax on the large veranda and enjoy small-town living. Well travelled hosts
delight in exchanging travel experiences with guests. Business travellers welcome. There is a
Maltese dog named "Codey" in residence. Gift certificates & special packages available. 〜 FOBBA

Gorrie　　　　　　　　　　　　　　*(east of Goderich; see also Clifford, Mildmay, Blyth)*

Bott, Larry & Shirley (Walk-A-Bott Creek B&B)　　　　☎ (519) 335-3234
RR1, Gorrie, ON　N0G 1X0

Phone for directions.
$40S　$50D　$5Child　$60F　🍽 Meals　　　　　▶ 8
🛏 Full　🏠 Farm, 2-storey, view from guest rooms, riverfront,
porch, quiet　■ 4D(upstairs)　⊨ 4D　⟋ 1Sh.w.h, plus
separate shower for guests)　★F,TV, paddle boat & canoe for
guests　🖐No smoking
🏃 Playground, walks on riverbank, canoeing, paddleboating
🚐 Kitchener, Goderich & Lake Huron beaches, Elora, Blyth Theatre
🚩 90-year old farm house situated on a hill overlooking the winding Maitland River. Relax under
the shade trees or in the gazebo and enjoy the tranquil scenery and wildlife. Savour meals in a
country-style atmosphere. There are also cozy gingerbread cabins. 〜B&B

Gravenhurst　　　　　　　　　　　　　*(north Orillia; see also Bracebridge)*

Bassett, Jim & Catherine (Breakfast at Tiffany)　　　☎ (705) 687-8343
210 Tiffany Trail, Gravenhurst, ON　P1P 1A6

Exit off Hwy 11 north into Gravenhurst and follow Bethune Dr. Turn left on Winewood, right on
Muskoka Beach Rd, left on Evans Ave, then right on Tiffany Trail.

$60S/D　　　　　　　　　　　　　▶ 6
🍳 July & Aug only　🛏 Full　🏠 Sub, 2-storey, swimming pool,
porch, deck, quiet　■ 3(upstairs)　⊨ 2T,1D,1Q　⟋1Sh.w.g.,
1ensuite,(whirlpool)　★ Air, guest sitting room, guest quarters
are separate, off-street parking　🖐 No smoking, no pets, children
min. age 13　〰 Spanish, French
🚐 Golfing, Muskoka Beach, Gull Lake Park, Bethune Memorial
House, Opera House, theatre, Segwun boat cruises, local artist &
antique shops, Huntsville scenic drives, summer sports
🚩 New home reflecting old-fashioned elegance with many antiques and wicker furniture,
surrounded by large private treed lot in a peaceful neighbourhood. Relax inside, on the front porch
or on the back deck, steps from the heated pool. There are twin daughters in the hosts family who
are active partners in the hospitality venture. All enjoy helping people and sharing information of
what to see/do in popular Muskoka Recreation Area. 〜B&B

Grimsby

(south-east of Hamilton; see also Beamsville, Vineland, St.Catharines)

Zimmerman, Roy & Victoria (Doran House B&B)   ☎ (905) 945-9882
470 Main St West, Grimsby, ON L3M 1T3

From QEW Niagara take Casablanca Exit, turn north (away from lake) to Regional Rd 81 (Main St.W.). Turn right for 1 km and look for house on right.

$75S $85D $20Child   ► 6A,2Ch
Cont.   Rural, res., hist, stone construction, 2acres, view of Niagara Escarpment from some guest rooms, swimming pool, patio, porch, deck, quiet ■ 4 (upstairs) 2S,2T,1D,1Q
1Sh.w.g., 1ensuite ★ F,TV,LF,off-street parking, large guest parlour, host quarters are separate ⑭No pets, designated smoking area ᴡᴡsome French
⚡ Bruce Trail, Stoney Ridge Winery
🚗 N.Falls, NOTL, wineries, Welland Canal, Hamilton, Royal Bot.Gardens, Niagara Escarpment
🚐 Historic home(ca1812 used as a hospital in wartime), furnished with antiques, artistic touches and elegant decor, on small acreage with many fruit trees and private water garden. On a warm evening enjoy a glass of Niagara wine on the floodlit pavillion by the pool. Book entire floor (exclusive use for one couple only), a favourite of newlyweds and anniversary couples. There is a friendly Springer Spaniel called "Reginald". ⟋B&B

Guelph

(west of Toronto; see also Kitchener, Rockwood, Cambridge)

Edwards, Jack & Lyn (Willow Manor)   ☎ (519) 763-3574, Fax (519) 763-4531
408 Willow Rd., Guelph, ON N1H 6S5

From Hwy 401, take Hwy 6 north for 13 km into town to Willow Rd. Turn left to 2nd house on left.

$85S/D   ► 8A
Cont. (Full on weekends)   Res., hist., acreage, view from large guest rooms, patio, swimming pool, quiet ■ 4D(main & upper level) 1D,2K,1Q 4ensuite with jacussi ★3F,TV in guest room, guest parlour, guest terry robes, separate entrance, off-street parking, host quarters are separate ⑭No smoking, no pets, no children
⚡ Stroll through the lush grounds framed in majestic pines, John McCrae House, MacDonald Stewart Art Gallery, downtown Guelph, shopping mall, restaurants
🚗 Elora Gorge and Mill Street, Kitchener Farmers Market, St. Jacobs, Toronto, Stratford, Elmira
🚐 1860 Georgian-style stone manor house set on 2 acres of lawns and flower gardens and located in charming 150-year old University town in the middle of southwestern Ontario. Elegant decor and inviting furnishings guarantee a pampered, relaxing stay.Visa ⟋CC

Garrett, John R. (Esperanza Farms B&B)   ☎ (519)763-6385,Fax(519)837-2211
4272 Watson Rd., Puslinch, ON N0B 2J0   E-mail: john.garrett@sympatico.ca, 1-800-504-2638

Phone for directions (map will be mailed/faxed upon reservation).
$45S $60D $85Ste 🍽 Meals   ► 6
Full   2-storey, stone house, acreage, view from guest rooms, deck with suite, quiet ■ 1D,1Ste(upstairs) 1D,2Q
1Sh.w.g., 1shw.h., 1ensuite, whirlpool in suite ★Air,LF,KF in suite, slippers & dressing gowns provided, guest sitting area, sep. entrance ⑭ No smoking, no pets, children min. age 12
ᴡᴡSome Spanish & French
⚡ Halton Region Conservation Area across road, walking, x-c skiing
🚗 Aberfoyle Antique Market, Guelph U., Elora, St.Jacobs, antique country
🚐 1872 Stone house lovingly renovated and surrounded by large farm. Enjoy the relaxed peaceful country atmosphere and generous breakfasts served in separate guest breakfast room. Watch the ducks on pond in front of house. Space may be available in the barn - for horses & pets. Hosts will arrange rental car & airport pickup with advance notice. Reg.Massage Therapist available. ⟋B&B

Haliburton
(west of Bancroft; see also Minden)

Cleeland, Bonnie & Ken (Sunnyside Bed & Breakfast) ☎ (705) 457-9173
Box 235, Sunnyside St., Haliburton, ON K0M 1S0

Take Hwy 35 or 11 north to Hwy 118 and east into Haliburton Village. Located on Sunnyside St &

Maple Ave (Hwy 118), first house on left.
$50-60S/D $10Add.person   ►6
🐾 Full, homebaked   🏠 Village, 2-storey, older, small acreage,
view, patio, quiet ■3D(upst) ◄3D ◢1Sh.w.g. ★F,TV,
parking ⓦ No smoking, no pets
🕇 Haliburton Village, public park, beach & boardwalk on Head
Lake, Haliburton School of Fine Arts, Sir Sam's x/c & alpine ski
resort, Lake ice skating, Rails End Gallery, shops, great dining
🚗 Bracebridge, Buckhorn Gallery on the Lake, Santa's Village, Algonquin Prov. Park
🐾 Comfortable, renovated farm house (ca 1905) located in popular Haliburton Highlands. Sit on
the front porch and enjoy the quiet sounds of being away from the city. Take the opportunity and
see Haliburton and its area from a more casual perspective. Perfect spot for people attending Sir
Sandford Fleming College. There is a small friendly resident dog.✓B&B

Hart, Barry and Heather Alloway (All-HART B & B) ☎ & Fax (705) 457-5272
RR2, South Kashagawigamog Rd., Haliburton, ON K0M 1S0

Take Hwy 35 to Minden and continue on Hwy 121 northeast to Haliburton. Just before entering
village, pass anitque locomotive & RCAF plane on display, then take next right (County Rd1) and
proceed 3km to County Rd18. Turn right and go 2km to house across from golf course.

$95S/D $25Add.person   ►6-9A
🐾 Cont.   🏠 Rural, hist., lakefront   ■ 3Ste(main and upper
floor) ◄ 2T(or 1K),1Q,1K,3R ◢ 3Ensuite (jacuzzi in one
suite) ★ Air,F, separate entrance, parking ⓦ No smoking,
no pets, no children ⌇French
🚗 Sports for all seasons, year-around activities in Haliburton,
excellent biking & hiking trails, School of Fine Arts
🐾 Unique guest quarters are an addition to the beautifully
restored original stone house landmark estate situated on the shore of Lake Kashagawigamog.
Enjoy the beach or relax in private guest lounge with Vermont fireplace. Host is an avid
bird-watcher and will direct guests to the "hot spots". A skier's delight in winter.✓B&B

Hamilton
(s/w of Toronto; see also Burlington, Waterdown, Dundas, Ancaster, Grimsby)

Hajas, Alex & Marvel (Westmount House B&B) ☎ (905) 388-2250
18 Eldorado Ct., Hamilton, ON L9C 2P9

From Hwy 403 exit at Mohawk Rd East and travel to Millbank Place (7lights). Turn right to

Lynbrook Dr, left to Montcalm and right to Eldorado.
$45S $55D   (Children welcome)   ►4
🐾 Full, homebaked   🏠 Res., 4-level-split, view, patio, porch
■3D(upstairs) ◄2T,2D ◢Sh.w.g. ★Air,TV,LF,off-street
parking ⓦNo smoking,no pets ⌇ Hungarian
🕇 Small Mall, churches, historic restored school museum
🚗 Beautiful views from Hamilton Escarpment (day or night),
downtown, McMaster U & Med Centre, hist Dundurn Castle
🐾 Charming and friendly home, centrally located on beautiful Hamilton Mountain. Congenial
hosts enjoy welcoming guests in their home and are happy to help with plans to see nearby
attractions. Relax in the lovely garden and patio after a day of travelling & sightseeing. Breakfast is
served in the bright/relaxing dining room. Pick-up from bus or train can be arranged. ✓B&B

Kennedy, Diana and Ron (Haddo House)　　　　　☎ (905) 524-0071
107 Aberdeen Ave., Hamilton, Ontario　L8P 2P1

From Hwy 403, take Aberdeen Exit and continue to flashing yellow light at Bay St South. Look for

yellow brick house on corner.
$75-105S/D　　　　　　　　　　　　　► 6
🍴 Choice　🏠 Downtown, res., hist., 3-storey large front porch,
quiet　■2D (2nd & 3rd floor)　⊨1D,1Q or 2T　🛋2Private
★TV,F, room air-conditioner, sparking　🚭No pets, restricted
smoking, no children
🏃 Downtown Hamilton, shopping, restaurants, Art Gallery,
Hamilton Place/Convention Centre, Copps Coliseum
🚗 McMaster University and Hospital, Dundurn Castle
🗯 Spacious turn-of-the-Century home with elegant eclectic decorlocated in one of the most
distinctive areas of the city. Silver service breakfast is served in formal dining room or large country
kitchen. Guest may relax in the cosy library or on the large front porch. Special wedding night
packages available. ✔B&B

Lehnert, Sharon (Inchbury Street Bed & Breakfast)　　☎(905)522-3520,Fax(905)522-5216
87 Inchbury Street,Hamilton,ON L8R 3B7　　　　E-mail: slehnert@networx.on.ca, 1-800-792-8765

From east on Hwy 403, exit at York Blvd, left at Rolph Gate (1st street past Dundurn traffic light),
right on Kinnel, left on Inchbury. From west on Hwy 403 go east on Aberdeen, north on Locke,
right on York and left on Inchbury.

$50S　$65D　$15Add.person　　　　　　► 4A,2Ch
🍴 Full, homebaked　🏠 Downtown, 2-storey, hist., quiet　■2D(upstairs)
⊨2D,1cot　🛋 1Sh.w.g.　★ Air,LF,TV in guest lounge, street parking
🚭 Smoking outside　〰 German, French
🏃 Historic Dundurn Castle and waterfront park, Copps Coliseum, Hamilton
Place, Convention Centre, downtown shopping, Art Gallery, restaurants
🚗 McMaster University, Royal Botanical Gardens, NOTL, Niagara Falls
🗯 Late 19th Century home decorated with distinctive family art and
English Garden, situated in a little enclave beside Dundurn Castle. Breakfast
is served in the large dining room. Hostess is a runner, sailor, skier and likes
to show guests the activities places in the area. Visa,MC ✔B&B

May, Gary & Anne (Galivants Rest B&B)　　　　　☎ (905) 575-5095
121 Dragoon Dr., Hamilton, ON　L9B 2C9

From Hwy 403 take Mohawk Rd Exit. At first stop light travel straight to Stone Church Rd. Turn
right on Upper Wellington. Turn left at Dragoon Dr. From Hwy 53 (Rymal Rd) turn on Upper

Wellington to Dragoon Dr.
$45S·　$55D　　　　　　　　　　　► 4A
🍴Full,homebaked　🏠Res.,2-storey,deck,quiet　■2(upstairs)
⊨1D,1Q,1R　🛋1Sh.w.g.　★Air,TV,F,LF, off-street parking
🚭No smoking, no pets, not suitable for children
🏃 Shopping, restaurant, bus routes
🚗 Hospitals, lookouts with spect.views of the city, downtown
McMaster U, Copps Coliseum, Mount Hope Airport, Bruce Trail
🗯 Large home located in the heart of Hamilton's mountain or upper city. Hosts enjoy travel,
birdwatching and theatre. ✔B&B

Mordue, Bruce and Betty (East Mountain B&B)   ☎ (905) 383-9517
61 East 43 St., Hamilton,ON   L8T 3B7

From Hwy 403 take Mohawk Road East Exit and stay to left for LINC (Lincoln Alexander Parkway).

Take Upper Gage Exit, go left and 3 km to end. Turn right on Concession St and right on East 43rd St to house on left.
$45S $55D   ⬛ Meals   ▶ 4
✠ Not July & Aug.   ⬛ Full, homebaked   🏠 Res., bungalow, quiet   ⬛1S,1D (main level)   ⊨1Q,2T   ⬛2Sh.w.h.   ★TV
🖐No smoking, no pets
🚶 Henderson General Hospital and Cancer Clinic, Mountain Brow, Bruce Trail, city bus routes

🚗 Convention Center, Copps Coliseum, Hamilton General, St.Joseph's Hospital, Dundurn Castle
🐾 Warm and friendly country-style atmosphere in cozy, quiet ranch-style home located one block from Mountain Brow, which offers a panoramic view of the city and Niagara escarpment.✍B&B

Ross, Jim & Barb (Bay South B&B)   ☎ (905) 528-1959, Fax (905) 528-8894
279 Bay St.S, Hamilton, ON   L8P 3J5

From Hwy 403 take Aberdeen Exit and proceed to Bay St. Turn left.
$45S $55D $15Child   ▶ 5
⬛ Full   🏠 Downtown, hist., patio, porch, deck   ⬛ 2(upstairs)
⊨1S,2T,1Q   ⬛ 1Sh.w.g.   ★ F,KF,LF,TV in guest rooms, air-conditioners, off-street parking   🖐 No smoking
🚶 Hamilton Place, Copps Coliseum, Dundurn Castle, shopping
🚗 McMaster U, Lakes Ontario/Erie shorelines, Niagara Falls, Toronto
🐾 Large home situated in old neighborhood. Professional hosts have excellent knowledge of local architecture and attractions. Breakfast is served in special guest breakfast room. There is a dog and a cat. Visa ✍B&B

Harrowsmith   *(north of Kingston; see also Sydenham, Inverary)*

Huntly, Roy & Muriel (Harrowsmith Farm B&B)   ☎ (613) 376-6056
3565 Stagecoach Rd., Harrowsmith, ON   K0H 1V0

From Hwy 401 take Hwy 38 (Exit 611) and proceed north towards Harrowsmith. Turn right at Murton Rd and right onto Forest Rd. At T-jct turn left and look for sign at first house on left.

$45S $55D $95F   ⬛ Meals   ▶ 4A,2Ch
⬛ Full, homebaked   🏠 Rural, hist., acreage, view from guest rooms, patio, quiet   ⬛ 3D(upstairs)   ⊨ 2S,1D,1Q,cot
⬛1Sh.w.g., 1sh.w.h.   ★ LF,F,TV, fans in guest rooms, off-street parking   🖐 No smoking
🚶 16 acres of woods and fields, access to the Rideau Trail,
🚗 Kingston, Frontenac Park, Sydenham/Loughborough Lakes
🐾 Warm welcome in Century home, surrounded by picturesque countryside. After a busy day of sight-seeing, hiking or x-c skiing enjoy the cozy warmth of the wood stove or soak in the whirlpool tub. English-style breakfast is served in guest breakfast room. There is a cat in residence.

Hastings

(east of Peterborough; see also Marmora)

Beamish, Sam & Jacqueline (Spring Valley Farm & B&B) ☎ (705) 696-2878
RR1, Hastings, ON K0L 1Y0

Take Hwy 401 east to Cobourg and take Hwy 45 (Exit 474) north to 11th line of Percy (app.40km).

$35S $50-60D $15child/Add.person   📷 Meals   ► 6
🍴 Full, homebaked   🏠 Farm (200 acres), rural, 2-storey, hist.,
view from guest rooms, patio, deck, quiet, pond   ■3D(upstairs)
⊢2T,1D,1Q,cot   ⊿ Sh.w.g.   ★ F,TV,ceiling fans, private entr,
playhouse for children   ⊕ Designated smoking area, no pets
🧍 Walks around pond area and in surrounding woods, back woods
picnics, tenting by the pond where (wildlife abundant), x-c skiing
🚗 Village of Hastings, fishing/boating on Trent River, golfing,
sugar bush, Lang Pioneer Village, Petroglyphs, museum, Peterborough Lift Locks
🔫 Warm welcome on sixth Generation farm (ca 1867). A delicious breakfast is cooked on Findlay
Coal Cookstove. Guests can relax in the newly added sunroom or by the fieldstone fireplace. Enjoy a
singsong around the piano. Children welcome (playhouse fully equipped with utensils & dress-up
clothes). There are 2 cats and a Golden Retriever called "Jasper" who love outside attention.

Hearst

(northern Ontario - west of Timmins; see also Kapuskasing)

Levesque, Rita (Northwinds Bed & Breakfast) ☎ (705) 362-4531
Box 2253, Lac Ste-Thérèse, Hearst, ON P0L 1N0

$55S $70D $10Child (free under age 12) $15Add.person   📷 Meals   ► 8A,3Ch
From TCH11 in Hearst take Hwy 583N for 12 km to Lac St-Thérèse.

🍴 Full,homebaked   🏠 Rural, res., ranch-style, view, 7 acres,
patio, lakeside, quiet, isolated   ■ 1D,2F   ⊿ 1S,2Q,1K,2R,
crib   ⊿ 1Sh.w.g., 1ensuite   ★ F,TV, facilities for the disabled,
off-street parking   ⊕ Designated smoking areas   ⌁ French
🧍 Private dock for swimming, canoeing, pedal boating, fishing,
snowshoeing, snowmobiling
🚗 Golf course, X-c Ski Club, boat rentals, marina
🔫 Architecturally designed lakeside home with huge octagonal
living area with fireplace and view onto the lake and walkout to large patio. Enjoy the breathtaking
Northern sunsets. Access to main snowmobile trails on lake below. Dock is also suitable for
aircrafts. Canoe & pedal boat at guests' disposal. There is a cat in residence.

Hillsburgh

(s/of Orangeville; see also Erin, Cheltenham)

Graham, Ken and Ann (Coningsby Brae) ☎ (519) 855-4685
RR1, Hillsburgh, ON N0B 1Z0

From Hwy 401 take Exit 328 and follow Trafalgar Rd. north (Halton Rd 3) to Hwy 24. Proceed 4 km
north on County Rd 24. Turn left on Erin Township SR 17 then 2km to No 9230 on right

$40S $50D   📷 Meals   ► 6
🍴 Full, homebaked   🏠 Rural, bungalow, acreage, view, quiet,
veranda   ■ 3D(main floor)   ⊢ 3D   ⊿1Sh.w.g., 1ensuite
★Air,TV,F,LF, parking, wheel-chair access   ⊕Restricted
smoking, no pets
🚗 Golf course, art galleries, hiking, cycling, fine country dining,
Forks-of-Credit Provincial Park and Conservation areas, arts and
craft and antique shops, Bruce Trail hiking, Caledon Ski Club
🔫 Enjoy the finest country hospitality and the spectacular view of the "Hills of Erin".CCards

Hillsdale
(north of Barrie; see also Elmvale, Phelpston)

O'Kane, Carol & Mike (O'Kane's Bed & Breakfast)   ☎ (705) 835-3554
General Delivery, Hillsdale, ON L0L 1V0

From Toronto, take Hwy 400 north to 400 Extension (to Sudbury/Parry Sound) and continue to Exit 121. Drive north on Hwy 93 for 3 km to Hillsdale and look for B&B on right at Albert St.

$35S $50D $5Child   🍽 Meals   ▶7
🛏 Full, homebaked   🏠 Village, 2-storey, hist., wrap-around porch, patio ■3D(upstairs & ground level) ⊢2T,1Q,1K,1P
🚗1Sh.w.g., 1sh.w.h.   ★F,TV, off-street parking ⚘Designated smoking area ∽Portuguese, Spanish
🏃 Antique and gift shops, pottery, honey factory
🚗 Midland, Penetanguishene Summer Theatre, Barrie, Horseshoe Valley & Mt.St.Louis downhill skiing, Hardwood Hills
📢 125-year old cottage-style home renovated with modern comforts and a large country kitchen, surrounded by picturesque farm and orchard lands and located midway between Barrie and Midland. Hosts have lived many years in Central & South America and are interested in people and their journey in life. ∽B&B

Hope Bay
(north of Wiarton; see also Red Bay, Lion's Head)

Strang, Bill & Nancy (Cedarholme B&B)   ☎ & Fax (519) 534-3705
Hope Bay, RR6, Wiarton, ON N0H 2T0

On Hwy 6 north of Wiarton, take County Rd 9 for 17 km. Turn right (east) and proceed 1 km.
$40S $45-50D $5Add.person   🍽 Meals   ▶6
🛏 Full, homebaked   🏠 Rural, 3-storey, acreage, view from guest rooms, patio,
quiet ■1S,1D,1F,1Ste(upstairs) ⊢2T,2D,1Q 🚗2Sh.w.g.,1ensuite ★F,TV, separate entrance, library, games, parking ⚘ No smoking ∽some French
🏃 Bruce Trail hiking, Hope Bay & sandy beach, volleyball/badminton court, Tea Room (May-Oct)
🚗 Tobermory, ferry to Manitoulin I., scenic caves, Sauble Beach
📢 Congenial hosts in spacious brick home on beautiful Hope Bay along the Niagara Escarpment. Ideal place to stop over on the way to catch the Chi-Cheemaun Ferry from Tobermory or on a Bruce Trail hike. There are also 4 winterized cottages available for families and pets. ∽B&B

Huntsville
(north of Orillia; see also Port Sydney, Baysville)

Barter, Rod & Ginny (The Carriage House B&B)   ☎ (705) 789-9434, Fax (705) 789-3222
22 Main St. West, Box 2245, Huntsville, ON P1H 2C3

From Hwy 11 north exit at Muskoka Rd 3 and travel towards town center. Look for house on left.
$50-65S– $65-75D $5Child(over age 10) $125F $10Add.person   ▶ 6A,4Ch

🛏 Full, Homebaked   🏠 Downtown, 3-storey, older, view from guest rooms, swimming pool, patio ■3D(upstairs) ⊢2T,1Q,2K, 2cots 🚗1Sh.w.g., 1ensuite ★ F,separate entrance, off-street parking, guest family room, guest quarters are separate, sauna
⚘No smoking, pets welcome (by prior arrangement)
🏃 Shopping, fine dining, Muskoka Pioneer Village, Recreation Centre, library, town waterfront, Mini Putt, boat tours
🚗 Golfing, tennis, downhill & x-c skiing, Algonquin & Arrowhead parks, hiking, canoeing, mountain biking, boating
📢 Beautiful 1920's Georgian-style home with spacious accommodation, indoor swimming pool and sauna near Huntsville's picturesque town centre. Enjoy a bayview breakfast before starting a busy day of outdoor activities or sightseeing. There is a dog and a cat in residence. Visa ∽CC

Carnochan, Pam & Jamie Honderich (Morgan House B&B & Wool Works)   ☎ (705) 789-1727
83 Morgans Rd., Huntsville, ON   P1H 1A2

Located east of Hwy 11 off Hwy 60, 8km east of Huntsville.
$40S $55D $10Child $20Add.person   ▶ 6A,2Ch
🍲 Full, homebaked   🏠 Rural, 2-storey, hist., acreage, view from guest
rooms, porch, quiet, pond   ■ 3D(upstairs)   ⊨ 2T,1D,1Q,1P
🚼1Sh.w.g.   ★ F,TV,private entrance, guest quarters are separate,
off-street parking   Ⓦ Designated smoking area, children welcome
🏃 Walk & ski trails, 77 acres of forests, meadows and ponds to explore
🚐 Algonquin Park, Pioneer Village, Arrowhead Park, town of Huntsville,
many local lakes, nordic & alpine skiing, excellent dining, fishing, golfing
🏠 Historic stone house (original Muskoka-style) filled with old country
charm, fieldstone fireplace & antiques. Enjoy the friendly farm atmosphere
and the resident sheep. The wool studio features wool products made from own sheep, including
handmade felt and homespun wool. The upstairs gallery displays local artists' works for sale. There
is an outside dog. ✔B&B

Cochran, Andy & Martha Mary (The Gingerbread B&B)   ☎ (705) 789-4115
882 Riverlea Rd., Huntsville, ON   P1H 1X5   Fax (705) 789-1272

From Hwy 11 turn onto Muskoka Rd 3 into Hunstville. Proceed through town and turn south onto
Brunel Rd (Muskoka Rd10). Continue 2.7km to N.Mary Lake Rd. Turn right for 2.8km (see signs).
$40S $50-75D $10Child/Add.person   🍴 Meals(lunch)   ▶8

🍲 Full   🏠 Rural, waterfront, 2-storey, view, porch, deck, quiet,
secluded   ■ 3D,1F(upstairs)   ⊨ 2T,2D,1Q,cot   🚼 1Ensuite,
1sh.w.g.   ★TV, canoe for guests   Ⓦ Smoking outside or in
garage, inquire about pets
🏃 Canoeing, driving range, trails (hiking, x-c skiing,
snowmobiling), swimming, boating, fishing, quiet road biking
🚐 Downtown, casual & fine dining on waterfront patios, shops,
Algonquin National Park, Arrowhead Prov.Park, Deerhurst Golf
Course, riding stables, Hidden Valley Alpine Ski Resort, Muskoka Lakes, boat tours
🏠 Charming rural family home with a beautiful view in all seasons, situated on the sandy shore
of the Muskoka River. Breakfast is served in the sunny dining room or on the deck overlooking the
water. Watch the loons, moose, mink, beavers as they drink on the far river shore. A hearty soup or
packed lunch available for day trips. There are 2 cats in residence. Visa ✔B&B

Collier, Ron & Margaret (Road's End Bed & Breakfast)   ☎ (705) 635-2634
1348 Walker Lake Dr., Box 292, RR4, Huntsville, ON   P1H 2J6

From Hwys 11 & 60 turn right for 12km to County Rd 8 (Limberlost Rd), turn left & proceed 2.5km
to Walker Lake Dr.Turn left again, stay left to end of road (3.5km).

$40S $50-60D $15Add.person   ▶ 6
🍲 Full, homebaked   🏠 Rural, view from guest rooms, lakefront,
patio, screened porch, deck, quiet   ■1D,1Ste (main & ground
level)   ⊨ 2D,1P,crib   🚼 1Private, 1 sh.w.h.   ★ F,TV/VCR,
sep.entrance, picnic table, dock   Ⓦ Smoking outside, no pets
🏃 Swimming from sandy beach, bass/trout fishing, canoeing
🚐 Huntsville, Algonquin Park, Hidden Valley alpine skiing, Arrowhead Pk x-c skiing (Hwy 11)
🏠 Retired, ex-Torontonians, in beautiful, spacious self-built home on quiet spring fed lake (no
waterskiing,no jet skies). Enjoy a congenial, tranquil atmosphere. There is a dog & a cat. ✔B&B

208   ONTARIO

Rye, Robert & Dawn (Fairy Bay Guest House)   ☎ (705) 789-1492, Fax (705) 789-6922
228 Cookson Bay Cr., Huntsville, ON   P1H 1B2   E-mail: fairybay@muskoka.com, 1-888-813-1101

Located 7km east of jct of Hwys 11&60, off Deerhurst/Canal Rd.
$75-135S $95-150D $25Add.person (plus taxes)   ► 18A,6Ch
🍴 Full, homebaked   🏠 Rural, lakefront, 3-storey. acreage, view
from guest rooms, patio, porch deck, quiet, secluded   ■9
incl.1Ste(main/upper/lower levels) ⊨4T,6Q,1K,3P,foam-pads
⊨1Sh.w.g., 8ensuite   ★Air,KF,F, exercise room, tennis, sauna,
indiv.climate control, private entrance, guest quarters are
separate   Ⓦ Smoking outside, no pets

🜊 Beach, dock, boating, bicycling, fishing, hiking/nature trails, Hidden Valley Highlands ski area,
Grandview, Deerhurst Highland Golf course, trail & dog-sled riding, snowmobiling, fine dining, pub
🚌 Muskoka Pioneer Village, town of Huntsville, shopping, Algonquin Park, Santa's Village
☛ New custom-designed country home, furnished and decorated as a B&B for the discriminating
traveller, and located on a quiet Bay with access to 40km of waterways in the heart of Muskokas
historic recreation region. Relax in the comfortable guest lounge or upstairs library, enjoy the view
of Fairy Lake through large windows, make use of the on-site equipment, or watch the Northern
Lights from the trellised deck. Breakfast is served in guest breakfast room. Visa,MC ✔CC

Yagel, David & Vanessa (St.George's Inn B&B)   ☎ (705) 789-4447, (705) 789-4143
400 Rowanwood Rd., Huntsville, ON   P1H 2K8

Take Hwy 11 to Rowanwood Rd until the road splits. Stay left and proceed to 5th driveway on left.

For snowmobilers: right of Hill & Gully Trail No2.
$65S $95D $10Child $15Add.person   🍴 Meals   ► 7
🍴 Full, homebaked   🏠 Farm, hist., riverfront, view from guest
rooms, quiet, porch, deck   ■ 1S,3D(upstairs)   ⊨ 1S,3Q
⊨1Sh.w.h.   ★ TV,ceiling fans Ⓦ Smoking outside, no pets
🜊 Shadow River on property leading to Mary Lake, canoeing,
paddle boating, 200 acres to explore, hiking & walking on Hill &
Gully Trail No2, private airstrip with 2500 grass runway
🚌 Santa's Village, Hidden Valley Ski area, Deerhurst Golf Club, Algonquin Park
☛ Spacious Victorian brick farm home (ca 1885) filled with antiques. Enjoy the quiet Muskoka
country atmosphere. Breakfast is served in the sun-filled breakfast area. Ideal place for reunions,
weddings, photographers & artists. Safe, covered parking for snowmobilers. Visa ✔CC

Kapuskasing   *(northwest of Timmins; see also Hearst)*

Grzela, Marc & Miling (The Northern Oasis B&B & Specialty Suites)
62 Riverside Dr., Kapuskasing, ON   P5N 1A9   ☎ & Fax (705) 335-4818, 1-888-299-9494

From Hwy 11, turn on Riverside Dr. Or phone for directions.
$65S $75-95D   🍴 Meals   (plus tax)   ► 6
🍴 Full   🏠 Downtown, res., 2-storey, porch   ■ 3Ste
(upstairs)   ⊨ 3Q,1R   ⊨ 3Private (with double heartshaped red
whirlpool tubs)   ★ F,air conditioners, TV/robes/hair dryers in
guest rooms, off-street parking, guest quarters are separate
ⓌNo smoking, no pets   ⋙ French, Fillipino, Spanish
🜊 Downtown, bus tours, Festival of Lights, Ron Morel Museum,
Train Stn, Spruce Falls Paper Mill, shopping, riverpark, leisure walks
☛ Friendly Northern hospitality in historic house, (one of first houses built in town) recently
renovated, with river view and situated across from park. Semi-retired hosts have travelled
nationally & abroad and are happy to share experiences with guests and always give champagne
welcome. Breakfast is served in main dining room or in guest room, if requested. Honeymoon, Red
Carpet & Silver packages available. Free shuttle service from and to airport. Visa,MC,Amex

Kenora
(n/w of Thunder Bay near Manitoba border)

Janke, Betty and Emil (Heritage Place)   ☎ (807) 548-4380, 1-800-562-9861
Longbow Lake, Kenora, ON   P0X 1H0

Located on Longbow Lake Rd, off Hwy 17 (TransCanada) 15km east of Kenora. Look for sign.
$35S $45-50D $5Child(over age 6) $10Add.person   📷 Meals   (Tax extra)   ▶ 16

🍴Full,homebaked 🏠Lodge, acreage, pond, view, balcony, patio, quiet ▦8D,F(upst) ⊨ T,D,R,crib, cots 🛁4Private,4sh.w.g. ★Air,TV,F,LF, pool table, camping hook-ups,playground 🖐No smoking, no pets ᴡᴡGerman
🕴 Cross-country skiing, hiking
🚙 Kenora, Lake of the Woods, fishing, boating, Int. sailing regattas, hunting, Lake cruises (M.S.Kenora), US border (Min)
🐾 Home offers family atmosphere in attractive and prosperous pulp and paper town and major tourist center both to the wilderness country in the north, and to the lake activities to the south. Hosts also operate a campground (K.O.A.) onsite. Visa,MC

Sprague, Barbara & Curtis (The Kendall House B&B)   ☎ (807) 468-4645
127-5th Ave South, Kenora, ON   P9N 2A3

Phone for directions.
$60S $70D   ▶6A
🍴 Full, homebaked 🏠 Downtown, hist., 3-storey, patio, porch, quiet ▦ 3D(upstairs) ⊨ 2T,2D 🛁 2sh.w.g. ★ Off-street & street parking, guests occupy 2nd floor 🖐 No smoking, no pets, not suitable for children
🕴 Downtown, Lake of the Woods & Harbourfront, Shopping Mall, museum, M.S.Kenora boat dock (cruising)
🚙 Kenora Airport, Bus station, Rushing River Prov. Park
🐾 Restored 1893 hist. brick home decorated and furnished to the late 1800's on extra large treed lot. Teacher & artist hosts are knowledgeable about the local history and are interested in antiques, nature and photography. Breakfast is served in guest breakfast room. There is a resident cat.

St. Hilaire, André & Eveline (Cozy Cove Bed & Breakfast)   ☎ (807) 468-6061
415 Lakeview Dr., Kenora, ON   P9N 4H3

Located 200 m south of TCH at 2nd bridge west of downtown Kenora. Phone for directions.

$70S $75D   ▶ 4
🍴 Full, homebaked 🏠 In town, duplex, view from guest rooms, lakefront, patio, deck, quiet, large gazebo, secluded ▦2D(ground level) ⊨2Q 🛁2Ensuite ★ LF,TV & pool table in lounge, private entrance, guest quarters are separate 🖐 No smoking, no pets, not suitable for children ᴡᴡFrench
🕴 Boat dock, walks along lakeshore to town
🚙 Norman Dam, boat rental, fishing, Paper Mill & tours, golfing
🐾 Retired teacher couple in comfortable home self-built by family members, with large deck and beautiful landscaped grounds on Lake of the Woods. Entire floor exclusively for guests. ✓B&B

Keswick
(north of Toronto on Lake Simcoe; see also Pefferlaw)

Eryavec, Amalia & Ivan (Bed & Breakfast By-The-Lake)   ☎ (905) 476-3624,
321 Lake Dr. North, RR1, Keswick, ON   L4P 3C8   Fax (905) 476-9692

$40-50S $50-60D   🍴Meals   (Moderate weekly & midweek rates available)   ▶ 6A,2Ch
Hwy 404 ends at Davis Dr (Newmarket). Make a jog east to Woodbine,
proceed 20km north (Keswick business area). At the Esso Stn turn left
(west) onto Church St which runs into Lake Dr North. If lost, call collect.
🍲 Full, homebaked   🏠 Cottage country, 2-storey, acreage, view from
guest rooms, private lakefront, patio, deck, quiet   ■2D,1Ste(upstairs)
🛏2Q,1K,1bunk,crib, playpen   🛁1Sh.w.g., 1sh.w.h., 1ensuite, jacuzzi
★Air,F,LF,TV in guest rooms, guest lounge with fridge, host quarters are
separate, guest mountain bikes & canoes, off-street parking   🚭No
smoking, no pets, safe place for children   ↝Croatian,German,some Italian
🏃 Swimming, canoeing, golfing, tennis, restaurants, marinas, ice-fishing
🐾 Warm welcome in new spacious home by the water. "Toronto Riviera on the southern shores
of Lake Simcoe". From the west-view sundeck on the private lakefront, a boardwalk stretches out to
clear and sandy bottom water. Relax and enjoy the sunsets. Guest pick-up from Newmarket or
Keswick GO Bus available. ↙B&B

Kincardine
(on Lake Huron north of Goderich)

McKean, Janice (Glory B&B)   ☎ (519) 396-7518
376 Nelson St., Kincardine, ON   N2Z 1X7

Phone for directions.
$40S/D   (monthly rates available)   ▶ 6
🍲 Full, homebaked   🏠 Res, 2-storey, hist., porch, acreage, quiet
■2D,1Ste(upst)   🛏2S,1D,1Q,2P   🛁1Sh.w.g.   ★TV,KF,LF,
sep.entrance, guest bicycles, off-street pkg   ↝French
🚌 Blyth Summer Theatre
🏃 Lake Huron (sandy beaches, swimming, walking fishing),
downtown, historic homes, museum, lighthouse, golfing, harbour
(famous Sat/night March of Kincardine Scottish Pipe Band - July/Aug)
🐾 Very quiet and peaceful 130-year old home surrounded by huge trees, flower gardens and
streams. Hosts have travelled world-wide and enjoy welcoming visitors from near and far. Breakfast
is served in guest breakfast room and includes produce from the veggie garden and local farmers'
market. There is a cat "Grey Bruce" who likes to curl up on visitors' laps. ↙CC

Kingston
(see also Amherst Isle, Wolfe Ilse, Inverary, Sydenham, Gananoque)

Bahri, Ruth & Marcel (Casablanca B&B)   ☎ (613) 546-2011, Fax (613)546-8577
1245 Hwy Two East, Kingston, ON   K7L 4V1

$50S $70-90D $15Add.person   (child under age 12 free)   🍴 Meals   ▶ 8A,2Ch
From Hwy 401, take Exit 623 and proceed south on Hwy 15 to Hwy
2. Turn east 5km on right immediately after King-Pitt Rd.
🍲 Homebaked (buffet)   🏠 Rural, 2-storey, view from guest
rooms, acreage, quiet, deck, secluded   ■ 1Ste,2D (main & upper
level)   🛏 2T,1D,1Q,1R,1P   🛁 3Private,   ★ KF in suite,
ceiling fans, air-conditioners, separate entrance, off-street parking,
guest quarters are separate   🚭 No smoking, no pets
↝French, German, Spanish, Arabic
🏃 Riding stables, canoe launch, pioneer burial ground, country walks, children's playground
🚌 Fort Henry, Communications Museum, 1000 Islands and boat tours, beaches, shopping, dining
🐾 Unique Mediterranean-style home with spacious layout surrounded by quiet countryside. Well
travelled hosts enjoy welcoming guests from everywhere. Gourmet dinners and box lunches
available upon request. Host is professional Chef. CCards ↙CC

Bruns, Ernie & Cynthia (Collins Lake Bed & Breakfast)   ☎ (613) 353-1593
RR1, 3458 Buck Point Line, Inverary, ON   K0H 1X0

From Hwy 401 take Kingston Exit 617 & Division St north 10.5km. Turn right at Buck's Corners

onto Holmes Rd then 2.2 km to Buck Point Rd & 1.5km to B&B.
$55S $65D $10Child $15Add.person   ► 6A,2Ch
🍳 Cont., homebaked   🏠 Rural, log house, veranda, view,
lakefront, quiet   ■ 3F (upstairs)   ⊢⊣2T,2S,2Q   ⊿ 2Sh.w.g.
★F,TV, launching facilities, canoe/rowboat for guest use   🖑No
smoking, no pets, children min. age 5   ∼German
🏃 Fishing (Bass, Muskie) x-c skiing on lake, skating
🚗 Downtown Kingston, shops, restaurants, University, Ft Henry
🐾 Log house with the ambience of a 19th Century country home with a beautiful view, situated
on grounds gently sloping to the lake surrounded by mature trees. Relax, enjoy the congenial
hospitality, watch the loons, herons and other lakeshore inhabitants. Hostess makes old-fashioned
jointed Teddy Bears.

Campbell, Clare and Tom (Chart House)   ☎ (613) 546-9026
90 Yonge St., Kingston, ON   K7M 1E6

Located across Olympic Harbour. Phone for directions.
$55-65S $65-75D   (Reservations recommended)   ► 8
🍳Full, homebaked   🏠Downtown, hist., view, patio, lakefront, very
quiet   ■4D(upst)   ⊢⊣2D,2T,1Q,crib   ⊿1Sh.w.g.,2ensuite, running
water in each room   ★2F,TV in guest room, parking   ∼French
🏃 Kingston Portsmouth Olympic Harbour
🚗 Old Ft Henry, 1000 Islands, Prince Edward County
🐾 Warm welcome and friendly hospitality in completely
renovated historic 1848-built home, tastefully furnished with period pieces and a beautiful
English-style garden. Relax on the patio, where breakfast is served. Enjoy the beautiful view of the
harbour & watch the activities. ✒B&B

Dubras, Ann & Pat (Stevie) Weyman (Ann Option B&B)   ☎ (613) 531-8074
91 Carruthers Ave., Kingston, ON   K7L 1M3   Fax (613) 531-1821

Located in the center of town at corner of College & Carruthers.
$45S $55-70D   ► 8A
🍳 Full, homebaked   🏠 City res., older, 2-storey, quiet
■3D,1Ste (upper & ground level)   ⊢⊣ 2T(K),3D   ⊿ 1Private,
1sh.w.g.   ★Air,guest TV room, parking   🖑No smoking,no pets
🏃 Downtown, Queens University, Lake Ontario waterfront,
McArthur College, park with tennis court across street, main city
bus route, annual International Boating Events
🚗 Old Fort Henry, 1000 Island tourist area, Prince Edward County, Sandbanks Prov. Park
🐾 Two women offer "Warm Canadian welcome, distinctly British style" in red brick home located
in quiet residential neighbourhood and in the heart of the beautiful 1000 Islands area. ✒B&B

Franks, Carol A (Painted Lady Inn)
181 William St., Kingston, ON   K7L 2E1

☎ (613) 545-0422

From Hwy 401 take Division St Exit south into Kingston. Left on William St.
$79S $89-145D   (plus tax)   (Corp.rates available)   ► 14A
🕮 Full, homebaked 🏠 Downtown, res., 3-storey, hist., older, patio, porch,
quiet ■ 7D(main & upper levels) ⊨ 2T,6Q ⊲7Private ★Air,F,TV
in one guest room, jacuzzis, private entrance, off-street and street parking,
host quarters are separate Ⓦ No smoking, no pets, no children
⌇Spanish, Thai, German
🕱 Fort Henry, 1000 Islands boat cruises, many restaurants, Bellevue House,
Queen's University, Royal Military College, museums
🚗 Gananoque, Smith Falls, US border
☛ Stately brick home (built in 1872) as a church manse and tastefully
furnished with antiques. Breakfast is served in the formal dining room. Luxury rooms have a
fireplace and jacuzzi. Relax on the Victorian front veranda, on the balcony or in the rose garden.
Lucury rooms have fireplaces & jacuzzis. Hostess is a former journalist, world traveller and trained
chef. Gift certificates available. Visa,MC,Amex ⌇CC

Grassby, Enid (Watersedge B&B)
4244 Bath Rd., Kingston, ON   K7M 4Y7

☎ (613) 634-2029

From Hwy 401, travel south on Rd 6 through Odessa and continue to Lake. Turn left and proceed
4.25 km to B&B.
$50S $75D $125F $10Add.person 🍽 Meals   ► 4A,2Ch
🕮 Full, homebaked, buffet   🏠 Res., sub., hills-side (ravine), view
from guest rooms, lake at back, patio, porch, deck, quiet
■1S,1D,1F (ground & lower level) ⊨ 1S,1D,1R ⊲ Private
★F,off-street parking Ⓦ Designated smoking area, no pets
🕱 Lake Ontario, park, bus to downtown
🚗 Downtown Kingston
☛ Comfortable home, decorated in a country Georgian style and nestled on the shore of Lake
Ontario. Relax on the private terrace or in guests sunroom and enjoy the beautiful lake views.
Breakfast is served on balcony or in the elegant dining room. There is a resident dog. Visa ⌇CC

Hart, Pam & Scotty (Hart's Haven B&B)
680 Hillview Rd., Kingston, ON   K7M 5C7

☎ (613) 384-3643
E-mail: hartwork@aracnet.net

Phone for directions.
$45S $55D 🍽 Meals & picnics-to-go   ► 2A
✚ May1-Sept1 🕮 Cont., buffet (full extra) 🏠 Sub, hillside,
2-storey, view from guest rooms, lakefront, deck ■1D(upstairs)
⊨1D ⊲1ensuite ★ LF,F,TV in guest room, ceiling fan, coffee
bar & minifridge in guest room. off-street parking ⓌNo
smoking, no pets, not suitable for children ⌇some French
🚗 Fort Henry, Royal Military College, Queen's University, John
A.MacDonald hometown (Bellevue house), Grand Theatre, Thousand Islands, boat tours, Wolfe Isle
🕱 Flea market and antique Emporium, restaurant, public bus to downtown, airport and train
☛ Spacious, unique custom-built house on large treed lot. Retired military couple enjoy sharing
their home filled with memorabilia from around the world and a beautiful view of Collins Bay.
Resident artist's own works are on display around the house. Pick-up from inter-city buses/trains
or planes, as well as transportation to city center or historic area tours available at a small fee.

Holland, Margaret (Baywinds B&B)   ☎ (613) 634-6045
4331 Bath Rd., Kingston, ON   K7M 4Z1

On Hwy 401, coming from west, take Exit 599 to Hwy 33 (Bath Rd) and turn left for 3km. Coming

from east, take Exit 615 to Hwy 33 and turn right for 5km.
$50-60S $60-75D $10Child   ▶ 6
✚ Summer only   🔊 Full   🏠 Res., older, 1-acre, view from two
guest rooms, deck   ■ 3D(main & upper level) ⊨2T,1D,1Q1R
🛁 2ensuite,1sh.w.h.   ★ Air,F,TV, off-street parking
🚬Designated smoking area
🚗 Downtown, Fort Henry, 1000 Island Tours, Bellevue House,
Queen's University, R.M. Academy, Olympic Harbour, St.Lawrence
College, fine restaurants & shops, golf courses, Fairfield Park swimming in Lake Ontario
🐾 Spacious "middle-aged" residential home facing Lake Ontario, located in historic town. Relax
in the comfortable guest sitting room or sun deck & gazebo and enjoy the gorgeous view. English
breakfast served in formal dining room. ✔B&B

North, Mary Ellen (The North Nook)   ☎ (613) 547-8061, Fax (613) 546-5857
83 Earl St., Kingston, ON   K7L 2G8

From Hwy 401 take Exit 615 and Sir John A.MacDonald Blvd south to King St. Turn left, proceed

to Earl St., turn left again.
$75S $85D $25Child   (plus tax)   ▶ 10A
🔊Full   ■Downtown, 2-storey, hist., balcony, quiet   ■4D,1F(upstairs)
⊨D,Q   🛁5Private   ★ Air,TV/ceiling fans in rooms,street parking
🚬No smoking, children min.age 12, small well-behaved dog welcome
🏃 Fort Henry, City Hall, Marine Museum, restaurants, 1000 Island Cruises,
Queens University Campus
🚗 Picton, Smith Falls, Brockville, Gananoque
🐾 Historically designated (ca 1849) home with exposed limestone & brick walls, tin ceiling in
living room, filled with antiques passed down through generations. Located in the heart of
downtown. Knowledgeable hostess is in her second decade of welcoming B&B guests. Breakfast is
served in guest breakfast room. Long-term rates from Sept to May available. There are 2 small
resident dogs. Visa,MC ✔B&B

O'Brien, Mary (The O'Brien House Bed & Breakfast)   ☎ (613-542-8660)
39 Glenaire Mews, Kingston, ON   K7M 7L3

From Hwy 401, take exit 615 (Sir John A.MacDonald) to Counter
St. Turn right, then left on Aberfoyle and right on Glenaire Mews.
Look for weathervane of horse.
$45-50S $55-75D   ▶ 10
🔊Full   🏠Midtown, res., hillside   ■3D,1Ste (upstairs & ground
level) ⊨1K,3Q   🛁2Ensuite, 1sh.w.g.   ★TV in guest rooms,
parking   🚬No smoking, no pets, children welcome
🚗 University, Military Academy, boat tours, shopping, dining
🐾 Colonial-style brick home with Irish hospitality designed & decorated especially for B&B, in
nice residential area backing onto parkland. Enjoy the relaxed atmosphere. Visa,MC ✔B&B

Sanders, Monique & John (Limestone & Lilacs B&B)   ☎ (613) 545-0222
1775, Hwy 38, Kingston, ON   K7P 2Y7   E-mail: john.sanders@sympatico.ca

Take Exit 611 from Hwy 401 and proceed north .5km on Hwy 38. Look for house on left.

$55-60S $65D $15Add.person   ▶ 6
🍳 Full, homebaked   🏠 Rural, 2-storey, hist.,acreage, porch,
quiet   ■ 3D (upstairs)   ⊨ 1D,1Q,2T   🚗 2Sh.w.g.   ★ Air,
F/TV/library in guest lounge, host quarters are separate   🚭 No
smoking, no pets   ⌇ French
🏃 Large acreage of nature land bordering Collins Creek
🚗 Kingston, 1000 Islands, summer festivals, Fort Henry
📷 Elegant, early 19th Century limestone farmhouse, lovingly
restored and nestled on 27 acres of picturesque farmland. Enjoy the close proximity to downtown,
while experiencing the space and tranquility of country living. Relax on the spacious wrap-around
porch or take a stroll by the creek. Hosts emphasize the importance of "breakfast" in B&B.
Excellent location for a stop-off point between Toronto and Ottawa/Montreal. There are 2 dogs and
a cat in back run area. MC ⌇CC

Smith, Maurice (Alexander Henry B&B)   ☎ (613) 542-2261, Fax (613) 542-0043
55 Ontario St., Kingston, Ont.   K7L 2Y2   E-mail: mmuseum@stauffer.queen.ca

Located on the Waterfront, 5 min to the Kingston downtown.

$38S $55-65D   ▶ 36
🌡Summer-Sept 30   🍳Cont.(fix your own)   🚢Ship (moored
icebreaker)   ■19 outside cabins with view   ⊨S,D (incl. upper
& lower bunks)   🚗Private (toilets),sh.w.g., sinks in some
cabins   🚭No smoking
🚗 Downtown Kingston, restaurants, shops, entertainment,
marinas, tourboats and other heritage attractions, car ferry to
Wolfe Isle and to US, Old Fort Henry
📷 "Floating B&B" on authentic working ship with basic no-frills cabins and built-in wooden
bunks (former Coast Guard Icebreaker on Lake Superior) operating as a B&B since 1986. Enjoy the
casual environment, ideally suited for families and guests who like to experience rustic
accommodations. Listen to the water and the restful lullaby of the waves washing against the hull.

Westenberg, Marion & Hans (Glen Lawrence B&B)   ☎ (613) 548-4293
1325 Hwy 2 East, Kingston, ON   K7L 4V1   Fax (613) 542-8141

From Hwy 401 take Exit 623 and proceed south to Hwy 2. Continue 5km east and look for B&B
sign right by small lane-entrance through trees.

$35S $60-65D $17Child $110F (in 2rooms)   ▶ 7A,2Ch
🌡 Summer only   🍳 Dutch-Canadian   🏠 Rural, hist., river
view from one guest room, river at back, tennis court, deck, very
quiet, secluded   ■ 3D,1S (upstairs)   ⊨ 1S,2T,1D,1Q,1R,crib
🚗2Sh.w.g. (one on main floor)   ★ F,TV in sitting room,
off-street parking   🚭 Designated smoking area   ⌇ French,
Dutch, German, some Italian
🏃 Swimming, hiking, horseback riding, canoeing, tennis, cycling, (good bike path all around)
🚗 Downtown Kingston, Old Fort Henry, 16 other museums, farmers market, 1000 Island tours
📷 Prof. couple in 150-year old limestone house with a European atmosphere, and eclectic mix of
European & Canadian furniture and art spanning three Centuries. Located in a beautiful country
setting on 48 wooded acres adjacent to the St.Laurence River. Guests are welcome to use the tennis
court. There are chickens for farm fresh eggs. There is a dog in residence. ⌇B&B

Kingsville
(south of Windsor; see also Leamington, Amherstburg, Comber)

Gelinas, Linda & Tom (The Wedding House B&B) ☎ (519) 733-3928, Fax (519) 733-9987
98 Main St.East, Kingsville, ON   N9Y 1A4

From Hwy 401 exit at Comber and take Hwy 77 south to Leamington. Turn right on Seacliff Dr and proceed 14 km to Kingsville. (Seacliff Dr becomes Main St).
$55S $60-75D $5Child $10Add.person   ◙ Meals   ► 9
🍴 Full, homebaked   🏠 Downtown, 2-storey, hist., swimming pool, porch, quiet   ■ 2D,2F(upstairs)   ⊨ 4T(2K),1D,1Q,1R
⊒ 1Ensuite, 1sh.w.g., 1shw.h.   ★Air,TV, off-street parking, guest quarters are separate   ⊚ No smoking, no pets
🏃 Ferry to Pelee Island, winery, shops, restaurants, churches
🚗 Point Pelee Nat.Park, Colasanti's Tropical Gardens, Heritage Village, Jack Miner's Bird Sanct., John R.Park Homestead, Holiday Beach, Windsor, casinos
🔫 Charming Victorian home, beautifully decorated and furnished with fine antiques and collectibles, including old family pictures. Relax in the home theatre with complimentary movies. Breakfast is served in guest breakfast room. There is a dog. Visa,MC ✓B&B

Kirkfield
(west of Fenelon Falls)

Scott, Joan & Paul (Sir William Mackenzie Inn) ☎ & Fax (705) 438-1278
Box 255, Hwy 48, Kirkfield, ON   K0M 2B0

Located in the village of Kirkfield on Hwy 48.
$65S $75D $20Add.person   ◙ Meals   (plus taxes)   ► 16
🔲 May1-Oct.20   🍴 Full, homebaked   🏠 Village,3-storey,hist., acreage, view from guest rooms, patio, porch, quiet   ■7(upstairs)
⊨3T,1D,3Q,2K,2P   ⊒ 7Ensuite   ★ F,TV,LF, parking
⊚Smoking area, no pets, children min. age 10   〰Sign language
🏃 Large beautiful grounds, conducted tour of 40 room Mansion
🚗 2nd largest liftlocks in the world, boat cruises, fishing, Casino
🔫 Very large, historic (ca 1888) mansion on 13 acres featuring sculptured garden and nature walk among spectacular 100-year old trees. Pick-up available for boating guests at Kirkfield Lift Locks. Facilities for conferences & receptions. Golf package available (2 for 1). ✓B&B

Kitchener
(west of Toronto; see also Cambridge, Guelph, St.Jacobs)

Findlay, Jo-Anne (River Breeze Bed & Breakfast) ☎ (519) 653-6756 Fax (519) 653-6249
248 Edgehill Dr., Kitchener, ON   N2P 2C9

From Hwy 401 take Exit 278 and Hwy 8 west to Kitchener. Exit at Sportsworld Dr. Continue through lights at King St and proceed to 2nd driveway on right.
$40S $75D   ◙ Meals   ► 6A
🍴 Full, homebaked   ■ Res, ranch-style, view, swimming pool, patio, porch, quiet   ■2D(ground level)   ⊨2T(K),2Q   ⊒Sh.w.g.   ★Air,TV,F,LF, direct access to pool & patio from each room, off-street parking   ⊚ Designated Smoking area, no pets, not suitable for children
🏃 Sportsworld, horseback riding
🚗 Farmer's markets, Oktoberfest, Mennonite Country, St. Jacobs, Elmira, Stratford Theatre
🔫 Unique U-shaped bungalow with extra-ordinary view of Grand River and Valley and large, tempting inground pool. Hosts are well informed of the area. Enjoy homebaked goodies and preserves for a tantalizing breakfast served indoors or out on the patio by the pool. ✓B&B

Holl, Frank and Maria (Austrian Home)　　　　　　　☎ (519) 893-4056
90 Franklin St.N., Kitchener, ON　N2A 1X9

From Hwy 401 take Exit Kitchener Hwy 8 West to Exit
Fairway/Weber. Turn on Weber to 3rd light. Turn right.
$35S　$50D　$10Child　　　　　　　　　　　▶ 4
🍴 Full　🏠 Res., patio　■ 2D (upstairs)　⊨2T,1D　🚿Sh.w.h.
★ TV, parking　⚓ No smoking, no pets　〰German
🕯 Restaurants, bank, shopping centre
🚗 Downtown, Bingemann Park, Waterloo University, Stratford
☛ Friendly Austrian-Canadian hosts welcome visitors to their
Austrian-style home with traditional handpainted decor, flower baskets, large backyard. Upper floor
is exclusive for guests. Enjoy the well-known October Fest activities in traditional style. ✓B&B

Krampitz, Alfred and Edith (Driftwood Home)　　　　　☎ (519) 745-8010
202 Driftwood Dr., Kitchener, ON　N2N 1X6

Located in the west end of the City. Exit Fischer-Hallmann or Trussler Rd..

$40S　$55-65D　$10Child　$15Add.person　　　　▶ 4A,2Ch
🍴 Full(German-style)　🏠 Res.,quiet　■ 1F,1Ste(main floor)
⊨2T,1Q,R,cot　🚿1Ensuite, 1sh.w.h.　★TV,F,LF, parking　⚓No
smoking, no pets　〰German, Polish
🕯 Sports Park, city of Kitchener, community trails, city bus stop
🚗 Waterloo University, Doon Pioneer Village, St. Jacobs/Elmira
(Mennonite country), Straftford, Niagara-on-the-Lake, Toronto
☛ Warm and friendly hospitality in raised bungalow Christian
home with large treed lot and located on a quiet street. Enjoy the night city view, relax in the back
yard or take a walk on the community trails. Waterloo Airport pick-up available. ✓B&B

Loney, Endla (Rockway Drive B&B)　　　　　　　　☎ (519) 741-8718
673 Rockway Dr., Kitchener, ON　N2G 3B5

Phone for directions. Located in the south end of town.
$45S　$60D　$15child　　　　　　　　　　▶ 4A,2Ch
🍴Full　🏠Res., 2-storey, older, quiet　■2D (upstairs)
⊨1D,2T(large)　🚿1Sh.w.g.　★TV,LF,F,TV in guest rooms,
off-street parking, guest quarters are on upper floor　⚓ No
smoking, no pets
🕯 Rockway Golf Club, Rockway Gardens, fine dining
🚗 St.Jacobs, Mennonite Country, Stratford (theatres), Chicopee
skiing, Cambridge (factory outlet shopping), African Lions Safari, Waterloo Universiities
✓ Comfortable home with cozy, warm atmosphere backing onto golf course & Rockway Gardens.
Well travelled hostess is retired (former Interior Decorator and builder) and a hobby sculptor. Her
works are displayed throughout the house. There are two small dogs "Tiny" & "Tay". ✓B&B

Mikolajewski, Gabi & Armin (Country House B&B)
35 Dodge Dr., RR2, Kitchener, ON   N2G 3W5

☎ & Fax (519) 748-6112

From Hwy 401 West take Homer Watson Blvd Exit and left on New Dundee Rd.

$40S $60D $100F $20Add.person   🍽 Meals   ▶ 4A,2Ch
🍺 Full   🏠 Sub., 2-storey, acreage, view from guest rooms, porch, deck, quiet   ■ 2(upstairs)   ⊨ 1Q,1K   ⬛ 1Sh.w.g.
★F,Air,TV,LF,KF, off-street parking, quest quarters are separate   ⑭ Smoking outside   ⌇ German
🕺 Pioneer Park Shopping Centre, Conestoga College Campus
🚗 Downtown Kitchener, Cambridge, Stratford, Toronto
🐎 Warm welcome in Christian based country house surrounded by mature nature setting with friendly German hospitality. Enjoy relaxation and comfort beside the fireplace or on the deck overlooking the garden.

Teal-Aram, Fay (Roots & Wings Bed & Breakfast)
11 Sunbridge Cr., Kitchener, ON   N2K 1T4

☎ (519) 743-4557, Fax (519) 743-4166

From Hwy 401, take Hwy 8 west & Hwy 86 north to University Ave E Exit. Turn right on Bridge

St, left on Bridle Trail, proceed to Sunbridge to first house on right.
$40S $65-80D $15Child   ▶ 8A,2Ch
🍺 Full   🏠 Sub., ranch-style, small acreage, view, swimming pool, quiet   ■4D(main & lower floor)   ⊨2T,1D,1Q,1K,1P,1R
⬛2Private,1shw.g.   ★F,LF,TV in lower level guest room, outside jacuzzi sep.entr, wheel-chair access, parking   ⑭Desig smoking
🕺 Walking trails to Grand River, spring fed ponds behind house (geese, heron & deer often seen)
🚗 Downtown Kitchener, popular farmer's market, shopping, restaurants, St. Jacobs, Elora
🐎 Retired School Principal in large comfortable home nestled in the heart of Central Ontario's tourist region and Mennonite Country. Enjoy the easy-going country atmosphere. Hostess loves motorcycling. There is a very gentle dog in residence. Children and pets welcome. Visa,MC ⌇B&B

Warren, Marg & Norm (Roses And Blessings)
112 High Acres Cr., Kitchener, ON   N2N 2Z9

☎(519)742-1280, Fax(519)742-8428
E-mail: nmwarren@golden.net

From Hwy 401, take Hwy 8 to Hwy 7&8 West To Fischer Hallman, left to Queen, left to Westheights, left to Blackwell to B&B.
$45S $50D $15child   ▶ 4A,1Ch
🍺 Full, homebaked   🏠 Res., back-split, patio, quiet   ■ 1D,1F
(upper and lower level)   ⊨ 1D,1Q,1R   ⬛ 2Private   ★Hot tub, air,TV,LF,F,KF,guest quarters are sep., exercise equipment, off-street parking   ⑭ No smoking, no pets   ⌇some French
🕺 Protected duck/wildlife pond, x-c ski trails, bus stop, plaza
🚗 Universities, farmers'market, Kitchener, St.Jacobs, Stratford, covered "Kissing Bridge"
🐎 Warm welcome in Christian home with cozy comfort and friendly hospitality. Breakfast is served in the dining room, in the kitchen or in the intimacy of the sunroom, featuring orchids & tropical plants. Relax by the fireplace, in the hot tub or work out on the exercise equipment. Hosts are happy to assist with excursions and information about the Mennonite community. Guests are provided with a special memento of their visit.MC ⌇B&B

Kleinburg

(north of Toronto; see also Nobleton)

Clark, John and Rosalind (Humber House) ☎ (905) 893-9108
10555 Islington Ave., Kleinburg, ON L0J 1C0

From QEW, take Hwy 427 north to the village. (Islington Ave is the main street). Look for B&B on right past main shopping area.

$35S $45D   ►5
🍳 Full   🏠 Village, older, patio, quiet   ■ 3D (upstairs)
▬1D,2T,1Q,P, crib   ☜1Ensuite, 1sh.w.g.   ★ TV   🖤No pets, non-smokers preferred
🧍 World renowned Art Gallery (McMichael Canadian Collection, with guest exhibits, dining room and gift shop), fine dining at (The Doctor's House) & other restaurants, gift shops, boutiques
🚗 Canada's Wonderland, Kortright center for Conservation, Toronto International Airport
🐾 Enjoy friendly hospitality in interesting 80-year-old home situated in charming village, very close to Toronto Metropolis. Hosts have been welcoming B&B guests from all over the world for many years. Enjoy the quaint village atmosphere. ╱B&B

Lakefield

(north of Peterborough; see also Lindsay)

Charlton, Elsie (The Elms Bed & Breakfast) ☎ (705) 652-7310
169 Queen St., Box 326, Lakefield, ON K0L 2H0

From Peterborough on Hwy 28 go 17km north to Lakefield & .8km north of shopping center.

$50-70S/D $10Add.person   ►9A,2Ch
✚ April1-Dec31   🍳 Full   🏠 Village, 2-storey, hist., .5acres, view from guest rooms, patio, front veranda, deck, quiet   ■4 (upstairs & street level)   ▬ 1S,2T,2D,1Q,1R,1P,   ☜2Sh.w.g., 3ensuite   ★ Air,TV in 4 guest rooms, private entrance, wheel-chair access from one room, off-street parking   🖤 No smoking, not suitable for small children
🚗 Trent U, downtown Peterborough, Curve Lake Indian Reserve
🧍 Lakefield College, downtown Lakefield, shopping, restaurants, marina and river shorewalks
🐾 Completely renovated 1875-built Century home with a relaxing village atmosphere. Hostess is an avid gardener. Breakfast is served in main dining area or overlooking the patio from the central hall. There is a small dog called "Wellington" in residence (not around until lunch hour). ╱CC

Crawford, Martha & Dan (Selwyn Shores Waterfront B&B) ☎ (705) 652-0277, Fax 3389
2073 Selwyn Shores Dr., RR3, Lakefield, ON K0L 2H0   E-mail: selwyn@ptbo.igs.net

From Buckhorn, travel south on Hwy 507/23 to Concession 20. Turn right, then right on 12th Line to Selwyn Shores Dr. Look for 3rd house on right.

$55-85D $10Add.person   🍽 Meals   ► 10
🍳 Full, homebaked (buffet)   🏠 Rural, backsplit, view from some guest rooms, lakefront, deck, quiet   ■ 4D,1F (main & ground level walkout) ▬3D,2Q,waterbed avail ☜2Sh.w.g.,2ensuite
★F(3),LF,TV in guest room, piano, guest quarters are separate, canoe/kayak/paddleboat for guests   🖤No smoking, no pets
🧍 Dock/boat launch, fishing on Trent Severn Waterway,x-c ski, skating, snowmobiling, Art Gallery, Selwyn Conservation area
🚗 Peterborough Lift Locks, Canoe Museum, Zoo, Trent University, Petroglyphs (stone carvings)
🐾 Spacious home and a friendly atmosphere, with great sunsets over Chemong Lake situated on the Trent Severn Waterway. Host is an expert professional bass fisherman who enjoys the tournament trail all summer & hostess is an occasional professional Caterer. Both are involved in many sports activities. Special diets accommodated with advance notice. Enjoy the huge collection of cookbooks. Access to fax and Internet provided. Corporate long-stay guests welcome. MC

Lancaster

(east of Cornwall; see also Apple H., Williamstown, Alexandria)

MacRae, Guelda and Robert (MacPine Bed & Breakfast) ☎ (613) 347-2003
Box 51, Lancaster, ON   K0C 1N0

Travelling on Hwy 401, take Exit 814 at Lancaster. Go east on South Service Rd (.75km from Esso
Gas Stn on the corner). Look for sign. Located 17 km from Cornwall.

$40S $45-50D $85Ste $15Child   ▶ 4A,2Ch
🍴 Full, homecooked 🏠 Farm,river-view, quiet ■S,D(upst)
⊨S,T,D,Q, cot, crib 🛏Sh.w.g. ★TV, sep.entrance, parking
🚭Restricted smoking, no pets
🧍 Private cottage on St. Lawrence River (swimming, canoeing,
fishing for Lancaster perch), China Warehouse Outlet, antique and
craft and art stores, Cooper Marsh nature walks
🚗 Golfing, Upper Canada Village, Montreal, Cornwall, Ottawa
🐾 Modernized Century home tastfully decorated with hosts' own handwork (pieces of Folk Art
etc.) with a view of the St. Lawrence River and surrounded by large pine shade trees. Relax and
watch the ocean boats go by. Breakfast served in sunroom overlooking St.Lawrence River &
mountains in the distance. ✒B&B

Leamington

(south of Windsor; see also Kingsville, Amherstburg, Comber)

Chase, Clair & Theresa (Park Gate Bed & Breakfast) ☎ (519) 326-3732
866 Pelee Dr., RR1, Leamington, ON N8H 3V4

Phone for directions.
$55-60S $60-65D   ▶ 4
⊞ Apr15-Oct15 🍴 Full, homebaked 🏠 Suburban, 2-storey,
lakeview from guest rooms, lakefront, deck, quiet ■1D,1F(upst)
⊨1S,2T(K),1D 🛏 2Sh.w.g.(on main floor) ★ Air,F,TV in guest
rooms, guest robes, one guest room balcony, off-street parking
🚭No smoking, no pets
🧍 Point Pelee National Park, sandy beach, swimming, canoeing,
fishing from beach, birdwatching, Fish Place Restaurant
🚗 Downtown Leamington, unusual shops/restaurants, Pelee Isle Ferry, Jack Miner Bird Sanct.
🐾 Unpretentious, but unique home on the beach with expansive decking for sunbathing and
watching beautiful Lake Erie sunsets. Well travelled hosts have many colorful stories to tell about
hunting & fishing in the North Country. Complimentary canoe is available (depending lake
conditions). Relax on the large deck and watch the beach activities or by the cosy fire on chilly
nights. House specialty is delicious rhubarb loaf and blueberry pancakes with strawberry sauce.
There is a dog on the premises. ✒B&B

Collings, Berit & Tony (Do Drop In B&B) ☎ & Fax 519) 326-5558
202 Seacliff Dr.W, Leamington, ON N8H 3Y6   E-mail: dodropin@mnsi.net

From Hwy 401 take Exit 48 and proceed south on Hwy 77 to Hwy 18 (Seacliff Dr. Turn right for
1.2km to Kenneth Dr. B&B located on corner. From Windsor take Hwy 3 to Leamington. At
Ruthven, take Union Rd south to Hwy 18, turn left for 5km to B&B.

$35-45S $50D $10Add.person   ▶ 5-7
🍴 Full, homebaked 🏠 Res, split-level, patio, quiet ■1S,2D
(upstairs ⊨ 1S,2Q,1P,crib 🛏 2Sh.w.g. ★ Air,TV,LF,
off-street parking, quest quarters are separate 🚭 No smoking,
no pets, children welcome 〰 Swedish
🧍 Seacliff Park Beach (swimming, boating), marina, restaurants
🚗 Point Pelee National Park (biking, birdwatching, canoeing,
hiking, swimming, sunbathing), Point Pelee-Sandusky (US) Ferry
🐾 Warm welcome in home with Swedish-English atmosphere, surrounded by trees, flower beds
and many birds, located near popular tourist attractions and nature parks in Canada's most
southerly point. Well travelled and informed hosts can provide help with itineraries.

Cowan, Margaret (Farm House B&B) ☎ (519) 326-8384
319 Rd#14, RR5, Leamington, ON   N8H 3V8

Located 10 km north of Leamington. By reservation only. Phone for directions.

$40S $45D   ► 6A,2Ch
🏠Full,homebaked 🐄Farm, view, patio, quiet ■3D,1S(upstairs)
⊨2D,2T,1S ⌐1Sh.w.g. ★Air,F,TV,parking 🐾No pets
🚗 Point Pelee National Park, Jack Miner's Bird Sanctuary, Colasanti's
Tropical Gardens, Pelee Isle Ferry, Windsor
🖐 Several generation family, spacious red brick farm home and
old-fashioned parlour with woodwork from Oak trees cut down on the
farm. Relax by the fireplace or in the beautiful large back yard and
enjoy warm hospitality, clean air and quiet countryside. There is a cat in residence. ✓B&B

Dyck, Richard and Irene (Leamington Bed & Breakfast) ☎ (519) 326-4378
92 Oak St.East, Leamington, ON   N8H 2C9

Phone for directions.
$45S $50D   ► 4-5A
🍽 Choice, homebaked 🏠 Res., split-level,patio, quiet ■2 (main
& upper level) ⊨2D,1R ⌐2Private ★Air,TV,LF,parking
🐾 No smoking, no pets 〰German
🧍 Beaches, stores, restaurants, marina, golfing, bus stop at door
🚗 Point Pelee National Park, Jack Miner's Bird Sanctuary,
Colasanti's Tropical Gardens, Pelee Island Ferry
🖐 Bright & cheery split-level home with a lovely large patio located in an area with many
beautiful atttractions. Enjoy a snack in the evening. ✓B&B

Fegarty, Barry & Diane (Marlborough House B&B) ☎ (519) 322-1395, Fax (519) 322-1444
49 Marlborough St.W., Leamington, ON   N8H 1V9

Located in central Leamington. Phone for directions.
$55S $70D   ► 6A
🍽 Full, homebaked 🏠 Res., 2-storey, hist., older, porch, quiet
■ 3D(upstairs) ⊨ 2T,1Q,1K ⌐ 2Sh.w.g., whirl-pool
★F,Air,TV in guest living room, ceiling fans, off-street & street
parking, guest quarters are separate 🐾 No smoking, no pets, no
children
🧍 Downtown area, shops, fine restaurants
🚗 Point Pelee Nat.Park (marsh boardwalk), Jack Miners Sanctuary, Tropical Gardens, wineries
🖐 Enjoy comfort and hospitality in a recently renovated Victorian home on a quiet, centrally
located and tree-lined street. Hosts are retired Diplomats who have furnished the home with
Chinese & Russian antiques. A sumptuous breakfast is served at guests convenience. MC,Visa
✓B&B

Sabbagh, Zirka & Elsie Stieglan (Home Suite Home) ☎ (519) 326-7169, Fax (519) 326-7383
115 Erie St., South, Leamington, ON   N8H 3B5   E-mail: hsuiteh@mnsi.net

Located 5 blocks south at main intersection of Erie St/Talbot. Look for sign on front lawn.

$55-65S $65-75D   ► 8A
❇ Not Feb. 🍽 Full(country-style) 🏠 Res., patio, glassed porch,
sundeck, large in-ground swimming pool ■4(upst) ⊨2D,2T,1Q
⌐4Private ★Air,F,TV, bicycle storage, entire 2nd floor for guests,
host quarters are separate, off-street parking in back 🐾No smoking,
no pets, no children 〰Ukrainian
🧍 Downtown, fine shops and restaurants, waterfront & harbour
🚗 Point Pelee Nat. Park and lovely beaches, Marsh Board Walk,
Tropical Gardens, marinas, boat launches, Pelee Island ferry
🖐 Spacious, traditional Victorian home, located on a shaded street with turn-of-the Century
homes, tastefully decorated & furnished in cozy country-style. Visa,MC ✓B&B

Lindsay

(west of Peterborough; see also Port Perry)

Barnes, Janet and Fred (Yellow Shutters B&B)   ☎ (705) 324-8158
31 Cambridge St.N, Lindsay, ON   K9V 4C6

Located 1.5 blocks from Town Hall in the center of town.
$40S $50D   ► 5A
🍴 Full, homebaked   🏠 Downtown, hist., patio, quiet
■1S,2D(upst) ⊨1S,2T,1D ⌂Sh.w.g.   ★off-street parking
🖐No smoking, no children, no pets
🧍 Kawartha Summer Theatre, Art Gallery, Trent Severn Locks,
beautiful parks, antique shops, downtown, hospital
🚗 Lindsay Central Exhibition (Sept), Haliburton Highlands, Sir Sandford Fleming College, Trent University at Peterborough, golfing, fishing, 2 auction rooms, fine restaurants, Skylark Tour Boat
☞ Retired hosts in designated Century home. The early history of the home is captured in the original antique furnishings and there are many crafts produced by the hosts. B&B was featured on TV's "Eye of Toronto". ⌐CC

Lions Head

(south of Tobermory; see also Dyers Bay, Red Bay, Hope Bay)

The Ashcrofts (The Cat's Pajamas)   ☎ (519) 793-3767
64 Main Street, Lions Head, ON   N0H 1W0

From Owen Sound, take Hwy 6 north to Ferndale. Turn east for 3.5km, then left at "T" on Main St.
$25-45S $30-50D $2.50Child $5Add.person   ► 6A,2Ch
🖐 May15-Oct.15   🍴 Full   🏠 Village, res., hist., patio, quiet
■2D,1F (upst) ⊨2T,1D,1Q,1P ⌂ Sh.w.h.   ★ TV,F, fans,
parking 🖐 No pets, restricted smoking
🧍 Sandy beach, swimming, marina, tennis, shops, LCBO, hospital,
antiques, restaurants, Bruce Trail hiking/climbing, biking
🚗 Bruce Peninsula, Tobermory (ferry to Manitoulin Island)
☞ Charming Century Home in a small village located on shore
of Georgian Bay. At the harbour, enjoy the unsurpassed view of wide sandy beach, colourful boats and sails at the marina, with a backdrop of cedar on limestone cliffs. Watch the world go by on the front veranda, or take a stroll through the "biggest little Metropolis in Ontario". ⌐CC

Taylor, Lynette & Jim (Taylor's B&B)   ☎ (519) 793-4853, Fax (519) 793-4682
31 Bryon St., Box 379, Lion's Head, ON   N0H 1W0

Phone for directions.
$40S $50D $15Child/Add.person   🍽 Meals   ► 9
🍴 Full   🏠 Village, split-level, deck, quiet   ■ 3(upstairs &
ground levels)   ⊨ 2S,2D,2Q,1P ⌂1Ensuite,1Sh.w.h. ★LF,TV,
off-street parking   🖐 Designated smoking area, no pets
🧍 Bruce Trail hiking, marina, sandy beach, shopping, ski trails
🚗 Tobermory, ferry to Manitoulin Islands, Owen Sound
☞ Warm and friendly welcome in comfortable home. Hosts are
members of Home to Home B&B. Ideal spot from which to hike the wonderful Bruce Trail. Hikers shuttle service available. Breakfast served in sunny dining room. Families welcome. ⌐B&B

Winters, Elinor & Bob (Winter's Wharf Bed & Breakfast)　　　☎ & Fax (519) 793-3875
Box 98, Lions Head, ON　N0H 1W0　　　　　　　　　E-mail: bwinters@compuserve.com

From Wiarton, take Hwy 6 north to Pike Bay Rd. Turn west to Whiskey Harbour Rd and north to Purgatory Point. Located near Pike Bay on the shores of Lake Huron (west side of the Peninsula).
$45S　$55D　$15Roll-away　$10Add.person　🍽 Meals　　　　　　　▶ 9
🍲 Full, homebaked　🏠 Rural, 2-storey, view from guest rooms, lakefront, private deck, quiet, isolated　■ 3D,1F (upstairs)　⊨1D,2Q,1K,1R　🚿1Sh.w.g., 1sh.w.h.　★ F,LF,TV in common room, 6ft whirlpool tub　🚭 No smoking, no pets, no children　🏃 Lake Huron, nature walks, fishing, birdwatching, boating　🚙 Bruce Trail hiking, x-c ski/snowmobile trails, Lion's Head, harbours, shopping, Georgian Bay beaches, Bruce Peninsula National Park, Tobermory Ferry to Manitoulin Islands
🐾 Comfortable home with 2 large decks overlooking the waters of Whiskey Harbour and Lake Huron. Enjoy the tranquil atmosphere and sleep to the restful sound of waves on the rocky shore. Breakfast is served on the wharf-like deck. There are 2 Golden Retrievers. ✔B&B

Listowel　　　　　　　　　　*(north/west of Kitchener; see also Newton, Millbank)*

Bowman, Bartley & Audrey (Bartlane Farms & B&B)　　　☎ (519) 291-1228
RR3, Listowel, ON　N4W 3G8　　　　　　　　　　E-mail: lab@wcl.on.ca

Located 5.6km east of Listowel on Line 86, Grid No 5224,
$35S　$45D　$60F　　　　　　　　　　　　　　　　　　▶ 4-6
🍲 Full　🏠 Farm, 200-acres, 2-storey, older　■ 1D,1F(upstairs)　⊨ S,D　🚿1Sh.w.h.
★Air,TV,KF,LF, separate entrance, air-conditioners　🚭 Designated smoking area
🏃 Trails (for snowmobiling, x-c skiing, snowshoeing and bikes), pond on farm grounds
🚙 Listowel (Paddyfest Irish Celebration), antique dealers & auction places, fine restaurants, golf course, Festivals (Stratford, Blyth, Drayton), Mennonite Country (St.Jacobs, Elora), fishing
🐾 Century red brick family farmhouse (ca 1863) with all of todays' comfort and yesterday's nostalgic atmosphere situated on large working cash-crop farm. Breakfast is served in the country kitchen or in antique furnished dining room. Tour around the pond, enjoy the herb & wild flower garden or relax under the shade tree. Guest are invited to trailer their snowmobiles, bring own skis or snowhoes or bikes and leave from the farm on groomed trail (guided tour available). There are 2 dogs outside and cats in the barn.

Ellingham, Enid & Frank　　　　　　　　　　☎ (519) 291-5217
165 Victoria Ave N, Listowel, ON　N4W 1S7

Phone for directions.
$40S　$45D　$50F　　　　　　　　　　　　　▶ 2A,2Ch
🍲 Full　🏠 Village, 3-storey, hist., patio, porch, quiet　■ 2 (upstairs)　⊨1Q,1P　🚿1Sh.w.g.　★TV,LF,F,off-street pkg　🚭No smoking,no pets　🏃 Downtown, shops, restaurants　🚙 London, Kitchener/Waterloo, Stratford Festival Theatre
🐾 Relax and enjoy the friendly environment in cozy older home with hospitable hosts.

London

(south-western Ontario)

Goodbrand, Stan & Verna (Goodbrand Retreat) ☎ (519) 453-2581
1172 Kaladar Dr., London, ON   N5V 2R5

Take Exit 100 from Hwy 401 W (Airport) and drive to Oxford St, turn west. Continue to Clark SRd and turn north. At 1st light, turn west on Cheapside St, right at Kaladar Dr.

$30S $50D   ▶4
🍲 Full, homebaked   🏠 Res., split-level, swimming pool, patio, quiet   ■2D(upstairs)   ⊨2D   ⏠ Sh.w.g.   ★Air,F,TV in one guest room, ceiling fans, off-street parking   ⊛Restricted smoking, no pets   ⁓ French
🕴 Fanshaw College, city bus
🚗 Airport, University Hospital, Pioneer Village and Fanshaw Conservation area, golfing, shopping malls

☛ Located in quiet northeast residential area of the city. Relax on the patio in park-like setting with coffee or tea in the evening. Hostess enjoys travelling, crafts and cooking for guests. ⌐CC

Herbert, Theresa (Terry) and John (Cosy Corner B&B) ☎ (519) 673-4598
87 Askin St., London, ON   N6C 1E5

Exit Wellington Rd off Hwy 401 (Exit 186). Turn left at Commissioners Rd, right onto Wharncliffe and right onto Askin.
$35S $40D   ▶5A
🍲 Full   🏠 Downtown, hist.   ■ 1S,2D (upstairs)   ⊨ 1S,1D,1Q
🚿2Sh.w.g.(original tigerfoot tub), one on main floor)   ★LF,guest kitchen, ceiling fans, electric blankets   ⊛No pets   ⁓French
🕴 Downtown shopping, restaurants, parks
🚗 Fanshawe/Springbank parks, Stratford Festival, Grand Bend, L.Huron
☛ Early retired couple in extensively restored 1871 spacious Victorian
home surrounded by many old churches & historic landmarks. Hosts are world travellers and enjoy charing travel tales with guests. Breakfast is served in cozy family kitchen or dining room. ⌐B&B

Humberstone, A. (Annigan's B&B) ☎ (519) 439-9196
194 Elmwood Ave. East, London, ON   N6C 1K2

From Hwy 401 take Exit 186 (Wellington Rd) and go north to Grand Ave. Turn left. Turn right at Ridout and immediate left onto Elmwood (one way). Then look for 3rd house from corner on right side).
$40S $55D   🍽 Meals   ▶6
🍲Cont., homebaked   🏠 Downtown, res., hist., veranda   ■3D(upstairs)
⊨2D,1Q (upstairs)   🚿1Sh.w.h., 1sh.w.g.   ★Air,F,TV, parking (off street)   ⊛No smoking, no pets
🕴 Downtown, Grand Theatre, Art Gallery, Thames Park, Galleria Mall
🚗 University of Western Ontario, Fanshawe College, hospitals, Stratford Festival, Port Stanley
☛ Charming, turn-of-the-century house with turret and interesting architecture owned by former Interior Designer. "A taste of home with a touch of class". Long-term rates available.

224   ONTARIO

James, Jesse & Joanne (James' Bed & Breakfast) ☎ (519)858-4106
543 Canterbury Rd., London, ON N6G 2N5

From Hwy 401, take Wellington Rd Exit North to Pall Mall, turn left, then right on Richmond.
Continue to Windemere Rd. Turn left 2 blocks to Canterbury Rd. Turn right to end.
$38S $48D   ►5
⬛Full 🛏Res., older, view from guest rooms, quiet, porch ⬛2(upst) ⊨2Q,1S ⌁1Sh.w.g.
★Air,TV in guest room, off-street parking Ⓦ No smoking, no pets, children min. age 6
🏃 University Hospital, University of Western Ontario
🚗 Storey Brook Gardens, golf courses, great shopping, restaurants, Grand Bend on Lake Huron
📣 Warm & friendly welcome in charming older home with very large guest rooms and dining
area situated in prestigious part of North London area. Hosts are active skiers and golfers. Relax in
the screened sunroom leading to the garden at the back of the house and watch birds and ducks
come to the large bird bath. ✔B&B

Quayle, Mike & Lou (Quayle's B&B) ☎ (519) 657-2726, Fax (519) 657-2118
118 Farmington Ct., London, ON N6K 3N9

From Hwy 401/402 exit onto Hwy 4 and proceed north to Comm.Rd. Turn right, continue up hill,
right on Cranbrook, right on Knightsbridge, left on Farmington Way, then left on Farmington Ct.

$40S $50D $15Add.person   ►5
⬛Full, homebaked 🛏Res., 2-storey, patio,, porch, secluded,
quiet ⬛2D,1S(upstairs) ⊨1S,2D ⌁1sh.w.g. ★Air,F,TV,LF,
off-street parking Ⓦ No smoking, no pets ⚋ French
🏃 Springbank Park, Storeybook & Rayner Rose Gardens, Guy
Lombardo Museum, Westmount Shopping Mall
🚗 Downtown, University & Hospital, public golf courses
📣 Warm and friendly welcome in lovely residential home on
quiet cul-de-sac, convenient to all major attractions. Enjoy the landscaped yard or relax in the
comfortable sitting room. Breakfast served in special guest breakfast room. There is a cat. ✔B&B

Rose, Doug and Betty (Rose House) ☎ (519) 433-9978
526 Dufferin Ave., London, ON N6B 2A2 E-mail: mperez@wwdc.com

Take Wellington Rd N Exit to Dufferin Ave. Turn right and 5 blocks past City Hall.
$40-65S/D   (Reservation recommended)   ►6
⬛Full 🏠 Downtown, 2-storey, quiet ⬛3D ⊨2D,1K
⌁1Ensuite, 1sh.w.h. ★Air, off-street parking ⓌNo pets,
children min.age 12, no smoking
🏃 Downtown shopping, City Hall, dining, London Grand Theatre,
Richmond Row, parks, Art Gallery, excellent public transportation
🚗 University of Western Ontario, Fanshawe College, Stratford
📣 Lovely, 130-year-old residence located in and area of historic
London homes. Active, retired hosts have been welcoming B&B guests from around the globe for
many years. Enjoy the congenial atmosphere and take a short stroll along tree-lined streets to the
downtown core. Visa,MC,Amex ✔B&B

Warren, Earl & Serena (Serena's Place)   ☎ (519) 471-6228
720 Headley Dr., London, ON   N6H 3V6

From QEW, take Exit 194 to Hwy 100 going north to Oxford St. Turn left and proceed west across

the City to Headley Dr., Turn left.
$30-50S/D   ► 7
🍴 Full, homebaked   🏠 Res., split-level, patio, summer room
■ 3 (upper level)   ⊨ 2T,2D,1R   🛏 1Sh.w.g.   ★ Air,TV
Ⓦ Restricted smoking
🏃 Springbank Park, shopping mall, restaurant
🚗 Downtown London
📷 Comfortable Oakridge Park home in prestigious residential
area of West London. Hosts have been welcoming B&B guests for many years. Hostess is the
founder of London & Area B&B Association. ✓ B&B

Mallorytown   *(south-west of Brockville; see also Athens, Gananoque)*

Chamberlain, Nicole & David (Nicole Bed & Breakfast)   ☎ (613) 923-5178
RR3, Mallorytown, ON   K0E 1R0

Located 1.5 km west of Mallorytown Ldg. Turn south on Vanston Rd toward St. Lawrence River.

$35S $45D $75F   ► 6
🍴 Full   🏠 Rural, split-level, acreage, view, lakefront, patio,
quiet   ■2D(main floor)   ⊨ 2D   🛏 Sh.w.g.   ★ TV,F,LF,
parking   Ⓦ No pets   〰 French
🏃 Canada's smallest National Park (Mallorytown Landing) in the
1000 Islands with water activities and picnic facilities, very long
bicycle path and x-country ski trail runs by the house
🚗 Rockport, Gananoque, boat tours, bridge to USA, Brockville
📷 Fully bilingual house with comfortable atmosphere, a beautiful view of the St. Lawrence River
and surrounded by over 100 trees. Relax on the large terrace and enjoy the friendly hospitality.
There is a dog in residence.

Manitoulin Island   *(north of Tobermory on Lake Huron/Georgian Bay)*

Arnelien, Barbara and Stan (Island Oaks)   ☎ & Fax(705) 368-2220 1-800-387-5723
Manitoulin I. Hwy 6, Sheguiandah, ON   P0P 1W0

Located 9km south of Little Current on Hwy 6 and 55km north of ferry dock in South Baymouth.

$45S $55D $70F $10Add.person   ► 8A,2Ch
🍴 Full, homebaked   🏠 Rural, ranch-style, 16 acres, quiet
■4(main & lower level)   ⊨1K,2D,2T, 2cots   🛏Sh.w.g.(whirlpool),
(wheel-chair access)   ★ F,LF,KF,TV, wheel-chair ramp   Ⓦ Pets
& children welcome   〰 Norwegian
🏃 Fishing, boat dock, historic village, swimming, hiking trail,
museum, antique store on property
🚗 Marina/beach,biking,horseback riding,museums,Pow-Wows
📷 Quiet guest home, decorated throughout in early Victorian splendor and surrounded by 16
picturesque acres in the hamlet of Sheguiandah. Truly a perfect retreat. Home is fully equipped for
the special needs of wheel-chair guests. Information on wheel-chair access places-to-go on hand.
Join the hosts at the round oak table and watch the natural beauty of small animals outside the
window while eating breakfast. A small dog called "Grizzly" is in residence.

Bowerman, Eunice and Richard (Happy Acres B&B)
RR1, Tehkummah, ON P0P 2C0

☎ (705) 859-3453
1-800-203-9028, Fax (705) 859-3687

Located 9km from South Baymouth ferry docks on Hwy 6, or 55 km from Little Current.

$40S $50D $60F $10Add.person ▶ 9
✚May-Oct. ◖Homebaked ◖Farm, older, quiet,
2-storey ■1D,2F(main &upper level) ◄1T,2D,2Q,1R,crib ★TV,
parking ◄3Ensuite ⑭No smoking, no pets
◄Museums, hiking trails, fishing, abundant wildlife, great native
crafts, annual pow-wow
◄ 3rd Generation family in completely renovated farmhouse
situated on popular vacation island. Children welcome (may be entertained by a marionette).

Daniels, Bob & Donna (Bay View B&B)
Box 137, Kagawong, ON P0P 1J0

☎ (705) 282-0741

Take Hwy 540 to the village and look for B&B at 165 Main Street.
$40S $50-55D $10Roll-away ▶ 7
✚May-Oct31(other by special arrangement) ◖Full,homebaked
◖Village, 2-storey, hist., view from guest rooms, lakefront, porch,
quiet, wrap-around deck ■3D (upstairs) ◄4T,1Q,1R
◄1Sh.w.g. ★Air(upper level), TV in guest living room, ceiling
fans, separate entrance, off-street parking ⑭Designated
smoking area, no pets, children min. age 8
✿ Lake across road with sandy beach, boat dock, swimming, fishing, marina, nature trails to Bridal
Veil Falls, tennis, library, restaurant next door
◄ Manitoulin Island Day Excursions, historic point, museums, golfing
◄ Turn-of-the-Century Victorian home with widow's walk balcony and wrap-around porch (for
guests only) overlooking the beautiful Bay and North Channel of Lake Huron & beach. Retired
hosts are avid fishing persons and are involved in community activities and local Economic
Development Committee. Explore the wonderful Manitoulin Islands from this central location.
Breakfast is served in private guest dining room. His-and-Hers mountain bikes and canoes for
guests available at nominal fee. There are 2 Min.Schnauzer (shedless) in residence.

McGregor, Ruth (Ruth's Bed & Breakfast)
73 Campbell St.W., Little Current, Manitoulin Island., ON P0P 1K0

☎ (705) 368-3891

Phone for directions.
$45S $50D $20Add.person ▶ 6
✚ Spring, Summer, Fall ◖ Full ◖ Res., hist., 1.5-storey,
view, patio ■ 2 (upstairs) ◄ 1D,1Q,2R ◄ 1Sh.w.g.
★parking ⑭ No pets
✿ Downtown Little Current
◄ Ferry docks at South Baymouth (Chicheemaun)
◄ Warm & friendly welcome in comfortable island home with
lovely view. Enjoy the perfect sunsets over North Channel.

Sheppard, Ron & Carol (Rockville Inn) ☎ (705) 377-4923, Fax (705) 377-5601
RR1, Mindemoya, ON P0P 1S0

From South Bay Mouth (ferry) on Hwy 6 turn left on Hwy 542, right onto Gibraltar Rd, right onto Rockville Rd. Continue through onto Demmy Rd and right on Albert Rd. Look for signs.

$65S $75D $85-95F $15child   (plus tax)   ▶ 10A,2Ch
🍳 Full,homebaked   🏠 Rural, ranch-style, acreage, view from guest rooms, lakefront, porch, quiet, secluded   ■ 6D,1F (main & upper level)   🛏 6Q   ⬛ 6Private   ★ F,KF/separate entrance (in family accommodation)   👋 Smoking outside, no pets
🏃 Hiking trail, boating, swimming, fishing, snowmobile trails
🚗 Restaurants, shops, golf course
📣 Completely up-dated and remodelled ancestral farm home (built by host's father in 1933) and situated on beautiful Lake Manitou with a spacious yard. Relax in the common room by the fireplace and enjoy the peaceful country atmosphere. There is a large country kitchen overlooking the lake. Rooms are decorated with nature themes i.e. "Morning Loon", "Maple", "Birdsnest", etc. Snowmobilers can get a group rating. Weekly rates available. ✔CC

Williamson, Harold and Sally (Mindemoya Lake View Farm) ☎ (705) 377-5714
Mindemoya, Manitoulin Island, ON P0P 1S0

From Hwy 17, take Hwy 6 to Little Current. Then take Hwy 540 to West Bay and Hwy 551 to Mindemoya. Take Hwy 542 west to Lake Mindemoya, turn right onto lake shore road and look for 5th house on the right with lake on left. From South Baymouth ferry docks take Hwy 6 to Hwy 542.

$40S $45D   ▶ 6A,2Ch
🍳 Full   🏠 800-acre farm, lakefront, patio   ■ 3D   🛏 3D, cot, 2cribs   ⬛ Sh.w.g.
★TV,F   👋 No pets, hunting guests welcome
🏃 Sandy beaches, fishing, swimming, beautiful sunrises & sunsets, Cup & Saucer hiking trail
🚗 Providence Bay, salmon fishing, Bridal Veil Falls, Ten-Mile Point scenic lookout
📣 Located on the South-East shore of beautiful Lake Mindemoya (world's largest fresh-water island) and home of The Great Spirit Manitou. Excellent deer hunting packages (including permission to hunt) on property available. ✔B&B

Manotick

(south of Ottawa; see also North Gower)

Chilvers, John & Heather (Chilvers B&B) ☎ (613) 692-3731
5220 NcLean Cr., Manotick, ON K4M 1G2

From Ottawa travel south on Hwy 16 to Rideau Valley Dr. Turn left and first left again on

Barnsdale. Proceed over bridge to 4th house on right.
$35S $45D   ▶ 4A
🍳 Cont., homebaked   🏠 Village, 2-storey, view from guest rooms, riverback, patio, deck, quiet, private   ■ 2D(upstairs)   🛏 1D,2T   ⬛ 1Sh.w.g.   ★ F,TV,LF, ceiling fans, separate entrance, off-street parking   👋 No smoking, no pets
🏃 Large park on Rideau River, boat access, restaurants, craft shops, art galleries, Canadian Guide Dogs for the Blind (tours)
🚗 Ottawa, Parliament Bldgs, Nat.Art Gallery, Byward Market (fresh flowers & local artisans)
📣 Comfortable home with view of extensive flower beds that sweep to the Rideau River. Enjoy the birds, ducks and Canada Geese and abundant wildlife while eating a hearty breakfast. Relax in the guest sitting room or join the family by the fireplace or on the deck. Hosts are active with Guide Dogs (in Manotick) and involved in community groups & Service Clubs. There is a dog in residence.

Davediuk, Faith and Fred (Long Island Bed & Breakfast)   ☎ & Fax (613) 692-2042
5607 Island Park Drive, Manotick, ON   K4M 1J3   E-mail: fdave@cyberus.ca

Take Bridge Street, then South River Dr (at Medical Centre) and turn left onto Island Park Drive.

$45-50S $55-65D   ▶ 6
🍲 Full, homebaked   🏠 Village, ranch-style, view, quiet, large
decks,riverside,back-split ■3(main & ground level) ⊨2T,1D,1Q
⛌1Sh.w.g., 1private ★Air,TV, ltd docking, parking ⓌNo
smoking, no pets ⌇Ukrainian, some French
🏃 Village of Manotick and charming local shops, Mill Museum
🚗 Ottawa (Capital of Canada), Parliament buildings
🗨 Spacious and comfortable home situated on the historic
Rideau River/Canal and located just outside of the Capital City. Enjoy the deck for a spectacular
river view and the "Feel right at home" atmosphere. Canoe available for guests. ✍B&B

Mansfield   *(south of Collingwood; see also Shelburne, Stayner, Alliston)*

Palmay, Sharon & Terry (The Palmay's B&B)   ☎ (705) 435-1556, Fax (905) 792-7175
RR3, Mansfield, ON   L0N 1M0   E-mail: palmays.bandb@sympatico.ca Bus.(905) 792-7163

From Toronto go north on Airport Rd (Dixon W). Cross Hwy 89 and proceed 2.5 km north. Take

1st left and continue .75 km . Turn right to 3rd house on left.
$50-65(S&D) $100F   🍽 Meals   ▶ 4
🍲 Full, homebaked (special diets accommodated) 🏠 Rural,
older, 2-storey, view, lakefront, patio, indoor swimming pool, spa,
quiet ■2Ste,1D(upstairs) ⊨2T,1Q ⛌1Ensuite,1Sh.w.h.
★TV,F,parking ♥ ⓌNo smoking ⌇French,Hungarian
🏃 Short walks around the pond or north to the Boyne River,
hiking/skiing/fishing and snowmobiling at door step
🚗 Numerous golf courses, skiing, antiquing, Bruce Trail hiking, arts and craft studios, fishing
🗨 Lovingly restored Victorian home offering charm, warmth, elegance and distinction in the
Hills of Mulmur. Enjoy a leisurely breakfast overlooking the pond, relax in the spa or do some
lengths in the indoor pool. There are resident Chinese Shar-Pei show dogs and a Vietnamese
potbellied pig. Kennel space may be available. Visa,MC ✍B&B

Markdale   *(south of Owen Sound)*

Brown, Monica and Iain (Cozy Nook B&B)   ☎ (519) 924-2063
RR7, Markdale, Ontario   N0C 1H0

Located exactly halfway between Flesherton and Markdale on the east side of Hwy 10.

$39S $56D $20Child(under age 12) 🍽Meals   ▶ 10
🍲 Choice, homebaked 🏠 Rural, village, hist., ranch-style,
acreage, patio, quiet ■S,D,F ⊨S,T,D,Q,R,P, cot, crib
⛌1Private,1sh.w.g.,1sh.w.h. ★F,TV,KF, separate entrance,
parking ⓌRestricted smoking, no pets
🏃 Cross-country and downhill skiing, golfing, boating, tennis,
Bruce Trail hiking, antique shops, boutiques
🗨 Warm hospitality in renovated and extended old schoolhouse
(built in 1821) with beautiful gardens, patios, courtyard and greenhouse, situated in the very
popular Beaver Valley area. Active hosts like golfing, tennis, cycling, swimming and skiing. ✍B&B

Markham
(north-east of Toronto)

Hall, Teil (Valley View House 109 B&B)   ☎ (905) 472-3163, Fax (905) 471-0643
109 Robinson St., Markham, ON   L3P 1P2

From Hwy 401, take Hwy 404 north to Hwy 7, proceed east to Hwy 48, turn north to Robinson St.
Turn left to 5th house on left.
$55S $65D $15child   ✔ 4-8
🍴 Full   🏠 Sub., res., split-level, older, view from guest rooms,
patio, deck, quiet, secluded   ■ 2Ste (lower level)   ⊨2T,1Q,2P
🛁2Private,2sh.w.g.   ★Air,F,TV,KF,sep.entrance,off-street
parking, hosts quarters are separate   Ⓦ No smoking, no pets
🚶 Markham Village shops and restaurants, library, museum,
town parks, fitness clubs
🚗 Markville Mall, Markham Theatre, Unionville Main Street shops/dining, Toogood Pond
🐎 Suburban bungalow with lower area built into a hill on a large secluded, quiet & private treed
lot in the centre of town. There is a small stream in shaded area with barbeque facilities. Breakfast
is served in Canadiana furnished dining room or on the deck. Relax and enjoy the small town
atmosphere in close proximity to the Metropolis. ✔B&B

Marmora
(east of Peterborough; see also Hastings, Tweed)

Morton, Douglas & Marion (Morton's Misty Meadows B&B)   ☎ (613) 395-0235
RR4, Marmora, ON   K0K 2M0

From Hwy 7 in Marmora, take Hwy 14 south for 8.9km, left .5km
$35S $50D $20Add.person   ► 6A,4Ch
🍴 Full, homebaked   🏠 Farm, 2-storey, 200acres, view, porch,
quiet   ■ 3 (upstairs)   ⊨ 1D,2Q,1R,1P   🛁 1Shw.g.   ★TV
Ⓦ No smoking, no pets
🚶 Leisure walks through fields and evergreens, hiking, horse-back
riding, x-c skiing, sleigh rides, skating on creek, abandoned railway
tracks (biking, snowmobiling),
🚗 Shopping, golfing, swimming, skiing, antiques & auctions, Indian arts & craft shops, fall fairs
🐎 Warm welcome in renovated Century home on working beef farm. Enjoy good old country
hospitality and relax on the sunporch while watching beautiful birds and pastoral views. Hosts
enjoy meeting people and invite guests to explore the farm and animals. ✔B&B

Mattawa
(east of North Bay)

Carriere, Colleen & Jennifer (Mi Casa B&B)   ☎ (705) 747-0032
Hwy 17E, Deux Rivieres, ON   K0J 1R0

Located approx.20Km east of Mattawa. Phone for directions.
$45S $55D $10Child/Add.person   🍽 Meals   ► 8
🍴 Full   🏠 Village, split-level, view from guest rooms,
riverfront, patio, porch, quiet, secluded   ■ 2D,1F(upstairs)
⊨4T,2D   🛁1Sh.w.g.   ★ TV,ceiling fans, separate entrance,
wheel-chair access, off-street parking, guest quarters are
separate   Ⓦ Designated smoking area, no pets   ⌣ French
🚶 Access to Algonquin Prov.Park, ferry to Prov. of Quebec
🐎 Friendly hospitality in large comfortable home with views of the Ottawa River. Relax in the
guest living and dining room and enjoy the friendly atmosphere and spectacular sunsets. ✔B&B

Levitan, Mrs. Mary (Bear Creek Farm)   ☎ (705) 744-2423
RR2, Mattawa, ON P0H 1V0

From North Bay, take Rt 17 East to Valois Dr in Mattawa. Turn right at 1st road after railroad trestle (250 ft). Continue for 5.75 km and look for hill with fork. Turn right to 2nd farm on left.

$50S $65D ◙ Meals (weekly rates available)   ▶ 4A
◐ Full, homebaked 🏠 260-acre sheep farm, older, view, patio, quiet ■2D,2S ⊨4T,futon ⬗1Ensuite,1sh.w.h. ★TV,F,KF 100 year old wood stove, spinning wheels, artesian well water Ⓦprefer non-smokers
🏃 Wool carding facilities on premises, hiking, bush
🚐 Town of Mattawa/dining/shopping, beaches at Lake Papineau
🐾 Spendid solitude in rustic Century-old log home with lots of antiques & casual charm, situated on scenic hill with large herb and organic vegetable gardens near the pretty town on the river. Former art teacher spins, dyes, weaves wool from own sheep raised on hillside. There is a unique in-house folkart collection. Ideal place for summer/winter sports. ↙B&B

Meaford   *(east of Owen Sound; see also Clarksburg, Thornbury)*

Allen, Joan and Doug (The Cheshire Cat)   ☎ (519) 538-3487
32 Nelson St.East, Meaford, Ontario N4L 1N6   E-mail: dallen@headwaters.com

Turn towards the Harbour at Townhall lights. Located next to Fire Hall(no siren).

$50-65S/D $15Add.person   ▶ 6A,4Ch
◐ Full 🏠 Downtown, older, harbour view, large old fashioned porch ■4D (upstairs) ⊨2T,3Q ⬗1Private, 1sh.w.g. ★F,LF,TV in guest lounges, 1st floor sitting room, parking in rear ⒲No smoking, no pets
🏃· Harbour & beach, downtown Meaford, summer theatre, restaurants, large craft show, antique and gift shops, museum, Summerfest (Owen Sound) Country Music Festival (June)
🚐 Blue Mountain/Beaver Valley (downhill skiing), scenic caves, Bruce Trail hiking & Georgian Trail cycling
🐾 Old country atmosphere in gracious old home with oak woodwork and leaded glass windows. Good location from which to explore the pretty town. There are 2 cats. Pick-up/drop-off for hikers on Bruce Trail.↙B&B

Avery, John & Bobbie (Irish Mountain Bed & Breakfast)   ☎ (519) 538-2803
RR1, Meaford, ON N0H 1Y0   E-mail: hugo@log.on.ca

From Collingwood or Owen Sound, take Hwy 26 to 5 km west of Meaford. Then take Grey Rd 112 north for 4.6 km. Turn left at top of hill to house on left along the cliff.
$45-75S $59-75D $80-100F $10Add.person $10Dog ◙ Meals   ▶ 8

◐ Full (Gourmet),(also available in suite) 🏠 Rural, split-level, acreage, fantastic view, swimming pool, patio, quiet ■1Ste,2D (upst & ground level) ⊨ 2S,3Q ⬗3Ensuite ★Air,F,LF,VCR, TV in guest room, hot tub on deck, separate entrance, facilities for the disabled Ⓦ No smoking, pets outside (kennel & fenced run) ∿some French
🏃 Great country restaurant, x-country ski & hiking trails, Irish Mountain Look-out, M.T.S.C. Meaford
🚐 Georgian Bay (swimming, fishing, sailing), downhill ski resorts, antique & gift shops
🐾 Spacious home (more California in style than rural Ontario) with soaring cathedral ceilings, large picture windows and magnificient views. Hosts are hospitality professionals who formerly operated one of the areas most popular restaurants, and well informed about hiking and eating places. Host leads guided tours along the Bruce Trail. There is a cat in hosts' quarters. ↙B&B

Bourne, Ann & Bill (Ash-Berry Hill B&B)　　　　　　　　　☎ (519) 538-2760
RR4, Meaford, ON　N4L 1W7

Take Hwy 26 to Meaford and 2km S (at lights) on Grey CtyRd7. Turn right (west) on John St (near top of hill) and right onto Penny Lane to end.
$45S　$55D　$15Child　$75F　$15Add.person　🍽 Meals　　　　　▶ 6A,2Ch
　　　　　　　　　　　　🍲 Full, homebaked　🏠 Rural, res., hillside, 2-storey, 5acres,
　　　　　　　　　　　　view from some guest rooms, patio, deck, quiet　■ 2D,1F(main &
　　　　　　　　　　　　lower level(walk-out)　🛏 3D,1Q　🛁 1Private,1sh.w.g.
　　　　　　　　　　　　★Air,KF,TV lounge with air-tight wood stove, guest quarters are
　　　　　　　　　　　　separate, wheel-chair ramp　🚭 No smoking, well-behaved pets
　　　　　　　　　　　　and children welcome
　　　　　　　　　　　　🔥 Bruce Trail & Georgian Trail, beaches, cycling, hiking, Meaford
　　　　　　　　　　　　Town Hall Opera and Play House (upstairs)
🚗 Collingwood, Blue Mountain & Talisman Ski Hills, Bruce Trail, beaches, scenic caves, Meaford
Harbour, good dining, golfing, boating, fishing, air tours, Owen Sound
🏃 A home with a view! Spacious modern retreat, decorated with a mix of antiques and
panoramaic view of Georgian Bay and countryside. Relax in the large music/sitting room with
grand piano, or in the cozy TV lounge. Breakfast is served in the comfortable country kitchen or on
the deck. Special diets can be accommodated. People-orientated hosts will provide pick-up from the
harbour, Georgian Trail or bus stop. There is a small dog and a budgie in residence. 3-7nights
special rate and seasonal rate available. ✔B&B

Franklin, Monika (Franro Farm & Bed & Breakfast)　　　☎ (519) 538-4597
RR2, Meaford, ON　N4L 1W6　　　　　　　　　　　　　　　Fax (519) 376-5996

From Meaford follow Grey County Rd 12 west to first stop sign. Turn left and proceed 1.5 km to
　　　　　　　　　　　　farm on right side.
　　　　　　　　　　　　$40S　$50D　$10Add.person　🍽 Meals　　　　▶ 6A,1ch
　　　　　　　　　　　　🍲 Full, homebaked　🏠 Farm, modern bungalow, 110 acres, view
　　　　　　　　　　　　from guest rooms, patio, deck, quiet　■ 3D　🛏 2D,1Q
　　　　　　　　　　　　🛁1Sh.w.g., whirlpool tub　★ F,TV,VCR, separate entrance
　　　　　　　　　　　　🚭No pets, no smoking
　　　　　　　　　　　　🔥 Fishing, trail rides
　　　　　　　　　　　　🚗 Wasaga Beach, boating, swimming, hiking, biking, golfing,
Summer Theatre, roadside markets, Owen Sound, excellent harbour, craft shows, Fall Fairs,
Collingwood, Blue Mountain skiing, scenic caves, farmers' and flea markets
🏃 Modern farm home surrounded by 2 acres of lawns & flower gardens on working farm in apple
country raising prize-winning Hereford cattle and modern Shetland Ponies. Enjoy the warm and
friendly hospitality. There is a small dog in residence. ✔CC

Prazmowski, Richard & Jan Smith (Belina House B&B)　　☎ (519) 538-3536
RR4, Meaford, ON　N4L 1W7　　　　　　　　　　　　　　　Fax (519) 538-3741

From Collingwood or Owen Sound, take Hwy 26 to Meaford. Take Grey Rd 7 south for 6.5km to
Griersville. Turn left on the Old Mail Rd and proceed 0.5km to B&B.
$45-60S　$55-70D　$10Child　🍽 Meals　(longer stay rates)　　　　▶ 6A,2Ch
　　　　　　　　　　　　🍲 Full, homebaked　🏠 Rural, 2-storey, view, deck, quiet　■3D
　　　　　　　　　　　　(upstairs)　🛏 2T,2Q,1P　🛁 1sh.w.g., 1ensuite　★Air,F,TV,
　　　　　　　　　　　　guest quarters are separate　♥ (on weekends)　🚭 No smoking,
　　　　　　　　　　　　no pets
　　　　　　　　　　　　🔥 Bruce Trail (hiking)
　　　　　　　　　　　　🚗 Beaver Valley, Georgian Bay, Georgian Trail (hiking, biking,
　　　　　　　　　　　　skiing), golf courses, snowmobile trails, antique shops, apple
　　　　　　　　　　　　orchards, local theatre, farmer's markets, downhill & x-c skiing
🏃 Modern country home located in the rolling hills of the Beaver Valley on the historic Old Mail
Rd, with the Niagara Escarpment at the front door. Relax on the back deck and listen to the wind in
the trees. Wake to the cooing of mourning doves. Hosts' interests range from painting and
photography to travel and theatre, from books and music to cooking and automobiles. Special
dietary needs can be accommodated. There is a dog and a cat in residence. ✔B&B

Merrickville   *(north of Brockville; see also Bishop Mills, Oxford Mills)*

Munroe, Sheila & Jim (Seven Gables B&B)   ☎ (613) 269-2545
RR4, Merrickville, ON   K0G 1N0

Located 4km north of Merrickville on CtyRd 2 Andrewsville.
$45S $55D   ► 6A
🈫 Full(country-style)   🏠 Rural, 2-storey, hist., acreage, view
from guest rooms, quiet   ■ 3D(upstairs)   ⊨ 2T,1D,1Q,cot
🛁2Sh.w.g.   ★ F,TV,KF,LF, separate entrance   ⊛ Designated
smoking area, not suitable for children
🕴 Rideau Canal at Nicholson's Locks, tennis court on property,
walking trails, fishing, canoeing, cycling
🚙 Merrickville (artist's village with antiques/crafts, glass blowers, leather shop, bake shops &
quaint tea rooms), Andrewsville (one of Ontario's ghost towns), Ottawa
🔺 1846-built stone farmhouse located in a quiet peaceful setting. Enjoy nature to the fullest,
unwind with a game of tennis, curl up by the stone fireplace in the parlour or simply "cloud gaze"!
Theme guest rooms are called "Equestrian, Nautical & Garden Rooms". There is a Golden Retriever
"Angus" in residence. Visa ✒B&B

Midland   *(on Georgian Bay; see also Penetang, Waubaush, Victoria Hbr)*

Bellamy, Eileen & Ron (A Place for All Seasons B&B)   ☎(705) 835-0048
RR1, Midland, ON   L4R 4K3   Fax (705) 835-2724

From Hwy 93 at Orr Lake turn onto McDonald Rd. Proceed 2km to stop sign. Cross Scarlett Line
and continue (Mcdonald Rd becomes 68/69 Side Rd). Turn into 2nd driveway on left (No 168)
$50S $65D $5Child(under age 7) $15Add.person   🍽 Meals   ► 11A,2Ch

🈫 Full, homebaked   🏠 Rural, 3-storey, view from guest rooms,
patio, porch, quiet   ■4 (upper & ground level) incl eff.unit
⊨1S,3D,1K,2P,1R   🛁1Sh.w.g., 1sh.w.h., plus 1private in
eff.unit   ★Air, F,TV in guest rooms, ceiling fans, separate
entrance, spa and fitness equipment, off-street parking, games
room, guest quarters are separate   ⊛ No smoking, no pets
🕴 Restaurant, golfing, hiking, picnic area/barbeque, Orr Lake
🚙 Midland, Barrie, Orillia, Wasaga Beach, Collingwood, fishing
🔺 Warm welcome in uniquely designed spacious country home with double turret, located in
centre of Huronia Tourism area. Ideal place for winter or summer, short or long term vacation.
Enjoy the 50km panoramic view of the lake, mountains and farmlands from the terrace. Breakfast
is served in special guest breakfast room. There is a dog in residence. Visa ✒B&B

Coulter, Marg & Mark (Mark & Margie's Bed & Breakfast)   ☎ (705) 526-4441
670 Hugel Ave., Midland, ON   L4R 1W9   E-mail: mcoulter@sympatico.ca, Fax (705) 526-4426

Follow Hwy 400 north to Hwy 93, turn right on Hugel Ave. (2nd
stoplight after Hwy 12 across from Mountainview Mall).
$55S $65-75D (Reservation, please)   ► 6
🈫 Full, homebaked   🏠 Village, hist., 2-storey, veranda   ■ 3
(upstairs)   ⊨ 2T,1Q,1K   🛁2Sh.w.g.   ★ Air,TV/VCR, guest
sitting room, off-street parking   ⊛ Smoking outside
🕴 Downtown Midland, shops, restaurants, Midland Docks, 30000
Islands Boat Cruises, Little Lake Park with sandy beach, churches
🚙 Marty'rs Shrine, Ste-Marie-Among-The-Hurons, King's Wharf Theatre, Discovery Harbour
🔺 Victorian Century Home in prime downtown neighbourhood with large veranda for relaxation.
Enjoy the warm and friendly atmosphere. Hosts are well informed about area activities, eating
establishments and local entertainment. There is a small Cocker Spaniel (Frankie) who makes
everyone feel welcome. Pick-up from bus station available. Visa,MC

Hébert, Mrs. Ruth (G & R Hébert Bed & Breakfast)   ☎ (705) 526-9474
Box 696, Midland, ON   L4R 4P4

Phone for directions. Located 1km from Town Center.
$30S $40-50D $5Child $10Add.person (Family rates
available)   🍽 Meals   ▶ 6A,5Ch
🍳Homebaked   🏠 Rural, bungalow, deck, quiet   ■ 4 (main
floor)   ⬜ 1Sh.w.h.   ⊨2T,1D,1Q,2R,1P   ★Air,TV,LF
🚭Designated smoking area, no pets   ⤳ French
🚗 Town Center, Georgian Bay (sailing, swimming, boating,
fishing), golfing, Saint Marie Among The Hurons, Martyr's Shrine,
Huronia Indian Village/Musum, 30000 Isls cruise, x-c skiing, snowmobiling, ice fishing
☛ Warm welcome in quiet comfortable home surrounded by 40 year-old pine trees. Relax and
enjoy the homecooked meals. Hostess has a collection of interesting bells. Pick-up from bus/town.
⤸B&B

O'Halloran, Suzanne and Tim (Kylemore B&B)   ☎ Fax (705) 526-6063
427 King St., Midland, ON   L4R 3N3   E-mail: kylemore@cryston.ca

Take Hwy 400 to Hwy 93, then east on Hwy 12 for 2.8km to King St. Turn left to 2nd stoplight,
then look for 4th red brick house on right.
$40S $55D (special rates for extended stays)   ▶ 5
🍳 Full, homebaked   🏠 Downtown, covered front porch   ■2D,1S(upstairs)   ⊨1Q,2T,1S
⬜1Sh.w.g.   ★F(fieldstone) in guest sitting room, phone in guest rooms, separate entrance,
ample parking   🚭No smoking, no pets
🏃 Little Lake Park, Huronia Museum & Huron Indian Village, downtown Midland (fascinating
murals), Georgian Bay waterfront, cruises
🚗 Ste.Marie-Among-The-Hurons, Martyr's Shrine, Wye Marsh Wildlife Sanctuary,
☛ Elegantly decorated turn-of-the-Century home furnished with antiques; situated in older
residential section of Midland. Breakfast is served in the formal dining room. Professional hosts are
happy to assist with suggestions for day trips in and around the Midland area. Computer, printer
and fax service available. ⤸CC

Mildmay   *(south-east of Kincardine; see also Clifford, Walkerton, Cargill)*

Culbert, Shirley & George (Whispering Brook B&B)   ☎ (519) 367-2565,Fax (519) 367-5434
7 Jane St., Mildmay, ON   N0G 2J0

Phone for directions.
$45S $50D $10Child/Add.person $60F   ▶ 4A,4Ch
🍳 Cont., homebaked   🏠 Res., village edge, split-level (3-storey),
2.5acres, patio, porch, deck, quiet, secluded   ■2F(main & upper
level) ⊨2D,2R, play pen with pad ⬜1Sh.w.g.,2sh.w.h. ★TV in
guest lounge, off-street parking 🚭Smoking outside, no pets
🏃 Stocked trout pond on property (watch 2 resident swans and
fish jump), feed deer in paddock on lawn, abandoned CNR rail-line
to explore,x-c skiing snowmobile trails, Village Christmas Lights Displays (well known)
🚗 Lake Huron beaches, ferry to Manitoulin Island, Blyth theatre town, Mennonite Country
☛ Warm welcome in comfortable, sunny cedar home in a park-like setting, situated in small and
friendly village ("where everyone knows everyone else") with interesting little shops and local crafts.
Relax in the park-like atmosphere & stroll among the flower beds. Sit on the lawn swing and watch
the deer. Breakfast is served in the country kitchen, on the large cedar deck, or in dining lounge.
Children welcome. ⤸CC

Milford

(south of Picton; see also Bloomfield, Wellington, Consecon)

Taylor, Al & Rita (Colleen Cottage)
68 Morrisons Pt.Rd., RR2, Milford, ON   K0K 2P0
☎ (613) 476-7346

Phone for specific details regarding routing from Picton.

$45-65S/D   ◧Meals (Reservations recommended) ►4
▣Full,homebaked   ♠Rural, res., split-level, view, patio acreage,
quiet, riverfront ■2 (main & upper level) ⊨2T(1K),1Q
⊐1Sh.w.g.,1ensuite   ★Air,F, TV/VCR in guest sitting room,
separate entrance ⊕No pets
♔ Black River Cheese Factory, cross-country skiing, excellent area
for cycling, walking, dock
🚗 World renowned white sandy beaches, Sandbanks Prov.Park

🔫 Award winning, beautifully landscaped modern home with extensive lawns hugging the bank of the Black River in a tranquil country setting on Morrisons Point Rd. Relax on the patio facing the river. Breakfast, including homemade granola muffins, is served in the dining room, overlooking the rose garden & river. Winter week-end specials available. Two cats "Sheba" & "Mister" make everyone welcome.

Millbank

(north of Stratford; see also Newton)

Henderson, Jack and Alveretta (Honeybrook Farm)
6662 Road 116, RR1, Millbank, Ontario N0K 1L0
☎ (519) 595-4604

Phone for specific directions and reservation.
$40S $55D $15Add.person   ◧ Meals   ►6A
▣Choice, homebaked (from extensive menue)   ♠160-acre farm,
hist., view, quiet ■2D(upstairs) ⊨2T,2D
⊐1Private,1sh.w.g.   ★TV,F,LF, indiv.heat control ⊕No pets,
no smoking, not suitable for children   ⇝Some French
🚗 Kitchener, Stratford & Drayton theatres, St.Jacobs, markets
🔫 Restored 1866 split granite house situated on rolling land by
the Nith River. Large comfortable rooms. ⌐B&B

Milton

(west of Toronto: see also Campbellville, Burlington, Oakville, Guelph)

Sandlohken, Horst and Ille (Red Maple House)
RR3, Milton, ON   L9T 2X7
☎ (905) 878-5716

From Hwy 401 take Exit 320 (Hwy 25) north and go 8 km to Reg Rd 15 (Service Station on corner). Turn left and look for house 2 km down road on left (No. 6190).

$30S $50D   ►2A
▣ Choice   ♠ 40-acre Maple Bush farm, ranch-style, tranquil,
isolated, swimming pool ■1D ⊨2T ⊐Ensuite ★Air,TV,F,
separate entrance ⊕ no pets ⇝ German
♔ Maple bush, Bruce Trail for hiking and cross-country skiing
🚗 Agricultural Museum, Glen Eden and Bronte Conservation
areas (summer and winter recreation), Crawford Lake restored
Indian village, Campbellville quaint village shopping

🔫 Contemporary, spacious country home with European atmosphere, tastefully furnished and situated on the Niagara Escarpment with own maple bush at backdoor. Watch maple syrup being made in the Spring and sold in March.

Minden

(south of Haliburton)

Howarth, Phyllis (The Stone House)
RR3, Minden, ON   K0M 2K0

☎ (705) 286-1250

Located 3 km north of Minden on Hwy 35. Phone for directions.
$85S $95D $25Add.person   ▶ 12A
❄ May15-Oct15   ☕ Full (hearty gourmet)   🏠 Rural, acreage,
view, quiet   ■2D,1Apt (main and upper floor)plus 2cottages in
the woods   ⊨T,D,K,Q   ⇗ All private, plus outdoor shower
★F,LF, 2guest kitchens, parking   ⓦNo smoking
🧍 Swimming and boating on lake or river, golfing, trail hiking
📢 Secluded rustic hideaway with walking trails thru woods.
Relax in a "real piece of paradise and island of tranquility". ✍CC

Pflug, Don & Jessie (Stouffer Mill Bed & Breakfast)
Hall's Lake, RR2, Minden, ON   K0M 2K0

☎ (705) 489-3024
1-888-593-8888

At junction of Hwys 35 & 118 (Carnarvon) proceed north on Hwy 35 for 9.3 km to Halls Lake. Turn
left on Stouffer Mill Rd., past old mill site 1 km to B&B.
$60S $65D $15Add.person   🍽 Meals   ▶ 6
☕ Full, homebaked   🏠 Rural, 2-storey 12-sided circular home,
acreage, view from guest rooms, swimming pool, patio, porch,
private deck, quiet   ■ 3D (upstairs)   ⊨ 2T,2Q   ⇗2Sh.w.g.
★2F,LF,TV in common room, separate entrance, canoe rental
ⓦNo smoking, no pets   〰 Some French
🧍 Walking, canoeing, fishing, swimming, x-c skiing, snowshoeing
🚗 Golfing, hiking, biking, boating, downhill skiing, Algonquin Park, dog sled races
📢 Unique, 12-sided circular home with suspended family rooms, rooftop solarium and a beautiful
view of Hall's Lake. Situated on 130 acres of peaceful and natural landscape in the Haliburton
Highlands. There is a dog in residence. ✍CC

Snyder, Nora (Minden House Bed & Breakfast)
23 North Water St., Box 136, Minden, ON   K0M 2K0

☎ (705) 286-4450

From Hwy 35 north, take first exit to Minden. Follow Main St over bridge, turn right immediately.
$60S $70D $10Add.person   ▶ 8A,2Ch
☕ Full, homebaked   🏠 Village, hist., 1 acre, view from guest
rooms, quiet, riverfront, porch   ■1S,3D(upstairs)   ⊨ 2T,1D,1Q,
2cots   ⇗Sh.w.g.   ★F,TV, off-street parking   ⓦPets welcome
(in cottages only)
🧍 Downtown, shopping, churches, walking trails
🚗 Haliburton Highlands, Dorset, Algonquin Park, golfing
📢 Century home (circa 1850) with wrap-around porch situated
on the Gull River in small village. Enjoy the cozy and friendly atmosphere. Also available: five
housekeeping cottages. There are 2 cats in residence.✍B&B

Mitchell

(west of Stratford)

Mikel, Ronald & Muriel ("Our Little Inn")   ☎ (519) 393-5521
RR2, Mitchell, ON   N0K 1N0

Take Hwy 8 west of Stratford 10km to Fullarton Twsp Rd145. Turn left (south) to 1st crossroad,

Line 32, then left to first farm on right.
$45S $50-60D $15Add.person   ► 4A,2Ch
🍽 Full, homebaked   🏠 Farm, older, 2-storey, quiet   ■3D
(upstairs)   ⊨1D,1Q,2T   ⌐Sh.w.g.   ★TV, parking   Ⓦ No
smoking, no pets
🕱 Apple orchard, lane to bush, various local area activities
🚗 Stratford Festivall Theatre, Grand Bend, antique & shops
🖙 Spacious, Century-old field-stone house on working farm
with peaceful country atmosphere, situated on 99 acres. Relax on the large veranda and watch the
sunsets. There are handcrafts and woodcrafts (made by the host family) to view and purchase.
House specialty is home-pressed apple juice, jams & scones.

Mountain

(south-east of Ottawa; see also North Gower)

Empey, Leroy & Barbara (That Added Touch)   ☎ (613) 989-5236/Fax (613) 989-2288
RR2, Mountain, ON   K0E 1S0   E-mail: lempey@sympatico.ca

Located on Hwy 43 between Kempville & Winchester. Phone for directions.

$55D $85 (Honeymoon package)   ► 4
🍽 Full, homebaked (with Champagne for honeymoon package)
🏠 Rural,res.,acreage,view,patio,swimming pool,quiet,isolated
■2D(upst)   ⊨2T,1Q   ⌐1Sh.w.g.   ★Air,F,LF,KF,TV in guest
room, sep.entrance   Ⓦ No pets   ⌁some French
🕱 Well-known local restaurant, apple orchard, walks in cornfield
by starlight, gift shop attached to house
🚗 Golf courses, Upper Canada Village, Bird Sanctuary, Rideau
Canal (boat rides, picnics, skating in winter), historic towns
🖙 Spacious Cape Cod home in a country setting with the upstairs totally for guests' use. Country
style breakfast can be served in guest room or private patio. There are pets in residence.
Honeymooners especially welcome. ✒B&B

Newboro

(north-east of Kingston; see also Westport)

King, Charlene & Bob (Newboro House Bed & Breakfast))   ☎ (613) 272-3181
31 Drummond St., Newboro, ON   K0G 1P0

From Hwy 401, take Exit 623 & Hwy 15 north. Turn left on Hwy 42 and go west 8 km to Newboro.
From Hwy 7, turn south on Hwy 15 at Carleton Place and proceed to Hwy 42 and Newboro.

$50-60 $55-65   (Picnic lunches)   ► 6
📅 May1-Oct.31   🍽 Full   🏠 Rural, hist., acreage, quiet
■3D(main & upper level)   ⊨ 2T,2D   ⌐ 1Private, 1sh.w.g.,
1ensuite   ★ Separate entrance, parking, secure storage for
bicycles   Ⓦ No smoking, no pets, not suitable for young children
⌁ some French
🕱 Historic blockhouse at Newboro Locks, canoeing/boating on
Rideau Waterway, popular cycling route, restaurants
🚗 Public golf courses, Foley Mt.Cons.Area (beach, self-guided walking tours, bird watching)
🖙 Second Empire Architecture home (1880) authentically renovated, with spacious rooms,
tastefully decorated and surrounded by lawns & gardens for relaxing and sunbathing. Enjoy the
warm and friendly atmosphere. ✒B&B

New Hamburg

(east of Stratford; see also Baden, Wellesley, Gadshill, Tavistock)

Cressman, Jeanette & Orval (Woodlot Acres Retreat) ☎ (519) 662-2089
RR1, New Hamburg, ON N0B 2G0   Fax (519) 662-6919

From Stratford take Hwy 7/8 East past New Hamburg and exit to Waterloo (Region) Rd3. Turn right and proceed 1km to B&B on right, or phone for directions.
$50S $65-95D $15Child 🍽 Meals   ▶ 6
🌷 Apr1-Nov30 ▥ Full, homebaked 🏠 Rural, 2-storey open concept, acreage, view from guest rooms, porch, deck, quiet ■3D (upstairs) ⊨ 2Q,2T(long), playpen ⌂1sh.w.g.,1ensuite (jaccuzzi) ★ Air,F,TV, piano Ⓦ No smoking, no pets
🥾 Maple syrup bush (operating in Spring), c-x skiing, hiking, pick your own blueberries in season
🚗 New Hamburg, Waterwheel, Ten Thousand Villages, Castle Kilbride, antiques/arts, golfing
🐾 Retired couple in fairly new tastefully decorated home with spacious grounds, on a quiet country road in Mennonite Country. Well travelled hosts are farm oriented, but no longer farm; are very involved with their family and enjoy welcoming guests. Relax by the fieldstone fireplace or on the deck after a hectic day of travelling and sightseeing. Business travellers welcome. ✒B&B

McMillan, Mrs. Ruby (Glenalby Farms) ☎ (519) 625-8353
RR1, New Hamburg, ON N0B 2G0

Situated 16.6 km east of Stratford. Phone for directions.
$70S $75-85D $115F   ▶ 10A,4Ch
▥ Full, homebaked 🏠 Dairy farm, hist. ■4D,F
⊨T,D,P,R ⌂3Sh.w.g ★ Air,TV,F Ⓦ No pets, no smoking
🥾 Conservation area (lake/picnic grounds/woodland trails)
🚗 Stratford, Mennonite country, antique auctions and shopping
🐾 Picturesque 6th Generation farm surrounded by hills and woods. Hot cider served by fieldstone fireplace. Hosts keep registered Lassie Collies & Clydesdale horses. Enjoy the English-style flower gardens. Hosts have welcomed B&B guests for many years.

Newton

(north of Stratford; see also Millbank, Listowel)

Streicher, Marlene and Ezra (Country Charm) ☎ (519) 595-8789
RR1, Newton, ON N0K 1R0

Located 0.75 km south of Newton. Phone for directions.
$30S $45D $5Child 🍽 Meals   ▶ 6A,2Ch
▥ Full 🏠 Farm, quiet ■ 3(upst) ⊨T,D,Q ⌂Sh.w.g.
★Separate entrance, parking, jacuzzi (in winter only) Ⓦ No smoking,no pets ～Pennsyl.Dutch
🥾 Sawmill and buggy shop, store
🚗 Stratford, Millbank, bakery/cheese factory, Kitchener
🐾 Warm welcome by Amish Mennonite family in large country home with new addition. Relax in the jacuzzi. ✒B&B

Niagara Falls

(see also NOTL, St.Catharines, Fenwick, Port Colborne)

Burke, Carolyn & Gary (Park Place Bed & Breakfast)   ☎ (905) 358-0279
4851 River Rd., Niagara Falls, ON   L2E 3G4

$65-140S/D $90-100CarriageHouse $15Child $20Add.person (2nights rates avail.)   ► 8A,2Ch
Take QEW to Hwy 420 and continue to Clifton Hill, turn left and proceed to River Rd., left again 1.9

km to house on corner of Ellis St (entrance on Ellis St)
❖ Summer only (by arrangement during off-season) ⬛ Full,
homebaked   🏠 Res., 2-storey, hist., view, riverfront, porch
■2S,1Ste (upstairs)   ⊨ 1D,1Q,1K,2cots   ⬛ 2Private,
1sh.w.h.   ★ F,private entrance for guests, jacuzzi/sauna,private
balcony, host quarters are separate, off-street parking ⬤No
pets, smoking on porches only
🕴 The Falls, Skylon Tower, Imax Theatre, Victoria Pk, bicycling
🚗 Floral Clock, Botanical Gardens, wine route, Marineland, boat/helicopter rides, Casino Niagara
🚌 Queen Ann-style Victorian home, designated historic and lovingly restored, with corner turret
and views of the Niagara River gorge, located on the Niagara River Parkway. Breakfast is served in
formal setting with silver, lace, linens and fine china. Special diets will be cheerfully accommodated.
Pick-up from train or bus station with prior arrangement. The carriage house can accommodate a
family and has cooking facilities. There is a large black Lab in residence. ✓B&B

Gardiner, Stan and Marg (Gretna Green B&B Guest House)   ☎ (905) 357-2081
5077 River Rd., Niagara Falls, ON   L2E 3G7

From QEW take Hwy 420 into Niagara Falls and turn left on Stanley Ave. At 2nd set of traffic
lights turn right onto Morrison St. Go to end and turn right onto River Rd.   ► 8A,2Ch

$45S $55-70D $5Child $10Add.person   (Winter rates available)
⬛Full   🏠Res.,older,view,quiet   ■3D,1F (upstairs)
⊨2S,1D,2Q   ⬛4Ensuite   ★Air, TV in guest room, separate
entrance, parking   ⬤No pets
🕴 Falls, Niagara Gorge
🚗 Skylon Tower, Rose Gardens and Floral Clock, Imax Theatre
🚌 Scottish hosts welcome visitors to their home with a view of
the Niagara Gorge. Bus/train pick-up available upon
request.✓B&B

Lambertson, Norma (Bed of Roses Bed & Breakfast)   ☎ & Fax (905) 356-0529
4877 River Rd., Niagara Falls, ON   L2E 3G5

From Hwy 420 take Stanley Ave Exit into Niagara Falls. Travel to
Bridge St, right to River Rd, right to Ellis St; house on corner.
$60S $85-95D $95-135F   ► 4A,4Ch
⬛ Full, homebaked   🏠 Res., 2-storey, hist., riverfront, porch,
quiet, view from one unit   ■ 2 units(upstairs)   ⊨ 2D,2P
⬛2Private ⬤ No pets   ★Air,TV,KF, private entrance for
each unit, off-street parking
🕴 Niagara Falls, Rainbow Bridge, Whirlpool, Floral Green house
🚗 Niagara-on-the-Lake, Shaw Festival theatres, Fort George, St.Catharines, Welland Canal
🚌 Retired couple in spacious home with two family B&B units, located between Rainbow &
Whirlpool Bridges. Breakfast served "room-service style" delivered on a tray to be enjoyed in
privacy. Enjoy the old-fashioned "Southern Hospitality" in busy tourist town.✓ B&B

Siciliano, Luciana (Butterfly Manor Bed & Breakfast) ☎ (905) 358-8988
4917 River Rd., Niagara Falls, ON   L2E 3G5   E-mail: b&bnotl@freenet.npiec.on.ca

From Toronto follow QEW to Hwy 420. Turn left on Stanley, right on Morrison, right again on Zimmerman and 2 blocks to River Rd. From Buffalo cross Peace Bridge and follow Niagara River Parkway to the Falls and to house 1.5 km north of Falls on the river.

$75S $85D $10Child $15Add.person   ► 8A,2Ch
🍲 Full, homebaked   🏠 Res., 2-storey, view from guest rooms, riverfront, quiet   ■ 4D (upstairs)   ⊨ 4D   ⛝ 4Ensuite ★Air,F, separate entrance, off-street parking   ⓦ No smoking, no pets   ～ Italian, German, French, Spanish
🏃 Mighty Falls, Niagara Falls/NY, downtown, restaurants, tourist attractions, shopping, shuttle bus, train/bus stations
🚗 Niagara-on-the-Lake, Buffalo, NY

🐾 Old Manor-type home with a delightful blend of old and new, overlooking the Niagara River, situated in convenient location from the Falls and other points of interest on both sides of the border. Breakfast is cooked and served in the very large open, modern kitchen with fireplace. Special Rates for longer stays. ↝B&B

Niagara-on-the-Lake   *(north of Niagara Falls; see also St.Catharines, Vineland)*

Blaney, Betty & Brock (Blaney House B&B) ☎ (905) 468-5362
177 Victoria St., Box 302, Niagara-on-the-Lake, ON   L0S 1J0

From QEW, take Hwy 55 and follow to end, which is Queen St. Turn right proceed 3 block to Victoria. Turn left to house on left.

$90-100S/D   ► 6A
🍲 Full, homebaked   🏠 Downtown, hist., patio, quiet   ■3D (main & upper floor)   ⊨ 2Q,1K(2T)   ⛝ 3Ensuite ★Air, off-street parking, guest quarters are separate   ⓦ No smoking, no pets, not suitable for children
🏃 All theatres, restaurants, galleries, shops, museum, Lake Ontario waterfront and park, riverboat cruises, golfing, horse-drawn carriage rides through town, Fort George
🚗 Niagara River Parkway, MacKenzie House, Laura Secord Homestead, scenic canal drive, Butterfly Conservatory, wineries and tours, Port Dalhouse, Niagara Falls, Botanical Gardens
🐾 Gracious, antique filled historic home (ca1816) located in the heritage district of historic town. Distinctive varied breakfasts are served in the elegant dining room overlooking the back garden. Hosts are avid auction-goers and collect & refinish antique clocks. ↝CC

Brown, Helen & Bill (Trillium House B&B) ☎(905) 468-5649
6 Christopher St., Box 995, Niagara-on-the-Lake, ON   L0S 1J0

From QEW take Exit onto Hwy 55 and continue 14km to Niagara-on-the-lake. Turn right on John St, right on Charlotte St and left on Christopher St.

$95-110D   ► 6A
➕ May-Nov   🍲 Full   🏠 Res., 2-storey, view from guest rooms, 0.5acre, swimming pool, patio, quiet   ■ 3D(upstairs) ⊨2T,2Q   ⛝ 1ensuite,1sh.w.g.   ★ Air,F, off-street parking ⓦNo smoking, no pets, not suitable for children   ～ French
🏃 Shaw Festival Theatre, Old Towne, shops, boutiques, galleries, restaurants, Fort George, lakeside park and walkways, bicycle and roller blade path linking up with Niagara Parkway to Niagara Falls, public transport
🚗 Golf courses, numerous wineries (wine tasting tours), Niagara River boat trips, Village of Queenston, Weir Art Gallery, Butterfly Conservatory, Welland Canal (viewing platform/museum)
🐾 Retired Professional couple in Williamsburg-style house with authentic decor and furnished with antiques. Enjoy the peaceful setting and relax in the sunroom-lounge or quiet sitting room overlooking the beautiful garden surrounding the swimming pool. Breakfast is served in the special guest breakfast room. Rental bicycles available. ↝B&B

Cummins, Bill & Lavender (Erinbeg Bed & Breakfast) ☎ (905) 468-0040, Fax 0039
Box 1273, 156 Gate St. Niagara-on-the-Lake, ON L0S 1J0 E-mail: cummins@mergetel.com

Situated right in the old town at the corner of Gate & Prideaux Sts and 1 block north of Queen St.

$75S $85-105D $25Add.person ► 7
🍴Full, homebaked 🏠Downtown, res., 3-storey, hist., view, porch,
quiet ■1Ste,2D (upst) ⊨1R,2T,2Q ⌁1Sh.w.g., 1ensuite ★ Air,
adjoining sitting room in suite, off-street pkg 🚭No smoking,no pets
🏃 Lake Ontario, 4 theatres, shopping, dining, golfing, Art Gallery
🚗 Niagara Falls, wineries (tours), St.Catharines, Marineland
📷 Elegant, bright historic (1890) home situated among mature trees
& view of Lake Ontario reflects hosts' love of antiques and pewterware.
House specialty is Irish Soda Bread as well as hot Gooseberry Sauce &
Yogourt for potato pancakes. Visa ⌐CC

Derry, Glenda & Bill (Cottonwood B&B Inn) ☎ & Fax (905)-468-1236, 1-888-663-3302
377 Johnson St., Box 1145, Niagara-on-the-Lake, ON L0S 1J0

From Toronto or US border, take QEW to Hwy 55 and follow signs to Niagara-on-the-Lake (old
town). Proceed on Mississauga Rd to Johnson St, turn left.

$112-124S/D (plus tax) ► 6A
🍴 Full 🏠 Downtown, res., 2-storey, quiet, secluded, porch
■3D(upstairs) ⊨ 2T,1Q,1K ⌁ 3Ensuite ★ Air,F, private
entrance, off-street parking, guest quarters are separate 🚭No
smoking, no pets, not suitable for childen
🏃 All Shaw Festival theatres, golf course (NA's oldest), historic
Fort Mississauga & Fort Niagara, historic Queen Street shopping,
fine dining, biking & hiking trails, picnic areas by the Lake
🚗 Estate wineries, Niagara Parkway scenic drive, Niagara Falls, Welland Canal, Casino Niagara
📷 Retired Professional couple in spacious home, specifically designed for B&B and inspired by
the romantic architecture of the USA's Old South, with full width columned gallery, entry fanlight,
arched dormer windows and carved mantels. Relax in the gracious guest lounge or on the wide front
porch. Breakfast is served in special guest breakfast room. Visa,MC,Amex ⌐B&B

Hernder, Pat and Art (Hernder's Country Home) ☎ (905) 468-3192
753, Line 3, RR2 Niagara-on-the-Lake, ON L0S 1J0

From QEW take Exit Hwy 55 and proceed to Four Mile Creek Rd. At Virgil traffic light turn right,
continue to Line 3 and then left to 1st house on right.

$75-80S/D $20Add.person ► 10
🍴 Full,homebaked 🏠 Farm (vineyard), 2-level, view, quiet
■4D,Ste(main & ground floor) ⊨1K/2T,3Q ⌁ 2Ensuite,
2private ★Air,F,large guest rec-room with
TV/fridge/microwave, large outside hot tub, screened gazebo
🚭No pets,child. min. age 10, smoking outside only
🏃 Conservation area, tennis, wineries (tours and tasting), cycling
🚗 Downtown, theatres, restaurants, Niagara Falls, Casino
📷 Spacious Colonial home viewing the Niagara Escarpment, situated on the wine route amidst
the cottage wineries, in the heart of Niagara's fruitland. Breakfasts always include fresh Niagara
fruits in season. Hosts'hobbies are handcrafted woodworks & Big-Band-Era memorabilia. ⌐B&B

Hiebert, Otto and Marlene (Hiebert's Guest House)   ☎ (905) 468-3687
Box 1371,275 John St., Niagara-on-the-Lake, ON   L0S 1J0

From QEW take Hwy 55 to NOTL. Turn left at John St to 3rd house on right.

$55-80S $60-85D   ► 6A,4Ch
🍴 Full, homebaked   🏠 Village, raised bungalow, patio ■3 (low.level)   ♥   ⊨T,Q,sofabed ⌂2Ensuite,1sh.w.g.   ★Air,F,TV in 2 guest rooms, private entrance for one room, parking ⓌNo smoking,no pets
🚶 Theatres, Main Street restaurants & shops, historic sites
🚗 Wineries, Niagara Falls, Artpark NY, Buffalo
🚐 Located in quiet peaceful setting. Guest accommodation is on separate floor overlooking garden. Hosts are natives of the Old Towne and well informed. ⌐B&B

King, Helen and Mike (The King's Way)   ☎ (905) 468-5478
308 Nassau St, Box 684, Niagara-on-the-Lake, ON   L0S 1J0

From QEW take the exit for N-O-T-L (Hwy 55) and follow through Virgil to Williams Street. Turn left, go 2 blocks to Nassau Street, turn right on Nassau St.

$55-80D $10Child $15Add.person   ► 6A,2A
🍴Full 🏠Res, acreage, patio, quiet ■3D(upst)
⊨3Q,2cots ⌂1Private, 2shw.g.   ★Air,F,parking, guest room balconies, guest parlor ⓌNo smoking, no pets
🚶 Shaw Festival Theatres, golfing, shopping, restaurants
🚗 Art Park (Lewiston), US border, Fort Erie, hiking, N.Falls
🚐 Enthusiastic host family in spacious modern home with walk-out balconies, located on a quiet street within strolling distance of downtown, theatres and shops. ⌐B&B

Krikorian, Donald & Julia (Innisfree on the Lake B&B)   ☎ (905) 468-1844
14 Firelane 2A, RR3, Niagara-on-the-Lake, ON   L0S 1J0

From QEW, take NOTL Exit 38 to Hwy 55 and follow to Virgil. Turn left on Four Mile Creek Rd and follow to end. Turn left on Lakeshore Rd, then take first right on Firelane 2 and right again on Firelane 2A.

$75S $90D $130F $20Add.person   ► 8
🍴 Full   🏠 Rural, 2-storey, view from guest rooms, lakeback, porch, guest deck, quiet secluded ■ 2D,1F(upstairs)
⊨3Q,2cots (if needed) ⌂ 1Sh.w.g.   ★ Air,TV, off-street parking, 2nd floor exclusively for guests, guest balcony Ⓦ No smoking, no pets
🚶 Lake Ontario, sandy beach, wine route, hike/bike along the breathtaking Niagara River
🚗 Niagara-on-the-Lake, Shaw Festival Theatre, Niagara Falls, Welland Canal, US border
🚐 Warm hospitality in charming Cape Cod country home overlooking Lake Ontario, located 3km from quaint little theatre town and surrounded by Ontario's wine region. Enjoy a full country breakfast while watching the splashing waves of Lake Ontario. Ideal place for bird watching enthusiasts. Guest balcony has view of Toronto skyline in distance. ⌐CC

Landray, Elaine & Phil (Linden House B&B)　　　☎ & Fax (905) 468-3923
389 Simcoe St., Box 1586, Niagara-on-the-Lake, ON　L0S 1J0　　E-mail: linden@niagara.com

Take QEW and Hwy 55 into NOTL. Turn right on William St and proceed to house on corner of
Simcoe St. From Lewiston-Queenston Bridge, follow Niagara Pkwy into N-O-T-L. From Queen &
King crossroads, follow Queen St to Simcoe St, left to William St. Parking from William St.

$75S　$90D　$20Add.person　　　　　　　　　► 6A
📅April 1-Dec1　🍴 Full　🏠 Res, 2-storey, deck, gazebo, quiet
■3D (upstairs private guest wing)　🛏 2T(or 1K),2Q (incl. brass
beds)　🚿 3Ensuite　★ Air,TV/VCR/books in guest lounge,
separate entrance, off-street parking　✋No smoking, no pets
〰some Spanish
🏃 Shaw Festival (3 theatres), Fort George, museum, bicycle trail
(50 km from NOTL to Fort Erie), downtown Queen Street & shops
🚗 Eight wineries, Niagara Falls, Welland Canal Lock 3 (viewing & museum),
🏴 Cape Cod style home was built in 1990 especially for B&B and, as such, affords privacy for
guests and hosts, located in the old town. Retired professionals have travelled extensively
world-wide. Enjoy a sumptuous breakfast featuring Niagara fruits (no need for lunch).✓B&B

Locke, Jane & Steve (Lakewinds Country Manor B&B Inn)　　☎ (905) 468-1888,
Box 1483, 328 Queen St., Niagara-on-the-Lake, ON　L0S 1J0　　　Fax (905) 468-1061

Located in the west end of NOTL, between Butler & Dorchester Streets overlooking golf course.

Take Hwy 55 to end (Queen St). Turn left.
$133S/D　(plus tax)　　　　　　　　　　► 8
🍴 Full(Gourmet)　🏠 Village, 3-storey, hist., acreage, view from
guest rooms, swimming pool, solarium, porch, large veranda,
quiet ■4D(upstairs)　🛏3Q,1K(2T)　🚿4Ensuite　〰French
★Air,F,TV,LF,separate entrance, off-street parking, guest lounge
with fridge, TV, billard table, indiv.temp control, guest bicycles
✋Smoking on veranda, no pets, children min. age 12
🏃 All Shaw theatres, restaurants, main street shops, golf course, lakeside park
🏴 Friendly and lively hosts in 1881-built Federalist-style home, renovated in 1994, tastefully
furnished with antiques and uniquely decorated guest rooms. Scrumptious breakfasts are served in
the dining room, or continental breakfast may be delivered to the guest room. After the theatre,
relax in the lounge or on the veranda, or have a dip in the pool. Hostess collects teapots. ✓B&B

McGraw, Hazel & Ron (Calabar House B&B)　　　☎(905)468-3349,Fax(905)468-1768
11 Confederation Dr.,Niagara-on-the-Lake,ON L0S 1J0

From jct Hwy 55 and Mary go 1.4km west on Mary (Lakeshore). Turn left on Garrison Village, 4th

left on Lower Canada, then first right on Confederation Dr.
$70S　$80-90D　$25Child/Add.person　　　► 8
🍴 Full, homebaked　🏠 Res., 2-storey, large veranda, quiet
■3(upstairs)　🛏 3K(6T),1P,1R　🚿 3Ensuite　★Air, TV/books
in guest parlour, guest quarters are separate, off-street parking
✋ Smoking on veranda, no pets, children min. age 12
🏃 Walking, jogging, roller blading, tennis, bicycle path to historic
area, shops, Niagara River, Lake Ontario
🚗 Niagara Falls, wineries (tours), Niagara bike/walking path (56km from Lake Erie to Lake
Ontario), Shaw Festival theatres, golfing, Casino, Butterfly Conservatory, Welland Canal, Brock U.
🏴 Large contemporary home situated in a quiet residential area with mature trees and beautiful
gardens. Breakfast, including Niagara fruit in season, is served in the dining room. Hosts are well
travelled, recent "empty nesters", who enjoy assisting their guests with local itineraries. Enjoy
comfort and quiet in the heart of Niagara. JCB,Visa,MC ✓B&B

McMorrough, Yvonne (Avoca B&B)   ☎ (905) 468-5217, Fax (905) 468-1702
RR3, G14, B63, Niagara-on-the-Lake, ON L0S 1J0

Located at 3 Sentry Circle on lakeshore site of area called Garrison Village.
$95-110D $10Child $30Add.person   (Senior Discounts on certain days)   ► 6A,2Ch

🍲 Cont.,homebaked 🏠 Res., raised bungalow, 0.5acres groomed gardens, lakefront-view, patio, porch, deck, quiet ■3 (ground & lower level) ⊨ 6T(K) 🛏3Private ★ F,TV,LF, electr. airfilter, 2 guest fridges, wheel-chair access in one guest room, off-street parking ⓦ Smoking outside, no pets ⤳French, Spanish, German
🕴 Golfing, tennis, Lake Ontario shoreline
🚐 Shaw Festival Theatre, Queen (Main Street shops, small theatres, restaurants), St.Catharines, Niagara Falls, US border
🐾 Elegant home with wheel-chair access (specially equipped and updated in 1995 by current owner). Relax in the peaceful garden or settle down in the well-stocked library/lounge. Ideal place for "literary addicts". Hostess has many years of exierience in hospitality & tourism (Ireland and Canada). Visa,MC,JCB(Japanese) ⤳CC

Moyer, Marybeth & Jay (House on the River B&B)   ☎ & Fax (905) 262-4597
14773 Niagara River Parkway, Niagara-on-the-Lake, ON L0S 1J0

Phone for directions.
$90S $95D $20Child (over age 12) $35Add.person   ► 6A
🍲 Full 🏠 Res., split-level, acreage, view from guest rooms, riverfront, swimming pool, patio, deck, quiet ■ 3 (ground level) ⊨3Q 🛏3Ensuite ★Air,F,separate entrance, patio doors in 2 guest rooms, guest bicycles, parking ⓦNo smoking, no pets
🕴 Niagara bike/walking path (56km from Fort Erie to the shores of Lake Ontario), historic village of Queenston, The Weir Museum & Gallery (Canadian Art)
🚐 Downtown shopping/dining, Shaw Festival Theatres, Niagara Falls, wineries (tours), golfing
🐾 Private and quiet home with a magnificient view overlooking the village of Lewiston NY and Art Park and situated high on the Niagara River bank. Breakfast is served on the river bank. Well travelled hosts are active in the Community and Shaw Festival Volunteer Group.Visa ⤳CC

Mullin, Marie & Ron (Chestnut House)   ☎ (905) 468-2235
Box 1119, 21 The Promenade, Niagara-on-the-Lake, ON L0S 1J0

Follow scenic Niagara Parkway along river to NOTL. Turn left at John St, then left on Charlotte St and continue to The Promenade.
$70S $90-100D   ► 4A
🍲Full, homebaked 🏠Res., 2-storey, quiet ■2D(upst) 🛏2Ensuite ⊨2T(K),1Q ★Air, parking ⓦNo smoking, no pets, no children
🕴 Shaw Festival Theatre, shops and restaurants, Bruce Trail
🚐Wineries, Welland Shipping Canal & Locks, Art Pk Lewiston
🐾 Well travelled, retired couple in modern home backing onto the Bruce Trail and Randwood Estate. There is a privade deck leading from large bedroom overlooking an English garden with gazebo and fish pond. Hosts are formerly from Toronto.

Owen, Bob and Beryl (Villa McNab)   ☎ & Fax (905)934-6865
1356 McNab Rd, Niagara-on-the-Lake, ON L0S 1J0

Located near Lock1 (north-east of St. Catharines near the Welland Canal). From QEW, take
Ontario St Exit47 north. Turn right at Lakeshore. Proceed to 3rd road on left after Canal Bridge.

$85-105D   ► 6A
🍳 Full(English)   🏠 Rural, Spanish ranch-style, acreage, 40ft
indoor swimming pool, quiet, ravine lot   ■ 3D (main level)
⇥2Q,2T(or1K)   🚗3Ensuite   ★ Air,TV in guest bedrooms,
private entrance, host quarters are separate, jacuzzi-sauna,
parking   ⌇ some French   🎋 Wineries, cycling
🚗 Niagara Falls, Port Dalhouse & picturesque harbour/marina
📣 Lovely Spanish-style villa, beautifully decorated, set in an
acre of lawns among orchards and vineyards of the Niagara Peninsula. Enjoy breakfast by the pool
surrounded by tropical plants and relax in the jacuzzi or sauna. There is a resident dog. ⮑B&B

Pellizzari, Imelda & Sergio (Comfort-on-the-Meadow B&B)   ☎ (905) 262-4112
976 Creek Rd, RR4, Niagara-on-the-Lake, ON L0S 1J0

From QEW take Exit 55. Turn right at light to follow York Rd to St.Davids. Turn left at 4-way stop
in St.Davids onto Four Mile Creek Rd. Look for 5th house on left past Line 6.

$65S $75-85D $20Child/Add.person   ► 6A,1Ch
🍳 Full   🏠 Rural, split-multi-level, acreage, view from guest
rooms, patio, porch, deck, quiet   ■ 3D(main & upper level)
⇥2T,2D   🚗1Sh.w.g.,1sh.w.h (ground level) ★Air,F,KF,LF,TV
in large guest lounge, ceiling fans, wood burning stove, separate
entrance, off-street parking   🚭Designated smoking area, no pets
indoor (kennel available)   ⌇ Italian, Spanish
🎋 Walks in gardens, orchards & vinyards
🚗 Old Town (Niagara-on-the-Lake), Shaw Festival Theatre,
Niagara Falls
📣 Bright and spacious home on 3acres of tranquil gardens & meadows and centrally located in
the Niagara Peninsula. Enjoy a bountiful country breakfast (may include homemade Italian
sausage) before starting a day of sightseeing, theatre-going or travelling. ⮑CC

Schankula, Mary (Amberlea)   ☎ (905) 468-3749
285 John St., Box 426, Niagara-on-the-Lake, ON L0S 1J0

From QEW, take Hwy 55 to NOTL. Upon entering town, turn left at first cross street (John St) and
look for 4th house on right.

$50S $85D   ► 6
🍳 Full   🏠Downtown, raised bungalow, patio, treed setting, quiet
■3D(lower level) ⇥1T,2K   🚗2Private, 1sh.w.h.   ★Air,F,TV in one
guest room, parking   🚭No smoking
🎋 Unique shops, Shaw Festival and Courthouse Theatres, historic sites of
Old Town, Lake Ontario picnic areas, walking, biking
🚗 Niagara Falls, Welland Canal, Ft Erie Race Track, Art Park (NY), Casino
📣 Located in a quiet, park-like area. Hostess is a history buff/art lover. Visa,MC ⮑B&B

Service, Peggy (Allayne's Kelmar House B&B) ☎ (905) 468-4982
399 Mississauga St., Box 622, Niagara-on-the-Lake, ON L0S 1J0

From QEW take Niagara-on-the-Lake off-ramp. At York St traffic light, turn left and follow NOTL road signs to Hwy 55 and into town. At William St, turn left, then right into B&B driveway.

$80S $95D $135(for 3)   ► 3A
🍴 Full   🏠 Downtown, res., 2-storey, terrace, quiet   ■ 1Ste (upstairs)   ⊨1Q,1P   🛏 1Private   ★ Air(with elect.air cleaner),F,TV,off-street parking   🚭 No smoking, child min. age 13   ∿ some French
🎭 All Shaw Festival theatres, NOTL Golf Club (rental clubs available), shops, dining, Lake Ontario waterfront parks, Fort George, Niagara Parkway bicycle path, The Yacht Club
🚗 Port Dalhousie, Niagara-on-the-Lake (township) wineries, Queenston Heights, Niagara Falls
🐎 Gracious and spacious home with fine original art works displayed throughout and situated among a lovely garden in a quiet part of town. Hosts are active members of the Int. Wine & Food Society and Shaw Guild/Shaw Festival. Relax on the terrace and patio of Italian porcelain tile. Breakfast is served in the cheery breakfast room overlooking the garden. Dietary needs are considered. Theatre tickets, dining reservations etc, can be arrranged either in advance or at the time of stay. ✓B&B

Wisch, Uwe & Thea (Brockamour Manor) ☎ (905) 468-5527, Fax (905) 468-5071
433 King St., Niagara-on-the-Lake, ON L0S 1J0   E-mail: brockamo@vaxxine.com

Take QEW to Hwy 55 and follow signs to NOTL. Turn right at traffic light (Mary St) and continue to last driveway at left before stop sign at King St. Look for large white house on corner.

$85-160S/D   ► 10
🍴 Full, homebaked   🏠 Res., hist., 1acre   ■5D(upstairs)   ⊨2S,3Q,2K   🛏5Ensuite   ★ Air,F in honeymoon suite and one guest room, separate entrance, parking   🚭No smoking, no pets   ∿German
🎭 Shaw Festival theatres, unique shops on Queen Street
🚗 Niagara Falls, Welland Canal, St. Catherines, US border
🐎 Quiet graceful elegance in lovely heritage Georgian home
(circa 1812) with romantic, historic past and a gracious present. Situated in beautiful park-like environment with huge old majestic trees among natural wilderness. Hostess produces beautiful creations from dried flowers and has her flower studio on site. Visa,MC ✓B&B

Nobleton
(north of Toronto; see also Kleinburg)

Gilbert, Daniel (Daniel's of Nobleton B&B) ☎ (905) 859-0060, Fax (905) 859-0216
12926 Hwy 27, Nobleton, ON N0G 1N0

Phone for directions.
$65S $75-125D $25Child $50Add.person   🍽 Meals   ► 10
🍴 Cont, buffet   🏠 Village, res., 2-storey (2 houses), porch   ■ 4D,1Ste(main & upper level)   ⊨2T,1D,3Q   🛏 5Private   ★ KF,LF,TV,ceiling fans, private entrance, off-street parking, guest quarters are separate   🚭 No smoking, no pets
🎭 Walking trails in parks
🚗 Golfing, Kortright Centre, Kleinburg McMichael Art Gallery, Wonderland, Albion Hills Conservation Area, downtown Toronto
🐎 Country charm and friendly hospitality in two newly renovated heritage homes, called the Waller House and the Goodfellow House, each decorated with original furnishings and the memorabilia of a bygone era. Gourmet cont. breakfast is served in the private dining room. Chef Daniel has operated his fine dining restaurant next door in the former Apiary building since 1980. Relax in comfortable surroundings and enjoy the ambiance and fine foods. CCards, ✓CC

North Bay

(northern Ontario; see also Powassan, Mattawa)

Persia, Marianne & Gary (Hummingbird Hill B&B)   ☎ (705) 752-4547
RR1, 254 Edmond Rd., Astorville, ON P0H 1B0   E-mail: mabb@vianet.on.ca, 1-800-661-4976

From Hwy17, take Hwy94 to Corbeil, follow signs to Astorville.
$50S $60-70D $15Child $20Add.person ◖Meals   ▶6+
◖ Full (Gourmet) ▮Rural, 3-storey, 6acres, patio, porch, deck,
quiet, secluded, screened gazebo ■3D(upstairs), plus loft
⊨2T,1D,1Q ◲1Ensuite, 1sh.w.h. ★ F,TV in guest rooms,
private guest sitting area, sauna, hot tub, solarium, off-street
parking ⊛No smoking
🕴 Birdwatching, beaches, boating, artisan tours, hiking,
snowmobile trails, x-c skiing, ice fishing, deer feed in yard
🚗 Chief Commanda Boat cruise on Lake Nippising, Dionne Quints Museum, downhill skiing
🖝 Unique, geometric dome house with spiral staircases, cathedral ceilings, skylights, cedar
interior & exterior and beautifully decorated; surrounded by extensive perennial beds and water
garden. Enjoy the relaxing, charming and elegant atmosphere, relax in the hot tub on deck or in the
solarium filled with many tropical plants - a sunny & private place, with nature at it's best. There
is a dog and a cat in residence. Ideal place for a spa weekend. Visa ✓B&B

North Gower

(south of Ottawa,; see also Manotik)

McDonald, Madeleine and Alfred (Carsonby Manor)   ☎ (613) 489-3219
Box 6035 RR3, North Gower, ON K0A 2T0

Phone for directions.
$40S $50-65D $8Child   ▶5
◖ Choice (dietary needs can be pre-arranged) ▮Rural, acreage,
quiet ■1S,2D (upstairs) ⊨1S,2D ◲1Ensuite,2sh.w.g.
★Air,F,TV in guest room, in-ground swimming pool, separate
entrance, parking ⊛No smoking, no pets ⌁French
🕴 Manderley Golf Course, cross-country skiing
🚗 Village of Manotick, restaurants, Ottawa, Stittsville (Canada's
largest flea market)
🖝 Large home in parkland setting with warm and friendly hospitality. Visa ✓B&B

Oakville

(west of Toronto; see also Burlington, Milton, Campbellville)

Caspary, Margaret and Guenther (Oakville Hideaway)   ☎ (905) 844-5513
1306 Napier Cr., Oakville, ON L6H 2A4

From QEW, take Exit 118 and Trafalgar Rd north to McCraney St. Turn left and then left again on
Sewell Dr. Follow Sewell to first street on right (Napier Cr). House is first property on right.

$45S $60D   ▶6
◖Choice,homebaked ▮Res.,sub.,split-level,patio,quiet ■3(upst)
⊨2T,D,1Q ◲1Sh.w.g.,1sh.w.h. ★Air,TV/stereo/books in guest
sitting room, off-street parking ⊛No pets, smoking outside,
children min. age 10 ⌁German
🕴 Sheridan College, Oakville Place Shopping center, Go-Station
(hourly commuter train to Toronto)
🚗 Downtown Oakville, Bronte Prov.Park, Glen Abbey golfing
🖝 Unhurried, uncongested lifestyle in quiet suburban home, comfortably furnished, located in
convenient area. Relax on the secluded patio & enjoy breakfast of homemade baked goods.✓B&B

Jordan, Marjorie & Colin (The Lamplighter B&B)   ☎ (905) 827-9363
116 Triller Place, Oakville, ON   L6L 6J1

From QEW take Exit 111 and travel south on Bronte Rd to Lakeshore Rd. Turn right over bridge and right again.
$40S $55-60D $80F   ► 4
🎫 Full   🏠 Sub., res., 2-storey, view, patio, quiet   ■ 2D (upstairs)   ⊨ 2T,1Q   🛏 1Sh.w.g.   ★ Air,TV,F, off-street parking   ⍟ Desig. smoking area, no pets, children min. age 10
🏃 Bronte Harbour with popular harbourfront, Bronte Village, shops and restaurants, fully restored historic Sovereign House
🚗 Oakville downtown & harbour, Commuter GO-Train to Toronto, Burlington, Bronte Prov.Pk
🐾 Warm and friendly hospitality in delightfull, well furnished home on quiet cul-de-sac, located on west side of Oakville. Well travelled hosts are originally from England. Relax on the patio and enjoy the close proximity to the Bronte Harbour activities and year-around festivals. ✓B&B

Sperber, Mrs. Elfriede (Elfy's Guest House)   ☎ (905) 827-2008
1301 Pinegrove Rd, Oakville, ON   L6L 2X2

From QEW, take Exit 116 and Dorval Rd south to Speers Rd. Turn right, proceed to next stop.

Turn left onto Morden Rd and right onto Pinegrove.
$40S $60D $6Child   ► 4
🎫 Cont., homebaked   🏠 Res., sub., bungalow, patio, quiet   ■ 2D (main level)   ⊨ 2S,1Q   🛏 1sh.w.g.   ★ Air, main level TV room, parking   ⍟ No smoking, no pets   〰 German
🏃 Public transportation, Lake Ontario
🚗 Downtown Oakville, major Shopping Mall, restaurants, Toronto, International Airport, Hamilton, Royal Botanical Gardens
🐾 Friendly German hospitality in cozy bungalow in west end of town. Enjoy an intimate B&B in the European tradition. Relax in the TV room or in the private backyard. There is a cat.

Ohsweken   *(south-east of Brantford; see also Cayuga)*

Johnson, Lisa & Tim (The Bear's Inn B&B)   ☎ (519) 445-4133, Fax (519) 445-0439
Box 187, Ohsweken, ON   N0A 1M0

Located on 4th Line Rd in Ohsweken. From Hwy 401, take Hwy 403 west and exit to Hwy 254 east toward Cayuga. Follow into the Six Nations Reserve. Turn right onto Chiefswood Rd, left onto 4th Line Rd. From St.Catharines, take QEW to Hwy 20 south to Hwy 53 west, to Hwy 6 south. Right on 4th Line Rd. Drive into Ohsweken and turn right at Inn.
$45-65S/D   ► 18A,8Ch
🎫 Full, homebaked   🏠 Village, 2 guest log homes, 3 acres, quiet, isolated   ■ 8Ste(main & upper floor), host quarters are in two separate buildings   ⊨ D,Q,cots   🛏 14Private   ★ Air,KF,TV in guest room, sep.entrance, reading rooms, fax machine access, exercise room, poole table, parking   ★ No smoking, no pets
🏃 Ohsweken shopping district, restaurants, sports complex, Six Nations Tourist Office, Pauline Johnson Home, golfing
🚗 Bell Homestead, Woodland Cultural Centre, Brantford, Hamilton, Niagara Falls
🐾 Experience Iroquois culture, art, history and hospitality in large white pine log homes located on Six Nations Indian Reserve of the Grand River. Each house has a breakfast room. Each guest room features a different theme dealing with Iroquois history & culture. Sightseeing tours to other parts of the community available. Conference rooms.Visa,MC,Amex ✓B&B

Orangeville
(north-west of Toronto; see also Hillsburg, Erin)

Country Host B&B Reservation Service & Ski Host   ☎ (519) 942-0686
RR5, Mono 5th LineEast, Orangeville, ON   L9W 2Z2

Lesley Burns, President
Rates: $45S $55-75D (including full breakfast)
The Country Host B&B Reservation Service & Ski Host consists of a great variety of houses, such
as Victorian, heritage and restored Century homes, estates and horse farms. They are situated next
to Provincial parks or trailways including the Bruce and Caledon areas for hiking, biking, and near
antique shops, country markets, festival and live theatre. Some homes have swimming pools, spas,
home studios or workshops. Homes represented are located in Belfountain, Caledon, Cheltenham,
Collingwood, Hockley Valley, Tottenham, Meaford and Mono Mills. There is also a Villa and an
apartment available. For reservation call the above. ⌐CC

Orillia
(north of Toronto; see also Waubaushene, Hillsdale, Elmvale)

Bridgens, Betty & Tony (Betty & Tony's Waterfront B&B)   ☎ 1-800-308-2579
677 Broadview Ave., Orillia, ON   L3V 6P1   Fax (705) 326-2262

From Hwy 12 in Orillia, take Couchiching Point Rd near Atherley bridge in the south-east end of
town and then turn right on Broadview Ave.

$59-65S $69-75D $10-15Add.person   🍽 Meals   ▶ 8A,3Ch
🍲 Full, homebaked   🏠 Res., modern 2-level custom built design,
view from guest rooms, 80ft Canal frontage, patio, deck, quiet
■3F(high lower level), plus pedal/sailboats at dock   ⊨2S,3D
⊇ 2Sh.w.g.   ★Air,LF,TV in guest lounge, library, guest coffee
counter, conference room (with copier, fax, computer), off-street
parking   ⓦ Designated smoking area, no pets   ⋙French,
Norwegian, some German and Italian

🕺 Stephen Leacock Museum, Tudhope Park, restaurants, pike fishing in canal, biking
🚗 Kirkfield Lift Locks, Big Chute Marine Railroad, Orillia (Casino & Opera House), boat cruises
🚌 Modern home on Trent Severn Canal & Waterway in upper class parklike neighbourhood,
filled with family heirlooms. Relax in solitude in one of the sitting rooms, or socialize with congenial
hosts and other guests in another area. Winemaking on premises (lessons available). Guided tours.
There is a cat (treated to be non-allergenic). Gift Certificates available. CCards ⌐FOBBA

Gregory, Judy & Freeman (Alexander House)   ☎ & Fax(705) 326-1119, 1-888-873-0062
7 Alexander Dr., Orillia, ON   L3V 5L7

From Hwy 400 North take Hwy 11 to West St Exit. Proceed to
Fittons Rd, turn right to Alexander, right to 3rd house on left.
$60-65S $70-75D   ▶ 6A
⊞ closed Dec24-26   🍲 Full, homebaked   🏠 Res., small town,
2-storey, older, patios   ■ 3D(upstairs   ⊨ 1D,2Q   ⊇1Ensuite,
1sh.w.g., (one jacuzzi)   ★ Air, TV in guest lounge,
air-conditioners, off-street parking, guest quarters are separate
ⓦNo smoking, no pets, no children

🕺 Shops, restaurants, churches, bus stop across the street, craft studio on premises
🚗 Horseshoe Valley/Mt.St.Louis Ski Resorts, Hardwood Hills x-c ski trail, Orillia Opera House
🚌 Unique Century Home (circa 1890) with many antiques, wicker, lace and collectibles. Enjoy
the elegance and charm of yesteryear with the convenience of modern day. Relax in the private
sitting room or on one of the outdoor patios overlooking lush gardens. Hosts are knowledgeable of
local attractions and happenings. Visa ⌐B&B

Guthrie, Pearl & Norm (The Verandahs Bed & Breakfast)   ☎ & Fax (705) 487-1910
RR2, Hawkestone, ON L0L 1T0

Take Hwy 400 through Barrie, then Hwy 11 toward Orillia. Turn
east on Oro Line 9 East and follow to end (3 km). House is on left.
$50S $60-70D   (Reservations recommended)   ▶ 6-7
🌞June 1-Oct15/Dec28-Mar31 🍳Full, homebaked 🏠Rural, res,
3-storey, view from guest rooms, porch, quiet ◼3D(upstairs)
🛏2S,1Q,1K,cot 🚿 1Sh.w.g.,1ensuite ★F/TV in guest lounge,
guest robes & slippers, guest bikes, off-street parking 🖐No
smoking, no pets, child min. age 12

🏃 Park & safe sandy beach, boat launch, icefish hut rentals
🚗 Ski resorts (downhill & x-c skiing), Barrie, Orillia, boat cruises, mtn biking, golfing, Casino
🐾 Victorian-style home with wide verandas on three sides, bright interior and welcoming
ambience, situated 150 ft from Lake Simcoe. Relax on the verandas and enjoy the cool summer lake
breezes; in winter snuggle up under goose-down duvets. Well travelled hosts are retired and enjoy
welcoming guests in their spacious house. There is a cat in residence. Visa,MC

Pidwerbecki, Mike (Siberi*inn Bed & Breakfast)   ☎ (705) 487-6456, Fax (705) 487-6459
RR2, Hawkestone, Oro, ON L0L 1T0   E-mail: siberinn@barint.on.ca

Located 9km south-west of Orillia. Phone for directions.
$40-60S $50-70D $5Child(age 5-10) $10Add.person   ▶ 11
🍳 Full, homebaked   🏠 Rural, 2-storey, acreage, view from guest
rooms, quiet, covered veranda ◼2D,1Ste 🛏3T,2Q,2D(futons)
🚿 1Sh.w.g.,1ensuite   ★TV/2F/microwave in guest lounge,
private balcony 🖐No smoking, no pets, child min.age 5
🏃 Ganaraska Hiking Trail, snowshoe/snowmobile & x-c skiing
🚗 Hardwood Hills/Horseshoe Valley/Moonstone/Mt.St.Louis &
Snow Valley ski resorts, equestrian farms, Casino Rama
🐾 Comfortable custom-built home with covered veranda surrounding the house and situated in
the woods atop a hill overlooking a beautiful hardwood forest. Ideal location in the heart of Central
Ontario's snowbelt. Unique decor includes Inuit souvenirs obtained by hosts on visit to Baffin
Islands. Enjoy the beautiful seasons including a great northern experience in the winter with plenty
of snow. There are friendly Siberian Husky pets, not allowed in guest rooms. ✓B&B

Reid, Rob & Tom Ruechel (Pine Tree House B&B)   ☎ & Fax (705) 329-0518
225 Matchedash St.N., Orillia, ON L3V 4V5

Take Hwy 400 and 11 north from Toronto and exit at Coldwater Rd. Proceed through 2 lights all
the way through downtown to Matchedash St N, turn left.
$55-65S $70-80D   ▶ 4A
🍳 Full, homebaked   🏠 Res., 2-storey, hist., view, quiet,veranda
◼2D(upst),guest quarters are sep 🛏2T,1D 🚿1Sh.w.g. ★Air,
F,guest slippers, parking 🖐No smoking, no pets 〰German
🏃 Couchiching Beach Park with wooden boardwalk, swimming,
Port of Orillia, Orillia Opera House, downtown, restaurants,
antique shops, golfing, waterfront
🚗 Hardwood Hills x/c skiing, Stephen Leacock Museum, antiques
🐾 Charming, traditional Victorian home, ca 1882, with charming interior. Enjoy Afternoon Tea
on the covered veranda overlooking the garden or rest in the cozy parlour by the fireplace. There is
a Mini-Schnauzer and a cat in residence. Visa,MC,Amex ✓B&B

Taylor, Sioux (Pan-O-Rama B&B)　　　　　　　　　　☎ & Fax (705) 326-1636
622 Moberley Ave., Orillia, ON　L3V 6R6

From Hwy 12 turn west onto Couchiching Point Rd. Look for 3rd house on right.
$70-80S　$80-90D　$20Add.person　📷 Meals　　　　　　　　　　　　　▶7
📺 Full, homebaked　🏠 Res., split-level, view from guest rooms, lakefront, deck, quiet　■3D
(ground & upper floor)　🛏 2Q,2T(K),1S　🛁 1sh.w.g., 1sh.w.h.　★ F,KF,TV in guest room,
gas barbeque on deck, boat dock (to 25feet), firepit and lakeside seating, off-street parking, guest
quarters are separate　🖐 Smoking outside, no pets, children by special prior arrangement only
🏃 Clean/safe swimming, boating on Trent-Severn Waterway, Stephen Leacock Home/Museum,
fishing, Gordon Lightfoot hiking/biking Trail, Tudhope Park and restaurant
🚗 Casino Rama, Orillia Opera House (music/theatre), golfing, crafts/antiques, skiing
🚐 Modern, comfortable lakeside home situated in classic cottage setting. Hostess is well
informed about local happenings and likes sharing her knowledge with guests. Relax and enjoy the
beautiful sunsets over Lake Couchiching from the spacious deck and the restful atmosphere. Boats
and canoe for guests. "Naomi" a friendly Black Lab in residence. Weekly rates. MC,Amex ✔B&B

Tuddenham, Brenda & Bob (Cavana House)　　　　　　　　☎ (705) 327-7759
241 Mississaga St. West, Orillia, ON　L3V 3B7

Phone for directions.
$60S　$75-80D　$25Add.person　　　　　　　　　▶6
📺 Full, homebaked　🏠 Downtown, 3-storey, hist., porches
■2D,1F(upstairs)　🛏 3D,1S　🛁 3Ensuite　★Air,F,TV in
guest rooms, off-street parking, host quarters are separate　🖐No
smoking, no pets, children min. age 12
🏃 Downtown shopping, theatres, Opera House (heritage building -
live theatre/music all year), Casino, farmers markets, bus/train
🚐 Traditional Victorian home decorated with anitques, old wicker and old paintings. Sumptious
breakfasts served in gracious dining room. Browse through the extensive library and enjoy Tea
served in the parlour decorated with traditional furnishings.✔B&B

Ottawa　　　　　　　　　　　　　　　　*(see also Hull & Aylmer (Quebec), Manotik)*

Bansfield, Anne-Marie and Irving (Le Gîte Park Ave. B&B)　　☎ (613) 230-9131
54 Park Ave., Ottawa, ON　K2P 1B2

Take Metcalfe Exit off Hwy 417 (Queensway). Turn right (east) on Argyle
and proceed 1 block to Elgin St(traffic lights). Turn left (north) and then
right at Park Ave.
$55S　$75D　$10Child　$20Add.person　　　　　　　▶7
📺 Full　🏠 Res., older, patio　■ 2D,1F(upstairs)　🛏 3Q,1D,1S
🛁2Sh.w.g.,powder room in one guest room　★Air,TV,F,LF, parking
🖐No smoking　〰 French
🏃 Downtown Ottawa, Parliament Buildings, National Art Gallery (Renoir
Exhibit June-Sept97), Museum of Civilization, lively Elgin Street, Rideau
Canal, Bus Station, Byward Market with countless flower and food stands,
cafés, restaurants and boutiques, popular Winterlude
🚐 Enjoy warm ambiance in 1904-built elegant home situated in charming
residential area and very central location. Well-informed hosts will gladly help with itineraries and
advise about local activities. Children welcome. Visa,MC

Bates, Renée C. (Paterson House B&B)
500 Wilbrod St., Ottawa, ON K1N 6N2

☎ (613) 565-8996, Fax (613) 565-6546
E-mail: paterson@cyberus.ca

From Hwy 417 (Queensway) exit at Nicholas St to Laurier, go east
to Charlotte St and first right at Wilbrod.
$135S $175D (plus taxes) ► 8
🍳 Cont. 🏠 Downtown, res., hist., view from guest rooms,
riverfront, porch, quiet ■ 4Ste (upstairs) ⊨ 1D,3Q
🛏4Ensuite ★ Air,F,TV in guest rooms, private entrance,
off-street parking & on site 🖐 No smoking, no pets, children
min. age 16 ⋙French
🏃 Ottawa River, park with bicycle/pedestrian paths, Embassies, Diplom.residences/stately homes
🚗 Parliament Hill, Rideau Canal, Byward Market, museums, National Arts Centre, shopping
🏴 Magnificient historic Heritage mansion, beautifully restored to original elegance. Enjoy a
tranquil and inspiring experience among traditional furnishings and Objects d'art. Deluxe Cont.
breakfast is served in sunroom. There is a Health Centre for total mind/body rejuvination on the
premises. CCards ⤳CC

Bickerdike, Christina & Brian (Mid-Towne Heritage B&B)
220 Lyon St., Ottawa, ON K1R 5V7

☎ (613) 236-1169,
Fax (613) 489-0246

From the Queensway (Hwy 417 in downtown), exit at Bronson. Go north to
Laurier Ave (flashing light). Turn right to Lyon Street.
$49S $85D $5Cot ► 8A,2Ch
🍳 Full, homebaked 🏠 Downtown, hist., res., 3-storey, hist., porch
■1S,3D,1F (main & upper level) ⊨ 1S,2T,1D,2Q,2cots 🛏 3Ensuite,
1sh.w.h. ★ TV,Air-conditioners, guest sitting areas, ceiling fans 🖐 No
smoking, no pets, children min. age 2 ⋙ French
🏃 Parliament Hill, downtown core (museums, shops, clubs, restaurants),
The Canal, Ottawa River, cycling, roller blading on local paths, athletic
facilities, craft & trade shows, Air-Porter & double-decker tour adjacent,
limosine service to the door, public transportation,
🚗 Casino, Steam Train, Gatineau Hills (fishing, hunting, river rafting, canoeing, skiiing, nature
trails), Petting Zoo, Agricultural & Horticultural Exhibits, antique & flea markets
🏴 Victorian home (ca 1890), faithfully preserved and authentically appointed, situated in
excellent downtown location. Enjoy a quiet and elegant escape. Victorian Hospitality Package and
museum/restaurants discounts available. CCards ⤳B&B

Brown, Irma & Zane (Brown's Bed & Breakfast)
539 Besserer St., Ottawa, ON K1N 6C6

☎ & Fax (613) 789-8320

From Hwy 417 (The Queensway) exit at Nicholas St and turn right on Laurier (which becomes
Charlotte going north). Proceed to Besserer, turn right to B&B on left.

$55S $65-75DF ► 6
🍳 Cont., homebaked 🏠 Downtown, res., 3-storey, older, porch,
deck, quiet ■ 3D(upstairs) ⊨ 2T,1D,1Q 🛏 Sh.w.g.
★Air, balcony off one guest room, TV/coffeemaker in each room,
host quarters are separate 🖐 No smoking, no pets ⋙ some
French, German
🏃 Downtown, Byward Market, Parliament Hill, Rideau Canal,
University of Ottawa, Art Gallery, Embassy Row, restaurants
🚗 Gatineau Hills, Museum of Civilization, Stittsville Flea Market, walking & cycling trails
🏴 Friendly and congenial hosts in 85-year old home with unique fireplace and situated in
beautiful older part of the city. Enjoy the quiet, comfortable atmosphere and relax after a day of
sightseeing or travelling. Visa,MC ⤳B&B

Dukic, Ante & Katarina (Maple House B&B)   ☎ (613) 569-1932, Fax (613) 567-3267
39 Goulburn Ave, Ottawa, ON   K1N 8C7

Located off Laurier Ave, and east of Rideau Canal.
$ 65S $85D   (plus tax)   ► 6
🍽 Buffet   🏠 Downtown, 2-storey, patio, quiet   ■3(upstairs)
⊨2S,2D   ⚲ 1Private, 1sh.w.g.   ★ Ceiling fans, separate
entrance, off-street & street parking, guest quarters are separate
🖐No smoking, no pets, children min. age 12
🕴 Parliament, centre of town, Rideau Canal, Nat.Gallery & Arts
Ctr., Bi-Way Market, theatres, University of Ottawa, bus No5/15
🚗 Ottawa River with parks, museums of Nature & Civilizaton, Gatineau Park, historic sites
🐾 Comfortable home with a blend of old and new and filled with works of local artists, providing
a cultural touch of Ottawa. There is an ongoing art exhibition in the house. Hosts have travelled
worldwide (including B&B) and enjoy exchanging travel experience with guests. Breakfast is served
in the special guest breakfast room.

Faubert, Nicole (L'Auberge du Marché)   ☎ (613) 241-6610
87 Guigues Ave., Ottawa, ON   K1N 5H8

Phone for directions.
$54-85S $64-85D $25Add.person   ► 8A
🍽 Full, homebaked   🏠 Downtown, older, duplex, view
■3D,1Ste (main and upper floor)   ⊨1D,4Q   ⚲ 1Private,
1sh.w.g.   ★KF,sep.entrance 🖐No pets, no children ⚭French
🕴 Parliament Hill, National Gallery, Byward Market, Rideau
Canal and River, National Arts center, Canadian War Museum, ND
Basilica, Major's Hill Park, specialty shops, restaurants
🚗 Skiing, walking,hiking in Gatineau Hills
🐾 Completely renovated turn-of-the-Century home beautifully decorated with truly Canadian
ambiance is located in the historic part of the city called "Byward Market", a 25-square-block area
containing all the interesting tourist attractions of Canada's Capital City. Hosts are in their 2nd
decade of welcoming B&B guests to their home. Guest quarters are in adjoining side of duplex.
Breakfast is served in host's quarters dining room. Visa,MC ⌐CC

Gervais, Richard (The King Edward Bed & Breakfast)   ☎ (613) 565-6700
525 King Edward Ave., Ottawa, ON   K1N 7N3

From Hwy 417, take the Nicholas Exit to Laurier Ave. Turn right, drive 3
blocks, then left on King Edward Ave. Located in the Sandy Hill District.
$59-69S $70-85D $10Add. person   ► 6
🍽Homebaked 🏠Downtown,hist.,deck,patio ■2D,1Ste(upst) ⊨1D,2Q
⚲1Private,1sh.w.g.   ★Air,LF,TV in each room, 2 private balconies, second
floor is exclusive for guests, parking   🖐No pets, no smoking ⚭French
🕴 Parliament Bldgs., Embassies, Byward Market, Sparks Street Mall, Nat.Art
Gallery, boat tours on Rideau Canal (also skating), UofOttawa, Nat.Arts Ctr.,
Museum of Civilization, Nat. Arts Centre, Cdn Mint, bicycle paths, restaurants
🚗 Governor General & Prime Minister's residences, Museum of Science &
Technology, Gatineau Park & Meech Lake (hiking, skiing, beaches)
🐾 Desig.heritage building, faithfully restored to its formal graciousness
offering a uniqueness of character & comfort found only in classic older homes, with spacious
interior, high ceilings & enormous bay windows in the tower. ⌐B&B

Glazer, Susan & Ron Holdway (Alanbury House B&B)   ☎ (613) 23-Guest(234-8378)
119 Strathcona Ave., Ottawa, ON   K1S 1X5   E-mail: alanbury@magma.ca, Fax (613) 569-5691

Phone for directions.
$90-100S $100-115D $149F   ► 6A,2Ch
🍲 Full, homebaked   🏠 Downtown, 3-storey,
porch ■3(upst)   ◄2T(K),2Q,2P   🛏 3Ensuite   ★Air,F,TV,
ceiling fans, access to Fax machine, off-street parking   🚫No pets,
smoking on front porch, children min. age 8   ∞ French
🏃 Rideau Canal (boat tours), Museum of Natural History, Parl.
Buildings, Nat.Arts Centre, restaurants, shops on Bank St, bus
routes, Ottawa Civic Centre, cycling, waterside parks
🚐 Hull Casino, Nat.Gallery of Canada, Cdn War Museum, Nat.Museum of Science & Technology
🎯 Spacious Turn-of-the-Century, fully modernized and inviting home with eclectic decor and
antiques, situated in the trendy area called "Glebe". Relax in the jacuzzi or by a blazing fire on a
chilly Canadian winter's day. Hosts enjoy meeting interesting people from around the world. There
is a resident feline friend called "Penelope". ✓B&B

Haydon, Mary and Andy (Haydon House)   ☎ (613) 230-2697, Fax (613) 233-7786
18 The Driveway, Ottawa, Ontario   K2P 1C6

Take Metcalfe Street Exit off Queensway to Somerset St. Turn right onto Somerset and to end.
House is at corner of Queen Elizabeth Driveway & Somerset St.W.
$55S $75D $15Child   ► 6
🍲 Cont.   🏠 Downtown, res., hist., canal-view, porch ■3D
(upstairs)   ◄2T,2D   🛏1Private,2Sh.w.g.   ★Air,TV,F,parking,
sep.entrance, private outdoor portico sitting areas   ∞French
🏃 Parliament Bldgs, Rideau Canal, Nat.Arts Centre, Nat.Gallery,
canal & river boat tours, Museum of Civilization, Ottawa U.
🚐 Embassies, Governor General/Prime Minister Residences
🎯 Victorian era mansion with traditional pine decor nestled in tranquil residential downtown
district, beside the historic and picturesque Rideau Canal (put skates on inside and walk over to the
longest skating rink in the world). There is a dog in residence.✓B&B

Hill, Charmaine (Chez Charmaine Bed & Breakfast)   ☎ (613) 733-7382
1543 Botsford St., Ottawa, ON   K1G 0P8

Phone for directions.
$55S $65D $25Child   ► 6A,2Ch
🍲 Homebaked   🏠 Res., 2-storey, older, patio, deck, quiet
■3D (upstairs)   ◄ 2T,1D,1Q   🛏 1Sh.w.g.   ★ F,Air,TV, safe
sport equipment storage, off-street parking   🚫 No smoking, no
pets, children min. age 6   ∞ French
🏃 Health Science Centre, quiet area for walking and jogging, bus
service to downtown
🚐 Parliament Bldg, downtown, Ottawa U., Rideau Canal & River, vast network of cycling paths
🎯 Warm & friendly hospitality in elegant home in ideal quiet location. Congenial Ottawa-native
hostess enjoys helping with sightseeing plans. Breakfast is served in the elegant antique filled
dining room. Dietary needs respected. Relax in the comfortable reading and music room or in the
large flower garden. Accommodtation is suitable for pleasure or business travellers.Visa

Hunter, John and Pat (Blue Spruces)　　　☎ (613) 236-8521, Fax (613) 231-3730
187 Glebe Ave., Ottawa, ON K1S 2C6

Take Bronson Exit off Queensway. Go south to Powell Street (first stoplight). Turn left and go to Percy Street, turn right and continue to Glebe Street, turn left.
$80S　$90D　　　　　　　　　　　　　　　　　　　► 6
🅓Choice, homebaked 🏠Downtown, older, quiet ■3D (one with glassed-in sitting room), 2nd floor exclusive for guests ⊨2T,2Q
⚄3Ensuite ★Air,TV guest sittings lounge with solarium, parking
🖐No pets, no smoking, children minimum age 10
🚶 Dow's Lake, Rideau Canal, Lansdowne Park, Carleton University, restaurants, antique shops, Civic & Conference Center, bus to downtown
🚗 Gatineau Hills, Fall Colour Spectacle, hiking, x/c skiing
🌾 Warm & friendly hospitality in newly restored Edwardian house, beautifully decorated, furnished with antiques and located in the Glebe (the heart of downtown).Visa,MC ↙B&B

Litchinsky, Gillian & Dan (Lampman House B&B)　　　☎ (613) 241-3696
369 Daly Ave, Ottawa, ON K1N 6G8

Travelling from east or west on Hwy 417 into Ottawa, take Nicholas Exit to Laurier. Turn right, then left at Chapel and right at Daly.

$45-55S　$55-65D　$10Add.person(over age 12)　　► 6-7
🅓 Full, homebaked 🏠 Downtown, 3-storey, hist., porch, deck, quiet ■ 2D,1F(upstairs) ⊨1S,1D,2Q ⚄ 1Sh.w.g.
★F,TV, roof-top deck and library for guests, street parking
🖐No smoking, no pets
🚶 Downtown core, Parliament Bldgs., Nat.Art Gallery, market area, major shopping centre, Sparks Street Mall, Rideau Canal (skating and boating)
🚗 Gatineau Hills (wonderful walking, hiking, skiing, out-of-way restaurants)
🌾 Heritage home (120 years old) with the original gingerbread carvings around the front porch and tastefully decorated throughout, was once occupied by the famous Canadian poet Archibald Lampman. Breakfast is served in special guest breakfast room. There is a cat in residence. Visa

---

Przednowek, Krystyna & Rafal (By-the-Way Bed & Breakfast)　　　☎ & Fax (613) 232-6840
310 First Ave., Ottawa, ON K1S 2G8

From Hwy 417 (Queensway) take Bronson Exit south to Powell Ave. Turn left to Lyon St, right to First Ave and right again to house on left.
$50-60S　$60-65D　$75-80Ste　　　　　　　► 8
🅓Full, homebaked 🏠Downtown, res., 2-storey, quiet ■3D,1Ste (upper & lower level) ⊨ 4T,2Q,1P ⚄ 2Private,1sh.w.g.
★Air,TV in guest room, kitchen & separate entrance in suite, central electronic filter, limited wheel-chair access, off-street parking 🖐No smoking, no pets, children min. age 5 ⌇French
🚶 Civic Centre, Parliament, Lansdowne Park, Dows Lake/Park (Tulip Festival), Rideau Canal (hiking, skating - winterlude), Bus Station, Carleton U.,museums
🚗 Gatineau Hills (hiking, skiing, cycling), Nat.Gallery of Canada & Arts Centre
🌾 Modern, smoke/pollen free, elegant house with warm and quiet ambiance located in the Glebe area, close to truly great amenities of downtown Ottawa - an ideal place for business or pleasure travellers.Visa,MC ↙B&B

Rivoire, Robert (Robert's Bed & Breakfast)   ☎ (613) 563-0161, 1-800-461-7889
488 Cooper St., Ottawa, ON   K1R 5H9

Located between Kent and Lyon Streets. Phone for specific directions.
$54S $64D $78Ste   ▶ 6
🍲 Full, homebaked   🏠 Downtown, older, patio, quiet   ■3D(upstairs)
╟═2D,1Q   ⊫1Sh.w.g, 1ensuite   ★ Air,F, guest sitting area, private
balcony, parking   🖑 No pets, no children
🏃 Parliament Hill, Byward Market, National Gallery of Canada & Canadian
Museum of Nature, Rideau Canal (skating and Winterlude), on bus route
🚗 Canadian Museum of Civilization, Gatineau Park
☞ Century home with much charm, lovely stained glass windows (three
are over 100 years old) and detailed woodwork. Breakfast is served in dining
room which has over 100-year-old church chairs from the province of
Quebec. ✓B&B

Tsui, Helen (Helen House Bed & Breakfast)   ☎ (613) 789-8263
168 Stewart St., Ottawa, ON   K1N 6J9

Located west of Parliament Hill. From Hwy 417 exit at Nicholas, turn east
onto Laurier and north on Nelson to Stewart.
$55S $68D $90(for 3)   (Long stays available)   ▶ 8
🍲 Full   🏠 Downtown, 3-storey, hist., quiet   ■ 2D,1F (upstairs)
╟═2T,2D   ⊫ Sh.w.g.   ★ Air,F,KF,off-street/street parking   🖑 No
smoking, no pets   ♥   ∼ Chinese, some French
🏃 Parliament Hill, Rideau Centre, Byward Market, National Gallery,
University of Ottawa, restaurants, shops, various public transportation
🚗 Gatineau Park, Hull/PQ, Jacques Cartier Park, Laurentien resorts
☞ Elegant Victorian home with warm ambience, located in the beautiful
surroundings of Sandy Hill district. Breakfast is served in bright eating area.

Waters, Carol and Brian (Australis Guest House)   ☎ & Fax (613) 235-8461
35 Marlborough Ave., Ottawa, ON   K1N 8E6

From Hwy 417, take Nicholas St Exit and turn right onto Laurier Ave East at first set of traffic
lights. After 1 km turn right onto Marlborough. From Hwy 416 take Hwy 417 and follow as above.
$50-75S/D $20Add.person   ▶ 11

🍲 Full   🏠Downtown, older, view   ■3 (upstairs)   ╟═4D,3S
⊫1Private,2sh.w.g.   ★TV   ♥   🖑No pets, no drinking
🏃 Downtown, Parliament bldgs, Ottawa University, tourist sites
🚗 Gatineau Hills (skiing, water sports, beautiful foliage scenery)
☞ 60-year-old home with fireplaces and leaded windows situated
in beautiful older part of the City with many Embassies, parkland
and the Rideau River. Congenial hosts are winners of Fall Harvest
Bake-Off Competition and hospitality Awards. Hostess has just
published a new B&B Cookbook "Breakfast Companion & Whispered Recipes". ✓B&B

Ottawa Bed and Breakfast   ☎ (613) 563-0161, 1-800-461-7889
488 Cooper St., Ottawa, ON   K1R 5H9

(Mr. Robert Rivoire)
Rates: $49S $59D $78Ste   (including a full homecooked breakfast)
Ottawa B&B offers a professional reservation service and represents older homes situated right in
the heart of the city, as well as suburban homes. The Agency represents 25 rooms in Ottawa and
surrounding areas. For information contact the above.

Westbrook, Shirley & Terry (Waverley House)
166 Waverley Street, Ottawa, ON   K2P 0V6
☎ & Fax (613) 233-0427

Phone for directions.
$55-65S $70-85D $10Add.person
► 8A,2-4Ch
🍽 Cont,homebaked   🏠 Downtown, hist., large balcony and porch, quiet
■3D,1Ste (upstairs)   ⊨2T,2Q,1P   ⚰ 1Sh.w.g, 1private,1powder room
★F,TV in each sitting room, ceiling fans in each room, parking   👋 No
pets, No smoking, children min. age 4
🏃 Parliament Hill, Byward Market, University, Nat. Gallery of Canada and
Arts Center, Rideau Center, Capital's Central business district
🚗 Gatineau Hills/Lakes/skiing/beautiful Fall colors
☛ Stately Edwardian home with elegant rooms situated in the heart of
Ottawa's most exclusive downtown area ("The Golden Triangle"). Suitable
for corp.travellers. ✔B&B

Whiting, Ermelinda & John (Flying Squirrel B&B)
1429 Lowen Dr., Gloucester, ON   K1V 1H3
☎ (613) 736-8060, Fax 1275
E-mail: ewhiting@flyingsquirrel.com

Located 4.6km south of Hunt Club Rd, corner of River Rd.
$60S $85D $15Child/Add.person   🍽Meals
► 6+
🍽 Full, homebaked   🏠 Rural, 3-storey, view from guest rooms,
swimming pool, patio, porch   ■ 1D,1Ste,1F(upstairs) incl. loft
above garage)   ⊨2T,2D,1Q   ⚰1Sh.w.g,2ensuite   ★Air,F,TV,
guest room air conditioners, off-street parking   👋No pets,
smoking outside, children min. age 12   〰French,Italian
🏃 Rideau River (canoeing, beautiful picnic spots), bus stop
🚗 Int.Airport (6min), downtown Ottawa, Parliament Hill, world's longest skating rink, Corel
Centre
☛ Warm & friendly atmosphere in Victorian setting situated on 0.30 acres surrounded by
farmlands and pastoral views. Hosts will delight in showing the area and directing to special
attractions the city has to offer. Breakfast is served in guest breakfast room. Access to computer,
fax & internet. Ideal place for the business traveller. Relax by the swimming pool after a busy day
in the city. Transportation to and from the airport & downtown can be arranged. There are birds in
the house. Visa,MC

Owen Sound   *(n/w of Toronto; see also Bognor, Meaford, Clarksburg, Thornburg)*

Breadner, Ron & Mickey (West Winds B&B)
RR3, Owen Sound, ON   N4K 5N5
☎ (519) 376-9003

Located south on 2nd Ave East and 3.4km from City Hall, just off Hwys 6/10. Phone for directions.
$55-65D $10Child/Add.person $75-100F   🍽Meals
► 8

🍽 Full, homebaked   🏠 Rural, bungalow, acreage, view from 3
guest rooms, swimming pool, patio, quiet, secluded   ■ 1D,1F
(main & upper floor)   ⊨ 2D,2Q,1S,1cot   ⚰ 2Sh.w.g.,
1ensuite   ★ TV in guest room, ceiling fans, guest patio, separate
entrance, guest quarters are separate   👋 Designated smoking
area, no pets, call regarding children
🏃 Bruce Trail hiking, Inglis Falls, city bus
🚗 Beaches, downhill skiing, snowmobile trails, golfing, ice &
salmon fishing, maple syrup & pumpkin festivals, museums, theatre
☛ Warm and friendly welcome in spacious home adjacent to very popular Bruce Trail. Kind and
caring hosts enjoy spoiling guests and love flower gardening, woodworking & crafts. Consideration
for vegetarians & food allergies. There is a very friendly (non-shedding) Schnauzer. ✔B&B

Buchanan, Bruce & Esther & Family (Highland Manor B&B)   ☎ (519) 372-2699
867-4th Ave A West, Owen Sound, ON   N4K 6L5

Phone for directions.
$50-55S $70-90D $15-20Add.p.   (off-season rates avail)   ► 10
🌙 Full   🏠 Downtown, res., 3-storey, hist., view from guest
rooms, porch, quiet   ■ 3D,1F (upstairs)   ⊨ 1D,5Q
🛏Private, 2sh.w.g.   ★ TV,LF,8F, guest quarters are separate,
elevator, off-street parking   🚭 No smoking
🕴 Theatre (live) downtown, shops, restaurants, library, Art
Gallery, harbour, hiking/cycling trails

🚗 Various beaches, Bruce Peninsula, Collingwood Blue Mountain Ski Resort, fishing, golfing
🐎 Spacious, 1870-built and restored Victorian home with high/ornate ceilings, orginal
woodwork, 8 fireplaces, elevator and central stairwell extending to 3rd floor orginal skylight.
Nestled in mature maple trees with a spectacular view and surrounded by very private grounds.
Breakfast is served in the elegant formal dining room. There is a dog in the family area.MC,Amex

---

Burritt, Richard & Sylvia (Rolling Acres)   ☎ (519) 376-5440, (813) 938-4368(USA)
RR5, Owen Sound, ON   N4K 5N7

From Hwys 6 or 10 at Owen Sound take Hwy 21 (Blue Water scenic Rte from Sarnia) to Alvanley
Cross Roads and proceed to B&B next to Sutherlands Farm.

$30S $45D $60F   ► 4
📅 May 24-Nov30   🌙 Full, homebaked   🏠 Rural, ranch-style
bungalow, acreage, patio, deck, solarium, quiet   ■ 2D (main level)
⊨ 2T,1Q   🛏 1Sh.w.g.   ★ F,LF,FV in guest room, separate
entrance, full size pool table in games room   🚭 No pets,
designated smoking area if necessary, children min. age 7
🚗 Bruce Trail and Niagara Escarpement, Southampton &
beautiful beaches, clean unpolluted lakes and rivers
🐎 Immaculate flower-filled home located in popular resort country. Enjoy the cosy and
comfortable atmosphere. Doll collectors welcome. Packed lunches for fishermen provided. Large
parking area for boats & trailers. Visa,MC 〰B&B

Moses, Bill and Cecilie (Moses' Sunset Farms Bed & Breakfast)   ☎ (519) 371-4559
RR6, Owen Sound, ON   N4K 5N8   E-mail: moses@bmts.com

From Hwy 26 turn south on 28th Ave.E (formerly 20thAve E)) and proceed 2.4 km. From Hwys 10
& 21, follow the hospital signs and proceed past hospital to T in road (28 Ave East). Turn right
(south) and proceed 1.5 km to house on left. Look for sign on mailbox (No 398139).

$40-50S $45-90D   ► 10A
🌙 Full (healthy, Gourmet)   🏠 Rural, at edge of town, 40-acres,
view, patio, peaceful   ■ 3 (main level)   ⊨ 3Q,1D,2T
🛏 2Sh.w.g., 1private   ★TV, guest robes, 3 woodstoves, picnic
area   🚭 No smoking, inquire regarding children
🕴 Bruce Trail, x/c skiing, skating, pond, creek, birdwatching
🚗 Sauble Beach, Bognor Wildlife Marsh, golfing, tennis, fishing
🐎 Owen Sound's longest established B&B. Spacious, antique
filled, well decorated home with unique antique brick floor in Quebec farmhouse-style kitchen.
Breakfasts are beautifully presented by Food Stylist hostess. Enjoy the gorgeous Autumn colours,
relax in the quiet reading room or by the cozy wood fires, picnic at the pond or on the patio. Cyclists
& hikers may leave vehicle parked. Drop-off & pick-up for hikers. There is an adorable dog. 〰B&B

Oxford Mills
(south of Ottawa; see also Merrickville, bishops Mills)

Morin, Margaret & Roger (Horse & Rider B&B)   ☎ & Fax (613) 258-7899
640 Jig St, RR1, Oxford Mills, ON   K0G 1S0

From Hwy 416 (formerly Hwy 16), go west on Hwy 20 and turn north on Hwy 18. Take first left (Jig St) and proceed 1km to farm on left. Look for sign.
$50-60S $70-80D   (plus tax)   ► 8
⬛Full, homebaked   🏠 Farm, 2-storey, older, view from guest rooms,quiet ■2D,1F(upstairs)
↦3Q,2cots ⬛ 1Shw.g.   ★ Air,TV in one guest room, separate entrance, 2nd floor exlusive for guests ⬤ No smoking, no pets, children min. age 12   ﹏French
🏃 Horseback riding, x-c skiing, snowmobiling, hiking, bird watching, spring-fed pond and creek
🚐 Ottawa, Merrickville (crafts/antiques & studio tours), Upper Canada Village, Fort Wellington, Rideau Canal & Lock System, 1000 Isle boat cruises, Limerick Forest & Trails
☛ Renovated farmhouse, decorated with local art as well as flowers from on-site green house, located on 100 acres with mutli-use trails. Guests are invited to bring their own horse, or ride one of the horses on the farm, or just enjoy the lovely countryside. Inquire about horseback riding packages. There are two cats and a very friendly yellow lab (outside or in basement). ✒B&B

Paisley
(south-west of Owen Sound; see also Cargill, Pinkerton)

Garton, John & Muriel (Gar-Ham Hall B&B)   ☎ (519) 353-7243
538 Queen St.N., Paisley, ON   N0G 2N0

Phone for directions.
$40-50S $55-65D $20Child   ► 10
⬛ Full, homebaked   🏠 Village, 3-storey, 2acres, patio, porch, quiet ■ 3D,1F (upstairs) ↦ 2T,1D,2Q,1P ⬛ 1Sh.w.g., 2ensuite ★4F(marble),TV in guest parlor, private entrance, off-street parking ⬤ Designated smoking area, no pets
🏃 Heritage walk, canoeing (two rivers meet), museum, antique shops, restaurants & tavern, specialty shops
🚐 Retired hosts in one of the village's prestigious Victorian homes elegantly decorated with antiques & collectibles. Enjoy friendly hospitality, good conversation.✒B&B

Pakenham
(west of Ottawa; see also Almonte)

Gillan, Maureen and Art (Gillanderry Farms)   ☎ (613) 832-2317, (613) 832-2556
RR4, Pakenham, ON   K0A 2X0   Fax (613) 832-2317

Located 4 km north-east of Pakenham off Regional Rd 20 (joins Hwys 17/29). Look for Dominion

Springs Drive at the corner of Kinburn S.Rd (Reg.Road20).
$35S $45D   🍽 Meals   ► 4A,3Ch
⬛Full,homebaked 🏠500-acre farm, hist., view, quiet ■2(upst) ↦2Q,2R,1S ⬛1Sh.w.g.,1sh.w.h. ★TV,F,LF
🏃 Dairy & crash crops, quiet country roads along Mississippi River, spring-fed creek with mineral springs
🚐 Pakenham, 5-span stone bridge, craft shops, Mt. Pakenham Ski Hill (downhill & x-c skiing), Pakenham Highlands golfing
☛ 7th consecutive generation family farm of Irish roots in 135-year-old, green-shuttered home of limestone. Hosts' hobby is collecting and restoring antique farm tractors (farm museum). Hostess is a "Decorative and Folkart Painter". Enjoy generous farm breakfasts and a homey atmosphere. Ideal spot to use as a base to tour the Nation's Capital. There is a resident dog.

Paris

(north of Brantford; see also Ayr, Troy)

Courtemanche, Judy & Rick (The St.Andrew Cottage)   ☎ (519) 442-1652
23 St.Andrew St., Paris, ON   N3L 2W8

Take Hwy 403 to Hwy 2 and then travel on Hwy 5 to Paris. Follow Willow St to downtown business section. Turn right on Grand River N to St. Georges St. Turn left and then left again on Baird St

and right to St. Andrew.

$35S $50D $10Add.person   🍴Meals   ▶ 5A,3Ch
🍷 Full   🏠 Res., extended bungalow, hist., deck, quiet   ■ guest cottage   ⊨3S,1D,crib   ⬡1Private,1ensuite ★LF,FK,F,TV in guest each room, cozy guest living room, separate entrance, private parking available, wheelchair accessible, tandom bike for guests 🚭Designated smoking area, no pets
🏃 Mary Maxim's, canoeing on the Grand River, boat rentals, Antique/Classic Car Assoc gathering, X-mas & crafts home tour 🚐 Adelaide Hunter Hoodless/Bell Homesteads, Sports Hall of Recogn., Wayne Gretzky Centre
🐾 1880-built, fully restored and extended (at back) home located in historic town. Spacious, separate guest quarters are in the beautifully restored "Brantford" style cottage with high ceilings and authentic furnishings. Hostess is an Interior Decorator and specializes in period decor and antiques. Hosts are involved with and store Antique Cars on the premises. There is a resident cat named "Toi". Children's room available. ✍B&B

Parry Sound

(west of Huntsville; see also Windermere, Port Carling)

Coomber, Sally & Rick (Pass The Thyme B&B)   ☎ 705) 746-8917
40 Cascade St., Parry Sound, ON   P2A 1J9

Travel north on Hwy 400 and Hwy 69 to Parry Sound. Turn left at McDonalds, continue to River St. Turn right, cross William St, then River St becomes Cascade St. Proceed to top of hill to B&B.

$50S– $60D $10Add.person   ▶ 6
🍷 Full, homebaked   🏠 Res., hist., 3-storey, quiet   ■ 3D,1Ste (2nd & 3rd floors)   ⊨ 2T,3D   ⬡ Sh.w.h., 1private   ★Air,TV, guest bicycles available, private entrance/kitchenette in 3rd floor suite   🚭 Smoking outside, no pets
🏃 Town beach, Festival of Sound, Rainbow Theatre, 30000 Island cruises.
🚐 Provincial parks, hiking, x-c skiing, snowmobiling
🐾 Teacher host in designated heritage home filled with many collectibles and located in a quiet, convenient area of town. Relax in the lovely gardens or on the porch. Pick-up from bus depot, train station or town dock available.

Douglas, Shirley and Cameron (Malkin House)   ☎ (705) 732-2994
RR3, Box 290, Parry Sound, Orrville, ON   P2A 2W9

From Hwy 69, at 3.2 km south of Parry Sound, take Hwy 518 and continue 16 km into Orrville.

Turn left and look for 3rd house on left.
$35S $45D $5Child $10Add.person   ▶ 8
🗓closed Nov-April 🍷Choice, homebaked 🏠Village, hist., quiet, acreage, screened/open porches ■3(main & upper floor) ⬡2Sh.w.g. ⊨4D,1Q,1P,crib ★TV,F, separate entrance, parking, handicap facilities 🚭Restricted smoking, no pets
🏃 Antique shop, lakes, private safe sandy beach, Sequin snowmobile & nature trail
🚐 Parry Sound (Festival of Sound, Rainbow Theatre), Lake Rosseau, 30 000 Island cruises, Algonquin International School of Music
🐾 Very cozy country atmosphere in restored Century home with huge country kitchen and surrounded by large pine trees and beautiful landscaped grounds. ✍B&B

Wallenius, Shirley and Anders (Evergreen)   ☎ (705) 389-3554
Box 223, Parry Sound, ON   P2A 2X3

Located 19km east of Parry S. on Hwy124; 1km south of McKellar.
$40S $50-60D $10Add.person   ► 10+
✚ May-Oct   🕭 Full   🏠 Rural, res., acreage, view, lakefront,
quiet   ■ 2D,2F(upstairs)   ⊨ 2T,3D,1Q,1S   ⬦2Sh.w.g.
★Guest lounge with TV, reading material, billiard room with
prof-size table, separate entrance   ⊘No pets   ⋯Swedish
🕴 Village of McKellar, beach with swimming, fishing
🚙 Parry Sound, Festival of the Sound, 30,000 Island Cruise
☛ Elegant cedar log home with spacious deck overlooking lovely park-like grounds on the shore
of Lake Manitouwabing. Breakfast served in bright summer room. Canoe/row boat for rent. ✔B&B

Wissel, Trudy (Blackwater Lake B&B)   ☎ (705) 389-3746, Fax (705) 389-3746
167 Blackwater Lake Rd., RR1, Parry Sound, ON   P2A 2W7

Take Hwy 69 to Hwy 518 and proceed east through Orrville to Blackwater Lake Rd.
$40S $60D $20Add.person   🍽 Meals   ► 8
🕭 Full   🏠 Rural, res., 7 acres, lake opposite, patio, quiet,
secluded   ■4(upstairs)   ⊨ 5S,1D   ⬦2Sh.w.h.,whirlpool
★TV,F,lakeview from 2 rooms,balcony   ⊘No pets, not suitable
for small children   ⋯German
🕴 Fishing, boating, swimming, canoeing
🚙 Hunting, hiking, Parry Sound (yearly Festival of the Sound)
☛ Art/craft-oriented hostess in very homey and comfortable
house. Relax in the sunroom or deck and enjoy the beautiful view to three sides at the lake. Pick-up
at bus stop available. Use of whirlpool, fishing and paddleboat at extra charge. ✔B&B

Pefferlaw
                (north of Toronto on Lake Simcoe; see also Kewick)

Andrews, Doug & Lois (The Log Cabin B&B on the Pefferlaw Brook) ☎ 1-800-465-4898,
536 Pefferlaw Rd., Pefferlaw, ON   L0E 1N0   Fax (705) 437-2722

Phone for directions.
$45S $75D $75F $35Add.person   🍽 Meals   ► 7
🕭 full   🏠 Rural, 3-storey, log house, view from guest rooms, riverfront, quiet   ■ 1D,2F (lower
level   ⊨1S,1D,2Q   ⬦1Sh.w.g. (sauna & whirlpool)   ★ Air,LF,TV in guest sitting room,
separate entrance, guest quarters are separate   ⊕ Designated smoking area
🕴 Pefferlaw Brook (boating, swimming, canoeing, fishing), Lake Simcoe & sandy beach, ice fishing,
snowmobiling, skating
🚙 Antique shops, Sharon Temple, Red Barn Theatre, Casino Rama, Sibbald Point Prov. Park,
St.George's Stone Church, Trent Severn Waterway
☛ Friendly hospitality in cedar log cabin house, built in 1932 with unique matched granite
fireplace and overlooking the Pefferlaw Brook. There is a resident dog.Visa,MC ✔B&B

Smrke, Debbie & Steve (Cobblestones B&B)   ☎ (705) 437-2330, Fax (705) 437-1736
2 Quinn Rd., Pefferlaw, ON L0E 1N0   E-mail: smrke@ils.net

Phone for directions.
$45S $75D $35Add.person   🅜 Meals   ► 12
🔟 Full   ■ Rural, 2-storey, riverfront, patio, deck, quiet   ■ 1D,3F(ground & upper level)
⊨5S,2D,1Q   ⊐ 2Sh.w..g., 1sh.w.h.   ★ LF,2F, separate entrance, guest quarters are separate
Ⓦ Designated smoking area, pets welcome (with notice)
🕺 Pefferlaw River, Lake Simcoe, sandy beaches, fishing, swimming, canoeing, ice-fishing, skating,
snowmobiling (OFSC Trails), x-c skiing along riverside
🚗 Casino Rama, Sibbald Point Prov.Park, St.George Stone Church, Trent Severn Waterways, Red
Barn Theatre, Sharon Temple & Commodore gift shop, golf courses, antique shops
📣 Large, comfortable home situated on the Pefferlaw River. Enjoy morning coffee on the deck
overlooking the river, arrange a boat cruise on family 27ft cruiser or order a special occasion cake
(custom decorated by the hostess). Relax in the 2-person jacuzzi. There is a friendly Yellow Lab
called "Cola" in residence. Visa ✓B&B

Pembroke   *(west of Ottawa; see also Cobden, Eganville)*

Lloyd, Debra (Hilltop B&B)   ☎ (613) 638-3041, Fax (613) 638-0343
RR1, Pembroke, ON K8A 6W2   E-mail: lloydkohls@renc.igs.net

$48S $55D $5Child $80F $10Add.person   🅜 Meals   E-mail: ✓ 6A,1Ch

Phone for directions.
🔟 Full, homebaked   🏠 Rural, 3-storey, hist., view from guest
rooms, acreage, porch, quiet   ■ 2D,1F (main & upper level)
⊨1S,2T,2D   ⊐1Sh.w.g., 1ensuite   ★ F,ceiling fans, separate
entrance   Ⓦ Smoking outside   ⌇ French
🕺 Walking/skiing along Ottawa River
🚗 Algonquin Park, Logos Land, whitewater rafting, The Chute,
Bonechere Caves, museum, Pembroke Murals
📣 Warm welcome and friendly hospitality in large, airy home with colourful, uncluttered
antiques and art. Hostess is a former chef and serves creative breakfasts in special guest breakfast
room. There is a well-used atlas in the house, which identifies guests' hometowns. ✓CC

Pilot, Bob & Lois (Pillars and Lace B&B)   ☎ (613) 732-7674
307 Maple Ave., Pembroke, ON K8A 1L8

From Hwys 17/41 exit on Paul Martin Dr (turns into River Rd). Cross over MacKay St and proceed
to Maple Ave. Turn left to 2nd house on right.
$45S $55D $10Cot   ► 6A
🔟 Full, homebaked   🏠 Downtown, 3-storey, hist., patio, quiet
■ 3D(upstairs)   ⊨ 3D   ⊐ 2Shw.g.   ★ LF,F,TV, off-street
parking, guest quarters are separate   Ⓦ No smoking, no pets,
not suitable for children
🕺 Historic Wall Murals (walk or tour-train), riverside walking &
cycling trail (bikes for rent), Music in the Park, city buses
🚗 Snowmobile & x-c ski trails, whitewater rafting, south entrance to Algonquin Park
📣 Edwardian (ca 1902) brick home, winner of 1994 Architectural Heritage Award, with original
stained glass and woodwork and filled with antiques, art. Relax in the wicker furnished sunroom or
in the library by the fireplace and enjoy the lovely ambiance. Hosts have considerable knowledge of
the area. Private river cruises available. Breakfast is served in special guest breakfast room. Ask
for Ottawa Valley Maple Syrup for breakfast. ✓B&B

Penetanguishene *(on G.Bay west of Orillia; see also Midland, Waubaushene, Vict.Hbr)*

Friedrich, Veronika (Villa Veronika)   ☎ & Fax (705) 533-1533
1347 Tiny Beaches Rd North, Lafontaine, ON   L9M 1R3

From Toronto take Hwy 400 to Barrie or Hwy 27 north to Elmvale. Continue north on Simcoe Rd6 through Wyevale to 16th Concession. Proceed through Lafontaine to Georgian Bay and to Tiny

Beaches Rd N and look for 1st house on north side.
$100D $30Add.person   ◙ Meals   ► 6A
◙ Full   🏠 Rural, 3-storey, 1-acre, view from guest rooms, lakefront, patio, deck, quiet, secluded   ■ 1D,2F(main & upper level)   ◄ 3Q,2P   ⌐ 3Private   ★ Air,KF,F,TV, pool-table & shuffle-board in upper level, air-conditioners, ceiling fans, private entrance, host quarters are separate   ⓦ Designated smoking area, no pets, not suitable for children   ∾ Slovenian, German

🕴 Town of Lafontaine, shops, restaurants, beach, forest walks, 4-storey Observation Tower with panoramic view of Georgian Bay
🚐 Penetanguishene, Midland, Indian Village, St. Mary's Shrine, island cruises
🖙 Uniquely designed spacious home with stained glass windows and beautiful garden. Breakfast is served at guests choice in the dining room, upper recreation room or on the outside garden patio with gazebo. Visa ✓CC

Maurice, Wendy (Chesham Grove Bed & Breakfast)   ☎ (705) 549-3740
72 Church St., Penetanguishene, ON   L9M 1B4   Fax (705) 549-5075

From Toronto take Hwy 400 north to Barrie & Hwy 93 to Penentanguishene. Turn right at 3rd light (Robert St), then left on Fox St and right on Church St.

$40-50S $50-60D $10Child   ► 4A,1Ch
◙ Full, homebaked   🏠 Downtown, res, bungalow, view from guest rooms, porch, deck   ■ 1D,1F (main floor)   ◄ 1Q,1D,cot   ⌐ 1Sh.w.h.   ★ TV/VCR, street & off-street parking   ⓦ No pets, smoking in sheltered area outdoor   ∾ some French
🕴 Town of Penetanguishene, shops, churches, restaurants, town dock, Penetanguishene Bay, 30000 Island Cruise Boat (Georgian Queen), Winterama (3rd wk/Feb), hiking/biking trails
🚐 Discovery Harbour (historic site & live theatre), Huronia Museum & Huron Indian Village, Wyemarsh Wildlife Center, Ste-Marie-Among-the-Hurons Martyr's Shrine, Awenda Prov.Park
🖙 Quaint fieldstone bungalow with a pleasant & casual family atmosphere. Breakfast is served in the breakfast nook overlooking McGuire Recreation Park & Penetanguishene Bay. Relax on the veranda and enjoy the beautiful sunsets from the deck. Hostess is an avid gardener and cat lover and would be pleased to assist with sightseeing plans. There are cats in residence. ✓CC

Robitaille, JP & Georgette (Chez Vous, Chez Nous Couette & Café & B&B)
160 Con16,RR3,Penetang(Lafontaine),ON L9M 1R3   ☎ (705)533-2237,Fax (705) 533-4610

Located in Lafontaine. Phone for directions.
$45-50S $60D $10Child $15Add.person   ◙ Meals   ► 21
◙ Full   🏠 Farm, village, 2-storey, older, view from guest rooms, deck, quiet   ■ 2D,5F(main & lower level)   ◄ 9S,5D,1Q,2cribs   ⌐ 3Sh.w.g.   ★ TV, separate entrance   ⓦ No smoking   ∾ English (household language is French
🕴 Farm grounds and farm animals, village craft shop
🚐 Beaches, historic sites, boat cruises, shopping malls, skiing

🖙 Spacious home with new extension for guest rooms (built by host), situated in a rare historic southern Ontario farmland environment and located in the heart of Huronia tourist country. After a busy day in the outdoors, relax and enjoy the friendly bilingual hospitality. ✓CC

Van Bruggen, Crista (No.1 Jury Drive Bed & Breakfast)   ☎ & Fax (705) 549-6851
1 Jury Dr., Penetanguishene, ON L9M 1G1

From Hwy 400 north exit to Hwy 93, follow signs to Penetanguishene & Discovery Harbour.

$50-70S $60-80D   ▶ 6A
✚ May-Oct.   🍳 Extended Cont.   🏠 Res., replica of Victorian-style
■3D (upstairs) 🛏 2T,1Q,1K ⬟ 1Sh.w.g., 1 ensuite, private vanity
rooms ★Air,F,LF, guest bicycles, canoe, parking 🚳 No smoking, no
pets, children min. age 10 👄Dutch, German, some French
🏃 Georgian Bay beach, park, Discovery Harbour, Kings' Wharf Theatre
historic sailing ships, restaurant, gift shop
🚗 Martyr's Shrine Church, Wye Marsh Wildlife Ctr, Island boat cruise
🐎 Gracious hospitality in charming home located at the entrance to
Discovery Harbour. After a wonderful Dutch breakfast, explore the Georgian
Bay area, either by car/bike or canoe. ✔B&B

Perth   *(south-west of Ottawa; see also Balderson)*

Leach, Rick & Claire (Drummond House)   ☎ (613) 264-9175
30 Drummond St. East, Perth, ON K7H 1E9

Phone for directions.
$55S $65-70D $15Add.person   ▶ 7A,2Ch
🍳 Full, homebaked 🏠 Downtown, 3-storey, hist., view from
guest rooms, riverfront, deck, gazebo ■3D(upstairs) ⬟3Ensuite
🛏2S,1D,1Q,1R ★ F, ceiling fans, TV in guest family room
🚳No smoking, no pets, children min. age 4 👄French
🏃 Restaurants, golf course, Tay River, downtown shopping, Great
Rideau Lakes Canal System
🚗 Ottawa, Westpoint Village, Lanark Mills outlets, Murphy Point & Silver Lake Prov. Parks
🐎 Spacious stone house (ca 1820), in the heart of beautiful historic town and featured in local
walking tour. Ideal place for boaters using the Rideau Lakes Canal System. There are cats.✔CC

McGuinness, Tom & Marty (Rivendell Bed & Breakfast)   ☎ (613) 264-2742
RR4, (Hwy 7), Perth, ON K7H 3C6   Fax (613) 264-1568

Located on Hwy 7, 1.4 km southwest of Perth.ph for directions.

$40-55S $50-65D   🍽 Meals & Victorian Tea   ▶ 5
🍳 Full, homebaked 🏠 Rural, log house, view, patio, porch,
quiet, acreage ■ 2D,1S(upstairs), host quarters are separate
🛏1D,1Q,1S ⬟1Sh.w.g., 1ensuite ★LF,guest lounge with library
2nd floor reading area, separate entrance, guest fridge, parking
🚳No smoking, no pets, children by special arrangement 👄French
🏃 Good restaurant, pond with aquatic wildlife on property, x/c
skiing, skating on pond
🚗 Lakes, parks, conservation areas, swimming, boating, hiking, fishing, downtown Heritage
Perth, factory outlets, antiques, museums, Lanark Rideau Cycle Trail (maps available)
🐎 Elegantly restored log house (ca 1830) with view of pond and creek, with antiques, numerous
wildlife prints, and large library reflecting hosts' interest. Enjoy the "charm of yesteryear with the
comfort of today". Breakfast is served in formal dining room. Safe bike storage. Pick-up & delivery
to Rideau Trail. There is a resident dog (not in B&B area). ✔B&B

Peterborough

(east of Toronto; see also Lakefield, Hastings)

Bottcher, Paul & Karen (Armour Road Studio)   ☎ (705) 745-2071, Fax (705) 745-2943
1308 Armour Rd., RR9, Peterborough, ON   K9J 6Y1

From Hwy 7 By-pass exit at Ashburnham Rd. Turn left at stop sign and left again at next stop sign.
Proceed to Maria St., turn left and cross over bridge, then immediately right at Armour Rd.

$40-50S $45-75D $10Add.person   🖵 Meals   ▶ 11
🔆 Apr-Nov 🌙 Full, homebaked 🏠 Sub. bungalow, view,2decks,
riverfront,sunporch ■5 ⊨1K,3Q,1D ⌂1Private/jacuzzi,
2sh.w.g. ★Air,TV,F,KF,LF,parking ⊛No smoking ∿French
🕴 Trent University, Riverview Park Zoo, river rowing, Sunday
afternoon concerts in the park, public route
🚗 Hydraulic Lift Locks, Buckhorn Art Festival, Petroglyphs
🐾 Home is situated on the Otonabee River near Trent University
within city limits. Relax in the jacuzzi and enjoy the peace and tranquility of the countryside. House
specialty: "A touch of French cuisine". Free pick-up from Ptb.Airfield, Bus or Trent Severn Locks
may be available. Visa,MC ✒B&B

Bowers, Sam & Mary (Dala Rose B&B)   ☎ (705) 742-0877
203 Dahousie St., Peterborough, ON   K9J 2M1

Take George St North past Holiday Inn. Turn left on Dalhousie to B&B on left side.

$35S $50D $10Child   ▶ 6
🌙 Full 🏠 Downtown, 2-storey, porch, deck, quiet ■2F (upstairs)
⊨1S,2T,1Q,1R ⌂ 1sh.w.g.   ★ TV in guest sitting room, KF in guest
quarters, private entrance, off-street parking, host quarters are separate
⊛Designated smoking area, no pets, children min age 10
🕴 Little Lake marina (waterfront Festival, lights showplace, concerts),
downtown, antiques, shops, restaurants, Bus Terminal
🚗 Peterborough Lift Locks, Zoo, Trent U., golfing, Canoe Museum
🐾 Comfortable home, situated in quiet part of downtown. . Hosts are
knowledgeable about local tourism and willing to help with itineraries and
attractions. Breakfast is served in the dining room and evening snack in the guest TV sitting room.
There is "Elsie" the resident cat. ✒CC

Buchanan, Anna Jean (McLeod House)   ☎ (705) 742-5330
486 Albertus Ave., Peterborough, ON   K9J 6A2

From Hwy 401 go north on Hwy 115 to Peterborough. Take Parkway exit and follow to end. Turn
right onto Clonsilla which becomes Charlotte St and continue to Monoghan Rd. Turn left and
proceed through 1st stoplight to Hopkins Ave. Turn left to Albertus and then right.

$40S $50D   (Discounts for longer stay available)   ▶ 5

🌙 Full, homebaked 🏠 Res., older, multi-storey, garden deck,
view, quiet ■ 1S,2D(upstairs) ⊨1S,2T,1D ⌂ 1Sh.w.g.,
1sh.w.h. ★ TV,F, parking ⊛ No pets
🕴 French cuisine restaurant, large park with hiking & ski trails,
good cycling, bus routes
🚗 Kawartha Lakes, Trent University, Hydraulic Liftlocks and
boat cruises, Trent-Severn Waterway System, Summer Festival of
Lights, Pioneer Village, Farmers' Market, Zoo & golf courses
🐾 Friendly hospitality in gracious older family home, tastefully decorated and situated on a quiet
street in the "Old West End" of the City. Transportation available to bus station & airport. ✒CC

Hunter, Ruth & Terry (Hunter Farm B&B)   ☎ (705) 295-6253
RR9, Peterborough, ON   K9J 6Y1

Travel 7 km east of Peterborough on Hwy 7. Then proceed 3 km
north on Hwy 134.
$40S $50D $15Child   🍽 Meals   ► 4A,2Ch
🍳Full, homebaked   🏠Farm,2-storey, hist., acreage, view from guest
rooms,porches,quiet,isolated   ■1S,2D(upst)   ⊨1S,2D,1R,1P
🛁2Sh.w.h.   ★TV,parking 🚭No smoking, inquire about pets
🏃 Riding stable, bird watching, skiing, skating, sleigh riding, biking,
boating & fishing in ponds (stocked with bass), sugar shack & walks
in maple woods and Christmas trees, large barns, Apiary and wildlife Sanctuary, hill with viewpoint
🚗 Country Store, antique shops, flea markets, galleries, Petroglyphs (Indian Writings), Trent U.
📣 Congenial middle-aged hosts in spacious 1879 solid brick home, updated to include modern
conveniences, while maintaining its original character and surrounded by 245 acre very private
farm setting of ponds, fields, woods & wetlands in the popular Kawartha Lakes tourist region.
Relax in the sunroom or on the large verandas and watch birds and wild animals in fields. Canada
Geese & black swans are on the pond. There are horse and buggy/cutter, dog, cats, sheep, miniature
donkey, goats and pigs. A perfect child's get-away! ✒B&B

Lindsay, Marlis (King Bethune Guest House)   ☎(705)743-4101,Fax(705)743-8446
270 King St.Peterborough,ON   K9J 2S2   E-mail: marlis@sympatico.ca, 1-800-574-3664

Located in downtown. From clock tower travel, south on George St., 1block, right on King St.
$55S $70-110D $20Child   (plus taxes)   🍽 Meals   ► 10A,2Ch

🍳 Full, homebaked   🏠 Downtown, 2-storey, hist., patios, porch,
quiet   ■ 2D,1Ste (upstairs and lower level)   ⊨ 1Q,2K,plus
1Q(futon)   🛁3Ensuite   ★ F,TV/VCR/dataports/Casablanca
ceiling fans in guest rooms, room door locks, outdoor hot tub and
private entrance for suite, garden fountain & fireplace, off-street
parking 🚭Designated smoking area
🏃 Local pub, library, restaurants, shopping, Little Lake (marina),
art galleries, Otonabee River, nature trails, Trent Severn Waterway
🚗 Provincial Parks, Burleigh Falls, many lakes, hiking, cycling, skiing
📣 Spacious Victorian house situated in the heart of downtown with a beautiful walled English
garden (featured in 1994 Art Gallery Garden tour). Breakfast is served in the dining room, kitchen
or on the roofed garden patio at guests' schedule. Relax, read or socialize in the comfortable
surroundings. Office facilities & meeting space. Business travellers & Christmas holiday guests
especially welcome. Cycling route maps available. ✒CC

Noack, Dean (The Elizabeth Davidson House)   ☎ (705) 749-6960, 1-888-417-1010
520 Dickson St., Peterborough, ON   K9H 3K1   E-mail: dnoackcaccel.net

From downtown Peterborough, go north on Water St to McDonnel. Turn right and continue to end
and to house directly on crest of hill.

$50-55S $55-65D   ► 8
🍳Full, homebaked   🏠Downtown,res.,hist.,view,patio,quiet
■3D,1Ste(upst)   ⊨2T,1Q,2K   🛁2Sh.w.g.,2ensuite
★Air,TV,F, guest robes, parking 🚭No smoking, no pets
🏃 Shopping, superb restaurants, antiques, art galleries, churches,
Peterborough Festivals, Lift Locks, YMCA, river fishing, nature
walks along banks of Otonabee River
🚗 Lang Pioneer Village, Cdn Canoe Museum, Buckhorn Wildlife Art Festival, Indian arts/crafts
📣 Magnificient 1877-built Victorian Heritage home beautifully restored, tastefully decorated
with antique furniture and fixtures, is a prime example of Tuscan-Style Italianate Architecture and
located centrally, yet in a tranquil ravine setting. There is a dog & a cat in residence. ✒B&B

Pollock, Elsie (By The River B&B)　　　　　　　　　　　　☎ (705) 742-7963
621 River Rd South, Peterborough, ON　K9J 1E6

From Hwy 7 take Lansdowne St West to River Rd South. From Hwy 115 proceed to Bensfort Rd.
Turn left to River Rd South and look for the sign of the rooster. Coming by boat, go south on East
Bank of Lock 19 on Trent Canal System and look for the sign of the ducks.
$40S　$45-50D　$5Child　　　　　　　　　　　　　　　　　　　　　　　► 7
🍽 Full, homebaked　🏠 Res., split-level, riverfront　■ 2D,1F(upstairs)　🛏 2T,1D,1Q, cot
🛁1sh.w.g.　★ F,TV,off, street parking, guest quarters are separate　🖐 No smoking, no pets,
children min. age 2
🏃 Peterborough Lift Lock, restaurants, fishing, swimming, boating, Festival of Lights, museums,
x-c skiing, sporting events, city bus route
🚗 Bethany Hills skiing, snowboarding, historic sites, art exhibits/gallery, churches
🎯 Spacious back-split suburban home situated on a large well-treet lot on the Trent Canal. Enjoy
the first cup of tea or coffee on the patio by the water's edge or wander through the gardens. In
winter warm up by the cozy fireplace.

Thompson, Sandra (Blue Willow B&B)　　　　　☎ (705) 742-1887, 1-888-742-BLUE
197 Perry St., Peterborough, ON　K9J 2H9

From Toronto, take Hwys 401/115 and follow Parkway to
Landsdown. Turn right to George St., left to Perry St & left again.
From Ottawa take Hwy 7 to Peterb. & turn right on George St.
$40-65S　$50-75D　　　　　　　　　　　　► 5A
🍽 Full　🏠 Downtown, older, porch, deck, quiet ■3(upstairs)
🛏1S,1D,1Q　🛁 1Private, 1sh.w.g, jacuzzi tub in one guest
room　★TV in guest rooms, gazebo, off-street parking　🖐 No
smoking, no pets, no children

🏃 Shopping, restaurants, Art Gallery, Little Lake Festival of Lights (free concerts), bus terminal
🚗 Peterborough Lift Locks, Curve Lake Indian/Native shops,Petroglyphs(native stone carvings)
🎯 Warm and friendly welcome in older home furnished with rustic and Victorian pieces and
located in "the heart of the City". Hosts have free passes & promotional material from local
merchants for their guests. There are 2 cats in residence. MC ✒F0BBA

Petrolia　　　　　　　　　　　　　(south-east of Sarnia; see also Camlachie)

Currah, Edgar & Carol (Wander Inn B&B)　　　☎ (519) 882-1849, 1-888-892-6337
4107 Catherine St., Petrolia, ON　N0N 1R0

Take Hwy 402 to Hwy 21 cut-off and continue 13km to Petrolia Line. Turn left and proceed through

Petrolia. Turn right on Eureka St and left on Catherine St.
$35S　$45D　$10Child/Add.person　$65F　　　► 6
🍽Full,homebaked　🏠Res.,hist.,2-storey,patio,quiet ■3D(upstairs)
🛏2T,3D　🛁 1Sh.w.g.(whirlpool)　★Air,TV,LF ceiling fans,
off-street parking　🖐 No smoking, no pets
🏃 Shopping, antique shops, Victorian architecture, live theatre
🚗 Oil Museum of Canada, working oil fields (Petrolia Discovery),
Chemical Valley, St.Clair River Parkway, golfing, bridge to US

🎯 Warm welcome in comfortable home filled with antiques and crafts and located on a tree-lined
street. Watch TV in the family room or relax on the veranda with a cup of coffee or seasonal
beverage. Breakfast is served in the dining room. There is a small dog in residence. ✒CC

MacLachlan, John and Becky (Rebecca's B&B)   ☎ (519) 882-0118, 1-800-530-9591
4058 Petrolia St., Box 1028, Petrolia, Ont N0N 1R0

Travelling on Hwy 402, take Hwy 21 south to Petrolia.
$35S $40-45D $10Add.person   ▶ 9
💮 Full   🏠 Res., older, 3-storey, porch, quiet   ▦3D(upstairs)
⊨2D,2T,cots,crib   ⊒1Sh.w.g.   ★Air,TV in 1 guest room,
century player piano, parking ♥ 🚭No pets, restr.smoking
🏃 Victoria Playhouse (live theatre), town arena & business area,
churches, restaurants, art gallery, antiques/crafts, unique library
🚗 Petrolia Oil Discovery (famous working oil museum), golfing,
x/c skiing or hiking, golfing, St.Clair Parkway (boating, public beaches), Sarnia
🐾 Young host family in spacious designated Century brick home situated in beautiful historic
town (Canada's first oil boom town). Hosts have been welcomeing B&B visitors for 10 years and are
knowledgeable about their small home town/area. Home was featured on the Southwestern Ontario
Travel Association brochure & Events directory (1996/7). ✓B&B

Phelpston   *(north of Barrie; see also Hillsdale, Elmvale)*

Van Casteren, Lynda & Nicholas (Nicholyn Farms B&B)   ☎ (705) 737-4498
3088 Horseshoe Valley Rd., West, RR2, Phelpston, ON L0L 2K0   Fax (705) 737-2972

Located 10km north of Barrie. Travel north on Hwy 400 to Horseshoe Valley Rd. Turn left 3km to
farm on right. From Hwy 27 turn right on Horseshoe Valley Rd. turn right 4km to farm on left.

$50S $60D $10Child/Add.person   🍽 Meals   ▶ 12
💮 Full, homebaked   🏠 Farm, 2-storey,view from guest rooms,
130acres, porch, deck, quiet   ▦ 2D,1F(upper & lower level)
⊨3Q,5R,crib   ⊒ 1sh.w.g., 1sh.w.h.   ★ F,TV,LF   🚭 No pets,
smoking outside, children welcome   〰 some Dutch
🏃 Cycling, hiking, walking, retail store on farm, bus route
🚗 Skiing, golfing, museum, zoo, theatre, antique shops, Georgian
Bay, Wasaga Beach, historic sites, Barrie, Midland, Orillia
🐾 Charming, completely renovated, spacious farmhouse surrounded by lawns, gardens and trees
in a parklike setting and situated on a working hog farm. Hosts also operate a retail outlet on
grounds, selling own products, fruitpies, pickles etc. Breakfast is served in special guest breakfast
rooms. Relax in country comfort and enjoy Ontario's popular resort area. Visa ✓B&B

Picton   *(south of Bellev.; see also Milford, Bloomf, Wellington)*

Dubyk, Pat & Ron (Ginkgo Tree Place)   ☎ (613) 476-1792,
352 Main St. E, Box 4219, Picton, ON K0K 2T0

For scenic road from Kingston, take Hwy 33 to Glenora Ferry.

$55-60S/D   ▶ 8
💮Full 🏠Res., older, patio ▦4D(upst) ⊨2T,1Q,2D ⊒2Sh.w.g.
★Ceiling fans, off-street parking, TV in guest sitt.room, 2 small
guest verandas   🚭No smoking, no pets, children min. age 10
🏃 Historic museums, shopping, yacht club, tennis, antique shops
🚗 Sandbanks beaches, excellent bicycling, ice fishing, skating
🐾 Classic, large Victorian home, beautifully decorated, in very
convenient location with large landscaped grounds and gardens
including a large "Ginkgo" tree. New owners welcome new and former B&B guests. ✓ CC

Grondin, Carolyn (Tall Pines B&B) ☎ (613) 476-7424
41 Ferguson St., Box 995, Picton, ON K0K 2T0

From West, take Exit 522 (Wooler Rd S) to Hwy 33 (Loyalist Pkwy). Turn left to Picton and right on Ferguson St. From East, take Exit 566 and proceed south on Hwy 49 to Picton. Turn left on

Ferguson St.
$45S $55D $15Add.person   ► 6
🏠Full 🏠Res, 2-storey, porch, quiet ■2D(upstairs) ⊨1S,2D
🚗1Sh.w.h.   ★ TV, window fans, off-street parking 🐾No pets, designated smoking area
🏃 Downtown area, restaurants, unique shops
🚗 Sandbanks Prov.Park, Lake Ontario beaches, tour route for bicycling/boutiques/antique shops, Lake on the Mountain

📣 Warm welcome in quiet, central home, built ca 1880, located in historic town of Ontario's only Island County which is surrounded by much history, winding roads & beautiful beaches. Delicious breakfast is served in the dining room. A perfect place for a great holiday. ✒CC

Hill, Jill and John (Travellers' Tales) ☎ (613) 476-1885
Box 376, 1109 County Rd.8, Picton, ON K0K 2T0

From Toronto, take Wooler Rd Exit off Hwy 401 and follow Hwy 33 into Picton. Located on

Waupoos Rd, 6km south-east of town.
$50S $60-65D   ► 6
🌼 May 24-Sept 🍴 Full, homebaked 🏠Rural, hist., acreage, patio, quiet ■ 3D (upstairs) ⊨2D,2T 🚗 1Ensuite,
1sh.w.g.   ★ Fans, parking 🐾 No smoking, no pets, children min.age 12 🗣Spanish, French
🏃 Cycling, walking, bird watching, book shop & book barn on site
🚗 Sandbanks and beaches, Lake on the Mountain, antique shops

📣 Antiquarian book dealers and world traveller hosts offer friendly hospitality in peaceful and charming 1870s Canadian farm house with antique furnishings. Enjoy the quiet beauty of the country location. Breakfast is served at the Quebec harvest table in the dining room. Join in for afternoon tea. Browse among many thousands of books in parlour and huge barn on property, including large section for children. A book-lovers Paradise! Visam ✒B&B

Musgrove, Elisabeth (Treefield House B&B) ☎ (613) 393-2149
RR1, West Lake Rd., Picton, ON K0K 2T0

From Hwy 401 in Belleville, take Hwy 62 or 49 south to Beaconfield. Follow signs to Sandbanks

Prov. Park. Look for B&B on County Rd12.
$60-70S $70-80D $10Child/Add.person   ► 8
🌼 closed Nov & April 🍴 Full, homebaked 🏠 Rural, 2-storey, hist., 3-acres, view, lakefront, patio, deck, quiet ■1S,1D,1Ste,1F
(upstairs & ground level ⊨ 1S,4T,1D,1P 🚗2Private,
1ensuite   ★ TV/fans in guest room, private entrances, full guest kitchen, host quarters are separate 🐾 No smoking, no pets
🗣German, French, Spanish, Italian
🏃 Sand Dunes, 2 fine dining establishments, boat launch, private tennis court
🚗 Provincial Park beaches, Belleville, Kingston

📣 1879 waterfront farmhouse, furnished with antiques and groomed grounds overlooking West Lake and famous Sand Banks Prov.Park. Enjoy the lilyponds and fountains or relax by the woodburning fireplace. Breakfast is served in guest breakfast room. Also cabin available. ✒CC

Timm, Rikki & Dieter (Timm's Grandview Manor B&B)   ☎ (613) 476-8875
RR2, Picton, ON K0K 2T0

From Hwy 401 exit to Hwy 49 and proceed south toward Picton. Watch for sign at waterside.
$70-120D $15Add.person   🍽 Meals   (off season rates)   ►8

🍴 Full   🏠 Rural, 2-storey, 3-acres, view from guest rooms, lake
at back, patio, quiet, secluded ■2D,1Ste(upstairs) ⊨4T,2D,1R
⊒1Sh.w.g., 2ensuite   ★ 2F,TV in some guest rooms, ceiling
fans ⚓ Smoking outside, no pets (pet accommodation nearby),
children min. age 12 ⁓German
🏃 Golfing, fishing, swimming, biking, picnics, restaurants, dock
🚙 Picton, Sandbanks Prov. Park, Lake on the Mountain,
museums, antiques, artists studios, tennis, fine dining

🐾 Elegant Loyalist-style home with panelled foyer and traverse hall leading to principal rooms.
Surrounded by parklike grounds and overlooking the picturesque shoreline of the Bay of Picton.
Breakfast is served in the solarium or in the formal dining room. Relax in one of the guest sitting
rooms or on the terrace or in the garden with the attractive vista of bay and hills beyond. Gourmet
dinners available. Two-night min. stay on weekends during July & August. ⁓CC

Whitney, Jean (The Poplars)   ☎ (613) 476-3513
RR2, Picton, ON K0K 2T0

From Exit 566 on Hwy 401 go south on Hwy 49 over bridge and immediately right on Northport Rd.

Proceed 1.5 km to large white house on right.
$45-60S/D $20Add.person   ► 8
🍴 Full   🏠 Rural, acreage, view, lakefront, patio, dock, quiet
■ 4D (upstairs) ⊨4T,1D,1Q,1R   ⊒1Sh.w.g., 1ensuite
★Air,TV,parking ⚓ No pets, no smoking
🏃 Excellent fishing, private dock for 4 boats
🚙 Belleville, Kingston, Picton, Sandbanks Prov.Park
🐾 Old-fashioned hospitality in renovated spacious Century home

surrounded by large poplar trees and expansive grounds reaching down to the water. Relax on the
upper deck and enjoy the tranquil atmosphere. ⁓B&B

Williams, Bob and Helen (Wilhome Farmhouse B&B)   ☎ (613) 393-5630
RR1, Picton, ON K0K 2T0   Fax: (613) 393-5108

Take Hwy 33 (Loyalist Parkway). Between Bloomfield & Picton, turn south on Cty Rd 32 for 1km,
watch for checkerboard road sign in yard.
$45S $55-60D $10Child $20Add.person   ► 6A,3Ch

❋ May-Oct.(other by reservation)   🍴 Full,homebaked
🏠300-acre farm, hist., deck ■2D,1F(upstairs) ⊨1S,2D,1Q,1R,
playpen for child's bed ⊒ 1Sh.w.g.,1sh.w.h. ★ TV,F, separate
entrance, parking ⚓ No smoking
🏃 Walk on country roads, cycling, birdwatching, Bloomfield
🚙 Picton, antique/craft shops, museums, Sandbanks Prov Park,
beaches, fishing, fine dining, Belleville, Kingston

🐾 Circa 1850 Loyalist home (with original pine floors and woodwork throughout and antiques
abound, including the original bake oven/fireplace in the kitchen). Situated on rolling farmland,
now part of a working farm settled by the host's family in 1814. Relax on the deck overlooking the
countryside and enjoy fresh produce and milk from the herd of Holsteins. There are two cats.

York, Marg (Log House B&B) ☎ (613) 476-5978
Box 413, 2 Henry St., Picton, ON K0K 2T0

Take Exit 522 from Hwy 401 (Wooler Rd South) and travel south on Hwy 33 to Picton. Upon

entering town limits, turn left on first street to house on right.
$40-50S $55-65D $10Child   ► 4A,1Ch
🍴 Full, homebaked   🏠 Res., 2-storey, log home, .5 acres, view
from guest rooms, porch, deck, quiet   ■ 2D (main & upper
floor) ⊨2T,1Q,cot ⫣2Ensuite, whirlpool bath ★Air,F,TV in
one guest room,off-street parking,sunroom 🖐No smoking,no pets
🏃 Downtown Picton, harbour, antique & craft shops
🚗 Sandbanks Provincial Park, extensive Lake Ontario shoreline
📷 New modern log home, built by hosts, with cathedral ceilings, open plan, lounge area with
fireplace and landscaped flower gardens. Retired couple are natives of the area. Breakfast special is
buttermilk pancakes served with fruit sauces, maple syrup; fresh preserves & sweet salsa. ✔B&B

Pinkerton   *(east of Kincardine; see also Cargill, Paisley)*

Garland, Ron & Koleen (Rose Hill B&B) ☎ (519) 366-9934
RR2, Cargill, ON N0G 1J0

Take County Rd 15 to Pinkerton, then north on Banting Line to No 50.
$75S/D   ► 2A
➕ May-Nov1 🍴 Cont, homebaked 🏠 Farm, rural, hillside, 2-storey, view from guest rooms,
acreage, patio, porch, quiet, secluded   ■ 1Ste (ground floor) ⊨ 1Q ⫣1Ensuite(jaccuzzi)
★ Air,KF,TV in suite, separate entrance, guest quarters are separate   🖐No smoking, no pets,
not suitable for children
🏃 Woodland bush and river on property, hiking, fishing, canoeing, bird watching, bicycling
🚗 Lake Huron beaches, Saugeen River, museums, farmers' markets, antique & craft fairs/shops,
theatre, Bruce Trail hiking, golfing, excellent dining establishments
📷 Large sheep and cash crop farm with the scenic Teeswater River Valley at front of property.
The tranquility and solitude provide a haven for walkers, wildlife enthusiasts and country lovers.
Hosts are avid gardeners and welcome guests to enjoy the many gardens. Ideal place for a weekend
or longer get-away.

Port Carling   *(west of Bracebridge)*

Mann, Wilsie & Bob (DunRovin B&B) ☎ (705) 765-7317
Box 304, Port Carling, ON P0B 1J0   E-mail: dunrovin@muskoka.com

Take Hwy 169 north to Mortimer's Point Rd (Muskoka Rd 26). Turn right and proceed 2 km to

B&B on left. Look for sign.
$80-90S/D   🍽 Meals (winter only)   ► 4A
🍴 Full, homebaked 🏠 Rural, hillside, acreage, view from guest
rooms, lakefront, sundeck on boathouse, quiet   ■ 2D(ground
level) ⊨ 2T,1Q (incl.romantic canopy) ⫣ 2Ensuite
★Ceiling fans, separate entrance, off-street parking, guest
quarters are separate   🖐 No smoking, no pets, no children
🏃 Swimming, canoeing, paddle boating, x-c skiing
🚗 Artisans shops, boat cruises, boutiques, scenic drives, theatres, museums, Segwun boat tours
📷 Picturesque home surrounded by a spacious deck overlooking the north bay of Lake Muskoka.
Guests who come by plane, boat or car are welcome to enjoy the warmth and charm of a cottage
with all the comforts of home. Relax in the hammock and watch the herons go by or in the hot tub
in the winter after a day on the ski trails. Breakfast is served upstairs in great room or on deck
overlooking the lake. Hosts are pilots and both know the local area well. ✔B&B

Nicholson, Terry & George (Nicholson's Bed & Breakfast)   ☎ (705) 764-1095
RR1, Port Carling, ON   P0B 1J0

Located on Hwy 118 and 18 km west of Bracebridge (8 km from Port Carling). Look for sign
opposite the Thom Wroe Rd.
$45S $55-65D   ► 6A
✚ not X-mas & New Years   ⬜ Full   🏠 Rural, 2-storey, quiet,
chalet-style,acreage, patio   ⬛2D,1Ste(upstairs)   ⊨2T,1Q,1D
⬛ 1Ensuite, 1sh.w.g.   ★ F,TV,parking   ⓌNo children, no
pets, restricted smoking, no food or beverages in guest rooms
🕅 Picnic area & beach on Lake Muskoka, boat launching ramp
🚗 Excellent restaurants, golf courses, steamship cruises
☞ Spacious home surrounded by many trees, virgin bush and unusual rock formations and
situated near a section of Lake Muskoka. Long time B&B hosts are originally from England and
have travelled the B&B route in many different countries. ✔B&B

Port Colborne   *(south of Niagara Falls on Lake Erie, Fenwick)*

Bisnette, Sandi & Brent (Ingleside Bed & Breakfast)   ☎ (905) 835-5062
322 King St., Port Colborne, ON   L3K 4H3

Phone for directions.
$60-75S/D   ► 4A+
⬜ Cont., homebaked   🏠 Downtown, 2-storey, hist., patio,
horsebarn & carriage shed   ⬛ 2D (upstairs) plus lakefront
cottage   ⊨ 2D   ⬛ 2Private   ★ Air,F,LF,TV, separate
entrance, parking   Ⓦ Designated smoking area, no children
🕅 Welland Canal, Showboat Festival Theatre,restaurant,gallery,
beaches, Sugarloaf Harbour Marina, docking facilities, bus stop
🚗 Niagara Falls, Niagara-on-the-Lake (Shaw Theatres), St.Catharines, Vineland, winery tours
☞ Stately Victorian home (built in 1867) completely restored for B&B and filled with Victorian
accent pieces, art work, fine furniture and ornate black iron fence surrounding the lovely garden.
Situated in a perfect area for history buffs. There are 3 very friendly dogs in residence. ✔CC

Port Dover   *(on Lake Erie, s/of Simcoe; see also Waterford)*

Ivey-Baker, Christine & John (Bed & Breakfast by the Lake)   ☎ (519) 583-1010
30 Elm Park, Port Dover, ON   N0A 1N0

Phone for directions.
$55S/D   ► 6
⬜ Full, homebaked   🏠 Village, ranch-style, view, lakefront,quiet
patio, porch, quiet   ⬛ 3D (host quarters are at other end of
house)   ⊨2Q,1D   ⬛ 1Sh.w.g.1sh.w.h   ★ Air,F,TV in guest
rooms, wheel-chair access, sep.entrance, parking   ⓌNo smoking,
no pets, child min. age 12
🕅 Lighthouse Festival Theatre (summer), Lake Erie (walking on
beach, fishing, swimming), hiking on Lynn Valley Trail, shopping, golfing
🚗 Art Galleries, museums, Long Point Biosphere, bird watching, Backus Woods nature walks
☞ Ranch-style home warmly furnished with antiques & art; situated in quiet residential area in a
private park overlooking Lake Erie. Lake Resort is well known for harbour activities and summer
theatre. Breakfast is served in separate guest breakfast room. Hosts can arrange Tee Times for
guests at nearby golf course. There is a dog in the backyard. Visa ✔B&B

Port Hope
(on Lake Ontario east of Oshawa; see also Cobourg, Colborne)

Harrison, Bob & Bonnie (Butternut Inn Bed & Breakfast)   ☎ (905) 885-4318
36 North St., Port Hope, ON L1A 1T8   E-mail: buttrnut@eagle.ca Fax (905) 885-5464

From Hwy 401, take Exit 461 & Hwy 2 into downtown. Turn left on Pine St & right on North St.
$70-85D $15Add.person   (plus taxes)   ⬟ Meals   ▶ 9

⬟ Full, homebaked (gourmet) ⬟ Downtown, res., 2-storey.
hist., view, patio, quiet ■ 3D,1Ste (upstairs) ⊨ 4Q,1P
⬟3Ensuite, 1private ★ 2F, TV in one guest room, wood stove,
private entrance, ceiling fans, off-street parking, guest quarters are
separate ⬟No smoking, no pets, children min. age 12
✠ Historic homes, many antique shops, downtown pubs &
restaurants, Capitol Theatre, Lake Ontario, beach, fishing, golfing,
museums, Lake Ontario Waterfront Trail
🚗 Ganaraska Forest, Lake fishing/boating, Presqu'ile Beach, Apple Route & Loyalist Trail
🐾 Delightful, restored 1850's home, luxuriously appointed to ensure peace and comfort. Curl up
by the fire in winter, explore the expansive secret garden in summer or watch the birds from the
skylit solarium. Indulge in a Gourmet Get-away Cooking Weekend or ask about other packages.
There are 2 downstairs cats in residence. Visa,MC ⬟B&B

McCormick, Diane and David Priest (Uppertowne Inn)   ☎ (905)) 885-5694
187 Walton Street, Port Hope, ON L1A 1N7

From Hwy 401 exit at Hwy 2 or Hwy 28 for downtown Port Hope. Look for house near top of the
Walton Street (Hwy 2) hill.
$45-55S $60-70D $10Child/Add.person   ▶ 9
⬟ Full ⬟ Downtown, hist., res., 3-storey, patio, quiet, large
ravine lot ■4D,1S(upst) ⊨S,T,Q,R ⬟2Sh.w.g. ★Air,F,TV
in guest room, parking ⬟No smoking
✠ Antique shops, fishing
🚗 Beaches in Prince Edward County, Ganaraska Forest, good
dining spots, civilized watering hole, excellent river/stream fishing
🐾 Gracious Georgian-style home dating back to 1857, (at the time serving as a hotel to horse and
carriage travellers), is situated in attractive town which is largely 19-Century without being in any
way artificial. Bicycle tours organized. There are 2 cats and a dog in the house. ⬟CC

Port Perry
(north-east of Toronto)

Heintzman, Merle (Landfall Farm Bed & Breakfast)   ☎ (905) 986-5588
3120 Hwy 7A, RR1, Blackstock ON L0B 1B0

From Hwy 401 take Exit 431 at Bowmanville and continue on Reg Rd 57 north to Hwy 7A. Turn

west 1.5 km to farm. Look for Antiques sign.
$40-45S $60D   (Childrens rates available)   ▶ 8
⬟ Full ⬟ Rural, 2-storey, hist., view from guest rooms, patio,
acreage, swimming pool, isolated ■3D(upstairs) ⊨2T,2D,1P
⬟2Shw.g. ★Air,TV,F, change house & washroom poolside,
parking ⬟May accept pets, designated smoking area
✠ Antique shop on premises, secluded pond, walking in fields
🚗 Golf course, tennis, fishing/boating, lake ice skating, Casino
🐾 1868 fieldstone farmhouse (desig.Heritage Site), surrounded by crop lands and extensive
lawns, large private pond. Located near Port Perry, a charming lakefront town on Lake Scugog in
Central Ont (noted for shopping). Relax in country comfort & contemporary surroundings.
Extended stays welcome.

Port Sydney
(south of Huntsville; see also Baysville, Windermere)

Chalmers, Joanne & Bill (Stone Cottage B&B)   ☎ (705) 385-3547
RR1, Port Sydney, ON   P0B 1L0

From Hwy 11, take South Mary Lake Rd to bridge. Turn right at Deer Lake Rd, proceed 1km south.

$55S $65D   ▶ 6
🍳 Full, homebaked   🏡 Rural, hist., acreage, view, sunroom,
quiet ■3D(upstairs) ⊨1D,2Q 🛏Sh.w.g. ∿some French
★Air,TV,F, separate entrance, parking 🚭No smoking, no pets
🏃 Fun golf course on property, x-country & alpine skiing, boating,
swimming, fishing, tennis, hiking, bird-watching
🚗 Pioneer Village, Santas Village, boat tours, craft studios
🐾 Century old stone house completely restored, decorated in
Canadiana with many antiques, situated on 32 acres of pine forest on North Muskoka River. Relax
in harmony with nature. Enjoy the riverfront facilities and trails on the property. Nutritious
specialties are featured for breakfast. ✓B&B

Powassan
(south of North Bay; see also Mattawa)

Hynd, Jo-Anne Elaine (Satis House Bed & Breakfast)   ☎ (705) 724-2187
RR2, 258 English Line, Powassan, ON   P0H 1Z0

From Powassan travel south on Hwy 11 and turn west (right) onto
English Line for 1.5km. Located 10km north of Trout Creek.
$40S $50D $25Add.person   🍽 Meals   ▶ 7
🍳 Full, homebaked 🏡Rural, 100 acres, view, quiet ■3(upstairs)
⊨3T,2D,1Q 🛏 1Sh.w.g., 1ensuite ★ TV 🚬Smoking
outside only, children min. age 10 ∿ French, Swedish
🏃 Excellent snomobiling, Powassan week-end market
🚗 Nipissing/Trout/Nosbonsing Lakes, beaches, museums, shops, Almaguin Highlands,
Algonquin Pk, North Bay waterfront attractions, Arts Center
🐾 Unique, new Georgian-style home with high ceilings and gorgeous view of open land & pine
forest growing on site. Enjoy "the best butter tarts in the North". There is a cat in residence. ✓CC

Priceville
(south of Owen Sound; see also Markdale)

Cambria, Jennifer (Glen Elg Country Inn B&B)   ☎ & Fax: (519) 369-2858
RR1, Priceville, ON   N0C 1K0

Located 1km south of Hwy 4 on Grey Rd23, between Durham and East Flesherton.

$65S/D $10Add.person   🍽 Meals   ▶ 6
🍳 Full, homebaked (buffet-style)   🏡 Rural, hist., acreage,
porch, quiet, secluded   ■ 3D(upstairs) ⊨ 2T,2Q,cot
🛏3Private ★ Ceiling fans, guest robes, host quarters are
separate 🚭 No smoking, no pets, children min. age 12
🚗 Beaver Valley skiing, Bruce Trail hiking, fishing, canoing,
kayaking, cycling, water activities, large arts community
🐾 Completely renovated 1853-built brick home, tastefully
decorated in Early Canadiana antique reproductions (by local handcraft furnitue makers), and
located on 40acres in beautiful Grey County. Breakfast is served in the glorious sunroom. Picnics
provided on request. Relax in the lounge and enjoy gourmet meals prepared by host-chef (with prior
notice). Weekend cooking packages available. There are 2 dogs. Visa ✓B&B

Red Bay

(west of Wiarton; see also Hope Bay)

Ford, Larry & Pat (Haven on the Bay)
RR1, 424 Huron Rd., Mar, Red Bay, ON N0H 1X0

☎ (519) 534-4002

Follow Hwy 6 north from Wiarton to Mar intersection. Turn left on Red Bay Rd passing scenic SkyLake to end of road. Turn right, proceed to Red Bay and look for sign on right side.

$45S $55-60D $12Add.person 🍽 Meals ► 15A
🍲 Full 🏡Village, rustic, 2-storey, large wooded grounds ■5
(upst) ⊨3S,4D,2Q 🛏2Ensuite,1sh.w.g. ★F,TV,VCR in great room, parking 🚭No smoking, no pets, no children
🦌 Lake Huron, excellent swimming, sailing, birding, star gazing, hiking, biking tour route, wildflower boardwalk at Petrel Point Nature Reserve, groomed x/c ski trails
🚗 Sauble Beach & Falls, Bruce Trail, Manitoulin Island ferry

🐾 Relax and unwind in Four Seasons landmark B&B near Lake Huron's sand beach in a peaceful hamlet. Enjoy complimentary fireside teas & candle light dinners. Gift Certificates available. Small groups welcome. There are cats in resident. ↙B&B

Ridgetown

(east of Chatham; see also Dutton)

Ure, Margaret & Glen (Ridgeland Bed & Breakfast)
RR2, Ridgetown, ON N0P 2C0

☎ (519) 674-2461

From Hwy 401, take Exit 101, proceed south on Kent Rd 15 for.4km & look for 3rd house on right

$45-55S $55-65D (Reservations please) ► 10
🍲 Full, homebaked 🏡 Farm, 2-storey, hist., acreage, swimming pool, patio, porch, deck, quiet ■ 3D (main & upper level)
⊨2D,1Q 🛏 1Ensuite, 1sh.w.g., whirlpool tub ★ Air,F,TV in guest room, separate entrance, large common room with player piano 🚭 No smoking, no pets
🦌 Surrounding cash crop farm grounds
🚗 Country auctions, Uncle Tom's Cabin, golfing, Rondeau Park

🐾 Century home (built in 1873) purchased by the host family and moved to their farm grounds, completely renovated blending 1800's charm with today's amenities and tastefully furnished with authentic antiques. Congenial hosts love to tell the storey and historic facts of the home. Guest rooms are separate from host quarters. ↙CC

Rockwood

(north of Kitchener/Waterloo; see also Acton, Ariss, Guelph, Elora)

Isbrucker, Jane (Country Spirit)
RR5, Rockwood, ON N0B 2K0

☎ (519) 856-9879

From Hwy 401, take Exit 312 north (Guelph Line) and continue for 16 km to Indian Trail (0.5 km past stop sign). Turn left and left again on Ash St to 2nd property on right side.

$40S (and up) $50D (and up) $20Add.person 🍽Meals ► 6

🍲 Full, homebaked 🏡 Rural, cedar home, country view from guest rooms, 5 acres, decks, quiet, pond, wooded area, secluded
■ 2 (main and upper floor) ⊨ 2Q,1D 🛏 1Ensuite, 1private
★ Air,TV, F, parking 🚭No smoking, no pets, not suitable for children 🗣French, Dutch, some German
🦌 Hiking, biking, x-c skiing, walks on country lanes & wooded acreage from back door
🚗 Exclusive boutique shopping, exc.dining, antiques, airport

🐾 Spacious, elegant and comfortable country home surrounded by virgin woods and pleasant gardens and pond. Situated at the edge of the village of Eden Mills in the beautiful Eramosa River Valley. A "hidden jewel" and ideal spot for a relaxed mini-vacation. Active hostess is well informed and involved in local activities and happenings. Ideal place for cyclers. ↙B&B

ONTARIO 275

Rossport *(on Lake Superior, east of Thunder Bay; see also Dorion, Wawa)*

Gordon, Linda D.& Paul (The Willows Bed & Breakfast) ☎ (807) 824-3389
1 Main St., Box 21, Rossport, ON P0T 2R0

Located 0.4 km off Hwy 17 on the Rossport Loop and opposite the main dock in town.
$65-110S $80-125D $15Add.person (plus tax) ▶ 8

Full Village, 2-storey, hist., view from guest rooms, lakefront, deck, quiet ■ 4D(main & upper level) 2S,3Q
4Private ★ F,TV,VCR/reading material for guests, whirlpool tub in 2 guest room, separate entrance, facilities for handicapped (on main floor), off-street parking No smoking, well behaved pets accepted
Excellent restaurants, gift shops, Charter Fishing, boat tours, local museum, pottery shop
X-country ski/snowmobile/hiking trails, fishing/hunting, Amethyst Mines, ice climbing
Newly renovated old Rossport Schoolhouse in central location on the rugged scenic North Shore of Lake Superior and overlooking a unique grouping of islands. Relax on the large deck and watch the activities of the Rossport main dock and harbour. Hosts may take guests out on their 27ft cruiser to the Rossport Islands for picnics and hiking. There are 2 little dogs named "Willi" & "Ami" in residence. Visa,MC ✓B&B

Sarnia *(on Lake Huron, west of London; see also Camlachie,, Petrolia)*

Simard, Rose (Lakeshore B&B) ☎ (519) 542-2025
1576 Mallah Drive, Sarnia, ON N7V 3R5

Phone for directions.
$25S $40D ▶ 9
Full, homebaked Res., older, 2-storey, sun deck, quiet
■3(upstairs) 1S,2T,1D,1Q 2Sh.w.g.,1sh.w.h. ★Air,TV,F, separate entrance,parking No pets,no smoking
Nice local beaches
Canatara Park (nature trails, animal farm, picnic areas), local tourist Information Bureau, Bluewater Bridge into USA
Warm welcome in home located in quiet residential area. Retired hosts love to play bridge. Enjoy good conversation and friendly hospitality.

Cain, Bev & Bern (Beverley's B&B) ☎ (519) 869-6502
2589 Westgate Cr., Box 233, Bright's Grove, ON N0N 1C0

Located approx 10km from Sarnia. Phone for directions.
$38S $48D ▶ 4A
Full,homebaked Sub.,split-level,view,patio,porch,quiet
■2D(upstairs) 2T,1Q 1Sh.w.g. ★Air,F,TV,off-street parking No soking, no pets, children min. age 12
Back gate on property leads to Wildwood Park and to shore of Lake Huron, walking/cycling path along lake, public library, art gallery, bus No 15
Bright's Grove, Sarnia, Blue Water Bridge to USA, golf courses, Huron County Play House
Warm welcome and friendly hospitality in charmingly decorated home, with antiques and art work and situated in serene parklike setting. Breakfast is served with quiet elegance in the dining room overlooking Wildwood Park. Relax and enjoy the magnificient summer sunsets over the lake. Hosts are happy to offer guidance for sightseeing and exploration planning. Ideal place for business travellers. Transportation from the train, plane or marina can be arranged. Visa ✓ CC

Ellis, Connie (Catalpa Tree B&B)　　　　　☎ (519) 542-5008, 1-800-276-5135
2217 London Rd, Sarnia, ON　N7T 7H2

From Hwy 401, take 402 westbound and Mandaumin Rd Exit. Proceed to County Rd 22 (old Hwy 7 London Line). Turn right and then 5km to B&B on left. From Hwy 402 eastbound exit at Airport

Rd to County Rd 22 Hwy 7 and turn left 2km to B&B on right.
$40S　$49D　$5Child　🍽 Meals　　　　　▶ 6
✴ Easter-Jan1　🐦 Full(gourmet)　🏠 Farm, Century home, 2-storey, porch, quiet ■3D(upstairs) ⊨2T,1Q,1D ⊐1Sh.w.g. ★Air,F,TV,LF, sep.entrance, guest quarters are separate, gas fireplaces in some guest rooms 🚭 Designated smoking area, children min. age 5　〰 some French
🕴 Golf Course across the road at end of lane

🚗 St.Clair River Parkway, Sarnia Bay, Lake Huron beaches, US border, Victoria Playhouse
📣 Victorian (ca 1894) home with a warm mix of contemporary and period pieces. Relax on the veranda, or play a game of croquet. Golf & gourmet weekends & interesting day tours can be arranged. Enjoy a Victorian Family Christmas stay. Breakfast is served in special guest breakfast room or on the veranda. Pick-up at airport/bus/marina can be arranged. There is a resident Mini Schnauzer "Penny" and cat "Skipper".Visa

---

Sauble Beach　　　*(on Lake Huron, north of Southampton; see also Red Bay, Wiarton)*

Jackson, Veronica and David (Jackson's B&B)　　　　　☎ (519) 422-3073
Box 24, RR1, Sauble Beach, ON　N0H 2G0

Located off County Rd 8 on Lakeland Drive. Phone for directions.
$40S　$45D　$10Add.person　(Child under age 10 free)　▶ 6
🐦Full　🏠Rural, acreage, 2-storey, patio, quiet ■3D(upst) ⊨3R,1R ⊐Sh.w.g. ★TV,F,KF,LF, parking 🚭Restricted smoking, no pets
🕴 Park beach, golf course, x-country/snowmobile trails
🚗 Southampton, Owen Sound, ski hills, Bruce Trail hiking
📣 Enjoy warm and friendly hospitality. Relax in the family room or on the large veranda/deck. Fishing equipment and charters available at the marina. ✒B&B

Sault-Ste-Marie　　　*(see also St.Joseph I., Bruce Mines, Blind Riiver)*

Brauer, Margaret & Bernt (Top o'the Hill B&B)　　☎ (705) 253-9041 Fax: (705) 946-5571
40 Broos Rd, Sault-Ste-Marie, ON　P6C 5S4　　　　　　E-mail: brauerb@sympatico.ca

From North on Hwy 17, turn right on Hwy 550(Second Line W). and proceed 7.4km to Broos Rd. turn right. From East take the Hwy 17 Bypass to Hwy 550 (Second Line and jct with Hwy 17 north (water tower). Follow Hwy 550 for 7.4km west to Broos Rd and turn right. House is up hill.

$45S　$65-95D　$15Child(under 16,free under 5)　　　▶ 6
✴ May-Oct　🐦Full, homebaked　🏠Sub., acreage, view from guest rooms, patio, quiet ■3D (upper level) ⊨ 2T,1K,1Q ⊐1Sh.w.g.,1ensuite　★F,TV, piano, parking, solarium with indoor fish pond　🚭No smoking　〰 German
🕴 Hiking and walking along creek and bush, Lily pond with fish
🚗 ACR Agawa Canyon Train, swimming, fishing, boating, hiking, Sault Locks

📣 Unique, large hill-top house with tranquil European ambiance and unhurried atmosphere is surrounded by picturesque gardens located in District 9, Algoma. Enjoy the spectacular autumn colours and afterwards relax in comfortable home which was selected for 1990 Art Gallery of Algoma House Tour. Breakfast is served in the center dining room. A small apartment also available. There is a Golden Retriever "Meggie" in residence. Reservations requested. Visa ✒B&B

Douville, Joe and Helen (Hillsview)
406 Old Garden River Rd., Sault-Ste-Marie, Ont. P6B 5A8
☎ (705) 759-8819 Fax (705) 945-1253
E-mail: douvillehj@sympatico.ca

Follow Hwy 17 (Second Line) to Old Garden River Rd (City water tower visible). Turn north-east
for 1 km to house on left side with brown brick with cream trim.
$40S $50-55D $15Child ▶ 6A,1Ch
Choice, homebaked Res., split-level, patio, quiet 3D
(main and lower level) 2D,1Q,1S 1Sh.w.g., 1sh.w.h.
★TV,F, guest fridge, large guest sitting room, parking No
pets, no smoking Restaurants, shopping
Agawa Canyon Tour Train, International Bridge, beach,
groomed x-c ski and hiking trails, boardwalk
Enjoy country living in the city in spacious, comfortable surroundings. Relax on the patio or by
the fireside in the guest sitting room. Conveniently located near Hwy 17, the Int. Bridge and the
Agawa Canyon Tour Train. B&B

Monaghan, Dennis & Deirdre (The Wabos Trails End)
Box 2, Searchmont, ON P0S 1J0
☎ (705) 781-1003

Located 58km from Sault-Ste-Marie at No2762 Lot 47, Wabos. Follow Hwy 17 north to Heyden.
Turn right onto Hwy 556 and continue to Searchmont (32km). Proceed through town and follow
Hwy 532 for 8km. Look for signs.
$50S $25Add.person Meals ▶ 6
Full, homebaked Farm, 42-acres, view from guest rooms, porch, deck, quiet, secluded
1D,1F(upstairs) 2D 1Private, 1ensuite ★ TV,F, ceiling fans, sauna
Designated smoking area, no pets, children min. age 10
Mountain biking, hiking, fishing for speckled trout, bird watching, x-c skiing & snowshoeing
Searchmont Ski Resort (downhill), Algoma Central Railway Tours, canoe/kayak/hunt
Hobby farm with newly renovated 70+ Finnish farmhouse situated on quiet hillside of Algoma
Country. Relax in the sauna or enjoy a walk with nature. Young hosts have studied Fish/Wildlife/
Forestry and like to share nature with their guests. Ideal place for a rest in every season of the year.

Tholberg, Lilja (Grand Oaks B&B)
9 Grand River Cr., Sault-Ste-Marie, ON P6B 3R9
☎ (705) 254-3797 1-888-625-6686

From Hwy 17E and Bypass Hwy 550 proceed to Black Rd. Turn left onto McNabb and onto
St.Georges. Turn right at Grand Blvd, left on Grand River Cr.
$45S $55-65D ▶ 5
Full, homebaked Res., bungalow, patio, quiet 1S,2D
(main floor) 1S,2D 1Sh.w.g., 1sh.w.h., access to
sauna ★ Air,2F,TV in one guest room, separate entrance,
off-street parking, guest quarters are separate No smoking,
no pets, children min. age 10 Finnish
Agawa Canyon Train Tour, St. Mary's River boardwalk, Roberta
Bondar Pavilion, fishing (Cohoe & King salmon), Bon Soo Winter Carnival, bus stop
Public swimming (Pointe des Chenes), Hiawatha ski trails, Lake Superior scuba diving, Locks
Warm welcome in cozy home with cathedral ceiling, quiet comfort, and centrally located.
Breakfast special is Finnish pancakes (crepes with fruit in season), including "Pulla" (Finnish
coffeebread) served in guest breakfast room. Relax and rejuvenate after a steamy sauna & Kalja.
There are cats in residence. B&B

Warren, Edie & Tom (Amadata Bed & Breakfast)　　　　☎ (705) 945-6171
376 MacDonald Ave., Sault-Ste-Marie, ON　P6B 1H6

From Sudbury on Hwy 17E, turn right on Lake St., left on MacDonald Ave. From Wawa (Hwy 17W becomes Northern Ave, Pim St), turn left at MacDonald Ave.

$35S　$40-45D　　　　　　　　　　　　　　　▶6
🍲 Cont.　🏠 Res., bungalow, patio, quiet　■ 3D(main and lower level)　🛏 2T,2D　🚪 1Sh.w.g., 1sh.w.h.　★ Air,TV in guest rooms, private entrance, guest fridge/microwave, off-street parking　👑 No smoking, no pets
🕴 Bellevue Park, Sault Locks, boat tours, harbour, shopping, fine dining, city bus
🚗 Agawa Canyon Train, downhill/x-c skiing, Kewadin Casino

🐾 Warm welcome in comfortable home with private guest sitting room. Recently retired hosts take pleasure in helping guests with sightseeing plans of local attractions. House specialty is "Edie's homemade muffins". There is a small poodle named Chandi in residence. ✔B&B

Shelburne　　　　　　　　　　　*(north of Orangeville; see also Mansfield)*

Anderson, Robert & Eleanor (Anderson's Hilltop B&B)　　　☎ (519) 925-5129
RR1, Blind Line #595438, Shelburne, ON　L0N 1S5

Take Hwy 10 north from Orangeville to Primrose. Proceed west on Hwy 89 to Line 2 WHS (2km.), & south 2.8 km to No 595438.

$45S　$50-55D　🍽 Meals　　　　　　　　　　▶10
🍲 Full　🏠 Farm, 2-storey, acreage, view, patio, porch, quiet
■5D(ground & upper level)　🛏 2T,2D,2Q　🚪 Sh.w.g. & private　★F,TV,LF,KF,wheelchair accessible, parking　👑 No smoking, no pets　〰 French
🕴 Wooded area hiking/wildlife viewing, small stream, x-c skiing
🚗 Shelburne (Old Time Fiddlers Contest), Orangeville, Medieval Festival, Fall Fair and art tours & Summer Theatre

🐾 Large modern, red brick home on 100-acre beef farm with a scenic country view, situated on a quiet gravel road. Relax and enjoy the rural atmosphere. Special arrangements can be made for transportation and vehicle placement for Bruce Trail hiking. ✔B&B

Simcoe　　　　　　　　　　*(south of Brantford; see also Waterford, Port Dover)*

Wares, Michèle & Les (Greens Corner B&B)　　☎ (519) 426-2285, Fax (519) 426-7177
973 Regional Rd.1, Simcoe, ON　N3Y 4J9

Located south of Hwy 3 between Simcoe & Delhi (3rd house from Greens Corner on north side).

$45S　$65D　$10Add.person　🍽Meals　　　　　▶2
🍲 Full, homebaked　🏠 Rural, pond, u-shaped ranch-style with courtyard, gazebo, acreage, view, patio, porch, deck, quiet, isolated　■ 1D　🛏 1Q　🚪 1Private　★ Air,F,KF,LF, guest sitting areas, TV/VCR, parking　👑 Smoking in allocated area, pet boarding can be arranged at nearby vets　〰 French
🚗 Superb restaurants, Port Dover, Turkey Point Beach/Prov.Park, golfing, fishing, Long Point

🐾 Country Retreat overlooking park-like grounds, sheltered from the bustling city and nestled in the heart of scenic Lake Erie tourist area. Lounge in the gazebo beside the pond which attracts varied species of birds/ducks/Canada Geese. Breakfast served in formal dining room.

Southampton
(on Lake Huron west of Owen Sound; see also Sauble Beach)

Higgins, John and Hazel (Hollingborne House)   ☎ (519) 797-3202
Box 324, 48 Grey Street North, Southampton, ON   N0H 2L0

Located in Southampton (3rd house behind hospital).
$35S $40-45D   ►4A
🗓April 1-Nov1 🛏Full 🏠Res., view, ranch-style ■2D
(main level) 🛏2T,1D 🚿Sh.w.g. ★TV, wheelchair access
🖐No pets, restr smoking, not suitable for children 〰Armenian
🔆 Inland Lake, nature walks, shopping areas, beautiful beach,
sunsets and Art School
🚗 Sauble Beach/swimming/boating, Bruce Trail hiking, skiing
☛ Modern home, furnished with antiques, overlooking beautiful Fairy Lake. Hosts are busy with
furniture re-finishing and caning chairs. Also available 3 cottages at the mouth of Saugeen River.
Book early to avoid disappointment. Guests taken by week. ✔B&B

St-Andrews West
(north of Cornwall; see also Williamstown, Lancaster)

Peachey, Norma & Jan (Winook Farm B&B)   ☎ (613) 932-1161
RR1 Concession VI, 16997, St. Andrews West, ON   K0C 2A0

From Hwy 401 take Brookdale Exit, turn right (north); from Hwy 417 take Cornwall Exit. Follow
Hwy 138 to St.Andrews West. Turn west on Con VI and proceed 2.4km to house on north side.
$35S $50D $15Child/Add.person 🍽Meals   ►6A,2Ch

🛏 Full 🏠 Farm, 2-storey, hist., 150 acres, view from guest
rooms, swimming pool, quiet ■3(upstairs) 🛏2S,2D,1R
🚿1Sh.w.g. ★TV,F, ceiling fans, separate entrance 🖐No
smoking, no pets
🔆 Farm grounds suitable for walks, snowshoeing, x-c skiing,
historic St.Andrews village with church/pub/restaurant
🚗 Upper Canada Village, Cornwall, Int. Bridge to USA, Maxville
Highland Games (Aug), Ottawa, St.Lawrence Park (nature trails,
bird sanctuary, golfing, fishing, cycling), Dinosaur Park
☛ Historic stone farm house (ca 1823), tastefully restored, containing several wood stoves for
extra comfort. Originally from Britain, hosts are widely travelled and interested in history and
weaving. They maintain a flock of sheep and are fulltime honey producers. There are friendly
Labrador Retrievers in their own area. ✔B&B

St.Catharines
(see also NOTL, Niagara Falls, Vineland, Beamsville)

Gale, Ross & Carol (Inn on the Henley Bed & Breakfast)   ☎ (905) 934-5146 Fax 646-3937
360 Martindale Rd., St. Catharines, ON   L2R 6P9   E-mail: b&b@innonthehenley.com

On QEW at St.Catharines take 7th St Exit. At stop sign turn right, then left and follow service
road to Martindale Rd. Turn left to house on right.
$80-125S/D   ►8A
🛏 Homebaked 🏠 Res., hist., 3 acres, view from guest rooms,
riverfont, swimming pool, patio, porch, deck, quiet ■4D(street
level & upstairs) 🛏1D,2Q,1K 🚿4Ensuite ★F,TV,
private entr, airconditioners, off-street parking 🖐Designated
smoking area, no pets, not suitable for children
🔆 Starting line of Henley Regatta, boating, fishing, canoeing,
swimming, Old Port Dalhousie, Martindale Pond with Canada Geese, bus stop at front door
🚗 Downtown, Brock University, N.Falls, US Border, x-c ski/bike trails, octagonal lighthouse
☛ 1840-built home, historically known as "Stokesdale", full of Canadiana antiques, overlooking
the Regatta Starting Line on a quaint harbour which cherishes and preserves its early association
with the Welland Canal. Well travelled hosts enjoy gardening/wood carving. Guests are invited to
create Twig furniture. "Leave the stress behind and take a walk with nature". Rates may increase
during the 1999 World Rowing Championship. ✔B&B

Bed & Breakfast Accommodations - St-Catharines & Niagara Region
28 Cartier Dr., St-Catharines, ON   L2M 2E7   ☎ (905) 937-2422 Fax (905) 935-0059
Evelyn Janke (Proprietor)   E-mail: bbassoc@chardonnay.niagara.com
$35-145S/D   (early reservations strongly recommended)

B&B Accommodations-St-Cahtarines & Niagara Region offers friendly, efficient and highly
personalized service in assisting guests in selecting and reserving B&B accommodations in
Fenwick, Fonthill, Jordan, Niagara-on-the-Lake, Niagara Falls, Port Coborne, St-Catharines,
Welland and Vineland. Warm hospitality in comfortable private homes varying in size, style, decor
and era (and priced accordingly) to suit particular preferences and needs. Some of the homes are
suited to and welcome children. All homes are smoke-free, although some offer designated smoking
areas. Special rates offered by some for extended stays. Personalized Gift Certificates available.

Janke, Evelyn (Cartier Place B&B)   ☎ (905) 935-9604
28 Cartier Dr., St.Catharines, ON   L2M 2E7

From QEW take Niagara St Exit and proceed north to Parnell Rd. Turn left and left again on
Cartier Dr. Located in the north end of the City between Port Dalhousie and NOTL.
$40S $70D $10-15Child $15Add.person   (Long term rates available)   ► 10

🍴 Full, homebaked   🏠 Res, split-level, patio, quiet, fenced
garden 🛏2D,2F (main & upper floor) 🛏 1S,2T,1D,2Q,1P
🚿 1Ensuite, 1sh.w.g.   ★ Air,LF,F, ceiling fans, private entrance
& wheel-chair access in one room, off-street parking 🚬 Smoking
outside 〰 German
🏃 Welland ship Canal, Walker's Creek Park, Lake Ontario and
beaches, public transportation
🚗 Downtown, Niagara-on-the-Lake, Niagara Falls, wineries

🐾 Family-style home with plenty of old-fashioned hospitality. Long-time hostess enjoys assisting
guests with information about places to go and where to eat/dine. Pick-up at bus or train can be
arranged. Hostess is Proprietor of B&B Accommodation- St-Catharines & Niagara Region. Rates
may increase during the 1999 World Rowing Championship in Port Dalhousie. ✔ B&B

Nunn, Ron & Barbara (Hayocks B&B)   ☎ & Fax (905) 934-7106
43 Ann St., St.Catharines, ON   L2N 5E9

From QEW at St.Catharines exit on 7th St North. Turn right on
Lakeshore Rd and proceed 4km to Ann St. Turn left.
$85-150D $20Add.person   ► 7
🍴 Full   🏠 Res., 2-storey, view from guest rooms, lakefront,
solarium   🛏3(upstairs) 🛏 2T,1Q,1K,1P   🚿 3ensuite
★F, air-conditioners, guest quarters are in separate wing
🚬Smoking outside, no pets, children min age 12
🏃 Old Port Dalhousie with lakeside park and sandy beach, craft
shops, restaurants, Henry Island, bus to downtown
🚗 Downtown, Niagara-on-the-Lake, Niagara Falls, Niagara Wine Rte, Welland Canal, Hamilton
🐾 Historic lakefront home (ca 1860) restored by present hosts, with period antique lighting
fixtures throughout the house, furnished with many antiques and located in the heart of Niagara
Wine Country. Relax in the solarium and enjoy the spectacular lake view. Well travelled hosts (he a
retired airline captain) enjoy meeting people. ✔B&B

Redman, Lawrence & Carmen (Lakeview B&B)
17 Mary St., St.Catharines, ON   L2N 6W8

☎ (905) 646-2010
E-mail: lakeview@npiec.on.ca

Located in Port Dalhousie. Phone for directions.
$45S $65D $10Child   🍽 Meals   ►4
🍲 Cont., homebaked   🏠 Res., raised bungalow, lakefront, view,
quiet   ■ 2D (lower level)   ⊨2T,1D   ⚓ 1Sh.w.g.   ★Air,F,TV
in guest rooms, street parking   ⛹ No smoking, no pets, not
suitable for children
🏃 Henley Regatta (Aug), Lake Ontario & park across the street,
shops, great walking trails

🚗 Niagara Falls, Niagara-on-the-Lake, Welland Canal, wineries, Toronto
🐾 Retired couple in comfortable home in quaint town located on the shores of Lake Ontario and home of the Worlds Rowing Competition in 1999. Host loves painting and his works are displayed throughout the house. A good place from which to explore the beautiful Niagara Peninsula and wine country. There is a dog in residence.

Versluis, Fran & Leo (Old Port B&B)
73 Main St., St.Catharines, ON   L2N 4V1

☎ (905) 934-5761

Located in Port Dalhousie. From QEW exit at Ontario St and go north to Lakeport Rd. Turn left and follow into Port Dalhousie. Turn left on Main St.

$75S $85D $10Child $15Add.person   ►6
🍲 Full, homebaked   🏠 Res., 2-storey, older, patio, porch, deck,
quiet   ■ 3(upstairs)   ⊨ 1S,1D,1Q, cot, crib   ⚓ 1sh.w.g.,
1ensuite   ★Air,TV,F, separate entrance, off-street parking
⛹No smoking, no pets   ✍ Dutch
🏃 Lakefront park (with beach, pier, restaurants, shops, antique
carousel ride), Rowing Henley course

🚗 Niagara Falls, ferry to Toronto (summer), Niagara-on-the-Lake, US border
🐾 Comfortable home situated in the heritage part of town, just steps from the grandstand at the finish line of the Henley Rowing course. Breakfast is served in guest breakfast room. Relax on the front or side porch or on the backyard deck. There is a young school-age boy in the host family. Discounts available for 3 nights plus.

St.Jacobs

(north of Waterloo; see also Elmira)

Doerbecker, Glen & Patricia (The Carpenter's House)
2 Isabella St., St.Jacobs, ON   N0B 2N0

☎ (519) 664-2451, 1-800-865-6162

At traffic light turn left down hill to bus.section. Look for house on corner of Front/Isabella Sts.
$45S $60D $30Add.Adult $10Child (age 8-16)(free under age 8)   ►7A,4Ch

🍲 Full, homebaked   🏠 Village center, historic, .5 acreage, view
from guest rooms, riverfront, patio, porch, quiet ■3D(upstairs)
including bridal suite ⊨ 3S,1D,1Q,cot, extra foam mattresses
⚓1Sh.w.g., 1sh.w.h.   ★ Air,TV,off-street parking   ⛹No pets,
no smoking
🏃· Scenic walks beside house, town center and main street shops
restaurants, bakery & mennonite products, walking & skiing path

🚗 Major farmers markets, Elmira & Mennonite Country, Ontario's first Outlet Mall
🐾 111-year old home, once a Miller's House a few blocks from major tourist attraction in pretty little Mennonite town. Hosts are artist/carpenter and the decor displays both their talents. Winter Rates & Specials available. ✓F0BBA

Feick, Lynne and Earl (Countryside Manor B&B)   ☎ (519) 664-2622, 1-800-476-8942
Box 500, 39 Henry St., St. Jacobs, ON N0B 2N0

From Hwy 401, exit on Hwy 8 and go north to Hwy 86 North. Exit on King St north and proceed to
St. Jacobs. Turn left at 1st street in town and continue over railway tracks to 1st house on left.

$60S $65D $15Child ►4
🔲Full 🏠Farm, older, patio, quiet,panoramic view ■2D(upst) in
separate guest quarters ⊨2S,1D 🚿1Sh.w.g. ★F,whirlpool,
guest sitting room, private balcony 🖐no pets 〜German
🏃 St.Jacobs, farmers' market, lovely shops, walks along Mill Race
🚗 Kitchener/Waterloo, hiking, covered bridge
📢 1917-built, renovated and tastefully decorated Victorian home
with manicured gardens in park setting, situated in the
heart of Mennonite country. Enjoy breakfast on the patio to the sound of the fountain. Ideal place
for Garden weddings. Visa ✓B&B

Frey, Amsey and Ina (Forestview Bed & Breakfast)   ☎ (519) 699-4668
RR1, St.Clements, ON N0B 2M0

From Hwy 401 take Hwy 8 North. Proceed to Hwy 86 North, exit on RegRd 15. Continue to
St.Clements. Turn right at main intersection onto Reg Rd 10 and 1km north to 2nd driveway on
left, past wooded area.

$40S $60D ►6
🔲Full,homebaked 🏠Bungalow ■3 (main & lower level)
⊨2S,2Q,1P 🚿1Sh.w.g.,1private ★TV,F,LF, easy access,
parking 🖐No pets, no smoking
🚗 St. Jacobs, Elora tourist area, Stratford Shakesp.Festival
📢 New bungalow, beside wooded area overlooking pond,located
central yet quiet in its setting in unique rural community. ✓B&B

Hill, Joyce & Neil (Village Bed & Breakfast)   ☎ (519) 664-2890
61 Queen Street, St.Jacobs, ON N0B 2N0

From Hwy 401 exit on Hwy 8 toward Kitchener/Waterloo. Take Hwy 86 to Waterloo & proceed to
1st exit to St.Jacobs, turn left into town. Queen St is 1blk west of main street.

$50-65 (S and D) $175Ste(2nights) ►8
🔲 Full 🏠 Village, res., older, 2-storey, quiet ■3D,1Ste (main &
upper level) ⊨2S,4D 🚿1Sh.w.g.,1ensuite ★ Air,
parking 🖐No smoking
🏃 Village of St. Jacobs, shops, Mennonite Interpr.Center, excellent
German/Mennonite eating places, walking trail, cycling, golfing
🚗 Mennonite farming area, only covered bridge in Ontario
📢 Retired professional couple invites guests to step into yesteryear
as the horse and buggies pass the window, while one block away the village bustles with visitors.
Minimum of 2 nights in main floor accommodation. ✓B&B

Noice, Anne & Barry (The Old Flax Mill B&B)
50 Glasgow St.N., Conestogo, ON N0B 1N0

☎ (519) 664-3600
E-mail: benoice@aol.com

From Hwy 401, take Hwy 8 north and continue on Hwy 86 north to Waterloo. Stay on Hwy to lights at Reg RD 17. Turn right to Conestogo (3 km). Turn left on Glasgow St, proceed to bottom of hill.

$60S $70D   ▶5
🍳 Full, homebaked   🏠 Village, 2-storey, 2-acres, view, quiet
▦2D (upst)   ⊨ 2Q   🛏1Sh.w.g.   ★Air, woodstove, parking
🚭No smoking,no children, no pets   💬French,German
🏃 Quiet sitting area by stream, old livery stables on property,
quiet walks in the village of Conestogo
🚗 Kitchener, Waterloo, St. Jacobs, farmers' market
🔑 Congenial hosts (retired teachers) in spacious Colonial-design
home with elegant decor, surrounded by tall trees and large property in a tranquil, park-like setting. There is a Labrador in residence.✓B&B

St. Joseph
(on Lake Huron south of Goderich; see also Bayfield)

Grusska, Pamela & André (Lilacs & Lace Tower B&B)
St.Joseph, RR2, Zurich, ON N0M 2T0

☎

Located in St.Joseph on Hwy 21, between Grand Bend & Bayfield.
$55-75S $65-95D   ▶7
🍳 Full, homebaked   🏠 Century home, 3-storey, hist.   ▦ 2D,1Ste
(upstairs)   ⊨ 1D,2Q   🛏 1Private, 1sh.w.g.   ★ F,TV, ceiling fans,
off-street parking   🚭 No smoking, no pets
🏃 Beach, ice-cream parlour, restaurant/lounge, St.Joseph private archives
🚗 Grand Bend Beach, Bayfield boutiques/antiques, Huron Country
Playhouse, Pinery Prov. Park, golfing, boating, x-c & jet skiing, drag racing
🔑 Landmark 19th Century home (as picture in "50 even more unusual
things to see in Ontario") with transom windows, and 3-storey turret, located
near Lake Huron on Ontario's West coast. A former pipe organ factory and ice house still stand on the spacious grounds. Home was a frequent stop for Brother Andre, the founder of the famed Oratory of St.Joseph in Montreal (guests may request to stay in the room where he slept). Stroll down to the beach and watch the most beautiful sun sets.

St.Joseph Island
(s/of Sault Ste Marie; see also Bruce Mines, Manitoulin Isle)

Campbell, Harold & Lynn (Outlook B&B)
RR1, Richards Landing, ON P0R 1J0

☎ (705) 246-3468

$35S $50D $10Add.person $5Child(first child free)   🍽 Meals   ▶ 5A,4Ch
Phone for directions.
🍳 Full, homebaked   🏠 Rural, 2-storey, older, 90acres, deck,
quiet, secluded   ▦ 3F(upstairs   ⊨ 3S,1Q,1K,cot   🛏 1sh.w.g.,
1sh.w.h.   🚭 No smoking, no pets
🏃 Hiking, snowmobiling, skiing
🚗 Sault Ste Marie (Ontario), Sault Ste Marie (Michigan)
🔑 Lovely country home, originally a rural post office serving
settlers, is now a secluded refuge for the host family and their
guests. Located amidst beautiful hardwood trees and evergreens. Hot refreshments served with fresh pie in the evening. Relax on the deck or enclosed veranda and watch various birds and small wildlife in the spacious yard with many flowers. There are a dog, a cat and 2 budgies ✓B&B

Higgins, Paul & Rilla (Sunset Bay B&B & Studios) ☎ (705) 246-2177, Fax (705) 246-0481
RR1, Richards Landing, St.Joseph Island, ON P0R 1J0

Phone for directions.
$35S $55D 🍽 Meals ► 6A,2Ch
🍴 Full, homebaked 🏠 Rural, 2-storey, view from guest rooms,
lakefront, quiet, deck, secluded ▥ 3D(upstairs) ⊨ 2T,2Q
🛏 3Ensuite,1sh.w.g,1sh.w.h. Ⓦ F,TV,guest balcony,
photography studio Ⓦ No smoking
🏃 Swimming, fishing, boating, cycling, hiking, views of shipping
(westbound lane)
🚗 Sault-Ste-Marie, airport, Soo Locks (tours), Agawa Canyon Rail Tours, historic Fort St.
Joseph, museums, shops, galleries, marinas, winter sports
🐾 Newly-built (1996) cedar home situated on 80acres. Relax in the scenic and serene atmosphere
with abundant birds and wildlife. Former Travel Agent hosts from Alberta enjoy meeting people,
love photography and are sports-minded. Relax in the sitting room/library or the indoor hot tub.
Indoor studio- or outdoor-portraits can be arranged as a special momento of the B&B stay. Airport
transfer service available for additional charge. There is a cat in residence. Visa,MC ➥B&B

Smith, Phyllis (The Anchorage) ☎ (705) 246-2221
RR1, Richards Landing, ON P0R 1J0

Phone for directions.
$25S $45D $12Add.person ► 10
🌞 Summer 🍴 Choice 🏠Rural, acreage, view, seaway-front,quiet
▥1S,1D,1Ste(upstairs) ⊨2T,2D,1Q,R,P,crib 🛏1Sh.w.g. ★TV
in guest rooms, private guest driveway ⓌRestricted smoking
🏃 Walking trails (wildlife), miniature golf, sandy beach (private)
🚗 Fort St. Joseph Nat. Hist. Park, Island Museum, "Soo Locks", famous Agawa Canyon Train
🐾 Quiet, friendly B&B home is on the Seaway where ships from all over the world pass right in
front. From the porch watch the water activities. Enjoy breakfast a stone's throw away from the
Captain's wheel. ➥B&B

St.Marys *(south-west of Stratford; see also Woodham, Centralia)*

Burgin Family (Burgin's Green Arbour B&B) ☎ (519) 229-6671, Fax (519) 229-8572
RR1, St. Marys, ON N4X 1C4

From Kirkton on Hwy 23 (north-west of St Marys), turn east on Perth Line 8 and look for 1st
farmhouse on north side (Fire No 5894)
$55D ► 4-6
🌞 Summer (other times by reservation) 🍴 Full, homebaked
🏠 100-acres farm, veranda, quiet ▥2D(upstairs) ⊨1Q,2T(1K),
cot 🛏 1Sh.w.g. ★ Air,TV Ⓦ No smoking, no pets
🏃 Sugar bush, village of Kirkton
🚗St.Marys & Quarry, Community Center with outdoor pool,
Stratford Festival, London, Blyth, Lake Huron
🐾 Quiet, homey Century farmhouse with veranda, renovated and lovingly maintained, set well
back from paved road on 3 acres of carefully tended lawns, and surrounded by hundreds of trees
planted on property by the family. Sour dough waffles with own maple syrup is a house specialty.
Hosts raise & train Llamas for caddying and hiking. There is a resident cat and a dog. Guests are
invited to bring suitable footwear to explore the 100 acre farm. ➥CC

St.Thomas
(south of London)

Held, Nadine & Don (Victorian Rose B&B) (pending)   ☎ & Fax (519) 633-3274
RR3, St. Thomas, ON   N5P 3S7

From Hwy 401 at London, take Exit 189 (Highbury Ave) south to Hwy 3. Look for B&B beside

Family Flowers Garden Centre east of St.Thomas.
$45-50S $60-65D $10Child $75F   ▶ 6A,3Ch
🍳 Full, homebaked   🏠 Hobby farm, 3-storey, hist.,porch
🛏1D,2F(2nd floor)   ⊨1S,2D,2Q,cradle (incl antique beds)
🛁1Sh.w.g.   ★ TV, ceiling fans   🚭 No smoking, , no pets
🕴 Large Garden Center (next door), farm land with fruit trees
🚗 London, Grand Bend, Port Stanley & Port Burwell beaches,
local estate winery, craft & antique shops, auctions
🐾 Edwardian home (ca 1904) filled with ornate antique beds in guest rooms and many antiques throughout. Relax on the spacious enclosed veranda, sit out in the large, sunny & tree-shaded backyard, or stroll around the gardens with roses and plants from British Columbia & Germany. Hosts create spectacular breakfasts for guests (choose from menu), served in guest breakfast room. There is a dog and a cat in residence (not in guest area).Visa,Amex ✔B&B

Moczulski, Joseph & Lorraine (Rosebery Place B&B)   ☎ (519) 631-1525
57 Walnut St., St.Thomas, ON   N5R 2Y7   1-800-878-6916

From Hwy 401 exit at Hwy 4 and procesd south into St.Thomas. Turn right on Stanley St at top of hill and continue to Walnut St. Turn right to house on left.

$50S $65D $10Child $10Add.person   🍽 Meals   ▶ 16
🍳 Full   🏠 Res., 3-storey, hist., acreage, porch, deck, quiet
🛏2S,5D,2F (upstairs)   ⊨2S,6T,1D,2Q,1K   🛁2Sh.w.g. ★TV,
off-street parking, wheel-chair access with lift & ramp, guest
quaarters are separate   🚭 No smoking, no pets
🕴 Main downtown area, Jumbo Elephant Statue, Pioneer &
Military Museums, old English hist. church, Art Gallery, Princess
Theatre, historic walking tour
🚗 Port Stanley (fishing port, antiques, boutiques, theatre), Hawk Cliff (bird migration), Sparta
🐾 Gracious Century home (late 1800's) located on "the Hill" in historic area of town surrounded by historic attractions. Relax in the cozy living room or the bright airy sunroom and enjoy the large library. Browse in the gift shop, or make an appointment for the Tea Room. Breakfast is served in the formal dining room or cheerful breakfast room. Ideal place for small weddings, workshops/seminars and meetings. Weekly & corporate rates available.Visa ✔CC

Stayner
(south of Collingwood; see also Creemore)

Gibson, Betty (Donet Bed & Breakfast)   ☎ (705) 428-3812
221 Louisa St., Box 148, Stayner, ON   L0M 1S0

Phone for directions.
$40S $50D   🍽 Meals   ▶ 4A,3Ch
🍳Full,homebaked   🏠Res., bungalow, patio, porch, quiet   🛏2
⊨2D,1Q,1R   🛁1Sh.w.g., whirlpool tub   ★F,TV, parking
🕴 Main street stores, antique shops, recreational and quiet parks,
country-style restaurant
🚗 Barrie, Wasaga Beach, luxury golf facilities, Collingwood (Blue
Mountain Pottery), downhill/x-c Ski Resorts, Bruce Trail hiking
🐾 Spacious, cozy home tastefully decorated and centrally located in quiet neighborhood of popular resort district. Seniors welcome.

Stratford *(west of Kitchener; see also New Hamburg,Baden,Tavistock,Gadshill,Wellesley)*

Blair, Richard & Nancy (Blair House B&B)   ☎ (519) 271-1830
240 Mornington Street, Stratford, ON   N5A 5G5   1-888-570-9924, Fax (519) 271-0082

In Stratford, take Ontario Street to Waterloo Street North and turn right on Mornington.

$84-105S/D $25Add.person   ▶ 7
🍴 Full, homebaked 🏠 Res., 2-storey, older, porch, large yard
■2D,1Ste (upstairs) ⊨ 1S,2T(1K),1D,1Q ⬛ 1Private,
2ensuite ★ Air,F,TV, off-street parking 🖐 No smoking, no
pets, children min. age 7
🎭 Three theatres, restaurants, shopping, Shakespearean Gardens,
Art in the Park, historic churches, public swimming pool library,
farmers market, city buses Nos 3/4

🚗 Kitchener/Waterloo, St. Jacobs, Mennonite Country, London, Lake Huron, Goderich
🐎 1905-built home filled with art painted by the host. Hostess is involved in volunteer work at
the Shakespeare Theatre and The Stratford B&B Association. Enjoy a different delicious breakfast
each morning. 2-nights minimum. Visa,MC ✓B&B

Bockus, Mary & Cran (Bockus House Bed & Breakfast)   ☎ (519) 273-7613
21 Caledonia St., Stratford, ON   N5A 5W4

Located in town, 2 blocks east of Huron St (Hwy 8).
$45S $65-75D   ▶ 6
🍴 Full, homebaked 🏠 Res., 3-storey, older, porch, deck, quiet
■3D(upst) ⊨2T,2D ⬛1Sh.w.g. ★Air,TV,F, one large
private sunroom, off-street parking 🖐No smoking, no pets
✎French
🎭 Three theatres (Annual Shakespearian Festival (May-Nov),
shops, restaurants, Stratford parklands, River Avon

🚗 Kitchener-Waterloo, Mennonite Country, farmers markets, quaint town of St.Jakobs
🐎 Congenial hosts in recently restored and renovated Century home with a country decor,
situated in quiet residential neighbourhood. Convenient location for theatre visitors. ✓B&B

Cook, Roger & Elaine (Double CC Farm & B&B)   ☎ (519) 271-1978
RR1, Stratford, ON   N5A 6S2

Take Hwys 7&8 between Stratford & Shakespeare. Turn north on Rd 110 and proceed 3.3km from
corner. Look for house No. 4335.

$70S $80D $15child 🍴 Meals   ▶ 2
🍴 Full 🏠 Farm, hist., view from guest rooms, riverfront,
porch, deck, quiet, secluded ■ 1Ste (main floor) ⊨ 1Q
⬛1ensuite ★ LF,F,TV, woodstove, ceiling fan, private
entrance, guest quarters are separate 🖐 No smoking, no pets
🎭 Hiking & x-c ski trails, skating on pond, Heritage Works
woodshop, miniature donkeys, farm animals

🚗 Stratford Festival Theatre, Shakespeare village, Mennonite Country
🐎 Heritage home (ca 1867) located on 200 acres farm. Award-winning hosts are very interested
in nature and conservation and have planted close to 10000 trees over the last decades. Watch them
work in the on-site workshop. Relax in the large screened-in porch or sit by the pond and take in
the tranquil country atmosphere and solitude. ✓B&B

Dunn, Verna and Allan (Dunn-Drae-Homes)　　　　　☎ (519) 273-0619
150 Douglas St., Stratford, ON　N5A 5P6

From Toronto take Hwy 7/8 west and enter Stratford on Ontario St. Turn on Huron St(Hwy 8), go

1 block to ESSO Canada Stn, turn left onto Douglas.
$41S　$45-67D　$96-106Unit　(plus tax)　　　► 16
🍴Cont., homebaked　🏠Res., hist., patio, quiet　■5D(main &
upstairs, plus eff.units)　⊨4T(or3K),3D,1Q,1R,1P　🛁4Ensuite,
1private, 3sh.w.g.　★Air,F,TV in 4 guest rooms, parking ⊗No
smoking, no pets, children minimum age 8
🏃 Festival Theatre, Shakespearean Gardens, uptown, River,
paddle boats/canoes
🚗 Shakespeare Antique Stores, x-c ski trails, Mennonite country, Montrose covered bridge,
📣 Large home, dating back to 1896, with each room in a different decor and hand quilted
bedspreads. Retired hosts enjoy cooking and baking breakfast goodies and have time to visit with
guests and help plan day trips to interesting sights in the area. Bus tours can be accommodated.
Relax in the little courtyard after a busy day. ✓B&B

Grose, Lloy and Allan (Cedar Springs)　　　　　☎ (519) 625-8182
RR1, Stratford, ON　N5A 6S2　　　　　　　　　E-mail: csprings@cyg.net

Located north of Shakespeare. Take Hwy 8 into Shakespeare (8 km east of Stratford). Turn north
at the traffic light. Go 4 km to Line 40, turn left at North Easthope Township Hall. B&B is on left
(1.5 km). Not visible from road. Look for sign and house No 2353.
$35S　$50-55D　$10Child　$5Infants　$15Add.person　🍽 Meals　　　► 6A,3Ch

🍴 Choice, homebaked　🏠 Rural, split-level, acreage, swimming
pond, patio, view, quiet　■5(main & upper floor),& trailer for
2-4　⊨2T,2Q,R,P,crib　🛁2Sh.w.h.　★Air,TV,F,LF, parking, full
handicapped facilities　⊗No smoking ♥
🏃 Nature trails and x-c skiing, hardwood bush with wild flowers,
pond, paddle boat, tree house, RV/tentsites, bird watching,aviary
🚗 Downtown, theatres, village of Shakespeare, antiques, Elora,
Drayton & Blythe Theatres, St. Jacobs Mennonite country
📣 Enjoy a tranquil park-like setting - a haven of natural beauty on large grounds. Hosts spent
several years in Kenya as missionary-educators and are active in the local, Nat/Intern.programs of
Habitat for Humanity. Special rates for small group retreats (church or professional).✓CC

Hrysko, Dianna & Mary Allen (Deacon House)　　　☎ (519) 273-2052, Fax (519) 273-3784
101 Brunswick St., Stratford, ON　N5A 3L9

Take Hwy 7 to Stratford (from London or Kitchener). Turn south on Nile St (at east end of town)

and proceed 2 blocks to Brunswick St. Turn right.
$85-105S　$95-115D　$30Add.person　(plus tax)　► 14
🍴Full,homebaked　🏠Downtown,res.,hist.,large front porch
■6D(upst, incl 1Ste)　⊨2T,3D,2Q　🛁1private, 5ensuite
★Air (in guest rooms),F,KF,TV in guest reading room, large guest
kitchen, private balcony in one guest room, ample parking on
site　⊗No smoking, no pets, children min. age 9
🏃 Three Theatres (Avon/Festival/Tom Patterson), downtown
📣 Well traveled hosts (Nurses) in large Queen Anne-style Heritage home with antiques &
Canadiana country whimsical details throughout. Escape packages available. There are cats in
residence. Visa ✓B&B

Watkins, Mathilde (Hildebob Guest Home) ☎ (519) 271-3303
136 Water St., Stratford, ON N5A 3C4

Phone for directions.
$75D $110F $15Add.person ► 7
Self-serve, homebaked · Res., view from guest rooms, patio, deck, quiet · 1D,1Ste (ground & upper level) · 3Q,1P,1P,cot · 2Private · ★ Air,KF, separate entrance, parking available with reservation, wheel-chair access, guest quarters are separate · No smoking, no pets, children min. age 5 · German
Festival/Paterson/Avon Theatres, shops, restaurants
Comfortable home in convenient location for theatre visitors. Relax and enjoy the large garden with gazebo. Hostess has been welcoming guests for many years. Breakfast provisions are supplied in guest TV/sitting area for guests' self-service.

Sudbury

(northern Ontario)

Brierley, Suzanne & Jim (The Brier Patch B&B) ☎ (705) 693-5034
27 Lindsley St., Falconbridge, ON P0M 1S0

Located in Falconbridge 15 km north-east of Sudbury. From Hwy 17 take Falconbridge Hwy through Garson and continue on Edison Rd to Lindsley St. Turn right and proceed to B&B on right.

$40S $50D ► 5
Full, homebaked · Village, 2-storey, patio, deck, quiet · 1S,2D(upstairs) · 1S,2D · Sh.w.h. · ★ TV,F,LF, off-street parking · Desig.smoking area, no pets, children min. age 12
Blueberry picking, x/c-skiing, Sudbury Snowmobile trail plan
Restaurants, Sudbury, Science North (IMAX theatre)
Hosts are knowledgeable about the North and the mining industry. Enjoy the friendly Northern Hospitality. Breakfast is served on the deck (weather permitting). There is a non-allergenic dog in residence. ✓B&B

Ross, Dan & Gail (Loonsnest Bed & Breakfast) ☎ (705 969-9852, Fax (705) 969-3227
5962 Onwatin Lake Rd., Hanmer, ON P3P 1J5 E-mail: loonsnest@hotmail.com

Approx 20km north of Sudbury, proceed to Val Caron (RegRd 80), continue 3km to Dominion Dr. Turn right 4.8km to end. Turn left and continue 5km to lake, turn left and look for the loon.

$45S $55-75D $10Child/Add.person · Meals ► 6A,2Ch
Full · Rural, 2-storey, view from guest rooms, lakefront, patio, porch, deck · 1S,1D,1Ste (upstairs) · 1S,2Q,1R,1P · 1Private, 2ensuite · ★ F,LF,TV in guest room, large common sitting room, sauna, warm gazebo, off-street parking · No smoking, children min. age 10 · French
Swimming, boating, canoeing, sailing, fishing, birdwatching, walking & hiking trails, horseback riding, x-c skiing, snowmobiling
Sudbury, Big Nickel Mine, Science North Science Centre, Laurentian University, theatre
Charming country home with a blend of elegance & simplicity on the shores of a small lake. Unwind, absorb and enjoy the peacefulness of nature and the beauty of the North. A good place to stop on the way north or south. Relax on the deck and wait for the loons. Special business or honeymoon packages available. There is a dog and a cat in hosts quarters. Visa ✓B&B

Sydenham

(north of Kingston; see also Harrowsmith, Inverary)

Preslar, Lillian   ☎(613) 376-3127
Box 19, Sydenham, ON K0H 2T0

From Hwy 401 take Exit 613 to Sydenham Rd. Upon entering Sydenham take Wheatley St between
schools and follow to stop sign. Turn right and go over bridge and railroad tracks. Turn right again
and proceed to 12 km sign to Frontenac Pk, make sharp left turn on Alton Rd and continue

to 2nd stone house with red roof.
$35S $50-55D   ► 6A,2Ch
🍽Choice   🏠100-acre farm   ■3D(upstairs)   ⊨1D,2T,1Q
🛁2Sh.w.g.   ★TV,F   🐾Pets
🎿 Conservation area, x-c skiing, Frontenac Prov.Park
🚐 Kingston, Old Fort Henry, Queen's U., Olympic sailing site,
1000 Island boat tours, many antique, craft shops & museums
🐎 Modernized 1837 Regency family stone house with the
Rideau Trail crossing the property. There is a little craft shop called "Summer Kitchen Crafts"
attached to the main house which offers diaphanous lampshades, & other crafts. Visa,MC ✓ B&B

Tavistock

(south of Stratford; see also New Hamburg, Baden)

Bauman, Gordon & Erma (Hendershot House)   ☎ (519) 655-2540
Box 583, 88 Hendershot St., Tavistock, ON N0B 2R0

From Stratford, travel 12 km east on Hwy 7/8 to Shakespeare. Turn south south on Perth County
Rd 107 (formerly Hwy 59) to Tavistock. At traffic light, turn left on Hope St East to Minerva

St, turn right to Hendershot St, turn left (18km from Stfd).
$50S $55D   ► 4
🍽Cont.or Full   🏠Village, 2-storey, patio, quiet   ■2D(upstairs)
⊨2D   🛁Sh.w.g.   ★Air,TV,upstairs balcony, separate entrance
🚭No smoking, no pets   ↝Pen.Dutch
🎿 Restaurants, Cheese House, golf course, gift & antique shops
🚐 Village of Shakespeare, Straford Festival, St.Jacobs, markets
🐎 Victorian-style brick home with warm oakwood throughout
and new tasteful decoration, surrounded by well-kept property and many flower beds. Busy hosts
enjoy many crafts including making quilts, which are used in guest rooms. Relax inside or on the
balcony after a busy day.

Birmingham, Jennifer (The Butternut Tree B&B)   ☎ (519) 655-3206
76 Hope St E, Tavistock, ON N0B 2R0

From Hwy 401, take Hwy59 at Woodstock, proceed into Tavistock.
$65S $75-85D $15Add.person   ► 10
🍽 Full, homebaked   🏠 Village, res., hist., swimming pool,
double front porches, large rear deck   ■2D,1F(upstairs)
⊨1Q,2D,2T,1P(Q)   🛁1Private,2ensuite   ♥   ★Air,TV,
parking 🚭No pets, no smoking, children min. age 10
🎿 Local antique shops, restaurants, churches, conservation area
🚐 Stratford Theatres, St. Jacobs/Elmira Mennonite Country,
🐎 Charming turn-of-the-Century Victorian home with double porches, original woodwork,
etched windows and antique furnishings reminiscent of another era. Relax around the inground
pool after a busy day of exploring and travelling. Hostess has had First Aid training and enjoys
hiking and the theatre. "George" the rabbit lives in host quarters. ✓B&B

Rudy, Bob & Joan (The Caboose B&B)
20 Holley Ave, Box 578, Tavistock, ON   N0B 2R0

☎ (519) 655-2691
E-mail: rrudy@orc.ca

$65S/D $90D(Caboose) $15Child/Add.person $95-120F   ►8

Located 14km from Stratford. Take Hwy 8 to Shakespeare. At lights, turn south to Tavistock, east at next lights to Holley Ave. ▓Apr30-Oct31 ▓Cont.(plus) ▓Village, 2-storey,swimming pool   garden view ▓1Ste(lower level), plus train-caboose (separate from main house) ▓2S,2D,1Q ▓Private ★Air,TV,off-street parking ▓No smoking, no pets ⚥ Cheese shop, golf course, gifts & antiques, country field walks ▓ Stratford Festival, Waterloo farmers' market, Octoberfest

☛ Warm welcome in contemporary home and separate caboose (built as a boxcar in 1913 and converted to a caboose in 1943) with the interior kept to original as much as possible. Enjoy the unique atmosphere and view the countryside from the Cupola. Breakfast is served in the solarium in the family home or in the large suite. Relax in the perennial gardens or swim in the heated pool. Caboose offers excellent privacy. Visa ✓B&B

Thornbury   *(east of Owen Sound; see also Clarksburg, Meaford)*

Blasdale, Carol & Arlene McDermott (The Golden Apple B&B)
78 Bruce St S., Thornbury, ON   N0H 2P0

☎ (519) 599-3850
Fax (519) 599-7751

Take Hwy 400 north from Toronto to Hwy 26 and proceed through Collingwood to Thornbury.

$55S $70D   ►6

▓ Full ▓ Village, 3-storey, older, quiet, porch ▓ 3D (upstairs - including turret room) ▓ 2T,2Q ▓ 1Sh.w.g.(on main floor)   ★ TV in guest den, private entrance, host quarters are separate, mud room for skiers, bicycle storage, off-street parking ▓ No smoking, no pets, children min. age 18 ⚥ Village shops, Georgian Bay, excellent dining, walking or cycling through fragrant apple blossoms in apple growing region ▓ Bruce Trail hiking, Summer Theatre, several Ski Resorts & trails. Tom Thomson Art Gallery.

☛ Victorian home with beautiful antiques & art, located in one of Ontarios prettiest country villages, where the Beaver River spills into beautiful Georgian Bay. Relax on the wide veranda and enjoy the main street activities. Art books are provided in guest sitting room to enjoy. Herbal & English teas are served daily. Hosts both enjoy hiking, skiing and cycling and are knowledgeable about the areas best facilities. There is a cat in residence.

Naish, Glenn & Karen (Glennkaren B&B by the Bay)
Box 613, Thornbury, ON   N0H 2P0

☎ (519) 599-2186

From Thornbury, on Hwy 26, go west 5 km to Christie Beach Rd. Turn right to 39th Sideroad, turn right down hill to Sunset Blvd, right again past Prime Shores Resort. Look for blue & white house

(No 285) on Bay side.

$45S $65D $5-15Child   ► 7,1baby

▓ Full, homebaked ▓Rural, side-split, view, Bay-front, patio, quiet ▓ 2 (upstairs & ground level) ▓ 1D,1Q,1P,1S (trundle) & traveltender ▓1Private, 1ensuite ★ TV, bicycles & skis available, separate entrance, parking ▓ No smoking, no pets ⚥ Georgian Bay & private beach, swimming, boating, surfing, Georgian Trail & Bruce Trail hiking, bicycling, x-c skiing ▓ Thornbury, good restaurants, Meaford, Collingwood, several ski resort, golf courses, fishing

☛ Unique home, with stained glass windows, , carved furniture, modern conveniences, country accents and homey ambiance. Situated on beautiful Georgian Bay. Relax on the private beach, or view gorgeous sunsets from the 2nd storey deck. In summer breakfast is served on the deck overlooking the Bay. 2nd night rates available.

Thunder Bay

(northern Ontario; see also Dorion, Rossport)

Aylward, Linda & Arnie (Captain's Quarters B&B)   ☎ (807) 475-5630
RR1, South Gillies, ON P0T 2V0

From Thunder Bay Airport, travel 20km south on Hwy 61. Turn right onto Hwy 608 for 8.3km to East Oliver Lake Rd., turn right, then left at first driveway.
$54S $69D $15Add.person   ▶ 4A,2Ch
🍳 Full, homebaked 🏠 Rural, 2-storey, log house, acreage, deck & veranda, quiet ■ 2D (main & upper level)) ⊨ 2Q,2T
🛁2Ensuite ★ Air,TV 🚭No smoking, no pets, inquire about children under age 12
🚶 Hiking and x-c ski trails, birdwatching, golf practice range
🚗 US border (Grand Portage Casino), amethyst mines, Kakabeka Falls, Old Fort William, Candy, Loch Lomond & Big Thunder Ski Resorts, Kamview x-c ski area
🏠 Modern, yet rustic log home assures rest and relaxation in the warmth and natural beauty of wood, highlighted by 20ft cathedral ceilings. Enjoy the flower beds which adorn the well-kept grounds in peaceful, picturesque setting. Choose from extensive gourmet breakfast menu. Cordial hosts offer helpful information on area attractions. ✓B&B

Ellchook, Sandy & Betty (Sunrise Farms B&B)   ☎ & Fax (807) 935-2824
4123 Oliver Rd., RR1, Murillo, ON P0T 2G0

Located between Murillo and Kakabeka Falls on the Oliver Rd. Phone for detailed direction.
$45S $55-65D $10Child (free under age 5) 🍴 Meals ▶ 4A,2Ch
🍳 Full, homebaked 🏠 Beef/cattle farm, ranch-style, quiet, view from guest rooms, isolated ■2(ground level) ⊨1D,1Q,R,crib
🛁1Sh.w.h.,1private ★TV,LF, ample parking, wheel-chair access 〰some Ukranian
🚶 Ponds, snowmobile trails, walking/hiking on farmland pastures, "This Old Barn" (Tea Room & craft shops)
🚗 Kakabeka Falls, restaurants, swimming, hiking & x/c-skiing
🏠 Comfortable open-concept hill-top home with a beautiful panoramic view of Thunder Bay region. Enjoy a delicious country-style breakfast and relax in tranquil surroundings. Hosts raise sheep and cattle. Bed & Bale for guest horses. Visa ✓B&B

Hall, Nancy (Archibald Arbor B&B)   ☎ (807) 622-3386, Fax (807) 622-1540
222 South Archibald St., Thunder Bay, ON P7E 1G3   E-mail: nthall@norlink.net

Take Arthur St. Exit off Hwy 11/17 to downtown. Turn left on Archibald St to house on right.
$40S $55D $5Child $15Add.person ▶ 6A,2Ch
🍳 Cont. 🏠 Downtown, older side by side duplex, quiet ■3D (upstairs) ⊨ 2D,1Q,1P,2cots,crib 🛁 1Sh.w.g.(incl deep-footed tub)
★ Air,TV,private entrance, street parking, guest quarters are separate
🚭No smoking, no pets
🚶 Thunder Bay Museum, restaurants, art galleries,International Friendship Gardens, bicycle rentals, farmers' market, unique downtown stores, McKellar Hospital, main Bus Terminal
🚗 Sleeping Giant Prov.Park, Old Fort William Historic Fort, Kakabekka Falls, Ouimet Canyon, Amethyst Mines
🏠 Comfortable character brick duplex with relaxing decor situated in convenient downtown location. Reflexology/Therapeutic Touch is offered as additional service in a treatment room. Breakfast is served in the bright and spacious guest living/dining room. There is a cat (not in guest area). Visa,MC,Amex ✓B&B

Isaksen-Sitch, Sonja (Sleeping Giant B&B)   ☎ (807) 475-3105
532 Cambrian Cr., Thunder Bay, ON   P7C 5B9

$50S $60D $85F   🍴 Meals   (special weekly rates available)   ► 4+
From Hwys 11/17 turn onto Harbour Expressway. Turn right on Golf Links Rd, right on James St,
right on Redwood Ave and right on Cambrian Cr.

🍴 Full   🏠 Res., bungalow, view from guest rooms, patio, deck,
quiet   ■ 2 (main floor)   ⊨ 1T,1D,1Q,1P   🛁 1Sh.w.g.,
1sh.w.h.   ★ F,TV,LF, off-street parking   🤚 Smoking on deck,
no pets, inquire about children   ⚓ Danish
🏃 Extensive walk/bike trail begins at Conf.College, city bus
🚗 Golfing, x-c & downhill skiing, airport, restaurants, fine dining
📣 Newly decorated, elegant & spacious home with French doors
leading to double-tierd deck, surrounded by award winning gardens, and situated on a quiet
tree-lined street. House specialty is Danish "abelskivers". World travelled hostess has a diploma in
travel & tourism administration, and takes pleasure in welcoming guests. Breakfast is served in
formal dining room. There is a Border Canary "Casey" in residence. Business travellers welcome.
Quiet work area available. Visa ✓F0BBA

Kennelly, Pat & Shannon McQuilter (At Your Leisure B&B)   ☎ (807) 767-6834
RR16, S2,C32, Thunder Bay, ON   P7B 6B3

From Hwys11/17 take Balsam St to Wardrope Ave & west to Onion Lake Rd. Turn north to ConIV
(follow signs), west to Pike Lake Rd, & 9 km north to B&B.

$90S $140D   (Reservations necessary)   ► 2
🍴 Full, homebaked   🏠 Rural, 2-storey, acreage, view from guest
room, lakefront, patio, deck, quiet, secluded   ■ 1Ste (ground
level)   ⊨ 1Q   🛁 Ensuite   ★ Air,2F,mini-dish TV/VCR in
suite, lower level walkout, terry robes, fridge & coffeemaker,
off-street parking, row boat & canoe for guests, plug-ins for
vehicles   🤚No smoking, inquire about children
🏃 Lake swimming, canoeing, hiking, biking, birdwatching
🚗 Old Fort William, Kakabeka Falls, Amethyst Mines, skiing/fishing/hunting, T. Fox Lookout
📣 Unique lakeside home with luxurious suite, nestled on 3 acres of gardens and woods. Relax in
the large private spa overlooking the lake. Ideal place for a get-away. Hosts are members of the
Horticulture Society and enjoy gardening, cooking, travelling and anitques. Extended stay discounts
offered. There is a friendly Irish Setter in residence. Visa ✓B&B

Weber, Armin & Sara Jeffrey (Pinebrook Bed & Breakfast)   ☎(807)683-6114,Fax8641
RR16, Mitchell Rd., Thunder Bay, ON   P7B 6B3   E-mail: pinebrok@baynet.net

On Hwy 17 and 4km east of Thunder Bay, turn north on Hwy 527 to Mitchell Rd (4km). Turn west
1 km, then south onto Pine Dr following B&B signs.
$45S $50D $10Child $20Add.person   (plus tax)   ► 16A,2Ch
🍴 Full   🏠 Rural, 2-storey chalet-style, view from guest rooms,
acreage, riverfront and back, deck, quiet   ■ 1D,4F (ground and
main floor)   ⊨ 6S,2D,1Q,3R,1P, crib   🛁 3Sh.w.g.jacuzzi
whirlpool   ★ F,TV,LF, woodfired Finnish Sauna by river,
workout gym, wheel-chair access, excellent reading/video library,
x-c skies/canoe/mountain bikes   🤚 Designated smoking area,
children and pets welcome   ⚓ German, French
🏃 Beaver pond, walking/mountain bike & ski trails, riverside
🚗 Old Fort William, Mt.McKay, Kakabeka Falls, Sleeping Giant Prov. Park, Ouimet Canyon
📣 B&B Chalet & property with a unique, friendly and tranquil environment, yet very close to the
city. Enjoy the quiet nights and truly relaxing retreat atmosphere. Retired teacher hosts have been
active in tourism and enjoy helping guests with itineraries. Also available one room for group
accommodation. There are 3 dogs and 2 cats in residence (all very friendly). Visa ✓B&B

Tillsonburg

(south-east of London; see also Simcoe; see also Waterford)

Nealon, Tina and Tom (The English Robin B&B) ☎ (519) 842-8605
19 Robin Rd., Tillsonburg, ON   N4G 4N5

Take Hwy 401 and Hwy 19 south to Tillsonburg. At 1st set of traffic lights, turn left on North St E and left on Woodcock Dr. Proceed to Owl Dr. Turn right and then left on Robin Rd. Travelling on Hwy 3 go north on Hwy 19 to North St E.

$50S $80D   ⦿Meals   ► 6
⬛Full (English)   🏠Res., bungalow, view, patio, quiet   ⊨2Q,2T
■3 (main level)   ⬅Sh.w.g.   ★Air,F, guest terry bath robes, tea coffe making facilities, hair dryer, sep.entrance, parking   ⑭No smoking, no pets
🏃 Community center, country walks
🚗 Downtown, shopping, churches, restaurants, hospital, local live theatre, museum, Annandale House, airport, London, Port Burwell, Lake Erie beach
🐾 Traditional English hospitality in spacious bright bungalow (built by hosts), in quiet suburb of "Rolling Meadows" north of downtown. Relax on the sheltered screened-in patio.↙B&B

Tobermory

(north of Owen Sound; see also Dyer's Bay, Lion's Head)

Buchanan, Libby & Allen Potvin (Dogwood Point B&B) ☎ & Fax (519) 596-2671
778 Eagle Harbour East, RR1, Tobermory, ON   N0H 2R0

From Hwy 6 (south of Tobermory), turn west on Warner Bay Rd. Proceed 7km to "T" intersection, turn left 3km to B&B.
$55S $60-75D $25Add.person   ► 11
⬛Full   🏠Rural, 2-storey, view, lakefront, patio, porch, deck, quiet, secluded   ■3D,1F,1Ste(main & upper floor)   ⊨3S,2D,2Q
⬅1Sh.w.g., 1sh.w.h., 1ensuite   ★ TV in guest common room, wheel-chair access, purified drinking water   ⑭ No smoking, no pets, not suitable for children
🏃 Swimming & snorkeling from lakeside dock in Lake Huron (on property), view bird/wildlife
🚗 Nature Reserve, William Henry Marsh, Tobermory (15km), Ferry Terminal, boat tours
🐾 Newly constructed waterfront home with quiet atmosphere, nestled in wonderful trees and rocks that make the Bruce Peninsula a unique "back-to-nature" experience. Relax on one of two level porches overlooking the lake, enjoy the sound of the waves, the smell of the balsam/cedar trees and the sparkle of the sun off the water. Guests are advised to bring old shoes for swimming (rocky shore) and hiking boots for exploring the Bruce. "And don't forget the camera!". Hosts will pick-up guests in Tobermory. There are 2 cats in residence. ↙B&B

Toronto

(see also Brampton, Kleinburg, Georgetown, Oakville, Markham, Whitby)

Boake, Audrie (King-Rie) ☎ (416)226-3283/484-0107 Fax (416)484-1510
163 Franklin Ave., Willowdale (Toronto),ON   M2N 1C6   E-mail: kbab@sympatico.ca

Located in the Yonge and Sheppard area, north of Hwy 401.
$50S $60D $10Add.person   ► 4
⬛ Full(provided - make yourself)   🏠 Res., bungalow, quiet
■1Ste(lower level)   ⊨2T,1P   ⬅Ensuite   ★ TV in guest lounge, KF, separate entrance   ⑭ No smoking, no pets
🏃 Yonge Street subway, shopping center, laundromat, restaurants, North York City Center
🚗 Golf Club, Science Center, Toronto Zoo, downtown, Airport
🐾 Cozy bungalow close to ravine with lots of flowers in the garden and an English-type front yard. Accommodation is self-contained. There are 2 cats ("Tiger" & "Miss Maple") in the house.

Buer, Carol & Paul (The Mulberry Tree B&B)   ☎ (416) 960-5249, Fax (416) 960-3853
122 Isabella St., Toronto, ON   M4Y 1P1   E-mail: mulberry@aracnet.net

From Hwy 401 take Don Valley Pkwy south to Bloor Exit. Proceed to Sherbourne,turn left, then

right on Isabella. From QEW take Jarvis St Exit north to Isabella & right.
$50-65S $60-75D $20Add.person   🍽 Meals   ► 8
🍴 Full, homebaked   🏠 Downtown, 3-storey, hist.   ■ 3D,1F(upstairs)
⊨1S,2T,3Q,2cot   ⚑2Sh.w.g.   ★ Air conditioners & ceiling fans in guest
rooms, TV and small balcony in guest lounge, off-street parking, guest
quarters are separate, in-room data ports/phone/desks   ✋ No pets,
designated smoking area, not suitable for children   ⌇ French, German
🏃 Royal Ontario Museum, Yorkville, Cabbagetown, Eatons Centre, Maple
Ref.Library UofT., restaurants, TTC
🚗 CN Tower, Harbourfront, Art Gallery, Toronto Isles, Chinatown
☛ Spacious heritage home, tastefully renovated and filled with original art
located in tree-lined neighbourhood downtown. Enjoy the friendly, homey atmosphere and relax in
the courtyard. There is a photography studio onsite. Breakfast may be served in the "butler's
pantry" area or in the "studio cafe". Well travelled hosts provide lively breakfast conversation. Ideal
place for business travellers with access to fax/laser printer/business services. There is a dog and a
cat. Visa,MC ⌐B&B

Buer, Michelle & Paul-Antoine (Les Amis B&B)   ☎ (416) 921-8512
31 Granby St., Toronto, ON   M5B 1H8   E-mail: les_amis@aracnet.net, Fax (416) 960-3853

Located 1 block south of College subway at Yonge St.
$50-75 $60-85 $15Child $20Add.person   ► 7
🍴Full   🏠Downtown, res., townhouse, deck   ■1S,2D(upstairs)   ⊨1S,1D,1Q   ⚑ 1Private,
1sh.w.g.   ★TV in guest rooms, guest quarters are separate, street parking   ✋No smoking
⌇French, some Spanish
🏃 College Park, Maple Leaf Gardens, Eaton Centre, shops, restaurants, theatres, College Subway
Station
☛ Young Parisienne couple, in quiet downtown neigbourhood, will help guests discover the
sites/sounds & tastes of the City. Hot Vegetarian dishes for breakfast are a house specialty and
served on the roof deck, weather permitting. B&B opening in June 98. Visa ⌐B&B

Carr, Judy (Palmerston Inn B&B)   ☎ (416) 920-7842, Fax (416) 960-9529
322 Palmerston Blvd, Toronto, ON   M6G 2N6

Situated 2 blocks west of Bathurst St and 4 houses north of College Street.
$55-70S $80-165D   ► 15
🍴 Full   🏠 Downtown, res., older, patio, quiet   ■2S,5D,1F
(upstairs)   ⊨ 5S,2D,1Q,1K   ⚑ 3Sh.w.g.,some private, wash
basin in most rooms   ★ Air,TV/reading material in lounge,
off-street parking   ✋ No smokers
🏃 Public transportation, Kensington Market, Chinatown, UofT,
Queen's Park, Eaton's Centre, CN Tower, Museum & Art Gallery
☛ Elegant Georgian-style mansion (ca 1906) flanked by large
white pillars and furnished with period pieces, situated majestically on a stately tree-lined boulevard
in downtown. A generous breakfast served on the deck weather permitting.

Charbonneau, Suzanne (Terrace House Bed & Breakfast)   ☎ (416) 535-1493, Fax 9616
52 Austin Terrace, Toronto, ON   M5R 1Y6   E-mail: terracehousebandb@sympatico.ca

From East on Hwy 401 exit at Bathurst and head south. From West on Hwy 401 exit at Allen Rd S
and go east on Eglinton, then south on Bathurst. From QEW exit at Spadina Ave, go west on

Dupont St and north on Bathurst.
$59S $75-91D $20Add.person   ▶ 6
🍲 Homebaked   🏠 Res., 3-storey, hist., deck, quiet   ■ 3D (upstairs)
🛏️2T(1K),2Q,1P   🛁 1sh.w.g., 1ensuite   ★ F,TV, airconditioner in
rooms, street & off-street parking, host quarters are on top floor 🚭No pets,
smoking, 8children min. age 8   ⟲English (household language is French)
🏃 Casa Loma, Forest Hill Village, Bloor Street cafes, subway station
🚗 U of T, ROM/AGO, Yorkville, downtown, Metro Zoo, Ontario Place
📷 1913-built home, richly furnished with antiques, stained/leaded glass
windows and scrolled living room ceiling, situated in Forest Hill, a quiet
residendial neighborhood in the Casa Loma area. Breakfast may consist of
quiches, fancy omelets, frittata, pancakes, french toast etc. Well travelled hostess has lived in
Europe and Africa and enjoys exchanging travel experiences and memories in front of the fireplace
sipping hot chocolate. There is a cat in residence. Visa,MC ↙B&B

Coxe, Jennie (Alcina's Bed & Breakfast)   ☎ (416) 656-6400
16 Alcina Ave., Toronto, ON   M6G 2E8

Located south of St.Clair and west of Bathurst.Phone for directions.
$65S(and up) $75-80D $10Child $15Add.person   ▶ 6A,2Ch
🍲 Cont.   🏠 Downtown, res. 3-storey, older   ■ 2D,1Ste (upstairs)
🛏️2T,2Q   🛁3Ensuite   ★ Sit-in garden, guest coffee-nook, off-street
parking   🚭 No smoking
🏃 Historic Casa Loma and Flower Gardens of restored Spadina House
(tours), exclusive Wychwood Park neighbourhood, St.Clair West Subway Stn,
Bathurst, bus, shopping
🚗 Downtown, University, Harbourfront, Science Centre, Yorkville, Theatre
district, Lake Ontario
📷 Gracious old Victorian house with "good bones", tastefully renovated and centrally located.
Enjoy the casual elegance of warm wood, stained glass, soft period furnishings in a bright and airy
setting with a quiet, private English flower garden. The loft suite is a delightful retreat. There is
"Cina" the resident cat.↙B&B

Dallimore, Rob (Dallimore Residence)   ☎ (905) 822-3540, Fax (905) 823-5212
2110 Varency Drive,Mississauga, ON L5K1C3

Phone for directions. Located in west suburb of Toronto.
$40S $60D   (Minimum stay 2 nights)   ▶ 6
🍲 Full   🏠 Res., sub., acreage, patio, quiet   ■ 3D (upstairs)
🛏️2T,1D,1Q   🛁Sh.w.g.   ★Air,parking 🚭Restr smoking
🏃 Large shopping Centre, good restaurants, excellent local bus
service to City Centre
🚗 Lake Ontario shoreline & parks, "GO" Commuter train to TO
📷 English-style hospitality in large modern home located on large treed property. There is a dog
in the house. Well travelled hosts enjoy discussing mutual adventures from all over the world.
Pick-up from Airport with advance bookings. Special rates for 7days or more. Airport pick-up with
minimum 3days stay. ↙B&B

Jarvie, May (Feathers' B&B)　　　　　　　　　　　　　☎ (416) 534-1923
132 Wells Street, Toronto, ON M5R 1P4

Located 2 blocks north of Bloor Street and 1/2 block east of Bathurst.
$50-65S $65-75D $15Add.person $5(extra for 1 night booking)　▶ 4A,2Ch
🚐 Cont.(lavish)　🏠 Downtown, older　■ 1D(upstairs), 1Studio
apt(downstairs for honeymooners or families)　🛏 2T(1K),1D,1T
🚿1Private, 1sh.w.h., 1private　★ Air,LF,TV in guest room, parking
🚫No pets,no smoking　💬Dutch,French, some German
🕴 Bathurst Subway and streetcar, Bloor Street dining and entertainment
area, Royal Ontario Museum, Casa Loma, Mirvish Village, antiques and
bookstores, bus stop on corner
🚗 Eaton's Center, Yorkville, Toronto Harbourfront, Science center
🔫 Charming Victorian family home situated in a super downtown location
called "Annex". Antique furniture, oriental tapestries and original artwork
lend a unique atmosphere to interesting and beautifully renovated house. Steps away from a
delightful area of affordably priced cosmopolitan restaurants and outdoor cafés. Studio apartment is
great for honeymooners or families. ↙B&B

Ketchen, Donna and Ken (Orchard View)　　　　　　　☎ (416) 488-6826
92 Orchard View Blvd., Toronto, ON M4R 1C2

Centrally located, 1block north of Eglinton Ave & 1block west of Yonge St.
$60S $70-75D　　　　　　　　　　　　　　　　　　　▶ 4A
🚐Full　🏠Uptown, res., 3-storey, patio, quiet　■2D(upstairs)　🛏2T,1Q
🚿1Ensuite, 1sh.w.h.　★Air,parking　🚫No smoking, no children
🕴 Subway Stn (Eglinton/Yonge 2blks) to City center & all major city
attractions, good shopping, excellent restaurants, library, North Toronto
Mem.Centre
🔫 Renovated, spacious 1911-built home is uniquely decorated for the
1990's and centrally situated . "Park the car and discover Toronto"! Friendly,
helpful hosts have been welcoming B&B guests for many years. There is a
resident cat called "Schubert". ↙ Travelinx

Kratochvil, V.J.　　　　　　　　　　　　　　　　　☎ (905) 889-6516
85 Garden Ave., Richmond Hill, ON L4C 6L6

Located just north of Hwy 7 and west off Yonge Street.
$45S $50D　　　　　　　　　　　　　　　　　　　▶ 2
🚐 Full　🏠 Res., sub., bungalow, swimming pool, patio, quiet
■ 1D(main level)　🛏 2S　🚿Private　★TV, parking　🚫 No
pets, no children　💬Dutch, Czech.
🕴 Public transportation to downtown Toronto
🚗 Wonderland, Pleasure Valley Ski center, Science center
🔫 Home is surrounded by towering evergreens and situated in
a quiet area in the North end of Toronto with a resort-like relaxing atmosphere.

Bed & Breakfast Homes of Toronto　　　　　　　　　☎ (416) 363-6362
46093, College Park PO, Toronto, Ont. M5B 2L8

Rates:　from $45S　from $60D　(including breakfast and parking)
Bed & Breakfast Homes of Toronto is an established B&B association with a difference: a
cooperative of 18 friendly, independent homes allows travellers to speak directly with the host
before booking. Standards are high, yet room rates are low. Call or write for free brochure
describing homes throughout the city.↙B&B

Maguire, Dorothy (Craig House) ☎ (416) 698-3916, Fax (416) 698-8506
78 Spruce Hill Rd., Toronto, ON   M4E 3G3

From Hwy 401, take Victoria Park Exit and go south to Queen St. Turn right and at 1st stop light turn right again on Beech. Proceed to Sycamore (first left) to Spruce Hill Rd. From Gardiner Expressway, exit at Lakeshore Rd and travel to Woodbine St. Proceed to Queen St, turn right,

continue to 3rd stop light, turn left at Beech, then as above.
$50S $65D $90Apt $15Add.person CAA/AAA discounts   ► 6A
🆁 Full 🏠Beaches Res., 3-storey, guest sundeck ■3D (2nd & 3rd level),1Ste(upst with lounge) ⊨2D,1R,2Q ⊰1Sh.w.g.,1private
★Air,F,sep.entrance,guest kitchen,parking ⓌNo smoking,no pets
🏃 Board-walk-by-the-lake, parks, pubs, boutiques, sidewalk cafés, 24hr public transportation on corner
🚗 Eaton Centre, C.N.Tower, Harbour-front, Sky Dome,
📣 Traditional Beaches home featuring stained glass and leaded bay windows, surrounded by flowers and a forest of stately oaks and located in a neighbourhood with the air of a small resort town by the lake. Breakfast is served in the dining room looking on to the garden.

McGregor, Gail (Marlborough Place Bed & Breakfast) ☎ (416) 922-2159
93 Marlborough Ave., Toronto, ON   M5R 1X5

Located north of Bloor/Yonge Sts. Phone for directions.
$50S $90D   ► 4
🆁 Cont.(lavish) 🏠 Hist., townhouse, 3-storey, decks on each level ■ 1S,1F (upstairs)
⊨1S,2T ⊰1Ensuite, 1sh.w.h. (jacuzzi) ★ Air,LF,TV, guest sitting & reading areas, private deck, parking Ⓦ Restricted smoking, no pets
🏃 Bloor Street, Yorkville, Royal Ontario Museum, Parliament Bldgs, Rosedale or Summerhill Subway Stations, excellent shops & restaurants, Toronto Lawn Tennis Club
📣 Comfortble, newly renovated 1900 Victorian townhouse with open staircase on third floor loft. Enjoy the view of the garden from the private deck. Long term rates available in winter. ⌐B&B

McLoughlin, Katya and Bernie (Beaconsfield B&B) ☎ & Fax (416) 535-3338
38 Beaconsfield Ave., Toronto, Ontario M6J 3H9   E-mail: beacon@idirect.com

Located near Queen & Dovercourt Streets. From Gardiner expressway, take Jamieson Exit and go

north to Queen. Turn right, past Dufferin to Beaconsfield Ave and left.
$59S $69D $99Ste $15Add.person   ► 6-8A,2Ch
🆁 Choice, homebaked 🏠 Downtown, res., hist., decks, front veranda
■2D,1Ste (upstairs) ⊨1S,2T(1K),2Q, 2cots ⊰1Private,1sh.w.g.
★Air,KF,LF,TV in guest room, Mexican honeymoon suite with tree-top terrace, parking ⌐Spanish, Slavic languages, some French
🏃 City transit streetcar (24-hour service), Queen Street West (trendy shops, ethnic restaurants), Canadian National Exhibition, Ontario Place
🚗 Eaton's Centre (10 min.trolley ride), Sky Dome, CN Tower, theatres
📣 Artist hosts (painting and film acting) in large 1882 Heritage home with imaginatively decorated rooms full of colour, art, books, antiques and plants ("eclectic, un-conventional and fun"). Well travelled and informed

hosts will help with itineraries for sightseeing, entertainment and dining. A generous breakfast is designed around guests' food preferences. There is a resident cat in host quarters. ⌐B&B

Toronto Bed & Breakfast Inc. ☎(416)588-8800/927-0354,Fax(416)927-0838
Box 269, 253 College St., Toronto, ON M5T 1R5   E-mail: beds@torontobandb.com

(Marcia Getgood, President)
Rates: 45-70S $60-85D   (including full breakfast)
A professional reservation service of quality inspected Bed & Breakfast accommodation, providing high level of safety, comfort, cleanliness & hospitality. Toronto's longest running urban B&B Service. Advance reservation recommended. Free brochure on request. CCards.

Perks, Dave & Adam Tanner-Hill (The House on McGill)   ☎ & Fax (416) 351-1503
110 McGill St., Toronto,ON   M5B 1H6   E-mail: mcgillbnb@hotmail.com

Located near intersection of Church & Carleton Street.
$50-70S $65-85D $15Add.person (discounts for long-term stay)   ▶ 9A
🍴 Cont+, self-serve 🏠 Downtown, 3-storey, townhouse, view from guest
rooms, porch, quiet   ■ 3D(upstairs)   ⊨ 3Q,1R,1P(incl. 4-poster)
⊿1Sh.w.g.   ★ Air,F, street parking, microwave/fridge/coffeemaker for
guests, bicycles on loan, guest quarters are separate   🦽 No smoking, no
pets, no children   ⌇ French, Australian
🧍 Eaton Center, University of Toronto, Maple Leaf Gardens, Yonge Street,
theatre district, Allen Gardens, St.Lawrence Market, Yorkville, Church
St.Village, Carleton Cineplex, Ryerson U., Cabbagetown, streetcar/subway
🚗 Ontario Place, ROM, AGO, Science Centre, Toronto Isls, Harbourfront
🐘 Elegantly restored 1894 Victorian Townhouse with stained glass windows and modern
conveniences, located in quiet shady enclave in the heart of the bustle of the City. Host will be
happy to guide guests in their own car on a tour of the city. Breakfast is served in special guest
breakfast room. Ideal place for business travellers. MC

Metropolitan Bed and Breakfast Registry of Toronto   ☎(416)964-2566
Ste 113, 650 Dupont St., Toronto, ON   M6G 1Z2

(Judy Carr, President)   Fax960-9529 8am-8pm
Rates $40-65S $50-85D   (Prices vary from home to home)
Metropolitan B&B represents Toronto's finest B&B homes located throughout the city and
suburbs. All of the homes are inspected and adhere to the Agency's high standards. Hosts provide
full breakfast, parking and easy access to all tourist attractions. Some offer honeymoon suites,
jacuzzis and other specialties. Call or fax for free booklet.⌐B&B

Snelson, Karen & Ken(Mayfair B&B)   ☎ (416) 769-1558, Fax (416) 769-9655
78 Indian Grove, Toronto, ON   M6R 2Y4   E-mail: ksnelson@compuserve.com

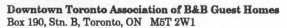

Located half a block south of Bloor Street and one block east of Parkside/Keele St.
$65-70S $75-85D $15Add.person   ▶ 8A,3Ch
🍴 Full, homebaked 🏠 Res., older, quiet ■ 3Stes (upstairs) plus effic.
suite ⊨2T,2Q,1cot ⊿ 4Ensuite ★Air,TV in guest room, parking
🦽no pets, no smoking
🧍 High Park, shopping and restaurants, subway stop
🚗 Downtown Toronto, Canadian National Exhibition, Ontario Place
🐘 Elegant, 1911 Edwardian home furnished with antiques and persian
carpets with many leaded and stained glass windows and beautiful oak
panelling. Located in a quiet residential area close to downtown. Congenial,
well travelled hosts enjoy helping guests with plans.Visa ⌐B&B

Downtown Toronto Association of B&B Guest Homes   ☎ (416) 368-1420/Fax 1653
Box 190, Stn. B, Toronto, ON   M5T 2W1

(Mrs. Linda Lippa, Co-ordinator)
Rates $45-65S $55-75D $80-120Stes   (Full/gourmet breakfast)
The Downtown Toronto Association & B&B Guest Homes is a professionsl reservation service,
representing Toronto's largest selection of fully inspected and privately owned Victorian homes in
downtown Toronto, all within 10 minutes of major tourist attractions. All hosts are active in the
arts or hospitality industries and proudly feature distinctive homes in downtown locations, with
access to 24 hour transit. Some homes offer fireplaces and jaccuzzis. Free brochure with map of the
city and home descriptions available. ⌐B&B

Vallance, Philomena & Dave (Philomena & Dave B&B)   ☎(416)962-2786,Fax964-8837
31 Dalton Rd., Toronto, ON   M5R 2Y8   E-mail: valladp@echo-on.net, 1-888-272-2718

Located near Bloor St & Spadina Ave. By prior reservation only.
$45S $70D   (Discounts for long stay & off-season)   ► 4A
🍽 Full   🏠 Downtown, res., 3-storey, quiet, deck   ■ 2D(upstairs)
⊨2T,1Q   ⊐1Sh.w.g.   ★ TV in guest rooms, guest kitchen for light
snacks with morning sun-deck, off-street parking   ★ Designated smoking
area, not suitable for children   ∾ German, Italian
🧍 Royal Ontario Museum, Chinatown, subway & streetcar, various
restaurants, University of Toronto
🚍 Friendly hospitality in comfortable home with stained glass, leaded
windows and original oak, located in the pleasant downtown community
called the "Annex". Enjoy the very quiet atmosphere, yet close proximity to
Bloor Street with large selection of stores and restaurants
operated by many nationalities. Breakfast is served in enclosed cozy sun room. There is a cat.⌐B&B

Vanderkooy, Joan (Vanderkooy Bed & Breakfast)   ☎ (416) 925-8765
53 Walker Ave., Toronto, ON   M4V 1G3

Phone for directions. Located in the Yong/St.Clair area.
$50-65S $70-75D   ► 6
🍽 Full   🏠 Downtown, res., 2.5-storey, patio, deck   ■ 3D (upstairs)
⊨ 4T(1K),1D   ⊨ 1sh.w.g., 1Ensuite   ⊐ Air,F,TV,off-street parking,
beautiful waterfall and pond in garden   🐾 Smoking outside
🧍 Popular restaurants and shops on St Clair Ave, Yorkville Ave & Bloor St.,
Summerhill Subway Station to downtown attractions
🚗 Ontario Place & Lake Ontario Harbourfront, Eaton Centre, CN Tower
🚍 Bright and cheerful home with a friendly, casual atmosphere and filled
with fine touches, including stained glass and original art. Breakfast is served
in open dining room overlooking the garden. Relax on the flower filled deck in
warmer weather. There is a resident cat. ⌐B&B

Walker, Susan & Garry (Clarence Square Bed & Breakfast Inn)   ☎ (416) 598-0616,
13 Clarence Square, Toronto, ON   M5V 1H1   Fax (416) 598-4200

Phone for directions.
$110-130S/D   ► 6A
🍽 Full   🏠 Downtown, 3-storey, hist.   ■3D(upstairs) ⊨2T,1D,1Q,1K
⊐ 3Ensuite (whirlpool tubs)   ★ Airconditioners, F,TV/phones in guest
rooms, off-street parking, fax service available, guest quarters are separate
🐾 No smoking, no pets, not suitable for children
🧍 SkyDome, Roy Thompson Hall, Harbourfront, R.Alex & P.of Wales
theatres, Queen Street West & Eaton Centre, restaurants, streetcar/subway
🚗 Black Creek Pion.Village, Roy.'Ont.Museum, Ont.Science Ctr, Niagara
🚍 Elegant 1879 historic home, combines grace of the past with modern
amenities and overlooks a pleasant park - a quiet oasis in the
heart of Toronto's entertainment district & ideal place for the discerning traveller. Hosts are
Torontonians who are happy to share their knowledge of local attractions, current happenings and
fine dining locations. Whether on business or pleasure, enjoy the enticing blend of historic and
contemporary living. Visa,MC,Amex ⌐B&B

Troy
(north of Brantford; see also Paris, Cambridge)

Cornell, Lillian & Carl (A Slice of Home B&B)   ☎ (519) 647-2082
1927 Hwy 5West, Troy, ON   L0R 2B0

Located 6.6km west of Peter's Corners and 16km west of Clappison's Cut.
$35S $45D   🍽 Meals   ► 5A,2Ch
🍳Full 🏠Rural, ranch-style, view from guest rooms, quiet ■3(main level) ⊨1S,1D,1K,1P,
2cots,3cribs 🛏 1Sh.w.h. ★ KF,LF,F,TV, off-street parking 🕊 No smoking, no pets
☛ Warm welcome and friendly hospitality in quiet country home comfortably decorated. Enjoy
the water gardens from the solarium and relaxing country atmosphere. There are 2 resident cats.

Tweed
(north of Belleville; see also Marmora)

Cooper, Margaret & Richard (Black River Country Inn)   ☎(613)478-6638,Fx(613)478-9956
225 Black River Rd., RR3, Tweed, ON   K0K 3J0   E-mail: blackriver@sympathico.ca,

$45S $55-80D $10child $15Add.person   🍽 Meals   ► 8A,2Ch
Located 4km west of Hwy 37 on Hwy 7. Turn south on Black River Rd for 0.5km to first house on
 right over bridge.
📅 April-Nov   🍳 Full   🏠 Rural, ranch-style, 66 acres, view
from guest rooms, riverfront, swimming pool, patio, porch, deck,
quiet, secluded   ■ 3 plus sleeping cabin   ⊨ 2T(K),3Q,1R
🛁2Shw.g., 1ensuite   ★ F,TV,private entrance   🕊 Smoking
outside, no pets
🚶 Walking trails on large private grounds, pond with paddle boat,
canoing, kayaking, fishing
🚌 Tweed, Belleville, Kingston, Peterborough, Bon Echo Park, Old Fort Henry, Trent Canal
☛ Warm and unpretentious hospitality in country home with modern facilities situated in a
picturesque and peaceful setting along the Black River. Walk about the large landscaped grounds,
have a picnic, settle down by the crackling camp fire or fireplace or relax in the whirlpool.
Breakfast is served in the elegant dining room or sunporch. Enjoy the special countrytime and
relaxed atmosphere. Ideal place for special occasions. Visa ✓B&B

Neumann, Lois & Harald (Inn Tweed B&B)   ☎ (613) 478-6242
Box 848, 359 Arthur St., Tweed, ON   K0K 3J0

From Hwy 401, take Exit 544 at Belleville and proceed north on Hwy 37 to Tweed. From Hwy 7
(east of Madoc) take Hwy 37 south to Tweed. Call or ask for directions in village.
                                     ► 6A
$45S $50-55D
🏠 Full, homebaked, buffet   🏠 Village, res., 2.5-storey, older,
patio, quiet   ■ 3D(upstairs)   ⊨ 2T,1D,1Q   🛏 1sh.w.g.
★Woodstove, off-street parking, guest sitting room on main floor,
quest quarters are separate   🕊 No smoking, no pets, not suitable
for children   〰 German, French
🚶 Footbridge over Moira River to village centre (with shops,
restaurants, tea rooms, antique, stores), Tweed Heritage Centre,
museum, beach at Stoco Lake, nature trails, scenic country roads
🚌 Belleville, Kingston, Perth, Bon Echo Prov. Park, numerous Conservations Areas, golf courses
☛ Congenial hosts welcome guests to their late Victorian limestone masonry brick home with
original custom woodwork, inlaid floors, leaded glass and a carriage house. Still known locally as the
"Louis Rashotte House" it is situated in quiet picturesque village. Nutritious breakfast served in the
bright dining room. Relax on the shady veranda or under the mature maples in the garden and
enjoy friendly small town hospitality. Amex ✓CC

Victoria Harbour
(north of Barrie; see also Midland, Penetang., Waubaushene)

Barron, Frank & Joyce (Daisy's Place) ☎ (705) 534-4600
7 Bayside Ave, RR1, Box 189, Victoria Harbour, ON L0K 2A0

Take Hwy 400 north to Hwy 12 West and to Victoria Harbour, Park St. Proceed to Davis Dr

(2nd on right) and then to Bayside Ave. Turn right.
$50S $60D $30Add.person   ► 6
▯ Full   🏠 Rural, bungalow, lakefront, patio, deck, quiet   ▮3D
(main & ground level)   ⊨ 2S,2D   ◪ 2Sh.w.g., 1ensuite
★F,TV,separate entrance   🐾 No smoking, no pets
🕴 Georgian Bay, country walks, x-country skiing, ice fishing
🚗 Moonstone & Mt.St.Louis Ski Resorts, Huronia Museum &
Indian Village, Martyr's Shrine, Wyemarsh Wildlife Centre
☛ Friendly hospitality in modern home on the water. Relax in the recreation room with pool table, TV, piano, games Enjoy breakfast in the dining room overlooking beautiful Georgian Bay. ↙CC

Vineland
(west of St.Catharines; see also Beamsville, Grimsby, N.Falls, NOTL)

Dunnink, Janet and Bert (Travellers Home) ☎ (905) 562-5656
RR1, Jordan, ON L0R 1S0

Location: 2924 Victoria Ave, Vineland. From QEW Exit 57, turn off on Victoria Ave towards
Vineland. Go through stoplight. After 5 km , look for house on corner of Springcreek Rd.

$35S $50D $5Child $10Add. person   ► 6A,2Ch
▯ Full   🏠 Rural, res., split-level, acreage, view, swimming pool,
patio, quiet   ▮1S,2D(lower level)   ⊨1S,1D,1Q,1R   ◪Sh.w.g.
★Air,F,KF,TV in guest room, separate entrance, parking, private
guest sitting room 🐾No smoking, no pets   ⚮Dutch
🕴 Balls Falls historic park, Bruce trail hiking, Prudhommes
Landing (Wet & Wilds), golfing, several wineries (tours & tasting)
🚗 Niagara Falls, Marineland, quaint town Niagara-on-the-Lake
☛ Spacious home with Dutch hospitality on quiet property located in Ontario's "Fruit Belt" with plenty of fruits in season. Entire lower level is for guests with bright, large windows and entrance through garage. There are pets around the house. Located 20km from Niagara Falls. Weekly rates.

Tieman, Jane & André (Tintern Vacations B&B) ☎ (905) 563-4000, Fax (905) 563-3446
2869 Tintern Rd, RR1, Vineland, ON L0R 2C0   E-mail: tintern.vacations@sympatico.ca

From QEW take Exit 57 (Victoria Ave/RR24) and proceed south to Spring Creek Rd. Turn right to

Tintern Rd and then left.
$45S $55-70D $10Child $15Add.person 🍽 Meals   ► 18
▯Full, homebaked   🏠Rural, village, bungalow, hillside,5-acres,
view from guest rooms, swimming pool, river at back, quiet, deck
▮2D,3F(main & ground level)   ⊨ 1S,2T,4D,1Q,1K,1P,crib
◪1Ensuite, 1sh.w.g., 1sh.w.h.   🐾 Designated smoking area
⚮some Dutch & French
🕴 Canoeing, cycling, golfing, country walks, churches
🚗 Two doz.wineries, Niagara Falls, Casino, Niagara-on-the-Lake, Bruce Trail hiking
☛ Fruit hobby farm with beautifully decorated large family home, situated on lush acreage in the heart of Niagara's wine region. Ideal place for outdoor enthusiasts. Explore the area by canoe or tandem bike (available for guests). There are teenagers in the host family. Host is an avid canoer and hiker. Hostess is Pres. of the newly-formed Niagara Wineries B&B Association. Breakfast is served in special guest breakfast room. There is a dog, cat and a talking parrot in residence and llamas, calves and rabbits on the grounds. ↙B&B

Walkerton
(east of Kincardine; see also Cargill, Pinkerton, Mildmay,

Huygen, Ruby (Silver Creek Bed & Breakfast) ☏ (519) 881-0252
17 Yonge St S, Walkerton, ON   N0G 2V0

In Walkerton, at junction of Hwys 4/9 proceed 1 block south of Main Street. Watch for signs.

$35S $45D   ▣ Meals   (Family rates available)   ► 6
⑥ Full, homebaked   🏠 Downtown,res.,older,.75acreage,quiet
▣3D(upst)   ⏩3D   🏠1Shw.g.,1shw.h.   ★TV,F,parking
♿Restricted smoking
🧍 Downtown shopping, parks, Saugeen River (canoeing, fishing),
Walkerton Ski Hills, cross country and snowmobile trails
🚘 Lake Huron and beaches, Kincardine, Blyth Theatre
👏 Comfortable country-style home near downtown surrounded
by spacious lawns and flower gardens with the Silver Creek running through property. Enjoy a
hearty breakfast with homemade jams and tea biscuits. There is a cat & a dog outside. ⎰B&B

Waterdown
(west of Toronto; see also Burlington, Hamilton, Dundas)

Wickens, Stan and Ann (Griffin House) ☏ (905) 689-5225
Box 282, 261 Mill Street North, Waterdown, Ontario   L0R 2H0

Take Hwy 5 to the village of Waterdown and turn north on Mill Street.

$50S $65D   ► 4
⑥ Full, homebaked   🏠 Village, hist., quiet   ▣2D (upstairs)
⏩1Q,1D,1P   🏠 1Sh.w.g.   ★ Air, stove in sitting room,
off-street parking   ♿No smoking, no pets, children min. age 12
🧍 Heritage area, antique shops, craft/collectibles, art
galleries/gift shops, excellent restaurants/tea rooms.
🚘 Hamilton, Burlington, Toronto Airport, Botanical Gardens,
Bruce Trail, Hidden Lake Golf Club, Christie Conservation Area,
Dundurn Castle
👏 Renovated Turn-of-the-Century house with country furnishings, antiques and reproductions.
Long-time B&B hosts are members of Torquay Pottery Collectors Society & interests include herb
& perennialgardens. Guests are invited to "discover Flamborough"! There is a cat "George".

Waterford
(south of Brantford; see also Simcoe, Port Dover, Ohsweken)

Kerr, Jean and Fred ☏ (519) 443-5165
150 Main Street S., Waterford, Ontario   N0E 1Y0

Located 3.2 km east of Hwy 24 on Reg Rd 24. Look for house opposite the Untited Church.

$45S $50D   ▣$3Each   ► 5
⑥ Choice   🏠 Village, hist.   ▣ 1S,2D(upst)   ⏩ 1S,2D,R
🏠1Sh.w.g.   ★F,TV,parking   ♿Restr.smoking, no pets
🧍 Park area, restaurants, craft & antique shops
🚘 Lake swimming, fishing, Bell Homestead (Brantford),
museum, Lake Erie resorts
👏 Designated Heritage House in small town in tobacco &
ginseng farm country, home of Pumpkin-fest.

Koch, Lena & Fred (Koch's B&B 📞(519-443-5205, Fax (519) 443-4520
RR4 Con7, Townsend #1644, Waterford, ON N0E 1Y0 E-mail: lenakoch@netroute.net

From Hwy 403 (Brantford) take Exit 24 south (Simcoe) and Con 6 to Coccos House Rd. Turn right
on Reg Rd 5, then left on Con 7 and proceed 6.6km to No 1644.
$50S $60D $10Add.person 🍽Meals (longer stay discounts) ▶6A,2Ch
📅 March1-Oct31 🍳 Full 🏠 Rural, bungalow, older, 7-acres, view, patio, porch, quiet, pond,
secluded ▦3D ⊨3D ⊿1Sh.w.g ★ TV/fans in some guest rooms, separate entrance,
guest quarters are separate 🚭 No smoking, ask about children and pets 〰 German
🚗 Swimming in pond on property
🚗 Brantford, Simcoe, Lakes Ontario & Erie, Camp Trilium, Hamilton, Kitchener, London
📣 Warm welcome in "gemuetliches" country home located in rural Southwestern Ontario area.
There is plenty of space for trailors and tents can be set up on the property. Tents are also available
for short overnight trips in the area and pick-up from Toronto Int.Airport available (both for a
small fee). There are 3 cats in residence. MC

Winkworth, Charlie & Harriet (Lorene's Place) 📞 & Fax (519) 443-7476
90 St.James St.South, Waterford, ON N0E 1Y0

Located 1.6km east of Hwy 24. Look for house on corner of St.James & Temperance Streets.

$45S $50D $5Child $80F ▶4A,2Ch
🍳 Full, homebaked 🏠 Village, 2-storey. older, patio, porch,
quiet ▦3(upstairs) ⊨2S,1D,1Q -⊿1Sh.w.g. ★Air,TV,
ceiling fans, separate entrance, street parking
🏃 Waterford Lakes (walking, fishing, picnics), Annual Pumpkin
Festival (Oct), museum, Legion Hall, restaurants
🚗 Brantford, Simcoe, Port Dover (Turkey Pt - swimming,
fishing), golfing, Bell Museum, Mohawk Chapel
📣 Warm welcome and friendly hospitality in beautiful, turn-of-the-Century home located in the
centre of the village and surrounded by well landscaped grounds. Relax on the patio or porch after a
busy day. Families are very welcome. There are 2 dogs and 1 cat in residence.

Waterloo *(west of Toronto; see also Kitchener, Wellesley, St.Jacobs, Baden)*

Mateyk, Bob & Hoda (Sugarbush Trail B&B - Executive Guest House) 📞 519) 725-3184
100 Blythwood Rd., Waterloo, ON N2L 4A2 E-mail: bmateyk@easynet.on.ca

From Hwy 401, take Exit 278 to Hwy 8, then to Hwy 86 north toward Waterloo. Take King St Exit,
turn left and then right on Weber St.N. then left on Blythwood Rd.
$50S $65-95D $15child(under age 12) $15-25Add.person (plus tax) ▶8+

🍳 Cont., homebaked, buffet 🏠 Res., 2-storey, view from guest
rooms, quiet ▦2D,1F (main & upper level) ⊨2T,3D,1Q,1P
(2futons) ⊿2Private, 1ensuite ★Air,LF,F,TV in guest
rooms, room air-conditioners, ceiling fans, off-street parking 🚭
Smoking on patio, no pets 〰 French, Arabic
🏃 Wilfred Laurier University, University of Waterloo, Sugarbush
Park next door to property, uptown Waterloo, museums
🚗 Farmer's Market, Factory Outlets, shopping mall, St.Jacobs,
Kitchener, Sportsworld, African Lion Safari, Mennonite Country
📣 European-style home nestled among the trails, located in the heart of Waterloo. Experience
the romance and sophistication, revel in the delightful mix of French elegance, Victorian charms &
Italian flair. Relax in the spacious parlour or rich library with stone fireplace. Breakfast is served in
special guest breakfast room. ✏B&B

Waubaushene *(on Georgian Bay, north of Barrie; see also Penetang.,Vict.Hbr.,Midland)*

Carpenter, Mary & John (Waubaushene Heritage House B&B)   ☎ (705) 538-1857
Box 429, 337 Pine St., Waubaushene, ON L0K 2C0

Take Hwy 400 and Hwy 69 crossing Hwy 12 into Waubaushene.Travel 1 block on Pine St to top of
hill and to B&B beside Waubaushene Heritage store.
$40S $50D   ► 6A,2Ch
🄳 Full, homebaked   🏠 Village, 2-storey, hist., lakeview, porch
▪ 2D,1F (upstairs)   ⊨ 2T,3D   ⚏ 1Ensuite, 1sh.w.g.   ★Air,
separate entrance, off-street parking   ✋ Smoking on front porch
🏃 Beach, boat rental, marina, churches
🚗 Discovery Bay (Penetanguishene), Big Chute (railway boat
crossing) on Severn Waterway
☞ Newly renovated 1881 house with a view of the lake in popular resort district. Hosts are well
informed about this historic area and enjoy helping guests with plans. Enjoy fishing or lunch on the
porch or a day at the beach. There is a dog in residence (not in guest areas).Visa,MC ↝CC

Wawa   *(northern Ontario; north of Sault Ste Marie; see also Rossport)*

Jones, David & Kay (Wawa Lakeshore Bed & Breakfast)   ☎(705)856-1709,Fax1785
1 Gold St., Wawa, ON P0S 1K0   E-mail: dhjones@onlink.net

Located 225km north-west of Sault-Ste-Marie on Hwy 17 north.
$45S $55D   ► 6
🄳Cont/deluxe 🏠Downtown, res., 3-storey, lakefront, view from
guest rooms, patio, deck, quiet ▪1Ste(upstairs) ⊨2D,1Q
⚏1Sh.w.g.   ★ F,KF,TV/VCR/phone in guest sitting room,
separate entrance, off-street parking, balconies, guest quarters are
separate ✋No smoking, one party only ↝Finnish
🏃 Lakeshore walkway displaying historic plaques, shallow sandy beach, snowmachine trails
🚗 Scenic High Falls, Agawa Pictographs, Magpie Valley Badlands, old mine sites
☞ Warm & friendly hospitality in lovely open-concept home located on the beach overlooking
scenic Wawa Lake. Guest quarters are in two upper floors with loft on third floor. Ideal place for a
family or up to 3 couples travelling together. Reduced rates for extended stays.

Paulencu, Cathie & Joe Lynett (Superior Avenue B&B)   ☎ (705) 856-7479
120 Superior Ave., Wawa, ON P0S 1K0

From Hwy 17 turn into Hwy 101 and follow into Wawa. Proceed
past Wawa Motor Hotel, turn left, follow curved street for 1km.
$40S $60D   ► 5
✚ May-Sept   🄳 Full   🏠 Res., bungalow, hillside, view from
guest rooms, patio, quiet   ▪ 1S,2D(main floor)   ⊨ 2D,1Q
⚏1Sh.w.g., 1ensuite   ★ F,TV in guest living room, off-street
parking   ✋ Smoking outside, no pets, not suitable for children
🏃 Public beaches, local parks, downtown, shopping
🚗 Golf Course, Lake Superior, scenic High Falls, old mine sites, hiking trails
☞ Brick bungalow, tastefully decorated overlooking public golf course. Hosts are knowledgeable
about the area and enjoy golfing, gardening, roller blading and good conversation. Breakfast is
served in the comfortable dining room.

Sanders, Dr. Norma & Ed Burford (Goose Down Inn)   ☎ (705) 856-7003
37 Klondike St., Wawa, ON   P0S 1K0

Turn off Hwy 17 and follow Hwy 101 into Wawa. Proceed past Wally's Restaurant & turn right onto
Klondike St. Look for white house with blue shutters & geese on the deck.

$40S $50D $60F   ▶ 4A,4Ch
✚ May24-Thanksgiving   (reservations required in winter)
💳Full,homebaked   🏠 Res., ranch-style, patio, quiet   ■3D
(main level) ⊨1Q,1K,1T,2R,crib ⊒Sh.w.g. ★LF, guest living
room, parking ⓌDesignated smoking area, no pets
🕇 Wawa Lake (spring fed), swimming, Wawa Goose Monument
🚗 High Falls, hiking trails, Lake Superior, miles of sandy
beaches Old Woman Bay, Lake Superior Park, Surluga Mine Road
🐾 Retired professional hosts in comfortable home decorated with family antiques and
collectibles. House specialty is homemade pork sausages and blueberry jam. Vegetarian breakfast on
request. Hosts are very knowledgeable of the area and its resources. There is a Hungarian Puli dog
named "Panya" in residence. ✓B&B

Wellesley   *(north of Stratford; see also Baden, Gadshill, New Hamburg)*

Hafemann, Adolph and Emily (Firella Creek Farm B&B)   ☎ (519) 656-2974
Box 99, RR2, Wellesley, ON   N0B 2T0

Take Hwy 401 to Kitchener and then Hwy 7/8 West. Turn right onto Rd 5 (just past Baden) and
continue to Wellesley. Turn left onto Queen St W. At the end turn right and proceed 1 km to farm.

$35S $50-55D $5Child   ⦿ Meals   ▶ 6A,2Ch and baby
💳Full 🏠98-acre farm,2-storey,view,patio,quiet ■3(upper &
main floor) ᾲGerman ⊨2T,1D,1Q,1P,crib ⊒1Sh.w.g.,1ensuite,
1private ★Air,TV,F, parking ⓌNo smoking, no pets
🕇 Trout pond, nature trails, wooded areas, stream, meadows and
wildlife, cross-country skiing and hiking on farm grounds
🚗 Local Cider Mill, Wellesley Apple Butter & Cheese Festival
Stratford theatres, St.Jacobs farmers' market
🐾 New comfortable house is equipped with climate control and located in the heart of Mennonite
farming country. Relax by the cheery fire with a hot apple cider. Hosts cater to special dietary
needs. Tour guiding available. Children welcome.✓B&B

Martin, John & Kathleen (Katies B&B & Books)   ☎ (519) 656-3498
78 Molesworth St South, Wellesley, ON   N0B 2T0

From Hwy 401 proceed to Hwy 7/8 west. turn right onto Rd5 entering Wellesley. Turn right on
Doering St, then left on Molesworth Street.
$60S $75D   ⦿ Meals   ▶ 2
💳 Full   🏠 Res., village, riverfront, patio, quiet ■ 1D(upstairs) ⊨ 1D ⊒ Ensuite
★LF,woodstove, separate entrance, off-street & street parking   Ⓦ No smoking, no pets, not
suitable for children ᾲ Pa Dutch
🕇 Downtown, shopping, park with dam, Apple Butter & Cheese Festival
🚗 Castle Kilbridge & Mennonite Relief Sale, largest Water Wheel, Stratford, popular Anna Mae's
restaurant, St. Jacobs farmers' market, Waterloo Universities
🐾 Warm welcome and friendly Christian hospitality in book lovers home. Hosts have collected
thousands of books and invite guest to enjoy them. Guest room can be converted to a fully equipped
Bachelor Apt on request for long term occupancy. There is a cat in residence. ✓B&B

Wellington

(south of Trenton; see also Consecon, Bloomfield, Picton, Milford)

Gander, Jeremy & Carol (The Ganders Bed & Breakfast)   ☎ & Fax (613) 399-1987
22 Beach St., Box 175, Wellington, ON K0K 3L0   E-mail: jcgander@connect.reach.net

Phone for directions.
$45S $65-80D $20Add.person   ►7
🍽 Full   🏠 Village, 2-storey, view from guest rooms, lake at
back, patio, porch, quiet   ■ 3 (upstairs)   ⊨ 3Q,1R
🚪2Ensuite,1Private(jacuzzi),1sh.w.g.   ★ Air,F,LF,private
entrance, off-street parking, small guest fridge, TV in library
🚭No smoking, designated smoking area, children min. age 6
🕴 Private beach on Lake Ontario, charter fishing, antiques/crafts
🚗 Sandbanks & Presqu'isle Prov. Parks and beaches, scenic drives, cycle route, x/c-skiing
🔫 Home is a reproduction of a traditional 19th Century country house, situated on .5 acre
waterfront with large gardens and located near the Loyalist Parkway. Hosts are retired
Professionals and invite guests to relax in the country atmosphere. Breakfast is served in the dining
room overlooking Lake Ontario. Ideal for cozy winter weekend getaways. There is a
Springer/Spaniel dog in residence. Visa ✔CC

Haeberlin, Elaine & Richard (Tara Hall Bed & Breakfast)   ☎ (613) 399-2801
Box 623, 146 Main Street, Wellington, ON K0K 3L0   Fax (613) 399-1104

From Hwy 401, take Wooler Rd (Exit 522) & Hwy 33 (Loyalist
Pkwy) south to Wellington.
$45-55S $62-72D   ►7A,3C
🍽 Choice   🏠 Village, hist., view, lakefront, patio, deck, quiet,
parking   ■1S,2D,1F(upst)   ⊨2T,1K,2Q,1R   🚪3Sh.w.g.
★Air,7F,LF,KF, TV in common & most guest room, jacuzzi
🚭No smoking indoors
🚗 Sandbanks Provincial Park, Lake on the Mountain, Picton
🕴 Lake Ontario sandy beach, fishing, boat launch, golfing, antiques/crafts, hist.sites, restaurants
🔫 Spacious, c1839 historically designated, majestic home. Rooms have luxury decor & fireplaces
& overlook Lake Ontario and West Lake. Hot breakfast served in formal dining room.Visa ✔B&B

Waterfall, Jean & Jim (Bridies Bed & Breakfast)   ☎ (613) 399-2376
307 Main St., Wellington, ON K0K 3L0

From Hwy 401E take Exit 522 (Wooler Rd) and proceed south on Hwy 33 into the village.

$45S $55D $15Add.person   ►8A,4Ch
🍽 Full   🏠 Village, res., 2-storey, hist., view from guest rooms,
lake at back ■2D,1F(upstairs)   ⊨3D,2R,1P,crib 🚪1Sh.w.g.,
1sh.w.h.   ★ TV, street parking   🚭 No smoking, no pets
🕴 Tea Room, numerous antique and craft shops, artisans and
historic museum, beach on Lake Ontario
🚗 Provincial Parks, Sandbanks, North Beach, pottery studios
🔫 Beautiful 1860-built house, once the village Doctors home,
situated in picturesque Lake Ontario village. Stroll down to the waterfront, sit on a bench or rock
and enjoy the breathtaking scenery. Hosts display precious Royalty plates and other collactables and
visitors may enjoy the model trains. Visa ✔B&B

Whittaker, Pat & Roger (Rose & Thistle Bed & Breakfast) ☎ (613) 399-1413
Box 615, 306 Noxon Ave, Wellington, ON K0K 3L0

From Hwy 401, take Exit 522 (Wooler Rd) and follow Hwy 33 to Wellington. Turn north off Main

St. at West St and proceed 1 block.
$45S $50-65D $15Add.person ▶ 6
🍳 Full, homebaked 🏠 Village, older, 3-storey, quiet, veranda
■3D(upst) ⊨2T,1D,1Q,1R ⟲1Sh.w.g.,1ensuite ★Air,TV,
upstairs library/den for guests, compl.bicycles & locked storage
🚭No smoking
🕴 Lake Ontario, beach and lakefront parks, craft & gift shops,
fishing, boating, cycling, antiques, museum, x/c skiing, hiking
🚐 Sandbanks & North Beach Provincial Parks, Bloomfield, Picton, cheese factory
🐾 Renovated and restored Queen Anne-style home with spacious guest rooms complete with
mini-libraries. Situated in the heart of the village two blocks from Lake Ontario, which offers an
everchanging scenery. Enjoy the breeze from the lake on the wrap-around veranda. Cycling tours
can be arranged. Two cats are unobtrusive co-hosts. Visa

Westport
(north of Gananoque; see also Newboro, Athens)

Bradley, Anne & Robert (A Bit of Gingerbread B&B) ☎ (613) 273-7848
27 Bedford St., Box 183, Westport, ON K0G 1X0

From Hwy 401 at Kingston, take Exit 617 and then Rte 10 north.
Located in the village.
$35S $45-65D $15Add.person ▶ 6A,1Ch
🍳Full 🏠Village,hist.,2-storey,quiet ■3D(upst) ⊨4T,1Q,1R
⟲1Sh.w.g.,1ensuite ★TV,library, separate guests quarters &
entrance, off-street parking 🚭No smoking, no pets
🕴 Rideau District Museum, historic village walking tour, harbour
& island picnic site on Rideau Waterway with marina, Rideau Trail, Foley Mt. Conservation Area,
Spy Rock Lookout, beach at Sand Lake, boutiques, antique shops, restaurants
🚐 Five Locks on Rideau Canal & historic Jones Falls Dam, hiking, cycling, canoeing
🐾 Century home in picturesque village. Ideal place for exploring the Rideau Lakes area.
Transportation to trails and excursions to places of interest or dining can be provided. Visa,MC
↙B&B

Cowan, Terry and Mary (The Cove Country Inn) ☎ (613) 273-3636
General Delivery, Westport, ON K0G 1X0

From Hwy 401, take Exit 617 (Hwy 10) north to Westport. Look for Inn on the corner of Main and

Bedford St on the water.
$50-120D(Summer) $40-95(Winter) 🍽 Meals ▶ 12
🍳 Full 🏠 Village, hist., view, lakefront, patio, quiet ■ 6D
⊨6T,3D,R ⟲ 4Ensuite, private ★ Air,LF,2F, ceiling fans in
guest rooms, hot tub and sauna, 4-jacuzzi seater, parking separate
entrance ♥ 🚭Restricted smoking
🕴 Boating, swimming, fishing, dining, entertaiment,
windsurfing,fish sanctuary, skating, sleigh rides, x-country skiing
🚐 Rideau Lake Locks, Old Fort Henry, historic Perth, Kingston
🐾 Antique and historic setting in popular vacation village. Cross-country ski packages, boat
cruises and bicycle tours can be arranged. ↙B&B

Fielding, Eleanor (Fielding House B&B) ☎ (613) 273-2661
16 Church St., Westport, ON K0G 1X0

Phone for directions.
$40S $55-85D $12Child $25Add.person 🍽Meals ▶ 8A,1Ch
🍲 Full, homebaked 🏠 Downtown, 3-storey, hist., porch 🛏4D
(upstairs) 🛏 2D,3Q,1R 🛁 1Sh.w.g.,2ensuite powder room
★ KF,TV, sep. guest quarters, off-street parking ♿ Designated
smoking area
🕴 Fine boutiques, good restaurants, museum
🚗 Golf courses, Foley Mountain Conservation Area, look-out

☛ Victorian elegance in charming Century house filled with collectibles and antiques. An array of life-size dolls are perched in odd corners, one dressed as a maid stands at the front door to welcome guests. Relax in the upstairs library, visit the hostess in her pottery studio. ✍B&B

Roach, Brian & Elaine (Spring Street Bed & Breakfast) ☎ (613) 273-5427
6 Spring Street, Westport, ON K0G 1X0 Fax (613) 273-4430

Located in the village centre, 1/2 block away from the dock.
$45S $55D (plus tax) ▶ 5
🍲 Full 🏠 Village centre, 2-storey, hist., acreage, view
🛏1S,2D (upstairs) 🛏 1S,1Q,1K 🛁 Sh.w.g. ★ F,TV in
guest living room, separate entrance, off-street parking ♿ No
smoking, children min. age 12
🕴 Marina on Rideau System, shops, boutiques, Foley Mountain
Lookout and hiking trails, Art Festival, antique show
🚗 Historic Kingston, Old Fort Henry, Olympic Harbour

☛ Charming 100 year-old house that has been lovingly maintained and nostalgically decorated. Host, a retired Golf Pro, serves gourmet breakfast. Visit the attached "Golf Emporium". Join the hosts for a glass of wine by the fireplace. There is a cat and a small dog in hosts' quarters only. Golf packages available. Visa,MC,Interac ✍B&B

Rothwell, Kathy & Margot (The Rothwells' Stone Cottage B&B) ☎ (613) 273-3081
Box 368, Westport, ON K0G 1X0

From Hwy 401 take Westport Exit & proceed on Hwy 10 to village
$55-85S/D $105F 🍽Meals ▶ 8A,2Ch
🍲 Full 🏠 Village, hist.,acreage, 2-storey, view, lakefront, oval
in-ground pool, patio, porch, quiet 🛏4(main & upper floor)
🛏4T,2D,2cots 🛁2Sh.w.g.,1ensuite ★Air,2F,LF,KF,TV in one
guest room, separate entrance ♿Designated smoking area
🕴 Hiking & x-c ski trails on lake & Foley Mountain, lake skating
🚗 Perth, Smith Falls, Kingston, Merrickville

☛ Historic home, decorated in an elegant style that befits its heritage and furnished with family heirlooms. Guests are welcome to sit on the screened veranda or on the tree-shaded patio overlooking the Upper Rideau Lake. Canoe available for lake exploration. Breakfast is served on the veranda in the summer. All inclusive weekends can be arranged for small groups. MC ✍CC

Whitby

(east of Toronto)

Stapleford, Ann & Alex Gillies (St.John's Inn B&B)　☎ (905) 666-4514
508 John St.W., Whitby, ON　L1N 2V6

Exit Hwy 401 at Hwy 12 (Brock St) and proceed to John St. Turn left and continue to Palace St.

Look for house on corner with 8ft hedge & entrance on Palace St.
$55-65S/D　$65Suite　▶ 5-7
✖ Spring-Fall　🍳 Full, homebaked　🏠 Downtown, res., hist.,
converted church, decks, quiet, isolated　■ 1S,2D (main & upper
level)　🛏 2S,1D,1Q,1R　🛁 1Sh.w.h., 1ensuite　★F,TV in one
guest room & in large upper level rec room, parking　🚭No pets
🐦 Lake Ontario, Whitby Hbr, downtown, restaurants, Pearson
Lanes shopping, Pickering Flea Market (Sundays), golfing
🚗 Cullen Gardens & Miniature Village, Yacht Club, Toronto Commuter Train, two ski areas
☛ Unique home (ca 1902), with 32 ft ceilings, stained glass windows and furnished with many
antiques, served as the Catholic Church until 1959. Enjoy the friendly casual atmosphere and relax
among extensive grounds. Hosts are well travelled and knowledgeable of Whitby's historic past.
There are two well-trained resident dogs who love children.

Wood, Mary & Ted (Ezra Annes House 1836)　☎ & Fax (905) 430-1653,1-800-213-1257
239 Wellington St., Whitby, ON　L1N 5L7

From Hwy 401 exit at Brock St/Hwy 12 and go north to Burns. Turn left to Annes St. Turn right
and continue north over Dundas/Hwy2 to Gifford. Turn left to Wellington and then right.

$75S　$85D　▶ 4
🍳Full, homebaked　🏠Downtown, res., 2-storey, hist., view from
guest rooms, stone terraces, quiet　■2D(upstairs)　🛏1D,1Q
🛁2Ensuite　★ Air,TV,F,LF, sauna room, off-street
parking　🚭No smoking, not suitable for children　〰some French
🐦 Lake Ontario shores, ravine and park
🚗 Cullen Gardens, Go-Train/bus to Toronto, Bird sanctuaries
☛ 1836-built home is filled with antiques, books and the grace
of a bygone era. The English perennial garden has stone terraces, a water garden and rose arbour.
Host is a Mystery Writer. Enjoy the elegant hideaway with gourmet breakfasts, afternoon tea on
the terrace, good conversation, and gracious, friendly atmosphere. Visa ✒F0BBA

Wiarton

(north of Owen Sound; see also Red Bay, Hope Bay, Lion's Head)

Christensen, Jorn and Elsie (Bruce Gables)　☎ (519) 534-0429/Fax (519) 534-0779
410 Berford St., Box 448, Wiarton, ON　N0H 2T0

Hwy 6 passes through Wiarton and is known as Berford Street. Located at the northwest corner of
Berford and Mary Streets. Parking off Mary Street.

$45S　$55D　$5Child　$10Add.person　▶ 9
✖ May-Oct　🍳 Full　🏠 Village, view　■ 3(upstairs)
🛏1D,2Q, cot　🛁1Sh.w.h.,1sh.w.g.　★F,TV,parking (off Mary
St)　🚭 No smoking　〰 French, German, Spanish, Danish
🐦 Bruce Trail, swimming in Colpoy's Bay, sailing, fishing, golfing,
restaurants, village centre
🚗 Bruce Peninsula National Park, Tobermory Island Ferry
☛ Spacious, turn-of-the-Century Victorian home restored to its Victorian splendour with bay
windows overlooking Wiarton and the clear blue waters of Colpoy's Bay, decorated with momentos
of hosts' stay in Switzerland and world travels. Enjoy the European atmosphere. ✒B&B

Cox, Gord & Ellie (Down A Country Lane B&B)
RR3, Wiarton, ON N0H 2T0

☎ (519) 534-3170
E-mail: gefcox@bms.com

Located in Oliphant. From Owen Sound, take Hwy 70 north to Hepworth and continue west to
Sauble Beach. Proceed on Bruce County Rd 13 north to Oliphant. Turn right to 5th house on right.
$45-55S $50-60D $10Child $10Add.person 🍽 Meals (weekly rates avail) ► 4A,3Ch

🍴 Full, homebaked 🏠 Rural, split-level, acreage, lakeview,
porch, quiet ■ 2F(upper level) ⊨ 2Q,1P,1R 🛏 1Ensuite,
1sh.w.h. ★ F,TV & ceiling fan in guest lounge, sep.entrance,
campfire area & barbeque 🖐No smoking, no pets
🏃 Walks through lawns with rose beds, country lane leading to
small barn, stroll around small lake across the road
🚗 Lake Huron shoreline, Sauble Beach, Wiarton, Bruce
Peninsula highlights. x-c skiing
🐾 Warm welcome in picturesque country home situated in very quiet, peaceful surroundings.
Relax on the covered wrap-around porch and enjoy the lovely view of Spry Lake and the beautiful
sunsets. Weekends only Sept-June. Also newly-renovated cabin available.

Cumming, Mary (Shoreline B&B)
RR1, Eastnor Twsp, Pike Bay, Mar, ON N0H 1X0

☎ (519) 793-4197

From Wiarton take Hwy 6 north to Pike Bay Rd. Turn left 6.6km to corner store. Turn left, then
right at 1st road to 2nd house on left.

$40S $50D $5Child $60F $15Add.person ► 8A,2Ch
📅July-Aug(other weekends only) 🍴Full, homebaked 🏠Rural,
2-storey, acreage, lakefront, patio, porch,deck, quiet ■3D,1F,1Ste
(upstairs) ⊨1S,1D,3Q,1P,2cots 🛏1Private,1sh.w.g.,1sh.w.h.
★Air,F,TV,KF, canoe & bicycles for guests 🖐Designated
smoking area, children min. age 5, small outside dog pen available
🏃 Lake Huron, canoeing, fishing, biking, nature walks, x-c skiing,
birdwatching, snowmobile trails
🚗 Sauble Beach, Bruce Peninsula Nat.Park, Tobermory (ferry to Manitoulin Isle), Bruce Trail
🐾 Spacious, comfortable home with large veranda and deck, located on 2.5 acres waterfront on
quiet cove off Pike Bay, overlooking Lake Huron. Ideal place for nature lovers to enjoy the rustic
beauty of the Bruce Peninsula. Breakfast is served in special guest breakfast room. Hostess loves
gardening and "lazy dog Jessica loves watching". ✍B&B

Last, Victor (Hillcrest B&B)
394 Gould St., Wiarton, ON N0H 2T0

☎ & Fax (519) 534-2262

Enter Wiarton from south and descend the hill. Turn left at Mary St. Located at 1st intersection

with Gould St (south-west corner)
$40S $50D (Children's rates available) ► 4
🍴Full 🏠Rural, village, hist. ■2D,F(upst) ⊨T,D
🛏1Sh.w.g. ★F, wrap-around veranda 🖐No pets, no
smoking 🗣French, some German
🏃 Bruce Trail, Niagara Escarpment, Colpoy's Bay, Bluewater
Park, Wiarton village center, restaurants, Bruce's Cave, Oxenden
🚗 Oliphant (sandy beach), warm shallow water
🐾 Spacious and comfortable, former (1880's) timber baron's house - a good base for interested
naturalists and travellers who would like to explore the many attractions in this part of the
Peninsula. Host is well informed about the area's history, geography and is active with nature
photography and field naturalist groups. ✍B&B

ONTARIO 311

Paquin, Doloris (The Green Door Bed & Breakfast)   ☎ (519) 534-4710
Box 335, 376 Berford, Hwy 6, Wiarton, ON   N0H 2T0

Travel on Hwy 6 through Wiarton (Berford St). Located 1/2 block north of Elm St on west side.

$45S $65D   ► 8
🔲 Full, homebaked   🏠 Downtown, village, historic, 3-storey,
view, patio   ■ 4D (upstairs)   ⊨ 2D,1Q,2T   ⏚ 1Ensuite,
1sh.w.g.   ★Separate entrance, parking   ⓦ No smoking
🏃 Antique shops, restaurants, park at Colpoy Bay (swimming,
walks), Bruce Trail hiking, hospital
🚐 Lark Whistle, the Caves, The Herb House, pottery shops
🚌 Red brick turn-of-the-Century home, restored to its original
Victorian splendor and tastefully decorated with antiques. Lounge in the spacious living room or sit
outside and enjoy the maple shaded deck and barbeque facilities. There is a resident dog.

Peer, Rosemary & Evelyn (Rosecliffe B&B)   ☎ (519) 534-2776
502435 Island View Dr., RR2, GMB5, Wiarton, ON   N0H 2T0   E-mail: roserep@bmts.com

Located 10km east of Wiarton on Frank St (Island View Dr.) across from Wiarton Golf Course.

$45S $55-60D $20Add.person   🍴 Meals   ► 8
🔲 Full   🏠 Rural, ranch-style, view from guest rooms, acreage,
lakefront, patio, quiet   ■ 1S,1D,1F (ground level)   ⊨ 2S,2D,2Q
⏚ 1sh.w.g., 1sh.w.h.   ★ TV,F in guest parlour   ⓦ Smoking
on outside patio, no pets, no children
🏃 Bruce Trail & Caves, cycle or stroll on scenic roads, swim or
beachcombe on private shore, visit potteries, antiques & artisan
studios/shops, Wiarton Blue Water Park & marina,
scenic lookouts at Skinners Bluff & Graham's Hill, seasonal stream/waterfall on property
🚐 Fathom Five Underwater Nat Park, Tobermory & Chi-Cheemaun ferry to Manitoulin Island
🚌 Spacious waterfront home nestled in a quiet woodland escarpment setting with a spectacular
view over Colpoy's Bay to Whitecloud Island. Simple, hearty country fare served outdoors on the
ledge-rock stone patio. Packed lunches available upon prior request. Mother & daughter host team
enjoy meeting international guests as well as folks with rural roots. Ideal place for hikers, cyclists
and naturalists. Gift Certificates available. Ideal place for hikers/small groups. ✍B&B

Veerman, Joanne (Long Lane B&B)   ☎ & Fax (519) 534-3901
RR2, Wiarton, ON   N0H 2T0

From Hwy 6 in Wiarton, turn east onto Frank St for 4.5 km. Turn right at Oxenden and proceed 7

km to "T". Turn left for 2 km and right to 2nd farm.
$35S $45-50D   🍴 Meals & picnic lunches   ► 6A,2Ch
🔲Full,homebaked   🏠Farm,older,deck,porch,quiet   ■1S,2D,1F
(upstairs)   ⊨2T,2D,1Q   ⏚ 1Sh.w.g., 1sh.w.h.   ⌐Dutch
★TV,Elmira wood stove   ⓦSmoking outside only
🏃 Bruce Trail hiking (Skinner's Bluff), bird watching, star gazing,
x/c-skiing, walking/cycling on country roads, Bruce Caves
🚐 Bruce Peninsula, Tobermory, Keppel Croft & Gardens
🚌 Lovely Century home "tranquility at roads end" surrounded by 104 beautiful acres, far from
any traffic or noise and easy to find. An ideal place for artists, hikers, birders and naturalists. Enjoy
the warm hospitality in the large farm kitchen, relax on the porch with morning coffee. Gift
Certificates available.There is an outside dog. Vegetarian fare available. ✍B&B

Vickers, Sally & Leighton
Box 298, RR4, Wiarton, ON   N0H 2T0

☎ (519) 534-3504
E-mail: sally-leight@log.on.ca

Located 7km north of Wiarton on Hwy 6 (on right side).
$35-40S $50-60D $10Child   🍽 Meals   ► 8A,2Ch
📺 Full   🏠 Rural, acreage, patio, quiet   ■ 2D,1F (upstairs &
ground level)   ⊨3D,1K,2cots   ⊇2Ensuite,1private   ★ TV,F,LF,
KF,guest lounge, parking   ⓦ No smoking
🏃 Walking & x-c ski trails on 50 acres of cedar bush at door
🚗 Tobermory ferry dock, swimming, boating, fishing, Bruce Trail
🐾 Large country home.Enjoy a visit or relax in upstairs sitting area. Dog oustide. ✒B&B

Williamstown   *(n/e of Cornwall; see also Lancaster, Apple H, Alexandria, St.Andrews W.)*

Caron, Mary & Michael (Caron House 1837)
Box 143, Williamstown, ON   K0C 2J0

☎ (613) 347-7338

From Hwy 401, take Exit 814 north to Lancaster Village and west on Pine St. Go 7 km (and 2
centuries) through Williamstown to four corners, turn left and continue over bridge, then left again
to 3rd house across from St. Mary's Church. Look for sign

$40S $50D   🍽 Meals   (Reservations recommended)   ► 4A
📺 Full (Gourmet)   🏠 Village, hist., acreage, veranda, patio,
gazebo, Victorian & herbal gardens, quiet   ■2D(upstairs)
⊨2D   ⊇ 1Sh.w.g.   ★ 3F,TV, parking, separate entrance,
parking   ⓦNo smoking, no pets   〰 French
🏃 Tennis court, village with historic sites, ideal for cycling
🚗 St.Raphael's Ruins (1821), Coopers Marsh, Upper Canada
Village, Montreal, Ottawa

🐾 Historic brick home with charming blend of the unpretentious and the sophisticated, offering
old-fashioned elegance, antiques, bright chintzes, candlelight gourmet breakfasts and
turn-of-the-Century hospitality in the finest tradition of a small elegant country inn. Weather
permitting, guests may dine alfresco in the gazebo or on the brick patio. Enitre upper floor for
guests only. ✒B&B

Wert, Wendy & Les (Capricorn Capers Bed & Breakfast)
5480 County Rd 19, RR2, Williamstown, ON   K0C 2J0

☎ (613) 347-3098
Fax (613) 347-1112

From Hwy 401, take Exit 814, turn left on Hwy 34 to Pine St (3rd after rail tracks). Turn left on
Pine (County Rd 17) for 7 km to village of Williamstown. Turn right on County Rd 19 (towards St.
Raphael), to 2nd house on left after leaving village.

$35S $60D   ► 6
🗓May-Oct   📺Full, homebaked   🏠Rural, res.   ■2D(upstairs),
1Ste (main level)   ⊨2T,1K,1Q, crib   ⊇ 3ensuite   ★F,TV in
study, separate entrance, parking, wheel-chair access   ⓦNo pets,
no smoking
🏃 Historic village of Williamstown, nature trails in sugar bush &
meadowlands, hiking, x-c skiing, cycling
🚗 Upper Canada Village, golfing, Cooper Marsh Visitor Centre,
fishing in St.Lawrence River, Cornwall, Ottawa, Montreal
🐾 A Glengarry welcome in comfortable stone-brick home with beautiful gardens and nestled in
the hardwoods of Eastern Ontario. A delightful spot for nature lovers & bird watchers. Families,
seniors, honeymooners welcome. There is a dog in residence.✒B&B

Winchester

(south-east of Ottawa; see also Mountain, Brinston)

Wall, Richard & Gillian (Sarah's House B&B)   ☎ (613) 774-0089
490 Caleb St., Box 928, Winchester, ON   K0C 2K0

Phone for directions.
$35S $55D $80F   ►4
🍳 Full   🏠 Downtown, res., hist.   ■ 2(upstairs) ⊨ 2S,1Q,1R
🛁Sh.w.g.   ★ TV,separate entrance, parking   Ⓦ No pets, designated
smoking area, children min. age 6   ⌇ French
🚗 Restaurants, Morrisburg, Upper Canada Village, Capital City of Ottawa
📷 Beautiful 1897 Victorian House with steep gables, built in the Queen
Ann style by a local lumber company as a show house. Enjoy the impressive
woodwork, tin ceilings, decorative hardwood floors and stained glass. There
are 2 cats in residence. Small babies welcome.

Windermere

(s/w of Huntsville; see also Pt Carling, Pt Sydney)

Dutton, Barbara & John (Top House Retreat B&B)   ☎ (705) 769-3338
Box 134, Windermere, ON   P0B 1P0   E-mail: tophouse@muskoka.com

From Bracebridge, take Muskoka Rd 4 to Windermere. Turn left at Longhurst Rd to 1st on left.
$50S $55-60D $10Child/$10Add.person   (over age 5)   🍴 Meals   ►7A,1Ch

🍳 Full, homebaked   🏠 Rural, village, 2-storey, older, 31 acres,
view from guest rooms, porch, quiet   ■ 3D,1F (upstairs)
⊨3Q,1P,crib   🛁 2Sh.w.g.   ★ F,TV,LF, off-street parking
Ⓦ Designated smoking area, no pets
🏃 Groomed walking trail on property (a Muskoka Heritage
Stewardship wood lot), tennis, golfing, public beach with rental
facilities, x-c skiing from door, snowmobile trails
🚗 Scenic roads, villages, beaches of Muskoka Resort region,
📷 3rd Generation Muskoka family home in park-like setting overlooking Lake Rosseau. "A house
that likes guests". Relax in the tranquil atmosphere and enjoy the great lookout view from the
covered porch. Hosts are world travellers and well informed about the local history & attractions
and will give guided tours & nature walks through the property. A naturalist's paradise. There is a
cat and a hedgehog. Visa ⌇B&B

Rowntree, Ruth & Gid (Rowntree Cottage)   ☎ (705) 769-3640/off season:(416) 231-6631
RR2, Utterson, ON   P0B 1M0   E-mail: rowntree@muskoka.com

Location: 1182 Dawson Rd. in Windermere, Muskoka. From Hwy 118 West, take Muskoka Rd 25
for 8.5 km to Dawson Rd. Or from Muskoka Rd 4 west, take Rd 25 for 1.2 km to Dawson Rd, 1km to

B&B. Seasonal address: 11 Herne Hill, Etobicoke, On M9A 2W9
$40S $70D $30Add.person   ►9
🗓Late Spring-Thanksgiving   🍳 Full   🏠 Rural, village, hist.,
acreage, view, lakefront, boat dock, quiet, screened/glass porch
■ 1D,2F(upstairs)   ⊨ 3D,3S   🛁 Sh.w.g., wash vanities in all
rooms   ★Air(in guest rooms), F,TV,video, free paddle boat/canoe
& horse-shoe pitch Ⓦ No pets,restr.smoking,child min.age 8
🏃 Lake Rosseau sandy beach swimming (1000 ft wooded
shoreline), free docking for boat (no jets),(bring windsurfer/bicycle), scenic nature walks
🚗 Resort area, golfing, tennis, gift shops, restaurants, Summer Theatre, boat/craft tours
📷 Charming, restored Century Victorian home, antique filled, Muskoka Cottage with stone
fireplace; situated on sparkling Lake Rosseau, has been in host's family for over 70 years, (the
original ice house, chicken house and stone root house are still on the property), and surrounded by
beautiful scenery and quiet elegance. Relax on the screened (glassed-in) porch overlooking the lake.
Hosts have completed their first decade of B&B hosting. A "Destination B&B"! Visa ⌇B&B

Windsor
(south western Ontario; see also Amherstburg, Kingsville, Leamington, Comber)

Diotte, Jeanne (Diotte B&B) ☎ (519) 256-3937
427 Elm Ave., Windsor, ON   N9A 5H2

Phone for directions.
$50S $60D $15Child   ► 6
💷 Full   🏠 Downtown, res., 2-storey, older, porch, quiet   ■3
(main & upper level)   ⊢ 2T,1D,1Q,cot   ⌐1Sh.w.g.
★ Air,KF, ceiling fans, separate entrance, parking in rear, guest
quarters are separate   ⓦ Smoking on porch, no pets   ⋙ some
French
🏃 Casino, University of Windsor, downtown, shopping, theatres,
restaurants, walking trail along Detroit River, bus route
🚗 Queen Elizabeth Gardens, Art-in-the-Park (June), Windsor Raceway, US borders
🎺 Warm welcome in cosy home with antiques and quality wholesome ambiance. There is a dog in
residence. Visa ✓ B&B

Wolfe Island
(south of Kingston; see also Amherst Island)

Caldwell, Beth & Greg (Queen Ann's Lace B&B) ☎ (613) 385-1710
73 South Shore Rd., RR1, Wolfe Island, ON   K0H 2Y0

From Kingston, take Wolfe Island ferry, then turn left to 12th Line. Turn right and follow road to
B&B. A Ferry also runs between Wolfe Island and Cape Vincent NY.
$70-90D $10Add.person   ► 7A
💷 Full   🏠 Rural, 2-storey, hist., acreage, view from guest rooms, river at back, porch, deck,
quiet   ■ 2D,1Ste(upstairs)   ⊢3D,1P   ⌐ 2Private, 2sh.w.g.   ★ F,TV in suite, guest rooms
are separate   ⓦ No smoking, no pets, not suitable for children
🏃 St.Lawrence River waterfront, St.Lawrence Seaway Ship Channel, restaurants, cycling on quiet
roads, scuba diving, fishing, hunting, bird watching
🚗 Kingston (with limestone architecture), boat tours, Queen's University, Royal Military College
🎺 Beautifully restored turn of the Century farmhouse, newly designed as a B&B and furnished
with antiques, surrounded by lovely pastoral scenery and magnificient view overlooking the
St.Lawrence River. Stroll along the adjacent waterfront property or relax on the cedar deck and
watch the passing ships. Gourmet breakfasts are served in the dining area or on the deck. Hosts are
avid gardeners and cyclists with extensive knowledge about the area. Visa,MC ✓ CC

Woodham
(west of Stratford; see also Centralia, Mitchell)

Miller, Earl & Marilyn (Country Haven Bed & Breakfast) ☎ (519) 229-6416,
RR1, Woodham, ON   N0K 2A0   Fax (519) 229-8606

From Hwy 401 at London, take Highbury Ave (Interchange 189) and travel north to Hwy 7. Turn
left and then right on Hwy 23. Proceed to Whalen, turn left onto paved Huron Rd 11 and 5 km
north to farm on right.

$40S $50D $5-8Child   🍽 Meals   ► 6
💷 Full, homebaked   🏠 Farm, 150 acres, view, quiet   ■3
(upstairs)   ⊢ 4D,cot   ⌐ 1ensuite,1sh.w.g.   ★ Air,TV,
parking   ⓦNo smoking
🏃 Stroll around farm grounds or through woods, x/c skiing
🚗 Stratford (Shakespeare Festival Theatres), Lake Huron &
Grand Bend (beach resort & summer theatre), London
🎺 Renovated Huron County farm house on working mixed crop/hog farm located in heart of
Ontario's prime farmland. Enjoy a nourishing breakfast in the warmth of the family dining room.
Floral crafts available. Ideal spot for families. ✓ B&B

Woodstock

Denton, Mrs. Joanne (The Dentons Bed & Breakfast)   ☎ (519) 539-8800
23 Summit Cr, RR7, Woodstock, ON   N4S 7W2

From Hwy 401, take Exit 232 and follow Hwy 59 through Woodstock. At north end of City, after crossing large bridge, take Pittock Park Rd on right and proceed to Summit Cr. Turn left.

$45S $50D   ► 2A,1small baby
🍳 Full, homebaked   🏠 Rural, 2-storey, acreage, view from guest rooms, porch, deck, quiet   ■1D(upstairs) ⊨1D ★Air,F,TV
🛁1Private   🚭 No smoking, no pets
🏃 Pittock Lake Conservation Area (fishing, sailing, canoeing, swimming, windsurfing)
🚗 Woodstock (historic sites, architectural splendour, Wood Show
📷 Large comfortable Colonial home surrounded by 2 acres of
mature evergreens, maples and willows. Relax on large front porch or back deck and enjoy the peaceful scenery or the fireplace in wintertime. Professional retired hosts have travelled extensively and enjoy the piano & classical music, gardening, crafts, hunting & fishing. "Sarah" the friendly yellow Lab. Retriever and "Amy" the timid cat are in residence. ✓B&B

Littlejohns, Ina & Harry (Heritage Guest House B&B)   ☎ (519) 456-8721
594766 Hwy 59 South, RR4, Woodstock, ON   N4S 7V8

From Hwy 401, take Exit 232 and Hwy 59 south for 0.5km. Look for sign and house on left.

$52S $63D   🍽 Meals   ► 4
🍳 Full, homebaked   🏠 Rural, res., bungalow, 0.3acres, quiet, secluded   ■2D (main floor)   ⊨1D,1Q   🛁1Ensuite,
1private   ★ Air,F,TV, separate entrance, off-street parking
🚭No smoking, no pets, children min. age 10
🏃 Public golf course, restaurants, specialty shops, artist's studio, candy making operation
🚗 Downtown Woodstock, Pittock Conservation Area, Trillium
Woods Prov.Park, Ingersoll, Paris, Stratford theatres, St.Jacobs, London, Lake Erie beaches
📷 Warm welcome in"1953 Cottage that has grown into an extended rural bungalow". Retired hosts in mediterranean-style home with comfortable antique country furnishings, enjoy welcoming B&B guests from worldwide. Relax in front of the fireplace in the large lounge/craft shop and breakfast area, which served until recently as a popular Tea Room. Watch the variety of birds in the secluded backyard from the bay-window area. Visa, ✓B&B

Wyevale

Lippert, Jane & Bob & Angela (A Wymbolwood Beach House B&B)
533 Tiny Beaches Rd South, RR1, Wyevale, ON   L0L 2T0   ☎ & Fax (705) 361-3649

$60S $70-75D $15Add.person   (special weekly rates available)   ► 10
From Barrie, take Hwy 27 north to Elmvale and continue north on County Rd 6 to Wyevale. Turn left at Con 5 to Tiny Beaches Rd. Turn right and look for sign.

🍳 Full, homebaked   🏠 Rural, split-level, hillside, view from guest rooms, patio, deck, secluded, lake across
■3D,1Ste,1F(main,upper and groung levels)   ⊨ 2T,1D,2Q,2R
🛁1sh.w.g., 1ensuite   ★ LF,F,TV in guest room, sauna, games room, off-street parking & indoor parking for RVs, turn of the Century piano in library-lounge, host quarters are separate
🚭Designated smoking area, no pets, inquire about children
🏃 Georgian Bay, sandy beaches, hiking trails, cycling, tennis, x-c skiing, snowmobiling
🚗 Midland, Penetanguishene, Wasaga Beach, Collingwood, historic sites, shopping, Casino-Rama
📷 Spacious home was recently designed and built by owner. A globetrotters retreat or a couples getaway paradise. Relax in the jacuzzi tub after a long day of travelling or sight seeing and enjoy the charm and easy living. Breakfast is served in special guest breakfast room. Phone and fax service available for the corporate traveller. There is a resident Bichon Frisé. Visa ✓B&B

Quebec

Gaspe →
Tourelle   ● Gaspe
          ●
                    →

                    Newport →
                           →
                    Paspebiac →
                    New Carlisle →
          Bic●   Bonaventure●

               Matapedia●

BaieSteCatherine●   ● Trois Pistoles

          ● Trois Pistoles
                         ●Cabano

Cap-à-l'Aigle ●
Pointe-au-Pic●   ●St-Andre-de-K.
               ●Kamouraska

          ●L'Islet sur Mer

Ile d'Orléans
Beauport ●   ●Beaumont
Quebec City●   ●Levis
Cap Rouge●

     Trois Riviere●
St-Severe●
Pointe-du-Lac ●
Louiseville●

●Mont-Tremblant
 ● Lac Superieur

          ●St.Adele   ●
          ●St-Anne-des-Lacs   St.Germaine
Prevost.●   ●Repentigny
ND-de-Sal●   ●   ●South Durham   ●Bishopton
●Wakef   ●St.Jerome   St-Hyacinthe   ●Cookshire
         Laval● Montreal
●Quyon ●   ●Montebello
Pontiac● ●Aylmer ●Hull   ●North Hatley
adysmith●
     ●Hudson
     ●St-Lazare   Sutton●
Papineauville

Tourisme Québec   toll-free 1-800-363-7777
CP 20000, Québec, QC G1K 7X2

*As of June 1988 telephone numbers for locations around Montreal are scheduled to change from area
code 514 to 450.*

Aylmer

(near Ottawa ON; see also Hull, Pontiac, Wakefield, Quyon)

Bergeron, Guy & Denyse (Maison Bon Repos)   ☎ (819) 682-1498
37 Cedarvale, Aylmer, QC   J0X 2G0

In Ottawa cross any bridge north to Quebec and turn left on Hwy 148 west into downtown Aylmer. Proceed 5km, turn left on Rue Terry Fox and right on Cedarvale.
$40-45S $50-55D $10Child   ► 6A,1Ch
🍴 Full   🏠 Sub., riverfront, quiet   ■ 3D(main & upper floor)   ⊨ 2Q,1D   🛏 2Private, 1sh.w.h.   ★ LF,TV in guest room, ceiling fans, storage for guests' sports equipment   ♿ Designated smoking area, no pets, children min. age 7
🕴 Restaurant, Ottawa River
🚗 Ottawa, Parliament Hill, cycling path, ski hills

🐾 Warm welcome in comfortable mezzanine home. Enjoy the magnificient view of the Ottawa River and the tranquil natural surroundings. Delicious breakfast served in the dining room.✓B&B

Charron, Lise & Rhéal (L'Escapade B&B)   ☎ (819) 772-2388
912 Aylmer Rd., Aylmer, QC   J9H 5T8

Located app.15 min. from Ottawa/ON. On Hwy 417 West take Exit 123 (Island Park Dr.). Crossing Champlain Bridge, turn left on Aylmer Rd. and continue 2km.
$50-60S $60-70D $10Add.person   ► 4A,1Ch
🍴 Full, homebaked   🏠 Res., sub., view   ■ 3D(upstairs)   ⊨ 1D,2Q, cot   🛏 1Sh.w.g.   ★ Air,F, parking   ♿ No smoking, no pets, children min.age 7   ⌇ English (Household language is French)
🕴 Golfing, biking and x-c ski trails
🚗 Ottawa (Capital City), Hull, Gatineau Park
🐾 Elegant traditional home well situated on large treed lot, a short scenic drive away from Parliament Hill. Winner of Agricotours Award of Excellence (96/97). Hostess serves full breakfast in dining room or on the terrace overlooking a lovely garden. Enjoy an all-season peaceful hideaway. ✓B&B

Rodrigue, Rita (Gîte Enchanté B&B)   ☎ (819) 682) 0695
32 Lakeview, Aylmer, QC   J9H 2A1

Via Ottawa: From Queensway, exit Island Park Dr North. Proceed across Champlain Bridge. Turn left on Aylmer Rd (148). After 3rd light, left on Lakeview.
$60-70S $65-75D $10Child   ► 4A,2Ch
🍴 Cont.   🏠 Res., 2-storey, 1acre, patio   ■ 2D(upstairs)   ⊨ 2D,2P   🛏 1Sh.w.g., 1ensuite   ★ F, separate entrance, balcony in one guest room, off-street parking   ♿ No smoking, no pets   ⌇ English (household language is French)
🕴 Restaurants, store, golfing, Outaouris River, walking/bike paths, parks, beautiful lakeview drive
🚗 Marina and beach, art galleries, skiing, theatres, Ottawa/Hull
🐾 Peaceful artist's home adorned with works of art displayed throughout the house. Enjoy breakfast on the terrace surrounded by trees and gardens or in the dining room aglow with morning light and view of landscaped backyard. There is a Finch in residence. ✓B&B

Baie-Ste-Catherine

(north side of St.Laurence, east of Malbaie)

Savard, Anne-Marie & Real (Gîte Entre Mer et Monts)
476 Rte 138, Baie-St-Catherine, QC G0T 1A0
☎ (418) 237-4391
Fax (418) 237-4252

From Quebec City, take Rte 138 east toward LaMalbaie & bridge to Tadoussac. Then proceed 2.8km to No 476. From Tadoussac, drive 4km from ferry.
$35S $45D $15Child $20Add.person Meals ► 10
Full, homebaked Village, bungalow, view from guest rooms, river at front, patio, quiet
2D,3F(upper and lower level) 3S,5D 1Sh.w.g., 1sh.w.h. ★ F,2V,2private entrances, off-street parking No smoking, no pets English (household language is French
Walks along St.Laurence riverbanks and woods and forests, picnic areas, horse-back riding, snowmobiling, x-c skiing
La Malbaie, Baie-St-Catherine, beach, Sagawney Fjord, parks, biking trails, Pointe Nova Beluga whale observation and Interpretation Centre, Tadoussac
Hostess is the proud owner of the regional Agricotour du Quebec Hospitality Award Winner and offers Quebecois Cuisines (table d'hote d'Anne Marie). There is a dog, Visa,MC B&B

Beaumont

(east of Quebec City; see also Lewis)

Fournier, Michèle & Jean L'Heureux (Au Gré du Vent)
220 Chm. St-Roch, Beaumont, QC G0R 1C0
☎ (418) 838-9020,
Fax (418) 838-9074

Phone for directions.
$40-50S $55-65D $15Child/Add.person ► 6A,2Ch
closed Oct and April Homebaked Rural, 2-storey, hist., patio, quiet, secluded 2D,1F(upstairs) 3D,1R,crib
1sh.w.g., sinks in 2 rooms ★ F,TV in guest living room, wood burning stove, guest quarters are separate, off-street parking
No smoking,no pets English(household language is French)
Ferry, Old Quebec, Gross Ile (Irish Mem Nat Historic Site)
Warm and friendly hospitality in bicentenary traditional Quebec-style home with country decor and period furnishing. Snuggle up by the ancient fireplace or wood-burning stove. Breakfast is served in the dining room. There is a dog and a cat in residence. Visa B&B

Beauport

(east of Quebec City; see also Ilse d'Orleans)

Roussel, Raymonde & Joseph De Rijck (La Grand' Maison)
2153 Ave Royale, Beauport, QC G1C 1N9
☎ (418) 660-8039

From Quebec City, take Hwy 40 east towards St-Anne-de-Beaupré. Take Exit 322 (Blvd. des Chutes). Turn left at traffic light, left at Morel St and right on Royal Ave to house on left.

$50S $60D ► 6A
Full Village, 2-storey, hist., quiet, porch 3D(upstairs)
3D 2Sh.w.g. ★ Separate entrance, reading room & lounge, guest quarters are separate, off-street parking No smoking English, Dutch, German (household language is French)
Manoir & Montmorency Falls, antique shop on premises
Golfing, Isle d'Orleans, Quebec City, St.Anne de Beaupré Shrine, Mont Ste Anne Ski Resort
Bright and cheerful 200-year old farmhouse converted to B&B overlooking St.Lawrence River and located in historic area east of Quebec City. Relax on the covered porch and enjoy the tranquil surroundings. There is a cat in residence. Visa

Bic
(east of Rimouski; see also Trois Pistoles)

Parceaud, Judy (Aux Cormorans Bed & Breakfast) ☎ (418) 736-8113, Fax (418) 736-4216
Box 627 Pointe-Aux-Anglais, Bic, QC G0L 1B0

From Quebec City take Hwy 20 past Riviere du Loup, then Rte 132 past Bic to "Aux Cormorans"
Exit (right turn). At the theatre turn left and follow B&B signs to the point. Look for last house on
left at seashore.

$40-55S $55-75D $10Child/$10Add.person   ▶ 12
🍴 Full, homebaked   🏠 Rural, 2-storey, hist., view from guest
rooms, oceanfront, porch, quiet   ■4D,1F(upstairs) ⊨2T,5D,2R
2Sh.w.g.,1ensuite   ★ F, guest quarters are separate, off-street
parking   Ⓦ Smoking on porch, no pets   ～French
🏃 Walks along the beach from the calm of the Bay to the wild &
natural coastline of the St.Lawrence Estuary
🚗 Bic Golf Club, Bic Provincial Park, Metis Gardens, Bic Theatre
🐷 Sea-side home (ca 1896) with cottagy decor, overlooking Massacre Island and snuggling close
to the south shore of the St.Lawrence River in Bic Bay. Relax on the encircling verandas and
observe a continuous spectacle of sea birds following the eternal ebb and flow of tides. Hostess is a
native of Windsor, England and has spent many years in Northern Quebec. Visa,MC～B&B

Bishopton
(north of Sherbrooke; see also Cookshire)

Roy, Maude (Aux Tournesols B&B) ☎(819)-884-5450, Fax(819)884-5639,1-888-884-5450
92 Rte 255 South, Bishopton, QC J0B 1G0   E-mail: mauderoy@multi-medias.ca

$45S $60D $15Add.person   🍽 Meals   (plus tax)   ▶ 10A,4Ch
From Rte 112 (Bishopton) take Rte 255 south for 5.2km. From Rte
108 (Bury) take Rte 255 north for 11km.
🍴 Full, homebaked   🏠 Farm, 2-storey, older, patio, porch,
quiet   ■ 5D,incl.1Ste (upstairs)   ⊨ 2T,3D,1Q,1P,crib
2Sh.w.g.   ★ TV,LF,guest quarters are separate   Ⓦ Pets
outside   ～ French
🏃 Hunting, fishing, snowshoeing, x-c skiing, walking, biking,
maple sugar house on property
🚗 Golfing, beach, Mount Megantic Observatory, Art Gallery, museum, historic buildings
🐷 Active farm home in peaceful country setting next to a small stream. Hosts are commercial
dairy farmers. Enjoy the traditional sugar camp (in season) with sweet smells and springtime in
Quebec. Walk in the woods and sample freshly boiled syrup or visit the dairy barn and observe
milking operations. At the end of the day relax by a soothing wood fire. Visa,MC ～CC

Bonaventure
(south-shore Gaspé; see also New Carlisle, Paspebiac, Newport)

Hall, Helen (Bay View Manor/Manoir Bay View) ☎ (418) 752-2725, (418) 752-6718
395 Bona.E., Box 21, New Carlisle, QC G0C 1Z0

From Quebec City follow Rte 20 and Rte 132 south to Matapédia and then east to Gaspé Peninsula.
Located beside Fauvel Golf Course in Bonaventure East.
$25S $35D $5Child (under age 12) $10Add.person   ▶ 15A,5Ch
📅 April1-Nov30   🍴 Full, homebaked   🏠 Rural, 2-storey,
hist., view from guest rooms, oceanfront, deck, quiet   ■ 1D,5F
(main & upper level)   ⊨ 5T,5D,1R, crib   1Private,2sh.w.g.
★ TV, picnic tables, camping on grounds   Ⓦ Smoking outside,
no pets, ideal place for children of all ages   ～ French
🏃 Fauvel Golf Course, picnic grounds, quiet private beach, corner
store, crafts, birdwatching, Bonaventure East lighthouse
🚗 Acadian & United Empire Loyalist Museums, Perce Rock
🐷 Comfortable home, once served as a country store and rural post office. Listen to the sound of
the waves washing up on the shore, view the spectacular sunrises, watchful lighthouse beacon and
breathtaking sunsets over the water. Hostess is a retired teacher. ～B&B

Cabano

(east of Rivière-du-Loup)

Emond, Roger (Au Ranch du Soleil Levant)   ☎ (418) 854-2983
69 Rte 232 Est, Cabano, PQ   G0L 1E0

Phone for directions. Located 1.6km from Trans Canada Hwy.
$40S $50D $5Child $10Add.person   ► 10
🍞 Homebaked 🏠 Rural, ranch-style, lakefront, patio, porch,
quiet, secluded ■ 5D (ground level) ⊨2T,4D ⬜ 2Sh.w.g.
★ TV,LF, private entrance, guest quarters are separate, off-street
parking 🖐Designated smoking area ᴡᴡ English, Spanish
(household language is French)
🚙 Golfing, fishing, hunting, restaurants

🏃 Hist.Fort Ingall, fishing, beach, bicycle path "Petit Temis" (130km along Lake Temiscquata)
☛ Congenial hosts in recently built ranch-home with country-style decor, surrounded by woods
and trees and facing gorgious Temiscouata Lake. Relax and enjoy the tranquil atmosphere. There is
a dog and a cat in residence. Ideal place for a short visit or a vacation.

Cap-à-l'Aigle

(north side of St.L.River east of Québec City; see also Point au Pic)

Villeneuve, Claire   ☎ (418) 665-2288
215 Rue St-Raphael, Cap-à-l'Aigle, QC   G0T 1B0

Located on north side of St. Lawrence River. On road 138 at La Malbaie cross the bridge, turn right
and continue to village and to St.Raphael St on right side.
$30S $50D $15Child (over age 5)   ► 11
🍞 Full, homebaked 🏠 Village, hist., view, riverfront, quiet
■4D,1F(upstairs) ⊨ 2T,4D,1S ⬜ 2Sh.w.g.,1shower only
★TV,KF, separate entrance, parking ♥ ᴡᴡ English
(household language is French)
🏃 St. Lawrence River, beach, wharf and marina
🚙 La Malbaie/Manoir Richelieu/Baie Ste Catherine, Casino
☛ Warm welcome in comfortable home with quiet and relaxing surroundings including the oldest
thatched barn in Quebec (over 150 years). Hostess enjoys welcoming guests from worldwide. ⌐B&B

Cap Rouge

(south-west side of Quebec City)

Denis, Yvan (L'Hydrangée Bleue)   ☎ (418) 657-5609
1451 Rue du Golf, Cap Rouge, QC   G1Y 2T6

From Hwy 20 at Quebec, cross Pierre Laporte Bridge and exit chm St.Louis West. Turn left on chm
Louis Francoeur and proceed on ch. St.Foy to the river. Turn right on Rue St.Felix and continue to
rue du Golf.
$40S $50D $10Child $15Add.person   ► 4
🍞 Full 🏠 Res., 3-storey, patio, quiet ■2D(upstairs)
⊨2D ⬜1sh.w.g., 1sh.w.h. ★ TV,LF, ceiling fans, off-street &
street parking 🖐 No smoking, no pets ᴡᴡEnglish (household
language is French)
🏃 Golf course, marina, x-c ski trail, St.Lawrence River banks
🚙 Shopping Centre, Old Quebec, Montmorency Falls
☛ Teacher hosts in large modern home situated on a quiet street. Enjoy the warm and friendly
atmosphere. ⌐B&B

Cookshire
(east of Sherbrooke; see also Bishopton)

Thomas, Ross & Brenda (Odana Shamut Bed & Breakfast) ☎ & Fax (819) 875-3317
77 chemin French, RR1, Cookshire, QC   J0B 1M0

From Hwy 10 take new Hwy to Hwy 55 toward Thedford Mines. Turn off at East Angus and take
Rte 253 to Cookshire. Turn left at lights, then right on Rte 212 and proceed 10 km to Chemin

French, turn right, go 3km to river and to B&B on right.
$25S $40D $10Child (over age 10)   ► 4A,4Ch
🍴 Full, homebaked   🏠 Farm, hist., 3-storey, 350 acres,
mountain views, deck, quiet, isolated   ■ 4D (upstairs)
🛏2T,2D,1R,crib   ⚓ 1Sh.w.g., 2sh.w.h.   ★ LF,KF,TV in guest
living room, parking   🚭 No smoking   ⌇ French
🚶 Eaton River, sugar bush (brunch at the camp & help gather the
sap - in springtime), barn with dairy & beef herds, x-c skiing
🚗 Golfing, downhill skiing, US border, covered bridges, museums, Mt Megantic Observatory
📷 Century home with new addition on 5th Generation working dairy/beef farm, decorated
country-style, occupied by 3 Generations and located in the center of a managed deer yard. In winter
watch the deer from the dining window. Second floor designated entirely for guests. There are 2
school children in the family and dogs & cats outside. Children & guest-pets welcome.⌐B&B

Gaspé
(Gaspé region; see also Newport, Paspébiac, New Carlisle, Bonaventure)

Beriault, Helen & Denis (La Canadienne) ☎ & Fax (418) 368-3806
201 Mgr. Leblanc, CP 1321, Gaspé, QC   G0C 1R0

Take Rte 132 or 198 to Gaspé. Exit at Jacques-Cartier or Rue De La Reine St to Gaspé Cathedral

where Mgr Leblanc St. begins.
$45S $55D $10Child/Add.person   ► 10A,2Ch
🍴 Full   🏠 Downtown, res., raised bungalow, patio, quiet
■5   🛏 2S,5D,1K,1P   ⚓ 6Private   ★ KF,LF,TV,private
entrance, off-street and street parking   🚭 No smoking, no
pets   ⌇ English (household language is French)
🚶 Restaurants, museum, shopping center, train & bus terminals
🚗 Forillon Nat. Park, Percé Village, Bonaventure Island
📷 Warm welcome in modern home situated in the beautiful Gaspé area with many activities and
interesting sights. Breakfast is served in special guest breakfast room. Visa ⌐ CC

Fortin, Blanche (Gîte Baie Jolie) ☎ (418) 368-2149
270 Montée Wakeham, Rte 198West, Box 1413, Gaspé, PQ   G0C 1R0

Take Rt 132 East all the way to Gaspé. At the Gaspé Bridge keep going straight for 1 km along the
Bay (198 Rd) to house on right side.

$35-45S $45-55D $10Child/Add.person   ► 9
🏕 May to Nov15   🍴 Homebaked   🏠 Res., view, bungalow,
patio, quiet   ■ 4D(main and lower level)   🛏3D,1Q,1R,1P
⚓2Sh.w.g.   ★KF,TV in 2 guest rooms, parking   🚭 No pets,
rest.smoking   ⌇ some English (household language is French)
🚶 Cathedral Christ the King, Jacques Cartier Cross, Soldiers'
Memorial Monument, museum, golfing, salmon fishing
🚗 Parc Forillon, Percé Rock
📷 Warm and friendly Québec Hospitalité in comfortable home situated on the Bay of
Gaspe(aigue09r). Relax and enjoy a lovely view of water and mountains. Hosts have many years
experience in the tourist trade.Visa ⌐B&B

Hudson/Heights

(west of Montréal; see also St.Lazare)

Henshaw, Naomi and Fred (Riversmead)
245 Main Rd, RR1, Hudson (Como), QC J0P 1H0

☎ (514) 458-5053

Take Hwy 40 west from Montreal towards Ottawa and any Hudson Exit to Main Rd.

$55S $65-75D $100(for 4)   (long stay reductions)   ▶ 6A
🍽 Full (English)   🏠 Village, acreage, hist., view, lakefront, patio, swimming pool, quiet ■ 3D ⊨2T,2D ⊴ 2Sh.w.g.
★ 2F, bicycles for guests 🚭No smoking ⚬ French
🕴 Fine restaurants, swimming, golfing, tennis, bicycling, riding, x-c skiing, shops, riding, sailing, maple syruping
🐎 Historic Georgian brick home filled with family antiques and situated on large grounds with access to Lake of Two Mountains. Delicious breakfast is served either on screened porch or in the Victorian dining room.

Hull

(north of Ottawa, Ontario; see also Aylmer, Pontiac, Wakefield, Quyon)

Hagedorn, Jacqueline & Marcel (Au Gîte du Parc Bed & Breakfast)   ☎(819)777-7981
260 St.Rédempteur, Hull, QC J8X 2T1   E-mail: jm.hagedorn@sympatico.ca, Fax(819)771-1621

From Ottawa's Parliament Buildings, take Alexandria Bridge and continue on St.Laurent Blvd. Turn right on St.Rédempteur.
$40-50S $50-60D $10Add.person   ▶ 6A,1Ch
🍽 Full   🏠 Downtown, 2-storey, view, deck ■ 3D(main floor) ⊨
1D,2Q ⊴ 1Sh.w.g.   ★ Air,LF,TV in guests room, separate entrance, off-street parking 🚭Designated smoking area, no pets ⚬English, German (French is household language)
🕴 Museum of Civilization, Casino, War Museum, Canadian Mint, Palais des Congrès, Hull-Arena, Ecomuseum, park & cycle trail
🚌 Ottawa (National Arts Centre, Parliament Buildings, Byward Market, Aviation/Nature & Science museums, Rideau Canal (ice-skating, boat tours), Gatineau Park, Meech Lake
🐎 Comfortable, renovated 19th Century home owned and decorated by professional Photographer. Host will organize fishing trips on Quebec's many lakes. ✓B&B

Ile d'Orléans

(in St. Lawrence River, east of Québec City)

Bouffard, Mariette & Jean-Marc (Aux Capucines B&B)   ☎ (418) 829-3017
625 Ch Royal, St-Laurent, Ile d'Orléans, QC G0A 3Z0

From Quebec City, take Hwy 40 east to Ile d'Orléans Exit. Proceed over bridge and continue 12km to house on riverside.
$50S $60-65D $15Child $25Add.person   ▶ 6A,1Ch
🍽 Full   🏠 Rural, acreage, river-view from guest rooms, patio, riverfront, quiet, secluded ■ 1S,2D,1F(upstairs)
⊨1T,1D,1Q ⊴1Sh.w.g.   ★ F, entire 2nd floor for guests
🚭 No smoking, no pets, not suitable for children ⚬ English (household language is French
🕴 Fine dining in historic building, golfing with beautiful scenery of St-Laurence River, shore walking trails, tennis, kayaking,artisans/crafts 🚌 Quebec City
🐎 Retired couple in very large, beautiful Colonial home, with a view of the St.Laurence River and set back from the road among mature maple trees and Nasturtium (capucines) beds. Hosts are well travelled & enjoy exchanging stories with guests. Experience the beauty of Ile d'Orléans. ✓B&B

Dumesnil, Yolande & Claude (Le Mas de l'Isle Bed & Breakfast) ☎ & Fax (418) 829-1213
1155 Chemin Royal, St.Jean, Ile d'Orléans, QC G0A 3W0   E-mail: sorciere@total.net

From Quebec City, take Rte 138 east toward St-Anne-de-Beaupre and Ile d'Orléans Exit. Travel over bridge, at traffic light continue for 17.5 km and turn left at B&B sign. Look for house on right.

$55S $60D $20Child(under age12) $30Add.person   ► 9
🍳 Full   🏠 Rural, view from guest rooms, quiet, deck   ■2D,1F (upstairs) ⊨ 1S,3D,2R ⊂ 1Sh.w.g., 1sh.w.h. ★F,TV, books & games ⊛ No smoking, no pets ⌇ English (household language is French)
🕆 Village of St. Jean (founded in 1679) with well established historic homes, boutiques, restaurants, 1732-built church and cemetery, 1858-built quay, beach, swimming pool

🚗 Historic villages on the island, Montmorency Falls, Cap Tourmente Nat Wildlife area
🐾 18th Century replica farmhouse situated on a cliff overlooking the St.Laurent River. Relax and enjoy the peaceful surroundings. Winter rates available.There is a resident cat. Visa ✓B&B

Lambert, Gérard & Lucie (Le Giron de l'Isle)   ☎ (418) 829-0985
120 Chm des Lièges, St-Jean, Ile d'Orléans, QC G0A 3W0   Fax (418) 829-1059

From the Island's Bridge, take Rte Prévost toward St-Laurent and St-Jean. Proceed 2.4km past St-Jean's church to B&B on right.
$35S $55D   ► 6A
🍳 Full, homebaked   🏠 Rural, 2-storey, view, riverfront, patio, quiet   ■ 3D(upstairs) ⊨ 1D,2Q ⊂ 2Sh.w.h. ★TV,F,LF, ceiling fans, jacuzzi ⊛ No smoking, no pets ⌇ English (household language is French)
🕆 Shore walks, art galleries, shops, pond fishing, bird watching

🚗 Quebec City, Mont St-Anne, Montmorency Falls, St-Anne de Beaupré Shrine, golfing
🐾 Newly built island home with modern comfort located by the majestic St.Lawrence River with its impressive boats and breathtaking sunrise and moonlight. Relax in the jacuzzi, on the veranda or patios. Retired hosts are knowledgeable about the region. A private tour of the beautiful gardens can be arranged. Visa,MC ✓B&B

Lapointe, Louise & Hughes L'Heureux (Le Vieux Presbytère)   ☎(418)828-9723
1247 MgrD'Esgly,Saint-Pièrre,Ile d'Orléans,QC G0A 4E0   Fax(418)828-2189

$50S $60-90D $10Child $15Add.person   🍽 Meals   ► 12
Take Rte 440 from Quebec City to Ile d'Orléans. After crossing bridge, turn left at traffic light. Go 2 km, turn left between two churches in the centre of village.
🍳 Full   🏠 Village, farm, hist., view, quiet   ■ 4D,1F(upstairs & ground level) ⊨2T,4D,1P,2R ⊂ 2Sh.w.g., 1private
★TV, parking ⌇English (household language is French)
🕆 Hist. church, craft shop, bicycle rentals, public pool
🚗 Quebec City, golfing, museum, skiing, Montmorency Falls
🐾 Large and beautiful ancestral residence (200-year old stone house) with warm and cozy atmosphere near the oldest church in Québec, located on large property with buffalo, wappitis, goats etc. Visa,MC

Lettre, Francoise (Jardin d'Antan)
556 Chm Royal, St-Laurent, Ile d'Orléans, QC G0A 3Z0
☎ (418) 829-3834

From Quebec City take Hwy 40 or 440 to Ile d'Orléans, cross bridge and proceed 12km.
$50S $60-65D $15Child(under age 12) $110F $20Add.person   ▶ 6A

🍽 Full, homebaked 🏠 Village, hist., acreage, view from guest rooms, swimming pool, patio, quiet, secluded ■ 3D(main & upper floor) ⊨ 3D ⊒ 1Private, 1sh.w.g. ★ TV in guest living room, sep.entrance, off-street parking ⊛No smoking,no pets ⌇English(household language is French)
🏃 Golfing, walking trails, handicraft & art boutiques, fine cousine in old Water Mill
🚗 Old Quebec, Montmorency Falls, Mount Ste-Anne ski area

🔫 Charming 17th Century stone house furnished with antiques and with a 4-sided roof that bears witness to the earliest French settlement. Enjoy the large old-style country garden and intimate atmosphere of yesteryear.

Kamouraska
(s-w of Rivière-du-Loup; see also L'Islet sur Mer, SteAndre de K)

Bossé, Nicole & Jean (Chez Nicole & Jean)
81 Ave Morel, Rte 132, Kamouraska, QC G0L 1M0
☎ (418) 492-2921

From Hwy 20, take Exit 465 to Kamouraska. In the village, turn left on Morel Ave (132 Rd) to 2nd house on left past church.

$40S $50D $10Child $20Add.person   ▶ 6A,2Ch
🍽 Full, homebaked (Gourmet) 🏠 Village, res., 2-storey, hist., view from guest room, riverfront,patio,wrap-around balcony,quiet ■1S,2D,1F(upstairs) ⊨1S,2T,3D,1R ⊒1Sh.w.g.,1sh.w.h.
★F,TV, parking, solarium, bicycles for rent ⊛No smoking, no pets,children min.age 5 ⌇some English (household lang French)
🚗 Rivière-du-Loup, La Pocatière, Saint Pascal

🏃 Restaurant, museum, dock fishing, bicycle/walking on panoramic path along the shore
🔫 Early retired couple in 19th Century home on south shore of the St. Lawrence River in 320-year old historic village with typical architecture. In K"amour"aska, nature lovers will be impressed by the sunsets over the water and the view of the surrounding fields and woods. Visa
↵B&B

Lac Supérieur
(north-west of Montreal; see also Mont Tremblant)

Lachance, Louise & Normand Sauvé (Chez Nor-Lou B&B)
803 Ch Lac à l'Équerre, Lac Supérieur, QC J0T 1J0
☎ (819) 688-3128
E-mail: norlou@intlaurentides.qc.ca

Phone for reservation.
$40-45S $55-65D $15Child   ▶ 7
❌ Not April or Nov. 🍽 Full, homebaked 🏠 Rural, 2-storey,

35acres, view from guest rooms, swimming pool, patio, porch, deck, very quiet ■ 3D (upstairs) ⊨ 2D,1Q,1R,crib ⊒1Sh.w.g., 1sh.w.h. ★ TV ⊛ Designated smoking area, no pets ⌇ English (French is household language)
🏃 Swimming (in pool or river), fishing, snowshoeing, x-c skiing, walking, hiking, bicycling, mushroom picking, forest with birds and wild animals
🚗 Mt Tremblant Int. Ski Resort and Park, Montebello, Mirabel Int. Airport
🔫 Country style home built by hosts in 1984 with plenty of wood and furnished with antiques, in natural surroundings of forest, river and peaceful countryside. Rest and observe Hummingbirds from May to September. Hosts operated youth hostels and outdoor activity centres before opening a B&B and enjoy welcoming guests from all over the world. There is also a small unique country home in the forest on the property, which is available for rent/no b'fast provided. ↵B&B

Ladysmith
(north/west of Ottawa,ON; see also Wakefield)

Cushing, Geoffrey & Joellen (Cushing Lodge B&B Nature Retreat) ☎ (819) 647-3226
197 Chemin Fierobin, Ladysmith, QC   J0X 2A0   E-mail: cushing@istar.ca, Fax (819) 647-6645

$71.50S $98D $22.50Add.person   (Child under age 10 free) (plus tax) ◙ Meals   ▶ 10A,10Ch
From Ottawa/Hull, take Hwy 148 west to Shawville and proceed north on Hwy 303 to Ladysmith.

Follow blue Tourism Hwy signs to Lodge.
🕮 Full, homebaked 🏠 Rural, hillside, 2-storey, view, 500acres, lakefront, deck, quiet, secluded ■ 5F(upper & ground level) ⊨5Q,5cots 🛏 5Private ★ Air,TV,F, guest quarters are separate Ⓦ No smoking, no pets ∿ French
🕺 Birds of Prey Center on property, skating on private lake, dog sledding, x-c skiing, hiking (guided nature discovery walks), fishing, swimming, canoeing, horse-back riding
🚗 Golf courses, down-hill ski resorts, scenic waterfalls, museums, scenic train excursions
🐾 Large comfortable log home on 500 acres nestled in secluded hills, a unique wilderness sanctuary for both wildlife and those who seek the tranquility of a truly natural setting. There is a wildlife sanctuary and birds of prey breed and release facility for eagles, hawks and owls. Ideal place for photography. Hosts are environmental science grads with appreciation for nature, conservation and earth stewardship. There 2 cats, a dog, and "Casper" the barn owl. Visa

Laval
(north-west of Montreal)

Trudeau, Louise (Gîte du Bord de l'Eau) ☎ & Fax (514) 625-3785
495 des Patriotes, Laval, QC   H7L 2L9

Located 8.5km east of Hwy13/Exit17, 3.5km east of Hwy15/Exit16.
$45S $60D $5-15Child $20Add.person   (plus tax)   ▶ 4
🕮Full 🏠Res., riverfront, 2-storey, swimming pool,deck,quiet ■ 1F(street level) ⊨ 2D plus foam mattress ⊨1Private (whirlpool) ★TV, off-street parking Ⓦ No smoking, no pets ∿English, Spanish (household language is French)
🕺 Canoeing/bicycling/fishing/skating/x-c skiing on property, restaurants in the old village of Ste Rose, bus from Montreal
🚗 Laval, shopping centers, golf courses, Space Science Center, Mille-Isle River Park, Montreal
🐾 Long time hosts have welcomed guests from many different countries over the years. Delicious breakfast is served with a wonderful view of the Mille-Iles River. Admire the truly spectacular sunsets. Babysitting can be arranged. Visit a truly French Canadian family and enjoy friendly atmosphere and good conversation.

Lévis
(across the river from Quebec City; see also Beaumont)

Pelletier, Véronique & Emile (Gîte Des Bosquets B&B) ☎(418)835-3494,Fax (418)835-0563
162 Rue des Bosquets,Lévis,QC G6V 6V7   1-888-335-3959

Phone for directions.
$30-35S $45-50D $15Child/Add.person $75F   (plus tax) ◙ Meals   ▶ 8A,4Ch

🕮 Full, homebaked 🏠 Downtown, res., townhouse, view from guest rooms, riverfont, patio, quiet ■ 1S,2D,2F(upstairs & lower level) ⊨ 1S,2T,5D 🛏 3Sh.w.g. ★ Air,TV, off-street & street parking, bicycle storage Ⓦ Desig.smoking area, no pets, child min.age 10 ∿English (French is household language)
🕺 Restaurants, public swimming pool, golfing, marina Summer Theatre, Fort de la Martiniere and Fort No1 (Nat.hist.sites - with mysterious tunnels, amazing blockhouses & caponiers), ferry station, Rue St.Laurent/riverfront, Memorial Park, cycle track, bus route
🐾 Comfortable home facing Old Quebec with a nice view of St.,Lawrence River and situated in a quiet area of historic town. Relax on the terrace and admire the dancing lights at night. Visa ✓B&B

L'Islet-Sur-Mer
(s/side of St.Lawrence east of Quebec;see also Kamouraska,)

Caron, Marguerite and Denis (Auberge La Marguerite)   ☎ (418) 247-5454
88 Des Pionniers Est, CP 101, L'Islet-Sur-Mer, QC G0R 2B0

On Hwy 20 East (from Montreal), travel past Quebec City and Montmagny and exit at Hwy 285
North (Exit 400). Travel 4 km through L'Islet village to intersection of Rt 132 (in village of
L'Islet-Sur-Mer), turn right and continue for 1 km to house on right side. Look for sign.

$60-120S $92-125D (Children's rates avail.) ▐●▌Meals ► 12A,2Ch
🕭 Full 🏠Village, historic, acreage, view, patio, quiet ■6
(upstairs,including family suite) plus 2 downstairs ⊨2T,2D,5Q
🛏8Private ★Air,F, comfortable guest sitting room, separate
entrance, parking ⌇English (household language is
French) 🚫No smoking, no pets
🕺 Scenic St.Lawrence River, historic church
🚗 Quebec City, artisan villages along the St. Lawrence

📢 Very spacious 180-year-old home, well-kept and pretty with large garden to walk, read, relax,
and located in the heart of a 300-year-old historic village on the St.Lawrence River. Rooms are
named after schooners built in the area. Meals are served in the bright large dining room.

Louiseville
(west of Trois Rivières; see also Pointe-du-Lac, St.Sévère)

Gilbert, Michel (Gîte de La Seigneurie B&B)   ☎ & Fax (819) 228-8224
480 Chemin du Golf, Louiseville, QC J5V 2L4

From Quebec City take Hwy 40 east and Exit 166. Take Rte 138 east to Rte 348 west. Turn left and
drive 1.5 km to 7th road on right.

$45S $55D $15Add.person ▐●▌ Meals (plus tax) ► 12A,4Ch
🕭 Homebaked 🏠 Farm, hist., quiet, isolated 🛏2Sh.w.g.
■1S,2D,1Ste,1F(upstairs) ⊨ 2S,5D,4R 🛏 2Sh.w.g., 1Private
in suite ★F, private balcony in suite 🚫 No smoking, no pets,
children min. age 12 ⌇English (household language is French)
🕺 Golf courses, cycling paths, farm activities, c-x skiing
🚗 Zoo, museums, Ste.Ursule Water Falls, St.Lawrence cruise

📢 Comfortable Victorian home (built in 1880) with Victorian Garden on 14 acres. Relax on the
veranda & enjoy country life with a calm/cozy atmosphere. House specialty: "forfaits" (inquire
please). Hosts are music & flower lovers. Artist Lithograph atelier on site. Also available
full-equipped separate house on property for longer stays. ⌐B&B

Matapédia
(north-west of Campbellton, NB)

Anderson, Lanny & Cathleen McQuiston (Notre Réve)   ☎ (418) 865-2505
114 Perron Ouest, Matapédia, QC G0J 1V0

Located on Rte 132 and 4km west of the village of Matapédia, and directly across the road from the
United Baptist Church of Mann Settlement.

$65S $75D $15Add.person ► 6A,2Ch
❊ Summer only 🕭 Full 🏠 Village, hillside, acreage, view,
porch ■ 3D(upstairs) ⊨ 3Q 🛏 1Private, 1sh.w.g.
★Ceiling fans, off-street parking 🚫 No smoking, no pets,
children min.age 12 ⌇ French
🕺 Matapédia River, walk and roam large property
🚗 Restigouche River and popular salmon fishing area, Gaspé
Peninsula, northern New Brunswick

📢 Notre Réve will open in the spring of 1999. Warm welcome in large modern home, situated on
80 acres of wooded land, with a view of the river in the beautiful Matapédia River Valley. Rooms are
decorated in Irish country style. Visa,MC

Mont-Tremblant

(north-west of Montreal; see also Lac Superieur)

Bourdon, Bob & Johanne Parent (The Inn at The Crossroads)   ☎ (819) 686-5289
4273 Des Tulipes, La Conception/Mt-Tremblant, QC   J0T 1M0

Take Hwy 15 north from Montreal and Hwy 117 north from Ste-Agathe. Turn right on MTEE Ryan (towards Tremblant), left on Principal, left on Chm Lac Mercier and right on des Tulipes.
$41-71S $55-95D $10Child(under age 13) $20Add.person   ◉Meals   (plus tax)   ▶ 24

▯Homebaked   ▮ Rural, 2-storey, hist., acreage, riverfront
▮6D,3F(upstairs)   ▭2S,4D,4Q   ▭ 7Private, 1sh.w.g.
★F,ceiling fans   ⓦ No smoking, no pets   ⌇ English
(household language is French)
♴ Swimming in warm and clean Rouge River, walks along sandy dunes or pine forest
🚗 Tremblant (best known & fastest growing year-round ski resort), cycling path (180 km long transformed railway line)

🐎 Large comfortable home built by hosts of red pine cut on land, reminiscent of a majestic "Seigneurie" farm house of the 1920's and appointed with natural fibers and antiques from that era. Hosts are a Herbalist and musician & wilderness guide. Breakfast is served in guest breakfast room. there is a dog and a cat in residence. Visa,MC ⌐B&B

Lachance, Pierre & Sylvie Senécal (Auberge Le Lupin B&B)   ☎(819)425-5474,Fax6079
127 Pinoteau, Mont-Tremblant, QC   J0T 1Z0   E-mail: lelupin@intlaurentides.qc.ca

From Montreal, take Hwys 15/117 north past St-Jovite. Turn right on Montée Ryan and continue to end. Turn left along lake to 2nd street on left. Look for B&B sign.
$50-90S $65-120D $12Child $20Add.person   (plus tax)   ▶ 18

✳ not Xmas holiday period   ▯ Full, homebaked   ▮ Resort town, 2-storey, log house, patio, quiet   ▮ 3F,6D (main, upper & lower levels)   ▭ 3S,9Q,2cots   ▭ 7ensuite, 2sh.w.g.   ★F,TV
in 5 guest rooms, wheel-chair access, off-street parking
ⓦDesignated smoking area, no pets   ⌇ French
♴ Lake (with limited beach access), boat cruises, golfing, tennis, Tremblant ski lift, hike/ski/bike path at door, dog-sledding

🚗 Mont Tremblant Park (trails/horseback riding), hydroplane tours, Fish Hatchery
🐎 Splendid log home (built in 1945) with spacious rooms and cozy atmosphere, nestled in the center of Mont Tremblant recreational playgrounds. Relax by the massive stone fireplace and enjoy a natural setting outside the window. There is a dog and a cat. Reservations recommended, inquire about summer rates. CC's ⌐B&B

Montebello

(east of Ottawa Ontario; see also ND de Salette, Papineauville)

Lacasse, Suzanne (À l'Orée du Moulin Bed & Breakfast)   ☎ & Fax (819) 427-8534
170 Joseph Lucien Malo, Papineauville, QC   J0V 1R0

Phone for directions.
$45S $55D $20Child $30Add.person   ◉ Meals   ▶ 6A,2Ch
▯ Full, homebaked   ▮ Village, 2-storey, hist., swimming pool, patio, porch, deck, quiet   ▮ 3D (upstairs)   ▭ 2T,2D,2cots,1P
▭ 2Sh.w.g.   ★ Separate entrance, off-street parking   ⓦNot
suitable for children, designated smoking area   ⌇ English
(French is household language)
♴ Ice-fishing on the Outaouais River

🚗 Chateau Montebello (largest log structure in the world), fine dining in village, Domaine Omega
🐎 Historic home built around 1850 beautifully restored with wrap-around porch and situated on the northshore of the Outaouais River. Visa

Montréal
(see also Hudson, Laval, Repentigny, St.Lazare)

Alacoque, Christian (Alacoque Bed & Breakfast)   ☎ & Fax (514) 842-0938
2091 St.Urbain, Montréal, QC H2X 2N1

Located west of St.Laurent & south of Sherbrooke Sts. Phone for directions.
$40S $60D $10Child $20Add.person (plus tax) ► 9
🍴 Full 🏠 Downtown, 3-storey, view, quiet ■ 1D,1Ste,1F (ground
level) ⊨ 4D,1Q,1R ⌐ 1Sh.w.g., 1private ★ Air,LF,KF,TV in guest
room, private entrance, off-street & street parking, (garage available), host
quarters are separate ⌣ English (household language is French)
🕴 Place des Arts, Chinese Quarter, Conference Centre, McGill U., Old
Montreal, Latin Quarter, subway station (St.Laurent/Place des Arts)
🚗 Botanical Garden, Biodome, Olympic Stadium
🔔 1830-built home with original wood finishes & elegant furniture.
Gourmet breakfast is served in the guest breakfast room. Visa,MC ✓ B&B

Allaire, Denise and Lucien   ☎ (514) 382-4807
10840 Avenue d'Auteuil, Montréal, QC H3L 2K8

From Metropolitan Hwy exit at St-Hubert St North and go to Henri Bourassa St. Turn left and
proceed to d'Auteuil Ave, turn right. House is next to bridge (Pont Viau Rivière des Prairies).

$35-40S $50-70D ► 6
🍴Full,homebaked 🏠Res., sub.duplex, quiet ■3D ⊨4T,1D
⌐1Sh.w.g. ★Separate entrance, parking, solarium ⓌNo pets, no
smoking, no children ⌣Some English (household lang.is French)
🕴 3 parks (Athuntsic, Nicolas Viel, Stanley), Rivière des Prairies,
Metro Henri Bourassa (subway to downtown), Laval bus station
🚗 Fall colour Festival (Eastern townships, Laurentiens), 8km ski
trail, 5km bike trail, Visitation Isle Reg. Park
🔔 Home is situated in lovely residential area called "Ahuntsic" and very convenient location.
Well-informed & long-time B&B hosts will gladly assist with sightseeing and entertainment plans.

Bertrand, Robert & Aline (Manoir Harvard B&B)   ☎ (514) 488-3570, Fax (514) 369-5778
4805 Harvard Ave., Montreal, QC H3X 3P1   E-mail: alrc@sympatico.ca

Located next to Decarie Expressway leading to Montreal Int.Airport (Dorval). Turn off at Cote
St-Luc Queen Mary, proceed west to Somerled. Turn left, then right on Harvard. House on corner.

$75S $85-105D $10Child/Add.person 🍽 Meals ► 11
🍴 Full 🏠 Res., hist., 3-storey, view from guest rooms, patio,
quiet ⊨ 4D,1F (main & upper level) ⊨ 1S,1D,4Q
⌐5Private ★ F,KF,ceiling fans, separate entrance, off-street
parking, guest quarters are separate Ⓦ Designated smoking
area, no pets ⌣ French
🚗 Downtown, Peel & Ste-Catherine (heart of Montreal), Casino
🕴 2 Subway Stns (Villa Maria & Snowdon), Village Monkland
with good multicultural eating restaurants and fancy shops & boutiques, public transportation
🔔 Victorian-style stone house with personal and elegant surroundings offering country living in
an urban environment, situated in the heart of N.D.G. Relax in the secluded private rose garden
and terrace. Computer with Internet & E-mail and fax are available. Breakfast is served in special
guest breakfast room. Visa,MC,Enroute ✓B&B

QUEBEC 329

Bilodeau, Pierre & Dominique Bousquet (Pierre & Dominique)   ☎ (514) 286-0307
271 Square St-Louis, Montreal, QC H2X 1A3   E-mail: pierdom@cam.org

Phone for directions.
$45-50S $65-75D $15Child   (plus tax)   ►7
🟥 Full, homebaked   🏠 Downtown, townhouse, hist., view from
guest rooms, quiet   ■ 1S,2D,1Ste(ground level)   ᴴ 1S,2D,1Q
🛏 Sh.w.g.   ★ TV,ceiling fans, private entrance, street
parking(free), guest quarters are separate   Ⓦ No smoking, no
pets   ᴡᴡ French
🕇 McGill University complex, UQAM, boutiques, restaurants,
theatres, museums, Palais of Congrès, Old Montreal Sherbrooke Metro Stn, Voyageur Bus Term.
🚍 Montreal Dorval Airport, Laurentian Mountains
☛ Warm welcome in the heart of the Latin Quarter in a charming Victorian house on the
Saint-Louis Square which has captivated several generations of poets and artists. Enjoy the
tranquility of the country in downtown and relax in the park to the sound of birds. Hosts are very
knowledgeable of the City and can provide "off-the-beaten-track" itinerary. ✔B&B

Blondel, Lena (Montreal Oasis B&B)   ☎ (514) 935 2312, Fax (514) 935-3154
3000 Breslay Rd., Montréal, QC H3Y 2G7

Follow directions to downtown/center-ville Montréal, do not take the Bonaventure Express Rd, but
exit at Atwater and continue to Breslay Rd/Chemin de Breslay, turn left to
1st house with turquoise door.
$55-70S $65-75D $10Child $25Add.person   ►8+
🟥 Choice, homebaked (Gourmet)   🏠Downtown, res.,large garden
■3D(upst)   🛏2Sh.w.g.   ★TV ⓌNo pets   ᴡᴡSwedish, French, some
Spanish, German
🕇 Various restaurants/fine dining (Crescent, St.Cahterine & Sherbrooke
Sts), Museum of Fine Arts, Cdn. Center for Architecture, Mt Royal Park (a
short hike up hill), Montreal Forum, Alexis Nihon Plaza (part of
underground City), Old Montreal, The Latin Quarter, subway stop
☛ Spacious home, decorated with Swedish & Quebec furniture, located in
downtown's beautiful "Priest Farm district" (once a holiday resort for priests). There are original
lead windows and slanted ceilings. Swedish hostess is world travelled and loves all kinds of music
and African Art. There is a beautiful blue-cream Siamese cat & a collection of Bergman movies &
videos. Hostess also operates "A Montreal Oasis B&BA" a small quality B&B Network.

De la Figueroa, Sylvia   ☎ (514) 489-8234
4772 Grosvenor Ave., Montreal, QC H3W 2L8

Located close to Mount Royal. Take Queen Mary Rd Exit, turn left and proceed 4 block. Turn right
on Roselyn Ave and right on Sunnyside, then right on Grosvenor.
$35S $65D $30Add.person   ►3
🌅Summer only   🟥 Full, homebaked   🏠 Res., hist., balcony, quiet   ■ 1S,1D (upstairs)
ᴴ1S,1Q   🛏 2Private   ★ F, off-street and street parking   Ⓦ No smoking, not suitable for
children   ᴡᴡ Spanish
🕇 St.Joseph Oratory, neighbourhood restaurants and shops, bus stop to downtown
🚍 Mount Royal Park, Laurention Mountains
☛ Artist hostess in home with leaded glass windows, french door to balcony, full of antiques and
paintings, situated in a lovely quiet neighbourhood. Well informed hostess will be pleased to provide
information about the city and area. Special longer stay and senior rates. There is a cat and a bird.

Durand, Lise & Jean Pierre (Gîte "Le 6400" B&B)   ☎ (514) 259-6400, Fax (514) 255-4692
6400 Rue Lemay, Montreal, QC H1T 2L5

From Mirabel Airport take Hwy 15 south to Hwy 40 East. Exit at Lacordaire Blvd and proceed
south to Rosemont Blvd. Turn right to Lemay. From Dorval Airport take Hwy 520 east to Hwy 40

East and continue as above.
$35-40S $55-60D   (plus tax)   ► 4
🛏 Full   🏠 Res., 2-storey, patio, swimming pool, quiet   ■2
(main floor)   ⊨ 2S,1D   🛁 1Sh.w.g.   ★ Air,LF,TV,street
parking   Ⓦ No smoking, no pets, not suitable for children
ᕝEnglish (household language is French)
🕴 Biodome, Botanical Gardens, Olympic Stadium & Tower,
mueum, golfing, cycle path, bus No131, Metro L'Assomption
🚐 Old Port (cruising jet-boating), Old Montreal, Cathedral, St.Josph Oratory
🖝 Warm welcome in comfortable home. Bicycles for guests available. Breakfast is served in the
salle à manger. Relax in the reading/ TV room or on the patios by the pool. ↙B&B

Filion, Hélène, and Emile Bédard (L'Anse du Patrimoine)   ☎ (514) 437-6918
475 Emile-Nelligan, Boisbriand, QC J7E 4H4   Fax (514) 434-5130

From Montréal, take Rt 15 N or Rt 13 N and Boisbriand Exit to La Grande Côte, (2 km) to Hubert
Aquin St, turn south, then east on Emile Nelligan.

$40S $60D $20Add.person   ► 10
🛏 Full   🏠 Sub., hist., stonehouse, acreage, swimming pool,
patio, quiet   ■ 1S,3F(upst)   ⊨S,D   🛁1Private,1sh.w.g.
★Air,F,TV,LF, parking   Ⓦ No pets   ᕝsomè English
(household languarge is French)
🕴 Nature Interpretation center
🚐 Museum, theatre, historic sites, golfing, skiing
🖝 Comfortable stone house steeped in 2 Centuries of history
situated on large secluded grounds along the Mille Iles River. Enjoy a savory breakfast and
exchange points of interest, relax in the solarium or spacious "salle d'eau". There is also a fully
equipped apartment (for 4) next to the main house.

Fischer, Alexander (Chez Alexandre Le Bienheureux B&B)   ☎ & Fax (514) 282-3340
3432 Hutchison, Montreal, QC H2X 2G4

Phone for directions.
$60-85S $75-95D $15Child/Add.person (plus tax)   ► 8
🛏 Full   🏠 Downtown, 3-storey, hist., quiet   ■ 2D,1Ste(upstairs)
⊨2S,2Q,1P   🛁 1Sh.w.g., 1sh.w.h.   ★KF,LF,2F,TV,fans in guest rooms,
private entrance, off-street and street parking, guest quarters are separate
ⓌDesig.smoking area, no pets, children min.age4   ᕝFrench,German
🕴 Downtown area and Underground City, Central Station, Bus Terminal,
museums, Place des Arts, McGill University, Chinatown, shops, restaurants,
Jazz Festival, trepidating nightlife, buses No24/80, Metro Stations
🚐 Laurentian Mountains, Eastern Townships
🖝 Quiet Victorian House with high ceilings and large luxurious interior, situated in the middle
of Cosmopolitan Montreal. Retired University Professor, assisted by his dynamic team of young
Montrealers, will make certain that guests enjoy and experience the well-being and happiness of
their stay. Breakfast is served in the elegant dining room. Relax in the quiet atmosphere by the
fireplace or in the little garden. Hosts live in lower level. Visa,MC

Gauthier, Nicole (Le Petit Bonheur)
6790 Lemay St., Montreal, QC H1T 2L9
☎ (514) 256-3630, Fax (514) 255-2782

$40-55S $50-65D $10Child $100-120F $40-55Add.person   (plus tax)   ► 5A,2Ch
From Hwy 40, take Exit 76 or 77 (Lacordaire South) and drive 1 km. Turn right on St-Zotique St, then right again on Lemay St.

🍴 Full   🏠 Res., townhouse, terrace, quiet   ▦ 1S,2D(main floor)   ⊨ 1S,2T,1D,P   ⊒ 1Sh.w.g., 1sh.w.h.   ★Air,KF,LF,TV, street parking, host quarters are upstairs   🚭 No smoking, no pets   ⚍ English (household language is French)
🏃 Biodome, Olympic Stadium, Botanical Gardens, restaurants, shopping center, bus to subway system (L'Assomption Blvd Stn)
🚗 Downtown, Laurentians and resorts
☛ Warm welcome in townhouse situated in peaceful residental neighbourhood. Breakfast is served on the terrace, weather permitting. Relax in the friendly atmosphere after a busy day. Separate kitchen available for guests. Transportation to and from airport, as well as bus and subway pass available. Special rates for 3 nights & more. ✓B&B

Hornby, Linda Michelle (Angelica Blue B&B)
1215 Ste.Elisabeth St. Montreal, QC H2X 3C3
☎ (514) 844-5048, Fax (514) 281-9288

Phone for directions.
$55S $65D $80F $10Add.person   ►15
🍴 Full, homebaked (self-serve)   🏠 Downtown, 3-storey, Victorian Row-house, patio, quiet   ▦4D,2Ste(upstairs)   ⊨ 2T,3D,5Q,3K,3P
⊒1Private, 2ensuite, 2sh.w.g.,1sh.w.h.   ★KF& microwave,LF,TV, ceiling fans, separate entrance, bicycles for guests, off-street & street parking
🚭 Designated smoking area   ⚍French, some Italian
🏃 Chinatown, Old Montreal (port), downtown shopping, Convention Centre, wonderful restaurants, underground shops, American Embassy, subway
🚗 Skiing, snowmobiling, Casino, Mt.Royal Olympic Station, Biodome
☛ Historic home (ca 1890) with spacious sunny rooms, recently decorated in different themes and located in the heart of downtown Montreal. Relax in the comfortable TV & sitting room. A scrumptious breakfast is served in cosy bistro. Children welcome. Visa,MC,Enroute

---

Jacques, Micheline & Fernand (Gîte Maison Jacques)
4444 Paiement St., Pierrefonds, QC H9H 2S7
☎(514)696-2450, Fax 2564
E-mail: gite.maison.jacques@sympatico.ca

From Hwys 20/40 exit at Blvd Saint-Jean (Exit 50N) and continue north to Blvd Pierrefonds. Turn left to Paiement St and left again.

$37-40S $53-55D $12Child   ► 6A,2Ch
🍴 Full, homebaked   🏠 Res., sub., bungalow, patio, porch, quiet   ▦ 1S,1D,1F (main and lower level)   ⊨S,T,D,R,cot
⊒1Private, 1sh.w.g., 1sh.w.h.   ★ Air,TV,F, off-street parking
🚭 No smoking, no pets   ⚍ French
🏃 Village center, restaurants, services, churches, shopping centers, recreational parks, skating rink, bus routes #68 & #215
🚗 Downtown Montreal, Mirabel/Dorval Airports, skidoo trails, Laurentians, St. Laurence Seaway
☛ Retired teachers in comfortble home located in a peaceful suburb in the "West Island" and in excellent proximity to the city and skiing/cycling areas. Enjoy the quiet seclusion and relax in the backyard, the lawn swing or the screened veranda after a day of sightseeing or travelling. Breakfast is served on patio weather permitting.C.Cards ✓B&B

Lauzon, Jean-Paul (La Maison de Grand-Pré)   ☎ (514) 843-6458, Fax (514) 843-8691
4660 Rue de Grand-Pré, Montréal, QC   H2T 2H7

Take the Main Street "St.Denis" north to corner of St. Joseph Blvd, turn right and around the
Metro Station to Gilford St. Cross St.Denis, direction west, to corner of Grand-Pré.

$50S $70D   (Off-season rates available)   ► 8
🍽 Full, homebaked   🏠 Hist, downtown, view 2-storey, quiet, two
balconies ■2S,3D(upst) ╾2S,2T,2Q 🚿2Sh.w.g.   ★Parking
〰English (household lang. French)
🚶 Famous St. Denis Street (fashion boutiques, cafés, terrasse jazz
concerts, Metro Laurier Stn to downtown
🚗 Old Montreal, City center, Mt. Royal, panoramic City lookout
📣 Cozy and quiet Century home located beside a park in French part
of Montreal with a view of Mount Royal. Former University teacher host
is known for his tasty French/Québécois breakfasts. ✐CC

Logan, Andrée (Marmelade B&B)   ☎ (514) 876-3960, Fax (514) 876-3926
1074 Rue St-Dominique, Montreal, QC   H2X 2W2   E-mail: marmelad@total.net

Phone for directions.
$60S $75-95D $10Child $14Add.person   (plus tax)   ► 16
🗓 closed Feb   🍽 Full, homebaked   🏠 Downtown, hist., 3-storey, older,
patio ■ 5D,3F(upper & ground level) ╾ 2T,4Q,1K,2R,1P   🚿1Sh.w.g.,
1sh.w.h.   ★ LF,2TV guest lounges, ceiling fans, separate entrance,
off-street & street parking   🚭 Designated smoking area, not suitable for
children 〰 English (household language is French)
🚶 Montreal & Old Port, Convention Center, Place des Arts, Chinatown,
sites of Jazz & Film Festivals, Latin Quarter, underground shopping,
riverfront bicycle paths, Metro Stations (subway), major bus routes
🚗 Botanical Gardens, Olympic Site, Casino, US Border, Laurentian
Mountains and resorts (skiing)
📣 Charming older (1830) home, recently renovated in contemporary style and tastefully
decorated, situated in the heart of downtown. Works of local artists are on display throughout the
house. Hostess is former Hospitality & Tourism Exec. and willing to help guests with itineraries.
Enjoy a hearty gourmet breakfast."Farley" the friendly resident Bearded Collie is eager to welcome
guests. Also apartment available for longer stay.Visa ✐CC

Messier, Nicolas (Au Gît'Ann B&B)   ☎ (514) 525-3938, Fax (514) 879-3236
1806 St-Christophe, Montreal, QC   H2L 3W8

From the Voyageur Bus Terminal exit on Berri St North, turn right on Ontario St, right again on
St-Christophe.
$40-45S $55-60D $10Child $15Add.person   (plus tax)   ► 5A,2ch
🍽Cont.   🏠Downtown, townhouse, quiet ■3(upstairs) ╾2S,2D 🚿1Sh.w.g.   ★KF,TV,
ceiling fans, off-street/street parking   ♥ 🚭Design.smoking area   〰 French,Spanish
🚶 Downtown core area with shops, boutiques, restaurants, entertainment, Universities, Congress
Center, Old Port of Montreal, subway station, bus connection to airport
📣 Active and knowledgeable young host in comfortable home located on a calm street in the
heart of the village. Enjoy the peaceful ambience. Children welcome.

Ritchot, Gilles (B&B Turquoise)　　　　　　　　☎ & Fax (514) 523-9943
1576 Alexandre de Sève, Montreal, QC   H2L 2V7

Located 1 block north of Ste Catherine St East and 2 blocks west of Papineau St.
$50S $70D $15Child　　　　　　　　　　　　　　　　　　　　　▶ 10
🍴 Buffet　🏠Downtown, 2-storey, older, patio, deck, quiet　■5D(main & upper floor)　⊨5Q
⊨2Sh.w.g.　★ Private entrance, street parking, guest quarters are separate　⑩Designated
smoking area, not suitable for children　⚐ French
🧍 Montreal's Gay Village (bars & restaurants), Latin Quarter, Old Montreal, downtown business
district, subway station
🚐 Bus Terminal, Olympic Park/Botanical Gardens, Casino, museums, Mount Royal Observatory
🐾 Colourful home with a quiet, warm and friendly atmosphere, Victorian interior situated in the
heart of the Gay Village. The exterior balconies lead to a sunny flower garden and goldfish pond.
Knowledgeable hosts will provide necessary information on cultural activities and sightseeing.
Breakfast is served in guest breakfast room. ╰CC

Rybinski, Stephanie and Ed (The Ecles)　　　　☎ (514) 457-3986, Fax (514) 457-3986
20799 Lakeshore Rd., Baie d'Urfé, QC   H9X 1S1

From Autoroute 40, exit at Rt 41 to Ste-Anne-de-Bellevue. Continue to Ste.Ann's St, turn left 1.5
km. From Autoroute 20, exit at Morgan Rd and go to Lakeshore, turn right.
$35S $50-60D $15Add.person   (discounts 5 nights & longer)　　　▶ 6A,2Ch

🍴 Full　🏠 Res, acreage, 2-storey, lakeview, swimming pool,
patio, quiet　■3D(upstairs)　⊨4T,1Q,3R　⊨1Sh.w.g.
1ensuite　★TV,LF, parking　⑩No smoking　♥
🧍 Ste-Anne-de-Bellevue, restaurants, John Abbott & MacDonald
College (McGill), bicycle & jogging paths
🚐 Downtown Montréal, skiing Laurentiens/Eastern Townships
🐾 Superb hospitality in friendly turn-of-the-Century house
situated in beautiful residential neighbourhood. Relax in the
old-world charm gardens or enjoy the comfortable family atmosphere. Very convenient location and
easy-to-reach from major highways. Beautiful pressed flower/nature handicrafts made by hostess
are on display/sale. There is a dog in residence.

Schilling, Rosemarie (The Gables)　　　　　　　☎ (514) 697-3609
56 Gables Court, Beaconsfield, QC   H9W 5H3

From autoroutes 20 or 40, exit at Saint Charles and go south to Beaconsfield Blvd. Turn right to
4th street then left to B&B.
$45-55S $65-80D $40Add.person　　　　　　　▶ 4A,1Ch
🍴 Full, homebaked　🏠 Res., hist., riverview from guest rooms,
private lakefront, swimming pool, tennis court, patio, quiet
■2(upstairs)　⊨2T,1Q　⊨1Private, 1sh.w.h.　★ F,TV in guest
room, parking　⑩No smoking, no pets　⚐French, German
🚐 Downtown Montréal, Laurentiens, Ottawa, Quebec, Vermont
🧍 Quaint village, boutiques, on bus route (No200/211) from City, McGill & McDonald colleges,
Fairview Center shopping, riverfront restaurants.
🐾 Home is situated in a private Country Club & decorated Laura Ashley-style with antiques &
paintings. Located on the St Lawrence River with its own swimming pool, tennis court and boating
facilities. World travelled hostess (a former Stewardess) is now an Art & Antique Collector.
Breakfast is served in the formal dining room. Min.2-nights stay. "Herzlich Willkommen!"

A Montreal Oasis Bed & Breakfast Network   ☎(514) 935-2312, Fax (514) 935-3154
3000 Breslay Rd., Montreal, QC H3Y 2G7

(Lena Blondel)
$40-80S $55-90D   (including breakfast - some gourmet)
A Montreal Oasis Bed & Breakfast Newtork is a small network of quality homes, situated in the heart
of the city, the "Latin Quarter", in the "Old City" or near the Universities. Hosts are artists,
composers, performers & professionals with many and varied interests and abilities. Some are native
to the city, others have come from different parts of the world. Each has been carefully chosen. Most
travelled worldwide & have a wealth of experience to tell. The Network will remain small in order to
maintain the quality service it is known for. For information/reservation call above.

A Bed & Breakfast Downtown Network   ☎ (514)289-9749,Fax(514)287-7386,1-800-267-5180
3458 Laval Ave., Montreal, QC H2X 3C8

(Bob Finkelstein, Co-Ordinator)
Rates $35-55S $45-65D $10Child $110F $20Add.person   (including full breakfast)
A Bed & Breakfast Downtown Network is in its 15th year of operation and represents 80 homes
(specializing in the center-city, Latin Quarter and Old Montreal. For reservation call the above.

New Carlisle   *(on Gaspé south-shore; see also Paspebiac, Newport, Bonaventure)*

Sawyer, Aaron (Bay View Farmhouse B&B)   ☎ (418) 752-6718/752-2725
337 Rte 132, Main Highway, Box 21, New Carlisle, QC G0C 1Z0

From Quebec City follow Rte 20 east and then Rte 132 to Gaspé Peninsula. Located on Rte 132.

           $25S $35D $5Child $10Add.person   ▶ 10A,5Ch
           ✚ May-Oct.   🍴 Full, homebaked   🏠 Farm, 2-storey, hist., acreage, view
from guest rooms, porch, deck, quiet   ■ 2D,3F (upstairs)   ⊨4S,5D
🛁1Sh.w.g., 1sh.w.h.   ★ TV, parking   🚭Smoking outside, no pets
🗣French
🚶 Beach, walking, birdwatching, but route
🚗 Tennis, boat cruises, Fauvel Golf Course, Acadian & United Empire
Loyalist museums, British Heritage Centre, St. Elzéar Archaeological Caves, Maguasha Fossil Site,
Percé Rock, Bonaventure Island Bird Sanctuary
☞ Warm welcome and quiet Gaspésien country hospitality in comfortable farmstead with
un-ending and breathtaking mountain-sea vistas. Memorable copious farm breakfasts served.

Newport   *(south shore of Gaspé; see also Paspebiac, New Carlisle, Bonaventure)*

Lambert, André & Guylaine Michel (Auberge les Deux Îlots)   ☎ (418) 777-2801
207 Rte 132, CP 223, Newport, QC G0C 2A0   Fax (418) 777-4719

$40-50S $50-65D $5-10Child $15Add.person   (plus taxes)   ▶ 12A,4Ch
From Quebec City take Hwy 20 east and Rte 132 to Newport. Look for B&B located west of church
on seaside facing the rest area which looks over the two islands.
🍴 Full, homebaked   🏠 Village, 3-storey, older, 34 acres, view from
upstairs guest rooms, oceanfront, quiet   ■3D,2F(upper level)
⊨5D,1Q,2R,crib   🛁 2Private, 2sh.w.g.   ★F,KF,TV in guest
sitting room, private entrance, guest quarters are separate, off-street
parking   🚭 No smoking, no pets   🗣English (household language
is French)
🚶 1km beach on property, La Boldue Museum, fishing harbour
🚗 Centre d'interpretation du Bourg de Pabos, Percé Rock & Bonaventure Island, Port-Daniel
☞ Spacious house, once the estate of a wealthy merchant, with old-fashioned charm, enchanting
decor and cozy comfort, situated on property including the most beautiful beach in the township.
Tucked between Percé and Bonaventure, an ideal place for a longer stay, quiet nights and days filled
with discovery. Breakfast ("a pleasure for the palate") is served in guest breakfast room. Visa 🖊 B&B

North Hatley

Fleischer, Ann and Don (Cedar Gables)   ☎ (819) 842-4120
Box 355, 4080 Magog Rd., Rt 108, North Hatley, QC   J0B 2C0

From Sherbrooke, Montreal points west and north, take Autoroute 55 South and exit Rt 108 East to house before center of village. From Eastern USA, take I 91 North to Quebec Autoroute 55 N

$64-104S $73-104D (off-season discounts)   ▶ 10-12
🍽 Gourmet(famous)   🏠 Res., village, older, view, lakefront, patio, dock, lakeside deck, sunporch   ■ 4D,1Ste (ground & upper floor)
🛏 4K,1D,P, futon   🛁 5Ensuite   ★ 3F,VCR, tape deck, piano, 2canoes, rowboat, parking, wheel-chair access to ground floor room
🗣 some French
🏃 English-style pub, village center, summer concerts, watersports, swimming, cycling, fishing, gourmet/casual dining
🚗 Piggery Theatre, 7 alpine ski areas, riding stables, Orford Festival, 2 Universities
📷 Large, tastefully appointed turn-of-the-Century home on Lake Massawippi in the beautiful Eastern Townships. Hostess is an expert spinner and weaver and has a few surprises, host is a brewer & winemaker. Visa,MC,Amex ✓B&B

Notre-Dame-de-la-Salette   *(north of Ottawa, ON; see also Wakefield, Montebello)*

Burda, Georges & Doreen (Domaine La Maison Blanche)   ☎ (819) 766-2529
Box 185, RR1, Notre-Dame-de-la-Salette, QC   J0X 2L0   Fax (819) 766-2572

Located in the village of La Salette. Look for large white house with six flags of different nations.

$50S $60D $15Add.person   ▶ 11
🍽 Cont.   🏠 Village, 3-storey, older,9 acres, patio, riverview from guest rooms, riverfront, deck, quiet ■1S,4D,1Ste (ground & upper level)   🛏 1S,2T,4D,cot   🛁2Shw.g.,1ensuite   ★Air, TV, separate entrances, parking, boats on location   ⓦDesignated smoking area, pet & children by special arrangement
🗣English(household language is French)
🏃 Fishing, tennis, snowmobile trail on property, bowling alley
🚗 Horseback riding, golfing, hunting, Ottawa/Hull region (45km)
📷 Spacious, charming old estate with oak interior and beautiful view of the Lièvre River and mountains. Relax on the large veranda and deck on 2nd floor and watch the boats go by. Hostess is an R.N. and host, Monsieur Georges is a proficient chef and serves culinary delights in the dining room. Excellent place for a special occasion. Reduced rates for longer stay. Visa

---

Papineauville   *(east of Ottawa/Hull; see also Montebello, N.Dame de Salette)*

Montpetit, Règeanne (Au Fil Des Ans B&B)   ☎ (819) 427-5167, 1-800-361-0271
228 Duquette, CP 808, Papineauville, QC   J0V 1R0

In Papineauville exit on Joseph-Lucien Malo St and proceed to Duquette. Look for house on corner.
$35S $55-65D $8Child $15Add.person   (plus tax)   ▶ 10A,3Ch
🍽 Full, homebaked   🏠 Village, hist., view from guest rooms, quiet ■ 1S,4D (upstairs)   🛏 1S,2T,3D,1P   🛁 2Sh.w.g., 1ensuite   ★ TV,ceiling fans, off-street parking, guest quarters are separate   ⓦ Designated smoking area, no pets   🗣English (French is household language)
🏃 Walks in woodlands
🚗 Hull, Mirabel Airport, Dorval Airport
📷 Old Victorian house, built in 1853. Breakfast is served in the solarium. Enjoy the peaceful and warm atmosphere and relax with a cup of coffee on the veranda or in the yard listening to sweet sounds of singing birds. Knowledgeable hostess will guide guests through the history of the house and the region. Visa

Paspébiac

(south-shore Gaspé; see also New Carlisle, Bonaventure, Newport)

MacWhirter, Anne and Gordon (Macdale B&B) ☎ (418) 752-5270
465 Rte 132, Hope Paspébiac, QC G0C 2K0

Phone for directions. Weekly rates available.
$45S $55D $10Child(under age 12) 🍽 Meals E-mail: ✒ 10
🍳 Full, homebaked 🏠 Farm, older, view, multi-storey, quiet,
oceanfront ■3F (upstairs) ⬛1Private(in loft), 3sh.w.h.
⊨2S,3D,1P,cot ★TV in guest room, parking 🚭No smoking,
pets outdoors only ᵥᵥFrench
🏃 River, beach, playground/park with mini golf, tennis courts,
canteen, fishing, churches, walking trail, ski-dooers welcome.
🚗 Historic site (Paspébiac), Acadian museum, Loyalist Village, golfing, Thallasotherapy
🍃 5th Generation farm with cow/calf operation along with chickens (which supply brown eggs).
Host is a retired High School Teacher, while hostess continue to teach Grade One. ✒B&B

Pointe-au-Pic

(on north side of St.Lawrence east of Québec City; see also Cap-à-l'Aigle)

Vermette, Raymonde & Adolf Frizzi (La Maison Frizzi B&B) ☎(418)665-4668
Côteau-sur-mer, CP 526, Pointe-au-Pic,, QC G0T 1M0
Fax (418) 665-1143

Phone for directions.
$60-70D $15Child $25Add.person ► 11
🍳 Full, homebaked 🏠 Village, res., Austrian-style, view, patio,
oceanfront, quiet ■2D,2F(upstairs) ⊨S,Q,cots ⬛2Sh.w.g.
★F,TV,LF, separate entrance, parking ᵥᵥEnglish, German,
Italian (household language is French)
🏃 Manoir Richelieu Hotel, restaurants, St-Laurent River, golfing,
museum & art gallery, swimming, sailing, fishing, riding
🚗 Whale watching tours, Hôtel Tadousac, Cap Eternité, Mont Grands Fonds (skiing, skating)
🍃 Typical Tyrolian-style house with very charming & friendly hospitality "à la Québecoise" and a
beautiful view of the St-Laurent River. Relax on the outside terrace where breakfast is served weather
permitting. Hosts' 15-year old daughter enjoys helping with B&B chores. There is a Golden Retriever
called "Max" in residence. ✒B&B

Pointe-du-Lac

(west of Trois-Rivières; see also Louiseville, Saint Sevère)

Piccinelli, Barbara and Jacques (Gîte Baie-Jolie) ☎ & Fax (819) 377-3056
11 Notre Dame, Rte 138, Pointe-du-Lac, Trois-Rivières, QC G0X 1Z0

From Montréal, take Hwy 40 East and Exit 187. Continue on Rte 138 east for 7 km. Look for B&B
sign. - From Quebec City, take Hwy 40 West. Exit to Hwy 55 and then take Notre Dame Exit and

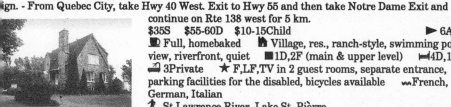

continue on Rte 138 west for 5 km.
$35S $55-60D $10-15Child ► 6A,4Ch
🍳 Full, homebaked 🏠 Village, res., ranch-style, swimming pool,
view, riverfront, quiet ■1D,2F (main & upper level) ⊨4D,1S
⬛3Private ★ F,LF,TV in 2 guest rooms, separate entrance,
parking facilities for the disabled, bicycles available ᵥᵥFrench,
German, Italian
🏃 St.Lawrence River, Lake St. Pièrre
🚗 Old Center of Trois-Rivières, cruises to Montréal and Québec, National Park of the Mauricie
🍃 Comfortable home with warm hospitality is situated on a magnificient site on the banks of the
St. Lawrence River and Lake St. Pierre, 10km away from the "old Center" of Trois Rivière. Relax in
the garden with picnic table & barbeque and enjoy a copious breakfast with delicious French pancakes,
maple syrup & homemade breads. There is a resident dog. Children welcome. ✒B&B

Pontiac
(west of Ottawa; see also Quyon, Wakefield)

André, Thérèse & Armand Ducharme (Au Charme de la Montagne)
368 Chm Crégheur, Pontiac (Luskville), QC   J0X 2G0   ☎ (819) 455-9158, Fax (819) 455-2706

From Hull proceed 17.5km north on Chm de la Montagne. Turn right on Chm Crégheur.

$45S $50-60D $10Child/Add.person   ► 6A,4ch
🍴 Full, homebaked   🏠 Rural, log house, bungalow, 3-acres, view from guest rooms, quiet   ■ 1D,2F(ground level)
🛏2T,1D,1K   🛁 2Sh.w.h.   ★ TV,LF,F,KF, ceiling fans, guest quarters are separate, wheel-chair access   ⓦ Smoking outside
⌇French, some Spanish
🏃 Museum & canoe building shop onsite, Luskville Escarpment look-out, rock climbing, voyageur canoe trips   🚗 Ottawa

🐾 Retired educators in loghouse with massive fieldstone fireplace in the centre of the living room and country decor mixed with an eclectic collection of pottery, skins and stuffed animals. Located at the foot of the Gatineau Park mountains. An outdoor enthusiast's paradise, both winter and summer. Hosts will guide guests in a rock climb to the escarpment summit and will take guests in their 12-man canoes on the river (following ancient trading routes). There is a cat. ✓B&B.

Fisher, Ken (Wanaki-on-the-Ottawa B&B)   ☎ (819) 455-9295, Fax (819) 455-9213
133 Ave des Plages, Pontiac (Luskville), QC   J0X 2G0

$45S $55D $5Child (under age 13) $70F $15Add.person   🍽 Meals   ► 10A,4Ch
Phone for directions.

🍴 Full (gourmet)   🏠 Rural, 2-storey, view from guest rooms, riverfront, 3acres, deck, quiet, secluded   ■2D,1F (ground level)
🛏6S,2T,1D   🛁 2Sh.w.g.   ★ Air,F,TV, LF,KF, indoor swim spa & exercise room, separate entrance, guest quarters are separate   ⓦNo smoking   ⌇ French
🏃 Extensive, private and secluded beach with view of open water, canoeing or x-c skiing on the river
🚗 Ottawa, Hull, Casino, Luskville Falls, Gatineau Hills, Prov. snowmobile trail

🐾 Large, new house surrounded by woods overlooking private beach and the Ottawa River. Sumptuous meals range from traditional to vegetarian. Relax in the swim spa or by the campfire. Breakfast is served in special guest breakfast room. Meeting room for 20 available. There are very friendly dogs in residence.

Prévost
(north of Montreal; see also Ste Anne des Lacs, Ste Agathe, St.Jerome)

Laroche, Francois (Aux Berges Fleuries)   ☎ (450) 224-7631, Fax (450) 436-5997
1028 Principale, Prévost, QC   J0R 1T0

From Montréal take Hwy 15 north and Exit 55. Cross bridge and turn right on Rue Principale. Look for B&B on left side.

$40S $60D $20Add.person   ► 8
🍴 Full, homebaked   🏠 Village, hist., patio   ■ 2S,3D (main floor)   🛏4S,1D,1Q   🛁 2Sh.w.g.   ★LF,TV in guest lounge, parking   ⌇English(household language is French)
🏃 Restaurants, flea market, art gallery, park (river & woods), hiking, canoeing, golfing at back door, cycling, fishing, x/c skiing
🚗 St-Sauveur (shopping, theatres) excellent downhill skiing

🐾 100-year old red brick country house located in quiet village at the beginning of the Laurentian Mountains. Rooms are named after important painters (Monet, Van Gogh, Renoir, Picasso, Cezanane). Experience the very special house breakfast, enjoy an ideal get-away from the hectic life in the city around the outside fireplace. ✓CC

Lavigne, P.& M. Sévigny (Chez Madeleine et Pierre B&B) ☎ (514) 224-4628
CP 92, Prévost, QC J0R 1T0 E-mail: bdaignau@marasuca.com, Fax (514) 224-7457

From Hwy15 North take Exit 55. Turn right on Rue Morin, cross bridge, left on Station Rd. Proceed 1km to Montée Sauvage, turn left to Du Sommet, right to De La Voie Lactée, right to B&B.

$40S $50-65D ► 4A
Jan15-Mar31 and June1-Oct15 Full, homebaked Res, rural, hillside, log home, view, quiet 2D(street level) 2T(K),1Q 1Private, 1sh.w.h. ★ F,TV,fans in guest rooms No smoking, no pets, not suitable for children
English, Spanish (household language is French)
Linear Park (200 km for biking/walking/x-c skiing), horseback riding, St.Sauveur Village, alpine skiing, golfing, waterslide, Flea Market and Antiquarians, bush walk/ski paths (developed by McGill Outing Club), bus to Montreal
Montreal, Laurentian Mountain Region (with lakes, panoramas, colorful autumns
Large Austrian/Swiss-style Alpine house, designed and constructed by hosts (inspired from trips abroad) with fireplaces in living and dining rooms. Relax in the solarium with jacuzzi and spa. Hosts are retired Professionals and have time to share their travel experiences and lovely home in the mountains with guests. B&B

Quebec City

(see also Ile d'Orléans; see also Cap Rouge, Beauport, Levis)

Blouin, Gilberte "Mimi" (Bienvenue Chez Mimi) ☎ (418) 524-9161, Fax (819) 843-7627
70, rue Fraser, Québec City, PQ G1R 2B6

Entering City on Hwy 20, cross bridge & take Blvd Laurier (becomes La Grande Allée). Turn left on Cartier and right on Fraser.

$50-60S $65-70D $15Add.person Meals ► 6+
Full, homebaked Res., 3-storey, hist., deck, quiet
1S,2D(upstairs) 1S,2T,1Q,2R 1sh.w.g., 1sh.w.h.
★Indiv. air-conditioners, TV in guest rooms, piano, parking No smoking
Center of Old Québec City, lively district of rue Cartier, hist. Plains of Abraham, easy access to buses #11 & #801
Chutes Montmorency, Ste-Anne-de-Beaupré, Ile d'Orléans, Mont St-Anne skiing, Charlevoix
Cozy, comfortable home with a wonderful balcony shaded by a stately maple tree, situated in central location. Breakfast is served in the dining room. Enjoy the friendly atmosphere.

Bourgault, Ginette (Bourgault Centre Ville) ☎ (418) 525-7832
650 Dela Reine, Quebec City, QC G1K 2S1

Phone for directions.
$55S $65D $85F ► 10A,2Ch
Full, homebaked Res., townhouse, 3-storey, patio, quiet
5D,1Ste(upstairs) 2T,1D,3K,cots 2private, 3sh.w.g. ★LF,KF with microwave,TV in guest room, bike rack, garage for motorcycles/canoes, barbeque, picnic table, parking English (French is household language)
Old walled city of Québec, Museum of Civilization, Art Gallery, restaurants and shops, train & bus station
Spacious renovated Century home with bright, large courtyard and flower garden in back. Also apt-studio available.

Côté, Odile and David Leslie (Gîte du Passant B&B)   ☎ (418) 648-8168
324,21E Rue, Québec, QC   G1L 1Y7

From Hwy 40, turn off at Exit 315 for 1ère Ave. Turn left onto 41st
St, then right on 4th Ave, right onto 21stE St.
$50S $60D $10Child $15Add.person ►5
🍷 Choice, homebaked   🏠 Downtown, res., patio, quiet   ■2D
(upstairs)   ⊨ 1D,1Q,cot   ⊴1Sh.w.g.   ★ F, parking at door
♥   ⓦNo pets,no smoking   ⚘ English
🏃 Cartier Brébeuf Park with replicas of Cartier's boat/Indian
settlement/Interpretation center, bus to Old Québec.
🚗 Historic Old Québec (5 min), Old Port with ferries, cruises.
🐎 Comfortable home on tree-lined residential street. Breakfast, organically grown & homemade, is
served to classical music. Tourist information available. Visa ⤙B&B

Du Sault, Francine (B&B Les Corniches)   ☎ (418) 681-9318, Fax (418) 681-4028
2052 Chemin St-Louis, Sillery, QC   G1T 1P4

Sillery is in the center of Quebec City. Cross the St. Lawrence River on Pierre Laporte Bridge, follow
Blvd Laurier to Maguire Ave. Turn right and proceed to Chemin St-Louis St, then right.

$50-75per room (off-season rates available) ► 7A,2Ch
🍷 Homebaked   🏠 Center Town, res. hist., 2-storey, view from
guest rooms, quiet, deck   ■ 2D,1F (upstairs) guest quarters are
separate   ⊨ 1S,1Q,2K   ⊴1Private, 1sh.w.g.   ★ F in TV
room   ⓦ Designated smoking area, no pets, children min. age 6
⚘ English (French is household language)
🏃 Historic plains of Abraham, St. Lawrence River, museums, fine
restaurants, shopping malls, cycling, walking, jogging
🚗 Famous Old Québec (walled historic site), revamped old port area with ferries/cruise boats
🐎 Lovely historic cottage with beautiful English-style interior and atmosphere of comfort and
elegance. Situated on large landscaped grounds with a variety of trees in one of the most attractive
neighbourhoods of the city. Relax on the outside deck or in the large family room with fireplace. Hosts
have longtime experience in hospitality and know the city extremely well.

Fleet, Stuart and Marie-Paule (Fleet's Guest House Bed & Breakfast)   ☎ (418) 688-0794
1080 Holland Ave., Sillery, PQ   G1S 3T3

North Shore Route: Take Autoroute 40 to Rte 440 Blvd Charest. Exit Ave St.Sacrament Sud which
becomes Holland Ave. South Shore Route: Take Autoroute 20 to Quebec Exit. Cross Pont Pierre
Laporte Bridge, turn right on Blvd. Laurier to Holland Ave. (3 km).
$35-45S $50-65D $75F $5Child $15Add.person   🍽 Meals ► 8A,3Ch

🍷Full,homebaked   🏠Res.,2-storey, quiet   ■3D,1F(upstairs)
⊨2T,1D,2Q, cots, crib   ⊴ 3Sh.w.g.   ★Air,LF,TV in guest rooms,
parking   ⓦNo pets   ⚘ French
🏃 Famous "Plains of Abraham", Citadel - Changing Guards
🚗 Old Quebec, Place Royal (proclaimed world treasure heritage)
🐎 Enjoy breakfast outside on the deck, in the solarium or dining
room of this spacious home. Hosts have many years of experience in
the hotel business. Entire upper floor is for guests only.

Lafleur, Gilles (La Maison Lafleur B&B)   ☎ (418) 692-0685
2 Rue de Laval, Quebec City, QC   G1R 3T9

From Hwys 20/40, follow signs to Old Quebec. Located inside Walls.
$60S $75D $115F $20Add.person   ► 8
🔲 Full   🏠 Downtown, 2-storey, view from guest rooms, quiet   ▣2D,1F
(upstairs)   ⊨ 2D,1Q,1R,1P   ⛴ 1sh.w.g., 1sh.w.h   ★ TV,off-street
parking   🚭No smoking, no pets   ⚫ French
🏃 Downtown area with tourist attractions, restaurants, services, bus/train
🚗 Ski resorts, Cote-de-Beaupre, Ile d'Orléans, maple sugar cabins
🚘 Comfortable home with stone walls and interior decoration of style and
harmony situated in peaceful location in the heart of the old Latin Quarter,
surrounded by exceptional views of 17th and 18th Century architecture.
Host is a longtime resident of Old Quebec and will gladly suggest many unforgettable places to visit
(all within walking distance). Visa,MC

Saint-Aubin, Monique and André   ☎ (418) 658-0685, Fax (418) 658-8466
3045 rue de la Seine, Ste-Foy, QC   G1W 1H8   E-mail: staubin@qbc.clic.net

From Montreal, take Hwy 20 east to Quebec City and Pierre Laporte Bridge. Exit on Laurier Blvd. At
1st traffic light turn right to rue Lavigerie, and right on rue de la Seine (3rd street).

$40-45S $50-60D $10Child(under age 12)   ► 9
🔲 Full   🏠 Res., multi-storey   ▣2D,1F(upstairs & main level)
⊨ 2T,2D,1Q   🚗3Sh.w.h.   ★ Air,TV,F,parking   🚭No
pets   ⚫English (household language is French)
🏃 Shopping Center, bus and railway station, Laval University
🚗 Old Quebec City, museum, Art Gallery, Summer Festival,
golfing, Zoo, downhill skiing, Ile d'Orléans
🚘 Comfortable Canadian-style home located in quiet residential
neighbourhood. Sightseeing tours and excursions can be arranged with pick-up at the house. ✓B&B

Saint Gelais, Marie Denise (A L'Etoile de Rosie"   ☎ (418) 648-1044
66 Lockwell, Quebec City, QC   G1R 1V7

From Pierre Laporte Bridge proceed on Blvd Laurier which becomes Grand
Allee. Turn on Turbull St, then on Lockwell.
$55S $75D $15Child   ► 8
🔲 Homebaked   🏠 Upper town, 2-storey, view from guest rooms
▣2D,1F(upstairs)   ⊨ 2S,2D,1R   ⛴ 1Sh.w.g., 1sh.w.h.   ★ Street parking
(4Pm to 10Am)   🚭 No smoking, no pets, children min. age 5   ⚫English
(household language is French)
🏃 Rue Cartier & Saint Jean Street shopping, Grand Theatre, Musee du
Quebec, Old City, Congres Centre, bus route
🚗 Chateau Frontenac, Citadelle de Quebec, Plaines d'Abraham, Parliament
🚘 Comfortable row-house (ca 1920) exuding great energy and situated on a quiet tree-lined street
near the artists quarters of Saint Jean Baptiste and Montcalm in an area with European atmosphere.
Breakfast is served in special guest breakfast room. Hostess is knowledgeable about the sites and
happenings in the City and will gladly help with plans. Visa

Tessier, Gaétan & Sylvie (B&B Bedondaine - Couette et Café)   ☎ (418) 681-0783
912 Ave Madeleine de Verchères, Quebec City, QC   G1S 4K7

Coming from Hwy 20 over Pierre Laporte Bridge procced on Blvd Laurier toward Quebec City.
Continue past Laval University, turn left on Blvd René Lévesque, then left on Ave Madeleine de V.
$40S $50D $10Child $15Add.person   (special rate for longer stays)   ▶ 2A,1Ch

🍲 Full,homebaked (selfserve) 🏠 Res., raised bungalow ■1D
(lower level) ⊨1D,crib 🛁1Sh.w.h. ★ F,LF, storage space
for guest bicycles and skis 🚭 No smoking, no pets ᴡᴡEnglish
(household language is French)
🏃 Jardin Coulange, Domaine Cataraque, Rue Maguire (Sillery),
restaurants, shops, Laval University, x-c skiing, tennis, bus route
🚗 Old City of Quebec, Ils d'Orléans, Chute Mont Morency, Mont
St.Anne downhill skiing, Museum de la Civilization
📢 Comfortable family home situated on a calm street. Enjoy warm and friendly Quebec hospitality.
Host is an English Teacher & hostess is a Librarian. Healthy breakfast is served in the dining room
with beautiful music. There is a cat in residence. Ask about pick-up in summer.

Tim, Guitta & Greg (Maison Historique James Thompson)   ☎ (418) 694-9042
47 Rue Sainte-Ursule, Old Quebec City, QC   G1R 4E4

Entering the City via 175 north, tun left on 2nd street inside Saint-Louis Gate.
$60S $65D $5child $10Add.person   (plus tax) 🍽 Meals   ▶ 10

🍲 Full, homebaked 🏠 Downtown, 3-storey, hist., quiet
■1S,1D,2F(upstairs) ⊨5D,1futon 🛁1Sh.w.g., 1sh.w.h - ★TV
in guest lounge, ceiling fans, off-street & street parking, guest
quarters are separate 🚭 No pets ᴡᴡ French
🏃 Chateau Frontenac, Citadal, fortified Old Towne, bus & train
station, harbour, horse buggyrides
📢 Historic home (ca 1793) located in the heart of Old Quebec.
Breakfast is served in the guest breakfast room.↙CC

Quyon   *(west of Hull & Ottawa,ON; see also Paspebiac, Ladysmith, Wakefield)*

Marcotte, Gilles & Christine (Hillside B&B - Lit et Gîte de la Colline) ☎(819)458-2324
315 Clarendon St., RR4, Quyon, QC   J0X 2V0

$35S $50D $15Add.person (child under age 5 free) 🍽 Meals (plus tax)   ▶ 8

Follow Hwy 148 west and 3.3km west of Quyon.
🍲 Full, homebaked 🏠 Farm, 2-storey, view from one guest room,
patio, quiet ■ 2F(main level) ⊨2D,2P,cot 🛁1Sh.w.g.,
1ensuite ★ Air,F,TV,private entrance, wheel-chair access, guest
quarters are separate 🚭 No smoking ᴡᴡ French
🏃 X-c skiing, snowshoeing, tobogganing, skidoeing trails (Reg &
Trans Quebec No13), hiking
🚗 Golfing, skiing, Luskville Caves, Gatineau Park, boating
📢 Large, newly renovated home with country decor and beautiful view of the Gatineau Hills. Relax
by the warm fire in the evening either outside or in. Enjoy the quiet and relaxing atmosphere after a
day of travelling or sightseeing or hiking in the bush. Browse through the on site gift/craft shop.
Breakfast is served in large central eating area. There is a resident dog (not in B&B area).

Repentigny

(north-east of Montreal)

Cloutier, Denise & Claude Neveu (La Villa des Fleurs) ☎ (514) 654-9209
45 rue Gaudreault, Repentigny, QC J6A 1M3

From Montreal or Quebec City on Hwy 40, take exit 96E and 640 east. Turn left on l'Assomption Blvd, right at Perreault St and left on Gaudreault. From Rte 138 in Repentigny, turn on Claude

David St and right at L'Assomption Blvd, then as above.
$40S $50D $10Add.person   ▶ 12
🔟 Full, homebaked   🏠 Res., sub., split-level, swimming pool, patio, deck   ■ 3D,1F (main, ground & upper level)   ⊨2S,3D,1Q
⌐ 2Sh.w.g.   ★ F,TV,KF,LF, off-street parking   ⓌDesignated smoking area   ⌁ French
🚶 Shopping, cinema, church, bicycle way, restaurants
🚗 Olympic Stadium, Botanic Garden Biodome, St. Helene Island
🐾 Warm and friendly welcome in large modern home. Enjoy the congenial hospitality. ⌐B&B

Saint-Hyacinthe

(east of Montreal, see also St German de Grant, South Durham)

Avard, Bernard & Carmen (Le Jardin Caché B&B) ☎ (450) 773-2231
2465 Ave Raymond, Saint-Hyacinthe, QC J2S 5W4

From Montreal or Quebec City take Hwy 20 and Exit 130 Blvd Laframboise to the Arch. Turn right on Bourdages, right on Bourassa, left on Raymond.

$35-45S $50-60D $15Child $80F   (plus taxes)   ▶ 6A,1Ch
🔟 Full, homebaked   🏠 Res., 2-storey, patio, porches, quiet
■3D(upstairs)   ⊨ 2T,1D,1Q,1R   ⌐ 2Sh.w.g.   ★F,TV,ceiling fans, separate entrance, off-street & street parking, spa, guest quarters are separate   Ⓦ Designated smoking area, no pets, English (household language is French)
🚶 Retro Rock/Roll Music Festival (Aug), Agricultural Fair, Int. Fibers Symposium (May98), golf courses, walking/cycling paths, x/c skiing, bus & train
🚗 Montreal, Dorval Airport, Drummondville Folklore Festival
🐾 "Young" Bell Canada pensioners and well travelled hosts in family ancestral home filled with antiques and paintings, located in the heart of the city. Proud winners of the Montérégie Hospitality Excellence Prize (96/97). Relax in the outside spa situated in the English garden and enjoy the fish pond. "Scrumptious breakfasts are worth the detour"! Visa,MC ⌐B&B

Sainte-Adèle

(n/w of Montreal; see also Ste Anne des Lacs, Prevost, Ste Adele, St Jerome)

Lamothe, Hannes & Diane Savard (Beaux Rêves B&B) ☎ & Fax (514)229-9226
2310 Blvd St-Adèle, Saint-Adèle, QC J0R 1L0   E-mail: welcome@beauxreves.com 1-800-279-7679

$50-65S $75-90D $15Child $90-120F $20Add.person   (plus taxes)   ▶ 8
From Montreal, take Hwy 15 north to Exit 67. Proceed on Rte 117 to Blvd Ste-Adèle, then 3.6km to stone house with blue roof.
🔟Full   🏠3-storey,view from guest rooms,riverback,patio,deck, quiet   ■3D,1F(upstairs)   ⊨3D,2Q   ⌐4Private   ★F,TV,separate entrance,ceiling fans, guest balconies, relaxation pavillion, massages, stone sauna/ext.spa, off-street parking   ⓌNo smoking, no pets, children must be supervised   ⌁English (French is household language)
🚶 Golfing, hiking, cycling, downhill & x-c skiing, snowmobiling, "Le Petit train du Nord", festivals, summer theatres, fine dining, gift & souvenir shop on site
🚗 Montreal, Mont Tremblant, Mirabel Airport
🐾 Warm and friendly welcome in old stone home with tastefully decorated rooms located on an enchanted river in the heart of the Laurentian mountains, offering a unique relaxing experience. Browse through the in-house gift shop, or watch the natural whirl pools.Enjoy a complete Canadian breakfast. An ideal place for a romantic get-away or special occasion. Visa,Amex ⌐B&B

Lelland, Huguette & Michel Ouellette (L'Auberge Bonne Nuit Bonjour)
1980 Blvd Ste-Adèle, CP2168, Ste-Adèle, PQ J0R 1L0 ☎ & Fax(514)229-7500, 1-888-229-7500

From Montréal take Rt 15 N to Ste. Adèle (Exit 67). Ask for directions at Tourist Kiosque

$65S $85D $15Add.person ▶ 14

🍲 Full, homebaked 🏠 Village, outdoor heated swimming pool, patio,quiet ■6D(main and upper levels) ■6D,3T ⬅4Private, 1sh.w.g. ★F,TV Den, glassed-in sitting room, parking ⓦNo smoking, no pets ᳭English (household language is French)
🏃 Ski resorts(x-c/alpine skiing), snowmobiling, golfing, sport center, bowling, historic village (Seraphin), summer theatre
🚗 Waterslides, ice-skating, pedal-boating, fine food restaurants
🔫 Tourist Award winning home is located in a wooded setting and projects a calm and serene atmosphere for relaxing. "Come, discover the old in the new & partake of warm hospitality". ↩ CC

St-André-de-Kamouraska   *(west of Rivière-du-Loup; see also Kamouraska)*

Robert, Yvon & Isabelle Poyau (Auberge La Solaillerie)   ☎ (418) 493-2914
112 Ave Principale, St-André-de-Kamouraska, QC G0L 2H0   Fax (418) 493-2243

$45-85S $54-90D $20Child $25Add.person 🍴Meals (plus tax) (Off-season discounts) ▶ 24

From Hwy 20, take Exit 480 toward St-André. In the village, turn right on Ave Principale. Look for house next to Post Office.
🔆 Summer only 🍲 Full 🏠 Village, hist. 3-storey, acreage, view from guest rooms, riverfront, patio ■ 11 (main & upper level ➡5D,6Q ⬅ 6Private, 2sh.w.g., footbath and sink in three guest rooms ★ Separate entrance, guest quarters are separate ⓦDesignated smoking area, no pets ᳭ some English (household language is French)
🏃 Hiking, golfing, summer theatre, boat cruise, horsback riding, bird watching
🔫 Spacious historic home built in 1853 with authentic period decor and view of the St.Lawrence River. Breakfast is served in the onsite period restaurant. Visa, MC ↩B&B

St-Germain-de-Grantham   *(south of Drummondville)*

Levasseur, Juliette (Le Madawaska B&B)   ☎ (819) 395-4318
644 Rte 239, St-Germain-de-Grantham, QC J0C 1K0

From Montreal on Hwy 20, take Exit 166. turn right onto Hwy 239 North. From Quebec City take Exit 166 and turn left onto Hwy 239. Proceed 3km.

$40S $55D $10Child ▶ 6

🍲 Homebaked 🏠 Rural, older, multi-storey, large flowered grounds, wrap-around veranda ■3D(upper & lower level) ➡2T,1D ⬅Sh.w.g. ★Parking ⓦ No smoking, no pets ᳭ English
🚗 Drummondville (historic village), Folklore Festival (July)
🔫 Large warm country home ca1916, with simple comforts and sunny atmosphere. Enjoy true warm Acadian-Québec hospitality. ↩B&B

St-Jérôme

(n/of Montréal; see also Prévost, Ste Anne des Lacs, Ste Adele)

Lemay, Marie-Thérèse et Gérard (L'Etape)
430 Melançon, St-Jérôme, QC J7Z 4K4

☎ (514) 438-1043

From Montréal or Mirabel Airport, take rte 15 north & Exit 43 east for St-Jérôme. Proceed along DeMartigny St to City center. Turn right on Blvd Labelle & just before the park in front
of the Cathedral turn left on DuPalais. Proceed to Melançon on left
$35S $50D $12Child $20Add.person ▶ 6A,1Child
💧 Full, homebaked 🏠 Res., older, large acreage, quiet
■3D(main and upper level) ⊨1S,4T,1K 🛏 3Sh.w.h.
★TV,F,LF,KF ⚓ Restricted smoking ⌇English (French is household language)
🕴 City center, Cultural Center, art galleries, popular concerts in the park, shops and restaurants, church, baseball/football field

🐦 Stone-brick house is a cottage in the New-England style with 2 columns framing the front door, built by a renowned architect and situated adjacent to a municipal park. Hosts are professional retirees and active in local cultural and sociological groups. ✒B&B

St-Lazare

(west of Montreal; see also Hudson/Heights)

Bisson, Lise & Leah Archambault (Halte de Ressourcement B&B)
2565.Chm St-Angélique, St-Lazare, QC J7T 2K6

☎ (514) 990-7825
Fax (514) 455-1786

From Hwys 20 and/or 40 take Exit 22 to St-Lazare. Turn left on Chm St-Angélique.
$45S $60D $15Child $20Add.person 🍽 Meals ▶ 16
💧 Full 🏠 Farm, ranch-style, view from guest rooms, 1.5 acres, patio, porch, quiet ■ 6S,5D(upstairs) ⊨ 6S,5Q 🛁1private, 2sh.w.g.,1sh.w.h. ★ KF,LF,F,TV,ceiling fans, off-street parking, guest quarters are separate, on-site yoga/meditation facilities
⚓No smoking ⌇ English (household language is French)
🕴 Equestrian facilities, alpine/x-c skiing, summer theatre, cycling path, dog-sledding, ice-fishing, long silent walks
🚗 Dorval International Airport, downtown Montreal

🐦 Large comfortable Cape Cod home; a very quiet and idyllic place, where guests are invited to relax, revitalize and participate in daily yoga and meditation practice. Breakfast is served in guest breakfast room. MC,Amex ✒B&B

St-Sévère

(west of Trois-Rivières; see also Louiseville, Pointe du Lac)

Héroux, Lise (Au Bourgainvillier)
83 Rue Principale, St-Sévère, QC G0X 3B0

☎ & Fax (819) 264-5653

Located halfway between Montréal and Québec City. From Hwy 40 take Exit 180. In Yamachiche at
flashing light, proceed towards Shawinigan and continue on Rt 153
for 3 km. Then follow signs to St-Sévère for 5 km.
$35S $50D $10Child $15Add.person ▶ 8A,3Ch
💧 Full 🏠 Village, older, quiet ■ 4 (upstairs) ⊨4D
🛁2Sh.w.g. ★ TV,LF, parking ⚓ No pets ⌇ English
(household language is French)
🕴 Watch farming activities, walking in village "promenade"
🚗 Art Gallery, museum, summer theatre, boat cruise, skiing

🐦 Sixth-Generation family (Héroux and Bourgainville) in rustic, spacious, 170-year-old home with antique furnishings situated in an agricultural village projecting a taste of yesterday. Relax on the wrap-around porch and enjoy the peaceful, quiet country atmosphere. ✒B&B

Ste-Anne-des-Lacs

(north-west of Montreal; see also Prevost, St Jerome, Ste Adele)

Martin-Garin, Gabrielle (Bed & Breakfast des Lacs)   ☎ & Fax (514) 224-8030
831 Chm Ste-Anne-des-Lacs, Ste-Anne-des-Lacs, QC J0R 1B0

From Montréal, take Hwy 15 north and Exit 57 at Ste-Anne-des-Lacs. Turn left, proceed 4km to

Chm des Ormes. Turn right to 1st house on right.
$40-45S $50-55D $10Child $10Add.person   ► E
🍴 Full, homebaked   🏠 Res.,2-storey, 1 acre, view from guest
rooms, patio, quiet, secluded   ■2(ground level)   ⊨1D,1Q,cot
⌐1sh.w.h.   ★ TV,F,LF, wheel-chair access, off-street parking
🚭No smoking, no pets   ⚬ English (household language is French)
🚶 Village, Lake Ste-Anne, woodland strolls, x-c skiing at door
🚗 Several major Ski Resorts, Montreal, St.Sauveur (restaurants, chic boutiques, Aquatic Centre)
🏹 Warm, quiet home located in popular Laurentien Mountains area, and excellent location for
summer and winter activities. Well travelled hosts (from France & Belgium) will gladly arrange tours
of the areas. Pick-up from bus/airport can be arranged. Hostess is a Massage Therapist ("parfait"
B&B massage available). There are 2 dogs in residence.

Swerdlow, Anne   ☎ (514) 224-5401
39 Chemin des Lilas, Ste. Anne Des Lilas QC   J0R 1B0

From Montréal, take Hwy 15 north and Exit 57 at Ste-Anne-des-Lacs. Turn left and proceed 5 km

to Chemin des Lilas (opposite gas station). Turn left.
$30S $35D $6Add.person   🍽 Meals   ► 4
🍴 Full, homebaked   🏠 Village, view, patio, lakefront, quiet
■2D(upstairs)   ⊨ 1S,2T,1D   ⌐ Sh.w.g.   ★ TV,F,KF, parking,
space for ski equipment   🚭No smoking
🚶 Lake directly in front of house, swimming, canoeing, woodland
strolls, x-c skiing
🚗 Several major resorts for winter sports, esp.downhill skiing
🏹 Well travelled hostess in very spacious comfortable family home overlooking the lake and
situated in beautiful wooded area surrounded by the Laurentien Mountains. Enjoy the close proximity
(7km) to popular St.Sauveur Ski Resort, jewel of the Laurentian ski area.

South Durham

(south-east of Drummondville)

Carson, Norman & Heather Lunan (La Sixième Génération B&B)   ☎ (819) 858-2539
415 Ch.Mooney, Durham-Sud, QC   J0H 2C0   Fax (819) 858-2001

From Montreal, travel east on Hwy 20 to Exit 147. Follow Hwy 116 east to Durham-Sud. Proceed
2.5km past village on Mooney Rd. From Hwy 10, take Exit 88 and follow Hwy116 to Mooney Rd.
$40-45S $55-60D $10Child $15Add.person   (plus taxes)   ► 6A,2-3Ch
🍴 Cont.,homebaked   🏠 Farm, 2-storey, hist., view from guest
rooms, swimming pool, patio, porch, deck, quiet   ■2D,1F(main &
upper level)   ⊨2T,1D,1Q,1P   ⌐ 1Sh.w.g.   ★ F,TV, guest
quarters are separate   🚬 Designated smoking area   ⚬ French
🚶 Children's play area, river/fields/woods, skidoo trails, x-c skiing
🚗 Historic Woolen Mill, museums, x-c ski club, concert halls,
golfing, antiquing, cycling
🏹 Warm welcome in enlarged & extended 1865-built home on
Sixth Generation farm, surrounded by peace & beauty. Ideal place from which to view exquisite fall
foliage. Join the host family in the original beam accented living room for social time. There is a cat
and a dog. Also farm stays available. ⌐B&B

Sutton

(south of Saint Hyacinthe near US border)

.eBaron-Watson, Pat & Allan Watson (Willow House)   ☎ (514) 538-0035
0 Western Ave., Box 906, Sutton, QC   J0E 2K0

'rom Montreal, take Eastern Township Auto Rt 10 and Exit 60 onto Hwy 139 to Sutton. Turn
right off Principale at Foyer Sutton to Western Ave.
$30S $50D $20Child $20Add.person   🍽 Meals   ► 8
🆎 Choice 🏠 Village, hist., view, patio, quiet ■4D(upstairs)
⊨4T,1D,1K 🛁Sh.w.g. ★TV,LF, guest den ✋ Designated
smoking area ⌇French
🚶 Boutiques, Art Sutton, library, antiques, fine restaurants,
gorgeous fall colours, public transportation to downtown Montreal
🚐 Mount Sutton ski hill, x-c skiing, Vermont Border, golfing

Lovely Old Loyalist home with a view of running brook and pond. Situated in the hub of artisans
nvironment with many arts/craft shops nearby. Enjoy homebaking for breakfast and afternoon tea.
'ets welcome. ⌐CC

Tourelle

(Gaspè, east of Matane)

1iville, Bibiane & Rino Cloutier (Le Courant de la Mer)   ☎ & Fax (418) 763-5440
Rue Belvedere, Box 191, Tourelle, QC   G0E 2J0   1-800-230-6709

.35S $50-75D $7-12Child $12Add.person   (longer stay rates)   ► 12A,3Ch
From Quebec City take Hwy 20 and Hwy 132 east to Tourelle. From the
Rest Area drive 0.2km and turn left at white house.
📅Mar-Nov 🆎 Full 🏠3-storey, patio, oceanfront ■3D,1F(upst)
⊨2S,2T,3D,R,P,cot 🛁 3Sh.w.g. ★ TV in guest room, off-street
parking ✋Smoking in Den, no pets ⌇English (household language is
French)
🚶 Stroll by the sea, stores, restaurant, Sea Food Canteen
🚐 Parc de la Gaspésie (Mont Jaques Cartier), Explorama, Mont Albert

Retired teacher/med.service hosts in large home by the sea with warm & friendly atmosphere &
superb view of the St.Laurence River. Relax by the rythm of the waves breaking on the beach &
njoy the peaceful environment. Visa ⌐B&B

Trois-Pistoles

(east of Rivière du Loup; see also Bic)

1ardy, Marcel & Jeanne Riverin (Au Gré des Marées B&B)   ☎ (418) 851-3819
25 Notre Dame Ouest, Trois-Pistoles, QC   G0L 4K0

Phone for directions.
$40S $50D $10Child $15Add.person   ► 6A,2Ch
🆎 Full, homebaked 🏠 Rural, res., 2-storey, older, view, porch,
riverback, patio, quiet ■2S,2D,1F (upstairs) ⊨2T,2D,1Q
🛁1Sh.w.g., 1sh.w.h ★ F,TV,ceiling fans ✋ Designated
smoking area ⌇ English (household language is French)
🚐 Summer Theatre, restaurants, golfing, salmon fishing, skiing
🚶 Old Car Museum, Basque Adventure Park, ferry to north shore,
xcursions (to Basque Island and whale watching on St.Lawrence River)
Warm welcome in spacious confortable home with a beautiful view of the St. Lawrence river and
cenic countryside. Enjoy a sumptuous breakfast. Pick-up at railroad or bus station available. There is
cat in residence. Visa ⌐B&B

Trois Rivière

(east of Montreal; see also Point du Lac, Louisville, Saint Sevèr

Huard, Mme Nicole (Le Gîte du Huard) ☎ (819) 375-877

42 rue St-Louis, Vieux Trois Rivière, QC   G9A 1T5

From Hwy 40, take exit to Trois Rivière Centre Ville (downtown) and proceed on St-Rock St South.

Turn left on Notre Dame St, right on Des Casernes St, left on Terrasse Turcotte and left on St-Louis St.
$30-45S $50-60D $10-15Child/Add.person   ► 1
🍽 Cont.   🏠 Downtown, 2-storey, hist., riverfront, porch, quiet
📺 5 (main & upper floor)   🛏 S,T,D,Q,K   🚿 5Private
★Air,KF,F,TV in guest rooms, ceiling fans, private entrance, street & off-street parking   🚭 No smoking, no pets   〰 English (household language is French)

🎣 St.Lawrence River and waterfront promenade, park with historic monuments, Quebec Museum of Arts, river cruises, skating, art shops, restaurants, local bus system

📣 Large home, former American Consulate (1880-82) located in the heart of the city's historic section with a panoramic view of the St.Lawrence River. Breakfast is served in special guest breakfast room. There is a small dog in residence.

Loisell, Michele (Le Gîte Loiselle) ☎ & Fax (819) 375-212

836 des Ursulines, Trois-Rivières, QC   G9A 5B9

Phone for directions.
$45-55S $65-75D $15Child   ► 1
🍽 Homebaked   🏠 Downtown, 3-storey, hist., patio, quiet
📺 4D,1F (upstairs & lower level)   🛏 3S,4Q   🚿 5Private
★Air,TV, private entrance, off-street parking, guest quarters are separate   🚭 No smoking, no pets   〰 English (household language is French)
🎣 Cruises on St.Maurice & St.Laurence Rivers, golfing, beaches, marinas, bicycle roads, antique dealers, shops, restaurants

🚗 National Park La Mauricie & historic site, Pulp & Paper Industry Exhibition Centre

📣 Large home built in 1899, restored over the years and located in the historic city area. Hosts are proud receivers of the City's Heritage Restoration Award. Visa,MC 〰CC

Richer, Sylvia (L'Emerillon B&B) ☎ (819) 375-101

890 Terrasse Turcotte, Trois-Rivières, QC   G9A 5C5

From Hwy 40 take exit to Trois-Rivières Centre-Ville (downtown) and proceed on St-Roch St South. Turn left on Notre Dame St, and right on Des Casernes St.

$55S $65D $10Child   ►
🍽 Cont, homebaked   🏠 Downtown, hist., 2-storey, view from guest rooms, riverfront, patio, quiet   📺 3D(upstairs)   🛏 3Q,1R   🚿 3Private   ★ F,TV,ceiling fans, separate entrance, billard room, off-street parking   🚭 No smoking, no pets   〰English (household language is French)
🎣 St-Lawrence River, waterfront park, historic monuments & buildings, Quebec Museum of Arts & Traditions, Pulp & Paper Museum, Quebec Archives, river cruises, skating, art shops, restaurants, local bus system

🚗 La Mauricie National Park, golf courses, Les Forges du St-Maurice National Park

📣 Distinctive colonial house furnished with fine English antiques, offering the charm and elegance of a bygone era with today's comforts. Located in the heart of the city's historic section along the waterfront promenade. Enjoy the panoramic view.Visa

Mercier, Madeleine and Jacques (Les Trois Erables)   ☎ (819) 459-1118
01 Riverside Rd., Box 852, RR2, Wakefield, QC   J0X 3G0

rom Ottawa, take MacDonald-Cartier Bridge across Ottawa River and Hwy 5 north to temporary
nd. Proceed on Hwy 105 to Wakefield (follow Maniwaki signs).

$55S $65D $80Ste   ► 8-10
❄ Closed Nov.and April ⬛Full 🏠Village, hist., 3-storey, acreage,
view, river, patio ⬛3D(upstairs),1Ste ⊨2T,3Q,1D
🛁4Ensuite ★ Air,F,TV in guest room, sep.entrance, parking
✋Rest. smoking ᴡᴡEnglish (household language French)
🏃 Gatineau River, Gatineau Park, restaurants, shops, x-country &
alpine skiing, lake swimming, windsurfing, canoeing, hiking,
mountain biking, nature trails, rhapsody of legendary fall colours

☛ National Capital Region Heritage home, built around the turn of the Century, tastefully restored
nd renovated to enhance the craftsmanship of years gone by and provides guests with superior
eeping and relaxing facilities. Enjoy a hearty breakfast with the sun filtering through the stained
lass windows or on cold mornings feel the warmth from the unique fireplace.MC ✓CC

New Brunswick

Petite Rocher
Robertville
Caraquet
Losier Settlement
Miramichi
Ste-Anne-de-K.
Grand Falls
Cape Tormentine
Bayfield
Port Elgin
Woodstock
Moncton
Sackville
Dorchester
Fredericton
Cambridge
Prince William
Hopewell
Gagetown
Sussex
Harvey
Alma
St.Martins
Saint John
St.George
St.Stephen
Back Bay
St.Andrews
Grand Manan

Tourism New Brunswick
Box 12345, Fredericton, NB   E3B 5C3

toll-free 1-800-561-0123

"Dial-A-Nite"

New Brunswick offers an In-Province Accommodation Reservation System:

This free telephone service is available only in Tourist Information Centres located in the province. It allows the traveler to make advance reservations with B&B hosts located throughout the province of NB.

Albert

(south of Moncton; see also Riverside, Alma, Hopewell Cape)

Tingley, Cyril and Mary (Florentine Manor)   ☎ (506) 882-2271 1-800-665-2271
RR2, Albert (Harvey), Albert Co., NB   E0A 1A0   E-mail: florainn@nbnet.nb.ca Fax (506) 882-2936

$55S $65-95D $10Child $99(Ste)   🍽 Meals   (plus tax)   ▶ 16A,4Ch
Take Rt114 at Moncton towards Fundy Nat.Park. At Riverside-Albert take Rt915 past old Bank of

NB for 3.5km. to No.915 at Harvey Corner on Fundy Coastal Drive. 🏠Full,homebaked 🏡Rural, acreage, hist. pastoral views from guest rooms, quiet ■6D,1F,1Ste (main & upper floor) 🚗Private (2 with whirlpool tub) 🛏6T,5D,2Q,2K,2R 🚭No pets, no smoking ★F,TV,LF,KF, private entrance in suite, guest robes, 🏃 Country lanes for leisure walks, prime birdwatching location 🚌 Shepody Bay Hemispheric Shore Bird Reserve at Mary's Point, Fundy Nat.Pk, Hopewell, Cape Rocks world's largest flower pots

🐾 Spacious (1860) house with extreme high ceilings (11ft), full of antiques, speaks of the grandeur of a past era when sailing ships were built and launched in the shipyards nearby. A "Customs Office" at one time and visited by Sea Captains from all over the world. Relax in the parlour and enjoy the lovely country atmosphere. Ideal place for large groups (biking, birding, hiking) and special occasions. Visa, MC ✍B&B

Alma

(south of Moncton; see also Riverside, Albert, Hopewell Cape)

O'Regan, Elsie & John (Captain's Inn)   ☎ (506) 887-2017, Fax (506) 887-2074
Alma, NB   E0A 1B0

Take Rte 114 at Moncton to Fundy National Park or Rte 114 Exit after Sussex.

$53S $69-74D $10Add.person   (plus tax)   ▶ 18
🏠 Full 🏡 Village, 2-storey, view from some guest rooms, quiet ■ 7D,1F (ground, main & upper level) 🛏 9Q 🚗9Private ★ Air,F,TV in guest rooms, separate entrance, off-street parking 🚭No smoking, no pets 🏃 Fundy National Park, world's highest tides at Bay of Fundy 🚌 Mary's Point Bird Sanctuary, Hopewell Rocks, Cape Enrage, Moncton, golfing, fishing, well groomed x-c ski trails

🐾 Very comfortable and quiet spacious house with a homey country atmosphere, overlooking the mighty tides of the Bay of Fundy (highest tides in the world), in quaint little fishing port close to East Gate entrance of Fundy National Park. Relax in the parlour or sunroom after a busy day outdoors. Hosts were born and raised in the village and are knowledgeable about the area. Visa,MC

Back Bay

(south of St.George; see also Grand Manan)

Matheson, Peggy & Murvin (The Beach House B&B)   ☎ (506) 755-2675
Box 68, Back Bay, NB   E0G 1B0   E-mail: peggym.nb.sympatico.ca, Fax (506) 755-3376

From Hwy 1 follow Route 772, and Deer Island Ferry signs for 11.6km to B&B. Look for sign.
$40S $60D $10Add.person   ▶ 9

🏠Full,homebaked 🏡Village,raised bungalow, hillside,oceanfront, acreage,view from guest rooms,patio,deck,quiet ■1S,2D,1Ste (main & ground level) 🛏3S,1D,2Q,cot 🚗1Shw.g.,1sh.w.h. ★TV,private guest deck,off-street parking 🚭Smoking outside 🏃 Ocean beach, stroll along water's edge collecting sea shells & driftwood, lobster pound, Sardine Canning Plant, fishing wharf 🚌 St.Andrews-by-the-Sea, Saint John, lighthouses, three islands ferries, Aquaculture sites, bicycling the "Quoddy Loop", US border

🐾 Large ocean home with waterfront deck. Watch the tides rise & fall in an everchanging panorama of beauty. Hosts know the area well, have been involved with the local fishing industry for 30 years and can tell many "sea lures and tales". Guests may join hauling lobster traps or repairing fishing gear. Boat tours available. A hearty Maritime breakfast is served on the deck or in the dining room while watching loons, cranes, eagles & ducks. Visa ✍B&B

Bayfield

east of Moncton; see also Cape Tormentine
(east of Moncton; see also Cape Tormentine)

Sloan, Eric & Debbie (Briggs Homestead B&B) ☎ (506) 538-2313
RR1, Bayfield, NB E0A 1E0

Located on Rte 955, 8km east of Murray Beach Provincial Park and 3km west of the Confederation Bridge to PEI.
$60S $69.50-77.50D $10Add.person ► 8
🍳 Homebaked 🏠 Rural, 2-storey, hist., farmhouse, 125acres, oceanview from guest rooms, porch, quiet ■ 4D(main & upper level) ⊨ 2S,2D,1Q,2cots ⇱ 4Ensuite ★ Air,TV,LF, guest quarters are in separate wing, separate entrance ⊛No smoking
🏃 Bicycling, children's playcentre, ponies, horseshoe pitch
🚗 Confederation Bridge to PEI, golf courses, Murray Beach Prov. Park, nature trails, Fort Beausejour, Moncton, Magnetic Hill, NS border
📣 Restored ca1860 family farmhouse on large acreage overlooking the Northumberland Strait. Host's great-great grandfather was the original owner and the rooms are furnished with antiques passed down through generations. House breakfast specialty is wild blueberry pancakes with pure maple syrup and served in guest breakfast room. There is a cat in host quarters. Visa ✔B&B

Cambridge Narrows

(west of Moncton; see also Gagetown, Sussex)

Steeves, Susan & Greg (Cambridge-Narrows B&B) ☎ (506) 488-2000
RR1, Cody's, NB E0E 1E0

From TCH 2 at Jemseg, take Rte 695 to Cambridge Narrows. Turn right before bridge (Rte 715). From east, take Rts 710/715 at Coles Isle, continue to Cambridge N. & then 1km on Rte 715.
$27S $38D $49Ste 5Add.person (inc.taxes) ► 6A,2Ch
🍳 Homebaked 🏠 Farm, acreage, 2-storey, view, lake across road ■ 2D,1Ste(upstairs) suite has loft ⊨1D,1Q,1K,R,P,crib ⇱ Sh.w.g., 1ensuite ★F,LF,KF,TV, separate entrance ⊛No smoking, no pets, families welcome
🏃 Restaurant, store, campground (beach, pool, dock, Rec Hall)
📣 Renovated older home, situated on a little hill overlooking Washadehoak Lake, surrounded by pastures & forests. Relax on the wrap-around veranda and enjoy the peaceful country atmosphere. Two-seater bike for rent. Breakfast in suite available at extra charge. Hosts operate the large campground and services on the property by the lake. ✔B&B

Waldow, Ursula and Achatz (Norwood Farms) ☎ (506) 488-2681
Cambridge Narrows, RR1 Cody's, NB E0E 1E0

Coming from west on Trans Canada Hwy 2, take scenic Rt 715 at Jemseg and proceed to Norwood Farms (18 km from Jemseg). Coming from east, take scenic Rts 710/715 to Cambridge Narrows, proceed 12 km to farm on Hwy 715 west.
$40S $50D $10Add. person (Weekly rates) ► 14
❌ Not Jan/Feb 🍳 Choice, homebaked 🏠300-acre farm, quiet, view ■4(upst), self-contained apartment ⊨2D,2Q,1R, crib ⇱2Private, 2sh.w.g.(basins in 2 rooms) ★3TV,F,KF,LF, private entrance ⚬German, Spanish, some French
🏃 Washademoak Lake, private sandy beach, concrete wharf, small private marina, swimming, boating
🚗 Scenic drives in southern New Brunswick
📣 Century-old colonial-style farmhouse beautifully kept and situated on shore of Washademoak Lake in central location in southern New Brunswick. Working farm specializing in beef. Large porch with beautiful view. Home was featured on cover of 1989 NB tourist Guide. ✔B&B

352 NEW BRUNSWICK

Cape Tormentine

(east of Moncton; see also Bayfield)

Trenholm, Garth and Joan (Hilltop Bed & Breakfast)   ☎ (506) 538-7747
Cape Tormentine, NB E0A 1H0

From Hwy 2 exit at Aulac onto Hwy 16 and follow all the way to new
Confederation Bridge. Coming from Shediac, take Hwy 15.
$30S $40-50D $6Child $10Add.person   ▶ 6A,4Ch
🔲Full,homebaked 🏠Village,acreage,2-storey,ferry view,oceanfront
■1S,2D(upstairs) ◄2S,2D,4R ◢1Private,1sh.w.g.,whirlpool
bath ★F,separate entrance ⓌNo smoking, no pets
🕯 Confederation Bridge to PEI, churches, beautiful beach,
lighthouse, watch fishing boats in harbour
🚗 Murry Beach Park, shopping in three different towns, recreation area
🐎 Comfortable home is situated on a hill overlooking beach, harbour and Northumberland
Strait. Reservations can be made for a tour boat to take guests out to see longest bridge
(Confederation Bridge to PEI) in the world.

Caraquet

(east of Bathurst; see also Losier Settlement)

Dugas-Landry, Martina E (La Maison Touristique Dugas)   ☎ (506) 727-3195,
683 Boul.St Pierre Ouest, Caraquet, NB E1W 1A1   Fax (506) 727-3193

Located on Rt 11 and 6.5 km west of downtown Caraquet.
$29.95S $34.90D $9.95Add.person   (plus tax)
🔲 Choice 🏠 Res., village ■ 8S,3D,2Ste(upstairs), including sep.
house, plus cabins ◄2T,15D,2cots ◢3Sh.w.g.,1sh.w.h.
★TV,KF, parking ⓌRestricted smoking 〰English
(household language is French)
🕯 Wooded road leading to beach, excellent swimming
🚗 Village Historique Acadien, Aquarium, Pope Museum
🐎 Comfortable, 1926-built, spacious family home still has the orginal woodwork and is furnished
with antiques. Relax on the old-fashioned front veranda. 〰CC

Dorchester

(south of Moncton; see also Sackville)

Mitton, Lorne & Lynn (Swisscot B&B)   ☎ & Fax (506) 379-1902
5016 Main St., Box 11, Dorchester, NB E0A 1M0   E-mail: swisscot@auracom.com

From TCH take Exit 522 (going east) at Memramcook or Exit 541 (going west) at Sackville.
Proceed onto Hwy 106.
$45S $55D $5child $10Add.person   ▶ 6A,3Ch
✠ Jan-Nov 🔲 Full, buffet-style 🏠 Village, hist., acreage,
view, deck, quiet ■ 2D,1F(upstairs) ◄ 3D,1S,1P,1R
◢1Sh.w.g. ★LF,TV/fans in guest room, off-street parking
Ⓦ No smoking, housebroken pets welcome (must not sleep on
beds) 〰German, French
🕯 Marked walking trails (along the fish ponds, over babbling
brooks through forest and village), Bell Inn Restaurant, two museums, craft shop
🚗 Bay of Fundy, Johnson's Mills (famous Sandpiper birds' prime stop July/Aug), Moncton,
Amherst, NS, new Confederation Bridge to PEI, International Airport
🐎 150-year old home located in historic village and peaceful and tranquil surroundings. Enjoy the
relaxation, savouring the village history, heritage and friendly hospitality. Ask for a map of trails. A
Fine buffet-breakfast is served in the spacious dining room or out on the deck (weather permitting).
There is a dog in residence.

Fredericton

(seee also Prince William)

Doherty, Gail (Hidden Valley B&B)   ☎ (506) 363-5105, Fax (506) 363-1014
1055 Rte 104, Burtts Corner, NB   E0H 1B0   E-mail: gcdoher@nbnet.nb.ca

Phone for directions.
$40S $55D $10Add.person   🍽 Meals   ▶5A
🍲 Full, homebaked   🏠 Rural, res., 2-storey, older, view from guest rooms, quiet, deck   ■1S,2D
(upstairs)   ⊨ 1S,2D   🛁 2Sh.w.g.(one on main floor)   ★ LF,F,TV,private entrance for guests,
off-street parking   🚭 Designated smoking area, no pets, not suitable for children
🚶 Canada Walking Trail, local farmers market, churches, restaurants, local skating rink
🚗 Mactaquac Prov. Park, Crabbe Mountain skiing, Water Theme Park, Woodstock, Fredericton
🏠 Charming older home with lovely, sweeping view of the valley. Relax in the family room with
library/TV or by the fireplace. Host has an extensive collection of license plates. Enjoy a full
country breakfast in the large kitchen & dining area.

Gorham, Frank and Joan (Carriage House Inn B&B)   ☎ (506) 452-9924
230 University Ave., Fredericton, NB   E3B 4H7   Fax (506) 458-0799

Located off Hwy 2 and 102. Take Exit 295. Phone for directions.

$55-70S $60-85D $15Add.person (plus tax)   ▶ 20
🍲 Full, homebaked   🏠 Downtown, res., hist., quiet, open and
screened verandas, adjacent river   ■D,S(main & upper levels)
⊨4T,8D,3cots 🛁8Private,3sh.w.g. ★Air exchanger,
TV,F,KF,LF,parking, solarium, fax/computer, phones in rooms,
🚶 Saint John riverfront biking & walking path, farmer's market,
Art Gallery, Prov. Legislature, Playhouse Trans Canada Trail
🚗 King's Landing (1780-1830 re-created village)
🏠 3-storey Victorian mansion, built in 1875, surrounded by huge Elm trees. Spacious rooms are
furnished with antiques. Gracious mahogany staircase winds to 3rd floor and new sky-lit library.
Breakfast is served in solarium. Children welcome. Visa,MC,Enroute ✓B&B

Hawkins, Kathleen and Lorne (The Hawks Nest B&B)   ☎ (506) 363-3645
150 Rocky Rd., Keswick Ridge, NB   E0H 1N0

From Trans Canada Hwy 2, take Exit 274 and cross the Mactaquac Dam. Turn into 2nd road on

right. Proceed up the hill to house on left (1km).
$40S $55D   ▶6
🍲 Full, homebaked   🏠 Rural, acreage, patio, quiet   ■3D(main
and upper level)   ⊨ 2D,1Q   🛁1Sh.w.g., 1ensuite   ★ F,TV,LF,
parking   🚭No smoking, no children
🚶 Mactaquac Provincial Park (boating, beaches, golfing, marina,
fine dining, c/c skiing, skating, sleigh rides), salmon/bass fishing
🚗 Kings Landing, Woolastook Park, Fredericton, Crabbe Mtn
🏠 Colonial country home situated near the beautiful St. John River in the most breathtaking
scenic area of NB. Enjoy a full country breakfast with all the homemade fixings. Host is active with
the large family building business, hostess is an experienced toll/art painter, and both are
knowledgeable about the area. Enjoy the lovely decor and the congenial and relaxed atmosphere.
House motto: "Come as a stranger, leave as a friend". There is a large friendly dog called "UBU".

Myshrall, Elsie (Appelot B&B) ☎ (506) 444-8083
No 1272, Hwy 105, Douglas, NB E3A 7K2

From Hwy 2, take Exit 274 across Mactaquac Dam and first right onto Hwy 105 south. Follow the river to house on left side (approx. 9km). Look for signs. From Fredericton, take Westmorland Bridge 105 North and continue approx. 14 km to house on right.

$45-50S $55-60D $15Add.person ► 6
🍴 Full, homebaked 🏠 Rural, older, riverfront, view, sunporch, quiet ■3 (upstairs) ⊨2Q,2T,(extra length) ⊒1Sh.w.g.,1sh.w.h., 1private ★ TV,VCR, fans, picnic table, gas BBQ, lawn swing, parking ⛔No smoking, no pets
🏃 Orchards and woodlands, St. John River
🚐 Kings Landg, Mactaquac Prov. Park, Beaverbrook Gallery, golfing
🐾 Completely renovated 1905-built attractive farmhouse situated on hillside with sweeping view of river and surrounding countryside. Full scrumptious breakfast served in spacious enclosed sunporch with view of the beautiful valley. Check Inns. ✓B&B

Gagetown
(east of Fredericton; see also Cambridge Narrows)

Teakles, Don & Donna (Doctors Hill B&B & Crafts) ☎ (506) 488-8989
Box 94, 16 Doctors Hill Rd., Gagetown, NB E0G 1V0

From Saint John, follow Rte 1 West to Rte 7 North to Gagetown (Rte 102 North). Located next to the Medical Clinic.
$40S $55D $10Child 🍴 Meals ► 9
🍴 Full, homebaked 🏠 Village, 2-storey, view, deck, quiet ■3 (upstairs) ⊨ 2T,1D,1Q,3cots ⊒ 1Sh.w.g. ★ Air,TV, guest quarters are separate, off-street parking ⛔ No pets, designated smoking area
🚐 Fredericton, Oromocto, Saint John
🏃 Tilley House Museum, Loomcrafters, Court House, bird watching, pottery shops, flower press
🐾 Comfortble home set among mature maples in historic riverside village. Rooms have been dedicated to special themes, reflecting hosts travels in Northern Canada & Europe. Enjoy the peaceful yesteryear setting and atmosphere. Decorative crafts and furniture made by hosts are displayed in the on-premises craftshop. Visa ✓B&B

Grand Falls
(south of Edmundston at US border)

Coté, Noel and Norma (Cote's B&B) ☎ (506) 473-1415, Fax (506) 473-1952
575 Broadway St., Box 2526, Grand Falls, NB E3Z 1E6

From Hwy 2, take Exits 75/76 or 81 to Broadway St.
$40S $65D $15Add.person ► 13
🍴 Full, homebaked 🏠 Downtown, res., older, 2-storey, patio, quiet ■4(upstairs) ⊨4Q,2P ⊒4Ensuite ★TV,KF,LF, ceiling fans & air-conditioners, sep entrance, 2private balconies, parking ⛔No smoking ⚑French
🏃 Falls & Gorge, Wells In Rocks, museum, swimming, tennis, ball field, gift shops, restuarants, downtown
🚐 Golf club, USA border, Danish Community (largest in Canada)
🐾 Home is situated in the quiet part of downtown. Enjoy a complete breakfast in the dining room, evening snack on the patio. Hosts have a collection of "Precious Moments", Decoupage artwork and needlepoint in the house. Visa,MC ✓B&B

Crawford, Rachel and Jim (Maple B&B)   ☎ (506) 473-1763
142 Main St., Box 1785, Grand Falls, NB   E3Z 1E1

From Hwy 2, take Exits 76 or 81 into Grand Falls.
$50-55S/D $15Child   ►8
🍳Full, homebaked 🏠Downtown, res., older, patio, quiet ⊢T,D,R
🛏3(upstairs) 🚿3Private ★ F,TV and sink in each guest room,
guest housecoats, ceiling fans, 1 private balcony 🚭 No smoking,
children min age 6
🚶 Restaurants, stores, gift shops, scenic Grand Falls and beautiful
Gorge with walking trails, swimming pool
🚗 Golf Clubs, tennis courts, Danish settlement, Madawaska Weavers, swimming pool
🔫 Congenial hosts in 1934-built home, with lots of charm and personality, uniquely decorated
and elegantly furnished - "a comfortable home away from home". Hostess likes candles and there
are many of them in the house. Visa B&B

Grand Manan Island   *(on south coast near St.George; see also Back Bay)*

Parker, Ed & Nora (The Compass Rose)   ☎ (506) 662-8570
North Head, Grand Manan, NB E0G 2M0   winter: (514) 458-2607, Fax (514) 458 3119

Take ferry from Black's Hbr to North Head on Grand Manan
Island. There are six crossings a day.
$74-85 $79-85D $20Add.person 🍽 Meals   ►18
⚱ May15-Oct.15 🍳Full 🏠Island home, seaview from all
guest rooms 🛏4D(upstairs in main building), 3D (upper & lower
level in Flagg house) ⊢ 5D,6T, cot, crib 🚿 7Private ★F
🚶 Whalewatching, nature hikes, birdwatching, ferry, seakayaking
🔫 Two restored, charming old houses by the sea. Experience a relaxed friendly island
atmosphere. Enjoy fish chowder, scallops, salmon & lobster rolls. Visa,MC,Interact

---

Hopewell Cape/Hill   *(south of Moncton; see also Riverside, Albert, Alma)*

Hawkes, Aiko M. (Aiko's Villa Bed & Breakfast)   ☎ (506) 734-3160
Box 45, Hopewell Cape, NB   E0A 1Y0

Located 1st right past Hopewell Cape Post Office and "Cannon"
monument, 5km. north of Hopewell Cape "Rocks".
$50D $10Add.person   ►3
⚱ Summer only 🍳 Full, homebaked 🏠 Rural, village, deck,
bungalow, 10 acres, quiet, isolated 🛏 1(main level) ⊢1K,cot
🚿1Private ★F,TV,parking 〰 Japanese
🚶 Albert County Museum, country gift shop, Post Office
🚗 Hopewell Rocks (famous flower-pot shaped rocks), Tidal Bore
🔫 Friendly hospitality in very quiet country setting abundant with beautiful flowers and trees.
Enjoy a vast variety of birds, including hummingbirds, from the patio. Ideal place for a rest from
hectic every-day life. B&B

Holmstrom, Stephen & Elaine (Peck Colonial House B&B & Tea Room)   ☎(506)882-2114
Hopewell Hill, Albert Co., NB   E0A 1Z0

Located on Rte 114 between Moncton & Fundy National Park and south-west of Rocks Prov. Park.
Near Broad Leaf Farms. Phone for directions.
$40S $45D $10Add.person   🍽 Meals   ► 6
🍴Full, homebaked   🐓Farm, 3-storey, hist.,view from guest
rooms,quiet,isolated   🛏2D,1F(upstairs)   ⛺2T,1S,2D,crib
🛁2Sh.w.g.   ★ TV, parking   🚭 No smoking, no pets
🚶 Walks in 340 acres of field and forest with small creek
🚗 The Rocks, Fundy Nat.Park, Mary Pt. Bird Sanctuary, Cape
Enrage lighthouse, Albert County Museum, covered bridges
☞ Comfortable 9th Generation 200-year old ancestral Colonial home (on original land grant),
filled with handwoven rugs (by hosts) and surrounded by gardens. There is constant restoration in
progress. Hosts are very knowledgeable about local history and events. Enjoy breakfast or a light
evening snack in the unique 19th Century cozy in-house Tea room, also featuring chowders. ✒B&B

Losier Settlement   *(east of Bathurst; see also Caraquet)*

Losier, Jocelyne (Chez Prime)   ☎ (506) 395-6884
8796 Losier Settlement, Rte 11, NB   E1X 3C1

Located on Rt 11 in the Acadian Peninsula and 5 km north of town Tracadie-Sheila.
$30S $40-45D $7Child   🍽 Meals(Acadian Foods)   ► 6A
🎏 July/Aug   🍴Full   🐓Rural, acreage   🛏4D(upstairs)
⛺2T,2D   🛁2Sh.w.h.   🚭No pets, no smoking   ∿English
(Household language is French)
🚶 Peaceful blueberry farm surroundings, country walks, country
store, Christmas tree plantation
🚗 Acadian village at Caraquet, Marine Center at Shippagan, Bird
Sanctuary at Miscou, public beaches, fishing, airport, train station
☞ 4th Generation Losiers (family has been on property since 1854), is taking great pride in
preserving their heritage and keeping the original decor in the house. There is a very old Thomas
Organ and a huge hat collection. Discover Acadian history and traditions firsthand.

Miramichi   *(south of Bathurst)*

Donahue, Troy & Carla Crawford (Sunny Side Inn)   ☎(506)773-4232,1-800-852-7711
65 Henderson St., Chatham, Miramichi East, NB   E1N 2R4

Exit 120 off Rte 11. Phone for directions.
$40-45S $50-60D $10Add.person   ► 10A
🍴 Full   🐓 Downtown, hist., view, quiet   🛏1D,3F (main & upper
floor)   ⛺3T,3D,2cots   🛁2Private, 1sh.w.g.   ★ TV,LF, barbeque
for guests, parking
🚶 Scenic waterfront, downtown, shopping, restaurants, public
swimming pool, playground
🚗 Kouchibouguac Nat.Pk, MacDonald Hist.Pk, famous salmon fishing on Miramichi River
☞ Majestic Gothic-style home, built in early 1870 by local ship-builders, now fully reconstructed
to the original architecture with comfort and spaciousness. There is an old English-style lounge in
basement level with seating for 40 guests. ✒CC

Moncton

Harrison, Jocelyn & John (Downtown B&B) ☎ (506) 855-7108
101 Alma St., Moncton, NB   E1C 4Y5

Situated off Main St and 2 blocks from City Hall & City Center.
$39-45S $49-55D   ▶ 6A,2Ch
🍲 Full, homebaked   🏠 Downtown, res., 3-storey, hist., deck, quiet,
sunroom   ■4D(upstairs)   ⊨2T,3D,2cots ⇩2Sh.w.g.   ★TV,LF,F,
street & off-street parking   🖐 Designated smoking area ⚋French
🕎 Tidal Bore, many fine restaurants, Champlain Place Shopping Mall
Crystal Palace Amusements, Moncton Museum, farmers' market
🚗 Parlee Beach (Shediac), The Rocks (Hopewell Cape), Magnetic Hill,
🐾 Spacious home built in the 1920's with large rooms, recently restored and elegantly updated.
Relax in the upstairs sunny guest lounge, enjoy a favoirte book and meet interesting guests from
around the world. Breakfast is served in separate guest breakfast room. Internet Access. There is a
resident Golden Retriever called "Zach". ↙B&B

Langille, Gladys and Carson (Park View B&B)   ☎ (506) 382-4504
254 Cameron St., Moncton, NB   E1C 5Z3

Going East on Trans-Canada Hwy 1, take Exit 488A and continue on Mountain Rd to Rte 106/114.
Turn right on Cameron St. Going West, take Exit 511A and continue on Rte 132 onto Main St
(15 km). Turn right on Cameron St.
$45S $55D $8Child $10Add.person   ▶ 6A,2Ch
🍲 Choice, homebaked   🏠 Downtown, older, view, quiet
■3(upstairs)   ⊨ 2S,2D,1Q   ⇩ 1Sh.w.g.   ★Air,F,TV,LF,
parking   🖐No pets, no smoking
🕎 Victoria Park, Moncton Museum, Thomas Williams House,
Tidal Bore, Acadian Museum, Art Gallery, Highfield Square
🚗 Magnetic Hill & Game Farm, Rocks Provincial Park, beaches
🐾 Spacious, Art Deco home located in the center of the City and across from beautiful Victoria
Park. Retired host is active in the local Duplicate Bridge Club and a painter, whose pictures and
that of other local artists are displayed throughout the house. Hostess is a teaches. Enjoy the
congenial atmosphere and a delicious breakfast served in elegant dining room. ↙B&B

Martin, Jeremy (Bonaccord House)   ☎ (506) 388-1535 Fax (506) 853-7191
250 Bonaccord St., Moncton, NB   E1C 5M6

$40-45S $50-58D   from$55Ste(for 2) $10Add.person   ▶ 16-18
Located in downtown at the corner of John St. From Main St turn north on Bonaccord St or from
Mountain Rd turn south on Bonaccord St.
🍲 Full, homecooked   🏠 Downtown, res., older, patio, upper and
lower verandas   ■5(main & upper levels)   ⊨6S,1D,4Q,1R
⇩2Sh.w.g.,3Private   ★F,guest slippers,parking 🖐No pets, no
smoking   ⚋French,some Spanish
🕎 Downtown, restaurants, theatre, Moncton Museum/Art
Gallery, shopping, University of Moncton, Victoria Park & Tidal
Bore viewing, hist.Thomas Willams House, farmer's market
🚗 Magnetic Hill, Hopewell Rocks, Shediac beaches with warmest water north of Carolinas
🐾 Large yellow, 3-storey, turn-of-the-Century residence with a double living room, complete with
fireplace and bay window, offering a convivial atmosphere in which to meet fellow travellers or just
sit quietly and read. Centrally located and an ideal place from which to explore downtown Moncton
and southeast New Brunswick. Visa ↙B&B

Petit-Rocher
(north of Bathurst, see also Robertville)

Landry, Laurina & Lionel (Auberge D'Anjou)   ☎ (506) 783-0587, Fax (506) 783-5587
587 Rue Principale, CP 1076, Petit-Rocher, NB   E0B 2E0

From Hwy 11, take Exit 326 to Petit Rocher. Licated on Rte 134.
$55S $60D $5Add.person   (plus tax)   🍽 Meals   ► 18
🛏 Full   🏠 Village, 2-storey, hist., deck   ■14D,1Ste,
kitchenettes in 3 buildings (main & upper levels)
⊨4T,14D,1Q,2P, cot   ⊒ 12private, 6sh.w.g   ★ Air,KF,LF,TV
in guest room, ceiling fans, off-street parking, host quarters are
separate   ⊕ Designated smoking area, no pets   〰 English
(household language is French)

🕺 Bay of Chaleur, mining museum, art gallery, beautiful church, fisherman wharf, tennis
🚗 Parc Atlas (trout fishing, scuba diving, cycle trail), Pabineau & Tatagouche Falls, Daley Point
(nature trails), canoe excursions, golfing, sandy beaches, Acadian historic village
🚌 Large hist.family resort buildings (large main building, small chalet & old convent) completely
renovated and located in picturesque village on the Acadian Coastal Drive. Breakfast is served in
the on-site restaurant. Hosts have an apartment in the former Convent. Visa,MC,Amex

---

Port Elgin
(east of Moncton; see also Bayfield, Cape Tormentine)

Flad, Albert & Anne (Indian Point B&B)   ☎ & Fax (506) 538-7586
Fort Rd., Box 12, Port Elgin, NB   E0A 2K0

$50S $55D $5Add.person   (Child under age 10 free)   (plus tax)   🍽 meals   ► 18A,6Ch
Situated 1.5 km from Hwy into Port Elgin.ph for directions.
🛏 Full, homebaked   🏠 Farm, bungalow addition to farm house,
view, oceanfront, quiet   ■ 2D,3F,2stes, host quarters are in main
building ⊨12D,2P,cot ⊒5Private,2ensuite ★TV,KF,LF,phone
in guest room, separate entrance, picnic tables, parking, barbeque
⊕Designated smoking area, no pets   〰German
🕺 Shallow beach on property, village shopping, restaurants,
walking trails connected to the property
🚗 New Confederation Bridge to PEI, scenic coastline of Northumberland Strait,
🚌 Enjoy German hospitality in the Maritimes. Accommodation is in large extension to the main
farm house, with a beautiful view across to Nova Scotia and located at the Green Bay ("the warmest
Bay north of Florida"). The atmosphere is one of peace and serenity. Breakfast is served in separate
guest breakfast room in the main house. There is a dog in residence. ⌐B&B

Prince William
(west of Fredericton; see also Woodstock)

Schriver, Vaughan & Bunny (Chickadee Lodge)   ☎ (506) 363-2759, (506) 363-2288
Prince William, NB   E0H 1S0

Located on Hwy 2 and 25km west of Fredericton and 2.5km west of Kings Ldg.
$45S $50D $10Add.person   (plus tax)   ► 10+
🌞Summer only   🛏 Full   🏠 Rural, 3-storey, waterfront, patio, deck, quiet   ■2D,1F(upstairs)
⊨2S,9D   ⊒ Sh.w.g.   ★ F(one in guest room),LF,TV,sinks in guest rooms, host quarters are
separate, dock for guests   ⊕ Designated smoking area
🕺 Private beach, dock, canoeing, hiking, country walks
🚗 Kings Landing Historic Settlement, Mactaquac Provincial Park, Fredericton
🚌 Spacious home built entirely of NB natural woods with a wonderful lodge atmosphere and
perched on a hill overlooking the lake. Relax on the large deck with a beautiful view and enjoy the
warm, natural environment. Canoes, boats & motors for rent. Visa,MC ⌐B&B

Riverside

(south of Moncton; see also Albert, Hopewell Cape, Alma)

Cail, Hazen and Eunice (Cail'swick Babbling Brook) ☎ (506) 882-2079
Riverside, Albert Co., NB E0A 2R0

Coming from Moncton follow Rt 114 to Riverside. From Sussex (on Hwy 1) take Hwy 114 and follow
all the way through Fundy National Park to Riverside.

$35S $45D $50F ► 10
🍳 Full, homebaked 🏠 Village, acreage, older, view, patio,
quiet ■2S,3D (upstairs) ⊨2S,3D ⬛3Sh.w.h. ★TV,F,
separate entrance, parking ⚞ French
🏃 Running brooks, trees, flowers and spacious land
🚐 Hopewell Cape Rocks, Nat. Fundy Park, Moncton, Bird Sanct.
🐎 Relax on the large patio of Century old Victorian home overlooking Shepody Bay. ↝B&B

Robertville

(north of Bathurst; see also Petit Riviere)

Desgagné, Rosella & Jocelyn (Auberge les Amis de la Nature) ☎ & Fax (506) 783-4797
2183 Ch.Cormier, RR1,S2,B23, Robertville, NB E0B 2K0 1-800-327-9999

Phone for directions. From Hwy 11, take Exit 318.
$60S $65D $5Child(under age 10) $80F $10Add.person (plus stax) ► 13A,2Ch

🍳 Full, homebaked 🏠 Rural, 2-storey, 46acres, view from
guestrooms, patio, deck, quiet, secluded ■ 2D,3F(upstairs)
⊨3S,5D,1Q.2R ⬛5Private ★ F,TV,LF, fans, guest quarters
are separate, separate entrance ⊛ No smoking, no pets
⚞English (household language is French)
🏃 Orchards, walking trails, x-c skiing, snowmobile trails
🚐 Beaches, River waterfalls, parks, scuba diving, Acadian village,
Marine Center, golfing, yacht club, museum, deep sea fishing
🐎 Warm and relaxing atmosphere in new home in a unique spot, hidden in nature. Enjoy the
quiet comfort of country leisure. Breakfast is served in lic.dining room, serveing vegetarian meals,
seafood & other fine cuisine. Massage therapist available (reservation). Visa,MC ↝ CC

Sackville

(south-east of Moncton; see also Dorchester, Amherst/NS)

Young, Bill & Jean (The Savoy Arms B&B) ☎ & Fax (506) 536-0790, 1-800-583-5133
47 Bridge St., Sackville, NB E4L 3N8

From TCH 2 take Exit 541 & Hwy 106 (Bridge St) to B&B on left.
$49.50S $55D (plus tax) ► 8
🍳 Full, homebaked(buffet-style) 🏠 Village, 2-storey, hist., porch,
deck, quiet ■4D(upstairs) ⊨2T,2D,1Q ⬛4Private
★F,LF,TV/VCR in three guest sitting rooms, private entrance,
piano/games in library/den ⊛ No smoking, no pets,
🏃 Sackville Waterfowl Park, Mount Allison University
🚐 The Rocks at Hopewell C., Parlee Beach, Shediac, PEI Ferry
🐎 Retired Prof. couple in beautifully decorated 19th Century home with elegant decor and with
theme relating to Gilbert & Sullivan operettas. Relax on the spacious deck, in the cozy upstairs
sitting alcove or in the the common rooms. Breakfast is served in guest breakfast room/lounge.
There is a cat in residence. ↝B&B

Saint John

Gates, Linda (Five Chimneys B&B)   ☎ (506) 635-1888, Fax (506) 635-8402
238 Charlotte St.West, Saint John, NB   E2M 1Y3   E-mail: ajdg@nbnet.nb.ca

Located near Digby Ferry Terminal. From Calais or NS/PEI on Hwy 1, take Exit 109 to Market
Place or Ludlow St and drive 6 blocks to Charlotte St. Hwy 7 from Fredericton runs into Hwy 1.

$60S $65-70D $15Add.Person   ▶ 6
🍴 Full, homebaked   🏠 Res., hist., 2-storey, quiet, deck   ■3D
(upstairs)   ⊨ 2Q,2T,cot   🛏 3Private   ★ Ceiling fans,
library, VCR, Fax,LF,TV in 2 sitting lounges, large desk for
business travellers   🚳 No smoking, no pets
🚶 Carleton Martello Tower, Reversing Falls Rapids, Bay of Fundy
🚗 Museums, restaurants, nature parks, Fort Howe Lookout
🚔 Fully renovated Greek Revival Home (1850's) with 5 chimney
stacks, Italianate dormer, stained glass windows and rooms furnished in period-style, set in the
heart of West Saint John. Relax in the large library containing more than 2000 volumes of
historical and science fiction novels or join the hosts in interesting conversation. Works of 2 local
artists are displayed in some rooms. Catering to allergies is not a problem. Early breakfast is
served for guests who have ferry reservations. There is a young teen-age son in the host family.
〜B&B

Harrison, Wayne & Ross Leavitt (Mahogany Manor Bed & Breakfast)   ☎ (506) 636-8000
220 Germain St., Saint John, NB   E2L 2G4

From Hwy 1, take Exits 111 or 112 into Saint John. Take Charlotte St to Queen St. Take Queen St
1 block to Germain St. Turn right to house on right.
$55-60S $60-65D $10Add.person   ▶ 6
🍴 Full   🏠 Downtown, 3-storey, hist., porch, deck, quiet   ■3D(main & upper level) ⊨2Q,1K
🛏 3Private   ★ F,LF,KF,TV, off-street parking, wheel-chair access   🚳 No smoking, no pets
🚶 Restaurants, shopping, theatre, museums, parks, harbour, ferry to Digby NS, historic walks
🚗 Provincial parks, historic events, beaches, scenic drives
🚔 Restored turn-of-the-Century manor featuring spacious living areas of the classic elegance of
its period, and quality craftsmanship of the original appointments of a bygone era, situated on a
historic & prominent residential street of Canada's Loyalist city. Special diets may be
accommodated. Good environment for allergy sufferers.Visa,MC

Holyoke, Ralph & Karen (Homeport Historic B&B)   ☎ (506) 672-7255, Fax (506) 672-7250
80 Douglas Ave., Saint John, NB   E2K 1E4   E-mail: stay@homeport.nb.ca, 1-888-687-7678

From City Centre & Harbour Station follow signs to Reversing Falls onto Main St. Proceed through
3rd set of light (past McDonalds) and take quick left onto Douglas Ave.
$70-100S $80-125D $10Child $15Add.person   (plus tax)   ▶ 8A,2ch

🍴 Full, homebaked (gourmet)   🏠 Res., 3-storey, hist., acreage,
view from guest rooms, river/ocean at back, patio   ■2D,1F,1Ste
(upstairs)   ⊨ 2T,3Q,cot, crib   🛏 Private, ensuite   ★LF,TV,
air-conditioners, fans, guest robes, fainting couch in one guest
room, host quarters are separate, off-street parking   🚳 No
smoking   〜French, German
🚶 City Centre, shopping, restaurants, Reversing Falls (world
famous) Tourist Centre, historic up-town walking tours, bus stop
🚗 Fundy coastal villages, swimming, adventure tourism, quiet country picnics, whale watching
🚔 Restored, spacious ship-builders mansion (ca 1858) richly furnished with period antiques &
local art, located centrally high on a hill with breathtaking views of city, working harbour, tidal flats
and Bay of fundy. Relax in the opulence of a by-gone era. "Rise & Dine" gourmet breakfast is served
in formal dining room with very formal table setting. There is a resident dog. Visa,MC 〜B&B

Marks, Diane (Garden House B&B)
28 Garden St., Saint John, NB   E2L 3K3

☎ (506) 646-9093, Fax (506) 652-8425

$45-50S $60-65D   7-10child/Add.person   🔲 Meals   (plus tax)   ▶ 10
Phone for directions.
🍴 Full, homebaked   🏠 Downtown, hist.   ▪ 1S,2D,1Ste (main
& upper level)   ◄ 2S,2D,1Q,1K,2cots   🛁4Ensuite ★ LF,F,TV
in guest rooms, ceiling fans   ♥ 🚭 Designated smoking area
🧍 Uptown area, City Market, walking tours, museum, Harbour
Station arena, Imperial Theatre, good restaurants
🚗 St.Martins, St.Andrews, Fundy Nat.Park, Irving Nature Park
☛ Friendly "downeast" hospitality in wonderfully appointed
1900's Victorian home, elegantly furnished with antiques and with high ceilings. Relax by the
fireplace or in the library. Breakfast is served in elegant surroundings and helps start a day the
right way. There is a cat in residence. Visa,MC ✓B&B

Mavis, Ross & Willa (Inn on the Cove)
1371 Sand Cove Rd., Box3113, StnB, Saint John, NB   E2M 4X7

☎ (506) 672-7799,Fax (506) 635-5455
E-mail: inncove@nbnet.nb.ca

Phone for directions.
$65-125D   (plus taxes)   ▶ 10A
🍴 Full, homebaked   🏠 Rural, res., 2-storey, hist., acreage, view
from guest rooms, oceanfront, patio, deck   ▪5D(ground & upper
level) guest quarters are separate   ◄1K,2D,2Q   🛁Private,
2-person jacuzzis   ★F,LF,TV in guest room, whirlpool, sep.
entrance, parking   🚭No smoking, no pets, children min.age 12
🗣 French
🧍 Sweeping Shingle Beach on Bay of Fundy, Irving Nature Park, trails along coastal shoreline
🚗 Rockwood Park, Digby Ferry, Saint John City Centre, Nation's first museum and archives
☛ Turn of the Century home with massive expanse of glass overlooking Sand Cove on large
oceanfront property with beautiful gardens, sitting/walking areas. Winner of "Best NB Heritage
Inn" for 97 Award. Located in a quiet rural setting and the only accommodation next to Irving
Nature Park. Watch the world's highest tides and ships passing by each day. Hosts tape the "Tide's
Table", Maritime TV Cooking Show at the Inn. Breakfast is served in special guest breakfast/tea
room. There is a resident dog called "Bosun", who loves to take guests on nearby trails. ✓B&B

Molloy, Linda & Gregg (Linden Manor B&B)
267 Charlotte St. West, Saint John, NB   E2M 1Y2

☎ (506) 674-2754
E-mail: molloy@nbnet.nb.ca

From Hwy 1, take exit 109 for 6 blocks to Charlotte St West. Turn right and proceed 2 block to
corner of Charlotte and Lancaster Sts. From Digby Ferry go 4 blks on Lancaster St.

$64S $69D $15Add.person   ▶ 6A
🍴 Full, homebaked   🏠 Res., hist., quiet   ▪1D,1F (main &
upper level)   ◄ 1K,2Q(incl.poster beds)   🛁3Ensuite ★LF,TV in
common area, parking   🚭No smoking, no pets
🧍 Nova Scotia Ferry Terminal, Carleton Martello Tower,
world-famous Reversing Falls & Rapids
🚗 Farmer's market, art galleries, museums, Loyalist House,
Cherry Brook Zoo, Rockwood Park, nature park, theatre
☛ Large Colonial home, built in the early 1800's with the ambiance of the old with modern day
conveniences. Stroll through the house and view original paintings and prints by the host-artist.
Enjoy good company in the large family kitchen, which has a huge cozy fireplace. Breakfast is
served in the formal dining room. Visa,MC ✓B&B

Shediac

Pyke, Pauline & Christopher (Auberge Belcourt Inn)   ☎ (506) 532-6098
112 Main St., Box 631, Shediac, NB E0A 3G0   E-mail: belcourt@nbnet.nb.ca, Fax (506) 533-9398

Phone for directions.
$79-109S/D (plus tax)   ► 14
🍽 Full 🏠 Downtown, hist., porch ■ 7D(main & upper
level) ⊨ 2S,4D,1Q 🛏 1Private, 2sh.w.g., 4ensuite
★off-street & street parking 🚭 Designated smoking area, no
pets, children min. age 7 🗣 French, Cantonese
🕺 Downtown area shopping, restaurants, canoeing, beaches,
marina, fish market, ocean cruises
🚗 Parlee Beach Prov.Park, Confederation Bridge to PEI, Hopewell Rocks, Bouctouche (board
walk) Fundy & Kouchibouguac Nat.Parks, Moncton (Tidal Bore/Magnetic Hill)
🗨 Elegant, spacious & meticulously restored Victorian home with stained-glass windows,
furnished throughout with period antiques and located in beautiful coastal town. Breakfast is
served on fine china in the oval dining room. House specialty is authentic home-cooked Chinese
meals. Enjoy the cozy, warm atmosphere provided by two large fireplaces and relax in one of several
elegant drawing rooms or on the veranda. Ideal place for corporate meetings and the perfect setting
for intimate and elegant weddings. CCards ✓ B&B

St. Andrews   *(west of SaintJohn;see also St.George,St.Stephen,Back Bay,Grand Manan)*

Everett, Jura & Robert Estes (Harris Hatch Inn B&B)   ☎ (506) 529-4713
142 Queen St., St.Andrews, NB E0G 2X0

Phone for directions.
$95S/D 🍽 Meals   ► 4
❄ Summer only (other on special request) 🍽 Full 🏠 Res.,
hist., 3-storey, patio, quiet ■2Stes(upst) ⊨2Q 🛏2Ensuite
★Air,LF,F/TV/coffee maker in each guest room, off-street &
street parking 🚭No smoking, no pets, not suitable for children
🕺 Downtown shops and galleries, museums, historic homes,
beautiful churches, waterfront, Kingsbrae Gardens
🚗 Ministers Island, Campobello Island, Passamaquoddy Bay Loop
🗨 Beautiful, stately brick home built in 1840 with high ceilings and recently completely restored,
blending modern conveniences with historic design. Breakfast is served in special guest breakfast
room. Relax in the living room or enjoy a stroll about town. Hosts also operate the St.Andrews
Lighthouse Restaurant and extend discounts for guests. Special arrangements for late arrivals.
There is a dog in residence. Visa,MC ✓B&B

St. George   *(west of Saint John; see also Back Bay, St. Andrews, Grand Manan)*

Dougherty, Eleanor and Harvey (Bonny River House B&B)   ☎ (506) 755-2248
Bonny River, RR3, St.George, NB E0G 2Y0   E-mail: bonnyriverbb@hotmail.com

From Hwy 1 exit at St. George onto Rt 770 (sign posted opposite church) and go north 9 km on
winding road over 3 bridges. Look for signs & No 960 at driveway. Follow the new Government

(blue/white) B&B signs.
$45-55S $55-65D   ► 6
🍽 Full, homebaked 🏠 Rural, acreage, view, riverfront, patio,
quiet, isolated ■3 (upst) ⊨ 2T,1D,1Q 🛏 3Private ★TV,
parking 🚭No smoking 🗣French
🕺 Canoeing and boating, fishing, birdwatching, beautiful fall color
spectrum, x-country skiing,skating, excellent hunting, cycling
🚗 Saint John, Fundy Isles, Calais (US)
🗨 Renovated turn-of-the-Century farm house on large acreage overlooking the Magaquadavic
River and grounds reaching down to the riverbank on three sides. Relax in peaceful and tranquil
surroundings on the water's edge or on the sunny patio. Ideal place for honeymooners "or get-away
from it all". Bring a bicycle (do the loop across a covered bridge & natural canal).Visa ✓B&B

St. Stephen

(west of Saint John, St. Andrews, St. Georges, Back Bay)

Whittingham, David (Blair House) ☎ (506) 466-2233, Fax (506) 466-1699
38 Prince William St., Box 112, St. Stephen, NB   E3L 2W9   1-888-972-5247

Located near Tourist Information center and 3rd house east of Christ Church.

$40-46S $48-56D $61+Ste $10Add.person   ▶ 6A,3Ch
🍴 Full, English (Vegetarian on request) 🏠 Res., acreage, hist.,
quiet, riverview   ■3D,1Ste (main & upper floor) ⊨1S,2T,2D
⊸3Ensuite ★F,TV, oof-street parking, ceiling fans 🖐No
smoking, pets outside only
🕈 Canadian-US border crossing (Calais/Me), Tidal River St. Croix,
fishing, boating, Duty-Free store, commercial St Stephen,
churches, library, Annual Int. Festival with Calais (Maine)

🚗 Fundy Tides (28ft), whale-watching beaches, ferry to Grand Manan, Moosehorn Nature Refuge
🐾 Spacious, elegant mansion standing back on treed grounds was built in 1850 and overlooks the
historic St Crox River. Ideal base for exploring Passamaquoddy Bay (on wheels or water), Fundy
Isles and the river system on both sides of the Int.border. There is a dog outside. Visa,MC ✔B&B

Hooper, Doran & Anne (Elim Lodge)   ☎ (506) 466-3521
477 Milltown Blvd., St. Stephen, NB   E3L 1K2

From traffic circle in St.Stephen drive 5km to Milltown Customs (border crossing) along King &

Milltown Blvd and look for B&B just before crossing to USA. From
Bangor, Maine, take Rte 9 to Calais, turn left at 1st traffic lights.
$40S $50-60D $10Add.person   ▶ 13
🍴 Full, homebaked 🏠 Small town, res., 3-storey, hist.,
riverside, ■3F (upstairs) incl.large suite ⊨ 4T,2D,1Q,1K,cot
⊸Ensuite ★ 6F,TV,LF, ceiling fans, pool table, piano, library,
canoe for guests, off-street parking 🖐 No smoking, no pets
〰 some French

🕈 Charlotte County Museum of local history, St.Croix River (Heritage River), boat landing, USA
border crossing, Milltown Generating Station (free tours), tennis court, parks, public pool
🚗 Island ferries, St-Andrew-by-the-Sea, golfing, kayaking, whale watching
🐾 Spacious 150-year old renovated Georgian home near the St.Croix River. A convenient
stop-over for international travellers. Restorations are ongoing with new surprises & added comfort
every year. Hosts are formerly from Toronto. Breakfast is served with down-home hospitality in the
huge country kitchen. Relax in the comfortable lounge by the fireplace or on the spacious closed-in
veranda. Take a guided historic walking tour of Milltown. Visa ✔B&B

Ste-Anne-de-Kent

(north of Moncton)

Caissie, Rita (Au Bord de la Mer)   ☎ (506) 743-5329
RR2, Ste-Anne-de-Kent, NB   E0A 2V0

From Moncton, take Rte 15 to Shediac, Rte 11 to St-Anne Exit 42 and Rte 505 for 3km.

$50S $55D   ▶ 4
❋ Summer only 🍴 Cont. 🏠 Rural, bungalow, acreage, deck,
porch, quiet ■1D,1Ste(lower level) ⊨2D,1P ⊸1sh.w.g.,
1sh.w.h. ★ Air,KF,TV in guest rooms, ceiling fans, private
entrance, guest quarters are separate 🖐Designated smoking
area, no pets 〰English (household language is French)
🕈 Sandy beaches, Pays de la Sagouine
🚗 Shediac, Moncton, Magnetic Hill, Confederation Bridge

🐾 Warm welcome and friendly hospitality in a country setting. French Acadian hosts enjoy
meeting people and take guests to points of interest. There is a cat in residence.

Sussex

(west of Moncton; see also Cambridge N.)

Cosman, Louise & Doug (Apohaqui Inn)   ☎ (506) 433-4149
Box 25, 7 Foster St., Apohaqui, NB   E0G 1A0

Write or phone for directions.
$35S $45D $8Add.person 🍽Meals (plus Tax)   ▶ 10A,8Ch
🍲 Full, homebaked   🏠 Village, hist., 3-storey, acreage, patio,
view from guest rooms, quiet ■ 7(upstairs) ⊨ 7S,3D,1R,baby
bed   🚿2Sh.w.g, 4private, 1sh.w.h.   ★Air, reading hall,
parking ⓦ Restricted smoking
🏃 Kennebecasis River (sea trout/salmon fishing), hunting (white
tail deer/bird or black bear), country walks

☞ Spacious Century home with 20ft pillars, wrap-around porch, in a picturesque village
enhanced by the quiet beauty of the country side. Rooms are named after famous covered bridges.
Enjoy the beautiful pastoral views and relax in the cozy guest meeting place.

London, Bertha & Lloyd (Jonah B&B Place)   ☎ (506) 433-6978
977 Main St., Sussex, NB   E0E 1P0

Phone for directions.
$50S/D 🍽 Meals   ▶ 6
🍲 Full 🏠 Downtown, hist., acreage, patio, deck, quiet,
secluded ■ 3D(upstairs) ⊨ 3D 🚿Sh.w.g ★F,TV,
off-street parking ⓦ Smoking outside
🏃 Downtown Sussex, shops, retaurants
🚗 Fundy Nat.Park, Hopewell Cape Rocks, Saint John, Moncton
☞ Charming home built in 1884 with original 12ft ceilings,
moulding and fireplaces, having maintained much of its original character. Enjoy a quiet evening on
the veranda surrounded by mature trees and garden. Breakfast is served in guest breakfast room.
There is a resident cat.

Woodstock

(north west of Fredericton)

Froehlich, Elfriede and Edgar (Chalet Swiss B&B)   ☎ (506) 328-6751
4064 Rte 105, Box 4205, Woodstock, NB   E7M 6B6

Take Trans Canada Hwy 2 and exit at Woodstock or Upper Woodstock. Cross the Saint John River
on Grafton Bridge, turn right (south) onto Hwy 105 and drive 9 km along river to Chalet. Look for
sign at access to drive up hill.
$45S $49D $10Child/Add.person   ▶ 7
✠ May-Oct 🍲 Homebaked 🏠 Rural, hillside, view, acreage,
quiet, secluded ■ 2F (ground level) ⊨2S,4T(K),2D 🚿
2Private ★TV,LF, separate entrance, hosts quarters are
separate, parking ⓦ Designted smoking area 〰 German
🚗 World's longest covered bridge (Hartland), Kings Landing
Historical Settlement, Fredericton, Woolastook Wildlife Park
☞ Enjoy a quiet and relaxing atmosphere in Swiss-style Chalet with typical European decor and a
"Kachelofen" in the comfortable living room. Situated high on the hill guests can enjoy the
commanding and breathtaking views over the Saint John River Valley from the windows or while
eating breakfast on the large sunny deck. There is a very friendly Miniaature Schnauzer in the
house. German hosts enjoy "serving special people in a special way". ✔B&B

Reid, Shirley (Shirley's B&B)
116 Parkwood Dr., Woodstock, NB   E7M 5G1   ☎ (506) 325-2756

From Rte 2 (TCH) take Exit 188 to Woodstock. Turn right on Parkwood Dr to 2nd house on right.

 $40S $45D $10Child $55F   ◙ Meals   ► 4A,2Ch
🍳 Full, homebaked   🏠 Res., raised bungalow, view from guest rooms, porch, deck, quiet, secluded   ■ 1D,1Ste (main & upper level)   ⊨ 1D,1Q,1P   ⟋ 1Private, 1ensuite   ★ F,LF,TV in guest rooms, ceiling fans, wheel-chair access, off-street parking
✋ No smoking, no pets
🏃 Golfing, swimming, farmers' market, boat tours on St.John River, small shopping mall, eating places

🚐 Kings Landing, US border, scenic drives
📣 Retired potato farmers and long-time B&B hosts in newly-built home and new location. Breakfast is served in the spacious dining room. Hosts are active with the Ladys Institute, church work & local Chamber of Commerce and enjoy meeting people from all over the world. Pick-up at bus stop and airport.

Prince Edward Island

- Tignish
- Alberton
- Park Corner
- Westpoint
- Elmira
- Cavendish
- Stanley-Bridge
- St-Eleanors
- Kensington
- S.Rustico
- Brackley Beach
- St-Peter's
- Summerside
- Albian-Cross
- Winsloe
- Marshfield
- Albany
- Charlottetown
- Millview
- New Perth
- Cornwall
- Montague
- Cherry Valley
- Victoria
- Earnscliff
- Brooklyn
- Little Sands

P.E.I. Visitor Services Division   toll-free 1-800-565-0267
"Dial-the-Island" and Marine Atlantic Ferry schedule   toll-free 1-800-463-4734
Box 940, Charlottetown, PEI   C1A 7M5

Marine Atlantic Ferry schedule (Cape Tormentine/NB to Borden/PEI)   (902) 564-7489

Northumberland Ferry schedule (Pictou/NS to Wood Islands/PEI)   toll-free 1-800-565-0261

Albany

(north of Borden; see also Victoria)

Muttart, Everett & Freda (Muttart's B&B)　　　☎ (902) 437-6403, 1-800-253-1749
RR2, Albany, PEI　C0B 1A0

Located on Rte 10 and 6km from Confederation Bridge at Borden.
$30S　$40D　$5Child　(plus tax)　　　　　　　　▶ 6A,2Ch
🍽 Cont., homebaked　🏠 Rural, bungalow, view, deck, quiet
■2D,1F (main floor)　◀ 2D,1Q plus air mattress　🚿1Sh.w.g.,
1sh.w.h.　★ TV,LF,KF, fans in guest rooms, separate
entrance,　🤚No smoking, no pets
🏃 Beach, swimming, clam digging, wind surfing, church
🚗 Summerside, Cavendish, Charlottetown, Confederation Bridge
📢 Warm welcome in comfortable home with a beautiful view of Northumberland Strait and
Confederation Bridge; surrounded by quiet countryside. Hosts enjoy welcoming guests from all over
the world. Guests are invited to join them in the living room for quiet time. Also available a deluxe
cottage at Gordon Point (with wheel-chair access). MC ✓B&B

Rogers, Jim & Sue (The Captain's Lodge)　　　☎ (902) 855-3106, 1-800-261-3518
Seven Mile Bay, RR2, Albany, PEI　C0B 1A0

From Borden Ferry, turn left on Rte 10 (Blue Heron Drive) and proceed 7 km to St. Peters Church.
Turn left at 3rd house past church, go on gravel road 1km towards water, turn right to green house.

$70D　(plus tax)　(Sen.discounts & off-season rates)　　▶ 6A
❄ June-Oct (other by special arrangement)　🍽 Full　🏠 Rural,
2-storey, hist., view from guest rooms, porch, quiet, veranda near
beach ■3D(ground & upper level)　◀2T,2Q　🚿1Private,
2ensuite ★F,TV room, guest robes/slippers, parking　🤚No
pets, no smoking, not suitable for children　~French
🏃 Walks to lovely red sandy beach, beachcombing, Seven Mile Bay
🚗 New Confederation Bridge, Hist.Charlottetown, live theatre
📢 Large home built by a sea captain, furnished with antiques, and beautiful rustic-elegant decor,
surrounded by potato, grain & clover fields and many flowers (spectacular Lupins in June/July), on
the quiet serene side of PEI, where the sea is warm and inviting. Relax on the cozy sunporch and
veranda or curl up by the wood stove and enjoy evening deserts and good conversation. There are
resident pets (Lab "Annie", cat "Ziggy", bunny "Precious". Visa,MC ✓B&B

Alberton

(south of Tignish)

Wells, Marilyn and Kennedy (Cold Comfort Farm)　　　☎ (902) 853-2803
Box 105, Alberton, PEI　C0B 1B0

Located on Matthews Rd just off Rte 12 and 3 km from Alberton.
$30S　$45D　$10Add.person　　　　　　　　▶ 6A,1Ch
❄ Mid/June-Mid/Sept　🍽 Choice, homebaked　🏠 Rural,
acreage, view, quiet, isolated riverfront　■1D,2F (upstairs)
◀1S,2T,2D, cot　🚿 1Sh.w.g.　★ TV, parking　♥　🤚Pets
~some French, German, Swedish
🚗 Golf Course, many uncrowded beaches, restaurants
📢 B&B name derived from an English Comic Novel, and is not a description of the hospitality.
75-year old home was built during PEI's Silver Fox Farming Boom, and furnishings reflect hosts'
long residence in Europe. Enjoy the peaceful country atmosphere and large library. Conversation &
solitude are equally available. Silver service breakfast served. Fine dining by arrangement. ✓CC

Albion Cross

(north of Montague; see also St. Peters Bay)

Foster, Fred (Needles and Haystacks B&B)
RR2, St-Peter's Bay, Albion Cross, PEI C0A 2A0

☎(902)583-2928, Fax(902)583-3160,
E-mail: ffoster@eyeor.ca, 1-800-563-2928

Located 500m off Rt 4 on Rt 327 in Albion Cross. Look for signs.
$65-110D ▣ Meals (plus tax) (Reservation preferred) (weekly rate available)   ▶ 8

✜May1-Oct31 ◖Full,homebaked 🏠Rural, 2-storey, hist., view, mansard roof, 5 acres, quiet ■4(upstairs) ⊨2T,3D ⬭2Ensuite, 1sh.w.g.,1sh.w.h. on main floor ★TV,KF,LF, two woodstoves, bicycles for guests, enclosed sundeck with hot tub, parking ⍟No smoking ⌇French
🏃 Apple orchard, bicycling, excellent for long walks
🚗 Lobster fishing ports, white sandy beaches ("singing sands"), Magdalen Islands Ferry, golf courses
🔫 Large 1880's home furnished with antiques provides romantic setting in Dundas farm country. Enjoy a cool drink in the orchard or on the swing with a book and relax on the sun deck with spa. House specialty: blueberry pancakes. Host is world-traveller and skier and involved in producing a travelling cassete for visitors of East PEI. Visa, MC ⌐B&B

Brackley Beach

(north of Charlottetown; see also South Rustico)

Zember, Em & David (Red Island B&B)
RR9, Winsloe, Brackley Beach, PEI C1E 1Z3

☎ & Fax (902) 672-2242
E-mail: zember@isn.net

Located on Rte 6 between Rtes 15 and 7.
$35S $45D $5Child/Add.person   ▶ 14
✜ June 1-Labour Day (other special discounts) ◖ Cont.plus (self-serve) 🏠 Farm, 2-storey, quiet ■ 1D,3F(upstairs) ⊨7D,cot,crib ⬭2Sh.w.g. ★ LF,TV in guest rooms, ceiling fans, private entrance, guest quarters are sep. ⍟No smoking
🏃 Walking trails on property and in wooded area, semi-private beach on Rustico Bay, bird watching, Country General Store
🚗 Brackley Beach, Charlottetown with shops, restaurants & theatres, National Park, Cavendish & Anne of Green Gables, Lobster Suppers, excellent golfing, airport, Confederation Bridge
🔫 Young family in large, remoddeled 19th Century farm home. Hosts are Professional dog trainers. Children and leashed pets are welcome. There is a cat and there are 2 very friendly and well trained dogs in residence, which are particularly good with children. Visa,MC ⌐B&B

Brooklyn

(south of Montague; see also Murray River, Murray Hbr.N., Little Sands)

Bates, Vera (Redcliffe Farm B&B)
Brooklyn, RR1, Montague, PEI C0A 1R0

☎ (902) 838-2476, 1-800-663-3799 (May-Oct)

Redcliffe Farm is located on Hwy 317 off Hwy 315. Look for sign at farm gate.

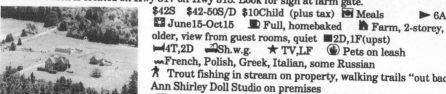

$42S $42-50S/D $10Child (plus tax) ▣ Meals   ▶ 6A,2Ch
✜ June15-Oct15 ◖ Full, homebaked 🏠 Farm, 2-storey, older, view from guest rooms, quiet ■2D,1F(upst) ⊨4T,2D ⬭Sh.w.g. ★ TV,LF ⍟ Pets on leash ⌇French, Polish, Greek, Italian, some Russian
🏃 Trout fishing in stream on property, walking trails "out back", Ann Shirley Doll Studio on premises
🚗 Montague, Charlottetown, Murray River, Panmure Island & beach, Wood Island Ferry to NS, golfing, restaurants offering fresh fish/lobster
🔫 1823-built home, expanded and completey renovated. Unwind and relax in the quiet and peaceful atmosphere. Browse through the doll shop with exquisite hand-made porcelan dolls. Hostess is gourmet cook and will serve home-made wine with dinner for in-house guests (reservation). Families, couples and retired persons are particularly welcome. ⌐B&B

Cavendish

(north-east of Kensington; see also Stanley Br., Park Corner)

Brewer, Ruth (The Country House Inn)   ☎ & Fax (902) 963-2055/1-800-363-2055
RR2, Hunter River, PEI C0A 1N0

Centrally located in Cavendish Nat.Park on the North Shore Gulf Shore Rd. Phone for direction.

$45-80D 🍽 Meals (plus Tax) (2-nighst min.)   ► 21
✠May-Oct. 🍴Full(buffet) 🏠 Rural, hist., acreage,oceanfront,
sea-view from guest rooms ■5, + 2 apts, 2nd/3rd level)
⊨42S,2T,5D,2P,cots (including canopy bed in studio) 🛏2Sh.w.g.,
1ensuite, 2private, 2shw.h.   ★KF, TV in guest room, jacuzzi
available, separate entrance for ground floor studio, small fridge in
3rooms, some facilities for the disabled, barbeques, bicycle rental,
free entrance to Park for house guests 🕲No smoking

🏃 Cavendish National Park, beaches, hiking, jogging, cycling, birdwatching, walks along the cliff
🚗 Cavendish, excellent golfing, theatre, Island sites, day trips in any direction of the island
🚐 Charming spacious old Island home, tastefully decorated with antiques and heritage furniture
and panoramic view overlooking the Gulf of St. Lawrence. Situated high on a hill on spacious
grounds in the National Park. Breakfast is served in sunporch facing the Gulf. Relax in the music
room or enjoy the large LM Montgomery library. Weekly rates avail. There is a resident cat. ✐CC

Dorgan, Gloria & Patrick (Wild Rose Country Home B&B)   ☎ (902)-963-3324
Cavendish Rd., RR2, Hunter River, PEI C0A 1N0   1-800-794-3324

Located on the Cavendish Rd., Rte 6 and 3km east of Cavendish intersection.
$75-85S/D $8Add.person   (Off-season rates Sept21-June21)   ► 18

🍽 Cont. 🏠 Rural, new, veranda, quiet ■ 6(upstairs)
⊨6D,2Q,2T 🛏 6Private ★LF,TV in guest rooms, barbeque,
separate entrance, parking 🕲 No pets, no smoking
🚐 National Park (great walking and cycling trails), Anne of
Green Gables House, Golf course, Cavendish Beach, Lobster
Suppers, restaurants, deep-sea fishing, Charlottetown
🚐 Modern, newly renovated home, a quiet country retreat
located in rural Cavendish. Enjoy the fantastic sunset view from
the veranda and friendly island hospitality. Visa,MC ✐B&B

MacLure, Naomi (MacLure Bed & Breakfast)   ☎ (902) 963-2239
Cavendish Rd., RR2, Hunter River PO, Cavendish, PEI C0A 1N0

Located on Rt 6 and 3 km east of Cavendish intersection and 15km from Hunter River.

$45-50 per room $5Add.person   🍽 Meals   ► 9
🍽Cont,homebaked 🏠Rural, older, patio, quiet ■3(upstairs)
⊨1S,4D,cot 🛏1Sh.w.g.,1sh.w.h.(on main floor) ★LF,TV in
guest room, sep.entrance, parking   🕲 No pets, no smoking in
bedrooms
🏃 Country roads for walking, National Park, great cycling area
🚐 Anne of Green Gables House, golf course, Cavendish Beach,
deep-sea fishing, restaurants, Lobster suppers, Charlottetown
🚐 Remodelled Century farm house, featuring a large sun deck, perfect for lounging, situated in a
tranquil farming community in fairly central location.

Morris, Edward & Ann (Willow Cottage Inn)   ☎ (902) 963-3385
Hunter River, RR1, Cavendish, PEI C0A 1N0

From Charlottetown go west on Rte 2 to Rte 13, north to Rte 6 and west to Memory Lane on left.
$60-90S $65-95D $10Add.person   (plus taxes) (off-season rates available)   ► 18

🔁 May15-Oct15   🍴 Full, homebaked   🏠 Rural, 2-storey,
quiet, older, acreage porch   ■ 7F,plus family suite(main & upper
level)   ⊨T,D,Q   ⏚ 1Private, 6ensuite ★Air, F/TV/VCR in
guest sitting room, refreshment counter in guest rooms, veranda &
TV in two guest rooms and suite, LF/service, separate entrance for
suites   🚭No smoking
🚶 Ann of Green Gables house (next door), tennis courts, golfing,
beach & dunes, hiking & bicycling (rental nearby)
🚗 Charlottetown, new Confederation Bridge, north/southshore beaches, good restaurants, fishing
☞ Cozy family-owned Inn decorated in homey old-fashioned Victorian manner. After a day of sun
/sand/exploring the enchanting Island, spend some lazy time in the charming guest sitting room or
on the shady veranda. Hosts are very proud of their Island and love to share this enthusiasm.
Breakfast is served in guest dining room. There is a dog & a cat in hosts' private area.Visa,MC

Charlottetown   *(see also Cornwall, Marshfield, Winsloe)*

Barnes, Lee, Peggy & Elaine (Taste of Home B&B)   ☎ (902) 566-9186
Box 6674, 33 Marianne Dr., York Point, PEI C0A 1H0   E-mail: barnes@isn.net

Located 1km off TCH. Turn towards York Point on Hwy 248 at the North River traffic lights.
$35-42S $40-47D $5Child(free under age 5) $8Add.person   (plus tax)   ► 12

🔁 May1-Nov30   🍴 Full, homebaked   🏠 Rural, split-level,
patio, quiet, secluded   ■2D,2F(main & lower level) ⊨2S,3D,1Q,
cot,crib   ⏚2Private,1shw.g.   ★KF,LF,F,TV in some guest
rooms, hot tub, ceiling fans   🚭Restricted smoking area, no pets
🚶 Nice quiet area for walking
🚗 Downtown Charlottetown, beaches, golfing, Cavendish and
northern beaches, Summerside, Confederation Bridge from NB,
Wood Island ferries to NS
☞ Warm welcome in modern comfortable home. Relax in the large (for 6) hot tub on the patio
and enjoy the large private backyard. Families welcome. Courtesy pick-up at airport and bus
station. There is a Highland White Terrier, but not permitted in guest quarters. ✔B&B

Campbell, Maida (Campbell's Maple Bed & Breakfast)   ☎ (902) 894-4488
28 Maple Avenue, Charlottetown, PEI C1A 6E3

From Borden on Hwy 1, turn left on Belvedere Ave through one
traffic light. Maple Ave is the next street on the left.
$50-60D $5Child $10Add.person   (plus Tax)   ► 8
🔁 May24-Oct31   🍴 Full, homebaked   🏠Res.,sub.,acreage,patio,
quiet   ■4(upper & lower level) ⊨S,D,cot ⏚2Private, 2sh.w.g.
(lower level) ★TV,F,parking
🚶 Shopping centres, restaurants, park
🚗 Charlottetown downtown, beaches & most Island attractions
☞ Situated in residential area, this suburban home has a large
backyard and deck for relaxation. Enjoy a comfortable home atmosphere and the company of
knowledgeable retired professional hosts. Courtesy pick-up at airport & downtown. Convenient
location upon entering the City. ✔B&B

Newcombe, Paul & Joyce (Reddin House Bed & Breakfast) ☎ & Fax(9-5): (902) 892-7269
90 Brighton Rd., Charlottetown, PEI   C1A 1V1   E-mail: pnewcomm@peinet.pe.ca

From Bridge, take Rt1 (TCH) to Charlottetown & North River Rd. Turn right on Brighton.

$60-65(S and D)   🏵 Meals   (plus tax)   ▶4
🍺 Full, homebaked 🏠 Res., hist., view, quiet ■2D(upstairs)
⊨2Q   ⚬ 1Private, 1sh.w.h.   ★ F,TV, fans, bicycles & tennis
racquets avail,parking ⑭No pets,restr.moking ∾some French
🏃 Walking trails, tennis courts, swimming pool, downtown area
🐾 Historic home built in 1915, near the harbour and nestled in
beautiful surroundings of Victoria Park. There is a Newfoundland
dog in residence. ↙CC

Stewart, Scott & Jayne Toombs (Hillhurst Inn) ☎ & Fax (902) 894-8004
181 Fitzroy St., Charlottetown, PEI   C1A 1S3

Located on the corner of Fitzroy & Hillsboro Sts. in the heart of downtown and 2 blocks east of

University Ave (Rte 1).
$85-135D $18Add.person   (plus taxes)   ▶ 23
🍺 Cont. + 🏠Downtown, hist., 3-storey, porch ■9(upstairs)
⊨4T,3D,4Q,2R,3P   ⚬9Ensuite   ★ 5F, separate entrance,
off-street/street parking ⑭No children ∾some French
🏃 Confederation Centre of the Arts, Province House, downtown
core and historic buildings, shopping, galleries, restaurants,
waterfront, Victoria Park, Rails-to-Trails, health clubs
🚗 PEI National Park, Cavendish, Green Gables House, beaches, lobster suppers, ferries
🐾 Beautiful and very spacious 1897 mansion, formerly occupied by University presidents, is one
of Charlottetown's grandest homes. Experience the elegance of this distinguished Heritage property
with its lavish woodwork, period furnishings and contemporary Island art. Relax in the comfortable
sitting and reading rooms and enjoy the gracious surroundings. Visa,MC

Cherry Valley   *(east of Charlottetown; see also Millview, Earnscliffe)*

Scheier, Elsie & Josef (Cherry Tree House Bed & Breakfast) ☎ (902) 651-2010
RR3, Vernon Bridge, PEI   C0A 2E0

Located .25 km off TCH 1 on Cherry Cove Road in Cherry Valley.
$38-44D   (plus tax)   ▶ 6
✖ Summer only   🍺 Cont, homebaked   🏠 Rural, 2-storey,
hist., acreage, view from guest rooms, deck, quiet   ■ 3D
(upstairs)   ⊨ 3D,1R   ⚬ 1Sh.w.g., 1sh.w.h.(on main floor)
★ TV,LF   ⑭No smoking, no pets   ∾ German
🏃 Anglican Church & graveyard , walks on country roads
🚗 Wood Island Ferry, Charlottetown, secluded beaches
🐾 Retired couple in 1870-built home cheerfully decorated and modernised with many original
features retained. Enjoy the tranquil farming area of Cherry Valley. Hosts are interested in
gardening, reading, outdoors, dancing and travels. There is a friendly dog in residence.

Cornwall

(south Charlottetown)

Gallant, Sandi and Paul (Chez Nous)   ☎ (902) 566-2779 fax (902) 628-3852
Route 248, RR4, Cornwall, PEI C0A 1H0   E-mail: cheznous@pei.sympatico.ca, 1-800-566-2779

Located west of Charlottetown on scenic drive off TCH 1. From Cornwall, take Hwy 248 (Ferry Rd),
look for house on left side with white picket fence (2 km).
$75S $99D   ► 8A,3Ch
🛏 Full, homebaked   🏠 Rural, view, patio, quiet   ■ 5 (main
and upper floor)   ⊨2D,3Q,1R   ⌐4Private (2jacuzzi)
★F,TV in all guest room, bike rentals, sink/vanity/phone/TV in
rooms, separate entrance ♥ ⌇French, some Spanish, Italian
🕴 Bonnie Brae Restaurant
🚗 Charlottetown Harbour, Cavendish and Brackley Beaches, Nat. and historic parks
🕭 Secluded retreat. Native PEI hosts in very spacious beautiful home with elegant and cozy
decor, nestled among tall birches, mature maples and surrounded by wide-open spaces in the heart
of PEI. Unique layout and deluxe decor. Enjoy bountiful breakfasts in the charming
solarium-enclosed dining room overlooking the flowering garden. Browse through the on-site
giftware shoppe "Serendipitous Sandi's". Ideal for honeymooners. Stay 3 nights and the 4th night is
half price (with coupon). ⌐B&B

Earnscliffe

(east of Charlottetown; see also Cherry Valley, Millview)

Mutch, Esther (Esther's Farm Home B&B)   ☎ (902) 651-2415
RR3, Vernon, Earnscliffe, PEI C0A 2E0

Located 15 km east of Charlottetown and 5 km off Trans Canada Highway 1.
$30S/D $5Child/Add.peron 🛏 $3Each (plus tax) (Weekly rates available)   ► 10
🛏 Full   🏠 185-acres farm, view, patio, quiet ■2D,1F
(upstairs) ⊨4D,2R ⌐ 1Sh.w.g. ★TV,KF
🕴 Orwell Bay and beaches
🚗 Wood Island Ferry, Charlottetown
🕭 Well maintained, 180-year old farmhouse has been in the
family for many years and is situated in quiet rural, very pretty
area. Hosts also raise pheasants and game. There are many small
farm animals/swings/games for children. Time permitting, hosts
will go clam-digging with guests and cook them up. 2 s/c units are also available. ⌐B&B

Elmira

(on north-east tip of PEI)

Rose, Elora & Robert (Lakeville B&B & Cottage)   ☎ & Fax (902) 357-2206
RR1, Elmira, PEI C0A 1K0

Travel east on Rte 2 to Souris, then Rte 16, left on Rte 16A to North Lake Hbr, 3rd house on right
$35-50S/D $50-75Ste $8Add.person 🍽Meals (plus tax)   ► 8A,2-4Ch
❄Summer only(off-season by special arrangement) 🛏Full,
homebaked 🏠 Farm, 2-storey, older, view, lakefront, oceanback,
patio, quiet ■3D,1Ste(main & upper level) ⊨1Q,2D,1S
⌐1Sh.w.g,1sh.w.h., 1private ★TV,KF,sep.entrance,
wheel-chair access for cottage ⓦDesignated smoking area
🕴 White sandy beach on property, fishing village, deep-sea (tuna)
fishing charters, Confederation Trail hiking and biking
🚗 Souris, Magdalin Island Ferry, Provincial park restaurants
🕭 Spacious home on potato & grain farm surrounded by lake and ocean with a wonderful view.
Hosts are happy to show guests around the 250 acre farm. There is a resident dog"Lindy".Visa

Kensington

(north of Summerside; see also Park Corner, Stanley Bridge)

Thompson, Valerie and Don (Thompson Tourist Home) ☎ (902) 836-4160
Kensington, RR6, Margate, PEI C0B 1M0   E-mail: thomtour@atcon.com 1-800-567-7907

From Rte 6 turn left on Thompson Point Rd and proceed 1.4 km. Located 5 km north-east of Kensington in Margate.
$30S $35D $70Ste $5Child $65F (Weekly rates) ▶ 10
✠ Summer only ☕ Cont. ♞ Farm, older, quiet, riverfront, multi-storey, view ■3D,1Ste(upstairs) ⊨3T,2D,1Q
⇔1Private, 1sh.w.g., 1sh.w.h. ★TV ⓌPets on leash
🏃 Small boat launch, beach, swimming, clam digging
🚐 Woodleigh Replicas, Lucy Montgomery Museum, deep-sea fishing, Cavendish National Park, Anne of Green Gables
🐾 Restored farm home in picturesque setting. Relax on the balcony and enjoy the scenic Southwest River. There are two cats in the house.Visa

---

Little Sands

(east of Woods Island Ferry)

Perkins, Don and Nancy (Bayberry Cliff Inn B&B) ☎ & Fax (902) 962-3395
RR4, Little Sands, Murray River, PEI C0A 1W0

From Wood I.Ferry turn right on Rt4 East 8km to house on right.
$85-125 per room 🍽 Meals ▶ 10+
⬤Full, homebaked ♞Rural, acreage, view, oceanfront, quiet
balcony ■5D(upstairs incl 3 with lofts) ⊨T,D,cots ⇔5Private
★Small guest fridge ⓌNo pets,no smoking
🏃 Private stairs leading to beach
🚐 Rossignol Estate Winery, Prov.Park, Wood Isle Ferry
🐾 Two post and beam Barns very uniquely decorated with antiques and marine art by artist hostess and situated on 40ft cliff above waters of Northumberland Strait with sweeping view of ocean. Relax high on the cliff behind the house and see the ferries crossing over to Nova Scotia from Woodland Ferry Terminal. ╰B&B

Marshfield

(north of Charlottetown; see also Winsloe)

Wood, Wallace and Doris (Woodmere) ☎ & Fax (902) 628-1783, 1-800-747-1783
Marshfield, RR3, Charlottetown, PEI C1A 7J7

Located 6 km from Charlottetown on Rt 2 East. Look for signs.
$75D $10Child/Add.person (plus tax) ▶ 12A,4Ch
⬤Full, homebaked ♞Horse farm, 2-storey, rose garden
■2D,2F (upstairs) ⊨ 4T,2Q ⇔ 4Ensuite ★ TV in guest rooms, separate entrance Ⓦ No pets
🏃 Mares and foals graze in pasture close to house, Hillsborough River, rose garden
🚐 Golfing, harness racing, Charlottetown, fine dining, airport
🐾 Spacious, new Colonial home was built especially for B&B, furnished with custon-made pine furniture from the Maritimes and situated on large grounds in convenient location. Long time B&B hosts raise standard bred horses. Horses love guests' attention. Enjoy the extensive rose gardens. Off season rates Sept15-June15. Visa,MC ╰B&B

Millview

(east of Charlottetown; see also Cherry Valley)

Smith, Mrs. Louise (Smith's Farm B&B) ☎ (902) 651-2728, 1-800-265-2728
Millview, Vernon Bridge P.O., PEI C0A 2E0

Located on Rt 3 and 3.5 km off Trans-Canada Rt 1, and 21 km east of Charlottetown.
$35S $40D $4Each $5Add.person   ▶ 10
Cont. plus   🏠 Farm   ■ 5 (main and upper floor)   4D,1S,
cots   1Private, 1sh.w.g.   ★ TV, sitting room ♥
🚗 Charlottetown, Montague, North Shore beaches, walking trail
🔫 Long time B&B hosts in 150-year-old farm house. Relax,
share a cup of tea, and enjoy a visit with 5th-generation farm
family. Guests are welcome to use organ and piano. ✐B&B

Montague

(east of Charlottetown; see also New Perth, Brooklyn)

Coneen, Al and Anne (The Pines Bed & Breakfast) ☎ (902) 838-3675
31 Riverside Dr., Box 486, Montague, PEI C0A 1R0

In Montague travel south along Main Street and turn right before bridge. Watch for B&B signs.
$50-60D $10Add.person Extra (plus tax)   ▶ 11A,1CH
Summer only (other by special arrangement)   Full,
homebaked   Res., hist., acreage, patio, quiet, veranda
■3(main & upper floor), plus suite   2T,2D,1Q,1P,1R
3Private   ★ T,TV,LF, separate entrance, guest sitting area,
bicycle storage, parking   🚭Smoking on patio or veranda
🏃 Montague River, large grounds with lawn games, picnic
facilities, museum, tennis courts, restaurants, marina, golfing
🚗 Beaches, boat tours, nature trails, Buffalo Park, Wild Fowl Sanct., seal watching cruises
🔫 Turn-of-the-Century Queen Anne Revival home, tastefully furnished and renovated on a 2
acre lot in quiet residential area close to downtown. Hostess is a quilter and her quilts are used in
the guest rooms. Quilting demonstration can be arranged. Weekly rates available.✐B&B

New Perth

(north of Montague)

Van Dyke, John & Lorraine (Van Dyke's Lakeside B&B) ☎ (902) 838-4408
New Perth, RR3, Montague, PEI C0A 1R0

Located on Hwy 3 and 12km from Montague. Look for round house on right just before the water.
$25S $25-50D $10Child (plus tax) 3.50Each (Full)   ▶ 12A,2Ch
☀ Summer only   Cont., homebaked   🏠 Farm, 2-storey,
view from guest rooms, 102 acres, lakefront, deck, quiet ■4D,2F
(upstairs & main level)   4D,2Q,2S   1Sh.w.g., 1ensuite
with jacuzzi, 1sh.w.h.   ★ TV,KF,LF, separate entrance, large
parking area, barbeque, host quarters are separate 🚭No pets
🏃 Wooded path along lake, trout fishing
🚗 Salt water beaches, historic Ch'town, Wood Island ferry
🔫 Newly renovated, enlarged 1885 house beside a quiet lake, with unique dining/living room (the
actual old house) and bright and cheerful modern guest quarters in new addition. Relax on the large
patio and enjoy breakfast in the beautiful surroundings. There are family pets outside. ✐B&B

Park Corner

(north of Kensington; see also Stanley Bridge)

Williams, Hank & Clara (Beds of Lavender Bed & Breakfast) ☎ (902) 886-3114
Park Corner, Rte 20, RR2, Kensington, PEI   C0B 1M0

Located in Park Corner. From Confederation Bridge proceed to Summerside and Kensington. After traffic light, turn left on Rte 101 and continue to Park Corner at end of road. Turn right on Rte 20, cross over Lake of Shining Waters to first house on right. Look for illuminated sign next to road.

$25S $40-50D $10Child   (plus tax) ► 6
🦋 Summer only ◗ Cont. plus 🏠 Rural, acreage, view from guest rooms, lakefront, deck, quiet ■ 1S,2D (upstairs)
🛏1Sh.w.g. ★ TV 🖐 No smoking, no pets
🏃 Sandy beaches, quiet walks along country roads or through Lavender Gardens on property, historic homes, fishing
🚗 Ch'town, Summerside, Cavendish Resort, Confederation B.
🔫 Friendly and informal new (1993-built) home with balcony off one guest room, furnished with Shaker-style furniture, overlooking Lake of Shining Waters in a quiet rural setting and in the heart of Lucy Montgomery historic country. Guest quarters are on 2nd floor. Experience the still evening from the deck and enjoy the beautiful smell of lavender in and around the house. Hosts are happy to share their knowledge of the island.

South Rustico

(north-west of Charlottetown; see also Brackley B., Stanley Br.)

MacDonald, Judy and Gary (Barachois Inn) ☎ (902) 963-2194
Box 1022, South Rustico, Charlottetown, PEI   C1A 7M4

Located in South Rustico on Church Rd (Rt 243).
$115-135D $25Add.person Deposit required ► 13
🦋 May 1-Oct.31 ◗ Full 🏠 Village, historic, acreage, view, quiet ■2D,2Ste(upst) ⊨2Q,2D,2S,1P(Q),cot 🛏Private 🖐No smoking,no pets ★Sitting rooms in suites,parking ∿French
🏃 Seashore, clam-digging, golfing, horseback riding, Farmers' Bank of Rustico (1869) and St. Augustine's Church (1838)
🚗 Charlottetown City center, theatres, Province House
🔫 Spacious Victorian house, located in a beautiful historic community, has lovely vistas including a view of Rustico Bay, Winter River and surrounding countryside. Built in 1870, and restored to its former graciousness without sacrificing modern comforts. ∕B&B

St. Eleanors

(west of Summerside)

Gallant, Muriel & Gerard (Paneau Bed & Breakfast) ☎ (902) 436-0543, 1-800-281-0171
11 North Drive, St. Eleanors, PEI   C1N 4E7

Take Hwy 1A past Summerside and continue on Hwy 2 to St. Eleanors. At flashing light turn left on North Drive and look for B&B sign. From Summerside, take Water St west to St. Eleanors.

$35-40S/D $10Add.person   (plus tax) ► 10A,4Ch
🦋 Summer only (to Nov 30) ◗ Full, homebaked 🏠 Village,,
2-storey, hist., acreage, deck, quiet ■5(upstairs) ⊨2T,1D,3Q,2R,
cots,crib 🛏 1Sh.w.g.,2sh.w.h.(on main floor) ★TV,KF,
parking ∿French 🖐Designated smoking area
🏃 Walks along country roads, Memorial Park next door
🚗 Charlottetown, Cavendish, Anne of Green Gables, Tignish
🔫 1816-built home played a great part in the history of St. Eleanors and hosts have interesting documented material on hand. Enjoy the friendly, genuine hospitality and stimulating conversation. There is a photo-wall with numerous pictures of house guests who have come from all over the world. ∕B&B

St.Peters Bay
(on northshore, west of Souris; see also Albion Cross)

Evans-Renaud, Seana & Rick Renaud (Crab'n'Apple Bed & Breakfast) ☎ (902) 961-3165
Box 9, St.Peters Bay, PEI   C0A 2A0   E-mail: renaud@auracom.com

Located on Hwy 2 and 1 km. east of jct with Hwy 313, east of St.Peter's campground facility.

$30S $45D $8Add.person   🍽 Meals   ► 8
❈May-Oct31(other by special arrangement) 🍵Cont. 🏠Village,
2-storey, acreage, oceanfront, view   ■ 3D (upstairs)   ⊨2T,2D,
2cots 🛁 Sh.w.g.   ★ F,TV,LF, off-street pkg   〜French
🚶 Camground with swimming pool, Rails to Trails
(biking/walking paths) from backyard (Confederation Trail)
🚗 Links Golf Course, spectacular secluded beaches
🐾 "Get away from the hustle and bustle" in Eastern PEI home
overlooking St. Peters Bay and mussel farms. Enjoy the spacious cedar sunroom for breakfast.
There are 2 young children in the family, a friendly Nfld dog & a cat. 〜B&B

Stanley Bridge
(north-east of Kensington; see also Cavendish, Park Corner, Rustico)

MacEwen, A.S.(Buddy) & Helen (Linden Cove Farms)   ☎ (902)836-3222
Stanley Bridge, Box 737, Kensington, PEI   C0B 1M0   Fax (902)836-3700 1-800-268-4783

Located on Rte 238, off Hwy 6. Phone for directions.
$50-80D $8Add.person   (plus tax)   ► 12
❈ Summer only   🍵 Cont, homebaked   🏠 Farm, 2-storey,
view, riverfront   ■4D,1F(ground and upper floor)   ⊨2T,5D,R,
crib   🛁1Private, 1sh.w.g.   ★TV in some guest rooms, parking
🚭Designated smoking area, no pets
🚶 Stores, Marine Aquarium, deep sea fishing boats, artist's
paradise surroundings, browse through the antique store on site
🚗 Restaurants, pub, craft shops, pottery studios, Summerside, Charlottetown, lobster suppers
🐾 70-year old ancestral home, well maintained and surrounded by huge Linden trees (same age
as the house) on 100 acre grain & potato farm. Relax on the shaded lawns and enjoy the superb view
of New London Bay. Housekeeping apartments & cottage also availaible. 〜B&B

Smallman, George and Helen (The Smallmans)   ☎ (902) 436-5892/886-2846
329 Poplar Ave, Summerside, PEI   C1N 2B7   E-mail: smallman@atcon.com

Located 3 km south of Stanley Bridge on Rt 254.
$33-43S $38-48D   ► 6A+
❈ June-late Sept   🍵 Full   🏠 Rural, bungalow, acreage, view,
patio, quiet   ■3D(main level)   ⊨ 2T,2D,crib, cot 🛁Sh.w.h.
🚭No pets   ★F,TV,VCR,BBQ, boat, picnic tables, parking
🚭No smoking
🚶 Walking, birding, swimming, private floating dock, boating
🚗 Cavendish, Green Gables, beaches, lobster suppers, golfing
🐾 Scenic, tranquil, hill-side setting with spacious grounds and fabulous view of the beautiful
Stanley River. Breakfast includes homemade jams, muffins etc. Also available 3 bedroom
housekeeping cottage with patio, barbeque & picnic tables. 〜B&B

Weeks, Adelaide (Blue Heron Tourist Home)   ☎ (902) 886-2319
RR6, Stanley Bridge, Kensington, PEI C0B 1M0

Take Rt 238 off Hwy 6 in Stanley Bridge. Turn by the Aquarium and follow signs and private road
all the way to house in the trees and by the water.
$25-30D   ▣ $2Each   ► 6A
✪ Reservation required after Sept.   ▣ Choice   ♠ Res., acreage, riverfront, view, patio
■3D (main and upper level)   ⊨ 3D   ⌐ 1Private, 1sh.w.g.   ★ F,TV in one guest room,
separate entrance, parking, pool table
⋏ Stanley River beach, Marineland Aquarium, licenced dining room
🚗 Cavendish, Lobster suppers (June-Oct), deep-sea fishing
☛ Long time hosts make visitors feel right at home in comfortable house by the river. Relax on
the large deck and enjoy the beautiful view overlooking the Stanley River and shallow beach. ✔B&B

Summerside   *(see also St.Eleanors, Kensington)*

Zambonin, Susan & Mario (Silver Fox Inn B&B Inn)   ☎ (902) 436-4033
61 Granville St., Summerside, PEI C1N 2Z3   1-800-565-4033

From Confederation Bridge take Hwy 1A, then Hwy 11 to Summerside. Turn north on Granville St.

$65-85S $70-90D $5Child $10Add.person   (plus taxes)   ► 12
▣ Cont.,homebaked   ♠ Res., hist., porch, deck, quiet   ■ 4D,2F (2nd &
3rd floor)   ⊨ 2T,3D,1Q,1R   ⌐ 6Private   ★ TV in guest sitting room,
off-street parking   ⊕ Desig.smoking area, no pets, children min. age 10
⋏ Live Theatre, Exhibition Centre, shopping, walking tour, antique & craft
shops, entertainment on Harbourfront, Museum
🚗 Golfing, north & southshore beaches, Confed.Bridge to NB, fishing
☛ New owners in 1892-built home lovingly restored and furnished with
antiques - a charming reminder of the past with its own
distinctive heritage and situated in central location to the business/shopping district. Previously
located in Ontario, hosts have been in the hospitality business for many years. There are 2 chool
children in the host family. Visa,MC,Amex ✔B&B

Tignish   *(north-west part of the Island; see also Alberton)*

Arsenault, Jackie & Elmer (Maple St. Inn Bed & Breakfast)   ☎ (902) 882-3428
216 1/2 Maple St., Tignish, PEI C0B 2B0

Turn left off Hwy 2 (runs into Phillip St.) onto Church St and proceed to Maple St. Go past

church and look for house immediately after Recreation Center.
$35S $45D $10Child/Add.person   (plus tax)   ► 8
✪June1-Sep.30 ▣Full, homebaked ♠Village,2-storey,3acres
■3D (upstairs)   ⊨ 2D,1Q,2cots   ⌐ 1Sh.w.g.   ★TV,LF,
guest sitting room, off-street parking   ⊕ No smoking, no pets
⋏ Museum across street, Roman Catholic Church, downtown
🚗 Fishing port, sandy beaches, tip of Province with longest
natural reef in Eastern Canada, wind test site
☛ School Teacher hosts in cozy & comfortable new modern family home, well decorated. Enjoy
the spacious guest quarters, friendly hospitality and congenial ambience. Relax in the cozy little
guest sitting room in the upper hallway. There are school children and a cat in the house. ✔B&B

Victoria

(east of Borden; see also Albany, Cornwall)

Wood, Kay (Dunrovin Lodge - Cottages & Farm)   ☎ (902) 658-2375
Box 40, Victoria, PEI   C0A 2G0

$35S $45D $6Child $55F $25Add.person   (plus tax)   📶 Meals   ▶ 10

Phone for directions.
✴ Summer only   ▣ Full, homebaked   🏠 Farm, 2-storey, hist.,
100acres, view from guest rooms, patio, quiet   ■ 4 (upper &
ground level), incl. tower room   ⊨ 2S,4T,2D   ⊿ 1Private,
1sh.w.g.   ★ F,separate entrance, guest quarters are separate
🚭 Designated smoking area, no pets in lodge, families welcome
🏃 Churches, playhouse & museum, Chocolate Factory, wharf
development, craft and art shops, lobster dinners, beaches, golfing
🚗 Charlottetown, Summerside, "Anne Country", Cavendish beaches, Int.Doll House, Car Museum
🎯 Warm and friendly Island hospitality in historic (ca 1802) Heritage home and only farm to
contain a village (Victoria). Hostess has welcomed many renowned guests over the years and is well
informed about local history. She is involved with various organizations and has received many
honours. Enjoy the many recreational facilities on the grounds, the warmer southshore waters and
take in the picture of rural life and its delights. There are 2 cats and a much loved Sally dog outside.

West Point

(on south-west coast, south of O'Leary)

MacDonald, Audrey & Lynwood (Stewart Memorial House B&B)
RR2, O'Leary, West Point, PEI   C0B 1V0   ☎ (902) 859-1939, (902) 859-2970

From Borden Ferry Terminal bear left on main Hwy to Coleman Corner or O'Leary Corner and
follow signs to West Point.
$50S $60-70D $100F   ▶ 7A,2Ch
▣ Full   🏠 Rural, 2-storey, hist., view from guest rooms, patio, quiet   ■ 4(upstairs)
⊨4D,2cots   ⊿ 3Sh.w.g., 1ensuite   ★ TV,LF,KF,separate entrance, wheel-chair access
🚭Designated smoking area
🏃 West Point fishing harbour & wharf, trail to Light House restaurant & gift shop, beautiful
Northumberland Strait beach area, newly erected World War II Memorial
🚗 Summerside, Mill River Golf Course & Resort, Alberton, O'Leary, Tignish
🎯 Large new modern house full of historic artifacts of West Point area. First Generation
Settlers, hosts (Mother & daughter team) and family live across the street, are very knowledgeable
of the area's geneology and involved with the first MacDonald Reunion (Aug1/2,1998). Help with
researching local roots is gladly offered. Host is a fisherman and docks his boat at the wharf a few
steps from the house. Visa,MC ✓B&B

Winsloe

(west of Charlottetown; see also Marshfield, Brackley Beach)

Hall, Norman & Phyllis (A Country Home)   ☎ (902) 368-2340, 1-800-265-4255
RR10, Winsloe, PEI   C1E 1Z4   E-mail: norman.hall1@pei.sympatico.ca, Fax (902) 892-3522

Located 0.75 km W of Charlottetown off Rte 1. Turn at Upton Rd to house on left. Look for sign.
$75-85D   📶 Meals   (plus tax)   ▶ 7
▣ Full (gourmet)   🏠 Farm, hist., multi-level, acreage, view,
quiet   ■ 4D(upstairs)   ⊨ 2T,1Q,2R   ⊿ 4Private   ★LF,TV
in guest rooms, separate entrance, parking, golf practise hole
🏃 Country gardens, rustic walking paths, golf practise hole,
licensed recreation room
🚗 Beaches, golfing, downtown shopping mall, Confederation
Centre, Cavendish & beaches, Anne of Green Gables attraction
🎯 Retired Professional couple in Century home, full of antiques & country charm & spacious
grounds, flower beds and mature trees. Owners keep Standard Bred horses, including mares and
foals. Enjoy country living near the city. Also garden guest house avail.(for 4).Visa,MC ✓B&B

B & B Travel Tips

B&B travelling can be most enjoyable, when it is planned ahead and when there is ample time to socialize.

When travelling B&B, you get more than just a bed to sleep in, because you are making a personal contact in a strange place.

Plan your trip at home in the comfort of your living room, researching the maps of the provinces you want to visit, and then write or phone the B&B hosts, to see if the room is available for you. When you have B&B confirmations, you will relax and enjoy your trip much more.

If you are on the road and decide to stay in a B&B, do phone ahead from a nearby phone (best: take a break at lunchtime and choose the B&B for the coming night). The hosts will appreciate your consideration and if their rooms are booked, they can also direct you to another B&B host. (This is not convenient, if you appear at the door in the evening without prior notice.)

Contacting the B&B hosts ahead of time is a big advantage. You will not only have a room waiting for you that night, but you have already "broken the ice." The hosts will be welcoming you at the door and you are not a stranger any more.

Do remember that you are entering a private house as a guest – (even though you are paying something) – the hosts are still doing you a favour by inviting you into their homes and you must observe whatever house rules exist. If you keep this in mind, your stay will be very enjoyable.

Do not expect the same service you usally get in a hotel. The service in a B&B is completely different. It is even better, because of all the little things the hosts will do for you and the information they will give you (many extras that cannot be bought in a hotel!). In fact, they will be happy and so proud to tell you all about the local attractions/events/history of their hometown.

Breakfast is almost always memorable! Most hosts will ask in the evening what you would like for breakfast and at what time (you can sleep in if you wish!). Go ahead and tell them if you would like porridge or something special. You will be pleasantly surprised.

On the day of departure, you should leave after breakfast and with all your belongings! It is not fair for the hosts to have to store your luggage, while you are making some side-trips before leaving town. Remember, they have to get the room ready for the next guests.

If you stay more than one night, you can go and come at your pleasure. But do let the hosts know when you will be back, especially if you plan to be late. They might even give you a key, and then you can let yourself in quietly.

As a B&B guest you have all the privacy you want in your own room. Hosts take the cue from you - if you do not want to socialize, they will understand.

All hosts are very obliging to special needs, but as a guest you must always remember that these extras are usually given by the hosts out of friendliness and a desire to please.

Most guests find it more convenient to pay in the morning at breakfast, when there is usually more time. Some hosts will ask for this to be settled upon arrival. It is wise to ask the hosts what they would prefer.

Do tell the hosts all about yourself and where you come from and what you do day in and out. They will be eager listeners. After all that's why they are inviting people into their homes – so the world comes to them!

Nova Scotia

(including Cape Breton Island)

Tourism Nova Scotia and Check Inns Reservation Services
Box 130, Halifax, NS B3J 2M7   toll-free 1-800-565-0000

Nova Scotia offers a free Accommodation Reservation Service. Bed and Breakfast homes which are registered with this service have such a notation in their listing.

Afton Station

(east of Antigonish; see also Auld's Cove)

Randall, Gordon & Joan (Chestnut Corner B&B)   ☎ (902) 386-2403, Fax (902) 386-2301
RR1, Afton Station, Antigonish Co., NS   B0H 1A0

$35-40S $40-45D $5Child $10Add.person
From TCA 104, take Exit 36A and proceed 3 km on Hwy 4 to B&B.
Located on the old Trunk Hwy to Cape Breton Island.   ► 7A,2Ch
✖ May15-Oct15   🍽 Full   🏠 Rural, 2-storey, hist., acreage,
view from guest rooms, porch, quiet   ■ 2D,1F (entire upstairs
floor for guests) ⊨2T,1D,1Q ⇱1Sh.w.g. ★KF,TV in guest
sitting area, sep.entrance Ⓦ No smoking, children welcome
🧍 Picnic facilities on property, country walks
🚗 Viewpoint and hiking trail, Bayfield Prov.Park and warm sandy beach, Antigonish Festival
📣 Retired teachers in large older family home newly renovated and located along the eastern
path of NS's Sunshine Trail among rolling tree-lined country roads. Tastefully decorated rooms
provide an intimate, relaxing environment. Enjoy the genuine NS country hospitality. Visa ✓B&B

Amherst

(near NB border; see also Sackville/NB)

Boss, Marilyn & Alpha Treen (Treen Mansion B&B)   ☎ (902) 667-2146
113 Spring St., Amherst, NS   B4H 1T2

Phone for directions.
$30-35S $45-50D $10Add.person   ► 7
🍽 Homebaked   🏠 Res., 3-storey, porch, deck, quiet   ■2D,1Ste (upstairs) ⊨2T,2D,
cot,crib ⇱ 1Ensuite, 1sh.w.g.   ★ F,LF,KF,TV in guest rooms, ceiling fans, off-street parking
♥ Ⓦ Designated smoking area
🧍 Golf Course, Cumberland Museum, downtown walk through (historic building)
🚗 Ann Murray Center, Miners Museum, beaches, Joggins Fossil Cliffs
📣 Warm and friendly Eastern welcome in comfortable Victorian home built in 1907. Browse in
the little craft corner. Evening snack will be served on request. Families welcome. Visa

Brander, Carl & Beatrice (Victoria Garden Bed & Breakfast)   ☎ (902) 667-2278
196 Victoria Street East, Amherst, NS   B4H 1Y9

Situated on the Sunrise Trail . From TCH take Exit 3 and proceed 3.5 km east.

$40S $50-60D $10Add.person   ► 7A,2Ch
✖ Summer only   🍽 Full   🏠 Downtown, 2-storey, hist., quiet,
acreage, view   ■ 1S,2F (upstairs) ⊨ 2S,2D,2Q,1R,1P,cot
⇱1Private, 2sh.w.g.   ★ F,LF,TV in guest room, separate
entrance, off-street parking Ⓦ Designated smoking area, not
suitable for children
🚗 Anne Murray Centre, Northumberland Strait, Joggins Fossils,
Parsboro, Sackville, rockhounding/swimming/boating, live theatre
📣 Majestic turn-of-the-Century Victorian Heritage home (built in 1903), furnished with antiques
and situated among other homes with turrets and spires and beautiful architecture in a character
neighborhood. Experience the elegance of an earlier era. House specialty is NS blueberry pancakes
served with pure NS maple syrup. Special diets accommodated with due notice. ✓B&B

Annapolis Royal

(west coast; see also Clementsvale, Barton, Digby)

Atwell, Fran & Gordon (English Oaks Bed & Breakfast) ☎ (902) 532-2066
Box 233, Annapolis Royal, NS B0S 1A0 E-mail: engoak@tartannet.ns.ca

Phone for directions.
$50-60S/D $10-15Child $15Add.person ► 10
Apr-Oct30 Full, homebaked Rural, hillside, 2-storey, acreage, view from guest rooms, riverfront, patio, porch, deck, quiet, fishing pond ■ 1D,2Ste(2D each) (main & ground level) 2T,1D,3Q,2R 2Private, 1ensuite ★F,TV No smoking
Historic Gardens, Fort Anne, boardwalk on river, historic town of Annapolis Royal
Wildlife Park, Upper Clements Theme & Kedgie National Parks, Bay of Fundy, scenic drives
Retired couple in spacious, custom-designed modern waterfront home with a panoramic view of Annapolis River, North Mountain and surrounding area situated in a park-like setting on beautifully landscaped grounds. Relax on the screened veranda. ✓CC

Lahey, Dorothy & Dick (The Turret B&B) ☎ (902) 532-2770
372 St.George St., Box 497, Annapolis Royal, NS B0S 1A0

Take Hwy 101 and Exit 22 North. Follow St.George St to traffic light. Look for house with B&B sign on right.

$45-55S $55-65D ► 6A
May-Oct (other by special arrangement) Full, homebaked
Downtown, village, hist., view, verranda ■3D(upstairs) 2T,2Q (incl.four-poster) 1Sh.,w.g., 1ensuite ★ TV,F, guest sitting alcove, off-street & street parking, host quarters are separate No smoking, no pets, not suitable for children
Annapolis Tidal Power Plant, Historic Gardens, Fort Anne, historic grave site with candlelight tours, restaurants, shops, bus route to Halifax
Port Royal Historic Site, Upper Clements Park, whale watching (Brier Island) Digby and ferry to NB
Retired couple in registered Historic home decorated and furnished to the Victorian era. Well travelled hosts were born in NS and are very knowledgeable of the local and Atlantic regions. Relax by the window in the little turret guest sitting room. ✓ B&B

McGinis, Jim & Jean (The Carriage House B&B) ☎ (902) 532-5156
643 Upper St.George St., Box 164, Annapolis Royal, NS B0S 1A0

From Hwy 101 take Annapolis Royal Exit and follow St.George St into town.

$60S $65D $8Add.person ► 5
May1-Oct31(other by special arrangement) Full,homebaked
Res, hist. porch ■ 2(upstairs 2Q,1R 2Ensuite
★TV,F, off-street parking No smoking, no pets
Annapolis Royal Historic Gardens, Fort Anne Nat.Park, Candlelight Graveyard Tour farmer's market, King's Theatre, Tidal Power Station., downtown (exquisite shops, fine dining, museums, waterfront boardwalk)
Kejimkujik Nat.Park, Upper Clements Wildlife Park, excellent bass fishing, wilderness hiking trails, whale watching, golfing, Lester B.Pearson Int.Peacekeeping Centre, Digby & ferry to NB
Retired R.C.M.P. Officer family in 1890's heritage home situated in small historic town at the mouth of the Annapolis River. Enjoy casual elegance & warm hospitality. Breakfast is served in the formal dining room. Relax in the screened sunporch or by the fireplace on a cool evening. Indoor storage available for bikes and motocycles. There is a resident cat (not in guest area). Visa ✓CC

Nightingale, Sandy & Jim (Nightingale's Landing)   ☎ (902) 532-7615, Fax (902) 532-7615
Box 30, 5305 Granville St., Granville Ferry, NS B0S 1K0

Located 2 km from Annapolis Royal on way to Port Royal.

$60-70S $70-80D $10Add.person   ► 7
✴ Summer only   🍴 Full, homebaked   👣 Village, hist., view from guest rooms, acreage, riverfront, porch, quiet   ■2Stes (upstairs)   ⊨1S,1D,1Q,1K,cot (including 4-poster beds)   ⊨2Ensuite   ★F,TV, parking   ⊛ Smoking on veranda only, no pets   ᴧᴧGerman
🏃 Explore quaint historic architecture in Granville Ferry, antique folk-art craft shop on premises
🚗 Habitation (Port Royal), Fort Anne & Historic Gardens (Annapolis Royal), Kejimkujik N.Pk.
🔫 Enjoy the peace & quiet of elegant living in old Victorian Gingerbread home (ca 1870), filled with antiques acquired by hosts from years of travel in Europe and Asia. Well travelled hosts have lived in Germany for several years. Browse through the wonderful in-house gift shop, which includes a large selection of Polish "Bunslauer" Pottery. Relax and enjoy the much photographed picturesque setting. There is a dog and a bird in residence. ✔B&B

Susnick, Donna and Michael (The King George Inn)   ☎(902)532-5286/(902) 425-5656
548 Upper St. George Street, Annapolis Royal, NS B0S 1A0

Turn off Hwy 101 at Annapolis Royal Exit or: off Hwy 1, 1 km from light.
$44S $49D $98Ste $7Add.person   ► 10
✴ June1-Sept30   🍴Full(country-style)   👣Res.,hist.,acreage,view   ■4,1Ste (upstairs)   ⊨S,D,T, cot, crib   ⊐2Sh.w.g.1P   ★F,TV/phone in parlour, classic movies, lawn games, bicycles   ⊛ No smoking   ᴧᴧ French
🏃 World's highest tides, wharf and waterfront walkway, restaurants, antique and craft shops, Fort Anne, Historic Gardens, Tidal Power Project.
🔫 1868 restored grand Victorian sea captain's home (designated a "Registered Heritage Property"), comfortably furnished with antiques, ornate fireplaces & leaded glass windows. Vacation packages. Whale watching tours can be arranged. Visa, MC ✔B&B

Wartenberg, Stefanie & Klaus (Falcon's Way B&B)   ☎ (902) 638-8429, Fax (902) 638-3190
17 Basin View Lane, Upper Clements, NS B0S 1A0

Located 10km from Annapolis Royal on Hwy 1 west and 4km west of Upper Clements Park.
$35S $45D $80F $10Add.person   (child under age 3 free)   ► 8

✴ May1-Nov30   🍴 Full, homebaked   👣 Village, 2-storey, contemporary design, acreage, view from guest rooms, deck, quiet   ■ 2S,2D (upstairs)   ⊨ 4S,1D,1Q   ⊐1Sh.w.g., 1ensuite   ★TV in guest rooms, plenty of parking   ⊛ No smoking, no pets   ᴧᴧGerman, Slovenian, Croatian
🏃 River shoreline and walking trail
🚗 Annapolis Royal, Digby (ferry to NB), historic sites, Botanical Gardens, Wildlife & Family theme parks, fishing harbour
🔫 Contemporary design home in a lovely country setting. Breakfast is served in sunroom or on the large deck with view of the Annapolis River Basin & north Mountain. Well travelled hosts are goldsmiths and love hobby cooking.

Antigonish

(east of New Glasgow; see also Afton Stn., Auld's Cove)

Bekkers, Sisca & John (Bekkers Bed & Breakfast) ☎ (902) 863-3194
Clydesdale Rd., RR2, Antigonish, NS B2G 2K9

Take Exit 32N to Main St., left at Hawthorne (Rte 245). Proceed 3km, turn left on Clydesdale Rd to B&B on left with sign.
$35S $45-50D $5Child ► 7
June1-Oct31 Full Rural, ranch-style, acreage, view from guest rooms, riverfront, deck, quiet ■ 3 (main & ground level) 2T,2Q,1P,crib 1Private, 1sh.w.g. ★ TV
No smoking, no pets Dutch
Canso Causeway to Cape Breton Island, Sherbrooke Village
Former Dairy Farmer hosts offer warm welcome in quiet country setting with scenic view of valley and rolling hills. There is a dog. ✓B&B

Auld's Cove

(west of Port Hawkesbury; see also Afton Station, Ile Madam)

Burton, Gardiner & Linda (The Bluefin Bed & Breakfast) ☎ (902) 747-2010
Auld's Cove, Box 119, Port Hastings, NS B0E 2T0

Located at Auld's Cove (Antigonish County) and .8 km west of Canso Causeway off Hwy 104. (Entrance same as Cove Motel).
$46S $51-56D $10Add.person (plus tax) ► 14A
Mid May-Oct31 Full Rural, village, raised bungalow, quiet ■1D,1F(lower level)
4D 2Sh.w.g. ★TV in guest rooms, separate entrance,parking No pets, no children
Gift shop and motel dining room on large property, boating
Golfing, museums, Bras d'Or lakes
Situated on a Peninsula surrounded by salt water in a quiet setting. A great place to start and finish a trip around the Cabot Trail. Breakfast is served in dining room by the water's edge in motel complex with very scenic surroundings. There is a resident dog. ✓B&B

Baddeck

(on Cape Breton Island - central; see also Christmas Isle)

Stephen, Murdena & Bob (The Stephen's B&B) ☎ & Fax (902) 929-2860
RR4, Baddeck, NS B0E 1B0

Located in North River Bridge. From TCH 105, take Exit 11 and proceed 19.2km north on The Cabot Trail to North River Bridge. Turn right onto Murray Rd and continue 2km.

$45S $55D ► 6A
May-Oct31 (off-season by special arrangement) Full, homebaked Rural, 2-storey, view from guest rooms, riverfront, porch with veranda, quiet ■ 3(upstairs)
2T,1D,1K(2T) 1Sh.w.g., 1sh.w.h. ★ F,TV,ceiling fans
Smoking on veranda, no pets, no children
Walks along the water (3km long), trout & salmon fishing, hiking, kayaking, sailing
Gaelic College, Baddeck, Alexander Graham Bell Museum
Retired, professional couple in beautifully restored country home with magnificient view overlooking the North River, located near famous Cabot Trail (a spectacular drive around the northern part of Cape Breton Island). Host is a retired member of the Royal Canadian Mounted Police. The beautful setting and house was featured by a BBC Television (Scotland) crew when shooting a Gaelic speaking programme (1993). Visa,MC ✓B&B

Theriault, Marj & Dan (Auld Manse Bed & Breakfast)   ☎ (902) 295-2362,1-800-254-7982
1351 RR1, Baddeck Forks, NS B0E 1B0

Phone for directions.
$35S $45-55D $10Child $15Add.person (plus tax)   ▶ 8A,2Ch
🔟 Full 🏠 Rural, 2-story, older, 26 acres   riverfront, porch,
deck, quiet   ■ 3 (upstairs   🛏 2S,,2D,1Q,1R   🚗 1Private,
1sh.w.g.   ★ F,TV   👋 No smoking
🚗 Cabot Trail, St.Ann's Gaelic College, Bell Museum, boat tours,
fishing streams, walking trails, golfing
🐾 Former Presbyterian manse, lovingly restored over the years
to its former Century old style. Congenial hosts enjoy socializing with guests and have a great sense
of humor and lots of stories to tell. Guest are invited to play the grand piano in the living room or
join in for informal sing songs. Breakfast specialty is blueberry pancakes or fresh trout in season.
special diets are considered. Visa,MC ✓B&B

Woodford, Patricia & Michael (Breezy Brae Bed & Breakfast)   ☎ (902) 295-2618/1700
1163 Baddeck Bay Rd., Box 566, Baddeck,NS B0E 1B0   Fax (902) 295-1700

Located 3.5 km from Baddeck on the Baddeck Bay Rd (Hwy 205) on left side. Look for sign.

$45S $50-55D   ▶ 7-8A
🌼 June15-Sept15   🔟 Cont.   🏠 Rural, 2-storey, older, 5acres,
view from guest rooms, quiet, veranda   ■ 1S,3D
(upstairs)   🛏 2S,3D   🚗 2Sh.w.g.   ★ 2F, host quarters are
separate   👋 No smoking, not suitable for children
🧍 Bras d'Or Lakes
🚗 Alexander Graham Bell Museum, Cabot Trail (beginning and
ending at Baddeck)
🐾 Beautiful, spacious, late Victorian summer estate home (ca 1894) with rustic/elegant
cottage-like decor. Relax on the 90ft long veranda, overlooking Bra's d'Or Lakes and enjoy the
peaceful country atmosphere. Breakfast is served in charming large breakfast room. Host family
members are experienced sailors and they live next door in the wintertime. Also available for rental
fully-equipped housekeeping cabin "Wee Brae" with access to private beach. ✓B&B

Barton   *(south of Digby; ses also Annapolis Royal, Tiverton, Clementsvale)*

Dechênes, Laurette (The Barton House)   ☎ (902) 245-6695
Box 33, Barton, Digby County, NS B0W 1H0

Located on Hwy 101 in Barton directly across the street from the Barton Post Office.

$45S $50D $85-100Ste $10Child/Add.person   ▶ 12
🔟 Full   🏠 Rural, hist., older, view from two guest rooms, patio,
quiet, oceanfront   ■ 1S,3D,Bridal Ste (main & upper floor)
🛏 4T,3D   🚗 1Ensuite, 2private, 1sh.w.g.   ★ TV in guest rooms,
LF,KF, deck with whirlpool, parking in yard   👄French
🧍 Beach and Provincial Park
🚗 Ferry to New Brunswick, Upper Clements Theme Park, Digby
museum, Digby Fleet shopping
🐾 Comfortable home with friendly atmosphere, situated in a convenient location overlooking the
ocean and beautiful St. Mary's Bay. Also available a self-contained log cabin (for 6) with use of
paddle boat. ✓B&B

Big Pond

(on Cape Breton Island west of Louisbourg, Christmas Isle)

Nelder, Keith and Patricia (Big Pond B & B)   ☎ (902) 828-2476 Fax (902) 828-3065
RR1, Big Pond Centre, NS B0A 1H0

Located on Rt 4, between the town of St-Peters & the City of Sydney, 7 km west of village store.
$40S $45-50D $5Child $10Add.person ✒Meals ► 6A,2Ch
✖ Summer only (other by special arrangement) ◖Full
🏠Rural, older,acreage, view, lake across road ⊨2S,2D,cot,crib
■3D (on main floor) ◁1Private, 1sh.w.g. ⊕No pets, no
smoking ∾French
🔥 Rita MacNeil's Tea Room, beach, dock
🚗 Fortress of Louisbourg, Alexander Graham Bell Museum,
ferry from North Sydney to Newfoundland
☛ Sailing family in enlarged old Cape Breton farm house surrounded by wood acreage and a
beach on the Bras d'Or Lakes. Hosts spent many years in the West Indies (Charter boats). There
are 2 children in the host family. Relax in the south-facing glassed-in living room. Charter boat &
guided Eagle viewing tours available. Visa,MC

Bridgetown
(west of Kentville; see also Paradise, Lawrencetown, Middleton)

Jay, John & Sharon (The Stitchers' Cottage B&B)   ☎ (902) 665-4009
Box 362, 377 Granville St., Bridgetown, NS B0S 1C0

From Hwy 101 take Exit 20 to Granville St in Bridgetown.
$45S $50D $10Add.person   ► 7
✖ March-Oct31 ◖ Full 🏠 Res., 2-storey, older, veranda
■ 3D(main & upper floor) ⊨ 2T,2D,cot ◁ 1Sh.w.g.,
1sh.w.h. ★ F,TV, off-street parking ⊕ No smoking
🔥 Cypress Walk (nature trail, board walk etc.), James House
Museum, Annapolis River (canoeing, boating), lawn bowling,
curling, skating
🚗 Valley View Prov. Park, Eden Golf Course, high & low tides of the Bay of Fundy, Annapolis
Royal, Oaklawn Zoo, Port Royal Habitation, Digby scallops & ferry to NB
☛ Warm welcome in comfortable 1921-built home with country decor and local art, reflecting
host's keen interest in needlearts (cross-stich) in the pastoral heartland of NS. Works by hosts &
local designers are on display throughout the house and for sale. Relax on the veranda or by the
cozy fireplace and watch hosts work on their latest creations. There is a resident cat. Visa ✒B&B

Brookfield
(west of Bridgewater)

Harlow, Les & Emma (The Big Oak Tree B&B)   ☎ & Fax (902) 682-2783
RR1, South Brookfield, Queen's Co., NS B0T 1X0

From Halifax on Rte 103, take Exit 13, turn right on Hwy 325, left on Rte 208 to North Brookfield.
Continue on Rosette Rd to Harlow Rd and follow signs.
$35S $45D $10Add.person (over age 12)   ► 6A,2ch
◖ Full, homebaked 🏠 Farm, hist., view from guest rooms,
lakefront, deck, quiet, secluded ■ 2D,1F (upstairs)
⊨3D,1Q ◁ 1Sh.w.g. ★ TV in guest sitting room, ceiling
fans, private entrance ⊕ Designated smoking area, no pets
🔥 Lake swimming with beach, canoeing, fishing, nature trails,
biking, Wilderness camping (island), 3 golf courses
🚗 Kejimkujik National Park, Bridgewater, Digby, Peggy's Cove
☛ 5th Generation ancetral farmhome (built in 1827 and completely renovated), located on a
Peninsula between Little and Big Tupper Lakes. Breakfast is served in special breakfast room.
Hosts are proud owners of an award given in 1992 for the largest hardwood tree in the province. (A
giant red oak located 75 ft behind the house). Visa ✒ B&B

Cape North

(on northern tip of Cape Breton Isle)

McEvoy, Hansel and Sharon (Oakwood Manor)　　　　　☎ & Fax (902) 383-2317
North Side Rd., Cape North NS　B0C 1G0

At Cape North, take road to Bay St.Lawrence for 1.6 km and Northside Rd (0.4 km).

$35S　$45D　$15Add.person　　　　　　　　　　▶ 14
✠ May1-Oct31　🍁 Full, homebaked　🏠 150-acres farm,
3-storey, view, quiet, isolated　■4D,2F(on 2nd & 3rd floor)
🛏7D,2S　🛁 1Sh.w.g.　★ Air,TV, sink in each room, host
quarters are separate, private entrance　🚭 No smoking, no pets
🚶 Enjoy the vast surrounding farmland and tranquil countryside
🏚 Large, unique home with rustic decor was built from local
wood milled by hosts' father situated at foot of mountain in
a pretty valley. Longtime B&B hosts are of Irish descent. Enjoy a stay "in the woods". Visa ✓ B&B

Chester

(west of Halifax; see also Mahone Bay, Hubbards)

Fraser, Suzan (Mecklenburgh Inn)　　　　　　　☎ (902) 275-4638
78 Queen St., Box 350, Chester, NS　B0J 1J0　　　　E-mail: frnthrbr@atcon.com

Located next to the Post Office. Phone for directions.
$50S　$59-69D　$115Ste　$20Add.person　　　　▶ 10
✠ May24-Oct31　🍁 Full, homebaked　🏠 Village center, hist.,
water view, covered balcony　■ 3D(upstairs)plus suite on main
level　🛏2T,2D,2Q,4P　🛁3Sh.w.g.,1private　★ 2F,TV,VCR,
bicycles available, private entrance for suite　🚭Smoking on
balcony, no pets, children min age 10　💬French
🚶 2blocks from ocean, tennis courts, golf club by the ocean, yacht
clubs, summer theatre, public wharves, ferry to Tancook Island
🚗 Airport, Mahone Bay, City of Halifax, Bluenose II, Peggy's Cove, Lunenburg Fisheries Museum
🏚 Large home (c.1890) in the heart of seaside village with cozy/informal atmosphere, painted
period furniture and paintings by local artists. Young hostess has spent many years travelling
around the world and is a Cordon Bleu trained chef and an experienced sailor. Visa,Amex ✓B&B

Christmas Island

(east of Sydney; see also Baddeck)

O'Handley, Leona (Lakeview Bed & Breakfast)　　　☎ (902) 871-2808, Cell 565-7290
RR2, Christmas Island, NS　B0A 1C0

Located at 4339 Boisdale Hwy. From Rte 105 exit at Little Narrows, proceed on Rte 223 to Boisdale.

Look for white number on red mailbox.
$40S　$50D　$10Child/Add.person　(plus taxE-mail: ✓ 4A,4Ch
🍁 Full　🏠 Rural, split-level, acreage, view from guest rooms,
lakefront, quiet　■ 2D (main floor)　🛏 2D,cot　🛁 1Sh.w.g
★ Air,TV,off-street parking　🚭 No smoking, no pets
🚶 Llama farm, hiking trails
🚗 Rita MacNeil Tea Room (Big Pond), Bell Museum (Baddeck),
Cabot Trail, Highland villages, Sydney, Louisbourg
🏚 Comfortable home with a view of Bras d'Or Lakes, Boularderie Island and mountains. Enjoy
friendly Cape Breton hospitality and CB Island video which is available to view anytime. ✓B&B

Clementsvale

(east of Digby; see also Annaplolis R., Barton)

Edwards, Fred & Helen (General's B&B)   ☎ & Fax (902) 467-4163
3486 Clementsvale Rd., Clementsvale, NS   B0S 1G0

From Hwy 101 take Exits 23/24/25 and directions to Bear River/Clementsvale. Watch for signs.
$40S $55D $5Child/Add.person   ► 8

✚ May1-Nov1   ☄ Full, homebaked   🏠 Village, 2-storey, hist.,
acreage, view from guest rooms, porch, deck, quiet, secluded
■3D,1F(upstairs)   ◄ 3T,3Q,1P,cots,cribs   ⬜ 4Ensuite
★TV,F,separate entrance, guest quarters are separate, off-street
parking   🖐 Designated smoking area, no pets, not suitable for
children   ⁓ French
🔥 Hiking trails on 105acres property

🚗 Kejimkujik Nat.Park, historic Annapolis Royal & Gardens, Champlain's Port Royal Habitation,
Upper Clements Theme Park, Fort Anne, Digby and ferry to NB, Brier Island Bird Sancutary
📢 Congenial hosts in charming country home, surrounded by fields, mixed forests, wetlands and
streams with a diverse habitat for birds and wildflowers. The house was once the estate of a retired
Army General. Awaken to the sounds of birdsong (not traffic). Breakfast is served in special guest
breakfast room. Guided tours of nature walks can be arranged by local naturalist, on request.
Special 2-day guided nature tour packages available. Visa,MC ⤳B&B

Clyde River

(east of Yarmouth; see also Pubnico)

Nickerson, Michael & Patricia (Clyde River Inn)   ☎ (902) 637-3267, Fax (902) 637-1512
10525 Main Hwy, Box 2, Clyde River, NS   B0W 1R0

From Hwy 103 take Exit 28. Look for B&B next to United church.

$45S $55D $80Ste $10child   ► 8
☄ Full, homebaked   🏠 Rural, 3-storey, hist., view, deck, quiet
■ 2D,1Ste(upstairs)   ◄ 1S,2D,2R (incl.pull-out antique
desk-bed)   ⬜ Private   ★ TV,LF,ceiling fans, guest quarters
are separate   🖐 No smoking
🔥 Sport fishing in Clyde River, golf course, horse trails, canoeing,
restaurants, daily bus route
🚗 Shelburne, Yarmouth, fantastic beaches, scenic south shore
📢 Recently restored former Stage Coach (ca 1880) furnished
with antiques and collectibles. Relax in the guest parlour overlooking the river or in the guest
sitting room of suite. Congenial and knowledgeable hosts are retired teachers. Breakfast is served
in guest breakfast room. Bike barn on property. There is a dog in residence. Visa ⤳B&B

Digby

(on west coast; see also Tiverton, Barton, Annapolis R., Clementsvale)

Bartson, Lester & Ed Reid (Thistle Down Country Inn)   ☎(902)245-4490
98 Montague Row, Box 508, Digby, NS   B0V 1A0   1-800-565-8081 Fax (902) 245-6717

$65-99S/D $15Child/Add.person   (plus tax)   🍴 Meals   ► 18A,4Ch

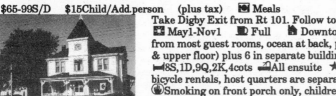

Take Digby Exit from Rt 101. Follow to end at water & turn left.
✚ May1-Nov1   ☄ Full   🏠 Downtown, 2-storey, hist., view
from most guest rooms, ocean at back, porch, quiet   ■ 12D(main
& upper floor) plus 6 in separate building by the water
◄8S,1D,9Q,2K,4cots   ⬜All ensuite   ★F,TV, separate entrance,
bicycle rentals, host quarters are separate, off-street parking
🖐Smoking on front porch only, children min. age 6   ⁓French
🚗 Golfing, ferry docks, Annapolis Valley, Digby Neck
🔥 Historic walking tour of Digby, Loyalist cemetery, downtown, shops, wharf & fishing fleet
📢 Lovely 1904 turn-of-the-Century home, beautifully preserved and gas lights adding to its
unique charm, located directly on the harbour with breathtaking views of Annapolis Basin, scallop
fleet & world famous high tides. Knowledgeable hosts will answer all inquiries. Breakfast cooked to
order from menu (House specialty:scallops omelette), and candle-lit dinners served in Queen
Alexandra Dining room (reservations necessary).. Also large guest building on property by the
water's edge. Off-season rates available. CCards

Cabana, Bob & Maria (Ocean Hillside Bed & Breakfast) ☎ (902) 245-5932
Shore Rd., RR3, Digby, NS B0V 1A0

Situated on road to Saint John Ferry (New Brunswick)
$50-65D (plus tax) ►4
❊ May-Nov1 🍽 Full 🏠 Rural, 3-storey, hillside, acreage,
view from guest rooms, ocean across road, patio, deck, quiet
■1D,1F,2Ste (ground & upper & lower levels) ⊨1K,1Q,2D,1S
🛏2Ensuite, 1sh.w.g. ★F,TV,LF, separate entrance ⊕ No
smoking, no pets, no children ⌇French, German, Dutch
🏃 Ferry Terminal, walks along shoreline
🚗 Digby downtown, Brier Island whale watching, French Acadian area and Port Royal Habitation,
Annapolis Royal Historic Gardens and Fort Anne, Upper Clements Theme Park, Scallop Fleet
🚗 Spacious home with Victorian decor and beautiful flower garden. House specialty: candlelight
gourmet breakfast with NS background music. Enjoy the congenial atmosphere. Convenient
location for early or late ferry crossings. There is a cat.

East Lawrencetown *(east of Dartmouth; see also Musquodoboit Harbour, Dartmouth)*

Jackson, Sheila & Barrie (Seaboard Bed & Breakfast) ☎ & Fax (902) 827-3747
2629 Crowell Rd, East Lawrencetown, NS B2Z 1P4 1-800-SEA-6566

From Hwy 207 (Marine Dr), turn onto Crowell Rd at eastern end of Lawrencetown Beach.

$40-45S $55-60D $15Add.person ►7
🍽 Full, homebaked 🏠 Rural, 2-storey, older, 4 acres, view from
guest rooms, seaside, porch ■ 3D (upstairs) ⊨ 2T,2D,2cots
🛏 2Sh.w.g.(1private available with key for extra charge)
★F,TV, ceiling fans, picnic table, barbeque, bicycles, canoe
⊕No smoking, pets by arrangement ⌇French
🏃 Atlantic ocean sandy beach (supervised swimming, surfing,
strolling beside sand-dunes & salt marshes, collecting tidal
treasures), Porter's Lake (fishing, canoeing, windsurfing), cliffs & abandoned railroad for
walking/jogging/cycling, birdwatching, skating, x-c skiing
🚗 Martinique (5 km long beach), Fishermans Harbour, Dartmouth/Halifax, Int.Airport
🚜 Retired couple in 1917-built farmhouse fully renovated with rooms named after Scottish
Dances (hosts favorite passtime), and located in a seaside rural setting across the road from famous
surfing beach with a fantastic panoramic waterview. Listen to the sound of the ocean and relax on
the large shaded wind-protected veranda. There is a dog in residence. Visa ✓ B&B

Folly Lake *(north-west of Truro; see also Great Village, Masstown)*

Younger, Angela (The Winnett House at Folly Lake) ☎ (902) 662-4197
Folly Lake, RR1, Londonderry, NS B0M 1M0

Phone for directons.
$35S $40-45D 🍽 Meals (plus tax) ►6
🍽 Full, homebaked 🏠 Rural, lakefront, 2-storey, older, acreage,
view from guest rooms, patio, porch, deck ■ 3D (upstairs)
⊨2T,1D,1Q 🛏 1Sh.w.g. ★ F,LF,TV/VCR, piano in guest
living/library room, indivi.thermostats ⊕No smoking, no pets
🏃 Folly Lake, hiking trails, loon nestings, Snowmobile Club
(Fundy) and trails, blueberry fields, maple sugar camp
🚗 Bay of Fundy (highest tides and Tidal Bore), beaches (clam-digging, rock-hounding, fossil cliffs
🚜 Older-style home furnished with antiques and country-style decor, overlooking Lake and Folly
Mountain. Hostess is originally from New Zealand and travelled many years before settling down in
this beautiful area. Relax on the deck or sunroom overlooking the lake and enjoy the spectacular fall
colours in season. Special diets considered with notice. Winter packages and rates for skiers and
snowmobilers are very popular. ✓B&B

Grand Pré
(east of Wolfville; see also Port Williams, Kentville)

Halbrook, John & Cally Jordan (Inn the Vineyard)   ☎ (902) 542-9554
Box 106, Grand Pré, NS B0P 1M0   E-mail: 101610.2263@compuserve.com

Located at 264 Old Post Rd in Grand Pré. From Hwy 101 follow Exit 10 and signs.
$54S $59-85D $10Add.person   ► 7
✥ Summer only ▣ Full 🏠 Village, hist., acreage, quiet ■3 (upstairs) ⊨ 1S,3D ⊐3Ensuite ★ F,TV,Parking ⓦ No smoking ⌇ French
🕴 Grand Pré Nat.Hist.Park, Covenanters Church, orchards
🚗 Wolfville, Acadia University, fine restaurants, elegant shops, Evangeline Beach, "tubing" on the Gaspereau River, Cape Split
🔫 Registered Heritage house, locally known as the "Stewart House", has been in host family for 200 years, with classic Colonial-style that retains its original layout, character and charm. Enjoy the relaxing atmosphere. Writer-host is well informed about the Annapolis Valley region.

Great Village
(west of Truro; see also Folly Lake, Masstown)

Michaud, Richard & Jan (Windflower Coach House B&B)   ☎ (902) 668-2780
RR1, Great Village, NS B0M 1L0

In Great Village, turn right on Wharf Rd or phone for directions.
$45S $55-70D $10Child/Add.person (plus tax)   ► 6A,3Ch
▣ Full 🏠 Village, hist., acreage, view from guest rooms, swimming pool, patio, porch, deck, quiet ■ 2D,1Ste (upstairs) ⊨ 1D,2Q,1P,1R ⊐ 1Sh.w.g., 1ensuite ★ 3F,TV,LF, off-street parking ⓦ No smoking
🕴 Highest tides in the world, Dyke and aboiteau, Laytons General Store and Museum, antique shops, Home of Elizabeth Bishop
🚗 Wentworth, Balmoral Grist Mill, Joy Laking Art Studio, Parrsboro Dinosaur Museum, Ships Company Theatre, Truro
🔫 Retired hosts in former stage-coach stop in the early 1800, elegantly furnished and overlooking the Cobequid Bay with world's highest tides. Be refreshed in the inground heated pool after a hot drive, enjoy a stroll in the old English-style garden, in winter relax by the fire after a day of skiing. Hosts enjoy welcoming world travellers in their house. Visa,MC ⌐B&B

Halifax
(see also East Lawrencetown)

Bowlby-Lalonde, Joe & Joanne Montgomery (Garden View B&B)   ☎ (902) 423-2943
6052 Williams St., Halifax, NS B3K 1E9   1-888-737-0778, Fax (902) 423-4355

Take Robie St Exit from MacKay Bridge to Halifax. Proceed through 4 stop lights along Robie St and turn right on Williams St.
$65-75D $15Add.person   ► 7
▣ Full 🏠Downtown ■ 3(upstairs) ⊨ 1S,2Q,1P,crib ⊐1sh.w.g. (incl watercloset) ★ Street parking, host quarters are separate ⓦ No smoking, no pets
🕴 Metro Centre, Citadel Hill, Old Town Clock, Public Gardens, Maritime Museum of the Atlantic, hist.properties on waterfront
🚗 Atlantic Theatre Festival, Annapolis Valley, Peggy's Cove, Lunenburg, International Airport
🔫 Old Victorian style home with lead glass front door, furnished with antiques and original art. Relax in the little backyard garden, on the front porch or in the cozy little den. Breakfast in bed is available at small extra charge. Shuttle service to airport express bus available. There is a dog in residence. Business travellers welcome. Visa,MC ⌐B&B

Ellis, Bruce & Anna (Caribou Lodge B&B)　　　　　　　☎ (902) 445-5013
6 Armada Dr., Halifax, NS　B3M 1R7

Phone for directions.
$55-65S/D　$10Child/Add.person　　　　　　　　　▶ 8
🍽 Cont., homebaked, buffet　🏠 Sub., 2-storey, hist., view from
guest rooms, patio, porch, quiet, secluded　▦ 1D,1F,1Ste(main &
upper level)　🛏 2D,1Q,1R　🛁 1Private,2ensuite　★ LF,TV
in each guest room, wheel-chair access, separate entrance & porch
in ground level suite, off-street parking, guest quarters are
separate　🚭 Designated smoking area
🏃 Hemlock Ravine Park, "Titanic" Cemetary, numerous restaurants, Art Gallery, Duke of Kent
Music Room (Nat.Hist.Site), bus routes Nos12/80/14
🚌 Downtown Halifax, Int.Airport, Acadian Museum, Peggy's Cove, Shubenacadie Wildlife Park
🐾 Spacious Century home with warm period furnishings and art gallery/gift shop. Watch
hostess(A.J.Scanlan) work at her easel in the gallery. Host offers professional expertise in both the
region's civilian and military heritage & reserves. Breakfast is served in special guest breakfast
room. Group & extended stay terms available. Perfect place for honeymoon and special occasions.
There are 2 dogs in residence. Visa,Amex

Grandfield, Bob & Bob Woods (Bobs' Bed & Breakfast)　　　☎ (902) 454-4374
2715 Windsor St., Halifax, NS　B3K 5E1

Located between North & Almon Sts. Phone for directions.
$50-60S　$60-75D　$15Add.person　(plus tax)　　　▶ 10A
📅 May1-Oct31　🍽 Full, homebaked　🏠 Res, 3-storey, older, patio
▦ 1S,3D,1Ste (upstairs)　🛏 1S,2T,1D,2Q(including poster bed)
🛁 1Ensuite, 2sh.w.g., 1sh.w.h.　★ F,TV, fridge in one guest room, grand
piano & organ, host quarters are separate, off-street & street parking
🚭 No smoking, no pets, not suitable for children
🏃 Shopping, restaurants, Casino, downtown area, historic sights, Bus Stn
🚌 Peggy's Cove, waterfront, harbour, beaches, Train Station, Int. Airport
🐾 Charming, large home with high quality furnishings & selected Nova Scotia Art throughout,
close to downtown Halifax. Relax on the patio or in the extensive flower garden. A sumptuous
homecooked breakfast is served in the formal dining room. There are 2 Sheltie dogs. MC

Hatfield, Elaine (Sea Watch Bed & Breakfast)　　　　☎ & Fax (902) 477-1506
139 Ferguson's Cove Rd., Ferguson's Cove, Halifax, NS　B3V 1L7

Located 7km from Armdale Rotary off Rte 253 (Purcells Cove Rd) at 139 Fergusons Cove Rd.

$65S　$75D　$10Add.person　　　　　　　　　　▶ 2A
🍽 Cont.　🏠 Rural, 3-storey, hillside, oceanview from guest
room, ocean across the road, quiet, deck　▦ 1Ste (ground level)
🛏 1D　🛁 1Ensuite　★ Private entrance and private deck,
TV/VCR/microwave/fridge in suite, street parking　🚭 No pets,
inquire about children
🏃 Ocean, nature trails, historic York Redoubt Fort, bus #15
🚌 Shopping malls, downtown Halifax, harbourfront, Int.Airport
(45km), Peggy's Cove, scenic southshore drives and villages
🐾 Young host family in large home with nautical decor and a panoramic view of Halifax Harbour
and McNabs Island, situated on a very quiet road 40ft from the waterside. Host was born and raised
in the Cove and is very knowledgeable about local history and the sea. There are school children in
the host family. Breakfast served in seashells in suite or on deck.

MacDonald, Innis and Sheila (Fresh Start B&B)   ☎ 902) 453-6616, Fax (902) 453-6617
2720 Gottingen St., Halifax, NS B3K 3C7

Located 1 block north of MacDonald Bridge, across from Maritime Command Museum.
$55-60S $60-65D $75-85Ste $10Add.person (Off-season Rates available)   ▶ 22
⬛Full, homebaked 🏠Downtown, 3-storey, hist. ■7D,1Ste (upstairs) ⊨4T,2Q,6D,2cots
⬛2Private,3sh.w.g. ★TV,F,KF, parking, meeting facilities ⬤No smoking ⌇some German
🏃 Maritime Command Museum, Citadel Hill, historic Halifax waterfront, shopping, fine
restaurants, site of Halifax Explosion, public swimming pool, Maritime Museum of the Atlantic
🚐 Picnic area, fresh/saltwater beaches, windsurfing, Peggy's Cove, Fundy Tidal Bore
🐚 Modest Victorian Mansion which has retained much original woodwork and glass. Though
close to downtown, the location is very quiet. Business travellers welcome.CCards ✔B&B

Nielsen, Judy & Dobbie (Brook Haven Court B&B)   ☎ (902) 860-0047
3440 Hwy 2, Fall River, NS B2T 1J2   E-mail: brook.haven@ns.sympatico.ca

From Hwy 102 (from Halifax) take Exit 5 and proceed north 2.3km to house on right side. From
Dartmouth, take Exit 14. Located south of airport (app 25km).

$45S $50D $8Add.person (Child under age 10 free) ▶ 10
⬛ Full, homebaked 🏠 Rural, ranch-style, acreage, patio,
quiet ■2D,1F ⊨ 2Q,2D,crib ⬛ 2Sh.w.g.
★LF,TV,KF,separate entrance, wheel-chair access, help-yourself
linen closet, high-chair, stoller, host quarters are separate
⬤Designated smoking room, no pets, children welcome
🏃 Shubic Canal, country walks, fishing, outside fireplace, nightly
bonfire, picnic site with barbeque
🚐 International Airport, Halifax, Dartmout, golfing, Prov. Parks, beaches,
🐚 Newly constructed ranch-style home, especially built with B&B in mind, surrounded by trees
and brook in rural setting. Ideal place for early or late flights at Halifax Int.Airport. Enjoy the
down-home comfort and hospitality. Breakfast is served in large bright country kitchen. ✔ B&B

Hubbards   *(west of Halifax; see also chester*

Zinck, Maureen (Blandford Inn B&B)   ☎ & Fax (902) 228-2016
Lighthouse Rte No 329, Blandford, NS B0J 1T0

From Halifax follow Hwy 103 to Exit 6, turn left toward Hubbards, then along ocean side to B&B.
$60S $72D $20Child 🍽Meals   ▶ 16
⬛ May-Oct ⬛ Buffet 🏠 Rural, village, hist., view from guest
rooms, deck, quiet, secluded ■ 4F(upper & ground
level) ⊨8D ⬛4Private ★ TV,F,LF, wheel-chair access in
ground floor guest room, bicycles and fishing rods for guests,
off-street and street parking ⬤No smoking, inquire about pets
🏃 Beautiful Bayswater Beach, oceanside meanders, horseback
riding, nature trails, hiking paths, fishing from the wharfs
🚐 Historic seaports of Chester, Mahone Bay, Lunenburg, dining, shopping
🐚 Charming Century house with a new addition located by the ocean providing a good place to
relax, unwind, relieve stress and restore the mind and body. Enjoy the tranquil and peaceful
atmosphere. Hostess was born and raised in the area and is knowledgeable of sites and events.
Breakfast is served in the sunroom overlooking the harbour. Small groups for weddings or special
occasions can be accommodated. Visa,MC ✔CC

Isle Madame

(on Cape Breton Island east of Hawkesbury)

Kehoe, Claire & George (Kehoe's Bed & Breakfast) ☎ (902) 226-2839
698 Rocky Bay Rd., Isle Madame, NS B0E 1K0 Fax (902) 226-1592

Take Rte 104 to Exit 46 and Rte 320 east to Isle Madame. Continue through D'Escousse to
Pondville, turn left for Rocky Bay Rd. Located 45km from Port Hawkesbury.

$35S $47D $12Child/Add.person 📷 Meals ▶ 8A,4Ch
🌙 Full 🏠 Rural, 2-storey, 5 acres, view, oceanfront, deck
quiet ■4 (upstairs) ⊨ 2S,1D,2Q,1K,crib ⟂ 2Sh.w.g.
★TV ⊛No smoking, no pets ∿ French
🏃 Private beach, bonfires, clam-digging, beachcombing, open air
cooking, walking trails, berrypicking
🚗 Golf Course, LeNoir Forge Museum at Arichat, restaurant
🔫 Cheerful home situated on the Atlantic coast of picturesque
Isle Madame. Enjoy the beautiful sea-side location & homemade breads and jams.

Jeddore

(east of Halifax; see also Musquodoboit Hbr, E.Lawrencetown)

Jonah, Dora & Bill (Jonah By the Sea B&B) ☎ & Fax (902) 889-3516
Lower West Jeddore Rd., RR1, Head Jeddore, NS B0J 1P0

Located east of Dartmouth at West Jeddore. Travel 10 km south on West Jeddore Rd off Hwy 7
(Marine Dr) to mouth of harbour. Look for B&B sign.

$45S $50D $10Cot (plus tax) ▶ 6
✜ May-Oct. 🌙 Homebaked 🏠 Rural, 2-storey, older, 215 acres, view
from guest rooms, ocean across road, deck, quiet, secluded ■ 3(upstairs)
⊨1D,2Q,R,cot ⟂ 1Sh.w.h. ★ TV in guest room on request, old
woodstove in huge country kitchen ⊛ No smoking, no pets
🏃 Beach (clam digging/beach combing), bird watching, harbour entrance,
fishing, scenic walks on large acreage or by the ocean, star gazing at its best
🚗 Railway Museum, Cities of Dartmouth & Halifax, airport, restaurants
🔫 1900's country home in quaint fishing village, built by a Sea Captain,
with scenic view of the Atlantic Ocean and surrounded by 210 acres of
grounds with flower & vegetable gardens, bordering the ocean. Relax in the cozy guest room window
seats and enjoy the many varieties of birds, the beautiful ocean view with Jeddore Rock & Light.
Trails are under construction. There is a cat in residence. Visa ∕B&B

Kentville

(see also Wolfville, Pt.Williams, Grand Pre)

Newcombe, John (Newcombe House B&B ca 1881) ☎ (902) 678-7486
997 Hwy 341, Upper Dyke, NS B0P 1J0

Located 5km north of Kentville on Hwy 341. Follow signs through Kentville to North Kentville.

$40S $50-60D $10Add.person (plus tax) ▶ 6A,2Ch
✜ May-Nov 🌙 Full, homebaked 🏠 Farm, 2-storey, older,
view, deck, quiet ■ 3D(upstairs ⊨ 2D,1Q,cot,crib
⟂1sh.w.g. ★ F,TV in guest rooms, private entrance, guest
quarters are separate ⊛ Smoking outside
🏃 Walk the dykelands on the property, local golf club in village
🚗 Scenic look-off, sandy beaches, world's highest tides, museums,
recreationsl facilities, Grand Pré Historic Park
🔫 Family Century homestead with Georgian-style architecture, overlooking the Canard
(Wellington) dykeland and situated on a working farm. Discover good old country hospitality and
congenial surroundings. Enjoy candlelit breakfasts. "Wag"s the poodle/terrior and "Buffy" the manx
cat in residence. Visa ∕B&B

Peerless, Darlene & Jim (Wickwire House B&B)   ☎ (902) 679-1188, Fax (902) 679-5196
183 Main St., Kentville, NS   B4N 1J6   E-mail: wickwire.house@ns.sympatico.ca

From Hwy 101, take Exit 12 to Kentville. Look for B&B on right when descending Wickwire Hill
into town. Or take Exit 13 to Kentville, turn right on Main St and look fo B&B on left.

$75S $85D $15Add.person   ► 4
✚ Summer only (other by special arrangement)   ▣ Full,
homebaked   🏠 Res., 3-storey, acreage, hist., riverview,
gazebo-porch, deck   ▪ 2D (upstairs)   ⊨ 1D,1K(2S),1P
🚗2Ensuite   ★ F,TV, Princess grand piano, off-street parking
✋ Smoking on veranda, not suitable for children
🏃 Downtown, Agricultural Research Stn (park setting), pubs,
restaurants, shops, Courthouse Museum, Tourist Bureau
🚗 Annapolis Valley, Bloomidon Lookoff, Halls Hbr & Lobster Pound, golfing, Cape Split hiking
☞ Stately Victorian Century home with elegance and coziness in prominent historic Main Street
location. Relax on the large ornate veranda with gazebo in front of the house. Breakfast is served in
separate guest breakfast room. Hosts are proud recipients of 95 & 96 awards for "Hist.Restortation
& Built Heritage". There is a small Lasa dog "Barney" who loves to greet guests. Visa MC

Snow, Richard & Sandra (The Grand Street Inn B&B)   ☎ (902) 679-1991
160 Main St., Kentville, NS   B4N 1J8

Phone for directions.
$65S $75D $10Child/Add.person   ► 10
▣ Full   🏠 Res., 3-storey, acreage, swimming pool, view, patio,
porch, deck   ▪2D,1F(upstairs)   ⊨ 2T,3D,1P,crib   🚗1Private,
1ensuite   ★F,TV, ceiling fans, separate entrance, off-street
parking   ✋ Smoking ouside, no pets   〰 French
🏃 Agricultural Centre, museum & nature trail, downtown,
shopping, dining, entertainment, Courthouse Museum
🚗 Hall's Harbour, Lobster Pond, Acadian University (Wolfville), Atlantic Theatre Festival, Bay of
Fundy (highest tides in the world), scenic drives, Halifax and Int.Airport
☞ Completely renovated spacious Queen Anne Revival Century home, tastefully decorated and
situated in the heart of the Annapolis Valley. Rooms are on 2nd & 3rd floor. Early retired Air Force
hosts were born in Newfoundland. Relax in the large common rooms. Breakfast is served in formal
dining room. There is a young school boy in residence. Children welcome. Visa,MC ⌐B&B

Larry's River
                                                (on south-east shore near Canso)

Uloth, Doug & Mary-Anne Casey (Cole-Harbour Bed & Breakfast)   ☎ (902) 358-2889
RR2, Larry's River, Cole Harbour, Guys Co., NS   B0H 1T0   1-800-565-9144

Located 30km west of Canso on Rte 316 and 42km east of Country Harbour. Phone for directions.
$45-55D $15Add.person   ► 6A,2Ch
✚ May-Oct (other by special arrangement)   ▣ Full, homebaked   🏠 Village, bungalow, 10 acres,
river & oceanfront, deck   ▪ 3D (main floor)   ⊨ 4D,cot   🚗 2Ensuite, 1sh.w.h.   ★LF,KF,TV
& fans in rooms, off-street parking
🏃 Beach, walking trails, birdwatching, trout fishing, restaurants, boat rides
🚗 Historic villages, beaches with boardwalks, ferry to islands, golf courses, fishing villages, parks
☞ New home with beautiful harbour view and peaceful, quiet atmosphere. Loons, deer and bald
eagles visit regularly. Host is a lobster fisherman with a 34 ft boat, available to take guests out to
see the seals on the islands. Relax on the deck and watch the harbour activities. Visa ⌐B&B

Lawrencetown
(west of Kentville; see also Paradise, Bridgetown,Middleton)

Jahn, Ingrid (Cricket's Harp Inn)   ☎ (902) 584-3388, Fax (902) 584-3389
7165 Highway 201, RR1, Lawrencetown, NS   B0S 1M0

$55S $65D $10Add.person   (plus tax)   📷 Meals   ► 10

Phone for directions.
💮 Full, homebaked   🏠 Farm, hist., acreage, view from guest rooms, patio, porch, deck, quiet   ■3D,1F(upstairs)   ⊨5D,cot
🚗2Sh.w.g.   ★ F,KF,LF,TV, fans available, host quarters are separate   ✋ Smoking outside, pets boarding across street ♥ 🚶German
🏃 Apple orchards, farm pastures with farm animals and woodland 🚗 Middleton, Annapolis Royal (Queen's historic Gardens), Bay of Fundy, Wolfville, (Atlantic Theatres Festival), Port Royal (Habitation), McDonalds Museum
🢂 Friendly hospitality in large 19th Century renovated homestead with a warm elegant ambiance, surrounded by apple and fruit orchards. There are school children in the house. Hostess also owns & operates a Lady's Fashion Boutique in the nearby town of Middleton. Enjoy a gourmet dinner with wine (at request). Relax on the lovely porch. Special packages available. There are outdoor pets. Visa,Amex ✓B&B

Louisbourg
(on Cape Breton Island south of Sydney; see also Big Pond, Sidney)

Brooks, Dorothy and Delmer (The Manse)   ☎ (902) 733-3155 or 733-3694
10 Strathcona St., Louisbourg, NS   B0A 1M0

Follow Hwy 22 straight into town of Louisbourg & continue down Main Street. Turn left at Esso Service Station to 1st house on right.
$40-50S/D $12Add.person   (plus tax)   ► 6A
💮 Full   🏠 Downtown, res., hist., view from 2 guest rooms, oceanside   ■ 3D (upstairs)   ⊨ 3D,3R   🚗 1Sh.w.g., 1sh.w.h.(on main floor)   ★ Parking   ✋ No children
🏃 Downtown, restaurants, shops
🚗 Fortress, city of Sydney, scenic lighthouse, historic beach
🢂 Spacious, turn-of-the-Century home with large rooms, many antiques, collectables and a panoramic view of harbour and ocean. There is a small dog. ✓B&B

Cross, Mrs. Greta   ☎ (902) 733-2833
48 Pepperell Street, Louisbourg, NS   B0A 1M0

Located in Louisbourg. Look for 2nd street on right side of Main St.
$35S $45D   Children welcome.   ► 10A,4Ch
💮 Full, homebaked   🏠 Downtown, older, view, quiet   ■3D,F (upstairs)   ⊨ 3D   🚗2Sh.w.g.   ★KF,LF, bicycle shelter, ample parking ♥   🚶 some French
🏃 Scenic view on hill overlooking Fortress and Harbour
🚗 Fortress of Louisburg
🢂 Enjoy warm hospitality in quiet area of historic town. "Ciad Mile Fialte" (One hundred thousand welcomes)! ✓B&B

Ferguson, Hazel (Sunlit Valley Farms B&B)   ☎ (902)562-7663,Fax 562-2222
821 Brickyard Rd., Albert Br., RR2 Marion Bridge, NS   B0A 1P0

From Port Hawkesbury, take either Rt 4 or Rt 105 to Sydney area. From Sydney take Hwy 22 tow.

Louisbourg, crossing the Mira River, take 1st left, then 3 km.
$35S $45-50D $16Add.person   ▶7
✣✣May 1-Oct.30   ⬛Full   🏠Farm, view, riverfront, quiet, deck
⬛4(main & lower level)   ⊨4D,1S   ⬛2Sh.w.g.   ★F,TV room
🚗 Fortress of Louisburg, Provincial Park, swimming beaches,
camping & picnicking, NFLD ferry, Glace Bay Miners Museum,
Marconi Museum, "Rita MacNeil Tea Room", Sydney,
☛ Very social and congenial atmosphere in comfortable Cape
Breton home overlooking the Mira River. Well-informed hostess will help with travel plans. ╰B&B

MacLeod, Harvey and Mona (MacLeod's B&B)   ☎ & Fax (902) 733-2456
5247 Hwy. 22 Louisbourg, NS   B0A 1M0

Located 10 km before Louisbourg on Rt 22 and 23 km from Sydney.

$30-35S $45-50D   ▶6
✣ May1-Sept30   ⬛ Full   🏠 Rural, acreage, patio, quiet   ⬛
3D (upstairs)   ⊨3D (upstairs)   ⬛1sh.w.g., 1ensuite   ★TV,F,
parking   ⓦRestricted smoking, no pets
🚗 Fortress of Louisburg, Miners Museum, Newfoundland
Ferry, Sydney Airport
☛ Ambassador Award-winning new Cape Cod home in a very
quiet area in the country.Enjoy the interesting birds on the
property. Very convenient location. Visa ╰B&B

Lunenburg   *(west of Halifax; see also Mahone Bay, Chester)*

Barrett, William and Sheila (Barrett's Bed and Breakfast)   ☎ (902) 766-4655
RR1, Feltzen South, Rose Bay, NS   B0J 2X0

From Hwy 103, take Exit 11 towards Lunenburg. Follow signs to Riverport. Turn left for "Ovens
Natural Park" off Rt 332 and proceed to Feltzen South (located 10km south of Lunenburg).

$45S $55D $85F   ▶8
⬛ Full, homebaked   🏠 Village, hist., rural, acreage, view, patio,
ocean frontage, isolated   ⬛4(upstairs)   ⊨ 4S,2D,cot
⬛2Sh.w.g.   ★ Separate entrance, guest fridge, guests' common
room (former cobbler's shop)   ⓦ No pets, children min. age 12,
restricted smoking
🏃 Ocean beach (swimming and clamming), Ovens Natural Park
and campground (once the site of NS's own gold rush), fishing
🚗 Lunenburg (shopping and fine restaurants), Fisheries Museum, Mahone Bay, Peggy's Cove
☛ Retired couple in renovated colonial home with pine-planked floors and lots of comfortable
country antiques, situated on Lunenburg Bay. Hosts are rug hooking & braiding artists and offer
lessons as well as sell. A charter fishing boat is available for rent and other boats and bicycles.
There is a Golden Retriever & a cat in residence. Visa,MC ╰B&B

Heubach, Merrill and Al (Blue Rocks Road B&B) ☎ & Fax (902) 634-8033
RR1, #579 Blue Rocks Rd., Lunenburg, NS B0J 2C0 1-800-818-3426 (Reserv.only)

From Hwy 103, take Exit 11 towards Lunenburg and travel on Rt 324S for approx. 10 km. At stop sign, turn left towards Blue Rocks. Turn left again at next stop sign, proceed to 4th house on left.

$45-55S $55-65D $20Add.person ► 6
� closed Nov-March ✪ Full, homebaked 🏠 Rural, res., hist., acreage, oceanview, quiet ■ 3(upstairs) ⊨2T,2D
⊂1Private,1sh.w.g. ⓌNo smoking,no pets 〜German
🕇 Bicycle shop on premises, Lunenburg Centre, fine restaurants, galleries, shops, scenic surrounding countryside, beautiful uncrowded beaches, fishing, whale-watching, sea-kayaking.
🚗 Mahone Bay, Halifax, Kejimkujik Nat.Park, Peggy's Cove
☛ Charming, comfortable 19th Century home with veranda overlooking Lunenburg Bay and surrounded by a cyclist's paradise. Enjoy awesome breakfasts and the friendly relaxed atmosphere. Hosts operate the Lunenburg Bicycle Barn (day-trip plans, maps, bicycle rental, accessories, full service available). There is a very friendly dog in residence. Visa ✓B&B

Jennings, Tom & Judy (Commander's Bed & Breakfast) ☎ & Fax (902) 634-3151
56 Victoria Rd., Box 864, Lunenburg, NS B0J 2C0 1-800-550-4824 (Reserv.only)

From Halifax, take Hwy 103 south-west toward Yarmouth and Exit 11. Continue on Hwy 324 to Lunenburg and proceed to house on left prior to harbour.

$60-90S/D $15Add.person ► 10
✪ Full 🏠 Village, hist., 3-storey, view, oceanfront, patio, porch, deck, quiet ■4F(upstairs) ⊨3Q,2T,4P 🚗 4Private ★F,3TV,LF
2lounges,Fax/photocopier/word processor, sitting areas in all rooms, library, iron/blower avail., parking ⓌDesignated smoking area, young adults 12 & over welcome
🕇 Sports Park, Exhibition grounds, tennis, swimming pool, picnic area downtown & historic district, restaurants, local craft shops Fisheries Museum, fishing.
🚗 Halifax, Mahone Bay, Peggy's Cove, scenic south-shore drives & coastal villages
☛ Elegant turn-of-the-Century home, retaining all of its original character. Interesting naval memorabilia collected by host during navy career, as well as an extensive library, ship/airplane models, working model railway & a unique "pig" collection. Visa,MC,Amex ✓CC

Mabou *(on Cape Breton Isle north of Port Hawkesbury; see also Port Hood)*

McIntyre, Kathy (Glendyer Mills Bed & Breakfast) ☎ (902) 945-2455
RR4, Mabou, NS B0E 1X0

Take Rte 19 to Rte 252 to Mabou. Proceed 2 km , turn left on Smithville-Glendyer Rd and continue 2km to B&B before bridge.

$45-55S $55-65D $20Add.person (plus tax) ► 9
✪ Cont.(Full at extra charge) 🏠 Farm, 2-storey, hist., riverfront, patio, deck, quiet ■ 1D,1F,1Ste (upstairs) ⊨
4S,3D 🚗 1Sh.w.g.,1sh.w.h. (main floor) ★F,LF,KF,TV/VCR in suite ⓌNo smoking, no pets
🕇 Walking and x-c ski trail on abandoned railroad line
🚗 Many beaches, beautiful hiking trails, Alexander Graham Bell Museum (Baddeck), local dances (step dancing to local fiddlers)
☛ Formerly the site of a bustling woolen mill (late 1800's) spacious heritage home, lovingly restored and filled with antiques - nostalgic of an other time - and nestled in a Glen surrounded by 8 acres bordered by a brook. Relax in the dining room or adjoining deck with a view of the gardens. Breakfast consists of farm fresh produce. Hostess lives in small house next door. ✓B&B

Mahone Bay

(west of Halifax; see also Lunenburg, Chester)

O'Brien, Rose & Allan (The Manse at Mahone Bay Country Inn) ☎ (902) 624-1121
88 Orchard St., Box 475, Mahone Bay, NS B0J 2E0   Fax (902) 624-1182

Approaching from the east look for house next to first of 3 famous churches. Look for yellow house
with white trim.
$85S $95D $15Add.person   ☑ Meals   (plus tax)   ► 10
⓪ Full, homebaked   🛂 Village, hist., view from guest rooms,
oceanfront, deck, quiet   ■ 4D(ground & upper level)incl.carriage
house   ⏩ 4T,2Q   ⌜ 4Private   ★ F,TV in guest rooms,
ceiling fans, off-street parking   ∾ French
♟ Shops, galleries, restaurants, fishing, sailing
🚗 Halifax, Peggy's Cove, Chester, Lunenburg, Wolfville
🔨 Elegant, restored 1860's manse (former parson's house) with all modern amenities, great art,
books, eclectic music and a wonderful view of the Bay, situated on a tree-lined street. Relax on the
deck or by the fireplace. Ideally suited for weddings and special occasions. Visa,MC ↰CC

Piccolo, John & Faith (Amber Rose Inn) ☎ (902) 624-1060
319 West Main St., Box 397, Mahone Bay, NS B0J 2E0

From Hwy 103 take Exit 11, turn right at Blockhouse and proceed 2km. From Mahone Bay Hbr.,
drive straight up from monument at main intersection, 1km.
$85-95S/D $15Child/Add.person   (plus taxes)   ► 8A
✝ May-Oct   ⓪ Cont.(cooked)   🛂 Village, 2-storey, hist., patio,
porch, deck   ■ 2D,1F (upstairs)   ⏩ 2D,2Q   ⌜ 3Private,
whirlpool tub   ★TV/fridge/coffee machine in guest suites, guest
quarters are separate, airconditioners in guest suites, private
entrance, guest robes   ♿ Designated smoking area, no pets, not
suitable for children   ∾ Italian
♟ Waterfront & harbour, shopping, park, wooded area with trails, restaurants, churches
🔨 Originally the General store, one of Mahone Bay's best preserved architecture of Heritage
buildings, has been renovated and expanded to modernize facilities, while maintaining the look and
feel of the original house. Enjoy luxury decor, spacious lawn & gardens. Browse in the craft shop on
premises, featuring apparel made by hostess. Breakfast is served in the guest breakfast room.
There is a cat. Visa,MC,Amex ↰B&B

Redden, Ron and Mabel (Sou'Wester Inn) ☎ (902) 624-9296
Box 146, 788 Main Street, Mahone Bay, NS B0J 2E0

Located in Mahone Bay on Hwy 3 West (towards Lunenburg).
$75D $15Add.person   ► 10
✝ May-Oct.   ⓪ Choice, homebaked   🛂 Res., oceanfront, quiet
■4D(upst)   ⏩2Q,2D   ⌜4 private   ★Parking   ♿No smoking
♟ Fine shops, collectables, antiques, exquisite dining
🚗 Halifax, Peggy's Cove, fishing hamlets, beaches, Lunenburg
🔨 Long-time B&B hosts in spacious seaside Victorian
shipbuilder's home. Quiet, friendly and gracious accommodation
with antique furniture and large guest rooms. A favorite spot for Honeymooners to Seniors. Relax
on the large front veranda, watch sailboats in the scenic Bay. There is a piano and there are books
& games for rainy days. Host sculptures graceful wooden whales in his workshop.Visa,MC ↰B&B

Margaree Forks
on CB Isle south of Cape North, see also Mar.Harbour)

Harrison, Robin & Marilyn (Harrison Hill B&B)   ☎ & Fax (902) 248-2226
Box 561, Margaree Forks, NS B0E 2A0

From Rte 19, turn right at T junction toward Baddeck. Continue past Fire Hall & Dept of Fisheries
to B&B sign. From Baddeck, follow Cabot Trail from Red Barn past Doyle's Rd to B&B sign

$55D $10Child/Add.person   (plus taxes) ⬢ Meals   ▶6
🍽 Full 🏠 Rural, village, 3-storey, older, acreage, view from
guest rooms, patio, porch, deck, secluded   ■ 2D,1F(upstairs)
⊢⌐2T,2D,1Q,P,R ⊿ 2Sh.w.h.   ★ LF,TV,off-street parking
🚭No smoking, no pets
🎣 Salmon fishing (Margaree River), beaches, on-site gift corner
🚗 Cheticamp (Acadian Village), Baddeck (Alexander Bell
Museum), Centre Bras d'Or Festival, Fortress of Louisbourg, Cape
Breton National Park

🎤 Elegant, romantic and old world charm in restored large older home with spacious grounds set
in tranquil surroundings of beautiful scenery. Relax on the wrap-around veranda. Concert Pianist
host' special interest is music, drama and travel. Enjoy the entertainment in the music room,
soirees or outdoor theatre in the back garden (Sat & Thurs evenings July15-Aug15). Visa,MC

Margaree Harbour
(on CB Isle south of Cape North; see also Margaree F.)

Taylor, Francis and Mary (Taylor's Bed & Breakfast)   ☎ (902) 235-2652
Margaree Harbour, Inverness County, NS B0E 2B0

Located 1.5 km south of Margaree Harbour bridge on Cabot Trail.
$35S $45D $5Child $10Add.person   ▶ 6A,2Ch
✜ June-Dec. 🍽 Full, homebaked 🏠 Farm, hist., view, quiet,
oceanfront, veranda ■ 3D(upstairs) ⊢⌐3D,2cots ⊿Sh.w.h
★TV, parking
🎣 Beaches, restaurants, gift shops, laundromat, hiking trail
🚗 Deep-Sea Fishing
🎤 Comfortable Century farm house overlooking St. Lawrence
Gulf/Margaree River. Native hosts are well informed, & happy to help with travel plans. ✔B&B

Wheeler, Jan & Bob (Chimney Corner B&B)   ☎ & Fax (902) 235-2104
Box 6, Margaree Harbour, NS B0E 2B0

From Canso Causeway take Ceilidh Trail (Rte 19) and proceed beyond Inverness. Turn left at Shore
Rd (Rte 219). Travel north for 13km and turn left into long driveway at B&B sign.

$55S $65D   ▶4A
✜ May15-Oct15 (other by arrangement) 🍽 Full, homebaked
(may cater to dietary requirements) 🏠 Rural, split-level 3storey,
25acres, view, oceanfront, deck, quiet, isolated ■ 2D (ground &
upper level) ⊢⌐2D ⊿ 2Private ★ F,TV,LF, beach towels
for guests, barbeque 🚭 No smoking, no pets, no children
🚗 Cabot Trail, AGB Museum (Baddeck), CB Highlands Nat.Park,
whale watching, salmon fishing, canoeing, boat tours
🎣 Wooded trails, private beach on grounds, Chimney Corner Beach (famous "singing sands")
🎤 Unique A-frame house built and decorated by hosts situated on the ocean. Each guest room is
on a separate level, adding to a feeling of privacy. Hosts are retired teachers with many and varied
interests and abilities. Ideal place for honeymoons, special occasions, anniversaries. Also on
property 2 self/cont. housekeeping cottages. Breakfast is served in special guest breakfast room.
There are 2 "user friendly" dogs. Reservations preferred. Visa,MC,Amex ✔B&B

Masstown
(west of Truro, see also Great Village, Folly Lake)

Eisses, James & Ellen (Shady Maple Bed'N Breakfast)   ☎ & Fax(902) 662-3565,
RR1, Debert, Masstown, NS B0M 1G0   1-800-493-5844

From Truro on Hwy 104 take Exit 12 to Masstown, turn on Hwy 2 and travel 5 km. Or from Hwy
102 take Exit 14A, turn left to Masstown and go 11.8 km to white farmhouse with 2 silos by barn.
$40S $50D $65Ste $5Child(free under age 3) $10Add.person   ► 8A,4Ch
🍴Full 🏠Farm,patio,quiet,inground pool & spa ■3D(upst) + 1Ste
⊨2D,1Q,1waterbed,cots,crib ⊲2sh.w.g.,1whirlpool bath ★TV,F,LF,Tidal
Bore Video ⊛No smoking ﹏Dutch
🚶 Woodland walking trails, extensive farm grounds, view of Bay of Fundy
🚗 World famous Tidal Bore viewing site, Halifax Airport, Parrsboro, Truro
🐄 Working farm with large recently renovated and restored Century farm
house, but still maintaining "that down home" feeling. Guests are
welcome to view and visit farm activities. House specialty is candlelit breakfast.

Middleton
(west of Kentville; see also Paradise, Lawrencetown, Bridgetown)

Griffith, Richard & Shae (Fairfield Farm Inn)   ☎ & Fax (902) 825-6989
10 Main St., Middleton, NS B0S 1P0   1-800-237-9896

Located in Middleton at west end of Main St on Hwy 1.
$45-65S $50-70D 🍽 Meals (plus tax)   ► 10
🍴 Choice 🏠 Farm (within town), hist.,110acres, 2-storey, mountain
view, patio ■ 5D (main & upper level) ⊨ 1D,3Q,1K ⊲5Ensuite
★Air-conditioners & ceiling fans, LF,TV in most guest rooms, separate
entrance, large guest kitchen, parking ⊛ No smoking, no pets, children
min. age 12
🚶 Annapolis River & Slocum Brook with trail for walking (on property),
historic Loyalist church across street, MacDonald Museum, galleries,
boutiques, restaurants, tourist bureau, meadows & woodland
🚗 Bay of Fundy shore, Port Royal, Kejimkujik & Grand Pré Nat.Parks,
Atlantic Theatre Festival, golfing, fishing, hiking
🐄 Elegant 1886-built Country Inn in completely restored, large Victorian farmhouse with period
antiques, situated on 110 acre property in the "Heart of the Annapolis Valley". Relax on the upper
or lower terrace and enjoy friendly Maritime hospitality with a wholesome country breakfast of
traditional Nova Scotia fare and fruits fresh picked from the garden. Ideal place for groups, retreats
and special occasions. Hosts live in separate building on property. CCards ✔B&B

Musquodoboit Harbour
(east of Halifax; see also East Lawrencetown, Jedorre)

Kent, Mildred and Ivan (Seaview Fisherman's Home)   ☎ (902) 889-2561
RR1 Musquodoboit Harbour, NS B0J 2L0

Located at Pleasant Point. Travel 12 km on the Ostrea Lake Rd off
Hwy 7 (Marine Drive) to road sign Kent Rd and to 2nd house.
$45S $50D $55Cottage $10Add.person (plus tax)   ► 6A,1Ch
🗓April1-Nov.1 🍴Full, homebaked 🏠Rural, acreage, view, quiet,
oceanfront ■1S,3D(upst) ⊨1S,1T,2D ⊲2Sh.w.g.,1powder
room ★TV,parking ⊛No smoking, no pets
🚶 Lighthouse on property, seashore, watch fishing boats come in
🚗 Two beaches, restaurants, Dartmouth/Halifax, historic sights, birdwatching, nature walks
🐄 Fourth and Fifth Generation home (built 1861) in pretty fishing village and very quiet
secluded island (20 acres) with a view of the sea from every room in the house. Hosts have been
welcoming guests for many years. There is a cat "little KIT" who accompanies guests on walks
along the trails made for guests to the lighthouse and around the vast shore property. Home has
been featured on TV NS-travel series. Enjoy the wonderful ghost stories told by congenial host. Also
small housekeeping cottage (for 2) and weekly rates available. ✔B&B

Skaling, Randy & Judy (Wayward Goose Inn - B&B)   ☎ & Fax (902) 889-3654
343 West Petpeswick Rd, Musquodoboit Harbour, NS B0J 2L0   1-888-790-1777

From Dartmouth, take Hwy 107 to Rte 7 at Musquodoboit Harbour. Turn right for 1.7 km to West

Petpeswick Rd and right again 1.7km to Inn.
$44-69S $54-79D $5Child $10Add.person (plus tax)   ► 6A,4Ch
🏠Full,homebaked   🏠Rural,2-storey,acreage,waterview,patio,
quiet,private ■3D(upst)incl.honeymoon ste & whirlpool bath,
guest quarters are seprate ⊨2T,2Q, foams and sleeping bags for
children ⊲2Ensuite,1private ★F,TV/VCR/stereo, canoe,
rowboat/daysailer, separate entrance ⓌNo smoking, no pets
🏃 Walking/cycling trails, water activities, birding, x/c skiing
🚌 Sandy beach, craftshops/antiques, restaurants, golfing, scenic drives along the coast, Halifax
🐎 Spacious, quiet Inn overlooking the magical Petpeswick (saltwater) Inlet. Enjoy traditional
Maritime Hospitality on Nova Scotia's undiscovered Maritime Folklore. Eastern shore. Hostess is a
water colour artist. Browse in "Judy's Art Works Studio" in the barn. Lessons available. Hosts are
very knowledgeable about local sights and events. Ideal place for honeymoon and special occasion.
Visa,MC ⸝B&B

Paradise   *(west of Kentville; see also E.Lawrencetown,Middleton, Bridgwater)*

Grimard, Kim & Claude (The Paradise Inn, B&B)   ☎ 902) 584-3934
116 Paradise Lane, Box 24, Paradise, NS B0S 1R0   E-mail: grimard.kc@ns.sympatico.ca

From Hwy 101 take Exit 19 and proceed on Rte 1 to Paradise Lane.
$45-55S $50-60D $15Add.person   ► 7
🎏 May15-Aug30 (other by special arrangement)   🏠 Full,
homebaked   🏠 Rural, village, 2-storey, hist., view from guest
rooms, deck, quiet ■ 3D(upstairs) ⊨ 2T,2Q,cot ⊲1Private,
1sh.w.g. ★ Guest robes, host quarters are separate, private
guest parlour, secure bicycle & canoe storage, off-street parking
Ⓦ No smoking, no pets, children min.age14 ⋙ French
🏃 Croquet, Eden Golf & Country Club, Annapolis Valley Exhibition (early Aug), Annapolis River
🚌 Brook running through property, Annapolis Royal, Fort Anne, King's Theatre, World famous
Bay of Fundy & tides, Oaklawn Farm Zoo, Macdonald Museum, Port Royal Habitation
🐎 Young hosts in unique home (ca 1876) situated next to the Annapolis River. Formerly called
the Paradise Hotel and used as an Inn for many years, now converted into a comfortable, luxurious
B&B. Located on the scenic Evangeline Trail in the heart of NS farmland. Breakfast is served in the
cozy dining room and evening refreshments are served in parlour. Browse through the craft
cupboard of tiny stitchery and crafts. Extended stay/business rates available.Visa,Enroute ⸝ CC

Peggy's Cove   *(west of Halifax; see also Prospect)*

Code, Dorothy and Tom (Oceanside Inn)   ☎ & Fax (902) 823-2765
General Delivery, Peggy's Cove, NS B0J 2N0

Located in West Dover, 5 km from Peggy's Cove. Take Middle Village Rd for 100yds, turn right
to house down Barringer Rd on the ocean.
$70-125S/D $15Add.person   ► 8
🏠Full,homecooked 🏠Rural,village,multi-storey,acreage,
patio,quiet, 3 gazebos ■3D(upstairs) ⊨1D,1Q,1K ⊲3Ensuite
1jacuzzi suite ★F,parking ⓌNo smoking,no pets ⋙French
🏃 Private sand beach, nature trails, comp. row boats, fishing
🚌Famous Peggy's Cove golden sunsets, photographer's heaven
🐎 Spacious modern mansion with 9 acres of lawns, forest &
beach overlooking quaint fishing village, situated on 900 ft ocean frontage on one of NS's most
famous Peninsulas. Enjoy a silver service breakfast in the elegant dining room overlooking cape &
ocean. Home was the proud host to the Imperial Japanese Delegation at the 1995, G7 World
Economic Summit. ⸝CC

Ellis, Sara (the Mermaid's Garden B&B)
139 MacDonald Pt Rd, Box 695, RR1, Seabright, NS B0J 3J0

☎ (902) 623-2227
E-mail: elliss@is2.dal.ca

From Hwy 103 take Exit 5 and take Rte 333 (Peggy's Cove Rd) to Seabright. Turn right onto McDonald Point Rd and proceed 0.5km. Located 14 km north of Peggy's Cove.

$55S $60D   (plus tax)   ► 6
🍴 Full, homebaked 🏠 Rural, 2-storey, older, acreage, view from guest rooms, deck, very quiet, secluded   ■3D(upstairs) ⊨2D,1Q   ⊿ 1Sh.w.g.   ★ TV, guest quarters are separate ⊕No smoking ∿ French
🕺 Ocean cove with small swimming beach, Seabright Smokehouse (famous for salmon and other seafare), pottery and art gallery, restaurant, berry picking in season
🚐 Whale & Puffin cruise, seaside walking trails, scenic villages, City of Halifax, Int.Airport
🐾 100-year old country home, tastefully decorated with antiques. Relax and read beneath the spreading chestnut tree. Hostess is a marine biologist and enjoys sharing her knowledge of local marine life. Whale and Puffin watch packages available. House specialty may be fishcakes and homebaked beans or Belgian waffles with NS maple syrup. Amble along back roads where postcard views are the norm. Breakfast is served in the cozy breakfast room. There is a resident cat.Visa

---

Klees, Gabriele & Anna-Maria Kroeck (The Old Fisher House B&B)
204 Paddy's Head Rd., RR1, Box 1527, Indian Harbour, NS B0J 3J0   ☎ & Fax (902) 823-2228

From Halifax, on Hwy 103 take Exit 5 and continue on Hwy 333 to Paddy's Head Rd in Indian Hbr. Turn left and follow coastline. From Peggy's Cove take Rte 333 to Paddys Head Rd, turn right.
$65S $70-78D $10Child $15Add.person   (plus tax)   ► 6

🔆 Summer only 🍴 Full, homebaked (European) 🏠 Fishing village, 2-storey, view from guest rooms, 1-acre, ocean at back, quiet,private decks ■2(upstairs) ⊨2Q,2cots ⊿1Sh.w.g.
★KF,F(also in one guestroom) ⊕No smoking ∿German
🕺 Private beach, swimming, walking trail, picnic area, Paddy's Head Lighthouse, Anne Murrays Beach, whale watching
🚐 Peggy's Cove, Halifax, Int. Airport, Chester, Lunenburg, studios of local artists & craftsmen, scenic coastal drives
🐾 Professional hosts from Germany in lovely, renovated 125-year old, Cape Cod-style former fisherman's house situated on picturesque peninsula surrounded by the sea and beckoned by Paddys' Head Lighthouse (where time stands still). Relax by the fireplace, admire the exceptional sunsets/sunrises and bountiful sea and wildlife. Diving and kajak packages available. Weekly or monthly rates can be arranged. There is also a motor home for rent. Visa

---

Webb, Karl & Shelley (Havenside B&B)
225 Boutilier's Cove Rd., Hackett's Cove, NS B0J 3J0

☎ & Fax (902) 823-9322, 1-800-641-8272
E-mail: webbk@atcon.com

$65-85S $75-95D $7.50Child (age 6-12) $15Add.person   ► 6-7A,2Ch

From TCH103 take Exit 5, follow signs to Rte 333 & Hackett's Cove. Located 10km from Peggy's Cove.
🔆 April1-Oct31 (other by special arrangement) 🍴 Full, homebaked 🏠 Rural, village, 1.5 storey, acreage, view, 3decks, oceanback, quiet ■3(main floor) ⊨3Q,1P ⊿3Ensuite
★F,LF,TV, gathering room, games room with pool table, square grand piano & organ, guest quarters are upstairs, ample parking ⊕No smoking, no pets
🕺 Walks in scenic area, sailing charters, whale & bird-watching, canoeing, swimming, deep-sea fishing, restaurants, churches, barbeques, picnics
🚐 Peggy's Cove, Halifax, South Shore, Mahone Bay, Chester, beautiful beaches
🐾 Spacious new home, tastefully decorated, overlooking picturesque cove. Knowledgeable and gracious hosts are retired educators and delight in welcoming appreciative guests from all parts of the globe. Ideal base from which to explore the historic and scenic area, and a wonderful retreat for those with relaxation in mind. Relax in the gathering room on the ground level or on the waterfront decks. Enjoy NS writings and art & crafts (some for sale). Breakfast (which makes lunch redundant) is served in the guest breakfast room. Visa,MC ∕B&B

Pictou

McCrone, Jean & Hugh (Strathyre House B&B) ☎ (902) 485-3495
2713 West River Rd., Lyons Brook, Pictou Co, NS B0K 1H0

From TCH 104, take Exit 20 or 22 and proceed on Rte 376 (West River Rd.)

$40S $50-55D ► 4A,2Ch
❊ June1-Sept31 ❤ Cont.(plus), homebaked 🏠 Rural,
2-storey, 45acres, view from guest rooms, riverfront, patio, quiet
▣ 1D,1F(main floor) ⊨ 1D,1Q,1R,crib ⬛1Sh.w.g. ★TV,
ceiling fans, private entrance, off-street parking, guest quarters are
separate ⚜ No smoking
🍴 Excellent restaurants, shops
🚗 Pictou, PEI Ferry

☛ New home surrounded by walking trail and lawns with pond, in a beutiful setting high on a hill with a commanding view of the surrounding countryside. Hosts are originally from Scotland and offer true Scottish hospitality in "New Scottland". Enjoy the quiet rural atmosphere.There are 2 dogs and a cat in residence. Visa ⊷B&B

Port Hood   *(on Cape Breton Isle north of Causeway; see also Mabou)*

Kargoll, Elvi & Uwe-Georg (Haus Treuburg Country Inn) ☎ (902) 787-2116
Box 92, Port Hood, NS B0E 2W0   Fax (902) 787-3216

$70-90S/D $10Add.person $110Cottage 🍴Meals ►14

From Causeway take the Ceilidh Trail. Located on main street.
❊ Summer only ❤ German Sunday Morning B'fast
🏠Heritage home, village, 2-storey, view from cottages, quiet,
oceanfront, private beach ▣2D,1Ste(upst) & 3 cottages
⊨5Q,2D ⬛6Private ★F in lounge & dining room, TV/phone in
rooms & cottages, separate entrance, bikes, parking ⌇German
🍴 Court House Beach in the center of town, supervised
swimming, restaurant with Italian and French Cuisine

☛ Friendly European hospitality with a German flair in pretty little Maritime fishing port with lovely sandy beaches and some of the warmest waters in Eastern Canada. Enjoy the beautiful view over the ocean to Port Hood Island. Inquire locally about boat tours and charters to Port Hood Island. Candlelight dinners served in cozy dining room. Visa,MC

Port Mouton   *(on south coast near Liverpool)*

Adams, Judy and John ("Apple Pie" B&B) ☎ & Fax (902) 683-2217
Box 32, Central Port Mouton, Queens Co., NS B0T 1T0   1-888-72-APPLE (722-7753)

Located 1.5 km off Exit 21 from Hwy 103. Look for sign.
$40S $50D $10Add.person 🍴 Meals ► 2+
❤Full 🏠Village, hist., 3-storey, oceanfront,quiet ▣1D(upstairs)
⊨2T(or1Q) ⬛1Private ★F,TV,LF, library, music room
⚜No smoking, no pets, unsuitable for small children
🍴 Beautiful white sandy Carter's Beach, birdwatching, hiking and
biking trails, family restaurant
🚗 Liverpool town, Kejimkujik Park, Halifax, Yarmouth

☛ Warm welcome in turn-of-the-Century home with a cozy pellet stove in the living room, overlooking Mouton Harbour and the Atlantic Ocean. Enjoy the pleasant atmosphere of a Victorian Country Tea Room in the bright and spacious sunporch (June-Sept) or browse in the little gift shop. Host is a cabinet maker & musician and the workshop is always open to visitors. House specialty: delicious lobster chowder & steamed mussels. There is a resident cat "Jupiter".Visa,MC

Port Williams

(west of Wolfville; see also Kentville, Grand Pre)

Buckley, Ron & Carol (The Old Rectory Bed & Breakfast) ☎ (902) 542-1815, Fax 2346
1519 Hwy 358, RR1, Port Williams, NS B0P 1T0   E-mail: orectory@fox.nstn.ca

From Hwy 101 take Exit 11 to Rte 1 and then to Hwy 358. Located 3 km beyond Port Williams.
$45-53S $55-65D $15Add.person   ► 8
✚ May1-Oct31 (other by special arrangement)   ◑ Full,
homebaked   🏠 Farm, 2-storey, hist., orchards, porch   ■3D
(upstairs)   ◄ 2T,1D,1Q,2R   🛏 2Sh.w.g.,1ensuite
★F,TV,LF, guest sunroom   ⓦNo smoking, no pets
🕴 Stroll or sit in the surrounding apple orchard
🚗 Look-Off, fishing village with "Lobster on the Rocks", hiking
trails, rockhounding, historic Prescott House, Grand Pré Park
🐾 Retired professional couple in spacious newly restored Victorian Century home nestled in tall
trees with 3 acres of orchard - located in the heart of apple growing and market gardening area.
Well informed hosts like to share their knowledge of the local area. Retired Geologist host will take
guests on geological tours in the area (at small fee). Visa ✒ B&B

McMahon, Mary (Carwarden Bed & Breakfast) ☎ (902)678-7827,Fax (902)678-0029,
640 Church St., RR1, Port Williams, NS B0P 1T0   1-888-763-3320

From Hwy 101 take Exit 11 to Rte 1 & right to Hwy 358. Proceed
4.4km to Church St, turn left and 2.2km to B&B.
$45-50S $55-60D $15Add.person   ► 8A
✚ May1-Oct31   ◑ Full, homebaked   🏠 Rural, 2-storey, hist.
view from guest rooms, 3 acres, veranda, quiet   ■ 2D,1F
(upstairs)   ◄ 2D,1R,1Q,1T   🛏 1Sh.w.g,2ensuite   ★LF,F,
separate entrance, large rooms, fans, off-street parking   ⓦ No
smoking, no pets, not suitable for children
🚗 Bay of Fundy shores (tides, agate, driftwood, lobsters), Cape Split hiking trail, museums,
galleries, Acadia University, Theatre Festival, golfing, antiquing
🐾 Restored 1910 Heritage home with great character. antique furnishings and beautiful view
across sweeping Canard Dykelands. Relax on the wide veranda, shaded by magnificient elms, a cool
& pleasant retreat for conversation, reading or idling. Savour a decadent breakfast in formal guest
dining room with fireplace, beamed ceiling - tea & crumbs in evening. Hostess is a former teacher,
30-year resident and thoroughly familiar with the area. There are dogs & cats. Visa ✒B&B

Prospect

(west of Halifax; see also Peggy's Cove)

Prsala, Helena & Stephen O'Leary (Prospect B&B) ☎ (902) 852-4493, 1800-7258-732
1758 Prospect Bay Rd., Prospect, NS B3T 2B3

From Hwy 103 take Hwy 3 and then Hwy 333 following signs for Peggy's Cove and Prospect.
Proceed to Prospect Village and continue all the way to end of road at the water. Look for B&B sign.
$60S $70-80D $10Add.person   🍽 Meals   (plus tax)   ► 12
◑ Cont., homebaked   🏠 Village, hist., 2-storey, view from guest
rooms, oceanfront, deck, quiet   ■ 3D,2F(main & upper floor)
◄ 1D,4Q,2S   🛏 5Ensuite   ★ TV, canoe & row boat for
guests   ⓦNo smoking, no pets   ᜑCzech, some German,French
🕴 Magnificient walking trails along coastline, small sandy private
beach behind house
🚗 Peggy's Cove, City of Halifax, deep-sea fishing, boat tours
🐾 Professional couple in unique, restored Century-old former Convent overlooking scenic
Prospect Bay and situated at water's edge in very quiet location. (featured in Nat.Geographic in
1975). Relax by the water or in the large sitting room and enjoy the pleasant informal atmosphere.
There is a school-age boy in the host family. Perfect place for honeymoon and special occasions.
Private Island picnics and Eco Adventure Tour packages can be arranged. Visa,MC ✒B&B

Pubnico

D'Entremont, Marie & Hubert (Chez Marie B&B) ☎ (902) 762-2107, Fax (902) 762-3575
Box 66, West Pubnico, NS B0W 3S0 E-mail: chezmarie@hairyfreaky.com

From Hwy 103, take Exit 31 and Rte 335 to Chemin de l'Allée. turn left to B&B.

$35S $45D $10Add.person(over age 10) ►8
🏳 Summer only (other by special arrangement) 🍵 Cont.,
homebaked 🛏 Rural, village, older, view, oceanfront, deck,
quiet ■ 2D,1F (upstairs) ⊨1S,2D,1Q,cot,crib ⚱ 1sh.w.g.,
1sh.w.h. ★TV,LF,KF,separate entrance, off-street parking,
guest quarters are separate ⓦ No smoking, no pets ⤬French
⚔ Water's edge (400ft from house), restaurant, shops
🚗 Yarmouth, theatres, light houses, airport, ferry terminal

☛ Remodeled ca 1845-built, cozy ancestral home with a beautiful waterview, built originally by host's grandparents. Congenial hosts invite guests to sit on the deck or in the living room where conversation often includes local history and geneology. Hostess gives courses in candle wicking. Enjoy the warm and friendly "granparent's house" atmosphere. Visa,MC ⤶B&B

Donaldson, Richard & Deborah (Yesteryear's B&B) ☎ & Fax (902) 762-2969
Box 16, Pubnico, Yarmouth Co., NS B0W 2W0

From Rte 103 take Exit 31. Located on the Lighthouse Route at junction of Rtes 3/335.

$35S $45D $10Child ►7A,1Ch
🍵 Full, homebaked 🛏 Rural, village, 2-storey, hist.. acreage,
porch, quiet ■ 1S,3D(upstairs) ⊨ 1S,3Q,cot ⚱ 1sh.w.g.,
1ensuite ★ TV/ceiling fan in guest room, private entrance,
off-street parking, guest quarters are separate ⓦ No smoking,
no pets, children min. age 5
⚔ Golfing, antique shop, walking trail, great seafood restaurants
🚗 Wedgeport (Tuna Museum), Yarmouth (ferry to Maine US),
Tusket (Canada's oldest courthouse), scenic coastal drives with fishing villages and wharves

☛ Majestic 90-year old Victorian country home, restored in keeping with yesteryears, but with modern cenveniences and furnished with antiques and collectibles. Host is a captain of a lobster fishing vessel. There is a school-age daughter in the host family. Enjoy an evening of friendly conversation on local history and learn about the local lobster fishing industry. Born & raised in NS, hosts offer the true flavour of Maritime hospitality. There is a resident cat. Visa,MC

Sherbrooke

Peck, Randy & Linda (Days-A-Go B&B) ☎ (902) 522-2983
15 Cameron Rd., Sherbrooke, NS B0J 3C0

Located on Hwy 7 along Marine Drive on the Eastern Shore.

$45S $50-55D $10Add.person ►7
🍵 Full, homebaked 🛏 Farm, village, 2-storey, older, view from
guest rooms, patio, porch, quiet ■ 2D,1F(upstairs)
⊨1S,2T,2D,1R ⚱ 2Sh.w.h. ★ F,TV,ceiling fans ⓦSmoking
outside, no pets, not suitable for small children
⚔ Farm grounds with farm animals, well preserved historic
Village of Sherbrooke (135 years of history), 3 restaurants
🚗 Antigonish, restaurants, shopping

☛ Warm welcome in comfortable home (ca 1920) located on the banks of the beautiful St.Mary's River, famous for its salmon fishing and frequent appearances by one of the area's most colorful old-timers. Relax on the rear sun deck or the enclosed porch. Guests may gather their own eggs for breakfast. Guide available upon request. Visa ⤶B&B

Sydney

(on Cape Breton Island)

McEwen, Evanel & Lloyd (Park Place B&B)
169 Park St., Sydney, NS B1P 4W7

☎ (902) 562-3518, Fax (902) 567-6618
E-mail: lemcewen@highlander.cbnet.ns.ca

From Hwy 125 take Exit 8 and turn right at 2nd set of lights. Turn left again at Park St and proceed up 3 blocks.
$40S $45-50D $5Child $10Add.person (plus taxes) ▶6
🍳 Full, homebaked 🏠 Downtown, res., 3-storey, hist.,patio
■3D(upstairs) ⊨2T,2D Sh.w.g. ★TV ♥ ⊛No pets
🏃 Bus Station, park, town/shopping center, hospital, Steel Mills
🚗 Louisbourg, Glace Bay, Miners Museum, historic North End
☛ Interesting 1905-built home with curved walls in front hall and living room. Congenial hosts have travelled and lived in many countries and display souvenir artifact in the home. Enjoy the warm, genuine hospitality. VIP Service. Visa,MC,JVC

Sydney Mines

(on Cape Breton Isle north of Sydney)

Matthews, Clifford J. (Gowrie House Country Inn) (pending)
139 Shore Rd,Sydney Mines,NS B1V 1A6

☎ (902)544-1050
Fax(902)736-0077,1-800-372-1115

From Rt 105 (Trans Canada Hwy) take Exit 21 and follow Rt 305 north for 3 km.
$89-119S $99-129D $129-139Ste $189Cottage 🍽 Meals ▶15+

🍴 May-Oct. 🍳 Full 🏠 Hist., acreage, quiet ■5D(upst),
plus deluxe caretaker's cottage ⊨2T,3Q,1K 4private
★Air,Parking ⊛ Small pets only
🚗 Nfld Ferry, Louisbourg Fortress, Glace Bay Miners Museum,
Nfld Ferry Terminal, Cabot Trail
☛ 1825-built home enhances the feeling of comfortable elegance.
Reserve dinner for 4-course repast which may include delicacies from waters, fields & gardens of NS. Visa,MC,Amex ⮕B&B

Tatamagouche

(north of Truro; see also Wallace)

LeFresne, Shelley & James (Train Station Inn)
21 Station Rd., Tatamagouche, NS B0K 1V0

☎(902)657-3222,Fax(902)657-9091
E-mail: train.station@ns.sympatico.ca

$68.75(Station) $98-118(Caboose) $5Child 🍳 (Full extra) (plus tax)
From Amherst, take Hwy 6 (Sunrise Trail) east.
🍳 Cont., homebaked 🏠 Village, 2-storey & railway car, view from guest rooms, 2nd storey deck, , acreage, riverfront, patio, porch, deck, quiet ■ 4F(upstairs), plus suites in 6 caboose
⊨5S,5D,6Q,3R(incl berths under the cupola) 10Private
★Air,TV,LF,KF, ceiling fans, separate entrance, air-conditioners, wheel-chair access, off-street parking ⊛ Smoking outside
🏃 Wander or cycle along abundant rail-trail beside the river, Train Museum, Fraser Culture Centre, Tatamagouche Creamery-Coffee House & Market, camp fires
🚗 Village of Tatamagouche, Pictou, Truro, vineyards, Northumberland beaches, golfing, skiing
☛ Historic Train Station, tastefully restored, furnished with beautiful antiques which capture the historical aura and relaxing ambiance overlooking the green hills and the Waugh River on NS's Scottish Sunshine Coast. Guest rooms are in the former telegraph rooms and the former waiting rooms are converted into a railway museum/cafe, where breakfast is served, while the station clock tick-tocks away. Breakfast may be delivered to the caboose. Caboose mini suites area ideal for a romantic get-away and family vacations. CCards ⮕B&B

Tiverton
(on Digby Neck, west of Digby; see also Barton)

Goodwin, Thomas (B&B-Gallery by-the-Sea)   ☎ (902) 839-2417
Box 719, Tiverton, NS B0V 1G0   E-mail: oceanexp@atcon.com

From Digby, take Hwy 217 west on Digby Neck to East Ferry and 5 min crossing (every 1/2 hr) to Tiverton. After dis-embarking, look for house on right.

$35S $40D $10Add.person 📷 Meals (plus tax) ▶6
✖ Summer only 🍴 Full 🏠 Village, older, acreage, view from guest rooms ■1D,1F(upstairs) ⊨1S,1D,1Q,1R ⊯Sh.w.g. ★TV in guest room,extensive library & video collection, separate entrance, parking ⓌNo smoking ⌁German
🎭 Nature Centre-Aquarium on site, local museum (history of fishing industry), in-house snack/gift shop, start point for famous "Balancing Rock", biking/hiking trails
🚗 Brier Island (excellent birding), Digby, Ferry to New Brunswick, restaurant
🐾 Modest house with skylights and simple furnishing in quaint little fishing village, owned and run by young marine biologist & photographer and his summer students, located in quaint little fishing village in the best whale watching area in Atlantic Canada. Enjoy the extensive wildlife library. Property overlooks Fisherman's Wharf. Watch fishing boats arrive in front of house. Breakfast is served in the new solarium. Special reduced whale/seabird adventure ("Zodiac") packages. Also cottage available.

Truro
(in center of province; see also Brookfield, Masstown, Great Village, Folley Lake)

Kelly, Betty (Elizabeth House B&B)   ☎ (902) 893-2346
401 Robie St., Truro, NS B2N 1L9

Take Exit 14 onto Robie St. Proceed past shopping malls.
$40-50S $45-55D $10Child (plus tax) ▶6
🍴 Full, homebaked 🏠 Downtown, res., 2-storey, deck ■3D (upstairs), host quarters are separate ⊨2T,2D ⊯1Private, 1sh.w.g. ★F,TV in guest room, parking ⓌNo smoking
🎭 Riverbed Tidal Bore (evening or night shows), Victoria Park with trails, museum, golf course
🚗 Northumberland Strait and beach area, Halifax airport, ferry
🐾 Warm welcome in friendly, cheerfully decorated house in small town with architectural interest. Enjoy the homey and comfortable atmosphere. There is a cat in residence. ⌐B&B

Van der Leest, Akke (At the Organery Bed & Breakfast)   ☎ (902) 895-6653
53 Farnham Rd., Truro, NS B2N 2X6

$45-50S/D $55-65Ste $5Child $10Add.person   ▶8A,2Ch
Located in the village of Bible Hill. From Hwy 102, take Exit 14A, turn right at traffic lights, then left to 5th house on left. From Hwy 104, take Exit 17 on Pictou Rd to 2nd traffic light, turn right and right again to house on left.
✖ May1-Oct31 (ste open all year by spec. arrangement) ▣Full, homebaked 🏠Semi-rural, village, older, acreage,2-storey,view, patio ■2D,1Ste(upst) ⊨2T,1D,1Q,1P(D) ⊯1Sh.w.h.,1ensuite ★TV,small library in sunroom ⓌNo smoking, no pets
🎭 Organery on property, NS Agricultural College,
🚗 Downtown Truro, beaches, Halifax, Tidal bore, Victoria Park, Exhibition Grounds, airport, Halifax
🐾 Comfortable, 90-year old home with a large garden for strolling and relaxing on the patio. Hosts give guided tours of the Organery (100+ antique Reed Organs for viewing or playing). There is a teenager in the host family who helps with B&B and enjoy it greatly. There is a dog and a cat and both are attracted to guests.

Wallace

(east of Amherst on northern shore; see also Tatamagouche)

Dominy, Daphne & Leslie (Jubilee Cottage Country Inn) ☎(902)257-2432,Fax 257-2510
Box 148 Hwy 6, Wallace NS B0K 1Y0 E-mail: j.cottage@col.auracom.com, 1-800-481-9915

Located on Rte 6 in the village of Wallace. Look for Civic No 13769.
$60-79D $15Add.person ⦿ Meals ► 7
✱ May-Oct ◑ Full ♠ Village, 3-storey, hist., acreage, view
from guest rooms, ocean at back, quiet ■ 3D(upstairs)
⊨2D,1Q,cot ⬢ 3Ensuite (incl.2whirlpool) ★ TV,F & ceiling
fans in guest rooms, private entrance, off-street parking, guest
quarters are separate ⓦ No smoking, children min. age 10
🕴 Wallace Bay, watch Blue Herons and Canada Geese

🚗 Natural wildlife area with hiking trail, Northumberland Links Golf Course, Jost Vineyard
Farm with winery store, Seagull Pewter Factory Outlet, Malagash Salt Mine Museum
☛ Tastefully decorated home (ca 1912) located in historic village on the Sunrise Trail near the
warmest salt water beaches north of the Carolinas. Relax in the screen house. Ask about romance
and golf packages. Hosts were nominated for 1997 Accommodation Award of Excellence for NS.
Five-course candlelight dinners a house speciality. Breakfast is served in guest breakfast room.
There is a cat in residence. Visa, MC ↙B&B

Windsor

(north-west of Halifax; see also Wolfville, Grand Pre)

Boegel, Sharon & Terry (Boegel's Bed & Breakfast) ☎ (902) 798-4183, Fax (902) 798-1063
145 Dill Rd., RR1, Windsor, NS B0N 2T0

Take Hwy 1 to Exit 5 & Hwy 14 west to Chester Rd, left on Dill Rd.
$35S $45-50D $10Child $10Add.person (plus tax) ► 6-8
◑ Full, homebaked ♠ Rural, split-level, acreage, view, patio,
deck, quiet ■ 3D (upstairs) ⊨ 2T,2D,2cots ⬢ 1Sh.w.g.
★ F,TV/VCR, barbeque, ceiling fans in guest rooms, ramp to front
door, host quarters are separate ⓦ No smoking, no pets
🕴 Walks by nearby pond with ducks, turtles & spring peepers
🚗 Annapolis V., Halifax, southshore beaches, highest tides
☛ Comfortable hillside home with a nice view of the valley, situated just outside the City on 1.75
acres and in a very quiet area. Relax in the sunroom and feel just like at home. Hostess is a hobby
quilter. Fax service available (fee charged outgoing). There is a cat in residence. Visa,MC ↙B&B

Connelly, Veronica & Dennis (Clockmaker's Inn) ☎ & Fax (902) 798-5265
1399 King St., Curry's Corner, Windsor, NS B0N 1H0

West from Halifax on Rte 101, take Exit 5 and follow King St. Look for house at jct14 (for Chester).
$40S $50D $10Add.person (plus tax) ► 10
◑ Full, homebaked ♠ Rural, res., hist., acreage, sunroom,
veranda ■ 4(upstairs) ⊨ 2T,4D,1R ⬢2Sh.w.g. ★ TV,F in
2guest rooms, bicycles, barbecue, large book & TV library, baby
grand piano ⓦ No pets, smoking in sunroom only
🕴 Beautiful grounds for pleasant walking, local museums, Fort
Edward Blockhouse (1750), Teddy Bear Jamboree (July), Giant
Pumpkin Weigh-off(Thanksgiving)
🚗 Tidal Bore, Haliburton House (Sam Slick Museum), Grand Pré Nat. Park, Halifax, Peggy's
Cove, windsurfing, swimming, golfing, canoeing
☛ Prof. retired couple in Grand Victorian (1894) home with stained glass windows, ornate
Victorian fireplaces, high ceilings and period furniture, situated in small historic town. There is
plenty of folk art displayed throughout the house. Visa,MC ↙B&B

Wolfville
(north-west of Halifax; see also Pt.Williams, Kentville, Grand Pre)

McKenzie, Brian & Lisa (Garden House B&B) ☎ (902) 542-1703
150 Main St., Box 412, Wolfville, NS B0P 1X0

From Halifax follow signs to Annapolis Valley on Hwy 101 and take Exit 10 into Wolfville. Look for
B&B 1 block from Tourist Information Centre.
$45-60S $50-65D $10Child/Add.person ► 6A,2Ch
⊞ May15-Oct31 (other by special arrangement) ⅅ Full ♙ Downtown,
res, 2-storey, hist., view, 1 acre, quiet ■ 3(upstairs) ⊨ 2D,1Q,1P
⊒1Private,1sh.w.g. ★TV in guest parlour, sep.entr., on-site parking ⓌNo
smoking, no pets, children min.age 10 ⌣French,German,Dutch
⩓ Downtown area, Acadia University, Atlantic Theatre Festival, shops,
restaurants, antiques, historic properties, dykes for bird watching, cycling,
walking, Acadia Bus Line and city bus
⬤ Various swimming "holes", beaches, hiking, historic Center Grand Pré,
40ft tides (world's highest), Cape Split Lookoff, Blomidon Prov.Park
▰ Professional hosts in comfortable heritage home (ca 1830) formerly a Minister's house,
nestled amids stately elms and a sunny cottage garden with a sweeping view over fields of hay,
Minas Basin and Cape Blomidon, and located close to center of town. Host also teaches B&B
courses in nearby college and hostess is an airline stewardess. There is a school-age boy in the
family. Breakfast is served in quaint guest breakfast room. Visa,MC ↙B&B

Premi, Loretta (Seaview House B&B) ☎ (902) 542-1436
8 Seaview Ave., Box 1465, Wolfville, NS B0P 1X0

From Halifax go west on Hwy 101. Take Exit 10 to Main St in Wolfville. Turn left at United Church
to Seaview Ave. Located 1 block past the Tourist Office.
$45-53S $49-65D $10Add.person ► 6-7
⊞ Summer only(other by special arrangement) ⅅ Full,
homebaked ♙ Downtown, hist., view, deck, balcony, quiet
■3D(upstairs) ⊨ 1D,2Q,cot ⊒1Sh.w.g., 1ensuite ★ F,TV
in guest lounge with balcony, off-street parking, host quarters are
separate Ⓦ No smoking
⩓ Acadia University, Atlantic Theatre Festival, Randall House
Museum, Robie Tufts Nature Centre, Acadia Nature Trail, local shops and park, restaurants
⬤ Grand Pre, Halls Harbour, The Lookoff, Kingsport, Blomidon Prov.Park, Windsor Tidal Bore
▰ Victorian home elegantly restored, with a lovely view of Blomidon and located in the heart of
town. Full, gourmet breakfast is served on pewter in the formal dining room. Enjoy daughter
"Nicole's truffle" each night and the warm and friendly hospitality. Visa ↙B&B

Yarmouth
(on south-west coast; see also Pubnico)

Semple, George & Joan (Murray Manor) ☎ & Fax (902) 742-9625
225 Main St., Yarmouth, NS B5A 1C6

Located across from Ferry Terminal and Tourist Bureau on the
main street in town.
$50S $60D ► 6A
ⅅ Full, homebaked ♙ Downtown, 2-storey, hist.,
acreage,historic, quiet ■3D(upstairs) ⊨2T,1D,1Q,1R (incl.
4-poster) ⊒2Sh.w.g.(incl.1on main level) ★ Separate
entrance, extensive library, harbour view from 2 guest room prayer
windows (Gothic), robes & towel/showermat caddy for each room,
off-street parking, secure garage for motorcycles and bicycles ⌣French (Acadian)
⩓ Ferry to Bar Hbr. & Portland, bus/airport terminals, shops, restaurants, on hist.walking tour
⬤ Lighthouse, Look-out/old Finnish cemetery, golfing, large shopping area, scenic coastal drives
▰ Retired military family & Yarmouth natives in beautifully maintained Gothic Regency
Heritage house (ca 1825), surrounded by lovely grounds with Rhododendrons (over 100 years) &
green house tucked in behind flowering shrubs & stone wall. Complimentary pre-dinner wine prior
to 6pm. A wonderful place for honeymoon and special occasions. Pick-up and delivery to airport,
bus & Halifax Shuttle. Visa ↙B&B

Newfoundland & Labrador

Cape Onion
L'Anse aux Meadows
St.Anthony

Engle

Portland Creek

Rocky Harbour
Woody Point
Roberts Arm
Twillingate
Fogo

Lewisporte

Corner Brook
Stephenville

Glovertown
Eastport

Trinity
Dunfield

Clarenville

Burgeo
Port-aux-Basques
English Hbr.West

St.John's

Government of Newfoundland/Labrador
Dep't of Development (Tourism Branch)   toll-free 1-800 563-6353
Box 8730 St. John's, NF A1B 4K2

For CN Marine Ferry schedules and rates contact:
Reservation Bureau, Maritime Atlantic   toll-free 1-800 341-7981 USonly

Box 250, North Sydney, NS B2A 3M3   (902) 794-5700

Burgeo

(on south shore, east of Port-aux-Basques)

Parsons, Anne & Bill (Burgeo Haven B&B)
Box 414, Burgeo, NF   A0M 1A0

☎ & Fax (709) 886-2544, 1-800-886-7171
E-mail: a.parsons@nf.sympatico.ca

From Hwy 1, near Stephenville, take Hwy 480 for 147 km south to Burgeo. (watch for wildlife)
$40S $50D   10Add.person   (child free under age 12 with parents)   📷 Meals   ▶ 8A,5Ch

🍴 Full, homebaked   🏠 Village, 2-storey, hist., view from guest rooms, oceanback, patio, porch, deck,quiet   ▦3F,1Ste (ground & upper level)   ⊨3S,3D,4R   ⊿1Sh.w.g.,1ensuite ★F,TV,LF,KF, ample parking   🐾Pets accepted on leash
🏃 Coastal boat services, ferry docks, fishing boats, miles of sandy beaches (Atlantic Ocean), picnic area
🚗 Major salmon river, ferry to rural outports of Ramea, Grey River & Francois

📷 Beautiful, attractive older house in a very peaceful setting with reading room overlooking the harbour of small fishing community. Back gate of yard opens to the water. Canoeists can "put in" on property, and hosts are offering guided canoe tours including soft adventure tours, hiking, picnics. Home cooked meals include moose soup, fresh fish, freshly baked breads, etc.. There is a small dog in residence. Visa,MC,Amex ✔B&B

Cape Onion

(northern tip of Nfld; see also St.Anthony)

Adams, David and Barbara (Tickle Inn at Cape Onion)
RR1, Box 62, Cape Onion, NF   A0K 4J0

☎ (709) 452-4321   (709) 739-5503

Take Rte 430 (Viking Trail) all the way north to Rte 436 (in direction of L'Anse aux Meadows) and continue past Pistolet Bay. After a short distance, turn left onto Rte 437, and then left to Raleigh and Ship Cove, Cape Onion. At Raleigh turn right and proceed 8 km to B&B.
$50S $55-60D $10Add.person   📷 Meals   (plus tax)   ▶ 8

❊ June-Sept.   🍴 Cont., homebaked   🏠 Rural, hist., 3-storey, 9-acre, view, oceanfront, quiet   ▦3D,1F   ⊨2T,3D,2cots ⊿2Sh.w.g.,1sh.w.h.   ★F,KF,LF,TV in parlour with antique organ, separate entrance, parking   🐾Smoking outside, pets (may be considered with special arrangement)
🏃 Beachcombe, watch whale/iceberg, nature walk/hike trails,
🚗 L'Anse aux Meadows (World Heritage Site), St.Anthony (Grenfell Museum, fishplant, outport communities

📷 Fourth generation family in historic home, attractively restored, traditionally decorated and located in beautiful pastoral setting on beachfront property. Enjoy the warm Newfoundland hospitality. Relax in the parlour around the Franklin stove and listen to the legends and music traditional to the area and Province. Fall asleep to the sounds of seabreezes and waves lapping the shore. House specialty: Local seafood dishes. Reduced rates for 2 or more nights stay. ✔B&B

Clarenville

(south-east of Gander; see also Trinity)

Devine, Patricia (Islandview Hospitality Home)
128 Memorial Dr., Clarenville, NF   A0E 1J0

☎ (709) 466-2062

Phone or write for directions.
$39S $45D $8Add.person $65F   ▶ 10
🍴 Hostess' choice   🏠 Res., older, view, oceanfront   ▦2D,1F (upstairs)   ⊨2S,3D,1Q,1cot   ⊿2Sh.w.g.   ★ F,KF,TV, sep. entrance, clock-radios in each guest rooms, paved driveway parking, guest quarters are separate   🐾 No drinking, no smoking
🏃 First Class snowmobiling, cross-country skiing, hiking and snowshoeing trail, good trout fishing
🚗 White Hills Ski Resort, Twin Rivers Golf Course, Cod fishing, boating excursions arranged
📷 Well travelled hostess is quite versed in the history/geography of the island home and the theme of their fishing culture runs throughout the house (cod jiggers, life preservers from long liner, etc.). Enjoy the nightly "mug-up" with good friendship and interesting conversation. An assortment of homemade breads and jams is house specialty. Visa,MC ✔B&B

Corner Brook

(on west coast of Province; see also Stephenville)

Swyer, Edna and Eldon (Humber Gallery Hospitality Home) ☎ (709) 634-2660
Box 15, Corner Brook, NF   A2H 6C3

Located 15 km east of downtown on the TCH (Exit 10) in Little Rapids at 26 Roberts Drive.
$40S $45D $6Add.person (child free under age 5) 🍽 Meals (Senior Discounts)   ▶ 6

⚜ June-Sept.(Jan-March for skiing) 🍺 Cont. 🏠 Rural, quiet,
acreagae, deck ▪ 3D (main and upper floor) ⊨1T,2D,1R
⤴Sh.w.g. ★F,KF,TV, barbecue ✋No pets 〰some French
🎋 Humber River, nature & x/c ski trails, fall colour spectacles,
U-pick strawberry farms
🚗 Corner Brook, Marble Mountain Ski Resort,beaches on Deer
Lake, Gros Morne National Park, Bay Island sites
☛ Very impressive home with Cathedral ceilings and finished in cedar, pine, BC Fir in the heart
of the Scenic Humber Valley Reserve. Excellent place for an overnight stop when going or coming
from Gros Morne Nat Park. Relax on the sundeck, enjoy the spectacular view. Guide for salmon or
trout fishing available. The Brit.Royal family has visited this area many times.Visa⟋B&B

Dunfield

(south of Trinity)

Beckett, Ed & Margaret (The Rolling Hills B&B) ☎ (709) 464-3344, (709) 368-9674
RR1, S2, Box 40, Dunfield, Trinity Bay, NF   A0C 2S0   E-mail: ebeckett@nf.sympatico.ca

Take TCH to Clarenville and exit on Rte 230 (Discovery Trail). Proceed 64km to Rte 239 and
continue 7km to Dunfield.

$75S/D   🍽 Meals   ▶ 8
⚜ May 24-Oct31 🍺 Full, homebaked 🏠 Village, 2-storey,
patio, deck, quiet, 1-acre ▪4D(upstairs) ⊨4Q ⤴4Private
★TV,F,KF,LF,off-street parking ✋ No smoking
🚗 Historic Trinity, newly restored Lester Garland Property,
Trinity Pageant, Fort Point Lighthouse, Mussle Bar, berry picking,
whale/iceberg watching and boat tours, Bonavista, Clarenville
☛ Newly restored 4th Generation home with some antique furnishings and surrounded by the
rolling hills of Dunfield. Hook-up for phone and TV in each room. Breakfast is served in guest
breakfast room. Visa,MC ⟋B&B

Eastport

(south-east of Gander; see also Glovertown)

Pinsent, Lillian & Walter (Pinsent's B&B & Art Studio) ☎ (709) 677-3021
Box 85, 17 Church St., Eastport, NF   A0G 1Z0

From TCH, take Rte 310 Exit to Eastport at west entrance to Terra Nova Nat. Park. Drive through
park and through Sandringham. Turn left at T-Intersection in Eastport enroute to Salvage and to
3rd house on right. Situated near Credit Union.
$40S $50D $10Add.person   🍽 Meals(Oct-Apr)   ▶ 4
🍺 Full, homebaked 🏠 Rural, village, older, 2-storey, salt-box
design home, view, patio, quiet ▪ 2D(upstairs) ⊨2D,1R
⤴1Sh.w.g. ★TV,LF, parking ✋Smoking area provided
🎋 Stroll on banks to 2 beautiful beaches, art-studio/frame shop,
Family Funland with Fairground tours & pond, over 100-year old
Anglican Church, x/c skiing from doorstep, camping
🚗 Gander Airport, Terra Nova Park, hiking, beautiful fjords, boat tours, whale watching, ferry
☛ Delightful, quaint saltbox house (ca 1905) is surrounded by whispering aspens and gardens
located where the mountains meet the sea. Enjoy the salt sea breeze rising from Salvage Bay. Enjoy
happy memories and a restful night. Hostess from Saskatchewan and host, an ex-mountie turned
artist, delight in "talking up Newfoundland". Guests are invited to view the studio exhibits in a
separate building on the premises. There is a resident cat. ⟋B&B

Stephan, Lynn & Larry (Laurel Cottage B&B)
41 Bank Rd., Eastport, NF   A0G 1Z0

☎ (709) 677-3138, Fax (709) 677-2979
E-mail: laurel@nf.sympatico.ca

From Trans Canada Hwy exit onto Rte 310 to Easport (road to beaches). Turn left at stop sign and proceed to ocean. Turn left on Bank Rd and watch for sign.

$52-54S $54-64D   🍽 Meals   ►6
🚪 Full   🏠 Rural, village, 2-storey, older, view from guest rooms, oceanfront, wrap-around veranda, porch, quiet   ■ 3D(upstairs)   ⊨ 2T,1D,1Q   ⚘ 1Private, 1sh.w.g.   ★F,TV,LF,guest bicycles available   ⓌDesignated smoking area,not suitable for children   🧍 Sandy beaches with lagoon (Eastport & Sandy Cove), beachcombing, surfing, canoeing, Summer Beach Festival, local arts & crafts, Art Gallery with artist in residence, hiking/snowmobiling/x-c skiing from doorstep   🚗 Gander Airport, Terra Nova Nat. Park, Twin Rivers Golf Club, White Hills Ski Resort, whale/dolphin watching tours, spectacular sea coast scenic drives, ferry to St.Brendan'Island   ☛ Lovingly restored English-style Cottage (ca 1920) with antiques and eclectic furnishings. An abundance of natural light that spills into the rooms combined with fine china & art work & fireplace create a memorable ambiance. Enjoy the spectacular view of the intrinsic beauty of the coastline. Breakfast is served in the guest breakfast room overlooking the ever-changing sea. Visa ✓B&B

Englee

(on north-east coast south of St.Anthony)

Reeves, Holly & John (Reeve's Ocean View B&B)
Box 217, 69 Church Rd., Englee, NF   A0K 2J0

☎ (709) 866-2531

From TCH take Rte 430 north to Plum Point and then travel east on Rte 432 and 433 to Englee.

$45S $50D $5Add.person   🍽 Meals   ►6
🚪Full   🏠Res, multi-storey, view from guest rooms, patio, quiet, oceanfront   ■3D(upstairs)   ⊨3D,1cot   ⚘2Ensuite, 1sh.w.h.   ★KF,LF,TV in guest room, parking   ⓌNo pets   🧍 Whale watching and iceberg viewing from front patio   ☛ Newfoundland hospitality in quiet and private surroundings. Relax and enjoy beautiful views. Hosts will take guests on a boat tour to photograph icebergs and whales. Visa ✓B&B

English Harbour West

(on southshore (Fortune Bay))

Petite, Debbie (Olde Oven Inn)
English Harbour West, Fortune Bay, Nfld   A0H 1M0

☎ (709) 888-3461, (709) 888-4402
Fax (709) 888-3441

From Trans Canada Hwy (Rte 1), take Rte 360 at the Bishop's Falls junction and travel all the way to Dept. of Hwys. Depot. Turn left onto Rte 362 and keep following the signs to Inn.

$40S $50D   (plus Tax)   🍽 Meals   (Rates for longer stays/off season)   ►8A
🚪 Cont.   🏠 Rural, older, view, patio, quiet, oceanfront   ■4D (upstairs)   ⊨ 4D,1R,1P   ⚘2Sh.w.g.   ★ LF,KF,TV in guest room, parking   Ⓦ No smoking   🧍 Hiking, rowing, berry picking, outdoor lobster boil-up avail.   🚗 Yarn Point Craft shop, trout & salmon fishing, lighthouses (St.Jacques, Sagona Isle.)   ☛ Built in 1920, charming home retains many of its original features with a super view of the harbour and located in a small pretty fishing community. Arrangements can be made to take guests out fishing for cod, lobster, salmon etc. Guests can also go on the private longliner to visit remote communities where the people were re-located. Pick-up to/from Gander airport available. CCards ✓B&BA

Fogo

(on Fogo Island - north of Gander)

Payne, Mrs. John (Payne's Hospitality Home)
Box 201, Fogo, NF A0G 2B0

☎ (709) 266-2359

Take Fogo Ferry (7 return trips daily in summer) to Fogo Island from Farewell (near Stoneville).

$28-32S $56D   ◖ Meals (included)   ▶ 7
⚡ Full   🏠 Townhouse, quiet, view   ■3(upstairs)   ⊨3S,2D
cot, crib   🛏1.5Sh.w.g.   ★TV   ⓦNo pets.
🏃 Store, church, watch fishing boats and icebergs (in season) from
nearby hills, whale watching,
🚗 Ferry dock, sandy beaches, crab factory tours
📯 Enjoy the Atlantic Ocean view and lovely breezes from the
hill tops in comfortable island home located in historic settlement on rugged, scenic Island. Guests
can participate in the local Folk Festival (August).

Glovertown

(east of Gander; see also Eastport)

Churchill, Doug & Linda (The Lilac Inn B&B)
Pinetree Rd., Rte 310, Box 221, Glovertown, NF A0G 2L0

☎ & Fax (709) 533-6038

$50S $55D $5Child(free under age 3) $65F $5Add.person   ▶ 9

From Hwy1 take Exit 25. Drive through town, keep right for 3km.
Turn left on Pinetree Rd.
⚡ Full, homebaked   🏠 Res., village, hist., 3-storey, view from
guest rooms, veranda, quiet   ■ 2D,1F (upstairs)   ⊨1S,3D,1R
🛏2Private, 1ensuite   ★ F,LF,TV avail.in guest rooms, ceiling
fans, off-street parking   ⓦNo pets, no smoking
🏃 Bird watching, "Whimsicals" store/café, Jaski's Restaurant
🚗 Terra Nova Nat.Park, scenic drive around Eastport Peninsula,
Splash'n Putt Amusement Park, Twillingate, whale watching
📯 Warm welcome and friendly Newfoundland hospitality in restored 75-year old Victorian home,
nestled in a lovely garden with lilac trees and old-fashioned rose bushes; situated on a quiet street in
the centre of town. Relax on the veranda and enjoy the beautiful ocean view. Special rates for longer
stays (3 nights or more). There is a cat in residence. Visa ↜B&B

L'Anse aux Meadows

(northern tip of NFLd; see also Cape Onion)

Hedderson, Thelma (Viking Nest B&B) (pending)
Box 127, Hay Cove, L'Anse aux Meadows, NF A0K 2X0

☎ (709) 623-2238

Follow Viking Trail Rte 430 heading north. Turn left on Rte 436 to
L'Anse aux Meadows. In Hay Cove watch for B&B sign.
$30S $38D $8Add.person   ◖ Meals   ▶ 8
✳ May1-Oct31 (other by special arrangement)   ⚡ Full,
homebaked   🏠Rural, bungalow, oceanfront, patio, view from
guest rooms,quiet   ■ 3 (main floor)   ⊨1S,1D,2Q,2R
🛏2Sh.w.g.   ★ KF,TV in guest room
🚗 Town of St.Anthony, Grenfell house, Jordie Bonie Murals
🏃 L'Anse aux Meadows Nat. Historic Park, Viking Boat tours, hiking & walking trails
📯 Warm and friendly Labrador welcome in comfortable home situated in small fishing village.
Spend a pleasant evening whale and iceberg watching or chat with fellow guests in the family room.
Experience traditional Newfoundland hospitality. Meals are traditional and consist of seafood
dishes. Family and weekly rates available. Visa,MC

Lewisporte
(west of Gander; see also Roberts Arm, Twillingate, Fogo)

Leschied, Carl and June (Northgate B&B)   ☎ (709) 535-2258, Fax (709) 535-2239
92 Main St., Lewisporte, NF A0G 3A0

Travelling on TCH from Grand Falls proceed to Notre Dame junction. Proceed 10km on Hwy 340 to Lewisporte. $40S $55D $10Add.person 🍽Meals ►8 ☻Homebaked(wholesome) 🏠Res.,view,older,1.5-storey, oceanfront ■1S,3D(upst) ⊨1S,2T,2D,1R ⊒3Private ★F,large veranda, parking Ⓦ No smoking ⌇German 🕴 Labrador Ferry Terminal, museum and craft shop, restaurants, whale watching and fishing tours
🚗 Two major salmon rivers, strawberries "u-pick" in July and August, Provincial parks, historic Twillingate (view icebergs in May and June)
📣 Large home decorated in country style, overlooking Lewisporte Harbour. Relax on the veranda and enjoy the harbour activities or warm up by the cozy fire on cool evenings. Hosts operate a 27 ft tour boat, featuring trips with lunch beside icebergs (in season), to Beothuk Indian Island haunts, cod jigging & island cookouts (overnight at remote island cabin).Visa ⌐B&B

Port-aux-Basques
(south-west of Corner Brook; see also Burgeo)

Gibbons, Elizabeth and Henry (Caribou Bed & Breakfast)   ☎ (709) 695-3408
Box 53, 30 Grand Bay Rd., Port-aux-Basques, NF A0N 1K0   E-mail: douglasg@nlnet.nf.ca

Located 5 min drive from the Gulf Ferry linking Newfoundland to the Mainland.
$43-45S $47-49D $6-10Child $10Add.person (Cots extra) ► 10A,4Ch

🎏 Summer only 🍲 Cont.(extensive) 🏠 Res., ranch-style, quiet ■ 4(main level) ⊨ 2S,4D,4R ⊒ 2Private, 1sh.w.g. ★ TV,F, parking Ⓦ No smoking 🕴 Shopping center, churches, seafood restaurants, Provincial Interpretation center, sea, beaches 🚗 Ferry to Nova Scotia, Regional Museum, ancient Rose Blanche Lighthouse, Dorset Eskimo Site, long stretches of Cape Ray beaches and large sand dunes, scenic Codroy Valley
📣 Convenient location at the Gateway to Newfoundland. Informative adult-occupied home is a great starting point for a trip to the rest of Newfoundland and Labrador. Breakfast is served in time to catch the ferry boat. Free brochure on request. Visa,MC ⌐B&B

Portland Creek
(north of Corner Brook)

Wylezol, P (Entente Cordiale - Country Inn)   ☎ (709) 898-2288
General Delivery, Portland Creek, NF A0K 4G0   Winter: (709) 634-7407, Fax 7495

From TCH 1 take Hwy 430 north at Deer Lake and drive all the way to Portland Creek. Located 1.5km off Viking Trail. Phone for directions.
$50S/D 🍽Meals ►8 🎏Summer only 🍲Cont. 🏠Rural, 2-storey, hist., acreage, view from guest rooms, oceanfront, quiet, secluded ■4D (upstairs) ⊨4D ⊒4Private ★TV in sitting room, fans in guest rooms, guest quarters are separate Ⓦ No smoking,no pets 🕴 Hiking on sandy beach and hillside trail, salmon fishing 🚗 Gros Morne National Park, Arches (scenic attractions)
📣 Large home with historic decor, situated on a sandy beach with sunsetting vista surrounded by large private acreage in secluded cove. Enjoy the genuine friendly Newfoundland hospitality. Meals are served in licensed dining room. Visa,MC

Roberts Arm
(north of Grand Falls; see also Lewisporte)

Warr, Evelyn and Bruce (Lake Crescent Inn)   ☎(709) 652-3067/3568, Fax (709) 652-3056
Box 69, Roberts Arm, NF   A0J 1R0

Located 26 km off Hwy 1 on Rte 380 and approx. halfway between Port aux Basque and St. John's.
Drive along the beautiful Beothuk Trail to Roberts Arm. (1st residence when entering town)
$32S $37D $10Add.person   🍽 Meals   ▶ 12A,2Ch
🍴 Cont.(healthfood conscious)   🏠 Rural, res., multi-storey, view, lakefront, patio, quiet
■1S,3D,1F(main and upper level)   ⊨ 2T,4D,1S,1P   ⚐ 2Sh.w.g.,1shower   ★ TV parking,
wheel-chair access, whirlpool   ✋ No pets
🕺 Crescent Lake Beach (see "Cressie, the Lake Monster"), Medical Clinic, stores, library
🚐 Icebergs (in season), whale-watching, fine dining
🔺 Enjoy sights of icebergs and the "Upside Down Tree" on your drive to the B&B. Modern home
overlooks Crescent Lake. Relax in the whirlpool and enjoy a quiet talk or visit the antique room. A
great place to use as a base from which to explore the beautiful area. CCards ╱B&B

Rocky Harbour
(north of Corner Brook; see also Portland Creek)

Major, Violet (Majors' B&B)   ☎ (709 458-2537, 1-888-999-2537
General Delivery, Rocky Harbour, NF   A0K 4N0

Located on Pond Rd in Rocky Harbour (on the Viking Trail).
$25S $40D $5Child   ▶ 8+
🍽 Full   🏠 Rural, 2-storey, view from guest rooms, patio, deck
■4 (main floor)   ⊨ 2S,2D,1Q,1K   ⚐2Sh.w.g.   ★TV,KF,LF,
wheel-chair access, off-street parking   ✋ Designated smoking
area, special room for guests with pets
🕺 Gros Morne Fun Park, walking trails, horseback riding, craft
stores, beach, swimming, daily bus to airport and for shopping
🔺 Warm welcome and friendly Newfoundland hospitality in large home, situated in the heart of
Gros Morne National Park (world heritage site) among spectacular scenery. Relax on the large
patio or backyard after a day of outdoor activities, and travelling. Take a boat tour, view the
majestic fiords and watch for whales, moose and cariboo. Ideal place for nature lovers and
photographers. Fresh brewed tea or coffee is always available. Breakfast is served in guest breakfast
soom. There is a dog and a cat in residence. Visa,MC

St.Anthony
(on northern tip of Province; see also Cape Onion, Portland Creek)

Budgell, Donna & Lester (Fishing Point B&B)   ☎ (709) 454-3117/(709) 454-2009
Box 726, Fishing Point Rd., St.Anthony, NF   A0K 4S0

Take the Viking Rt (Hwy 430) up the west coast to St Anthony. Arriving on West St, proceed
through lights to Fishing Point Rd. (last house on edge of town).
$35S $40D $6Add.person   ▶ 10
🍽 Extra   🏠 Res., hist., view from guest rooms, 2-storey, hillside, oceanfront, deck, quiet
■3D,1F(ground level)   ⊨4D,1P,1R,cot,crib   ⚐ Sh.w.g.   ★ KF,separate entrance, off-street
parking, guest quarters are separate–   ✋ Designated smoking area
🕺 Lightkeepers Cafe (seafood specialties), Danny's Airbus, Fishing Point Park with boardwalks
and lookouts, whale/iceberg watching
🚐 L'Anse aux Meadows (Home of the Vikings)
🔺 Friendly & helpful hosts in old homestead (built in early 1900s), uniquely renovated, decorated
to give total and peaceful and memorable relaxation. Enjoy the "million-dollar" panorama of the
harbour view from the living or dining rooms with ships passing by and magnificient icebergs and
whales entering the harbour's mouth. Breakfast is served in guest breakfast room. Visa ╱B&B

St. John's

Badrudin, Trish (Waterford Manor) ☎ (709) 754-4139, Fax (709) 754-4155
185 Waterford Bridge Rd., St.John's, NF A1E 1C7

Phone for directions.
$80-165D   (plus tax)   ► 14
🍴 Full   🏠 Res., sub., hist., river at back, quiet   ■ 3D, 3Ste
(upstairs)   ⊨ 4D,2Q,1K   ⇛ 3Private, 3ensuite(jaccuzi)   ★F
(in suites), TV in guest rooms, table fans, off-street parking, guest
quarters are separate   🚬 Designated smoking area, no pets, not
suitable for children
🚗 Downtown, shopping mall
🕴 Park-like setting with gazebo and river on property, bus route, Bowering Park
🐾 Victorian-style B&B in authentic Heritage house built in 1870 with period furnishings and
conducive elegant atmosphere. Ideal place for special occasions and meetings. Breakfast is served in
special guest breakfast room. CCards ✍B&B

Bell, Ann (Bonne Esperance House) ☎ (709) 726-3835, Fax (709) 739-0496
20 Gower St., St. John's, Nfld A1C 1N1   E-mail: bonne@wordplay.com

Phone for directions.
$50-120S/D   ► 14+
🍴 Homebaked   🏠 Downtown, central, hist., multi-storey   ■ 10,2Stes(upstairs)   ⊨ T,D,Q,R
⇛All ensuite   ★ F,TV in each guest room   🚬 Smoking
🕴 Signal Hill, downtown, harbourfront, museums, historic churches, restaurants
🚗 Cape Spear (North America's most easterly point)
🐾 Historic Victorian home with 10ft ceilings, antique furnishings and collections of Nfld books
and situated in old St. John's. Relax and enjoy fabulous breakfasts.✍B&B

Clarke, Len (A Gower Street House) ☎ & Fax (709) 754-0047,1-800-563-3959
180 Gower Street, St.John's, NF A1C 1P9

Located in the centre of the City's Heritage area.
$50S $65D   (Off-season rates available)   ► 8
🍴 Full   🏠 Downtown, historic, view   ■ 4D(upstairs)   ⊨ S,Q
⇛Ensuite   ★LF,TV,Telephone,private parking   🚬 No smoking
🕴 Harbourfront, Signal Hill, museums, restaurants, antique & handicraft
shops, Government House, Cathedrals, Provincial Library, City Hall, live
theatre, Quidi Vidi Lake, Pippy Park, University, Rennies River hiking trail,
Hotels Newfoundland and Delta
🚗 Marine Laboratory, Bird Island, Marine Drive, Airport, scenic villages,
beautiful Conception Bay
🐾 Fully renovated, 1893-built Heritage home, filled with extensive art collection, has retained
much of the orginal floor plan situated in the core of the City's historic properties area and 2000 ft
from "Mile 0" of Trans Can Hwy. ✍B&B

Holden, Bob and Cindy (Compton House)   ☎ (709) 739-5789
26 Waterford Bridge Rd., St. John's, NF   A1E 1C6

Located downtown and west of water street. Phone for directions.
$59-189S $69-199D $15Add.person   ► 16A

🍲 Full, homebaked   🏠 Downtown, res., hist., patio, acreage, quiet   ■ 5D,3Ste (main and upper floor)   ⊨4D,5Q,2P,2R
🛏1Private, 5ensuite ★9F,Air,KF,3whirlpools, separate entrance, TV and phones in guest rooms, parking, sunroom   🚫No pets, no smoking, no children
🏃 Downtown St. John's, shopping, business section, restaurants and night life on George St., Harbour Charters and boat tours, Bowring and Victoria Parks, on main bus route
🚗 Cape Spear and Signal Hill National Historic Pks, Bird Island and Cape St. Mary's Bird Sanct.
🐾 Designated a Heritage home, elegant Victorian Mansion is set in a large garden and has been beautifully restored and furnished with antiques. Full English-style fireside breakfasts are elegantly served in the formal dining room. Hosts are very knowledgeable about local history and their home town and welcome any inquiries. CCards ⬿B&B

Keating, Patrick (The Roses B&B)   ☎ (709) 726-3336
9 Military Rd., St. John's NF   A1C 2C3

From Hwy 1 take downtown Exit; from airport go to Nfld Hotel & look for B&B 2 blocks west.
$60S $75-85D $10Add.person   (plus tax)   ► 16

🍲 Full (self-serve weekends)   🏠 Downtown, hist., view from guest rooms, patio, porch, quiet   ■ 2D,3F (main, upper & lower levels)   ⊨8D
🛏2Private,2ensuite,1sh.w.g.   ★ F,TV in guest rooms, separate entrance, off-street parking   🚫No smoking, no pets
🏃 Downtown, churches, museum, waterfront, Colonial Bldg. restaurants, walking trails, Quidi Vidi Lake, Commissary House, bus stop
🚗 Signal Hill, Cape Speer, Quidi Vidi Village, harbour & waterfront
🐾 Classic turn-off-the-Century home fully restored maintaining its originality & furnished with many antiques, situated in central location.
Enjoy the beautiful view of the St.John's Harbour from the top floor. Breakfast is served in guest breakfast room. CCards ⬿B&B

Stephenville   *(south of Corner Brook)*

Billard, Myra and George (Harmon House - Billard's B&B)   ☎ & Fax (709) 643-4673
Box 656, Stephenville, NF   A2N 3B5   1-800-644-4673

Location: 144 New Mexico Dr. From Hwys 460 or 490 proceed into Stephenville and follow hospital signs. Past hospital turn right on Pennsylvania Dr, then left on New Mexico Dr.
$42S $54D $10Add.person (Child under 5 free)   ► 10A,4Ch

🍲 Cont.   🏠 Res., hist., cape-cod-type, Bay-view, front & back patios, quiet   ⊨2T,2D,2Q,1R,cot,crib   ■3D,1F (main & upper floor)   🛏 2Sh.w.g.   ★ Library of NF books, phone avail. in guest rooms, parking   🚫 No smoking, no pets,
🚗 Hunting (in season - Moose, Caribou, Bear), salmon fishing, golfing, horse-back riding trails (Point au Mal), Joey's Lookout, Abitibi Paper Mill, shopping mall, College of the North Atlantic
🐾 Comfortable home is located on the former US Air Force Base. Relax and enjoy a selection of Newfoundland paintings. Tours and local visits to other points of interest can be arranged. Fax/Copier/Computer service avail. at extra cost. Visa,MC ⬿ B&B

Trinity

(south of Bonavista; see also Dunfield)

Gow, Tineke (Campbell House Bed & Breakfast) ☎ (709) 464-3377
High Street, Trinity, Trinity Bay, NF A0C 2S0

From TCH in Clarenville, turn onto Rte 230 (Discovery Trail) and proceed 70 km. Take Rte 239 to
Trinity Bay, turn left and follow road to village.

$75S $89D $10Add.person (plus tax) ► 10
🎏 May-Oct 🍲 Full, homebaked 🏠 Village, 2-storey, hist.,
older, acreage, view from guest rooms, oceanfront, patio, deck,
quiet ▪ 3D,1Ste (upstairs) ⊢ 1S,2T,2D,2Q 🚿 3Private,
1ensuite ★ F,KF,TV,separate entrance, off-street parking
🐾No smoking, no pets, children min. age 7 ∿ Dutch
🎐 Walking trails with breathtaking views of land and seascape,
restaurants, craft shops, museums, Interpretation Centre, wharf
🚗 Abandoned fishing villages, local boat tours to view Nfld marine wildlife.
🐾 Heritage home, built in 1840, completely restored, furnished with period pieces and
magnificient view of the ocean, located in the centre of the village. Hosts are ardent gardeners &
musicians and have often shown guests a real Nfld "Time" with a healthy repertoire of traditional
fiddle music. Icebergs may be seen from the guest room windows. Ideal base location from which to
explore the Bonavista Peninsula. CCards

Saint, Dolores (The Haven B&B) ☎ & Fax (709) 464-3373
Box 27 Trinity, TB, NF A0C 2S0

Travel west from St. John's on TCH1. Take Rte 230 and Rte 239 to Trinity.
$45-54S $63-72D 🍽Meals (Discounts for 3 nights or longer) ► 4
🎏 May-Nov (other by special arrangement) 🍲 Full 🏠 Village, 2-storey,
hillside, view from guest rooms, oceanfront, secluded ▪2D(upstairs)
⊢2D plus futon 🚿 1Sh.w.g.,plus main floor powder room ★TV,LF,
off-street parking 🐾 No smoking, no pets, children min.age 8
🎐 Hist. village of Trinity, waterfront/tides, whale watching, boat tours,
museums, restaurants, shops, Garland House (Pageants/Plays - July/Aug)
🚗 Bonavista Lighthouse, Ryan Premises, Trinity Loop, Easton Beach, The
Dungeon, Canada Goose Sanctuary, skiing
🐾 Comfortable home situated on a hill in historic Trinity Village proper, with a spectacular view
in all directions. Relax in the well stocked library with books, and puzzles and games. Breakfast is
served with the fabulous view to enjoy. A very private, quiet and tranquil atmosphere. Special diets
can be accommodated. There is a cat in residence. Visa,MC ⮕B&B

Twillingate

(north of Lewisporte, see also Fogo)

Pardy, Margaret & Martin (Beach Rock B&B) ☎ (709) 884-2292
Box 350, RR1, Little Harbour, Twillingate, NF A0G 4M0

Located in Little Harbour, 4km south of Twillingate off Rte 340. Phone for directions.

$35S $40D $5Child $10Add.person 🍽 Meals ► 9
🍲 Cont. 🏠 Village, 2-storey, view from guest rooms,
oceanfront, quiet ▪ 4D,1F(upstairs) ⊢ 1S,4D,R
🚿2sh.w.g. ★ TV 🐾 No smoking, no pets
🎐 Walks around Little Harbour community, view fishing stage,
oldtime saw mill, local boat building, hiking trail on property
leading to National Park, partridge and blueberry picking in season
🚗 Twillingate, Lewisporte, museums, lighthouse, craft shops
🐾 Warm welcome and true Newfoundland hospitality in traditional Newfoundland home built in
1904 by host family's ancestors. Enjoy the peace and beauty and spectacular views of Notre Dame
Bay and the occasional iceberg. House specialty: homecooked traditional fish dishes.⮕B&B

Woody Point

(north of Corner Brook; see also Norris Point, Daniels Hbr, Rocky Hbr)

Parsons, Jenny & Stan (Victorian Manor Hospitality Home)   ☎ (709) 453-2485
Gros Morne National Park, Box 165, Woody Point, NF   A0K 1P0

$50-125S/D $7Add.person   ▣$4.75Each   ◨Meals (winter)   ▶ 8

At Deer Lake on TCH1, take Rt430 to Wiltondale then Rt431.
Located in Gros Morne Nat.Park, a World Heritage Site.
▣Choice,homebaked   ⌂Village,hist.,acreage,view,oceanfront,
sunporch ■7 ◪6D,1Q ⇦4Private,2sh.w.g.,1jacuzzi ★F,TV in
guest room, sep.entrance, parking ♨No pets, no smoking
⚕ Seashore, whale watching tour boat
🚗 Lookout Hills Trail, Gros Morne Mountain & trails (Green
Garden's Trail with Sea Caves/Tablelands trail & rare plants)

🐾 4th Generation owners in unique Victorian Home still contains many artifacts and is rich in
history and Newfoundland culture with scenic panorama of Gros Morne and Bonne Bay. Fishing
and boat excursions can be arranged. ✒B&B

When to stay in a B & B ?

You can stay in a B&B anytime of the year. Of course, it is most popular when on vacation. And there are many more B&B's available in the summertime.

You can stay in a B&B if you are a single traveller (on business or pleasure). Then, you are in the company of others, and socializing with strangers is so much easier.

You can stay in a B&B for a weekend. You might want to go to the country for a good rest, or you might want to go to the city for a shopping spree or a cultural event.

You can stay in a B&B when visiting friends and relatives (if they do not have enough room for you). There is probably a B&B around the corner.

You can stay in a B&B when attending a wedding in another town. Many churches have lists of B&B's located nearby.

You can stay in a B&B when visiting a sick relative or friend in another town. It makes for very comforting and convenient accommodation. Many hospitals keep lists of nearby B&B's for out-of-town relatives.

You can stay in a B&B even if you are not travelling by car. Many B&B homes are situated near excellent public transportation and many hosts will pick up and deliver from bus terminal, railway station or airport, sometimes at no charge.

You can stay in a B&B even if you are on a camping trip. Give yourself a treat and sleep in a comfortable bed once in a while, especially if the weather turns miserable and the gear is soaking wet.

You can stay in a B&B if you travel with your own trailer. Many B&B's have ample room and a hook-up for that purpose, and they usually welcome guests to join them in the house for breakfast.

You can stay in a B&B when you are hiking the trails. In Ontario there are many B&B's along the famous Bruce Trail and some of these hosts may even forward your car and gear for you to the next B&B on the trail.

You can stay in a B&B when taking part in acitivity groups, such as whitewater rafting, bicycling and wilderness tours etc. Ask for information when signing up for a trip.

You can stay in a B&B when relocating to another city. Is there a better way of getting the feeling of a new area than talking to the local people?

NOTES